AMY LOWELL

A Chronicle

AMY LOWELL

AMY LOWELL

A Chronicle

With Extracts from her Correspondence

BY

S. FOSTER DAMON

ARCHON BOOKS
HAMDEN, CONNECTICUT
1966

FOR

A. D. R.

TO WHOM ALL THE BOOKS
ALSO THE BIOGRAPHY

CONTENTS

ILLUSTRATIONS

INTRODUCTION

'A great man can stand complete revelation

THE biography of Amy Lowell should have been an autobiography. None but she could have written it adequately.
The qualities of her poetry were also the qualities of her
life; she fulfilled Milton's noble dictum 'that he who
would not be frustrate of his hope to write well hereafter
in laudable things ought himself to be a true poem; that
is, a composition and pattern of the best and honorablest
things.' Many a generation will pass before we shall see
again such a composition of great heart, deep imagination,
brilliant poetic genius, and endless courage to fight for
beauty and truth against the rulers of the darkness of this
world, against spiritual wickedness in high places.

She had promised herself the fun of writing it. 'When
I get along in life, and my vein of poetry begins to run
thin, I'll do it,' she would say. The files of her correspondence and the scrapbooks of clippings were kept up against
that time; then, when the conflicts would have cooled and
the perspectives would have lengthened, she planned to
picture herself and her times as she had done for Keats
and thought of doing for Emily Dickinson. But the vein
of her poetry never ran thin; old age was not for her; and
after her premature death, in her files the folder labeled
'Autobiography' held not a page of her project. What a
book it would have been! She alone had the necessary
gusto and verve, the insight and background, the common sense and sense of fair play, and the knowledge and
the kindliness and the truthfulness to write it.

That unwritten book, I fear, may overshadow my attempt to replace it. But so vivid was she that, even
though those who knew her may feel that I have fumbled

many places, something of her reality must penetrate even the dullest prose.

Her life was essentially the triumph of the spirit over the tragedy of the body. She was a sick person from her early girlhood, yet her energy exceeded that of a dozen minor poets. Every obstacle except poverty blocked her path. She was twenty-eight when she wrote her first poem, thirty-eight when she published her first book, and only fifty-one when she died so abruptly. Yet in those thirteen years of public literary life, broken though they were by illnesses and eyestrain and a series of operations, she rose, through bored indifference, through ridicule and controversy and hatred, to complete victory, dying 'at the zenith of her fame' (as every newspaper phrased it: meaning simply that her powers had not started to wane, were still increasing).

Those thirteen years, in which she proved herself poet, critic, biographer, scholar, and controversialist, coincided with a great revival of poetry in the United States. America had reached a point in civilization where the arts were bound to flourish; and so vigorously did they do so that a World War with its subsequent inflation and depression was unable to stunt them. It was the time-spirit alone that caused Amy Lowell to publish her first book in that surprising year 1912; but her championing and development of the Imagist tenets in 1914 speedily made her the center of a storm which ventilated and refreshed all American literature, experimental or conservative, verse or prose; and her own literary achievements soon conquered a continent and left her one of the two or three leading influences in the poetry of a nation.

Such a full and public life in such times as those is best recorded chronicle-wise; and the calendar on which this biography is based was drawn chiefly from the files of her correspondence — eight full cabinet drawers of letters sent and received. While this calendar is reasonably complete, it cannot be guaranteed perfect. The files do not really begin until 1914, although many important documents before that time were preserved; and there is a gap in them from June through August, 1914 — those momentous months during which she took her last trip to England. The 'correspondence sent' consists simply of carbon copies of all the letters she dictated — unsigned, and lacking any impulsive postscript perhaps jotted at the last moment, and lacking also any corrections by pen-stroke. Fortunately Miss Lowell wrote very few letters with her own hand (like many another author, she found that additional labor almost impossible); and when ownership of such letters has been traced, copies have been requested, to be filed with the other letters. Doubtless many are still missing. Sometimes it has proved impossible to fix a definite date for engagements made by telephone; and when Miss Lowell went to New York, she commonly made her unofficial engagements that way. Then, especially in the 'correspondence received,' letters were often misdated, particularly at the beginning of the year; and still more letters were not dated at all. Another possible source of error was not discovered until the biography was nearly finished. In a letter to Sara Teasdale dated '30 January 1924,' she ended: 'Now, dear Sara, I must stop this very long letter and dress for Eva Gauthier's concert.' But this concert took place on January 29. Evidently Miss Lowell dictated the letter on the evening of the 29th; but it was typed, dated, and signed on the 30th. Whenever possible, these dates have been checked by the newspapers; references to 'last Friday' have been checked by a calendar; but there are still other references to 'last night,' which may be off by a day or two, as I found no way to correct them.

The narrative of these years has been supplemented by Miss Lowell's scrapbooks of newspaper-clippings, continued after her death by Mrs. Russell. Into these scrapbooks went everything about Amy Lowell or the 'New Poetry' which the clipping-bureaus furnished her; nothing, however silly or vicious or vulgar, was excluded. Each of these many volumes has been provided with an elaborate index. Scantier, but often richer in vivid details, are the chapters in books by various authors dealing with American literary life of recent years; for no one could write of these times and leave out the most striking personality of them all.

For the earlier years, there are numerous diaries, journals, school themes, school notebooks, and other materials of various sorts, including her earliest attempts — I mean this literally — at writing, and perhaps even earlier, for some of them are paper dolls and paper doll-houses. I have also interviewed many people who knew her in these years, and some of them have most kindly written out their reminiscences for my use.

To supplement all this manuscript and printed material, I fortunately have had my own memories to draw on. The New Poetry first interested me in the winter of 1912–13; my friendship with Miss Lowell started in the spring of 1916. As I was in Cambridge or its environs most of the time thereafter until her death (with the exception of the academic year 1920–21), I was able to attend many of her local readings, or hear about her trips immediately on her return. Every once in so often I was invited over to dinner at Sevenels. Sometimes I read her my latest batch of poems, always valuing the criticisms with which I often disagreed; and when I was working at a book on Blake, she delighted in hearing even the long textual commentaries (on which occasions I would read to her till three or four o'clock of a summer morning). It was she who placed the book for me, and I dedicated it to her. When we were not discussing literature, our talk would run on everything under sun and moon; incidentally, she told me much about her early life. I labor this point, so that the reader

will understand that all direct quotations ascribed to Miss
Lowell which are not extracted from some paper source
are not irresponsible fictionizing on my part: they are my
own memories of events at which I was present, or of
which she told me herself.

I have also used a few anecdotes from eye-witnesses at
events when I was not present; but these I have treated
with caution, as Miss Lowell was the kind of person whom
legends ringed round with extraordinary rapidity. I remember once, when she was going to a reception given by
Miss Alice Longfellow, she stopped her famous claret-
colored automobile at Harvard Square to enquire the way
to Craigie House. The traffic cop replied that the Craigie
House was the Longfellow House; to which she replied
again that she knew as much, but how did one get there?
Within an hour the tale was running through Cambridge
that her retort had been: 'And who the hell is Longfellow?' The *grande dame* is entitled to an occasional oath,
and Miss Lowell was aware of her privilege; but no lady
ever indulged in the cheap and perpetual profanity that is
one ear-mark of the Lowell mythology. Another ear-
mark is the threat or even actuality of tears.

Whenever feasible, I have told Miss Lowell's story in
her own words, using many extracts from her letters. It
has seldom been convenient to print entire letters; instead,
I have made selections of those passages which describe
events, outline literary theories, criticize books, shed light
on her personality, or whatever else seemed necessary to
illustrate the whole woman. A partial picture would have
been an injustice; indeed, when Mrs. Russell first offered
me the privilege of writing this biography, I refused at
once to undertake an 'official' one, and Mrs. Russell
agreed at once that an 'official' biography would be undesirable. Amy Lowell wrote of Keats, 'A great man can
stand complete revelation,' and of herself, 'You may come
with spade and shovel when I'm safely in the tomb.' If,

therefore, the reader thinks that I have been indiscreet or brutally frank, I can only reply that I have tried to do what I know she wanted — tell the whole truth and nothing else.

What is truth? Pilate was not wrong in asking; but he was wrong in not staying for an answer, in not recognizing that answer as it stood before him in human form. Channing said a century ago: 'The sayings and actions of a man, which breathe most of what was individual in him, should be sought above all things by his historian ... Sometimes one anecdote will let us into the secrets of a man's soul more than all the prominent events of his life.' [1] Every biographer should be beyond judgments of good and evil: he is concerned with 'faults' only in a geologic sense.

Such completeness of portraiture requires a considerable background of the times, and a frame of friends and enemies.

The times were thrilling and complex: after a long dry winter of decadent convention, the arts suddenly acquired meaning again. The American architects discovered the first new architectural principle since the Romans discovered the dome, and were converting New York into the most fantastic of modern cities. The American popular dance-music was imposing American rhythms on the ballrooms of the world. The great French painters were developing a new sense of form and color; the great French and Russian composers were doing the same in music; and the Russian Ballet, taking full advantage of these advances, was inventing ballets that were authentic expressions of the human imagination. All the arts were reviving in a tumultuous aesthetic spring; and in this spring the American 'New Poetry' burgeoned with fresh forms, colors, ideas, rhythms.

[1] William Ellery Channing: 'Christian Worship,' *Works*, stereotype ed., IV, 354.

The personalities of those years I have tried to represent as they appeared to Miss Lowell; the opinions about poets expressed in this book are hers, not necessarily mine. Sometimes these opinions shed more light on her than on the poet named, especially at the end of her life, when reaction was apparent in some books, and new lines of experimentation in others. But these epistolary opinions, often struck out in the heat of the moment, were always subject to change. Miss Lowell never cried out, with Job, 'Oh, that mine adversary had written a book!' If someone she had underestimated wrote a good book, she was among the first to proclaim it.

But with few exceptions, her enemies were persons more valuable as enemies than as anything else. Unable to keep their footing in the ranks of intellectual battle, they resorted to whispering campaigns. Envying her success and her wealth, they usually tried to explain the one by the other. In recording the controversies, however, I have tried to set forth all the essential facts, as I find them stated in the documents. Occasionally these documents tell a somewhat different story from versions already in print. Consequently, though I have tried to be absolutely fair to all parties, with malice towards none, probably no one will think I have wholly succeeded, some may deny that I have even tried, while others will be well aware what reserve I have practised in certain cases. I have been frank about Miss Lowell; but I have often been reticent about her opponents.

Exigencies of space have severely curtailed my treatment of Miss Lowell's many friends, with whom she held delightful correspondences for years. It has proved impossible to do more than select a few pungent paragraphs here and there, generally on literary topics. Reluctantly I had to make a rule to exclude letters from living persons. As representative, however, of these epistolary friendships, I have drawn heavily on the letters of D. H. Lawrence, which consequently bulk large in this volume. I felt doubly bound to do so as they themselves are of great literary value, and as Mr. Aldous Huxley overlooked them in editing Lawrence's *Collected Letters*, New York, 1932. They are a splendid specimen of the affectionate honesty of two writers who had become lifelong friends after knowing each other in the flesh for a mere month. The letters from Thomas Hardy represent another like friendship, the result of a single meeting only, although in this case, as the remove of a generation lay between him and Miss Lowell, their relationship was rather that of master and admirer. These two are presented as representative friendships rather than special ones. I regret that I had not room to quote more than one or two letters from other well-known writers. In the case of women writers, I have used their literary names throughout: 'Sara Teasdale' instead of Mrs. Ernst B. Filsinger; 'H. D.' instead of Mrs. Richard Aldington; and so on.

In discussing Miss Lowell's works, I have not treated them separately from her life, but have rather tried to show them in relationship to that life, after the method which she herself used in dealing with the French and American poets. Such an elaborate study, however, as she gave to the poems of Keats was out of the question: the time has not come for that. I have limited myself chiefly to telling what her poems are, and to quoting what she said about them herself.

Her letters have been transcribed from the carbons in her files. Once in a long while, when necessary for clarity, I have repunctuated lightly, though without seeking to follow academic standards. Miss Lowell's grammar was idiomatic, and she punctuated according to cadence; so particular was she that her published works exist exactly as she wanted them. But the punctuation in her letters was her secretary's; and I have felt no qualms in the few essential changes I have ventured. I have taken no such liberties with the letters written to her. Summaries of and quotations from her lectures have been made from the original typescript; whenever these were published, Miss Lowell often modified the text considerably, as she was using a different medium.

For all misprints, errors, and omissions, inevitable in a work the preparation of which has extended over so many years, I crave the indulgence of a generous public.

I am indebted to so many people that I can hardly thank them all adequately.

Particularly I am indebted to Mrs. Harold Russell, Miss Lowell's helpmate and literary executor, who accompanied her on all her trips, and who has read and commented on the entire manuscript of this book. She has added much, explained much, and suppressed nothing. Her patience and kindness and toleration I cannot praise enough; nor will the world ever appreciate how much it owes to Mrs. Russell for making the path smooth for Amy Lowell.

Mrs. William Lowell Putnam, Mrs. Francis Ayscough, Mrs. William Howard White, and John Gould Fletcher have written memoirs for my use, which have proved invaluable. Among other persons who have contributed reminiscences, either by letter or word of mouth, I must thank Conrad Aiken; Professor A. Joseph Armstrong, of Baylor University; Leonard Bacon; Miss Louise Winsor Brooks; Professor Ben C. Clough, of Brown University; Grant Code, of the Brooklyn Museum; Malcolm Cowley, of the *New Republic*; Louis A. Holman, of Holman's Print Shop; Carl Engel, president of G. Schirmer, Inc., Music Publishers; Gabriel Farrell, Director of the Perkins Institution; Mrs. Lyman W. Gale, founder of the Toy Theater; Professor Charles Gott, of Tufts College; Governor Theodore Francis Green of Rhode Island; Professor Raymond Dexter Havens, of Johns Hopkins; Professor and Mrs. Edward Burlingame Hill; Professor Robert Hillyer; Mrs. Frank L. Hinckley; Alfred Kreymborg; Miss Olga Lingard; John A. Lomax, Curator of Folk Music at the Library of Congress; Mrs. Lindsley Loring; Professor and Mrs. John Livingston Lowes; Miss Harriet Monroe, editor of *Poetry*; Miss Margaret Münsterberg; Miss Annie Endicott Nourse; Mrs. Charles Bruen Perkins; the late Professor A. Kingsley Porter, of Harvard; Professor Royall Snow, of Ohio State University; Mrs. Edward Clark Streeter; Miss Julia Sully; the Reverend Arthur Washburn; Edward Weeks, of the *Atlantic Monthly*; and Mrs. Edmund March Wheelwright.

Mrs. Thomas Hardy has most graciously granted the privilege of publishing the letters from her husband to Miss Lowell; Mrs. D. H. Lawrence has been equally generous with her husband's letters. For permission to include two letters from Sara Teasdale I am indebted to Miss Margaret Conklin; for a letter from Josephine Preston Peabody, to Professor Lionel S. Marks; for a letter from Barrett Wendell, to Mrs. Barrett Wendell; for a letter from Elinor Wylie, to William Rose Benét; and for a letter from Katharine Lee Bates, to Mrs. George S. Burgess. Although to date I have been unable to discover the literary executor of Donald Evans, even by appeals through the press, I have made so bold as to include a letter from him, since it sheds such a splendid light on the dead poet. Mrs. Robert J. Wyman has allowed me to use part of the record of Miss Lowell's session with Patience Worth; and Carl Sandburg has generously let me print a fine poem of his about Miss Lowell. To all these people I express my sincerest thanks.

I am indebted to the officials of the Harvard College Library, especially to Mr. George M. Kahrl, Curator of the Poetry Room, and to Mrs. L. H. Hall of the Theater Collection; and to the officials of the Brown University Library, especially to Miss Elizabeth Spicer, Custodian of the Harris Collection, and Miss Edith Blanchard, Assistant Librarian, who has patiently answered many hasty queries by telephone. The staff of the Providence Athenæum has also been exceedingly helpful; and Mr. C. K. Bolton, of the Boston Athenæum, put himself very graciously at my service.

Portions of my manuscript have been listened to by F. Munroe Endicott (of whose death I have just learned with great regret), Professor H. B. Grose, Professor John Curtis Reed, and Winfield T. Scott, whose suggestions have been most helpful. And here I must particularly express my gratitude to my wife and her brother, John Brooks Wheelwright, for their continual assistance and encouragement.

Professor Alphonso de Salvio, of Brown University, has translated Duse's letter for me. Miss Gertrude Whittemore prepared a most elaborate and painstaking index for my use. The 'List of Publications' was begun by Mrs. Winfield T. Scott and finished by George M. Kahrl, with the assistance of Miss Mary Hagopian. And I must also acknowledge the assistance of Miss Alice Duckworth, whose speed and accuracy under pressure of time was a very present aid.

S. Foster Damon

Brown University
September 2, 1935

AMY LOWELL

A Chronicle

CHAPTER I

ENVIRONMENT

'... certainly it is mine.'

AMY LOWELL was born in Brookline, Massachusetts; as a child she customarily added 'of Brookline' to her name; as a woman she made her home there, in her father's house; she died there; and the word 'Brookline' appears on her tombstone. Yet this rebellious attitude of hers against Boston was caused and conditioned by the fact that she was so thoroughly, inescapably, and proudly a Bostonian. Her family was of the older Bostonese, with a house on Commonwealth Avenue; she was educated in Boston (whether at the private schools or the Athenaeum); she 'came out' there; she was intimately connected with many phases of Boston life; and there she made her first and last appearances as a reader of her own poems. She loved Boston as heartily as any other Bostonian, and scolded about it, as all the best Bostonians do; but in Brookline, only four miles from the State House, was her home.

Spiritually, of course, Brookline was merely a country suburb, refusing to be absorbed into the growing city, though entirely surrounded by it, refusing even to become a city itself, content to keep the traditional Town Meeting and to be known as the richest town in the world. It was characteristic of Miss Lowell that she should have made this slight rebellion by identifying herself with the place that meant so much to her. But she never dreamed of denying that she was a Bostonian.

Boston is a perplexingly individualistic city, which has been more revered and more attacked than any other city in America. Its character was predetermined by its founders, whom history caused to be of one spiritual type and of one purpose. The purpose was to establish the

perfect community, the 'City of Saints'; and through all
the changes that have since come about, the place has
never lost its idealism, with its accompanying conviction
that Boston is really better than any other city in the
world, or at least in the New World.

The social system that developed there sprang directly
from Calvinistic theology. The discrediting of kings and
saints, in the attack on hierarchies, produced a democracy
on earth as in heaven. At first, to be sure, the franchise
was limited to church members; but after the Reverend
John Wheelwright, exiled for antinomianism, founded the
first completely democratic church at Exeter, New Hampshire, the other New England settlements insensibly followed suit, until every man had his voice and vote in Town
Meeting. Unmodified democracy, however, tends towards
envious levelling; this danger was checked by the doctrine
of Providence, which produced the cult of Individualism.
In practice, this doctrine meant that God had distributed
talents according to a higher plan of his own; to further
that divine purpose, these talents should not be hid under
a bushel, but should be developed. Not only were gifts to
be cultivated: the mere perception of an evil was the divine command to right it. Who does not do so is opposing
God's will; unhappiness follows automatically. But who
does so has full right to the authority and place that he
earns. However, Individualism also has its danger —
pride or selfishness; this in its turn was checked by the
doctrine of Predestination, which taught that as talents
were divinely bestowed, one deserved no credit for them.
They were given to further God's providence; whoso used
them for selfish ends simply brought misery upon himself.
Even the attempt to gain heaven or avoid hell was useless,
as all our fates had been fixed before the Creation; furthermore, as it was self-seeking, it was essentially evil.

Thus the Calvinistic theology strove for the perfect
community by developing a democracy which gave the

fullest opportunity to the individual, who was to use his powers for the community. Rising from the place in which one was born socially, to the place for which one was fitted mentally, was considered right and even divinely ordained. The intellectual and the social aristocracies often were all but identified and usually were allied. Community and Individual thus were made to serve one another, while the average citizen was taught moral and intellectual courage. Of course the scheme never worked perfectly; but this balance of opposed forces (as in Böhme's deity) ensured dynamism, progress. And the significance of Puritanism (as contrasted with Catholicism) lies in its tendency, its movement, rather than in what it might be at any given moment of time. Its own heretics are its saints.

Progress was thus made inevitable, but it was not made easy. The very stubbornness of revolt provoked stubbornness of resistance. The divine command operated on both sides. And when liberalism triumphed at last, it soon was defending itself to the end against newer ideas. The lava from one eruption hardened and became the crater for the next eruption. Therefore, while Boston history reads as a series of advanced ideas, we always find its great figures complaining of the city's bitter conservatism. The surprising thing seems to be that Boston continued to produce its great figures constantly and for so long: men and women both, for Anne Hutchinson and Anne Bradstreet were only the first two of its famous women.

Like citizen, like city. Historically, Boston proved itself to be revolutionary, though in a curiously conservative way. Its passionate belief in Christian Liberty more than once made it stand upon its rights and thus shape the world of the future. The English royalists complained of its influence in bringing about the Puritan Revolution of 1642; in the Glorious Revolution of 1688 it did not await official action, but had a private revolution of its own against Governor Andros; in 1774 it made itself the focus of the conflict which initiated the American Revolution; in the days of Mr. Jefferson's embargo and Mr. Madison's war, it was amongst those who considered secession; and its part in the Civil War was also a leading one. Not that Boston was ever unanimous in these matters. There was always hard pamphlet-fighting before the city could be carried. Even in the earliest days, amongst the immigrants were those who came for economic, not religious, reasons; in the Revolution, long after the surrounding countryside was Whig to a man, the Boston Tories remained powerful; the quarrels of families inspired by the War of 1812 still sputter faintly in odd corners; and in the next generation there were those who mobbed Abolitionists and hissed negro regiments.

The Conservatives never lost wholly, however; at least they ensured that Boston liberalism sprang from conservative roots. The original Puritans looked back to Scripture in their claim of re-establishing ancient liberties; the revolutionists of the eighteenth century reasserted the principles of 1688; the Abolitionists took their stand upon the Declaration of Independence; and its present liberals look back to the Civil War.

Their spiritual history was like their political history. Their creed proved progressively self-destructive in the direction of further liberalism. Having argued themselves out of Romanism and Anglicanism, they reached the conclusion that truth was still in process of revelation, and thus continued arguing themselves out of Calvinism into Unitarianism and finally Agnosticism.

The influx of university men soon made Boston one of the most intensively educated spots on the face of the globe.[1] Within six years of its founding it had established its school of higher learning, Harvard College, to educate the sons of the Boston gentry and also to prevent 'an il-

[1] Samuel Eliot Morison: *Builders of the Bay Colony*, Boston, 1930, p. 184, gives the statistics.

literate Ministery'; and the famous Massachusetts School Act of 1647 provided for a grammar school to each township of one hundred families or more. Thus the state took the lead in American education which it has held ever since.

Intimately allied to the Puritan passion for education was the Puritan passion for books. Boston was preordained a literary city. The Bible itself was a book, for the possession of which they had fought; and every New England child read in his primer:

> My book and heart
> Shall never part.

The seal of Harvard showed three open books inscribed 'Veritas.' Books were the great weapons in the search for truth, for liberty.[1] The Puritan college was named for him who left it his library. In the president's house was set up the first printing press north of Mexico City; that and the Foster press in Boston were for many years the only ones in the colonies. For nearly a century (1658–1747) a library stood on the site of the present 'Old State House.' The King's Chapel Library — a collection of two hundred theological works sent over by William III in 1698 — was another memorable early library; it is still preserved in the Boston Athenaeum. By 1700 Boston was next to London the chief literary center of the British Empire. The descendants of its citizens were bound to be literate; and

---

[1] This devotion to books was part of the reaction against the Roman policy of wiping out rival cultures whenever possible. The early Christian zealot Valens destroyed Roman libraries wholesale; the Genoese crusaders are said to have destroyed thousands of books at Tripoli; Torquemada, head of the Spanish Inquisition, was a famous book-burner; Cardinal Ximenes burned eighty thousand Arabic manuscripts in the public square of Granada; the early bishops of Mexico destroyed absolutely all the Aztec records there. When in 1643, the English Parliament established a censorship, it was the Puritan Milton who replied with his *Areopagitica*: 'unless wariness be used, as good almost kill a man as kill a good book: who kills a man kills a reasonable creature, God's image; but he who destroys a good book, kills reason itself, kills the image of God, as it were, in the eye.'

before the gifts of Andrew Carnegie, every city and every town of Massachusetts had its public library. Other literary centers eventually sprang up in America, but the advent of Transcendentalism and the New England poets ensured Boston's leadership until after the Civil War.

The other arts also flourished. The Bostonians of the seventeenth and eighteenth centuries enjoyed music; [1] the cult culminated in the choral Handel and Haydn Society (which flattered Herr Beethoven once by ordering an original composition) and the Boston Symphony Orchestra. Their taste in buildings can be seen in their churches — as fine a display of Georgian architecture as can be found anywhere. The portrait-painting of a hundred years came to flower in Copley and Stuart. Theaters were not allowed until after the Revolution; but plays were quite another thing — the Harvard undergraduates wrote and acted plays before the Revolution, possibly before the eighteenth century, without raising the slightest protest; indeed, one of the features of the Commencement came to be comic dialogues performed in costume. And when the Boston Museum stock company demonstrated that actors need not be customarily immoral, the last objection vanished.

After the storm-clouds of the Civil War had passed, the sun shone golden upon Boston again. A new era had come. Its poets were the glory of America, and in their light the whole city basked, collapsed into a remarkable complacency. It had solved the problems of heaven and earth. All its enemies were conquered — Archbishop Laud, George III, Satan, Simon Legree; and its crusaders (including the 'strong-minded women' supposedly a peculiar product of the city, along with 'thoughtful girls'), with-

[1] *The Puritan and Music in England and New England*, by Percy A. Scholes, Oxford, 1934, should kill forever the vulgar error that the Puritans prohibited the pleasures of life. His evidence as to such things as dancing-schools and maypoles in Boston is quite conclusive. But no thorough study has been made as yet of the eighteenth-century musical activities there.

out a common enemy to unite them in one grand moral purpose, diffused their energies in a hundred charities or causes. Religion was no longer an outlet. Soul-searching had dwindled to a painful self-consciousness; deity itself manifested only in 'the New England conscience.' 'High thinking and plain living' were still ideals, though any thinking that led to undue action was somewhat suspect, while the plain living might be very rich indeed if it were not ostentatious. Good morals had simply become good manners; convention was crystallizing; insensibly the clergy were losing their intellectual leadership. Moses and Darwin were set at loggerheads no longer. Unitarianism and Trinitarianism were equally respectable, and the agnostic was indistinguishable from the others when on fine Sundays they all walked down Commonwealth Avenue to King's Chapel or Trinity Church, the gentlemen gracefully removing their silk hats in the weekly greetings.

But the city was getting to be a real city. Hitherto, it had taken only ten minutes to get anywhere. The sudden dimming of the gas in every parlor had indicated that the chandelier of the Boston Museum was lighted, and that it was time to go to the play. But now the big coves and the space south of the Mill Dam (that extension of Beacon street across the salt marshes to Brookline) were being filled in rapidly, and the crowded town was overflowing on to the newmade land. Suburbs were being absorbed: Roxbury in 1868, Dorchester in 1870, and Brighton, Charlestown, and West Roxbury in 1874 (the year of Miss Lowell's birth). There were getting to be more carriages than one could recognize.

But the expansion did not mean cosmopolitanism. Boston, no longer on the road to anywhere except the North Shore, was expanding only from inside pressure; it grew, but remained itself. The Brahmins still lived on the water side of Beacon Street or the sunny side of Commonwealth Avenue; they still dined at two and had 'tea' at

six; they read the *Atlantic* and the *Transcript*, held four re-
ceptions a year, escaped from the Egyptian heat of summer by moving to the North Shore; sent their sons to
Harvard and their dead to Mount Auburn. Their ex-
clusiveness, as Russell Sturgis noted, was 'as by a law of
nature.' Since all the families composing Boston society
had reached the city before the War of 1812 at the latest,
they had now grown to clans, each privately thinking itself really much better than the others. Perhaps because
the Puritans raised no objections to the marriage of first
cousins, each family had acquired strong characteristics of
its own, which sometimes were summed up in local sayings.
One was 'always distinguished and always poor, always rising to resist persecutions they supposed were being aimed
at them'; another was 'a tribe living in or about Boston,
with customs but no manners'; a third had taste and ran
to swells; a fourth was always witty and charming without ever being intellectual; a fifth combined churchiness
with worldliness; another had a curse that drove every
twentieth child insane.

They addressed each other by their first names, even
nicknames. They valued friendships deeply, but could not
be bothered with acquaintances. They repeated family
jokes and preserved family feuds; were very independent
and yet horribly afraid of each other; were very self-satis-
fied and self-distrustful at the same time; were given to
introspection; were quite unpretentious and purse-proud;
were thrifty sometimes to the point of avarice, and yet
handsomely generous in behalf of any good cause or any
good friend. They were serious about their pleasures,
which had to be 'improving,' even ruthlessly 'good'; balls
and theaters actually could not compete with the Lowell
Institute. They disapproved of dressiness; but there were
many who achieved a striking picturesqueness in their
clothes, which was more appropriate to themselves than to
the fashions. They were unadaptable: when abroad they

dressed and acted as though they were still in Massachusetts. They were much concerned with Good Form, and accepted eccentricities as wholly natural. They avoided visible emotions and original ideas; they encouraged talent, disliked genius in the making, adored it when it was proved, and boasted of it when it was established.

Everybody was somebody, distinguished if not brilliant. The New England Conscience caused Bostonians to disapprove flatly of wasting either time or money on frivolities; the celebrities of the Saturday Club pitched the intellectual level high; consequently every person strove to be notable for something — administering a charity, painting china, collecting books, or even leading the german expertly. Less was expected of the women, but when they broke loose, they did so in remarkable ways. They might become sportswomen, like Louisa Wells; astonishing hostesses, like Mrs. Gardner; or artists, like Mrs. Whitman; or they might vie with the men as wits, like Rufus Choate's daughters, Mrs. Pratt and Mrs. Bell.

Genealogy was a very popular hobby; and at every social gathering were many who could announce the precise degree of relationship between any two persons there. Yet, curiously, they were all but unanimous in detesting their Puritan ancestors, who they vowed were as dismal and dour-faced a lot as ever existed. They blamed them for everything they were not, or fought against. The founders of the Bay Colony, they insisted, were narrow-minded, hypocritical, cruel, and superstitious fanatics who combined all the worst traits of the Dark Ages and Victorianism in a general onslaught against innocent pleasures. The Puritan practice of frankness, of the public confession of sins, as a means of improving their status, furnished what seemed like historical justification. Massachusetts had led the world in getting rid of witchcraft; but Judge Sewall's public admission of error gave the Bostonians a reputation of being witch-hunters, while other communities, not having repented their executions so openly, pointed the finger of scorn at Boston. Massachusetts had also led the world in abolishing hell-fire; the controversy was so heated that to this day the sulphur-fumes seem to hang peculiarly thick over the Puritan past. So the Bostonians after the Civil War felt very humble and broadminded in condemning their ancestors.

They were also enjoying quite a little fad of Anglophilism. In their first century and a half, they had customarily called England 'home'; then, after having started the War for Independence, they had become violently pro-English again during the War of 1812; and now again, after their horror at England's attitude during the Civil War, they had reverted to their original love. They believed, and said repeatedly, that they were of purer English stock than the English themselves. They preserved the broad *a* in their speech and the *u* in their spelling. Only the English were their social equals. They protected their daughters against the nobility from the Continent; and it is told — and believed — that one great lady, on being informed that she was to entertain visiting royalty on a Thursday, replied that she was sorry: Thursday was the cook's day out. But it is also told, that when a Bostonian was fatuously regretting that he was not a subject of the British Crown, Tom Appleton asked: 'Why do you want to be a subject when you are already such an object?'

But no love of London interfered with their believing in their heart of hearts that Boston was the Hub. They adored their sun-faded city, and kept it a town of rosebrick rising gently to the golden bubble of the State House dome. The narrow streets still follow the tortuous wild-deer paths of Shawmut, as trodden out by William Blackstone's bull. Bostonians preserved the little houses on the Hill, with their black iron-work balconies (so pretty after a snow-fall), preserved the little panes of glass purpled with age, preserved the local ivy. They moved an old church three feet to one side, to preserve it in an epidemic of street-widening. They decapitated a hotel that presumed to rear its head a couple of yards above the official sky-line. They dammed the Charles for a boat-race basin and an esplanade, and turned the Fenway into a park, planting Stony Brook with iris and bordering it with bridle-paths. They set the first example in America for the systematic preservation of natural beauties; and for many years they had the largest park area of any city in the world. They got the world's greatest artists (chiefly American) [1] to decorate their new Public Library, and fought fiercely the question whether a nude bacchante belonged in the courtyard or in the Art Museum. One could hardly cut down a tree without pros and cons in the *Transcript*. Resenting all criticism from outside, they scolded together constantly because the place was not perfect; and one distinguished citizen concluded a commination with the sad confession: 'I'd move away — but where could one move to?'

[1] When Whistler gave up the task of decorating the hall, Puvis de Chavannes was given the job.

CHAPTER II

HEREDITY

'... a name which honors all who bear it ...'

ONE important strand in the history of Massachusetts is the history of the Lowells. It is the story of a family with excellent blood that came over with the earlier colonists, of course starting at the bottom with everyone else; which then rose into the professional world, concentrating its full genius in the loins of one man and his only son, whose descendants then filled Boston with distinguished persons, some of them geniuses, until a popular epigram (which asserted that 'the Cabots speak only to Lowells and the Lowells speak only to God') [1] recorded their eminence at the very pinnacle of Boston society. It was a ruling family composed of individuals who were astonishingly indifferent to the opinions of others, who were much given to public benefactions and public controversies, and who tended to be manufacturers and merchants; judges; poets, scholars, and critics; and horticulturists. To understand Amy Lowell, one must know something of her forebears, for not only did they bulk large in her own consciousness, but actually she was what they made her. Genius is only apparently an exception to the law of predestination; and Amy Lowell — poet, critic, scholar, expert merchant of her own wares, public controversialist, and horticulturist — was a Lowell through and through.

In June, 1639, on the *Jonathan*, Percival Lowle, aged sixty-four, reached Newbury, on the North Shore of Massachusetts Bay, with his wife, children, and grand-

[1] For the history of this poem, which dates back to 1880, see the *New York Times* editorial, 'An Immortal Poem,' July 6, 1923. Miss Lowell once quoted the epigram to a correspondent in China; but her version was unique — in it, the Cabots and Lowells had exchanged places.

children.[1] The first influx of immigrants had cleared the ground; now a better class was coming over. Percival Lowle was a gentleman, in the technical sense of that word: his arms were 'Sable a hand couped at the wrist grasping three darts two in saltire and one in pale all silver. Crest: a stag's head cabossed gold and between the attires a pheon azure.'[2] He was of Norman blood, being tenth in descent from William Lowle of Yardley, County Worcester, England; his mother was a daughter of Edmond and Elizabeth (Penthuit) Percival, of Weston-in-Gordano, and seventeenth in descent from Eudon, Sovereign Duke of Brittany, first cousin to Robert, the father of the Conqueror. Percival Lowle himself, founder of the American Lowell family, was born somewhere in Somersetshire, England, in 1571. At the age of twenty-six, he was Assessor of Kingston-Seymour. He was also a Bristol wholesale merchant, the head of *Percival Lowle and Company*.

In 1639, Charles I and Archbishop Laud were well committed to their fatal scheme of forcing all Britain to conform to the Anglican Church; an army was vainly being dispatched against covenanting Scotland in the 'First Bishops' War'; young John Milton was hurrying home from his interrupted Grand Tour; and the Puritans were being driven across the Atlantic by the thousands. The emigration had its economic side, however; there were

[1] The material in this chapter is taken chiefly from Delmar R. Lowell's *Historic Genealogy* of the Lowells of America, Rutland, Vermont, 1899; Mary Caroline Crawford's *Famous Families of Massachusetts*, Boston, 1930; Lewis Chase's 'Amy Lowell, a Biographical Sketch' (which contains original material furnished by her) in the *English Student*, Shanghai, April 1, 1926; and Miss Lowell's correspondence, especially a letter to Archibald MacLeish, October 16, 1924.

[2] *N.E. Hist. & Gen. Register* (LXXXII, 153) April, 1928. Miss Lowell (letter to MacLeish, Oct. 16, 1924) said that the Lowells were 'one of the thirteen families in New England that have a right to their coat of arms.' That number was augmented to sixty in the first installment of the 'Roll of Arms' registered by the Committee on Heraldry of the New England Historic Genealogical Society (*Register, op. cit.*); many other genuine coats have not yet been authenticated; and there are plenty of American coats outside New England.

those who had more worldly reasons; and old Percival
Lowle with his family was traditionally among those who
came as a result of economic pressure. 'They emigrated
to this country not for any religious reason, but simply because they could not stand the taxes in England,' wrote
Miss Lowell.[1]

In America, Percival Lowle wrote a poem. He was not
very proud of it; but he had it printed, for it celebrated the
death of a friend who was also a famous governor. It was
called *A Funeral Elegie (written many years since) on the
Death of the Memorable and Truly Honourable John Win-
thrope, Esq.*;[2] it ends:

> Here you have *Lowells* loyalty
>   Pen'd with his slender skill,
> And with it no good poetry,
>   Yet certainly good will.
> Read these few verses willingly,
> And view them not with *Momus* eye,
> Friendly correct what is amiss,
> Accept his love that did write this.

A good man, though not a good poet, wrote these lines; the
mixture of learned conceits and halting meter and bad
rhymes does not cancel its earnest sorrow.

On January 8, 1665, the grand old patriarch died at
Newbury, aged 93, bequeathing to his descendants at
least the beginnings of the poetic instinct, along with his
social position and his mercantile ability.

His son and grandson, John and John, Jr. (both born
in England), and his great-grandson Ebenezer (born in
Boston) were remarkable more for the size of their families than anything else. The colony called for progeny,
and they responded handsomely. John, Jr., a cooper, first
brought the family name to Boston. Ebenezer was a cord-

---

[1] Letter to MacLeish, *op. cit.*

[2] Oscar Wegelin: *Early American Poetry*, 2d ed., New York, 1930, vol. 1, p. 51,
no. 252. Winthrop had died at Boston in 1649. The poem was printed as a
quarto broadside at Cambridge in 1665.

wainer, who died at the early age of thirty-six, leaving only six children. It was these children, however, who started the ascent of the family. Ebenezer, Jr., and Michael in their maturity sported the gold-headed canes that befitted prosperous Boston merchants. But the star of the family was John, who became one of the eminent men of his day.

John Lowell, fifth in descent from Percival Lowle and sixth in ascent from Amy Lowell, was the first of the family to go to Harvard, whence he graduated, aged seventeen, in 1721, receiving his A.M. three years later. After two years of preaching, he was ordained in 1726 as pastor of the third church of Newbury (the first in Newburyport) before he was twenty-two. He remained pastor there, in the town of his great-great-grandfather, until his death forty-two years later, in 1767.

The Reverend John Lowell, A.M., distinguished himself in the highest career then open to a Puritan. He was a minister noted for liberality and highly esteemed for scholarship. He was also 'a thrifty man financially and was frequently a purchaser of property, as the records abundantly attest.'[1] He found no inconsistency between worldliness and spirituality. That he believed in the joys of life is abundantly proved by the painted over-mantel which he ordered for his house at Newbury. The left half of the picture represents a romantic landscape of mountains descending to waters, on which float three boats and six swans. The right half of the picture represents an unexpected interior. At a long table sit seven Puritan ministers in wigs, bands, and gowns, all very smiling and jolly. On the table are pipes and tobacco dishes, an open Bible, an inkstand, and manuscript. Once each minister was furnished with an ale-pot, but where those utensils once stood there are now traces of overpainting.[2] An arch,

[1] *Lowell Genealogy, op. cit.*, pp. 22–23.

[2] James Russell Lowell, the Reverend John Lowell's great-grandson, acquired the panel and removed it to Elmwood, where I examined it, by the courtesy of the late Professor A. Kingsley Porter. For a reproduction, see Louise Karr's 'A Council of Ministers,' *Antiquities* (XI, 45–46), January, 1927.

supported by a Corinthian column, frames the scene; on it is inscribed: 'In necessariis unitas: in non-necessariis libertas: in utrisque charitas.' Unity, liberty, and charity in the mid-eighteenth century! His only son learned the meaning of those words.

That son, John Lowell, Jr., graduated from Harvard in 1760 at the age of seventeen. George II died that October; Governor Bernard suggested that Harvard issue an anthology of academic tributes to the late and the new kings; and it was John Lowell's 'honest tribute of an infant muse' that won the guinea prize for the English poem in 'long verse.' *Pietas et Gratulatio Collegii Cantabrigiensis apud Novanglos* appeared at last most handsomely, with a prefatory apology for its tardiness, and much talk of Liberty; John Lowell's poem is the seventh:

> While thro' the british world great GEORGE'S name
> With mournful accents fills the voice of fame,
> Remotest nations catch the doleful sound;
> And groans re-echo at the deep-felt wound:
> The muses' fav'rite sons in clouds arise,
> And trace his shining passage thro' the skies:
> The bards their temples crown with mourning weeds,
> And cypress to the laurel-wreath succeeds,
> While they in plaintive verse their loss deplore:
> For GEORGE their prince and patron is no more....

The times were changing, however. As the Congregational pulpit was now conscientiously abstaining from politics, lawyers were no longer regarded as mere pettifoggers who profited only by stirring up discord. John Lowell, Jr., was one of the young men who foresaw the careers that might open in that sphere; the minister's son was admitted to the bar in 1762.

His cousin Elizabeth married the brother of John Hancock; her sister Anna's husband, Dr. Alline, was a member of the Boston Tea-Party; a third sister, Mary, married the patriot Captain John Barnard. John Lowell himself became an officer in the Newburyport militia, and in 1776 was elected Representative of the General Court from Newburyport. The Evacuation of Boston purged the city of its conservatives — the Hutchinsons, Olivers, Leonards, Chandlers, Coffins, eleven hundred altogether — thus leaving the city free in its liberal tradition for another century. The Whig gentry in the surrounding country moved in to replace them; from Essex county alone came the Parsonses, Pickerings, Lees, Jacksons, Cabots, Lowells, Grays, and Elbridge Gerry.[1] John Lowell, however, was hardly a newcomer; though he had not been born in Boston, there were three generations of Bostonians behind him; and he had uncles and cousins in the city.

He had been a member of the Colonial Congress, and when that body was dissolved by order of Parliament, a member of the Provincial Assembly of Massachusetts which defied England. In the 'Bill of Rights' of 1774 he inserted that proud sentence: 'All men are born free and equal, and have certain natural, essential, and inalienable rights, among which may be reckoned the right of enjoying and defending their lives and liberties' — a sentence better known through Jefferson's rephrasing it in the Declaration of Independence. This sentence, as the courts decided later, abolished slavery in Massachusetts forever; and John Lowell offered his services free to any negro who needed them.

In 1778, he became Representative of the General Court from Boston. In 1782 and 1783 he was a member of the Federal Congress. From 1784 till 1802 he was a Fellow of Harvard College. He was one of the founders of the American Academy of Arts and Sciences, and also of the Massachusetts Agricultural Society, of which he was president for many years. In 1789, President Washington appointed him the first Judge of the United States District Court of Massachusetts. In 1792, Harvard bestowed

[1] Henry Cabot Lodge: *Boston*, London, 1892, p. 167.

upon him the honorary degree of LL.D. In 1801, President Adams appointed him Chief Justice of the United States Circuit Court, which in those days covered four states. The next year he died at Roxbury.

The Honorable and Judge John Lowell, LL.D., had three wives, and by each wife a son: John III, the great-grandfather of Amy Lowell; Francis Cabot, for whom the city of Lowell was named; and Charles, the father of James Russell Lowell. These men and their descendants are those who (virtually without exception) fill the Lowell drawer in library catalogues. In spite of Mendel, the ways of heredity are still obscure; and biographers usually pay gallant tribute to the mothers of great men; but, as one of the Lowells later remarked, 'the family has proved a singular instance of prepotence in the male line, while the temperament has been as strikingly a maternal gift.' [1]

The merest listing of the achievements of the two younger sons and their children and grandchildren would bulk too large here, and would merely leave a confused impression that the high places of Boston were permeated with Lowell poets, manufacturers, diplomats, judges, historians, ministers, and educators. We must limit ourselves therefore to the single line of John Lowell III.

John Lowell III was born at Newburyport in 1769; when he was seven, the family removed to Boston, in the wake of the retreating Tories; he graduated from Harvard in 1786; and following his father's profession, was admitted to the bar when he was twenty-one. He worked so hard at law that his health failed in 1803, but he had been so successful that he was able to retire and travel in Europe for three years, where Irving wrote of meeting him on October 14, 1804.

Returning, he plunged at once into public affairs, and became one of the leading Federalists. The great conflict

[1] Percival Lowell: 'Augustus Lowell,' *Proc. Amer. Acad. Arts & Sci.* (xxxvii, 635), August, 1902.

between Napoleon and England was on. America was the only important neutral nation; its merchant-marine (almost entirely from New England) prospered richly; and presently the English began their seizure of American sailors and ships on various specious pretexts. As usual, Boston was bitterly divided — so bitterly that one still finds traces of those ancient quarrels in and between families whether to sympathize with French liberalism (overlooking the execution of Louis XVI and the coronation of Napoleon) or to regard England as the bulwark of civilization against the all-destroying principles of Jacobinism (overlooking her hostilities past and present). The *Leopard* fired upon the *Chesapeake;* the country went crazy; and John Lowell defended England in a speech that alienated John Quincy Adams forever from Federalism.[1] Another of his opponents was Edward Everett. President Jefferson attempted to prevent further trouble by the Embargo of 1807, which stopped American ships from sailing; he closed Boston harbor as effectively as George III had done. Merchant vessels rotted at their wharves, the ship-yards were closed, the fisheries were abandoned, the populace soon was starving. Five years later, the Embargo had scarcely been repealed, when President Madison declared war on England, whose raiding ships then might be seen daily from Boston roof-tops. John Lowell's articles and pamphlets, signed 'The Boston Rebel' or 'The Norfolk Farmer,' voiced New England rage. His advocacy of Secession paved the way for the Hartford Convention;[2] but its resolutions did not reach Washington until the war was ending and the trouble was virtually over.

[1] James Truslow Adams: *The Adams Family*, Boston, 1930, p. 136. Miss Lowell, who regretted the fall of French liberalism (see 'Sea-Blue and Blood-Red'), did not sympathize with her great-grandfather's politics. 'He opposed the War of 1812 and affirmed England's right to impress American seamen — a singular point of view,' she wrote, in an unpublished manuscript of 1916.

[2] Samuel Eliot Morison: *Maritime History of Massachusetts*, Boston, 1921, p. 210.

There was more work awaiting the 'Boston Rebel.'
The city, sick of the Angry God, hell-fire, and an over-
elaborate supernaturalism in general, was rapidly going
Unitarian. In 1782, the congregation of King's Chapel
had declared itself converted (it was the first American
church to do so); the Episcopalian Church claimed the
building; and a famous law-suit let the congregation keep
both the old building and the new creed on condition that
the Episcopalian liturgy be used as far as possible. In
1804, the Unitarian Dr. Ware was given the Hollis
Professorship of Divinity at Harvard. John Lowell
entered the controversy by pamphleteering for the liberals.
To Jedidiah Morse's test question, 'Are you of the Boston
religion or of the Christian religion?' he retorted Yankee-
wise: 'Are you a Christian or a Calvinist?'

The 'Norfolk Farmer' was also known as 'the Colum-
ella of the Northern States.'[1] His interest in scientific
agriculture was so great that eventually he was recognized
as 'the principal promoter, if not the founder, of scientific
agriculture and horticulture in New England.'[2] He
succeeded his father as president of the Massachusetts
Society for Promoting Agriculture; both were among the
founders of the Massachusetts Horticultural Society; and
John III was one of the leading promoters of the Botanic
Garden of Harvard University. 'Broomley Vale,' his
country estate in Roxbury, was laid out in long walks and
filled with specially grafted trees; according to Miss
Lowell, 'he invented many new species — flowers and
fruit-trees.'[3] His greenhouses were reputed to be the first
in the United States.

> The first orchids grown in America were grown in his
> greenhouse, though not, I think, until after his death.
> The family is still in possession of a number of large azalea

[1] *Hist. Mass. Horticultural Soc.*, Boston, 1880.
[2] *Proc. Am. Acad. of Arts & Sci.* (IX, 408), 1882.
[3] Letter to MacLeish, October 16, 1924.

bushes brought to this country by the famous French landscape gardener, Michaux, to beautify the Middleton place in Charleston, South Carolina. Some of these azaleas he gave to my great-grandfather for his greenhouse, and they still bloom profusely every spring.[1]

John Lowell III was of public service in yet other ways. He was one of the founders of the Boston Athenaeum, that library for shareholders which is one of the city's landmarks. As the first Treasurer he saw it safely through the War of 1812; he then became successively Vice-President and President; and during his lifetime it grew until it was the fifth greatest library in America. He was also a prominent promoter of the establishment of the Massachusetts General Hospital and of the Provident Institute for Savings. Harvard College, of which he was Fellow (1810–32) bestowed on him an LL.D. in 1814. His private charities were so extensive that he employed an almoner to discover 'worthy objects.' His legal talents were offered to the poor gratis. His house at Roxbury was constantly visited by 'the most noted men of science and culture at home and abroad.' Suddenly, while reading a newspaper at his home, on March 12, 1840, he dropped dead.

His only son, John Amory Lowell, also became an 'Honorable' and an LL.D. He was born in Boston in 1798. From 1803 to 1806 he lived in Paris, during the excitement of the First Empire; he particularly remembered the return from Austerlitz. Like his forebears, he kept abreast of the times, for after graduating from Harvard in 1815, he abandoned the family profession of law for the new business of cotton manufacturing.

His uncle, Francis Cabot Lowell, while travelling through England and Scotland, had understood the Industrial Revolution sufficiently to appreciate the need of manufacturing cotton at home. Having seen spinning jennies at work, he returned home and, without mechan-

[1] Amy Lowell: unpublished *ms.*, 1916.

ical drawings or any other aid, he re-invented the machine,
as it were; and these machines of his were the foundation of
the factory system of New England.[1] The town of East
Chelmsford was renamed 'Lowell' in his honor. Though
Jefferson had ruined Massachusetts trade, the State
merely turned its energies into this new field.

John Amory Lowell built the Boott Cotton Mills, of
which he was treasurer and president, and the Massachusetts Cotton Mills, of which he was treasurer and director.
He was president of the Pacific Mills for six years, and an
official of the Suffolk Bank for fifty-nine.

In 1837 he became a Fellow of Harvard College, a position he held for forty years; he was the fourth of his family
to become a member of the Corporation.

The Honorable John Amory Lowell, LL.D., was most
distinguished for his devotion to the Lowell Institute. Its
dying founder, his half-cousin John, Jr., wrote his will sitting
among the ruins of Thebes. He deliberately put the fate
of the Institute into the power of a single trustee, who was
to be absolute autocrat; he did this with John Amory
Lowell in mind. The result was all that he could have
hoped for. The will needed interpretation; the trustee did
so with wise liberality. He fixed the unit of payment as the
current market price of wheat, so that whatever fluctua-
tions might occur in the value of money, the lecturers
would be paid handsomely. Agassiz was only one of the
distinguished foreigners whom he introduced to America
through the Lowell Institute, the successful career of
which was universally acknowledged to be due to the
genius of its first trustee.

Like his father and grandfather, John Amory Lowell
was a controversialist. The pamphlets of his warfare with
Edward Brooks over the disposition of the Boott pro-

---

[1] The family tradition overlooked the Cabot cotton mill at Beverly, Massachusetts, which Washington inspected on October 30, 1789; also the Byfield
factory at Newbury; also the mills at Pawtucket, Rhode Island, which started
with Sam Slater's machinery on December 20, 1790.

perty are still extant. He agreed with Agassiz that Darwin was wrong. He was also the author of a *Memoir of Patrick Tracy Jackson*, the partner of Francis Cabot Lowell, and the builder of the Boston and Lowell Railroad (a scheme popularly ridiculed as 'visionary').

John Amory Lowell's two passions, however, were algebra and botany. He was always setting himself mathematical problems, and the manuscript of a book written by him on that subject is in existence. Soon after he left college, he took up his father's interest in flowers and fruit-trees; eventually 'he was known not only at home but abroad, and was on terms of correspondence, not to say criticism, with botanists of his day.' [1] About 1845 he began his herbarium and fine botanical library. But the financial crisis of 1857 remanded him to business; he gave the books to Harvard and the herbarium to the Boston Society of Natural History.

He was notably well read in the Latin and French literatures, and also was acquainted with the literatures of Germany and Italy. He was a member of the Linnean Society of London, a member of the American Academy of Arts and Sciences, a successful merchant, and was 'connected with many other public, literary, and benevolent enterprises.'

He died at Boston on October 31, 1881, when his granddaughter, Amy Lowell, was seven years old. She always remembered the painted panels of fruit in his dining-room ceiling. Why did they never fall through? What fairy world was behind? What secret passage might lead there? When she acquired her own house, she had those panels set over the doors of her dining-room.

Augustus Lowell, son of John Amory Lowell by his second wife, Elizabeth Cabot Putnam, was born at Boston on January 15, 1830. He was brought up on the Roxbury place, his father driving him in town daily to the Boston

[1] Percival Lowell, *op. cit.*, p. 637.

Latin School. In 1850 he graduated from Harvard. He was not a scholar, however; and this lapse from family tradition troubled him so that, years later, when his son Lawrence was taking the entrance examinations, he had a nightmare. He dreamed that it was his duty to take the college course over again; then, at the end of a year, he realized he could not possibly pass the examinations, although the whole city expected marvels of him. 'At this awful moment he woke — to the pleasing consciousness that his son, not he, would have to pass them on the morrow.'[1]

After graduation, Augustus travelled abroad for a year, after which he went into cotton manufacturing. On June 1, 1854, he married Katherine Bigelow Lawrence, the youngest daughter of the Honorable Abbott and Katherine (Bigelow) Lawrence of Boston. Her family claimed descent from Sir Robert Lawrence, who was given armor by Richard Coeur de Lion for his bravery in scaling the walls of Acre in 1191. Her father had just returned from his post as American Minister at the Court of St. James's. The two centers of the nascent cotton industry of New England were Lowell and Lawrence, one named for Augustus's great-uncle, the other for his father-in-law; doubly involved in the business by birth and by marriage, he became the president or treasurer of many of the mills in the two cities.

The Lawrences, into whose family he had married, were an old north of Boston family, though comparatively late in reaching the city. That arrival, however, had been spectacular: it was the visible proof of the democratic dream that the poor boy, if honest, moral, and earnest, shall inherit the earth. Miss Lowell remembered the tale as follows:

[1] Percival Lowell, *op. cit.*, p. 638. Miss Lowell was dubious about her brother's including this dream in the obituary; he replied August 30, 1901 (see p. 146), having modified the story to avoid giving the impression that their father was idle in college.

Now as to my mother's family, they came over about the same time that my father's came over, and settled in Groton, where they were farmers. Sometime in the late eighteenth, or very early nineteenth, century, I do not now remember which (I am too lazy to look it up, and you cannot use all this stuff anyway), the oldest son of the family went to work in the village store. At that time it was the custom to keep a punch bowl on the counter, from which everyone who came in helped themselves. Amos Lawrence was so profoundly impressed with the viciousness of this habit, that he swore never to touch a drop of liquor himself, and I believe he never did. Some years later [in 1807] he came to Boston and went into another shop there, and, after a year or two, started in business for himself with a capital of [blank] dollars. He immediately sent for his much younger brother, Abbott Lawrence, who was my grandfather. The two were very energetic men; their business was importing English goods to this country, and their credit was so excellent that when the War of 1812 knocked that business on the head, they were able to obtain credit to tide them over until peace was declared.

Immediately upon the advent of peace, Amos Lawrence shipped Abbott over to England, to buy a consignment of English goods, which Abbott did, but arrived with them at the port, where the vessel was to embark, just as the anchor was being drawn up. Abbott hurried his bales and boxes into a row boat, or row boats, and managed to get to the ship before she got under way; but the captain informed him he could spare no sailors to get the goods aboard. Whereupon Abbott climbed up to the deck, seized hold of the hauling tackle himself, and by his personal energy and hard work, got all his things on board in time for the vessel to take them home. By this means A. & A. Lawrence & Co.'s consignment reached America before any other English goods did.

An old business friend of my father's told me that in his boyhood the firm's business literally spanned the globe; that he remembered being down in South America, which was then an almost untravelled region, and seeing a train of pack mules winding along a little foot-path in the Andes bearing bales labelled 'A. & A. Lawrence & Co.'; and the other day I came across a letter from Smyrna in the early nineteenth century by one of the Dabney family, in which the writer said that he had felt quite at home on landing at Smyrna by seeing on the wharf a large pile of boxes labelled 'A. & A. Lawrence & Co.'

Abbott Lawrence was a self-educated man, as he had no time for college, but he educated himself to enormous purpose. When he was still a comparatively young man, he was sent to Congress as a member of the House of Representatives, and eventually became Minister in England — we had no ambassadors in those days — which post he held from 1850 until 1853. My mother was his youngest daughter, and grandfather believed so firmly in the education that he had not had, that my mother spoke seven languages, played five instruments, and sang. I wish the same regimen had been handed out to me; it was not.[1]

The Lowells and the Lawrences, being prominent manufacturers, were inevitably 'Cotton Whigs,' as opposed to the 'Conscience Whigs.' They were aware that the problem of slavery confronting America was not a simple moral one: statecraft and economics, the legal points of the constitution, and justice to property owners, were also involved. Moreover, they were not inclined to believe the worst of people they met at Newport and whose sons at Harvard they entertained. The Honorable Abbott Lawrence, bosom friend of Webster's, was one of the leading anti-Abolitionists. (Amy Lowell, who heard all the arguments still warmly debated at the family dinner-table, and whose great-grandfather had once advocated the secession of New England, always retained a strong sympathy for the South.)

The first child of Augustus and Katherine (Lawrence) Lowell was Percival, born March 13, 1855, and named for the immigrant ancestor ten generations back. The second

[1] Letter to MacLeish, October 16, 1924.

KATHERINE LAWRENCE LOWELL

AUGUSTUS LOWELL

child, Abbott Lawrence Lowell, born December 13, 1856, was named for his maternal grandfather. The twins, Elizabeth and Roger, were born February 2, 1862. Little Roger, however, died on August 31, 1863, from an illness contracted at their summer place in Beverly; Mr. Lowell sold it, and bought another at Lynn. Mrs. Lowell was also dangerously ill, from a strange malady later diagnosed as nervous exhaustion. Consequently in 1864 the family went abroad for two and a half years, wintering in Paris and travelling in the summer. Not till the second summer, under the treatment of a village doctor in the Austrian Salzkammergut, did Mrs. Lowell begin to mend; she never recovered wholly.

When they returned, in the autumn of 1866, the estate in Roxbury was about to be mutilated by a railroad; Augustus Lowell therefore bought a small estate in Brookline, on the western slope of Heath Street. Originally the land had belonged to Loyalists, who fled during the Revolution, after which it was given to the Heath family. In 1800, Mr. Stephen Higginson, who then owned it, and whose sister was Augustus Lowell's great-grandmother, had it laid out by some forgotten expert in landscape gardening, so that the small place looked much larger than it really was. From Heath Street, then a country road, an avenue curved through a wooded park to the front door; on the left were the stables, on the right the sunken garden. The old colonial mansion was pulled down by a subsequent owner about 1863, who put up a modern house which he no doubt thought handsome. He lived in it hardly a year, however, before he sold it to Mr. Lowell.

Here Augustus Lowell was able to express the love of horticulture which he had inherited from his father and his grandfather.

> He covered it with beautiful and exotic flowering shrubs, brought from all parts of the world, and many rare and lovely flowers. The planning of his garden was entirely

done by himself. He never allowed anyone else to make any arrangements or decide upon any matter of change or addition. Some idea of his fondness for flowers may be given when I say that he got up at six o'clock every morning and cut his favourites, the roses, with his own hands. I well remember one occasion when he cut a thousand roses in three days.[1]

In the rear were two greenhouses — about sixty running feet, which supplied the fruit and vegetables for a household of sixteen people.

> Two hot-houses of grapes helped to shield the [sunken garden], which lay in a hollow open to the south. Natural embankments enclosed it on the east and west, and a raised roadway, shut off from view, made artificial protection on the north. Clipped evergreens stood for sentinels along a terraced path, ending in an arbor which fringed one side of it, and a corresponding row faced them upon the slope opposite. In this sheltered spot he spent much of his time. Pruning his shrubs, tying up his plants, and attending generally to the welfare of his flowers, he was almost as much of an inhabitant of the place as they. It was a world in which he found infinite satisfaction. His roses were his chief delight. And fine they were — no finer than the feeling with which he showed them off. But nothing vegetal was alien to him. He would point out with almost as much zest, punctuated by a wink, a foreign thorn-tree, which flanked the avenue, a platted mass of thorns a foot long, the despair of squirrels and cats.[2]

Here was his home; houses in Boston were merely townhouses, which were successively abandoned as soon as the growth of the city made them unattractive.[3] In Brookline

---

[1] Amy Lowell: unpublished *ms.*, 1916.

[2] P. Lowell, *op. cit.*, pp. 643-44.

[3] According to the Boston Directories, Augustus Lowell lived at 7 Pemberton Square (1852-53); 131 Tremont Street (1854-57); 10 Park Square (1858-61); 61 Mt. Vernon Street (1862-63); Brookline (1864-77); 97 Beacon Street and Brookline (1878-79); and 171 Commonwealth Avenue and Brookline (1880-1900).

were the garrets where things could be stored away permanently; the stables for the horses and cows; the countryside for the children to ramble over; and the gardens that one could cultivate from decade to decade.

Besides business and botany, there were various educational institutions for which Mr. Lowell, as one of the family, had certain responsibilities. On the death of his father in 1881, he became the single trustee of the Lowell Institute; his practicality kept it far above any necessity for the customary begging. Yet 'almost all the famous foreigners in science, literature, or art who have been in this country have owed their personal introduction to it to the trustee of the Lowell Institute.' [1]

Of still greater international importance was the Massachusetts Institute of Technology, which had been founded in 1861. Mr. Lowell was elected a member of the Corporation in 1873; and so valuable was his influence that he was elected a member of the executive committee ten years later, a position he held until his death. His petition a year earlier to resign from the Corporation was answered by a unanimous memorial of protest. He was also treasurer and then vice-president of the American Academy of Arts and Sciences, and a member of the American Association for the Advancement of Science, of the Massachusetts Historical Society, and of the Colonial Society of Massachusetts.

Though of slight physique, Augustus Lowell possessed immense energy and it was his habit to rise at four o'clock in the summer and at four-thirty in winter. The before-breakfast hours in summer he used to employ in a swim during the months that the family passed at their country home in Lynn. He 'went in swimming every summer day until he was 80; and he never wore an overcoat!' according to the testimony of his daughter, Elizabeth Lowell Putnam.[2]

[1] P. Lowell, *op. cit.*, p. 646.
[2] Mary Caroline Crawford: *Famous Families of Massachusetts*, Boston, 1930, I, 146.

Mr. Lowell's character was outlined in the sketch of his life by his son Percival, from which we have already quoted so much. He was, like his father and his grandfather, unmistakably a Lowell. 'He inherited the quality of his name. Mentally he was the son of his father; as a matter of fancy as much as of fact, his mother's share in him being chiefly physical.' Everything he did, he did whole-heartedly, and he always 'acted for results.' In him was 'a singular wedding of energy in deed, with dislike of its external trappings,' for he was always self-effacing.

In practical, not in theoretical matters, he was great. Widely read as he was, he never seemed to care to theorize. He enjoyed highly the theories of others, when they did not collide with the puritanism which, as I have said, he inherited doubly distilled. Even this was perhaps as much due to the society in which he was brought up. He was educated before the modern movement in thought took place, and Boston of sixty years ago was even behind the rest of the world in this stirring of the waters of stagnation.

Like his father, he disbelieved in Darwin to the end of his days, nor would he allow a volume of Shelley in the house. He took his pleasures seriously; but he preferred work. Will, ability, and integrity he possessed notably; he was trusted with his many high positions because he was shrewdly right and reliably effective. He could put a point so clearly that the intelligent were converted instantly; for the others, he used tact and persistence. Self-effacing, he was never self-seeking; his cause absorbed him completely. He had, however, a sternness which did not tend to popularity. 'Those qualities compounded of sociability and forth-puttingness, however unintentional, which make for instant distinction among one's fellows, were not his by nature.' He once overheard himself described as 'a hard man but absolutely honest.' This reputation of hardness was perhaps due to the sternness of his countenance when in repose, for actually he was very tender-hearted. 'Few suspected him of the kindnesses he was constantly doing, so unostentatiously were they performed, and almost no one credited him with the affection he felt.' He was, in short, 'too strong a personality to be generally popular.'...

Through these words of his son, we can discern the splendid man, too strong to seem kindly, too proud to seek affection, content to serve his family and his city, knowing that generous work well done requires no recognition, no gratitude.

Meanwhile there was his home in Brookline, with his boys and his girls and his garden. Another little girl, May, was born on May 1, 1870, only to die the same day. Four years later, on February 9, 1874, the last of his children was born: Amy. His family was complete: he named his home 'Sevenels,' for now it sheltered seven Lowells.

CHAPTER III
THE CHILD
'Just a little nearer, moon.'

On Monday, February 9, 1874, Amy Lowell was born at the Lowell place on 70 Heath Street, Brookline, Massachusetts. Her mother had been suffering from an old complaint, and the late birth was somewhat precarious. Little Amy was very much the youngest of the five children: Percy (nearly nineteen) was a sophomore at Harvard; Lawrence (seventeen) was a freshman; and her two sisters were respectively sixteen and twelve. They nicknamed her 'the Postscript'; and in future years, when she constantly found it impossible to be on time, they assured her it was really not her fault — she was born late.

The parents named the baby after her great-aunt Amory, who had died two months before; 'Amory,' however, was softened to 'Amy,' somewhat to the annoyance of Miss Lowell later on.

> I object strongly to my own name of Amy, but as it happens to be my name, and as I have never cared for the *nom de plume* attitude, I wrote my first book over that name, and now, although I should like to adopt a different Christian name (one to which I am really entitled) I find myself brought up against the fact that I am known as Amy Lowell, so I have decided to stick to it. The reason that this is peculiarly annoying is that I was named after an aunt of my father's, whose name was Rebecca Amory Lowell. This combination was, I think, fine and strong, but the poor lady was always called Amory, during her life, and as my mother did not like a surname as a Christian name for a girl, she took a name which she thought sounded like Amory. It is a foolish, fancy name, and utterly unlike me, and I wish now that I had published my first book under the name of Rebecca Amory Lowell; but, as I did not, and as I am now known, it is too late to change.[1]

[1] Letter to Winifred Bryher, November 4, 1918.

The little girl was christened 'Amy Lowell' on July 5 at St. Paul's Church, Brookline, by the Reverend William H. Newton, the sponsors being her brother Lawrence and her two sisters Kate and Elizabeth. She was to be brought up an Episcopalian: the Lawrences were all devout members of that church; and her second cousin William was already well on the way to succeeding Phillips Brooks as the Bishop of Massachusetts.

When she was two years old, she drove the pair of horses to and from church, one fine Sunday. The coachman, of course, hung the reins on his finger, lest they slip from her tiny grasp.[1] It is the first act of hers that we can date; like all her acts, it was typical of her, for to the end of her life she loved animals, and she adored driving, until the automobiles spoiled that pleasure, even at Dublin, N.H.

Sevenels was the setting of her childhood. An imaginative child can make an Eden out of almost any place on earth; very few, however, have the privilege of growing up in such a place as the Brookline estate. Amy Lowell's entire life was suffused with her home.

Sevenels makes a corner where two roads join. They are streets now, with numbers, but I remember them as unfrequented country roads. The place is surrounded by a wall of uncemented pudding-stone over which predatory boys have made it impossible to grow vines. There is an entrance on each road flanked by heavy stone posts, and just inside the wall runs a wide belt of trees, mostly elms, but with just enough evergreens to keep the whole inviolate from the eyes of passers-by.

Within this belt of trees runs a wide meadow, kept for mowing, in June a glory of daisies and buttercups nodding in the wind, a paradise to a child, as I well remember. On the inner side, this line of trees is brightened by clumps of red-buds and hawthornes, in Autumn two or three copper

[1] Mrs. William Lowell Putnam: 'A Glimpse of Amy Lowell's Childhood by her Sister' (ms.).

beeches and several crimson maples keep colour always playing against the wall of green.

Beyond the meadow begins the grove. A little handful of land so cunningly cut by paths and with the trees so artfully disposed that one can wander happily among them and almost believe that one is walking in a real wood. In earliest Spring, snowdrops begin to glisten in the sunny spots under the trees to be followed by such masses of crocuses that I never see them without thinking of Chaucer's 'pied mead.' These give place to great drifts of daffodils in the hollows, and patches of lilies-of-the-valley, and under the beeches is a colony of painted trilliums. Later in the summer, the little stars of the potentilla mingle with wild strawberry blooms, and that abominable nuisance, bishop's weed, a great mass of marching white flowers, is really beautiful here, although it must be cut down before it seeds. Under the horse-chestnut trees, by the avenue, monkey-wort makes a soft trailing carpet and native rhododendrons are clumped here and there in the shade. One could put the whole grove in one's pocket, but as a child it seemed to me limitless, and many are the Indians I have shot when out scouting with my bow and arrows as they peered for a moment behind a distant tree trunk, and, in spite of a little confusion in my mind as to whether I were Robin Hood or the Last of the Mohicans, I delight to record that I never missed my man.

On the lawn beside the avenue grows the largest pink horse chestnut I have ever seen. I used to call it the bee-tree, for bees frequent it so assiduously that it sounds like a hive in blossoming time.

The house itself stands in the midst of lawns and grass terraces. The South Lawn, fringed by trees and bordered with hybrid rhododendrons and azaleas, drops sheerly down to a path, at one end of which is an old-fashioned arbour covered with wisteria and trumpet-vine, and two flights of stone steps lead into a formal sunken garden. But the real entrance to the garden is by a gradually descending path from the avenue.

I do not know if the garden was artificially blasted out,

or if the designer made use of a natural basin, but now it lies some twenty feet below the South Lawn, its surrounding terrace planted with alternate clipped hemlocks and flowering trees. It is so warm, and sunny, and protected here, that everything blooms early and blooms much. But all gardeners will appreciate the difficulties when I say that one can walk all round every bed, and that the garden must be kept in perennial bloom from April until October.

On the other side of the house, lawns, shrubberies of magnolia and lilac, and a pine plantation lead to the hot beds (so called because they are cold frames) which is really a cutting and vegetable garden, and a fruit garden runs up the side of the hill where grow apple and pear trees, more vegetables, strawberries, and all the thousand and one experiments to be set out near the house later on....

Having been brought up with flowers I should know something about them, but alas! I always took them absolutely for granted. Now that I have the ordering of them, I am unreasonably annoyed at both my own ignorance and nature's caprices. Why, for instance, will clematis Jackmani flourish year after year on two of my trellises and die annually on the third?...

... It is all tiny, as things go nowadays, but it is also very cosy and compact, and an object lesson as to what nine and a half acres can be made to do. There is no view, no pond or brook, no long sweep of park land, but I know every tree, every rock, every flower, as only children know these things and that is something which if forfeited can never be captured again.[1]

To a correspondent she once wrote: 'A mocking bird is my earliest recollection, for my father adored them, and we always had one in a cage, poor creature, when I was a child.'[2]

She also adored the carved wooden animal heads in the front hall, which she was lifted up to pat on the way to and

[1] Amy Lowell: 'Sevenels, Brookline, Massachusetts,' *Touchstone* (VII, 210–18), June, 1920.
[2] Letter to Richard Hunt, May 27, 1918.

from dinner. When she redecorated Sevenels she left the hall as it was, for the sake of those heads; and all her life the nose of the animal nearest the dining-room showed the shine which her constant patting had given it.

The stables were part of the attractive out-of-doors at Sevenels. The mysteries of the dark building, the fascination of the great animals, the tumult preceding a drive — all these stirred deeply the imagination of the little girl. When at last the carriage appeared, little Amy was sure to be perched on the box beside Burns; indeed, it was a Boston joke that 'Amy Lowell was brought up by the coachman.'

Burns was a character. In youth he had been a jockey at Newmarket; now his increasing years and weight had made the coach-box more appropriate. He served the Lowells from 1867 until his death many years later. 'He knew more about horses than anyone I have ever seen, and though, if he could read at all it was very little, association with him was, in its way, quite a liberal education. Amy was brought up with good horses.... All she knew about horses, and she knew a great deal, was learnt from him.' [1] There is a tale that once, when the two sisters were going for a drive, Bessie, with the authority of twelve additional years, bade Amy get her a coat, and Amy refused. Burns, however, repeated the command, and Amy obeyed promptly. When she was asked why she obeyed the coachman and not her sister, she replied earnestly: 'Oh, Burns was *born* to command.'

On Bessie, the youngest sister, fell the task of disciplining Amy. According to her account:

> It is almost certain to be hard for the youngest of a considerable family, for they are apt to be spoilt by the parents and likely to be 'picked on' by the other children. Amy was too much younger than the rest to suffer much from the latter trouble for it arises usually from jealousy, and

[1] Mrs. William Lowell Putnam: *op. cit.*

you are not jealous of a baby if you are nearly grown up, unless you are a very silly child indeed. She did suffer from the spoiling, however, and, from what is even worse, from spasmodic discipline. Parents who have devoted much time and energy for many years to bringing up a family are tired and want to rest, and so a belated child is not apt to be disciplined except when he or she annoys the weary parent. This was very much the case with Amy, and she was never taught self-control unless it affected their personal comfort. I do not blame them for this, for they were not young, and my mother, before long, developed the disease which, after invaliding her for many years, caused her death. The disease was one to make the sufferer intensely nervous and often irritable and unreasonable, and this could not but worry my father, and was, of course, hard for all of us, but particularly hard for a child, who, because she was a child, was likely to be constantly at home.

Almost the only discipline Amy got was what I gave her when we happened to be alone together at home. I well remember one occasion when I told her that if she did or did not do something she could not go to a neighbor's party the next day, which she counted on going to. I forget what the prohibition was but it was probably connected with her devoted and long suffering nurse, to whom she yielded but scant obedience, although they adored one another. Amy did the forbidden thing, and great were her surprise and disgust when no entreaties prevailed the next day and she was obliged to stay at home from the party. We often laughed about this episode in later years, and I suspect that I laid the foundation then of her affection for me, which was I believe peculiarly deep and tender, for Amy was able to see things very fairly and justly....

It was partly Amy's cleverness that caused her lack of discipline for she was very amusing, which sometimes made discipline difficult. If there was a joke at supper which made everybody laugh and so caused general good feeling, Amy would ask, 'On the strength of that, can't I sit up later tonight?'

Little Amy, in fact, suffered the privileges and dis-
advantages of arriving between generations, as it were.
Three of her four grandparents were born in the eighteenth
century; and though the two Lawrences died before she
was born, the two Lowells lived until she was seven. Nor
did their influence end then, for the books given them and
also those they had chosen for their children were passed
down to her. Her parents were half a generation too old to
discipline her; they had brought up too many children, to
respond to the novelty of coping with a new and stubborn
personality. Her brothers and sisters were grown men and
women by the time she was ten; and always they were too
old and too engrossed in their own interests to give her the
salutary bullying which most children in large families get.
Besides, the Lowells were individualists: each believed in
doing what he or she liked best, as long as it was done
worthily; consequently it was wrong to interfere in the
deeds of another. Only too often a genius is born into a
conventional circle, where conformity tries to crush out
his 'eccentricities'; but the Lowells had learned to let each
other alone, and to cultivate their own particular excellences. They believed in positive attainments and preferences; each one chose his career of writing, judging,
preaching, or what not, regardless of and unassisted by the
others; and they showed absolutely no fear of loneliness
from not running with the crowd. So little Amy ran wild
at Sevenels, where there was nobody near her own age;
she was let do much as she pleased; she bent her wits to
getting round grown persons (a habit she retained all her
life). She evaded difficulties, explored the greenhouses,
haunted the stables, teased her adoring nurse, grew up
out-of-doors. She played among the flowers; she hunted
ghosts and Indians in the grove; she rode with Burns on the
coachman's box. At the elaborate family dinners she
listened to them talk (the Lowells were famous for their
brilliant conversations) and joined in with an occasional
joke of her own.

One subject often recurred: the Civil War. In the earlier Abolition days, the Lowells and Lawrences were 'Cotton Whigs,' or Southern sympathizers; but naturally, when the war broke out, they went solidly on the side of the North, and it would seem that their attitude was confirmed by the reports of Southern atrocities on the battlefields and in the prison-camps of Libby and Andersonville. Writing to John Drinkwater (October 9, 1919) about his *Lincoln,* she said:

> Somehow I have never been able to touch the Civil War, or anything approaching it, in my work, perhaps because it was the nightmare of my childhood. I was not born until ten years after it was over, but I was surrounded by stories about it, and feeling in my family still ran high although the war was over. I was brought up on war songs, and the whole thing assumed at once the horror of actual happening and the mysticism of a legend. To this day, I cannot see a uniform of the period without a feeling of distinct fear; and last year, when I was in Richmond giving a reading, and went through the old museum there, it seemed to me as if those old Confederate uniforms would walk out of their cases and I should feel the touch of a yellow, gauntleted hand upon my shoulder. It is curious how these impressions last. I cannot make the Civil War a thing of flesh and blood; it always seems to be a war of demons and angels, and to this day the Southern accent fills me with terror, as something sinister might, all of which is nonsense as I have known many Southerners and liked them; but this seems to be the effect of the early impression.

She was supposed to rise promptly, although she was never in a hurry to obey her father's stern schedule and leave the land of dreams; she was scolded for reading in bed at night; she heard visitors told sternly that they ought *never* to blot on a big clean blotter; she watched her father and the boys playing billiards, watched her brothers study, watched them writing. Sometimes they unbent and played jackstones with her; at other times they waved her away, saying that she was too little to play chess. There were distinguished visitors: relatives, particularly the great Cousin James, and famous men from abroad came to lecture at the Lowell Institute. But in Sevenels there was nobody near her age; whereas the playmates she eventually acquired, from the neighboring estates, were brought up under somewhat newer ideas. Consequently she was precocious and yet late in developing, old-fashioned and yet eventually a leading modernist.

When she was four, Mr. Lowell took 97 Beacon Street for his town-house; thereafter the winters were spent away from Sevenels, to which they returned about May Day, when the gardens really began blooming again.

On February 4, 1879, she was five years old; from that time the anecdotes begin to multiply.

> Amy was, of course, a very clever child and my father was very proud of her intelligence. One day on his return from Lowell, where he had been to inspect a mill of which he was then Treasurer, he told my mother of a visit he had paid at the agent's house, where he had seen his little daughter of five, just Amy's age. He commented on the child's stupidity, for he found that she did not know her own age. To show Amy off to himself, he called her to him and asked her how old she was; and it was quite amusing to see how his opinion of the other child changed when he found that Amy knew no more than the other child how old she was.[1]

One of the events of this year which must have filled the little girl with rapturous excitement was the marriage of her brother Lawrence to Anna Parker Lowell (a third cousin, also descended from the Honorable and Judge Lowell), on June 19, 1879, at King's Chapel, Boston.

And if at five one begins to remember things, it was perhaps in this year that her 'educationally-forethoughted parents' took her to a dinner-party, 'to see the great ones of the earth.' It was an event for her: 'Mr. Longfellow

[1] Mrs. William Lowell Putnam: *op. cit.*

carried me round the table in a scrap-basket, and the recollection of that ride is quite as vivid as though it were
yesterday.'[1]

In these early years, she would be called downstairs to
amuse her mother's guests. She did her part to sustain the
family tradition of brilliant conversation, with a series of
really clever puns. After the guests had laughed awhile,
she would inquire brightly: 'Want to hear any more puns?'
If they said they did, she would oblige; but more often
they said no, whereupon she ran away.

Of course, a Lowell, even though a girl, required education; and Amy, like many another child in or near Boston,
was 'always taken to everything that was supposed to
have any educational value.'

> Once upon a time, when I was a little girl, I was taken to
> a Mechanics' Fair, or something of that kind... and a
> specimen box of spools of coloured silk took my fancy.
> One particular colour, which as I remember was a pecu-
> liarly fascinating cherry red, I lost my heart to so com-
> pletely that I persuaded my mother to buy a spool of it in
> order that I might have it with me all the time and feast
> my eyes upon its tint.[2]

The episode was characteristic of her — characteristic
not only for her passionate devotion to 'things' (which
later expressed itself so handsomely in her jewels, books,
furniture, and paintings), but also for her fondness for red,
which was offset by her hatred of magenta. No magenta
flower was ever allowed in her garden.

But she did not always get what she wanted. She remembered bitterly the day when she was given a tricycle,
for a small boy who lived near was given a velocipede at
the same time. Indignant at this discrimination against

[1] Amy Lowell: 'Early Years of the Saturday Club,' New York Times, March
23, 1919.
[2] Letter to MacLeish, October 16, 1924.

her sex, she bullied him into swapping, and was still more indignant when her parents refused to allow it.

When she was five or six, she began to learn reading and writing from her governess, an Englishwoman, who, however, could never teach her to spell, although Miss Lowell insisted on the *-our* ending throughout her life.

The earliest examples of her handwriting are to be found in *The Holiday Painting Book* (*n.d.*), in which the outlines are filled in quite carefully, with surprising success at not going over the edge. The pictures themselves are further described in a large and painful hand:

> [Title-page] This little boy has mad this raft and now is plaing on it. His frinds ar coming to play with him.
>
> ['A Native'] This little boy has leved her all his lif so he nos the plas. He has mad a big fort hav you ever ben to the sea?
>
> ['A Visitor'] This little girl has never plyd in the sand befor. She liks to romp. She is goin to a parte.
>
> ['In the Fields' — a girl holding a bunch of wild flowers.] This girl is plying in the fealds. She has gardes thes forars.
>
> ['In the Orchard'] This boy is eightn appels in the orght. he is goin to walk now.

In 1880, the Beacon Street house was given up, and the family removed to 171 Commonwealth Avenue for winter quarters.

It was about this time, perhaps on her sixth birthday, that she began collecting books with a copy of *Rollo Learning to Read*. It was not actually the first book she ever owned, for in 1878 two books had been given her: Watts' *Divine and Moral Songs*, printed on linen for children, and *Merry Elves or Little Adventures in Fairyland* — an oddly assorted pair. But *Rollo Learning to Read* was the first book she ever craved passionately to own; it was the first book she acquired for herself; it was therefore, spiritually if not technically, the first of the twelve thousand volumes she accumulated.

I perfectly remember the awakening of the acquisitive instinct for which it was directly responsible. The book... had been given to my mother when she was six years old, and on her mother's birthday, as an inscription in the pointed, careful writing of my grandmother duly testifies. I suppose it was brought out for my amusement, but it aroused such a passion of covetous desire in my small mind as to shake it to its foundations. The mere touch of that straight-grained morocco was a delight, the old wood-cuts, coloured with crayons doubtless by my mother, were to me gems of the purest art. I do not know that any pictures since have been quite so enchanting as those wood-cuts. Could I read at that date? I doubt it. But I demanded the stories again and again, I verily believe I could repeat them by heart now, if I were put to it. Obviously the book was given to me, for when a tenacious heart knows its goal few can withstand it, certainly not an affectionate and sympathetic mother.

The best of Rollo was that there were so many of him. There they were in a long line behind the glass doors of a high bookcase in the middle hall. Between them, my father and mother had been given the whole set as they came out, and before this bookcase it was my delight to sit most precariously upon a strange old arm-chair, which turned upside down and opened into a pair of library steps, and fumble for them behind more important volumes. The chair had an unpleasant habit of shutting up suddenly and catching one's foot, which was extremely painful, but this added a spice of danger to the proceeding which was not without charm. As Jason won the Golden Fleece, passing through many perils, so I won the Rollo books, at the cost of many a pinch and bruise.

But I won them, inside and out! One by one, I read them all, and acquired them through the child's immemorial right of wheedling; and, one by one, they passed from the middle hall to the hideous and beloved ash bookcase in my nursery.

But her friends refused with scorn to like Jacob Abbott's books.

> I used to try to make them, I used to read select passages out loud to all my small acquaintance, but they never 'took.' Yet obstinate little creature that I was, the scorn of my fellows did not in the least tarnish my admiration...
>
> ... I found no strangeness in the Rollo atmosphere; my friends did.... I can only account for my 'getting' Rollo, by the fact that I was surrounded by so many of his things, as it were. In 'Rollo Learning to Read,' the little boy is taught by means of round cards, with a picture on one side and a letter on the other. This must have been a favorite plaything, for my mother had just such a set of cards, and I inherited them as I had the books. In 'Rollo's Vacation,' the children make little folded paper packages to hold the flower-seeds gathered in the garden. Many is the time I have watched my father make these folders, and gone out with him gathering seeds. It was all true to life as I knew it.[1]

Miss Lowell's admiration for the Rollo books never waned; it was the life of real New England children, with everything except the imagination; and even there she remembered particularly 'a delightful passage where Rollo, going up to his room at night to get a book, encounters the moon' — indeed a vivid passage, especially vivid to her who loved both moon and books; to be found by the curious in *Rollo's Vacation*.

On September 17, 1880, was celebrated the two hundred and fiftieth anniversary of the founding of Boston; surely the little girl of six remembered something of the parades. In the next year (the year of Garfield's assassination) her two Lowell grandparents died: Mrs. Lowell on February 12, and John Amory Lowell on October 31, 1881.

By now the child's year was in full swing: New Year's;

[1] Amy Lowell: 'That Bookcase' (*ms.*); published in New York *Evening Post*, September 18, 1920. In this chapter I have also drawn upon 'Books I Liked as a Child,' *Evening Post*, November 8, 1919.

her birthday and valentines and the dog show and Washington's birthday in February; April Fool's Day and Easter; May baskets and the May festival and the moving out to Sevenels; the summer vacation at Lynn, where Mr. Lowell had taken a summer cottage — he bathed every morning before breakfast; Fourth of July (the perihelion); the return to Sevenels when the September leaves changed; the moving back to Commonwealth Avenue when it got really cold; Hallowe'en; the Thanksgiving dinner; then the secret making and buying of Christmas presents, the performance of the *Messiah* by the Handel and Haydn Society, and at last Christmas Day itself (aphelion of the child's year).

By the age of six, Amy must have been going to dancing school; many children started earlier. *The* Boston dancing school was Papanti's, with its spring floor which could emit such clouds of dust on great occasions. All the lights were controlled by a single valve, which daring boys loved to shut off. Mr. Papanti himself was a little old gentleman in a wig, who fiddled while he demonstrated the steps. One kept on going to Papanti's until one 'came out.'

Directly opposite Papanti's was the Boston Museum, now Boston's oldest and proudest theater. It had actually begun as a museum of those curiosities which reached the old seaport; attached was a 'lecture room' in which the first American vaudeville was performed as an added attraction. When it became a regular theater, the old name was retained, partly to placate the godly who still thought the stage essentially evil; the cynics who saw through the device nicknamed the place 'the deacons' theater.' The famous stock company produced the best plays, old and new, that were proper for young and old; it became virtually a family institution. The Lowells were habitual theatergoers; and little Amy accompanied them as soon as she was able to behave. The Boston Museum became one of her favorite spots, not only for the plays but for the col-

lections, then still to be seen: the portraits of almost all the
Boston clergy, Sully's huge 'Washington Crossing the
Delaware,' the stuffed animals, the mummies, and best of
all the dusty wax figures: the murder of Jane McCrae, the
murder of the drunkard's wife, the rake's progress, the
pirates' cabin, and other moral-pointing subjects. Besides
the plays at the Boston Museum, Amy was taken regularly
to hear all the great actors and singers.

In this period of struggle with the double difficulties of
calligraphy and orthography, she made one of her bright
remarks, which eventually got into print, and probably
gave her her first taste of the joys of publicity. It appeared
as a joke in *Life*, entitled 'A Short Way Out of It.'

> Papa — But why do you sign it: 'Your loving son, Amy?'
> Amy — Why, of course mamma will know, and I couldn't
> spell daughter.[1]

In 1882, Amy started a 'Private Book,' which contains
her first character sketches — brief but stinging comments
on friends, who are disguised under classical names, then
identified by a key several pages further on. There we
learn that 'Medusa' (or more briefly 'Mu') was Miss May.

Mu's caracter

> Mu. is my nerse she is very funny and a big bore when she
> comes after me we sometimes run away then she gets mad
> and scolds when she gets mad it is great fun when you have
> somebody with you but when you get home it is not so
> much fun.
>   That is all about Mu.

Over 'Pomona,' or Eleanor Payson, however, she waxed
enthusiastic.

[1] A clipping of a reprint of the joke was found in one of her childhood books.
John Tyler Wheelwright probably sent it to *Life*. A charter editor of the *Harvard Lampoon* (founded 1876), to which Lawrence Lowell contributed some puns,
Wheelwright was naturally interested in *Life*, which was founded in 1883 by
ex-Lampooners. Wheelwright constantly sent Boston jokes to *Life*, sometimes
to the dismay of his friends who did not expect the publicity.

Pomona's caracter

Pom is the girl I lick best she said she liked me the best of any except her one cousens I think. I even think her nicer than Me [a friend characterized elsewhere] words canot express my ~~fleeinngs fleeings~~ feelings towards her. That is all about Pom.

On page 21 we find later comments:

Why are children such fools? Amy Lowell, 1890
Are they such fools, I wonder? I am inclined to think not. Amy Lowell. 1905.

In the summer of 1882, the parents and the girls toured Europe, dashing through Scotland, England, France, Belgium, Holland, Italy, Germany, Norway, Denmark, and Sweden, 'travelling at a fearful rate of speed.' Hitherto the little girl had been allowed to do pretty much as she wished — her parents, as she later claimed, had spoiled her until she was eight; but wilful ways and European tours are incompatible; and it was probably on this trip that they changed their tactics and 'went to the other extreme.' It was Bessie, however, who as next of age was immediately in charge of her; and she has preserved the following memory:

... Paper dolls... beguiled many a long railroad journey. My father and mother took their three daughters abroad when Amy was only eight years old and I used to make these dolls for her in the train, following most minute directions from her as to details of themselves and their appurtenances. We made, by the hour together, every conceivable adjunct for the comfort and welfare of these families, from dust pans and brushes to umbrellas and things which it taxed my ingenuity to construct. Amy loved these dolls and they went everywhere with her. As they were small, and could all, together with their belongings, be put in an envelope, they made excellent traveling companions; and a pencil and piece of paper, a pair of scissors, my watercolor paint box — which I always carried with me anyway — and some paste made her independent of any other amusement. These dolls she always preserved and they are, I believe, now at Harvard in the bookcase where she always kept her childhood treasures.

One memento of the trip was a glass bead, made for her at Venice, with her initials and the year on it. Another memento was 'Amy's Journal,' a small, dutiful record of daily occurrences occasionally illustrated with small German decalcomanias. It begins on 'July 30th, Sunday' at Berlin. Evidently it was written under supervision as the calligraphy is painfully clear and the spelling perfect. The only entry of interest is: 'August 2. I read the Stokesley secret till 5 o'clock' — this book being Charlotte M. Yonge's tale of the trials of a very correct and Anglican governess with a brood of children so unattractive that one is forced to conclude that Miss Yonge hated children. After eleven pages of impersonal facts, the Journal stops on August 19 at the Lake of Como. Then promptly the little girl, released from facts and supervision, burst forth into fiction:

the horse and the cat.

there was once a horse and a cat the horse weas good and the cat was bad. they had a fight the horse beet. that is all.

But the most vivid impression of the whole trip was made by the notorious 'Iron Virgin' at Nuremberg, that supposed relic of the Middle Ages, which was actually constructed of tin in 1867.

My brain was so stimulated by the sights I saw, and by this rate of travel, that I was fearfully ill. An injudicious governess having taken me to see the tortures at Nuremburg, for months afterwards my nights were made horrible by visions of the Iron Virgin. The return home, however, and the tranquil life which ensued, averted what I think might easily have been a serious nervous breakdown, if not brain fever, although it was many years before I recovered my nerve and before I ceased to be afraid of the dark.[1]

The family returned home in the fall, and on December 5, 1882, Katherine was married to Alfred Roosevelt (first cousin to Theodore Roosevelt, later President) at St. Paul's, Brookline.

It was when she was eight years old — that is, probably in 1882 — that she went to a party, where a large plate of rice was set before her. Her brother dared her to eat a second plate — she did — but when they prepared to go home, her coat would not button across her stomach. 'And it never buttoned again,' Miss Lowell said, describing the episode. It was the first manifestation of her physical maladjustment.

In the spring of 1883 she was taken out west, and again she was persuaded to begin a journal, entitled *Notes of my trip to and from California*. She began dutifully by jotting down things she saw from the window of the train, such as a sign which read 'Billiards.' But in the description of the first night in the Pullman we find the first genuine evidence of literary ability.

> After supper we came back to the car, and Bessie, Miss Hodges, Miss Chapman and I played whist. Bessie and I were partners, and Miss Chapman and Miss Hodges. I think they beat but I am not sure.
>
> Then I went to bed and I think the others followed soon. It was very hot and the sheets were course, so sleep forsook me at first. I felt thirsty so Bessie got me some water, then as we had had supper at about half-passed five I was very hungry and had to have a cracker before I could go to sleep. But by the time the others were ready for bed I was ready for sleep.
>
> I pulled up the shades of one of my windows (you know there are two in every birth) and looked out it was very dark and I could not see much except at the stations which are of course lighted up at one (which I found out

Amy Lowell: *ms.*, 1916.

in the morning was Rotterdam Junction,) we staid an awfully long time, and as I could not go to sleep with my shades up I said I would pull them down when we started but we did not start for so long I was obliged to give in. I woke up in the night and the moon was beautiful. The country seemes very flat as I found out in the morning before I got up.

Somehow all of the first night in a Pullman is there. So direct are the observations and so clear the style that the single *cliché*, 'sleep forsook me,' is an amusing shock. Everything essential is there: the fatigue and excited sleeplessness; the heat and the coarse sheets of the berth; the constant peering out to see what is happening in the flat, dark landscape; the waiting at lighted stations; and finally the moon — thousands have experienced these things and never got them on paper. Incidentally, this is Miss Lowell's first mention of the moon, her lifelong love.

The strain of composition was too much for her, however, and when the next morning they walked across the suspension bridge at Niagara Falls, she was content to add to her bare record of the fact that it was 'very nice.' Soon the diary becomes little more than a list of eating places; but once in a while there is a comment. On the third day, they reached Chicago, and that afternoon visited Pullman: 'It reminded me very much of the English towns being very neat and nice.' On the eighth day she pronounced the Toltec Gorge 'supurb' and noted her first prairie dogs. On the tenth day, a Sunday, they went shopping in Santa Fé, where she bought for herself a pack of Mexican cards, and presents for others. Thirty years later (September 16, 1922) she wrote to D. H. Lawrence of her vivid memories of the 'Indians on donkeys [which] rode down the streets of Santa Fé arrayed in gaudily striped blankets and feathers'; that she had two sunstrokes here did not interfere with her delight. On the twelfth day, at Williams, they 'were delayed by the burning of a bridge. Went to see some horses in a pen, and saw one lassoed.' The next day at The Needles 'we saw lots of horred Indians.' They reached Los Angeles on their fourteenth day; on the seventeenth, they 'took stages to go into the Yosemite,' where they remained twenty-four hours. Two days later the Journal stops abruptly; all that is known of the rest of the journey is that they visited Monterey.

The trip was, Miss Lowell wrote later,

> a somewhat rough journey in those days, but certain aspects of it — the lassoing of a horse in a corral, and the wild dash in a coach along the steep roads of the Yosemite — delighted me, and I have never forgotten them.[1]

Several times in the course of her life, Miss Lowell stated that the first poem of which she had any record was written at the age of nine; and we find one at the end of this Journal.[2] Like a true modernist, young Amy chose an up-to-date American subject for her first poem; and like herself, she ended with praise for her own home-town. I do not think that the fame of her later work will be hurt by the publication of this first effort.

> *Chacago*
> Chacago. ditto
> the land of
> the free.
> It is on lake
> Mich'gan, and
> not on the sea.
> It has some
> fine houses
> in the suburbs
> I'm told

[1] *Ms.*, 1916.

[2] Possibly there was another, about the sun, but this is the only one written at this age which seems to have survived. Some entries, dated 1887 and 1888, intervene between the Journal and this poem; but as it is immediately preceded by a record of the number of dogs, cowboys, buffaloes (none) and sheep she had seen, and as the handwriting is the same, we must conclude that the poem was written on this western trip.

And its people
are rolling in
silver and
gold.
In the city
it'self there
are
warehouses
large.
The folks go
on the lake
in sail boat
and barge.
But for all
of its ~~beauty~~
I'de rather
go home.
To Boston,
Charles River,
and the
State houses
dome.

From 1883 to 1893, Percival Lowell lived chiefly in
Japan. The glamour of the Far East had just begun to
permeate the occident; already various Bostonians were
travelling westward to observe and even experience life in
those strange lands opened by Perry. Sturgis Bigelow
gave up medicine and went to Japan in 1882 for seven
years, during which time he gathered the collection of
Japanese art that was the beginning of the great collection
now in the Boston Art Museum. Percival Lowell went the
next year, in 1883. It was not till 1885 that Whistler published his famous *Ten O'Clock*; not till 1886 that Henry
Adams and John Lafarge went for a year; whereas Lafcadio Hearn was not inspired to go till he read Percival
Lowell's *Soul of the Far East*, 1888.

Soon after Percival's arrival in Tokyo he was appointed

counsellor and foreign secretary to the special mission from Korea to the United States. As his own secretary, he brought back with him the seventeen year old Tsunejiro Miyaoka, with whom the nine year old girl was promptly fascinated. 'I remember so well,' she wrote him years later (January 13, 1921), 'sitting in your lap and pulling your hair, and being reprimanded by my mother for over-familiarity. But you were so good to me and played with me so delightfully, how could I resist considering you a play-fellow of my own age!' To the family she was still 'the baby'; to him she was an eager sympathy in a foreign land; to her he was a strange being whom she was making her own, a laughing familiar voice from new realms of imagination, telling her long, fascinating tales, probably of fox-sprites and spider-demons and two-sworded nobles and camellia-trees that walked and sobbed. This boy-and-girl romping was her first vivid contact with the Far East; and she who was later to be called the first thoroughly American poet to take full advantage of European culture, thus early counterbalanced the civilizations across the Atlantic with those across the Pacific.[1]

Percy returned very soon to the Far East; for ten years he wrote his little sister letters on Japanese decorated note-paper; 'every mail brought letters, and a constant stream of pictures, prints, and kakemonos flowed in upon me, and I suppose affected my imagination, for in childhood the imagination is plastic.' Thus in later years she explained to a Japanese admirer how she was able to describe his country so vividly. 'Japan... seems entwined with my earliest memory'; these books and pictures showered upon her 'all through my childhood made Japan so vivid to my imagination that I cannot realize that I have never been there.'[2]

[1] When Dr. Miyaoka returned to the United States in August, 1918, he made efforts to call upon 'the baby,' but was unable to do so; on June 28, 1924, however, on another visit, he and his wife called at Sevenels.

[2] Letter to Paul K. Hisada, August 13, 1917.

It was when she was eight — in the fall of 1883 — that she first went to school, one of the private schools in Boston, where she became aware of a discipline stricter even than that at home. She was, in fact, that terror of many a teacher: a child precocious, well-informed, a tomboy, quick at retort, spoiled, and impatient of drudgery. Few children deign to learn from teachers whom they do not respect intellectually. Spelling and arithmetic were beyond her bother. From eight to twelve she went to 'various children's schools' in Boston; evidently the teachers despaired, and certainly the statements that Amy was 'the ringleader in fun and mischief' may have had something to do with her changes.

Probably for the first time she was seeing a good deal of a number of other girls.

> I remember that when I was a little girl my stock questions on being confronted with other children were always: 'How old are you?' 'What time do you go to bed?' 'What are you reading?' On their answers hinged my entire future relationship with them.[1]

She amused them, bossed them, won their devotion by her own, angered them, answered them back. Her outspoken admiration for any accomplishment was not to be resisted; and her enthusiasm continued until the subject was completely absorbed and exhausted; then, likely as not, the friendship would suddenly be shattered in a clamorous quarrel. Her increasing stoutness was a humiliation which proved steadfast. Her inmost heart wanted beauty and charm, which she envied so frankly in the other girls; but as the hope grew more and more impossible, she imitated her idolized brothers instead. At least in out-of-door sports she could be somebody; in 'Prisoner's Base,' the favorite game at the Cabots', or in the immortal game of Indians, for which the Lowell park (or 'jungle') was perfect. There they stalked, crept, whispered 'See!' 'Where?'

[1] Letter to Howard Willard Cook, August 9, 1919.

'No: there: see —!' until it was a wonder they didn't see something. In winter there was 'punging,' that childhood sport whose name goes back to Indian times, and which the automobiles have ended in the cities. 'Punging' meant going out in a bunch to get brief, free rides on the rear-ends of the slow sleighs that replaced the grocery-wagons when snow filled the streets, with the added excitement of knowing that there would be perhaps one driver in ten who was surly about it and could be teased. Amy punged with the rest; one friend remembers how her coat caught on a hook, and how she was dragged, screaming, feet uppermost, down the Avenue, at the tail of a slow-pacing pung.

When she was not at school or romping with other children, she was probably reading or playing with her games, especially in the evenings and on rainy Saturdays. Both her father and mother had been taught to be so careful of their books and toys, that they were able to give Amy quite a collection, which she preserved as carefully as they. There were beautifully colored cards of all sorts — animal alphabets, the 'Landscape Alphabet' of 1830, costumes, foreign views; there was a panoramic game of London, the box of which opened up into an elaborate peep-show; there were games French, German, English, even Dutch; games teaching history, geography, music. 'The New Royal Game of Goose' was evidently a great favorite, as it has fallen apart at the folds; moreover, the poet mentioned it later in her 'East, West, North, and South of a Man.'

Her two parents read aloud very well; regularly they read to her, but when they didn't, she was apt to try it herself, regardless who else was in the room. Rollo was succeeded by another creation of Jacob Abbott: Marco Paul, who travelled about the United States; but both of them were imaginative only about practical things. To atone for their deficiencies came the fairy-tales. It was the Walter Crane period; books illustrated by him were constantly given to her, but she disliked them all.

I always had a fancy for the books of an older generation, and again I think this was largely because of the illustrations — at least it was the illustrations which drew me to the books originally, although it was certainly the simple and straightforward texts which kept me enthralled. The illustrated books for children which are published nowadays seem to me to fail by a too involved arrangement of lines. The background does not stay back and the child is confused; it is almost like a puzzle picture. I remember feeling this way very strongly myself in regard to the illustrations of Walter Crane. At the time, I did not of course know what was the matter with them, but somehow they seemed false and unimaginative. They did not stir my imagination in the very slightest degree, and unfortunately I grew up just at the period when books illustrated by Walter Crane were very much the fashion. [1]

Cruikshank's fairies were the only real fairies, to her; she first encountered them in *Gammer Gretel's Fairy Book*, a softened selection from Grimm; but Grimm in the original versions she thought far too brutal and violent for children. Far better were the tales of Hans Christian Andersen, especially 'The Shepherdess and the Chimney Sweep,' 'The Top and the Ball,' 'The Constant Tin Soldier,' and 'The Darning Needle.' She liked also Jean Ingelow's charming *Mopsa the Fairy*, Mrs. Molesworth's books, and the books by Jane Austen's nephew, Lord Brabourne ('rather terrifying, some of them, full of witches and deep forests, but I braced myself up to read them and trembled and enjoyed in about equal degrees'), and a volume by Robert Saint John Corbet, called *Mince-Pie Island*. *Alice in Wonderland* and *Through the Looking-Glass* she found too confusing to be enjoyable; but Charles E. Carryl's *Davy and the Goblin*, which was avowedly written on the same pattern, gave her much pleasure. She was particularly fascinated by George Macdonald's symbolic

[1] Letter to Howard Willard Cook, August 9, 1919.

tales, *At the Back of the North Wind* (how she envied little
Diamond, who slept in the stable and flew with the North
Wind!), *The Princess and the Goblins*, and its sequel, *The
Princess and Curdie*. Inspired by the last two books, Amy
searched Sevenels itself for the secret stairway which would
lead her up to Princess Irene's grandmother and her bath
of stars and her fire of red and white roses. There was a
sham door, in the hallway on the left, under the main staircase, put there by a meticulous architect to match a real
door on the other side; she almost persuaded herself that
this door would really lead to the turret-stairs. At other
times, she crawled about under the eaves, listening 'for
hours' (as she said) to the water dripping in the large
tanks.

> But, dearest of all, was a slim volume entitled 'Moon-
> folk,' which I have read so many times that I have lost
> count. A lonely little girl makes the acquaintance of a
> delightful person, a chimney-elf, and under his guidance
> drifts away to sea in a rowboat over the broad glade of the
> full moon. But the 'moon-glade' takes them straight to the
> moon, where she meets all the persons of child literature,
> even to King Arthur and his knights. So deep an impres-
> sion did this story leave, that even today, when I see a
> wide path of moonlight over the sea, I invariably think of
> Rhoda drifting to the moon in her dory, with the irresistible
> Chimney-Elf sitting in the bow. Most of these fairy-
> stories were English and had an English setting, but 'Moon-
> folk' carried the advantage of being pure Yankee, since it
> was written by Jane G. Austin, a writer well known at one
> time for her novels of colonial life.[1]

A lonely girl... the moon... the friends in books: it is
clear enough why *Moon-folk* fascinated her beyond all the
other fairy-tales.

It will be observed that she liked either practical,

[1] Amy Lowell: 'That Bookcase,' *op. cit.* Her copy of this book was inscribed
'Aunt Amy from Elfrida, Xmas 1886' (Elfrida Roosevelt being just three); we
have included it here, however, for convenience.

sensible stories that told her how to do and make things, or else imaginative stories about little boys and girls who escaped out of reality entirely; but she did not like sentimental stories, of which there were plenty in the 1880's.

All her books she kept locked up in her own private bookcase. Whether originally hers or originally her parents', they are still in remarkably fine condition. One or two have slight scribbles, three or four have decalcomanias stuck in, and in five or six the illustrations are carefully hand-colored; but throughout the entire lot there is not a dog-ear, not a tear, not a finger-mark. One of the books is inscribed 'J. Augustus Peabody Lowell, a new year's present from his aunt Amory, Jany 1st, 1836'; Amy found others of her father's books also given him on New Year's. This puzzled her; nobody had ever thought of giving her a present on that day; so she asked why they had done it then. His answer was perplexing: in the 1830's, more conservative people still considered Christmas presents somewhat popish, so they delayed their gifts a week.

She showed the same taste in dolls that she showed in books. The ordinary French doll left her quite indifferent, nor did she even care to play with the paper dolls she enjoyed so much making. One of her early friends testifies: 'Mrs. Lowell thought Amy should be more feminine and tried to interest her in dolls and sewing, things which Amy abhorred. It was an act of self-sacrifice that after I had met with a slight accident, Amy came every day to play paper dolls with me because she knew I liked them.'[1] But 'Apple Pie House,' a brown-covered note-book of twenty-four pages, was a splendidly designed and executed paper-doll house: the first page was the façade, the other pages being painted to represent rooms, with doors cut through; and these rooms were elaborately furnished with pictures, utensils, tables and chairs, even animals and flowers, cut out of magazines and pasted in; then the whole thing was

[1] Katherine Dana White: 'Recollections of Amy Lowell in Childhood' (ms.).

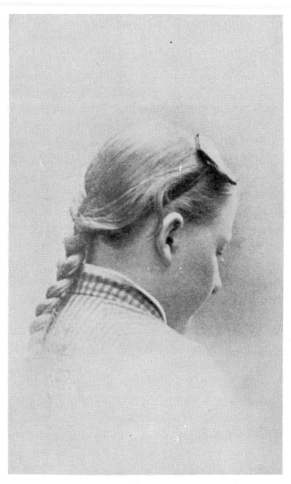

AGED EIGHT YEARS

colored. There was another similar note-book, intended to be inhabited by a paper-doll family named Perry, according to their door-plate; but only ten of the rooms of their mansion were ever finished. And there was another doll-family she had, which Cruikshank would have delighted in: a family of wishbone-dolls, made by Bessie from chicken wishbones, with children of the wishbones of pigeons, partridge, or grouse, and a grandfather of a turkey. Bessie dried the bones, made a head of sealing-wax, with beads for eyes, then dressed the dolls in fragments of gorgeous scraps.

One more event remains in 1883; on December 22 Katherine's first child, Elfrida, was born. Amy had a niece who was nearer to her in age than her own brothers and sisters.

By 1884, Amy's literary ambitions were definitely functioning. The proof lies in *The Monthly Story-Teller*, a mimeographed magazine, which ran for two issues, in an edition of at least four copies each.[1]

'A Day of Misfortunes, by A. Lowell,' is a wholly realistic story concerning one Tinky Rogers of Rollinsville, on the 3d of July. In Rollinsville, the boys have a custom of sleeping out with their chums, in barns or anywhere else, on the eve of the 4th, presumably so that they may rise at dawn without disturbing their parents. But the miserable Tinky suffers such a series of misfortunes, not wholly accidental (indeed, some of them are due to a carelessness caused by ill-temper), that his father finally forbids the great adventure; and Tinky tragically sleeps at home.

Vol. I, no. 1, contained the first installment of this story, also the first installment of another story, 'Helen's Birthday,' by L. Davis, evidently a co-editor, although the

---

[1] One of the stories, 'Helen's Birthday,' contains a letter dated 'Tuesday July 18th 1884'; this is the sole evidence as to the date of the magazine. One supposes that the author wished to be up-to-date, and therefore accepts the year as correct. But it is also true that the July 18th of that year fell on a Friday; one must conclude that realism yielded to laziness in consulting a calendar.

editorial office was at 171 Commonwealth Avenue. Young Amy also contributed a poem 'Spring is coming,' under the pseudonym of 'a born poet,' the third stanza of which runs:

> Spring is coming, spring is coming, sings the little wren,
> Spring is coming, spring is coming, echoes back the hen,
> Now let all some praises sing,
> Praises to the bright sweet spring.

She is also credited with a brief essay:

George Washington
by a deep thinker.

The dogs are barking, the bells are ringing. Tis the eve of Great Washington's Birthday. Think deeply of the great conquerror.

Vol. I, no. 2, contained simply the conclusion of the two stories.

On August 23, 1884, she wrote a fairy-story. It seems that she was ill, and confined to the house; so she turned to the 'Amy's Journal' of 1882; and at the end she added, in her more mature handwriting: 'I stayd in the house all day and playd with my Grocery store being sick.' The grocery store provided the information, and the tale followed:

Part 1.

The goblins and the grocer.

Once oponea time three ~~there~~ thir wass a grocer who was very industrious but though he worked and worked he could not get anough to live apon he stayd in his shop all day but there were outher grocers and no one came except one or two [erased] who did not buy much. One night he and his wife were together in there little kitchen when Jack ¹ ~~sade~~ said Anna I can not provide enough for us and little Zitta well said his wife we must do our best. The next morning Jack

¹ that was the grocers name [written across the bottom of the two pages]

went in to his shop and looked round but what was his surprize when he saw a tumbler of currant jeley on the shelf now all his customers had wandered thier and every where he looked he saw jelly jelley. That day the people kept coming in and going out and Jack made 20 $ more than usual. It went on every day till Jack had more than 100 $. I wonder what mafes them come sade said Jack. I know said little Zitta. What said Jack. The goblins said Zitta. and Zitta was right Jack lived happily ever for ever.

Part 2.

The elves in the grocery store.

One night a lot of elves went in to a grocery store Autumn the captane of the elves said we must do some good here. All right said Spring. Do you know what Jack wants said Autumn Yes said Spring. What said Autumn currant jelley said Spring. So the elves set to work and put jelley every where then laughed and went away till the next night. —

The End.

Yet another accomplishment of 1884 was 'The Private Scrap-book' which was 'Arranged by Amy Lowell' with the name of 'Lowell & Co. Sky-parlor. Sevenels.' on the title-page as publishers. It is chiefly notable as containing the first of Miss Lowell's provocative prefaces.

Preface

Amy Lowell.

The contents of this book are made up chiefly of scraps cut out of different magazines, quotations, & one or two original peaces. The compiling of this book has taken a good deal of time, care, and property. This book will probably interest nobody but myself, so do not imagine naughty reader that you will like it because you won't. I must now stip because the dinner-bell has rung.

Amy Lowell.

On the other side of the leaf is another.

Preface

> In a pretty cottage at the end of the world lives Dame Nature and her twelve children.
>
> The cottage is couvered with climbing roses and there is a wood, and a pond, and an orchard near it in fact it is the prettyest cottage that ever was.

On the next twelve rectos are twelve pictures, cut from *St. Nicholas* for 1884, representing Mother Nature and her twelve children, the months. She intended to select or write a poem appropriate to each month, and copy it in opposite the picture. January is fitted with lines 240–49 of 'The Vision of Sir Launfal'; March and April are furnished with brief poems, the authorship of which I do not know (perhaps they are the 'one or two original peaces,' but I doubt it — the spelling is perfect, for one thing); and the other months have no text at all.

After this pageant of the year comes a new title-page:

Sevenels Farm.

> Is a Pretty Farm in New England the following are Illustrations of it.

Thereafter the book becomes another paper doll-house, incomplete, though with pencilled inscriptions showing that the place was to be fitted with a theater, billiard room, two or three wood paths, a toboggan slide, carriage house, men's room, hayloft, and so on, to a terminal candy-shop.

1885 was chiefly notable in the family for the publication of Percival Lowell's *Chosön*, an account of his travels in the Far East, and for the birth of James A. Roosevelt on February 23, her first nephew, only a few days after Amy's eleventh birthday. And it was about this year that her friendship with Katie Dana began.

> My first recollection of Amy Lowell is of a very round roly-poly little girl with a brown spaniel named Buff.

From the time we were eleven years old we were close friends, living on adjoining places in Brookline, and running back and forth through a gate in the fence....

As an incident of her dislike of authority, I recall an incident in our early days. The Lowell family having gone away for a week, I was asked to visit Amy. One day we decided that we would get up the next morning to see the sunrise. This was a very unprecedented thing for Amy, as she always hated early rising. However, the 'powers that be' refused to allow us to do it (I cannot remember why). I abandoned the idea, but Amy just happened to wake up at dawn. She then just happened to wake me up. I suggested that we might see the sun rise from our beds, but Amy pointed out with perfect truth that this was impossible, as the windows of our room faced south and west. She then ascended to the roof where she got a clear view. (I believe this was the part which was especially forbidden.) After that we decided to go with Mike McGraill to the Lowell's cow pasture about two miles away, to watch him milk the cows. We were greatly disappointed on our return to find that no one had missed us, as all supposed that we were still in bed.

Amy was deeply grieved that she was not a boy. She always tried to walk exactly like her brothers Percy and Lawrence, striding along with her head down and her hat crammed over her ears. She loved dogs and horses. Her black cocker spaniel Jack was her inseparable companion. Though not fond of riding horseback, she loved to drive, and her father gave her a horse of her own as soon as he thought her sufficiently skilled to handle him....

As I look back on our childhood, I can see Amy driving her dog Jack in harness over the place, or sliding down the hay in the barn loft, or struggling to play baseball, or maybe reading aloud out of the immortal Rollo books. The adjective which would best describe her in those days is 'obstreperous.' I well remember the exasperations of our French teacher at school, how she would beat on the table and say, 'Ne riez pas des bêtises d'Aimée.' Amy had an impish desire to shock people, which remained with her

in later life, but at heart she was sound and would cut off
her right hand rather than do a dishonorable action.

She was one of the younger members of our 'crowd' of
boys and girls, who always played together. When she
became too exasperating, we would rise up, with the strident
shout of 'Shut up, Amy Lowell!' which she always took
with good nature. Our great game was 'prisoner's base,'
an invention of the Cabot family, which remained popular
with us for years. Amy often referred in later life to the
good times had by 'our crowd,' citing their superiority to
the more elaborate pleasures of modern children.

Amy was always a clear thinker, seeing through the
shams and pretences, and not impressed by the fads of the
moment. She was a loyal friend. I never heard her say a
word behind a person's back which she would not say to his
face. On the other hand she never hesitated to express
her thoughts, whether it was tactful to do so or not. She
was a good sport, full of fun, but equally fond of long serious
talks with a friend till far into the night. Her courage was
great....[1]

Katie Dana was one of the co-editors of the *Sevenels
Gazette*, which was 'edited by A. L. & K. D.' It is not
dated; only the one number ever appeared; and that consists entirely of a Christmas ghost story (author not
named) and a page of burlesque want ads.

The Bloody Hand

'Twas the night before Christmas & all through the house
everything was stirring even to the baby in arms who was
yelling & screaming because its nurse had gone to get the
smallest Christmas stocking.

The house was so small that it would not hold all the
guests as well as the family, & I being the youngest son was
of course the one to be turned out....

The hero goes to a lonely hotel and is directed to his lonely
room by a toothless landlady who, as he afterwards recalls,

[1] Katherine Dana White: 'Recollections of Amy Lowell in Childhood' (*ms.*).

does not lead him there herself. As he has been reading Bulwer's *Haunters and the Haunted*, he cannot get to sleep at once. A black shadow and a chill frighten him; so that when he sees a luminous bloody hand in the dark he faints, not recovering consciousness till morning.

The explanation is simple. Once a guest suffered so from drafts in that room (the chill) that in revenge he painted on the red wall-paper, in red luminous paint invisible by day, a bloody hand. Thus the room got its reputation of being haunted.

There were other girls in the neighborhood, who went to the same schools: Bessie Hamlen, who lived on the adjoining estate behind Sevenels; Polly Cabot across the street; Mabel Cabot further up Heath Street; and Amy Cabot, who also lived near. There was Charlotte Cochrane, who once was inveigled by Amy into locking a sister up in a closet, and who remembered her in the evening, after Amy had gone home. And some time during these years, while they were in their town house, she met Florence Ayscough (then Florence Wheelock).

> My earliest recollection of Amy is that of a rather square little girl, with a very fresh colour, who came to see me one afternoon when I was recovering from pneumonia. I had been very ill indeed, and my physician, Dr. Charles Putnam, had told his cousin — Amy's mother — about the little girl from China who was lying at death's door just across 'the Avenue,' as Commonwealth Avenue was always spoken of; and Mrs. Lowell had very kindly sent me cream every day during my convalescence. Then when I was able to see people, Amy came up to my room.[1]

Another memory, not datable exactly, though of this period, relates to one summer, when Mrs. Lowell took Amy and a friend to the hotel at Rye Beach for a few days, as a change.

> There Amy invented a new game which seems to me to show considerable imagination. They caught snails (which

[1] Florence Ayscough: *Reminiscences of Amy Lowell (ms.)*.

was not in itself a difficult task) — the use they made of them, however, was quite unusual. They kept the snails in water in the soap dishes in their room, and every day, when they went down to the beach, they took the snails down with them and raced them on the beach. The only incentive which they had I understand was the gentle spur of a blade of grass. The idea of a racing snail seems to me worthy of record....[1]

By now a new world of reading had been opened to her — the world of adventure. Her father had started reading Scott to her when she was nine; by the time she was fourteen, she had read nearly all his novels.

Strange to say, it was not the historical novels which most children seem to prefer which gave me the greatest pleasure. It was the Scotch ones, and most of all, 'Rob Roy.' I fairly worshipped Diana Vernon. (So strongly does the old feeling linger that it seems an impertinence to call her Di.) The mystery hanging over her and the house never lost its spell, even when I knew quite well, from many readings, just what it all meant. Even the strange happenings in 'Woodstock' never so enthralled me.[2]

Katie Dana remembered: 'Her music teacher said that Amy would be perfectly good and tractable through the lesson if afterwards she might read aloud from "The Monastery" and "The Abbot," which were her favorites that summer.' And the first set of books she ever bought was the first collected edition of Scott. Mr. Lowell also used to read to her the *Leatherstocking Tales*; but she 'obstinately preferred' Cooper's sea-stories. Dickens she devoured from twelve to fourteen. The first non-classic tale of adventure she read was *Marmaduke Merry, the Midshipman*, a volume which 'through some lapse of technique' on her part, she never came to own.

[1] Elizabeth Lowell Putnam: 'A Glimpse at Amy Lowell's Childhood by her Sister' (*ms.*).

[2] Amy Lowell: 'That Bookcase,' *op. cit.*

But with another, R. M. Ballantyne's 'Fighting the Flames' I was more successful. I read it over and over, not at all troubled that this story of the London Fire Department depicted conditions as obsolete as Noah's Ark. The same author's 'Dog Crusoe' started me following the long lines of emigrant trains across the Western Prairies. No wonder the book was good, I glanced at it again the other day and it is an almost verbatim steal from Catlin's 'North American Indians.' The dog was added, but the episodes were identical.

Then came the sea. 'Marmaduke Merry' had no more than brushed it; with Marryat's 'Poor Jack' came its full force. My copy of 'Poor Jack' is illustrated by Clarkson Stanfield, and perhaps for that reason I have always preferred it to all others of Marryat's books.[1]

I simply revelled in that volume which I have read again and again, and it led me on to 'Midshipman Easy' and 'Peter Simple' and the whole long line of Marryat's books, which, somewhat later, turned into the broader interest of R. H. Dana's 'Two Years Before the Mast,' and Bullen's 'Cruise of the Cachalot.' Sea stories have been a real passion with me, and I read them today with almost as much pleasure as I did when I was a girl.[2]

Jules Verne became a particular favorite, so much so as to be notoriously potent as a bribe.

Some tales were almost too terrifying. There was Austin's story of Peter Rugg that had already become a legend, and about which she later wrote her 'Before the Storm.'

'Before the Storm' was an abiding fear of my childhood. How often have I driven through the hush which precedes a thunderstorm, all of a tremble lest I should meet the old man and his child in the yellow-wheeled chaise.[3]

Indian stories always frightened me, but charmed me at the same time, although I am bound to say that I think the

[1] Amy Lowell: 'That Bookcase,' *op. cit.*
[2] Letter to Howard Willard Cook, August 9, 1919.
[3] Amy Lowell: *Legends*, p. xiii.

fear rather overcame the charm, particularly after I had been taken to Buffalo Bill's Wild West show and seen real Indians pursuing a real old desiccated Deadwood coach.[1]

But Howard Pyle's *Robin Hood* got intermingled with Indians when they were playing with their bows and arrows in the 'jungle'; she never was quite sure which she was; and Pyle's *Robin Hood* she recommended without reservation.

In 1885, she first began adding extensively to the little collection of books in 'that bookcase.'

In a spelling and copying book, used at school, is a letter, evidently an assigned composition, but containing material which is probably authentic enough.

> Boston. May 21st
> 1886

Dear Ledie,

It must be very stupid at Hyde-Park now and you know (or at least you ought to know) what good fun we have out here, we play tennis every afternoon and sometimes have lemonade, but by the way Mamma wants you to come and spend Sunday with us, Mamma and Papa are going to Ashvill, L[aurence], A[nna], and B[essie] is abrod. while A[lfred], K[atherine], E[lfrida], J[ames] and the small unknown are in New York, but you and I will have an out & out good time (if out & out is slang.) Mamma has written to your mother to ask if you can come, so if you don't want to come you had better telegraph emmediatly to your mother and tell her so.

I hope you will want to come.

> Your Loving Frend
> Amy Lowell

1886 was the year of Percival Lowell's second book, *The Soul of the Far East*; it was natural enough, then, that his little sister should also be engaged in literary composition. The fairy leaven was working, and found laborious expression in *Lowell's Thurd Reader*, which in 1884 had

[1] Letter to Howard Willard Cook, August 9, 1919.

probably been a *First Reader* but in 1886 was docked of its first leaves, renamed, and made the repository of the adventures of one Jack with some wooden soldiers. As we shall see later, this tale was evidently part of one of Bessie's bedtime narratives, recorded with genuine gusto (though with painful spelling and chirography) by her adoring sister.

Other events of this year can only be guessed. But surely on 2 P.M. of Wednesday, December 15, 1886, the whole family attended the crowded commemorative services celebrating the two hundredth anniversary of King's Chapel. The children and grandchildren of the donor of the Munich glass windows could easily have got their share of the 1150 tickets of admission, even if Lawrence had not been Treasurer of the Chapel and a member of the subcommittee on the speakers for the occasion. The chapel was decorated with a series of colonial and Revolutionary flags, with portraits of the eight Royal Governors who had worshipped there, and their coats of arms, and also with portraits of other distinguished worshippers, and a series of escutcheons emblazoned with the arms known to have hung in the original chapel (Andros, Belcher, Bellomont, Burnet, Dudley, Foxcroft, Hamilton, Shute) besides others belonging to pre-Revolutionary members of the congregation. On the communion table were displayed the historic pieces of the church's silver, presented by James II and George III. The original Governor's Pew had been reconstructed; in it sat the present Governor, the Mayor, President Eliot, Dr. Holmes, Bishop Brooks, and the other speakers. The music (on the organ chosen by Handel) illustrated the development of church music in America. Dr. Holmes read a poem written for the occasion. Among the addresses, Amy would particularly have noted that of the Reverend Andrew Preston Peabody, who praised her grandfather:

> John Amory Lowell, toward whom there seemed a perpetual gravitation of trusts of the highest moment, that

would have weighed down almost any other man, but which only brought out into the clearer relief his wisdom, his fertility of resource, and his unsurpassed fidelity.[1]

An English notebook for the school-year 1886–87 contains analyses of sentences and of Figures of Speech, notes on a lecture by one Mr. Dalzell, themes on such subjects as 'Inconveniences of Horse-car strikes,' and just one personal note in 'A Discription of Something I did in the Easter Vacation. Year 1887 A.D.' It seems that she went to a fair, where 'I bought a pound of chockelet-creems (which by the way proved to be very stale) and we managed (between us) to finish them before we left the Fair which probably accounted for my being sick the next day.'

She always liked chocolate; forty years later she was to recall a gift of French chocolate.

> In those days, chocolate cakes used to be slipped into little pictured cartons of pasteboard, but the unusual thing about my box was that the cartons were changed into paper-covered French books — real little glazed bookcovers of different colours, only when you turned back the cover, instead of printed pages there lay a neat oblong of chocolate delectably wrapped in tinfoil.[2]

It was some time in 1887 — or at least, when she was thirteen — that her first poem was published.

> A poem of mine appeared when I was a child in a Worcester newspaper.... It was a joke, because the father of a friend of mine happened to be the editor and saw the poem in a little childs' magazine we got up for a few months, of which I believe every copy has perished.[3]

On August 18, Katherine Lowell Roosevelt ('the small unknown,' now Amy's second niece) was born.

[1] *The Commemoration by King's Chapel, Boston, of the Completion of Two Hundred Years since its Foundation*, Boston, 1887, p. 136.

[2] Amy Lowell: 'A Breaker of Moulds,' *New York Times*, March 26, 1922.

[3] Letter to William Van R. Whitall, May 22, 1923. This poem, to which Miss Lowell made several references, has not been recovered.

Toward the end of the year, Amy Lowell started a new book, entitled simply *Fairy Story Book*, in which she made a fresh start at transcribing stories Bessie told her, and also some of her own invention. It was hard work, writing; and Mrs. Lowell, observing her labors, was struck with the thought that it would make a charming object to sell at the Perkins Institution Fair. So with her daughter's en-raptured assistance, she set to work producing the book which Amy Lowell later kept all but completely from the knowledge of a world only too eager for any news about her.

CHAPTER IV

DREAM DROPS

THE Perkins Institution and Massachusetts School for the Blind is one of the boasts of Boston. Incorporated in 1829, it obtained for its first director Dr. Samuel Gridley Howe, warrior in the Greek struggle for independence, and militant reformer. The exhibitions of his first pupils roused all New England to contribute the necessary funds for continuing the work, and the great Faneuil Hall Fair of 1833 was long remembered as the first 'fancy fair' ever held in Boston. But it was the case of Laura Bridgman that made the Institution famous internationally. When the world learned (through Dickens and others) that Dr. Howe had established intelligent communication with a person lacking sight, hearing, the sense of smell, and the power of speech, it seemed like one of the major discoveries of the modern age.

By 1887 it had become obvious that the Institution should be enlarged by the addition of a kindergarten. To take one case: a Mrs. Keller in Alabama had read Dickens's *American Notes*, and had appealed to them on behalf of her six-year-old daughter Helen; they had sent down a teacher that March. But a kindergarten would be far more effective than sending out individual teachers; so another Faneuil Hall Fair was planned, to raise the necessary funds.

It was at this point that Mrs. Lowell became aware that her youngest daughter was the author of *Lowell's Thurd Reader, Consisting of Selections from juvenile books highly entertaining and instructive*, also of an *Amy Lowell Fairy Story Book*; and she conceived the idea that the proceeds of these stories, written by a child and sold by the author in person, would be a charmingly appropriate contribution to the kindergarten.

But though the stories were complete in Amy's head, writing them down was slow and painful labor; therefore Mrs. Lowell took up her own pen. Only four pages of the latter notebook had been covered; Mrs. Lowell rapidly filled the rest, evidently from dictation. *Dream Drops, or Stories from Fairy Land, by a Dreamer*, was the title, which she explained in an introductory paragraph, 'Where the Stories Came From.' The first story, 'Jack's Adventures,' was a continued bed-time tale of Bessie's, so highly prized by Amy that she had written most of it in *Lowell's Thurd Reader*, and then started to rewrite it in the *Amy Lowell Fairy Story Book*. 'Rosa,' which followed, was a similar tale of Mrs. Lowell's invention, 'the only story my mother ever told us when we were sick, or for any other reason.' But the next two were entirely Amy's: 'Harry's Travels in Fairy Land' and 'What Made Willy Bright Like to Go to Bed.' Then Mrs. Lowell wrote a last paragraph as epilogue.

But the manuscript was still too small to make a good-sized pamphlet, so Mrs. Lowell filled it out with 'The Good Little Henry' and 'The Little Grey Mouse,' translations of the second and fourth tales in the *Nouveaux Contes de Fées* by Mme. la Comtesse de Ségur née Rostopchine.

On November 2, 1887, Cupples and Hurd submitted an estimate of the cost of printing; the books were delivered on December 19 and 20 (250 copies, 99 bound in half white and half flowered cloth, the rest in brown paper); and on January 1, 1888, they sent in the bill.

The plans for the Faneuil Hall Fair fell through after all; but some sort of bazaar was held none the less, at which Miss Amy Lowell, gay in a fancy costume, sold her own writings, and took in $56.60, which was sent to the Perkins Institution.[1]

---

[1] *Second Annual Report of the Kindergarten for the Blind*, Boston, 1889, p. 73. The copy of *Dream Drops* at the Perkins Institution contains a confirmatory in-

The first of the two tales in *Dream Drops* by Amy
Lowell, 'Harry's Travels in Wonderland' (or 'in Fairy
Land,' according to the index and running title) was brief
but vivid. He went there in a sleigh that came to his bed
on a moonbeam which turned into a snowy road. On his
arrival, there was dancing; then a feast was announced:

> The supper was in a hall dressed with icicles, and one
> entered it through an arch of a single rainbow. They had
> iced dew-drops, and humming-birds' eggs, and roasted
> lunar moths for supper, and angel-cake, with bottled
> lightning for those who wished for something hot to drink.

Afterwards he was given a present to take home and open
the next day; and he was warned never to use it at night.
It was a pair of wings, with which he went calling freely on
the birds. At last he disobeyed the injunction to use them
only in the daytime, and an owl chased him home, tearing
his wings from him. His family, with all the brutal scepticism of families, insisted that he had been dreaming all
the while.

As Amy's other composition, 'What Made Willy Bright
Like to Go to Bed' was her favorite in after years, and as
the volume is so rare, we shall reprint it in full. A few obvious misprints have been corrected.

WHAT MADE WILLY BRIGHT
LIKE TO GO TO BED

Willy Bright was a small boy who lived with his father,
and mother, in a pretty village in the North of England,
and their cottage was the prettiest in the village. Though

scription, stating that the money was received in January, 1888. Miss Lowell
always concealed the fact of this book's existence; but when Mr. W. Van R.
Whitall acquired a copy in later years, she wrote him (June 20, 1923) an account
of its genesis, which I have expanded from the evidence in the original manuscript, the printers' correspondence, the inscriptions in her own copies of the
book, and the photographs of Miss Lowell in her fancy costume. The book was
never published, and never put on sale except at the fair.

generally very good, he had one very tiresome fault: he never was ready to go to bed. One day he was very naughty in refusing to go when he was called, he slapped his nurse, and spoke most improperly to his mother who finally said: 'You cannot take your wooden horse to bed, Willy, unless you go at once'; and at this dreadful threat he went, for this horse was his greatest treasure.

When he had been some time in bed, he heard a voice, saying to him, 'Willy, you know you have not been a good boy, but hoping you will improve, I will give you a pleasure.'

Willy promised to behave better in the future, and the horse (for it was he who spoke) said, 'Get on my back'; which Willy did, and they trotted along to the fireplace, and went up the chimney.

Arrived in the middle, or about half way to the top — the horse said, 'Get down,' and changed into a young man about five inches high, and Willy found that he had become small in proportion.

Looking round, Willy found that he was in a charming little country village, with tiny houses and gardens, and pretty gables and latticed windows peeping through over-hanging vines. Bright flowers were blooming everywhere.

Everything was small, and suited to his size. 'This is Chimneytown, and very few mortals know it,' said his guide, 'look at your friends yonder.'

Willy beheld to his great wonder, two children driving a pig, in whom he recognized, 'Johnny and Betty Pringle.'

Soon after another boy and girl on horseback passed by, along the road, and bowed to him. 'Who are they?' said Willy to his guide. 'Little Lord Fauntleroy and "Alice in Wonderland"' was the answer. They walked along the street, and passed a garden where two boys were playing horse, and a man pruning trees; and Willy saw that they were Rollo and Nathan Holliday, and their faithful servant, Jonas.

Still farther on they came to a lovely cottage, the porch covered with red and white climbing roses.

The guide knocked at the door, which was opened by an old woman, whom his guide addressed as 'Gammer Grethel.'

They entered a tiny hall, decorated with miniature deers' antlers, hunting whips and hunting horns of all kinds.

'Would you like to hunt?' said the guide. 'Whoever is in at the death not only gets the brush, but something nice inside of it. The meet today is at Mother Goose's Square, so come on.'

They went to a stable, got two horses, mounted them, and rode away.

They saw many people, among others, 'Richard and Robin,' and little 'Jack Nag'; and arrived at the Square, saw a busy throng of people marketing. And as it was a fine day, the little barometer woman was out in front of her door, looking very happy and smiling, while her husband stood scowling at her inside. A shooting-match was going on and Willy saw that one man always beat, so he went up to him, and recognized Leather Stocking, with Killdeer in his hand.

Just then, however, his guide called him, the huntsman wound his horn, off went the hounds, away galloped the hunters, and Willy with them, riding as fast as he could, until he found himself far in front, and saw before him a small red object, upon which the dogs threw themselves.

He drew a knife he found in his belt, killed the fox, and cut off his brush.

By this time the hunters had all ridden up and congratulated Willy, who then followed his guide, along some pretty lanes, overhung by beautiful trees, and at the end of one they stopped at the door of a thatched cottage, embowered in roses, and from the porch hung a sign, with 'The Peacock Inn,' in green letters. His guide took hold of the brass knocker on the door, and gave a sounding rat-tat-tat.

When out rushed a little woman crying, 'Oh! lawk a mercy, this can't be I, but I've a little dog at home, and he'll know me.' 'Why not?' they asked. 'Because I never had any customers before.' They asked for a private room, and so were shown into a cozy wainscotted parlor, with a bright sunny bow-window, the honeysuckle hanging in wreaths over it and scenting the air deliciously with its fragrance.

Through its festoons, they saw beautiful peacocks marching about, their plumage shining in the sun, some with dark rich coloring, and some snowy white, with golden eyes in their tails. From them the inn derived its name. After a substantial repast of milk and sponge cakes, they cut open the fox's brush, and discovered a little box, which contained some little white pellets, and inside the cover was written, 'When you do not wish to go to bed, take a pellet, shut your eyes, count ten, open them, and see what happens.'

Willy put the box in his pocket, they remounted their horses, and rode back to Chimneytown.

They went to the garden they had first seen, and while walking about Willy discovered some peaches growing on a high wall, at one end. He picked them, and eat all but one which he put in his pocket.

They went into the house and his guide asked him to play chess, and he accepted, though he remembered, afterwards to his great confusion, that the only time he had ever seen a chessboard, his older brother and sister were playing, and had told him that he was too young to learn.

His guide produced a board of ebony and ivory squares; the men red and white and exquisitely carved. The Knights were on horseback holding spears, the Castles which fascinated Willy especially, were men on elephants, and to his surprise he won all the games he played. At last the guide proposed going to bed, and taking a quaint little lamp, he led Willy up a winding staircase to a little bower of a room, under the eaves, with a pretty bed with a rosy quilt. He crept into the fragrant sheets and went to sleep.

When he woke, he was in his own bed, and the pellets under his pillow, and the peach, now no bigger than a pill. All that day he was so excited and anxious for bed-time that it surprised his mother and nurse.

When the time came he rejoiced, and quickly got into bed. After his nurse left him, he put a pellet in his mouth, shut his eyes, counted ten, opened them again, and found himself standing in front of a beautiful coral building under the sea, pretty soon he heard a voice behind him saying, 'Halloo, what's your name?' and turning he saw a little

boy about his own age, seated upon a sea-horse. 'My name
is Willy,' said he, in answer to this boy's question. 'What's
your name?' 'My name is Tom,' was the reply. 'Come
along and have a ride, I'll trust you,' so Willy followed him
along a road, and soon came to a stable, built of mussel
shells, with the name 'A. Whale, Hack and Boarding stable,
Sea-horses and Nautilus Shells to let.' They entered and
found everything in confusion, men rushing about and sea-
horses being harnessed to all kinds of shells, and beating
the water into foam, with their fins, in their impatience.

It must be explained that these people looked on land
like sea-urchins, but under the sea, where Willy now found
himself, they became men and women, and children with
seaweed for hair, tails for feet, and hands and heads like
mermaids. Tom ordered a horse saddled at once, and one
soon came, which Willy mounted, and they both rode off.

The roads were made of shining sands and bordered with
many-hued sea-anemones. Once Willy saw a curious object
in the water, and showed it to Tom, who crying 'Run, run,
for your life,' urged the horses faster, but in vain, for the
object came towards them, caught them up, and whirled
them up to the surface of the water, together with thousands of little fishes.

At length with a great splash and gurgle it was drawn
up to the surface, and over the side of a boat. Then Willy
for the first time realized that this was a net, and that they
were the prizes of some lucky fisherman. The fisherman
sorted the fishes, and finally seeing the urchins and sea-
horses, he took the latter, and said, 'These will amuse my
little girl: — but the urchins are good-for-nothing'; and
tossed the boys overboard. They fell down, down, and
finally came to a pretty road bordered with sea-weed trees,
when Tom began to cry. 'Oh! dear, oh! dear, what shall I
do, I've lost the horses, and mother's poor, and father's
dead, and I shall have to pay for them, oh! dear, dear, dear,
what shall I do?' Willy tried to cheer him, by advising him
to go at once and confess all to his mother, which Tom did
at last. They walked a long way and at last arrived at a
house built of Conch-shells, with their pink mouths outside,

but Tom only dared to enter the kitchen, where he sank upon a settle, dreading his mother's anger.

Presently in came a nice-looking woman, who appeared much surprised to see Tom crying on the settle, and Willy standing near him. 'Why, who is this? and why are you crying?' she asked. Tom told her all, and that Willy was admiring the Coral Palace when he found him. 'Well,' said she, 'he won't have much time to go sight-seeing, and he'll never be here again, so he had better be about it.'

Tom then took him to the Coral Palace, where he went from room to room, each new one more beautiful than the last, the walls lined with shells of every form and color, with pendants of flashing gems, from the deep sea mines; and one with the soft radiance of moonlight, composed of softly tinted pearls, of every shade of color. The one which pleased him most, was hung with cloth woven from the iridescent lining of the Abalone shells, of indescribable delicate rainbow tints. In one room was a child's cradle made of a boat-shell hung from razor shells of great beauty, and a large mussel shell near by, seemed so soft, with its bed of sea-moss, that Willy laid down in it, and was soon sound asleep.

The following day, he woke at home, and was very restless till evening, when he took a pellet and went through the formula of shutting and opening his eyes, counting ten, and going to sleep; and woke to his great surprise in his own bed. He got up, went to the window, and found a little fleecy cloud resting on the sill outside. — It gave a little bob, as much as to say, 'How d'ye do.' So he took the hint, and got on it. After a little ducking motion, away sailed the cloud with him. Presently other clouds came along, filled with little men and women; all wore little pointed caps, with a gold or silver bell on top. They all bobbed their heads at him and rang their little bells, making the sweetest music, and looked with astonishment at him for not bowing in return.

He discovered that only the nobles had golden bells, and other people silver.

The cloud bobbed and ducked so much, that he felt seasick, and was glad when they finally arrived at an immense cloud-bank, which supported an enormous palace of the same soft material. Everyone went into the palace, through great halls and rooms of cloud, some rosy, some violet, or deep red — and some shaded through the palest green and straw color to a pale bluish gray. The whole was lighted with stars, and the effect was magnificent. After walking about and enjoying the spectacle, and the sweet chords of so many musical bells, the King proposed to his guests to go and see how a thunderstorm was made.

'It will soon be ready, Sire,' said the Master of Ceremonies, Lord Snow Cloud, 'and your Majesty had better start now.' Accordingly they all walked out of the palace, over the huge cloud-bank, to an immense tank which was larger than the earth, and when they wished to make a thunder-storm, the little men pulled a string, and out poured the water through millions of holes, upon the earth.

Willy saw many little men setting fire to an enormous box, which seemed to contain rockets, only they shot downwards towards the earth, instead of upwards.

At the same time, many other workmen were turning a crank, which made a frightful rumbling noise, and thus was made a thunder-shower.

Everyone now returned to the Palace and stretched themselves upon the filmy floors, soft as down, and Willy followed their example, and woke up at home.

We shall leave him there, and as he had many pellets left, he is probably trying new adventures, equally interesting.

Of course children ignore various academic rules of plot-construction, yet one overlooks all such lapses in such a delightful caprice. But for freedom of fantasy, richness and exactness of vocabulary, clarity of sensorial effects (sight, sound, touch, scent, taste), whimsy and wit and vivid originality, this story is really remarkable. There are no hints of remembered reading, which so frequently mar other little girls' compositions. Instead, the creative imagination is rejoicing in its own powers, exploring the five senses and the four elements, gaily flouting science and schoolbooks as it spins little worlds out of stables and beaches and chimneys — little worlds complete in themselves and functioning perfectly, once you grant their fantastic premises. Nothing is proved but the joys of creation. Vivid, vigorous, original, unconventional, and unsentimental, without the least trace of eccentricity or affectation or effort, these stories, with their hard bright pictures, prophesy of the poet to be.

CHAPTER V
GIRLHOOD TO WOMANHOOD

*'I have had my own struggles to escape.... I sloughed off some of
my swaddling bands in the early twenties...'*

THE appearance of *Dream Drops* coincided with the open-
ing of a larger life — that of society. On the very day the
first copies of the book reached Sevenels, she went to the
Christmas Theatricals of the Hasty Pudding Club at
Harvard: *Zwei Bier; or, a Ghost's Ghastly Holiday* — the
last show given on the cramped stage in the old Jarvis
Field house. She was sufficiently impressed by this riotous
farce to write in a book acquired that day (*Crackers for
Christmas*, by E. H. Knatchbull-Hugessen, later Lord
Brabourne): 'Amy Lowell, Night of the Pudding Theatricals, 1887.' [1] One went to the Pudding Shows because one's
beaux and cousins were in them. Though she was still
reading fairy-stories, she was in the way of becoming a
young lady.

Indeed, her next literary effort was frankly aimed at
fashion. The first and last issue of *The Wall Flower Society
Mirror*, published by herself at her own home, appeared in
May, 1888.[2] The feature article was 'Ball-room Notes,' an
account of an entertainment at one Mr. L. Halbot's.
There is also a story, 'The Dagger of Krakminster or Why
She Laughed,' which breaks off in the middle of the most
exciting sentence: 'he saw ——' and ends with a demure
(to be continued).' The advertisements are parodies, of

---

[1] The '87 members, as their 'Senior Farewell,' had given *The Talisman; or,
the Maid, the Monk, and the Minstrel* on April 5, 1887; and on 'Strawberry
Night,' June 23, the '88 members gave their first show, *Fizz; or, If you don't like
it get up and git.* But *Crackers for Christmas* and 'Christmas Theatricals' coincide so evidently that I have assumed she went to the third performance of the
year.

[2] 'Weather Indications' mentions May; the book-review indicates 1888.

course. But the choicest morsel is Miss Amy Lowell's first book review:

The Editor's Book-Shelf

One of the latest, and also one of the most interesting, literary productions of the year, is the charming little book, by Miss Lowell, entitled 'Dream Drops by a Dreamer.' We understand that Miss Lowell is to be one of the writers for this paper, and as she is, perhaps, the greatest of the century's geniuses, we hope that this sheet will be patronized by many of the fashionable set.

On May 3, she started French II at school. Her mother had been teaching her French in the summer vacations; but now it was a question of irregular verbs and dictations and unattractive literature. In her copy of Jules Bué's *Philosophe sous les Toits* she wrote 'Ug. I am mad.' There were six other girls in the class, who well remembered Madame's difficulties with the 'enfant terrible,' and her repeated 'Ne riez pas des bêtises d'Aimée!'

An English composition book, surely of this year, also exists; it contains exercises in grammar and sentence-construction, paraphrases of Irving's 'Voyage' and other Stories, and a dull original essay on 'The Companionship of Books,' which, however, reveals at least one personal touch. In a very long sentence the reader is assured that you must like some book better than another; that nine books out of ten are not absorbing; but the tenth —

this you take up and curious fact the dinner is late, just in a most exciting place, Eliza comes up to tell you that dinner has been ready for a quarter of an hour, and your mother wan'ts you to come right down.

The teacher's favorite comment in this book is 'Spelling, Construction, Punctuation,' often with exclamation points.

On June 9, 1888, Bessie was married to William Lowell Putnam, a third cousin, at St. Paul's Church, Brookline.

It was probably near the end of the school year, on June 29, 1888,[1] that she saw James Russell Lowell for the last time. The reverence with which the rest of the family regarded him was somewhat tempered in Amy. To be sure, amongst the treasured books of her childhood was one of his own juvenile possessions, which he probably gave her (Walter Ferguson's *My Early Days*, Boston, 1827, inscribed 'James Russell Lowell from Father May 3th 1828'); and one of the only two poems she adored as a child was his 'What is so rare as a day in June?'; furthermore, as he was the most distinguished member of her family, she was bound to feel great pride in him. But when she began to earn her own fame as a writer, she got bored explaining that she was not his granddaughter; and for a while it seemed as though his reputation were antagonistic to her own, so that she informed one correspondent that he was not a real poet at all, and to another (J. B. Rethy, of the *International*) she wrote on May 3, 1917:

> I am grateful to you for comparing me with James Russell Lowell to the detriment of the latter. This may sound unkind, but if you had had that elderly gentleman held in front of you as a model and a shining goal all your life, you would realize the delight I take in reading such words as yours.

Later still, of course, she came to value, and imitate, his *Fable for Critics*. But in 1888 'Cousin James' was still somewhat resented.

> I remember so well that last time I saw him, standing in front of the fire at my Aunt Mary Putnam's (who was also his sister). I was a young girl then, very young, and most

---

[1] She was on the way to a college boat race, at which 'her side' lost. This was surely a Harvard-Yale boat race, as in 1876 those two colleges had made their agreement to row each other annually, excluding other colleges. Yale won on July 2, 1886; July 1, 1887; and June 29, 1888; all three dates are possibilities, but the last seems likeliest. In her diaries for 1889 and 1890 she did not mention the event; Harvard won in 1891; and shortly after that, Lowell died.

impressed to be en route to a college boat race. Our party
convened at Aunt Mary's, and I was hauled into the library
to say how do you do to Mr. Lowell. I was frightened to
death and he was obviously bored; had we but known it, it
was the old and the new meeting in furious conjunction,
but we did not know it. I was afraid of his grandeur and
his reticence, and he considered me a poor little girl whom
he had to speak to. I went on to my boat race, where my
side lost (I shall never forget that), he went on his slow and
stately way to the grave, and the stars went on their courses
— to what end, I wonder, alas! I wonder.[1]

After the summer vacation, she went back to the school
at 57 Chestnut Street, to continue the customary grind:
English History, French, a little Italian, and Literature.
'My family did not consider that it was necessary for girls
to learn either Greek or Latin, and I have found this ignorance of the classic languages a great handicap.'[2]
From her themes of this year, one learns that the emphasis
was on poetry — but not on 'modern' (nineteenth century) poetry. She wrote about *Beowulf*, Gray's Life,
Gray's personal qualities, his 'Elegy,' and paraphrased
'On the Death of a Favorite Cat'; she wrote about Goldsmith's poetry and again about his 'Traveller'; she sum-
marized the life of Burns and paraphrased the first stanza
of the 'Cotter's Saturday Night' and again the third,
fourth, and fifth stanzas, after which she wrote and rewrote a theme on Burns's poetry; then she did the life of
Cowper. Irving's 'Rip Van Winkle' (paraphrased) was
her nearest approach to contemporary literature. She also
made an analysis in elaborate outline form of the *Merchant
of Venice*. Only one theme in the entire year afforded the
least scope for self-expression. 'Man's Inhumanity to
Man' was the assigned topic; and in four flaming pages,
Miss Amy mentioned Cain and Abel, New Testament

[1] Letter to Elizabeth Cutting, August 2, 1920.
[2] Letter to Winifred Bryher, June 13, 1918.

persecutions, the tortures of the Middle Ages (with special reference to the Iron Virgin of Nuremberg, which had terrified her so, seven years before), Dionysius (a trifle misplaced chronologically), the French Revolution ('Blood! that was what the people wanted'), slavery, the labor of women and children in mines, ending at last with the women who still work for cheap clothing-houses. The teacher commented:

> A very good aspect of the subject, to present. There are many others. I should have been glad, had you elaborated the last topic, furthur, [sic] as it is a practical one at the present day; also to have had you begin the subject by a general statement, showing that you realize there are many other inhumanities, beside those treated here. — Penmanship and punctuation faulty.

Some years later, Amy Lowell wrote:

> We all hate the poetry we learnt in school. Why? Is it because it was in school that we learnt it, or is it because the conditions were such that we never really learnt it at all, the fine inner sense of it and its beauty of expression were both hidden from us? [1]

Outside of school she read as she pleased, however. From Dickens she went on to Thackeray, and was fascinated by his knowledge of the world that was just opening for her. At the same time, she kept up her interest in less sophisticated literature. Her parents had originally prohibited the books of Louisa May Alcott, as ungrammatical and untrue to life (an opinion in which she later concurred); but eventually — probably about this time — she read them, as all her friends had done so. It was about this year, then, that in her *Complete Composition Book* she took down the following questions from dictation and filled in the answers, thus making a character-sketch of herself:

[1] 'Poetry, Imagination, and Education' (*Poetry and Poets*, p. 40).

Name? Amy Lowell.

Resedence? Brookline.

What is your favorite moral caracterestic? Self controll.

Which one do you most dislike? deceat.

What is your favorite extrravegence? [*unanswered*]

What is your favorite exercise? books.

Who is your favorite hero in American history? Benjamin Franklin.

Who in the history of other countrys? Alfred the Great.

What caracter (male) in all history do you most dislike? Nepolian Bonaparte.

Who is your favorite heroin in American history? Barbera Friche.

Who in the history of other countrys? ~~Grace Dar~~ Josephine.

What caracter (female) in all history do you most dislike? Joan of Arc.

What are your reasons for your reasons for your likes and dislikes [?] Joseph's husband illtreated her [.] Joan of Arc was too masculin

Who is your favorite novelist among men? Thackeray

Who among women? Louisa. May. Alcott.

What is your favorite work of fiction? Little Women.

Who is your favorite hero in fiction? Diamond in 'At the Back of the North Wind.'

Who the most disliked? Steve (in 'Rose in Bloom')

Who is your favorite heroin? Jo (in 'Little Women.')

Who the one most disliked? Aunt Mira (in 'Eight Cousins')

Who is your favorite poet? James Russel Lowell.

What [is] your favorite poem? The vision of Sir Launfall.

What is your idea [of] misery? Not to be allowed to tobbogan.

What is your idea of happyness? To be loved.

What quality do you like best in a man? Manliness.

What do you most dislike? Cowardliness.

What quality doe you like most in a woman? Modesty.

What do you most dislike? imodesty.

What six books (Bible excepted) would you most desire to have with you if you were cast on a desert island? Little

Women, Webebsters unabridged Dictionary, Moon folk,
Boys a[t] Chequasset, Marco Pauls adventures on the
Erie Canal, & At the back of the North Wind.

But her character is depicted most vividly in the diary
she started with the New Year, 1889. Complete honesty
is rare in any diary; but she was unsparingly frank with
herself, even though she was in that gawky age (her fifteenth birthday fell in February) when her friends, with
lengthened skirts and lacing, were consciously developing
their flowerlike qualities in unacknowledged preparation
for marriage. Amy Lowell, awkward and stout, already
despaired of such happiness, and was becoming increas-
ingly subject to attacks of despondency. 'I was a fool *as
usual!!*' is a characteristic entry. She despised herself
for 'a great rough masculine, strong thing.' At another
time she noted: 'If I were not so self-conscious I would
be much better. Everybody thinks I'm a fool (& it's
true) & nobody cares a hang about me.' Dancing school
(she was now in the 'Friday Evenings,' for sub-sub-debs
and Harvard Freshmen) was no solace ('I was left over
in the German *as* usual!'). Riding-school brought no
exhilaration. She envied the freedom of her brothers and
their Harvard friends; she envied the other girls their
attractiveness; possessing neither quality, she was desperately lonely. On May 23 she wrote:

> I feel very much in need of a *very* intimate friend, a
> friend whom I should love better than any other girl in the
> world, & who would feel so towards me. To whom I could
> tell all that is in my heart & who would do so to me.
> We should love to be alone together, both of us.

But without beaux or friends of her own sex, nothing was
left for her but to accomplish something — what, she
could not guess.

> Jan 2 ... I could go to the theater every night, the lights,
> the people, the play, everything it is delightful....

Jan 13... What would I not give to be a poet. Well day-
dreams are day-dreams, & I never shall be a poet....
Jan 22... I feel as if I must have a talent for something, &
I cant help thinking it is photography....
Jan 23... I like to write as if somebody was going [to] read
this. I would not have them read it though. *You bet.*...
Feb 21... Just at present I am rabid about coaching and
inns...
March 19... I should like best of anything to be literary.
Ah me! I am afraid I never shall be...
March 28... I feel more and more drawn towards History
& Literature. Oh! if I could only write like Scott....

On April 17, she tried her hand at a poem, 'Morning in
Heaven'; the next day she tried another, 'Sunrise.' After
all, why should she not write? Both her brothers were
publishing books; and on June 27, Percy, back temporarily
from the Orient, delivered the Phi Beta Kappa poem in
Sanders Theater.[1]

But between the lines of the diary we can read that all
was not gloomy: there are plenty of traces of laughter
and fun of all sorts — games, jokes, theaters, dances
(which she was coming to like). She went to the D.K.E.
and Pudding shows, and got crushes on Jim P. and on
Phil S., which doubtless they never suspected. Once she
won a tennis tournament, playing doubles with Paul H.
But in the evenings, when she was tired and alone in
'Sky Parlour,' she confided to her diary all her depressions.
And always she recorded faithfully her hour of rising and
the phase of the moon.

On June 4, 1889, Bessie's first child, George Putnam,
was born.

The summer was spent chiefly in visiting, at Peterborough, Cotuit, Manchester, and the Cabots' island in
Maine.

[1] 'Sakura No Saku,' in heroic couplets, was published in the *Boston Post*,
June 28, 1889. Another of his poems, in blank verse, is 'Ontake,' printed in the
Liber Scriptorum, of the Authors' Club (New York), 1893, pp. 365–375.

School began again in October. On the 18th an attack of eyestrain relieved her, no doubt, from studying, but did not prevent her from going the next night to see Charles Wyndham in *David Garrick*. The play impressed her so much that she wrote the entire plot into her diary, and two weeks later recurred to its effectiveness. 'There is a spot in my heart that nothing had ever touched until I saw that play.' Meanwhile she had fallen in love, and recorded that event on October 28.

> Do you know I was 'struck all of a heap' the other day by discovering that I love Paul H*****.
>
> How long I have loved him I don't know. But I must have loved him for some time.
>
> It is so silly; but when Paul askes Mabel to walk with him I feel just like going off alone somewhere & crying. This feeling is mixed by a kind of a wish to hit Somebody.
>
> If there was any chance of Paul's ever loving me it would be different & I should not be ready to pound myself for being such a fool as to love him.
>
> But I am ugly, fat, conspicuous, & dull; to say nothing of a very bad temper.
>
> Oh Lord please let it be all right, & let Paul love me, & don't let me be a fool.

A few days later, after recording certain sarcasms because Paul talked to someone else, she noted 'I have given up letting Polly read this. It's too private'; and still a few days later we learn that she herself is writing a play. But on November 20, the Lowells moved to their town house, and, missing Paul, she found herself again alone in the world. 'I have no faculty for making friends.... Paul!' On the 24th she wrote:

> I don't think that being all alone, in here, is good for me. In fact I have been building my-self castles in the air, and thinking, thinking!
>
> I think that to be married, to a sweet, tender, strong & good man, would be the nearest approach to perfect happi-

ness, of course provided that you love the man. To be his sole, & whole, confident. In short my ideas of what a husband should be are very exalted.

No! I shall be an old maid, nobody could love me I know. Why, if I were somebody-els, I should hate my-self.

I am doomed, for how can it be different —? to see the man I love marry somebody-els.

Private.

Bessy H***** take pity on me for you love Fred.

But you are loveable, He may, will, love & marry you. But Paul! Oh! I feel queer! But, but Goodnight!

She felt that she was stupid at school, too, and on December 13 indulged another fit of self-castigation.

It doesn't make any difference to me. I am rough and strong and can bear anything that would bear down sweeter and more delicate natures. But somehow I can't seem to bear it very well. I hate to hear Patty and that kind of sweet girl getting sat on, & I have got into the habbit of thinking myself cast iron. I don't like to find I'm not.

Lotty told me last Sunday that I affected hoydeness, & was really the opposite, I did not like to let on but I knew it was true.

For the next year, 1890, she acquired another *Excelsior Daily Journal,* but though the moods recurred, the general tone was livelier. There was much more theater-going. On January 12, she commented on the day's sermon.

Mr. Parks gave a sermon on the fact that 'You are God's Child.' Well that was very nice but he said that one's aim in life was to 'Save your Soal.' Now I don't think it is. I think that is a very selfish view to take of life. I believe that you had better not think at all about your hereafter, [but] do what you think you ought to do in that particular instance and trust to God for the rest. Pray to Him for all you want. I tell Him everything.

But though she was soon in the dumps again, a more typical entry is that of February 13: 'Went down town with Dolly Brooks. Met Mabel Cabot there. She was too funny; kept Dolly & I in a roar of laughter.' Dolly Brooks and she at this period were partners in adoration of Miss Sheridan, the leading lady at the Boston Museum, who was particularly delicious as Lydia Languish. They wrote her letters, but alas! it was Dolly who got an answer; and Amy was further upset when she saw some of Miss Sheridan's poetry, which emphasized sentimental uplift. However, the theater was always magic; and March 3 was spent working on her play, which now had acquired a title, *Plot and Counterplot*. On the 14th, she was again in raptures:

> I am in! for the 'Saturday Evening'[1] next year. Oh Joy!! I don't know why I'm glad; of course I shall be an awful pill, as I was at the 'Friday Evening' last year. I think that I should like parties quite well if only I could dance well & was sure of having a *very* good time. But, of course, I am doomed to be a dreadful pill; doomed to blush very visibly, & waste my sweetness in the vicinity of the wall. But then, you know, I don't care a rap!

The next day she was forced to admit 'Really, you know, I am appaulingly fat.' A couple of days later, she went to see some old books brought over by 'a Mr. Quarritch,' the well-known London book-dealer, who eventually sold her many a handsome volume.

On March 20, she was confirmed, her knees shaking terribly; on April 3, she took her first communion at Trinity Church. How long her religion lasted cannot now be guessed; but in her first book, twenty-two years later, she made it clear that she had renounced conventional Christianity. Convinced by her own sufferings, and even more by the sufferings of others, that the god of this world, if there were one, was a devil, she had no hesitation in

[1] The dances for sub-debs and Harvard sophomores.

rejecting the formal proofs of deity, life after death, and so forth; and if occasion demanded, she would declare herself flatly an atheist. But she was never really a belligerent, or even an obstinate one; she recognized in herself the deep aspiration which is the root of religion; and the forgiveness of sins was the basis of her entire ethics.[1]

Three days later, on April 6, she wrote a poem to Louly W*******, which she admitted was 'a good deal in the style of "Nursery Rhymes"'; presently explaining 'I cannot help admireing, & generally falling in love with, extreme beauty.' But her admiration did not prevent her intelligence from acknowledging flaws in her latest 'crush': 'They say that she doesn't care for society, that is queer for I don't believe that she has got any brains.'

On April 29, she sprained an ankle — our first record of that very common event in her life. (In December 1918, she mentioned to a correspondent that she had sprained one ankle nine times and the other ten, and that she had cracked the bone of one leg three times.)

In May, a group of her friends were planning to produce *She Stoops To Conquer*; she was cast as Tony Lumpkin; but 'Mamma does not want me to act as a man, so we have given the play up.'

But by this time, school was ending; there was a tennis tournament; then on June 30 she went visiting at Dublin, where in the midst of high jinks the diary ended abruptly on July 12, 1890.

[1] To illustrate her attitude, I may recall here a conversation in which I remarked that the testimony of the mystics was the best proof of deity that we had. Her thoughtful acquiescence was followed by the positive declaration that she had no mysticism whatever in her nature. I countered with Blake's statement that everybody felt something of it, and quoted his quatrain, 'To see a world in a grain of sand' as something that only a mystic could understand, and yet which everybody understood. She admired the poem, said she understood it, and denied that sympathy with mysticism was necessary to understand it. I defied her to explain it in rational terms; she retorted that it meant just what it said and nothing else. I do not remember how the conversation continued, but I suspect that the subject was changed, by me.

Of her schooling this year, there is little to be said. Her themes (pure drudgery) and notebook indicate that the class in Literature II returned to *Julius Caesar*, studied the *Merchant of Venice* intensively for vocabulary and structure, and analyzed or paraphrased essays by Addison, Steele, Carlyle, and Ruskin. She also wrote two compositions on Thackeray. Under the heading 'Verse' she noted simply: 'It is language arranged in metrical lines.' About this time she stopped writing poetry entirely, not to start again until twelve years had gone by.

In the fall of 1890 she returned to school for her last year. Two episodes alone are traceable. On December 5, Katherine Lawrence Putnam, Bessie's second child, was born. And Miss Amy wrote a series of poison-pen portraits, which she endorsed 'Sketches of my teachers — Made during History recitations at School. Winter 1891.' They are merely the impertinent and thoughtlessly cruel attempts at wit which young ladies of her age are accustomed to pass to their fellow-pupils in defiance of discipline. In her 'Poetry, Imagination, and Education,' [1] however, she tried to explain her teachers' failure. The keynote of the essay is to be found in three sentences:

> Imagination is behind all the great things that have been said and done in the world....
> And yet imagination must take a second place to-day and give room for the learning of so-called *useful* things!
> ... the chief stimulators of imagination are the arts — poetry, music, painting: the humanities as opposed to the materialities.

Presently she comes down to her own case:

> For the last two years of my school course, I attended lectures on Shakespeare by an eminent Harvard professor. I remember those lectures very well; they made an indelible impression. We learnt everything about the plays we studied except the things that mattered. Not a his-

[1] *North American Review*, November, 1917; reprinted in *Poetry and Poets*.

torical allusion, not an antiquarian tit-bit, escaped us. The plays were mines of valueless information. Out of them we delved all sorts of stray and curious facts which were as unimportant to Shakespeare as to us. Not once in those two years were we bidden to notice the poetry, not once was there a single aesthetic analysis. The plays might have been written in the baldest prose for all the eminent professor seemed to care.

But she was equally frank in admitting her own short-comings as a pupil.

I learned nothing at school except reading and writing — I am still learning the multiplication table. I did learn something round the school curriculum, if I may so express it, but that was because I became interested in the subjects on their own account and used to read the whole of books in which only one chapter had been assigned. Some people can have knowledge pumped into them, I suppose, but I never could. I cannot be taught — I have to learn — and reading has been my education.[1]

Indeed, she could not be taught. Her spelling remained uncertain to the end of her life. Although she had vague impulses towards writing poetry, she learned nothing of its principles or practices in school, and what little poetry she read there she never admired in after years. Her prose at school was mediocre. She never really learned German, gave up Italian as beyond her, and in spite of her mother's tutoring in the summer vacations, she did not master French until later. At seventeen, she left school for good; 'and that has been the extent of my formal education; it really did not amount to a hill of beans.'[2]

She educated herself by browsing in her father's library, and also in the Boston Athenaeum, where she spent many an afternoon, climbing painfully the little spiral stairs, to reach some retired alcove, there to sit on

[1] Interview attached to letter to Miss Felice Davis, May 7, 1924.
[2] Letter to Archibald MacLeish, October 16, 1924.

the dusty floor, alternately reading and dreaming, while the sun shifted through the trees of the Old Granary Burying Ground or the winter snow slanted downward upon the graves. From Thackeray she had gone on to the discovery of Charlotte Brontë, Trollope, and Jane Austen. But the great discovery of these years was poetry and Keats.

One day [1] in her father's library she came across Leigh Hunt's *Imagination and Fancy; or, Selections from the English Poets, illustrative of those first requisites of their art; with markings of the best passages, critical notices of the writers, and an essay in answer to the question 'What is Poetry?'* This book 'opened a door that might otherwise have remained shut' and 'turned me definitely to poetry.'

> I did not read it, I devoured it. I read it over and over, and then I turned to the works of the poets referred to, and tried to read them by the light of the new aesthetic perception I had learnt from Hunt.
>
> So engulfed in this new pursuit was I, that I used to inveigle my schoolmates up to my room and read them long stretches of Shelley, and Keats, and Coleridge, and Beaumont and Fletcher. Guided by Hunt I found a new Shakespeare, one of whom I had never dreamed, and so the plays were saved for me, and nothing was left of the professor's lectures except an immense bitterness for the lost time.
>
> I have often thought that in this book of Leigh Hunt's we have an excellent text-book for what should be the proper teaching of literature, and especially of poetry. Poetry is an art, and to emphasize anything else in teaching it is to deny its true function.[2]

Although the child had scribbled verses and although as late as January, 1889, she was still troubled by the aspira-

[1] When she was 'about fifteen,' according to a letter to William Lyon Phelps, December 31, 1917; but in her 'Poetry, Imagination, and Education' she places the discovery after the lectures on Shakespeare. Evidently it occurred between July 12, 1890 (end of diaries) and June, 1891 (end of schooling).

[2] 'Poetry, Imagination, and Education,' *Poetry and Poets*, pp. 53–54.

tion to be a poet, her instinct had been starved. If we
make a list of the greatest and truest English poets, excluding Shakspere, we discover that she knew nothing
of any of them — nothing of Chaucer, Spenser, Marlowe,
Jonson, Donne, Milton, Blake, or the *Lyrical Ballads*,
or any poets after that, including Emerson, Poe, Whitman,
and Emily Dickinson. 'My father read very little of
what was considered in those days "modern poetry,"'
she explained to Professor Phelps (December 31, 1917);
on the evenings Mr. Lowell read aloud he evidently chose
other books. In 'that bookcase,' besides the customary
volumes of verse written for (or at) children, there were
only four books of adult poetry, and two of those were
mere curiosities: a *Longfellow Birthday-Book;* Frances
Ridley Havergal's abominable *Morning Bells;* Caroline
Gilman's parlor-game, *Oracles from the Poets;* and J. J. G.
Wilkinson's experiments in automatic writing, published
anonymously as *Improvisations of the Spirit.* We need
hardly be surprised that Amy Lowell liked only two
poems in her childhood: 'What is so rare as a day in
June?' and William Allingham's fairy 'Up the airy
mountain, down the rushy glen.' The Gray, Goldsmith,
Burns, and Cowper studied in school were perhaps the
worst choice possible for one of her temperament, and
indeed were completely left out of Leigh Hunt's book.
That book was her sudden introduction to the literature
of the imagination.

It told her that poetry was the utterance of the imaginative passion for truth, beauty, and power; it defined imagination as 'images of the objects of which it treats'; it
exhibited the variety of the poetic resources, including
'whatsoever of painting can be made visible to the mind's
eye and whatsoever of music can be conveyed by sound
and proportion without singing or instrumentation'; it
attacked wordiness, inversions, and worn-out epithets;
it explained the modulation of cadence in metrical verse.

Then, not content with winnowing the best of poetry for illustrations, it gave copious extracts from the great poets, italicizing and commenting on their happiest passages.

Though she had given up even the idea that she might write poetry some day, no better book could have been found for the training of the future Imagist. The essentials of Hulme's theories and the Imagist manifestoes are all here. To Amy Lowell, it taught what poetry was, who the great poets were and what they had written, and furnished a model for her own critical works. It also introduced her to Keats.

Shelley, being an atheist, was not in her father's library; but Keats was. And Keats was the poet predestinate to her discovery. He not only revelled in the five senses, he also established for her the fundamental values of life. A sceptic, he was 'certain of nothing but the holiness of the heart's affections and the truth of imagination'; this virtually became her creed. *Endymion* set her turbulent adolescence right about the related values of the physical and the spiritual in love, and taught her that both are essentially pure, essentially one. The love scene in the second canto affected her particularly: 'How many boys and girls have found solace and joy in this passage!' she wrote many years later.[1] And in this poem she also found her own adoration of the moon expressed so exquisitely that the symbolism was to run through her own poems, from the first poem in her first book to the posthumous volumes.

The summer vacation was interrupted by two deaths: that of Alfred Roosevelt, Katherine's husband, on July 2, and that of James Russell Lowell on August 12. Surely she attended the first funeral; as her mother attended the second, at which her brother Lawrence was a pallbearer, she was probably there also.

In the fall of 1891 she 'came out' formally.

[1] *John Keats*, I, 383.

If she learned anything from Boston society, it was the art of light conversation. The Bostonians prided themselves on their wit; they cherished well-turned retorts and epigrams. Tom Appleton ('the first conversationalist in America,' Emerson testified) [1] was famous for his 'cold roast Boston,' 'mutual admiration society,' and 'good Americans when they die go to Paris' — a sentence appropriated by Holmes for his Autocrat, and still later by Wilde. Rufus Choate's two daughters, Mrs. Bell and Mrs. Pratt, were sought everywhere for their wit: the envious suspected them of planning their repartee beforehand; but what little of it has survived is so extremely occasional that it must have been impromptu. People remembered how the two held the conversation up to an exhausting pitch of laughter, but could not remember what they laughed at. However, at least one of Mrs. Bell's remarks became a gift to the nation: 'The automobile is speedily dividing mankind into two classes: the quick and the dead.' [2] She took a warm interest in Miss Lowell, who saved twenty-four letters from her, all undated. 'I have always been thankful that you were born,' one of them begins. To Mrs. Bell, Miss Lowell read her first poems; when at last one of them appeared in the *Atlantic* (August, 1910), Mrs. Bell was on the watch, and wrote her an enthusiastic appreciation. A couple of other notes express concern over a serious fall which Miss Lowell suffered on leaving Mrs. Bell's house.

Another locally famous conversationalist was Sarah Wyman Whitman, of French descent, round whom inevitably a salon gathered. She painted a great deal, having studied under William Morris Hunt; wrote letters that were cherished, and could turn a neat sonnet; she made the stained-glass window in memory of Bishop

[1] Julia Ward Howe: *Reminiscences*, Boston [1889], p. 432.
[2] Paulina Cony Drown's *Mrs. Bell*, Boston, 1931, is an attempt to preserve some of her evanescent brilliance.

Brooks for Groton, and also two windows in Memorial
Hall at Harvard; she did jewelry, wood-carvings, sculptures, picture frames and bookplates, and set a high
standard of design in book-binding. But her greatest art
lay in bringing people together, and making them all con-
verse on a high plane. To some overtalkative authority
she would say: 'There you go, holding forth again!' and to
a shy girl: 'Of course I want you: you're ornamental.'
She liked to gather groups from the younger generation
to meet some distinguished guest. She was sympathetic
and intelligent, frank and tactful, all at once.[1]

Miss Lowell was one of those she invited to her eventful
gatherings, and Miss Lowell entertained her in turn at
Sevenels. One of her stained-glass pieces, a waterlily, was
hung in the library window at Sevenels; and Miss Lowell
kept five undated notes from her. One note accompanied
a gift of two quill pens, to provide inspiration for the young
writer; another invited her 'dear Book-lover' to meet
Mrs. LaFarge at dinner; a third addressed her as 'kind
Keeper of the Keys to so many histories.'

The coming generation had its own standards of conversation. Wilde's comedies furthered the native impulse
toward epigram; and the Harvardians were cultivating
that mixture of wit, exquisiteness, and boredom which
inspired the epithet 'Harvard Indifference.' The very
youngest generation, however, was devoted to the fantastic slang which O. Henry later made national.

The Decadence was plentifully picturesque in Boston.
It was the period of Huysmans and Laforgue, with
Howells writing a preface to Stewart Merrill's *Pastels in*

---

[1] Her *Making of Pictures*, twelve short talks with young people, was published
at Chicago in 1886. *Letters of Sarah Whitman* [edited by Sarah Orne Jewett]
was printed at Cambridge in 1907. *A Record of the Service held in Memory of
Mrs. Henry Whitman by her friends and neighbours, at the Baptist church, Beverly
Farms, on Sunday afternoon, July the seventeenth, 1904,* is also in existence. John
Jay Chapman's *Memories and Milestones*, New York, 1915, contains a chapter
on 'Mrs. Whitman of Boston.'

Prose, and with the two Harvardians, Stone and Kimball, publishing the *Chap Book*, so that America might not miss Verlaine and Maeterlinck and Mallarmé. Jules Bois came over and lectured triumphantly. It was the period of Beardsley and the *Yellow Book* (and of its echo, Gelett Burgess's delightful *Lark*), of Wilde's comedies and his fall. There was a rage for *fin-de-siècle* little magazines, for exquisite editions of exotic books, for collections of the more fugitive pieces of the minor authors fashionable amongst collectors. The myth of Murger's bohemia was revived by *Trilby*. And certain Bostonians carried their poses into extravagant actions which today seem little credible.

Was there actually a White Rose League dedicated to the Jacobite cause? Did its members constantly remark that the best of the Stuarts had come to America, the proof lying in the person of Mrs. Jack Gardner? Did a certain lady have a room lined with black velvet, in which she posed nude before a select company of gentlemen? Did she repent something else by washing the steps of the Advent one Good Friday? Was a Boston publisher photographed as the crucified Christ? and did his friends once appear in the South Station robed as Apostles? Did another gentleman actually burn off the hand that had slapped a friend's face? Those who should know swear that at least some of these things are true.

A debutante, however, would hardly join in such frolics; and furthermore, Miss Lowell always detested affectations. To Huysmans, probably the greatest genius of the movement, she later wrote a poem, which emphasizes his tragedy and not his poses. The manuscript of Wilde's *Sphinx* was once offered her, but she refused to buy it, and used to tell scornfully how the margin was covered with groups of rhymes which he worked into the poem; though she admired the comedies. Of the poets published by Copeland and Day, in their brief and brilliant career, she knew nothing; even Crane's *Black Riders*, with its orchidaceous cover, she did not discover till many years after.

There were too many other things to interest her. Intercollegiate athletics, in the first flush of their popularity, were inducing the whole nation to exercise; and in Boston, Louisa Wells (national golf champion) made sports fashionable among the debutantes. Bustles went out as the 'safety' bicycle came in; tailored suits, with daring ankle-length skirts, followed, and bloomers were revived. The bicycle freed women from the more artificial fashions, and also gave them means for getting away from the house on a summer afternoon — it was the beginning of their emancipation. All the Lowells rode; Mr. Lowell, sitting bolt upright, went as fast as any scorcher.

But Miss Lowell was a young lady now, and furthermore the most popular debutante of the season. No fewer than sixty dinners were given in her honor. She had learned to dance, and so well, that she enjoyed it as much as ever Jane Austen did. Like many stout persons, she was very light on her feet; and her boisterous good spirits and wit made an excellent substitute for the romantic glamour of other girls. She was always the center of a group of men; when she danced, she was fairly snatched from one partner to another, while she joked at the top of her lungs and shouted to other couples as she whirled past.

There was a certain ritual about balls in those days. The young men who engaged the German in advance sent bouquets; the girls arrived accompanied by their maids, unless they took Kenny & Clark hacks (the coachmen, in dark green coats with silver stag-headed buttons, were sufficient chaperons to any Boston ball). There were round dances: the waltz, which was resolving into 'the Boston'; the two-step, newly invented to go with Sousa marches and coon-songs; also the polka, the schottische, and the riotous mazurka. There were square dances, of which the most popular were the Portland fancy and the lancers. But the climax was the German, in which the gifts of little 'favors' were sure index of a girl's popularity. The last dance was invariably a waltz, to the 'Blue Danube.'

The smartest balls in Boston were the two solemn Assemblies held at Copley Hall, later at the new Somerset; as they were run for the older people, only six debutantes were ever asked; and Miss Lowell, of course, was one of the six in 1891. There were other subscription dances, nicknamed the 'Bachelors' Ball,' the 'Cinderellas' (which stopped short at midnight), and the 'Cheap and Hungries' (which, being inexpensive, served few refreshments).

All her life — until the operations made it impossible — she never missed a chance to waltz, especially at informal gatherings.

Besides dances, there were sleighing-parties, for which fifty or sixty people crowded on the two long plush-covered seats of a huge boat-shaped sleigh, and were driven to some place, singing and joking all the way, while they kept their ankles warm in the straw. There was tobogganing on the slide at Corey Hill; or skating at any number of ponds. There were also lunches and theater parties and concerts.

When one came out, one became automatically a member of the 'Sewing Circle.' The Sewing Circle was one of the unique features of Boston. It had begun with the purpose of persuading the fashionable young ladies to sew for the poor; presently, however, the young ladies discovered that the sewing was done much better if they paid someone else to do it; and by the time Miss Lowell joined, only the president worried about sewing — the Circle had become simply a lunch-club which met once a week at some member's home.

She was free to invite these friends to come stay with her;

now that her brothers and sisters were married, she had the whole top floor of Sevenels at her disposal. The meals were 'as good as a play,' Bessie Ward, from New York, testified, especially if the brothers and sisters were there, for the Lowells were famous conversationalists.

> As they gathered for the over-abundant meals of the era, it seemed to the stranger quite possible that the art of listening might be dispensed with, having become superfluous. Any two members of this family could talk and listen simultaneously, effecting a great economy in time and patience, for conflicting opinions might be stated, registered, and answered at the same moment. New England reserve did not prevail at that large table. No Latins or Slavs could have discussed more fervently, or with more expressive gesture, the local happenings or larger questions of the day.[1]

Another visitor, Louise Winsor Brooks, was there once during the excitement over the Borden murder trial. In the midst of dinner, the Lowells suddenly began to act it out: Percival was the prosecuting attorney, while Lawrence, in a brilliant speech, proved that the axe committed the double murder all alone, then went and buried itself in the garden. Guests, except for Lowell Institute lecturers and their peers, usually found the Lowell conversations a trifle terrifying.

But the brothers and sisters brought this vivacity with them.

> When this distinguished middle generation had gone about its engrossing interests, and the house was left to the parents and the two girls, reserve descended like a fog carried by the local east wind. The mother's invalidism, the father's stern conventions as to time and order, even in the conventional nineties, left non-conformist youth without sun or sun-warmed air to breathe. Unaccustomed terror

[1] Elizabeth Ward Perkins: 'Amy Lowell of New England,' *Scribner's Magazine* (LXXXII, 329), September, 1927.

fell upon the visitor, a spoiled only daughter, when a port-folio left on a forbidden table, or arrival late for breakfast, shadowed the hospitable spirit of the house and lowered the temperature.[1]

The solution was to get out of the house; and the girls went buggy-riding all over the neighborhood. Miss Lowell already had formed a theory that Fanny Brawne was not the silly, heartless creature that Keats's biographers sup-posed her to be; she and Bessie Ward would take a volume of his letters with them and thrash the matter out, pausing only when some other carriage made an ill-advised attempt to pass them. Or they would discuss religion, as Miss Ward was a Roman Catholic; and those who overheard them (for this discussion continued as long as they lived) said that Amy was always excited with a cold intellectual flame and Bessie always calm, even when Amy cried out, 'You're talking the jargon of a sect!'

Florence Wheelock, not yet Florence Ayscough, also visited in Brookline.

One of my greatest pleasures was to go out to 'Sevenels' and, starting from there, drive for miles through the woods with Amy. As you know, she handled a horse most beauti-fully, and as we drove we talked — talked about every-thing imaginable. Her keen common sense and very true sense of values often came to the fore. I remember very well an occasion when my girlish fancy had been rather taken by quite a charming youth and I was trying to decide what my course should be. Amy was most definite: 'No, my dear, never marry any man *unless you can't help it.*' I can-not imagine better advice.

I am not sure whether the autumn days, when the dry leaves sizzled under the wheels of the buggy, or the spring days, when tiny flowers glimmered in the pale sunshine, remain with me most vividly; at all events those drives in what was then the open country beyond Brookline, are very vital memories to me. [2]

[1] Elizabeth Ward Perkins, *ibid.*
[2] Florence Ayscough: 'Reminiscences' (*ms.*).

Miss Lowell often went visiting in turn. She was particularly fond of staying with the Lewis Cabots in Dublin, New Hampshire; Monadnock and Dublin Lake fascinated her, as well as the fashionably artistic people who summered there — Joseph Lindon Smith, the painter, whose place, 'Loon Point,' was full of things from the Orient; George DeForest Brush, Abbott Thayer, and Alexander James (son of William), who were also artists; Mrs. Charles MacVeagh, who gave theatricals; Eugenia Frothingham, who wrote books and sang charmingly; and other old friends, Mary Hutchinson and Mrs. Thomas McKittrick. Miss Lowell also visited Dolly Brooks at the famous Francis Brooks estate in West Medford;[1] with the original Indian deed, the kettle from which chocolate was served to the soldiers from Lexington, and the magnificent old gardens with the painted lead statues of Paul and Virginia. These gardens, among the oldest in America, vied in friendly rivalry with the Lowell's at Sevenels and the Sargent's, also in Brookline. Beyond the Brooks gardens was a field filled with fringed gentians, which Mrs. Francis Brooks never allowed the children to pick, as there were plenty of flowers in the beds. She was the author of *A Year's Sonnets*, Boston, 1885, and of the first English translation of *Heidi*. She kept open house; to Amy Lowell this constant coming and going of any number of guests, all in high spirits, was something like a revelation after the comparatively restricted atmosphere of Sevenels. She went driving a great deal with Dolly Brooks, whose constant delight in details of the countryside stimulated her tremendously. But the Brookses were puzzled by one problem: how it was that Amy Lowell, whose father was so notably strict about meal-hours, could never get down

[1] For a description of this place, since taxed out of existence, see Richard B. Coolidge: 'The Brooks Estates in Medford from 1660 to 1927,' *Medford Historical Register* (xxx, 1–20) March, 1927. The lead statues, which inspired Miss Lowell's 'The Statue in the Garden,' also inspired 'Paul and Virginia' in John Wheelwright's *Rock and Shell*.

to dinner on time. They made a game of it, pointedly waiting for her, then not waiting at all, or ignoring her tardiness, then commenting on it. But nothing worked; she was imperturbably late and always sweetly apologetic, and then just as late next time.

When she was not visiting, there were always her nephews and nieces, now growing up rapidly, who adored their young Aunt Amy. She remembered all their birthdays, and gave them the best presents; she played games with them outdoors and in; she read *Robin Hood* aloud to them, or got them to singing Gilbert and Sullivan (she knew all the songs by heart); and even unlocked her private bookcase for their browsing.

> I well remember racing with one of my nieces, when she was about twelve years old, to see which of us could learn Poe's 'Raven' first, and then we used to recite it out loud together with tremendous expression, and if one of us made a slip which the other could correct, the delight of the corrector knew no bounds. I used to keep a bookcase in my room full of books — poetry, fairy stories, everything — for my nieces and nephews, which they could come to whenever they wanted, and many is the time I have come in and found them grouped round the room, all reading, and then there would be the cry, 'O Aunt Amy, listen to this.' [1]

Her sister Katherine did not recover quickly from the shock of her husband's death, so Miss Lowell spent much time with her children.

> As a young girl she was driving one day with her little nephew, James Roosevelt, when the horse ran away. Amy told me afterwards that the one thought in her mind was, 'Katie has lost her husband; now I am killing her boy.' The horse was stopped by a wonderful feat of strength and skill on the part of her brother Lawrence just before they reached the dangerous sharp turn at the entrance gates of Sevenels. [2]

[1] Letter to Mrs. C. H. Goddard, November 27, 1917.
[2] Katharine Dana White: 'Recollections of Amy Lowell in Childhood' (*ms.*).

And when Major James Roosevelt died on the transport coming home from the war, Amy Lowell mourned: 'I practically brought him up, as my sister was an invalid, and he was almost like my son.' [1]

Datable events of these busy years of the debutante are not many, although it can be taken for granted that she was present at every event of any importance, whether ball or drama or college game; many girls envied her this ubiquity.

The first event was the filling of her private bookcase and the acquiring of a second, to hold the first set of books she ever bought, just after Christmas, 1891.

> My Christmas present from my mother was always in the form of a cheque which I might spend how I would. Needless to say, it always went for books. One Christmas, I was debating what I should buy, and my brother suggested that I should get 'some really good books' at a second-hand shop in Cornhill. He volunteered to take me there, and one morning, bright and early since he was on his way to his office, we set out. That shop!— many a sleepless night do I owe to it. But on this December morning it was perfect. As we entered the door, stacked upon the floor inside were a number of beautiful gold and leather books. They were a complete set of Sir Walter Scott. A complete set, do I say: *the* complete set, the first complete set ever published! Each volume had two engravings in the front; the sides were blind tooled in diamond-shaped lozenges, soft and comfortable to the fingers; the backs were brave with black and gold. What was it to me that the books were 'rebacked,' I loved them on the instant; but the price, of course, surpassed my cheque. How I waited and suffered while my brother reasoned with the proprietor; I had no hope, and an almost unbearable longing. My experience of shops had not included a double price, I dared not think. But the cheque, the cheque was there to prove what I had thought my wealth, my poverty. My

[1] Letter to Winifred Bryher, May 28, 1919.

brother was an able pleader, and I got the books. Got them, and read practically nothing else for months.[1]

In March, 1892, the Vincent Club, another institution peculiar to Boston, was founded. Mrs. Vincent for years had been a leading member of the Boston Museum Stock Company; after her death, a gift of money in her memory was used to build the Vincent Memorial Hospital for wage-earning women and girls. The building was erected in January, 1891; but further funds were needed; so the Vincent Club was founded, to provide the money through theatricals given by the Boston debutantes. These performances eventually became original musical comedies, modelled discreetly after the Pudding Shows; and that the proprieties might be observed, no men were admitted, until the World War. The only exceptions were the firemen, whose presence was required by law; so they wore masks, that the young ladies might not be embarrassed by recognizing them in some chance encounter outside. Miss Lowell was a charter member; but it is not remembered that she ever acted. She was, however, busy on the committees.

When she was eighteen, she had her portrait painted in her ballgown, by Miss Sarah Putnam, a second cousin. For many years, this portrait was her only likeness, and was used for publicity until she began lecturing.

In April, 1893, Duse on her first American tour came to the Globe Theater, which proudly boasted that it was 'Illuminated by the Edison Incandescant Light.' Duse gave *Camille*, *Fedora*, and a double bill of *Cavalleria Rusticana* and *La Locandiera*, all in Italian of course. Miss Lowell went, and felt something of the greatness of her acting, though not until the tour of 1902 did Duse become the overwhelming vision that started Miss Lowell writing poetry.[2]

[1] Amy Lowell: 'That Bookcase.' The set is at Harvard, with the date of purchase written in.

[2] In two letters written May 27, 1924, after Duse's death, Miss Lowell re-

On May 11, 1893, Percy wrote Amy his last letter from
the Far East, then returned home to stay. That winter,
he lectured at the Lowell Institute, his brother Lawrence
having lectured there the winter before. Percival then
turned to astronomy, founding the Lowell Observatory
in Flagstaff, Arizona, but spending his odd hours in
finishing *Occult Japan* (1894), a fascinating account of his
experiments in Japanese popular religions.

On December 19, 1893, Bessie's third child, Roger
Lowell Putnam, was born; there was also a twin sister who
died.

In May, 1894, Mounet-Sully, the great French actor,
came to the Tremont Theater; Miss Lowell saw him on
the ninth in the title-rôle of Ruy Blas, and a new world —
that of French literature — was opened to her.

> What queer things children are! I hated to study, but if
> I wanted anything, no effort was too great for me to make
> to bring it within reach. Part of my education consisted
> in being taken to see eminent actors. On one occasion,
> Mounet-Sully came to Boston, and I saw him in Hugo's
> 'Ruy Blas.' I came home walking on air and demanded
> of every one I saw information as to what Victor Hugo had
> written. Some one said, 'Notre Dame de Paris,' and
> 'Notre Dame' I got out of the library the next day. French,
> having hitherto been a hated study, I had, of course, ac-
> quired as little of as I could and stay in my class. But I
> wanted to read 'Notre Dame.' Many a night did I sit up
> in bed, reading by the flickering light of two candles, and
> looking up every word I did not know in the dictionary lest
> I lose some of the beauty of the descriptions. I believe
> Victor Hugo woke me up to the meaning of style. I was

ferred to this tour. In a letter to Louis Untermeyer she mentioned 'my reactions over a period of thirty years. I think I have told you what she has been
to me: how she started me in writing poetry and how she has been to me an
artistic ideal ever since I was eighteen.' To be precise, Miss Lowell was nineteen
when Duse came, thirty-one years before her death. In a letter to Hervey Allen
written the same day, Miss Lowell repeated that Duse had been 'my artistic
ideal for thirty years.'

lifted on the wings of a great poetry; although, so little had poetry been a thing which I considered, I did not know it was that...

Victor Hugo opened the doors of poetry for me, but through his prose. I did not then advance to his poetry, because — because — another Christmas came, and my now periodic visits to the Cornhill bookshop yielded Moxon's editions of Shelley and Keats. There indeed was my Waterloo, I surrendered completely to poetry, and with that surrender the chapter of my childhood definitely closed.[1]

Indeed, Keats was in the air; for on July 16, 1894, the first Keats memorial on English soil was unveiled on the parish church of Hampstead. It was a bust of the poet, made by the Boston sculptor, Anne Whitney, and was given by Charles Eliot Norton and other American men of letters.

A year later, on April 1, 1895, Amy's mother died, after a long siege of Bright's disease that antedated Miss Lowell's birth and that had kept Mrs. Lowell an invalid for many years.

Miss Lowell was now twenty-one, and inevitably she thought of authorship. Percy had published four fascinating books on the Far East, and in 1895 issued his *Mars*, the first of his astronomical books, in which by reaffirming Schiaparelli's reputed discovery of the Martian canals he was to cause great speculation.[2] Lawrence had published a book on government, and was just finishing another. Her sister Bessie also wrote, though she did not publish.[3] So Amy Lowell also played with her pen, trying

[1] Amy Lowell: 'That Bookcase.' The date of Mounet-Sully's performance has been established by the programs and newspapers; it was his first tour, so there is no question about the date. Miss Lowell was twenty at the time; looking back, she remembered herself as younger than she really was.

[2] Percival Lowell's calculations indicating an unknown planet led to the discovery after his death of Planet X in 1930.

[3] *Twenty-Eight Sonnets*, by Mrs. William Lowell Putnam, was published in 1929; *Odours of Hyacinth* in 1930; besides three prose volumes.

her hand at plays, novels, and short stories, none of which
satisfied her, and all of which were eventually destroyed.
She had written no verse since she was fifteen or sixteen:
not that she had given it up; she had simply lost interest
and forgotten all about it. Despairing of original compositions, she planned an elaborate biography of Matthew
Arnold.

> In my early twenties I conceived the idea of writing a life
> of him, and to that end read everything he wrote, including
> the school reports and everything I could lay hand on about
> the period, but a merciful providence prevented my touch-
> ing pen to paper.[1]

Although she filled two small notebooks with jottings,
she never actually began the writing of the book, and
eventually lost her first full enthusiasm for the man. In
later years she admired his essays, referred to him as 'a
very fine if somewhat attenuated poet,'[2] and in her *John
Keats* (II, 125) wrote of him still more severely:

> Matthew Arnold, for all his culture, his reiterated cry for
> 'sweetness and light,' was an arch-snob. His attitude to-
> ward the people he met when he toured America, lecturing
> under the auspices of P. T. Barnum, is one proof of this,
> and there are many others scattered through his letters.

In the summer of 1896 she went abroad again, with
Katie Dana and one of the Miss Dabneys, for six months,
'this time taking the Southern route to Naples, and going
through Italy, Austria, Germany, France, Holland, and
England.'[3] She fell absolutely in love with Naples, then
again with Venice, as appears from a letter she wrote Mrs.
A. Lawrence Lowell at the end of June.

[1] Letter to Stanley T. Williams, January 23, 1923. In this letter she also
quotes the opening of one of her early sonnets, now lost:
Dear Master, it is years since first my mind
Came under sway of thine....
[2] Letter to Stanley T. Williams, January 23, 1923.   [3] *Ms.* (1916).

AMY LOWELL AS A DEBUTANTE

HOTEL BRITANNIA, VENICE
Friday, June 26th, 1896

DEAR ANNA,

At last I have a moment to write in. A heavy storm, one cannot possibly write here under any other circumstances; mornings, afternoons, and evenings we are out of the house. I have never seen such a delightful place in all my life, I have enjoyed every minute of it. It was such a nice change after Florence.

Oh how we did work in Florence. The things we saw were most beautiful, but how we did bustle round seeing them. Then I was taken with a new and strange disease called Apthee or some such thing, so that my last week in Florence consisted largely of my own room. It (the disease) consists of a mixture of tonsilitis and cankers, thank Goodness it has gone. Then we came on here, and I do hope heaven will be like this, though it would seem a pity to have those back streets paved with gold and there aren't any others. I love every street and stone of this place, or rather every wave and ripple. We are having a moon, the very best moon that ever was, and we 'gondle' way out in the lagoon and have the moon on one side and the lights of the city on the other.

Wednesday we did a delightful thing; the Lowells, the Schieffeliens and ourselves went to Torcello. The Putnams had gone a few hours earlier and we were to meet them there. We got as far as St. Francisco in Deserto and then a large black thundercloud loomed up in front of us. We therefore camped out on the grass there and eat our supper. Then we decided to go on, much against the will of the gondoliers. It was magnificent when we started, the thundercloud was a sort of lurid yellow, and the water had colors in it such as I never have seen before. We got to Torcello all right and the storm passed round us. We found the Putnams ignominiously eating their supper in the house. We went over and saw as much as we could of the church by the light of one candle. It was quite ghostly. Then Eleanor Schieffelien & Miss Mary went up the campanile. It must have [been] very lovely up there, the moon was just rising round and red. I stayed down below to com-

fort Mrs. Schieffelien, who was rather worried and anxious.
Then we came home and the storm had gone, and the
moon was there and big wind-blown clouds. Oh what a
night!!! We were going to Malamocco this afternoon, but
it is a big, big storm.

Tell Lawrence that I spent hours looking at the St.
Ursula in the Accademia, and Tintoretto simply carries me
off my feet. We are not sightseeing worth a cent here, we
cannot do it somehow. We have seen a good many things
once, but when the weather and the city and out of doors
generally is so very enchanting, there hardly seems to be
room for anything else. I have Elly Lee's gondolier Tita,
he regards himself as an old family servant, and I am
so proud in the possession of my first manservant. In fact
I feel rather proud of our menage here, anyway....

I have been learning how to 'gondle,' it is the most
fatiguing thing I have ever done, I did it for about two
hours yesterday. Tita said there was 'molto vento,' & I
should rather think there was. We 'gondled' straight into
the teeth of a booming gale. The consequence is that it
seems to me as if I had developed about fifteen brand-new
muscles, and my hands are quite sore & blistery, but Tita
thinks I am *very* strong & that my perseverance is splendid,
'just like Signor Lee,' which is the highest compliment he
can give.

Miss Frothingham & Miss Fuller are here, and we have
such jolly times together. We sat up in their parlour this
P.M. and I read out loud some of Miss Fuller's new book,
'A Venetian June.' It was such fun reading it on the spot,
with the Salute & San Giorgio Maggiore peeking at us
through the windows.

Oh how fond I am of them both and how I am going to
miss them. But go we must, we shall have been here two
weeks and a half, & on Wednesday next we leave for Cortina. This climate does not suit Katie Dana, but I hope the
Tyrol will send her up again. I shall be desperately homesick, 'Venice is the land for me.'

I went to the Curtis's to dine the other night, & wore my
one balldress. It is quite romantic, going out to dinner in

a gondola. The butler waited at table assisted by one of the gondoliers in full gondola tog, of white flannel trimmed with red, it struck me a little like having a groom in breeches & top boots. The C's have been most polite & attentive & really affectionate. Tomorrow we go to their garden, a high honor I believe....

Naples and Venice always remained her two favorite Italian cities. From Interlaken Miss Lowell wrote Anna again, on August 10; but by this time as they had taken up the whirl of sightseeing again, her letter was chiefly an excited itinerary.

... From Cortina we went back to Innsbruck, and there quite unexpectedly we met the Putnams on their way to St. Moritz. We saw them for a few hours, and then left and went on to Munich, where we stayed over Sunday; and when I tell you that we went to a popular concert on Sunday evening and drank black beer out of mugs with pewter tops that lovingly enveloped one's ear while one drank, you can imagine that I have taken kindly to European customs, and ruthlessly deserted the traditions of my ancestors. From Munich we went to Nuremburg, and from there to Bayreuth. Oh Bayreuth, Frank Bullard and I agreed that it was an era in one's life to be there. It was almost like a religious ceremony, and so impressive; but it was almost too exciting, people were very much unstrung by it.

From Bayreuth we came back to Nuremburg, and there was a telegram from Katie saying she was to be in Nuremburg, and a letter from Papa saying he was to be in Lucerne with Margaret and Lizette before joining Katie. Well, I took a carriage and went to every hotel in the city. No Katie. At length a brilliant inspiration came to Miss Dabney and we telephoned to K's hotel in Munich, only to find that she had gone to Dresden!!! Well, an afternoon wasted and gone, to say nothing of my temper, which I seemed to have lost on the road. But Papa was still left, at least I fondly thought so, and Katie's family were in Interlaken, and I had promised that I should spend a week with them, and Lucerne was on the way. So to Lucerne we went, but the banks and hotels all shook their heads when I asked for Papa. At last I discovered Lizette, & Margaret & Lawrence, but when I asked for Papa, they said he had gone to join Katie. So I have given them up in despair, and content myself with writing and telegraphing invectives and any little biting thing I can think of. I thought Margaret seemed uncommonly well and happy, though the whole party hated Lucerne, and I should think they might. Then we came on here, & gave Katie to her family.

LEUKERBAD, *Wednesday*

Miss Dabney and I are on a five days' trip through the high mountains while Katie sees her family at Interlaken. We came over the Geninna Pass today, with horses, and then down on foot. I distinguished myself when we were almost down by spraining my ankle. Such a new departure for me. So here I am lying on the sofa with my foot all bandaged up, as usual, and wondering when I shall be able to walk nicely again.

But coming over the Pass was the most wonderful thing, with clouds and flying mists, and great splashes of sunshine, and the most beautiful view of the valley through the mists all round us. And sometimes we rode through great drifts of snow. Tomorrow we go on to Zermatt, and then over the Furca & the Grindel back to stupid old Interlaken to pick up Katie, and then to France, to drive through Picardy, Touraine, & Brittany....

In September she was at 57 Rue de Lille, Paris, writing the date and address in books she bought: Georges Frage-rolle's 'epopée lyrique,' *Le Sphinx*; the 'mystère,' *La Marche à l'Etoile*; and *L'Enfant Prodigue*. She also went to London, where she bought books of, and made a friend of, E. H. Dring, of Bernard Quaritch, Ltd.[1] Whistler's wife had

---

[1] She wrote him on March 3, 1920: 'I cannot tell you how disappointed I was not to see you, since this is the first time you have come to America in the twenty-four years since we have known each other.'

died that May, and he had gone to London, to live with Mr. W. Heinemann. Mrs. Heinemann took Miss Lowell to visit the great painter in his studio; there she bought a picture, and was always convinced that he was secretly pleased by the perspicacity of her choice.

> I am afraid nobody has ever directed anything where I am concerned. I cannot remember ever to have taken advice on buying anything of any kind. My grand experience in that line was when I was twenty-two and was taken by a friend to see Whistler in his studio. I bought a picture on that occasion, the little one you have seen hanging on the chimney-breast in the library. Mr. Whistler informed me that it was not as good as another picture of the same size and price, but I maintained that I preferred this one (I was very ignorant). However, I took the one I wanted, and I think Whistler was rather pleased that I did for other reasons than that he had the better one still to sell. What is more strange is that I have never regretted my choice.[1]

Then she returned home again.

On April 29, 1897, the Vincent Club departed so far from its traditions as to give 'Wax-Works,' a series of living pictures, in Copley Hall. The groups (one of which was a 'Judgement of Paris') included young men; the general public was admitted. Miss Lowell was head of the Committee, and also acted as usher.

On August 30, Harriet Putnam, Bessie's fourth child, was born; the number of Amy Lowell's nephews and nieces was finally completed with the birth of Augustus Lowell Putnam on June 25, 1899.

There remains one more episode in her life of the early twenties — an episode undatable, but which perhaps occurred in 1897. A young Bostonian proposed marriage; as she was deeply in love with him, she accepted; and the engagement was all but announced. Unfortunately he

[1] Letter to A. Edward Newton, November 10, 1921.

became entangled elsewhere, and the Lowell alliance was broken off.[1] Too proud to give outward sign, Miss Lowell secluded herself for days in her room, emerging only for meals.

Perhaps this event was one cause for the decision that she should spend the coming winter abroad.

[1] Miss Lowell received several proposals, now and later; 'A Communication,' in *Ballads for Sale*, was addressed to one of these admirers.

CHAPTER VI

THE BOAT OF THE RISING MOON

'The day is fair. In the clear Egyptian air...'

WHETHER or not her real reason for spending the winter of 1897–98 in Egypt was simply to get away from Sevenels and Boston, the ostensible reason was banting. She was abnormally stout. Medical science in those days knew nothing of glandular troubles and the like; the fact that her hands, feet, and head were perfectly normal did not affect the doctors' opinion that the whole trouble lay in her food. It was expected that the Egyptian heat and a diet of nothing but tomatoes and asparagus would correct the trouble.

Her father had to be persuaded — it would be her first Christmas away from home — but finally it was arranged. Polly Cabot, who was in France with a nurse, also would benefit from the trip, and could probably be persuaded to go. The two Dabney sisters would be the chaperons, Miss Frances as far as the train to Paris, and Miss Ellen from Paris on. In November, 1897, Miss Lowell bade farewell to her family, promising to write her father every Sunday; then with her maid Mary and Miss Frances Dabney and all her luggage, including a kodak (she was an enthusiastic photographer), and a new bicycle for use in France, she got off.

She wrote as regularly as she had promised; all but one of the twenty-three letters to her father have been preserved. The first six (November 14 — December 19, 1897) deal with the uneventful preliminaries. From England she went to France for 'a perfectly delightful week in that beloved Paris,' then on to Hyères for a couple of weeks, where she joined Polly Cabot and made the final arrangements for the trip up the Nile. They sailed from Marseilles to Alexandria, taking the train there to Cairo, where their little dahabeah *Chonsu*, named for the God of the rising moon, awaited them, with its two slanting, slender, triangular sails. Before embarking, they went to see the Pyramids and the Sphinx. Then, according to custom, they planned to ascend the Nile as rapidly as possible, anticipating the falling river and the rising thermometer; and to explore the temples at their leisure on their way back. This scheme had the added advantage of leaving many of the best ruins for the end of the trip. They did not, however, go up to the Second Cataract, but when they reached Aboo Simbel, decided to make that the turning point.

[VII]   Dahabeah 'Chonsu.' Sunday, December 26th, 1897, near where Memphis was once.

Here we are really on our own dahabeah at last. Our dragoman seems to be very nice; his name is Michael Abdu, a Syrian. He has worked for Cook for a number of years, and all the crew are men that have been on Cook's boats before, so that they are known all about.

They are most of them Nubians, with two Egyptians. The numbers we require seem quite ridiculous. Ten sailors, a captain, a steersman, a cook & a cook's assistant, a waiter & a waiter's assistant, and finally a dragoman. Seventeen men to take five women up the Nile.... The dahabeah herself is a little dot of a thing only 75 ft. long, but delightfully fitted up. There is a little saloon where we dine and three single state rooms, and a double one in the stern, which Miss Dabney and I have. The upper deck is all fitted up with sofas and long chairs and Turkish rugs and plants. Cook is most liberal in the way in which he fits up his boats, there is nothing that one could possibly want that is left out....

I never imagined anything so beautiful as it is. It is just as everyone has always said it was. Perfectly wonderful, a pink most of the time, mixed with purple. It is not too hot yet, in fact when the sun sets it is really quite cold, and also in the early morning. But the sun has tremendous power. The others are simply wild, and sketch all the time. It is the most delightful climate, and, in short there is so much that is beautiful that I cannot possibly describe it.

We are not going to see sights on the way up, because we want to push on to Aboo Simbel as fast as possible, so as to be sure to get up before it is too hot or the river too low. And we are going to do our sightseeing on the way down....

It seems to me that the color that best expresses the Nile is my pink diamond. It is really just like that....

Part of the ritual of the trip on the Nile was the singing of the crew, for which the passengers were expected to provide the crude musical instruments necessary for the accompaniment — a tambourine, drum, and a cocoanut fiddle. The noise that ensued was such that most tourists could hardly endure it; but Miss Lowell, though she did not mention it in her letters, recalled it years later with great pleasure.

> I remember, twenty years ago, when I was on the Nile, being greatly intrigued and delighted by the strange and difficult rhythms of the songs sung by the crew of our dahabiah as they rowed.[1]

She had plenty of opportunity to listen to this music during the first two weeks of the trip, before they reached Denderah, where they saw their first temple.

[VIII]   Dahabeah 'Chonsu,' Upper Egypt.
Sunday, January 2nd, 1898.

There does not seem to be much to write about this week, for we have not got to the part of the Nile where the temples are yet. Tomorrow we hope to reach Assiut, and after that the most interesting part begins, though we do not expect to see very much till our return journey.

Today we have been coasting the mountain of Gebel Abu Fadah. It is a magnificent cliff of some soft yellow stone,

[1] 'Some Musical Analogies in Modern Poetry,' *Musical Quarterly* (VI, 127–57), January, 1920.

sandstone, I suppose, and the scenery today has been the finest that we have seen so far. Miss Edwards in her 'Thousand Miles Up the Nile' says that somewhere on the face of the cliff she saw two royal ovals and the remains of an immense bas-relief. So of course we spent all the morning gazing at the cliffs with a glass, and ruining our eyes trying to discover these things. Miss Dabney and I thought we discovered the bas-relief, but I am sorry to say that Polly laughed at us, but the ovals were nowhere to be seen.

I posted my last letter to you at such a strange little place called Bibêh. It was our first introduction to a small village, seen from within and not from the water. I have come to the conclusion that I prefer the latter method. We proceeded through Bibêh like an army, in Indian file, Michael leading the way, all of us women in the middle, and a sailor at the end as rearguard, and so we wound round through this singularly dirty though extremely picturesque village in search of the postoffice, for we landed for the sole object of posting our letters. I hope you got it, the letter I posted to you there, for the postoffice did not look as if anything either came into it or went out.

A day or two later we stopped at Minieh to get some provisions etc. Here Michael went ahead to bargain for eggs, poultry etc. and we followed in the charge of the sailors. They are so funny when they have to escort us, these sailors, they evidently consider it a great honor, and are very proud in consequence. This day Polly wanted to buy some blue cotton, so we stopped in the bazaar to get some. And it was so funny, neither the sailors nor the shopkeeper spoke a word of English, and it is needless to say that our Arabic is not fluent; so we gesticulated, and the sailors gesticulated, and the shopman, and the whole town which gradually collected behind us, at last Michael came to our aid, master of both Arabic and English, and the bargain was completed. Michael seems to be a very good dragoman, he seems to have a faculty with beggars, for no one ever even suggests that we should give them backsheesh. The whole voyage is delightful, and the coloring simply wonderful. And I have never seen the stars so brilliant anywhere else. The climate is delightful and the air cool and exhilarating. It is COLD in the morning, but the sun is very powerful, and changes what had started as an autumn day into a summer one, when the sun sets there is a curious chill, which lasts half an hour or so, and then it becomes warm again, growing colder some time during the night. I suppose this is the way it does in all eastern countries, I never tried one before....

[IX]   Dahabeah 'Chonsu.' Beyond Den-
                                     derah, Upper Egypt. Sunday, January
                                     9th, 1898.

We have seen our first temple! And far from being dis-appointed we were more than surprized. Michael told us that we should get there at twelve o'clock, but of course the wind fell and we did not get there till three. Then we mounted donkeys and rode the two miles to the temple.

It is so entirely surrounded by the debris out of which it has been excavated, that you can only see a shapeless mound until you are close upon it; then the corner emerges and then at last, a gateway. Here you dismount. Then we went along a short avenue of crude bricks. Here you de-scend some steps into the temple, for the inside has been fully excavated, but the outside not. The first is the Hypostyle Hall, with twenty-four Hathor headed columns. This tem-ple was sacred to Hathor, the goddess of truth, beauty, and goodness. It is a late temple, Ptolemaic, and is conse-quently somewhat influenced by the Greek. It is a most beautiful temple, and we had read up about it everything that we could lay our hands upon. The Ptolemaic temples were consecutive in design, which the Pharaonic were not. And in the bas-reliefs at Denderah you can see exactly what the King did at the sacred festivals and you can follow all the processions just as they were, even up the stairs to the roof, for they are sculptured on the walls. On a certain day the shrine of Hathor was taken up to a little temple on the roof, and one can follow the whole course of the ceremonies. Most of the rooms are perfectly dark, but we all had candles and Michael had some magnesium wire and we saw very well indeed. We went back again this morning and just stayed there for about four hours, Miss Dabney sketched and Polly and I roamed round, and I studied the sculptures minutely by candlelight, and I do not know when I have enjoyed anything more or been so much interested. Lawrence and Anna ought to come, they would enjoy it so much. But they must come by dahabeah, for the tourist boat must be something awful, and although the postboats must be much better, still they only give you about an hour or two at places, and that is NEVER ENOUGH. While we were there appeared an influx of Gaza tourists, forty of them hounded through the temple by a portly dragoman; that is one thing about Michael, he is not portly and he is always on hand when we want him, and he does not bother at all when we don't, but lets us do just as we please, and does not even seem to mind, which is odd in a person in his position....

... The view over the desert from the roof of the temple was superb. I wish I could make you see it all. I am constantly reminded of the Gleyse pictures, and I never realized how good they were before. He has got the exact coloring....

Next time I shall be able to tell you about Karnak....

Her description of Karnak, however, was written in a letter to Mrs. A. Lawrence Lowell.

Dahabeah 'Chonsu,' Upper Egypt.
Friday, January 14th, 1898.

I have developed a new branch lately, namely cartouches. The charm of this particular game is that you stand for hours, book in hand, searching for the particular cartouche on the wall in front of you. You never can find it exactly, but you can find it very nearly in those of about five different Kings, which is discouraging.

I think that Karnak impressed me more than any building I ever saw in my life. It is all in ruins of course, but I am inclined to think even more impressive for that reason. The Hypostyle Court is, I am sure, more beautiful as it is, with most of the roofing stones gone and the sun checkering the pillars and the floor. I was almost disappointed at first, I had heard so much about it, and the effect of the immense size is much taken away by the debris piled in the side aisles, almost to the tops of the pillars. But the second day I spent some time just sitting on the ground against one of the side pillars, and just looking at the light and shade, and the immense size of the centre columns. And this time I was not disappointed. The sculptures are beautiful throughout the whole temple. I could not have believed that they would have been so much better than those at Denderah; but they were, and I see now why everyone said that the Ptolemaic art was so inferior to the Pharaonic. The firmness and purity of line in these bas reliefs were beautiful. And there is a great deal of color in many parts of the temple. The principal colors are yellow, a brick red, and a sort of blue green exactly like an old turquoise that has turned. A very queer but delightfully Egyptian combination. And the temple is built of all kinds of materials, pink and blue granite, sandstone, etc., and all this with the intense blue of the African sky above it, & flooded by the more than intense African sun. We wandered round book in hand reading the translations of the hieroglyphic inscriptions, and much interested. Imagine coming up on a tourist steamer, and being hounded through in no time, while a guide tells palpable untruths to credulous fools. I was sitting the second day at the foot of two broken columns in front of the sanctuary, reading; when a Cook's tourist party came through in detachments; and everyone was told by the dragoman in turn that a lotus on one of the columns was papyrus, and *vice versa* for the other column; the dragoman always throwing in as a choice bit that the papyrus was the most beautiful column that he had ever seen in his life. Of course one does not see Karnak in an afternoon and a morning, but we are coming back to spend a long time there. Just now we are on the dead rush to Aboo Simbel, our goal. And we can stop to see nothing on the way. Denderah and Karnak were irresistible but wicked exceptions. We had not had a good wind for a week till this morning, so we started at 5:30 and hope to reach Edfoo tonight, and there we can post our letters....

At Karnak, Miss Lowell saw what she always remembered as the most beautiful piece of Egyptian sculpture she ever saw: the Kiss of Amon Ra and Thutmosis IV, carved in relief on a doorway of blue granite. She photographed it, of course (she brought home five albums of snapshots), and in 1905 commissioned Joseph Lindon Smith to make a large painting of it.

Her letter to Anna Lowell left little to say in the tenth letter to her father: their watches by now were all quite different, and there was no way of telling which was right; they had run into the Putnams — the first white people they had seen for three weeks; yesterday a wind sprang up at last, 'and we have been spinning up the river, past the temple of Esneh, past the temple of Edfu, past the tombs of El Kab, and the quarries of Gebel Silsileh, and last but by no means least, perhaps even first, the newly excavated and most beautiful little temple of Kom Ombo.'

The eleventh letter, that of January 23, must have been written, as she mentions mailing it at Korosko on the following Thursday; but it is now lost. It undoubtedly described the twenty-four hour wait at Assouan, while the crew baked its supply of bread; the ascent of the three mile stretch of rapids called the 'First Cataract'; and the visit to Philae at the head, where Egypt ends and Nubia begins. The loss is to be deplored, as undoubtedly the letter was lively. The local natives who hauled dahabeahs up the Cataract always dramatized the event decidedly, with an eye to extra backsheesh; and Amelia B. Edwards, in her *Thousand Miles Up the Nile* (which Miss Lowell had been reading) described unnecessary difficulties and costly delays that were ended only when one of her party uttered a choice Arabic malediction. Thus warned in advance, Miss Lowell was prepared to stand no nonsense.

Apparently the first part of the ascent went smoothly

enough. While the craft was being hauled up from pool to pool by the Cataract Arabs, Miss Lowell sat placidly on deck, writing with that recent invention, a fountain pen. The Arabs, she observed, were mightily awed by the way the ink kept flowing magically, although there was no ink-pot.

Then came the outburst, the details of which were doubtless unintelligible. But Miss Lowell advanced to-wards the crowd, her mysterious pen held high like a wand, threatening them with death. The terrified Arabs instantly became docile, and hauled the boat the rest of the way.

Then the crew of the *Chonsu* obstinately refused to take it over to the island of Philae. So Miss Lowell, her dander thoroughly roused by this time, took the dahabeah over herself. Thereafter she had not the slightest trouble with the crew.[1]

A few days later they reached the objective of their trip. 'Never shall I forget Aboo Simbel as our dahabeah swung round the curve in the river and those four colossal figures sat gazing calmly down upon the blue river with that bright orange tumble of sand beside them.'[2]

[XII]   Aboo Simbel. Sunday, January 30th, 1898.

To think that we are really here seems too good to be true. This has been our goal ever since we started, and I never supposed that we should really get here. It seemed too impossible, and too far away, it is 762 miles from Cairo, and as there is only one steamer a week, it seems far, far away from civilization.

---

[1] Information from Professor Royall Snow, to whom Miss Lowell told the story. She also wrote, in a letter to Miss Winifred Bryher, July 28, 1919: 'Some day I will tell you about a row I had with the Cataract Arabs when we went up the Nile, and how I took the dahabeah across to Philae myself, to the surprise and consternation of the natives, and my consequent ascendency over them for the rest of my trip. I was just your age at the time, and was running a party consisting of an invalid friend and fifteen recalcitrant natives.... I saw Philae before the dam was built and when the colors were still bright on those wonderful capitals.'

[2] Letter to Winifred Bryher, July 28, 1919.

I posted my last letter to you from Korosko on Thursday. And there the river takes a big bend, so the splendid North Wind that would have been gloriously fair anywhere else, was dead against us, and it took us two days and a half to track eight miles.

There is one nice thing about Nubia, versus Egypt, and that is the dearth of population, there are so few people that one can really walk on shore with pleasure, and without being surrounded by horridly dirty people, and having 'Backsheesh' continually buzzed into one's ears.

The coloring is quite different from that of Egypt, there it is pink; everything is pink; but here it is a variety of colors, the Libyan desert is a bright orange, and the chain of volcanic hills that run along it are an equally bright purple. The Nile is blue or brown, the lupin that covers the bank is blue, the palms and grass are green, and the castoroil bushes a mixture of red and green. Miss Dabney and I took several walks in the Libyan Desert, while the dahabeah poked along. The view was simply beautiful, but walking in a desert is not unmitigated pleasure, the amount of sand I poured out of my shoes would make a small desert on its own account. One day we explored a very small, and very exquisite temple called Amâdah. It was such a little gem of a temple for the bas-reliefs are finer than any we had seen except in Karnak, and the coloring remarkably fresh. And the view! Miss Dabney & I spent several hours there, and walked or rather scrambled back to the boat, over the bank. One of the rules of Egyptian travelling is that you never stir from the boat, without at least one sailor, who carries an enormous pole as weapon. We find the man useful as coat-rack, stepping-stone, and bugbear to begging children. Then yesterday afternoon we rounded that fateful bend, and set sail again, and got here this morning. And this far exceeds anything I ever imagined, and I have been imagining for weeks. You know that the temple is carved out of the solid rock. On the facade are four gigantic colossi, also carved out of the rock, and the temple is a huge, and wonderfully decorated cave behind them. There they sit facing the quick running

river; quietly, their hands on their knees, their faces stern
and calm, and thus they have sat watching the same river
for thousands of years. Inside, the temple has exquisite
bas-reliefs all relating to a certain battle that Rameses II
had with the Kheta. They are cut deep into the sandstone
rock, and when the morning light falls on them one can see
the traces of color. The others are infatuated by them, and
have each planted their easels in a corner and are copying
away for dear life.

Besides ourselves we found here a compatriot, a snuffy
photographer from New Jersey. He is waiting for the down
steamer, which has not come up yet, and he attacked Polly
and asked if he could not buy some condensed milk and eggs;
we thought the poor thing must be starving, and almost forgave him for having taken up his abode in the temple; we
sent him various things, and of course would not let him
pay, but our eyes were opened as to his begging propensities,
by his asking Michael for some magnesium wire, now one
has a right to ask for necessities but not for luxuries, and
we felt that one could live for years without magnesium
wire, so we refused. Besides the photographer, the Marquis
of Northampton's dahabeah has just moored beside us.
All these people disgust us, we had so much rather have the
place to ourselves. The Marquis came up to Mary in the
temple this afternoon, and said that as their dahabeahs
were so close together he should like to make her acquaintance. Mary said that she was the maid — Tableau! We
think it rather a good joke on his sociable lordship. Poor
Lady Northampton is paralyzed, but has a very sweet face,
and there are three little children. But we have not spoken
to any of them yet. Lord Northampton is doubtless afraid
he may strike another maid.

We are not going on to the second cataract, for there is
nothing to see beyond this, and one cataract is much like
another. So we are going to stay here a week instead. It
is so nice that we are really going to have time to see a
temple, at last....

They spent all the next week at Aboo Simbel, studying
the temple 'in all lights, by sunrise and sunset, in the broad

light of midday and at dusk, and flooded with tropical moonlight; and I have seen the Southern Cross rise from behind the hills on the opposite bank of the river.' This constellation could be seen only between two and four in the morning; nevertheless they all saw it several times. In the evenings they sailed and drifted in the moonlight, 'and moonlight on the Nile is even more beautiful than I have ever seen it anywhere else.' The arrival of two dahabeahs of 'roaringly vulgar' Americans drove them into the desert for lunch one day; 'it was perfectly beautiful sand, stretching inland in billowy reaches.' Too soon their week was up; at dawn, February 6, from within the temple they watched the sun rise, then they started back down the river.

The next week was 'not at all eventful, not even very temply.' On the twelfth they reached Philae; the next morning before breakfast they descended the cataract, an event which she described the same day, in her fourteenth letter:

> People write about descending the cataract as if it were a really exciting and dangerous adventure, and of the 'big bab,' or first rapid, as though it were deserving of the name of cataract. They talk about 'its foaming, roaring waters, which surge over the lower deck and cover the upper deck with spray.' In a canoe it might be very exciting, in a dahabeah, it is very good fun; the famous 'bab' is a short, narrow, moderately fast rapid. No Americans would make anything of taking anyone down. But these idiotic, cowardly Arabs, make it out a tremendous undertaking, partly in the hope of more 'backsheesh,' partly because they do not know what real danger is. They put two men at the helm, and another at the stairs of the upper deck, who shrieks and waves his arms, and winds, and unwinds, and rewinds his turban. To an American it is most irritating. Our second waiter was so frightened that he turned perfectly white, and hid his head, and moaned. It was despicable, and I said 'coward,' quite loud, and remembered

afterwards that happily he could not understand English. Tonight the 'Chonsu' is to be illuminated, because we have passed that terrible cataract in safety. But it will look very pretty, I think, for they have put palm branches on both sides of the deck, and colored lanterns everywhere.

I am glad I am an American, and was brought up like a boy, and I am glad for every single time that I have been spilt out of a carriage. There!...

...

A second letter to Mrs. A. Lawrence Lowell contains her vivid description of the temple at Edfoo.

> Dahabeah 'Chonsu,' Upper Egypt,
> Saturday, February 19th, 1898.

It seems very strange to think that we have left Nubia, and are on our way back through Egypt, and that to-morrow we shall be at Luxor again. Luxor is Thebes, you know, and that is a perfectly brain-extracting thought, for the ruins at Thebes are many and large, & very beautiful, and the amount of studying they require is painful. I have not been on deck since I came back from the Tombs of El Ka this morning and the interval has been spent with Thebes. It is funny how you learn to eliminate when you have been here some time. We have learnt to eliminate everything that dates from Ptolemaic or Roman times. It is really strange how sculpture degenerated in the time of the Ptolemys. Architecture was beautiful, though it had become too ornate, but their proportions were exquisite; but oh! their bas-reliefs. Meaningless & in many cases absolutely vulgar. And from the mere decorational stand-point they fatally missed just what they were trying to achieve. The massiveness and grandeur of the ancient Egyptian temples was spoiled by putting in too much minute detail, even though that detail was very beautiful by itself. Yesterday we saw the most splendid of all the Ptolemaic ruins — The Temple of Edfoo. This is almost complete, almost 'as good as new.' And for its proportions and the capitals of some of its pillars is a pleasure. But the bas-reliefs! We will draw a curtain over them, or rather we

will not lift the curtain of blackness by means of a magnesium lamp. Just inside the pylon is a large colonnade court
with thirty-two columns. A sort of cloister between the outside world, and the Hypostyle Hall. And the birds fly
round this court, half in sun, half in shade, and the hum of
the village comes faintly through the big door in the first
pylon. The view from the roof is beautiful. From there you
look for miles over the land of Egypt. Miles of something
that is a brilliant green & ripples, with the river winding in
and out, and the desert beyond the green on either side.
Right below, clustered round, and almost touching the
girdle wall that runs round the temple, is an Arab village.
We look down on the roofs, and into the yards. Dirty, disgusting, picturesque and squalid, as they all are. And some
children seeing us, even though so many feet above them,
cry shrilly 'Baksheesh.' And above everything, children,
village, temple, and ourselves, circle hawks, lots of them,
squeaking and soaring in the sun....

The next day she continued her journal to her father.
From then on, there was so much to see that Miss
Lowell could write home little more than a list of the
temples they were visiting so efficiently. Even though
they spent all of the first week of March at Karnak, she
found time to say only that it was 'a perfect quarry of
beautiful things.' After that, the pace slackened; and the
trip to their last temple, on March 11, she was able to
record with some detail.

[XVIII]   Dahabeah 'Chonsu,' Upper Egypt.
                                     Sunday, March 15, 1898.

... The only exciting thing that has happened this week is
Abydos, our last temple, which we went to on Wednesday.
When I tell you that we spent four hours that day in the
saddle, you can judge how *much* better Polly is.

The dahabeah moors at the little village of Ballianah,
and from there you ride to Abydos. Some guidebooks say
that it is eight miles from the river, others say eight and a
half, but all agree that it is far, in which we entirely agree

with them. Polly said that she *could not possibly* go so far
in her chair, but she thought that she could go on a horse,
were such a thing procurable. The Sheik of the village was
therefore sworn at and bullied until he promised to provide
horses. The next day he appeared with an escort of the
usual howling arabs, a train of donkeys, and two arab
steeds. These latter were two very small and very meek
little horses, tortured by the very cruelest bits that I have
ever seen. Then began the usual endeavor to get ungalled
donkeys, accompanied by the usual yelling and general
confusion, and the kaleidoscopic manoeuvres of the donkey
boys, whereby the donkeys you have just rejected, suddenly
appear among those you have carefully selected, and you
have to begin all over again. This time the usual scrim-
mage was enlivened by a new feature, a hand to hand fight
between two Arabs. It must have been some personal
affair, for they were merely among the bystanders. I suspect it was merely what the Egyptians call 'Fantesîa,' for
nothing happened.

At last we all got off, quite an imposing cavalcade, with
Polly and Miss Dabney on horses, and the rest of us on
donkeys. It was such a pretty ride, for our road lay through
fields of wheat, barley, or beans, with here and there
patches of white clover mixed with yellow mustard. Wad-
ing in this up to their bodies, were buffalo, cows, sheep,
donkies, horses, every kind of animal; and men, women and
children. The latter as soon as they saw us would come
floundering through the tall barley with the inevitable shrill
cries of 'baksheesh.' Every now and then in the fields there
would be a 'sakîyeh,' or water wheel.

The road was raised a little from the fields on each side,
& along it came camels laden with sugar cane, donkeys
carrying sacks, donkeys carrying people, women with
bundles of straw on their heads, children in all sorts of costumes & lack of costume, offering every thing for sale, or
merely contenting themselves by demanding 'baksheesh'
without even pretending to offer an equivalent. It was the
kind of thing one reads about in books. Children with
slings of the pattern David used, were killing the birds that

threatened the crops. They were also threatening our lives, by letting them off under our noses in hopes of enchanting us sufficiently to induce us to purchase largely. It is needless to say that we did not buy one. Perhaps it is also needless to say that we have since repented our virtue.

We got there at last, and found the temple full of 'Kings,' in the shape of the respective parties of the Marquis of Northampton, & the Earl of Leven. The temple was one of the most beautiful temples that we have seen, and it well repaid us for our trouble.

But alas! 'the best laid schemes of mice & men,' & the wind began to blow, and wind on land in Egypt means unbearable, blinding, dust. We stood it as long as we could, but at last it became intolerable and we had to give up and come home....

Miss Lowell had planned to go to Spain after leaving Egypt; but these last days on the Nile brought news which made that trip impossible. The battleship *Maine* had been blown up in Havana Harbor on February 15; on March 21, the court of inquiry announced that it had been done by an external explosion. Meanwhile the American newspapers had been working up a war-fever, while the European continent expressed unanimous and unmitigated horror at this evidence of imperialism.

On March 24, the party left the *Chonsu* at Cairo, to sail on the 29th for Naples, which Miss Lowell found as fascinating as ever. They drove over to Sorrento, saw the Blue Grotto, visited Pompeii and Paestum — all new to Miss Lowell; and from April 17 to the 27th they were at Rome, where Miss Lowell had never been before. Among the other sights, she visited the Piazza di Spagna, to see the house where Keats died, 'and worshipped in true disciple form before its barred gateway.'[1]

The last letter of the Journal was written at Rome on the day of her arrival; but Miss Lowell remained in Europe at least a month longer. After Miss Cabot sailed from

[1] Letter to Mrs. George C. Riggs, May 22, 1920.

Genoa, Miss Lowell and Miss Dabney went back to Paris, where she saw the Salon; she was in this city when the real news of the Battle of Manila Bay reached the world, and it became evident that America had come of age. From Paris, Miss Lowell went over to London, where she visited the Quaritch bookshop.

Years before, as a child, she had loved to look at the colored books by William Blake which the Hooper family owned; and she had then vowed silently to buy some for herself when she could afford them. Now, reacting against the hieratic formalism of Egypt, she remembered that vow, and asked if they had any Blake books. They had three. She bought them at a price to boast of in future years, then sailed for home.

CHAPTER VII

YEARS INDETERMINATE AND DETERMINATE

*' ... one of the greatest handicaps that any one could possibly have.
I belonged to the class which is not supposed to be able to produce
good creative work....'*

THE winter in Egypt, intended to improve Miss Lowell's
health, was worse than a failure: it was a disaster. The
banting had undermined her constitution so that for
the next seven years she had nervous prostration — 'the
real thing, the kind where you live with a perpetual headache, and the slightest sound jars you all over.'[1]

The rest of the spring and the summer of 1898 passed
without event. In the autumn she went visiting at Dublin
again. Florence Wheelock was there; in a few months she
would be Mrs. Ayscough; and Amy Lowell rejoiced at her
fortune.

> ... I ... remember ... a picnic we had to Black Top the
> autumn before I was married. Amy was much interested in
> the prospect of my going to China to live. Later still during
> that autumn, Mary [Hutchinson] and I went to stay with
> her in Brookline and a great ceremony was indulged in à
> propos of my engagement. An altar with candles, and
> Frank's picture in the centre, was arranged and all sorts
> of jollifications took place, but Amy was not well, and
> when my wedding actually came off on December 23rd,
> 1898, she was in California.[2]

She had quite broken down, in fact; so it was thought
best to send her to California for the winter, where the
climate would be temperate, and where the excitements of
sightseeing would be impossible. The Dabneys owned
'Fayal Ranch'[3] in Jamacha, San Diego County, about

---

[1] Letter to John Farrar, October 24, 1921.

[2] Florence Ayscough: Reminiscences (*ms.*).

[3] Named after Fayal in the Azores, where, for eighty-five consecutive years,
three generations of Dabneys served as American consul.

twenty miles north of the Mexican border; next to it was another fruit ranch with a house adequate for Miss Lowell, and her chaperon, maid, and cook.

The journal of seventeen letters, which runs from December 7, 1898 (written 'En Route') to April 2, 1899, lacks the vigor and vividness of the Egyptian journal; it is occupied almost entirely with small talk, and an occasional description of scenery and flowers. On December 15, she wrote that she had arrived, and found the house 'very pleasant, with orange trees and pomegranates round it, and a garden in front, & yellow jasmine and roses climbing over it.' The next letter was dated 'Christmas Day' — her second Christmas away from home.

> ...Here the day has been perfectly beautiful. Miss Dabney found the first wild flowers today. Wild flowers on Christmas, doesn't that seem ridiculous?... I feel really better already, the climate is simply delightful, and the life quite perfect for me now....

But she was not really better. Two weeks later (January 8, 1899) she wrote:

> ...I find that riding tires me very much now, so I have to do it only occasionally, & not far. We drive a good deal, & I spend a large amount of time sitting on the piazza. Which seems to agree with me better than anything. Last Monday we went on a picnic, with the Kendalls, way up in the hills where there were beautiful views, and we could even see the sea, twenty miles away....

The Kendalls were a pleasant English family in the vicinity, who were interested in wood-carving. There was also a Browning class, which Miss Lowell attended. Only once was there anything exciting in a letter home.

Jamacha, California,
Sunday Jan. 15, 1899

DEAR PAPA,

We have had another side of California this week. A very interesting side, if not as beautiful a one. We have had a

winter rain! That sounds mild, but I wish you could see
it. It began mildly enough on Tuesday morning. On
Tuesday afternoon Miss Dabney & I drove over to El
Cajon to meet Miss Alice Dabney at the train, for she has
been in town several days. It rained steadily all the way
over and all the way back. When we got back to their home
where we were to take tea, we consulted as to whether
we had better not go right home. But as tea was ready
there, and we had no tea waiting for us at home, we decided
to have it & start as soon as it was over. Which we did.
It was a pitch black night, & the rain was pouring in tor-
rents. I held the lantern high over Miss Dabney's head,
while she drove. The light of the lantern was reflected back
from the rain, & made it look dense, we felt as though we
were enveloped by a thick sheet of water. It is only a mile
from their house to ours, & a little more than half way the
road forks, & either goes to our house.

As we came near the fork we heard rushing water loud to
our left. We knew that when it rained very hard the water
did pour down there, but it had been *absolutely dry* in the
morning.

We could not see anything, but we drove splashing along
at a foot pace. We knew that the stream must cross both
roads, & when we had gone a little way on the lower road
(which we usually take, as it is somewhat shorter, & much
less steep) I got out & went ahead with the lantern. After
I had gone a little way I came upon the water, tearing
down a little hill & foaming across the road.

There was no crossing there, so we turned round & went
back to the upper road. Here the water was also rushing
across the road, & the sides were terribly soft. There is
great danger of getting mired here when it rains, & we did
not know whether it was safe or not. So we went back to
the house & got José, Mr. Dabney's man, to come with us.
He said that it was safe & helped us over. But the next
morning he told us that if we had been a little later, we
could not have gone home at all, for going back through
the olives the water was rushing down the hill, & up to his
knees.

It rained more or less for three days, we have had over two inches. People say that if we had had three inches there would have been a flood. But now the sun is shining again, & everything is coming up. We found a hyacinth in bloom in the garden this morning & the roses are all out over the Dabney's piazza. The blue ipomeas that came from the same seed as mine have been flowering profusely.

Did the ones that Norton had in the greenhouse ever flower? I should like to know.

Your loving daughter
AMY LOWELL.

Evidently she thought the event an experience, as for once she signed the letter with her full name.

The last letter written from Jamacha is dated March 26, 1899; the next (the last of the series) was written from Monticello, California, where she was visiting Polly Cabot. It states that she expected to be home by May 1.

But though the Journal reveals little enthusiasm, in later years Miss Lowell wrote a correspondent that she enjoyed it hugely and would never forget it. 'We used to ride over the trails and the hills all day long and live a wonderful life in the open air amid flowering roses and orange blossoms.' [1]

The summer of 1899 she went abroad again, with Miss Frances Dabney, to spend the summer in Devonshire, 'as the mild climate of that place was supposed to be good for the nerves.' [2] Her letters were not preserved, and only once in her other correspondence did she refer to this period: a reference to the fuschias that used to hang over the walls of the house.[3] A notebook given her by Miss Dabney, dated 'Harbor Heights, Sept. 9th, 1898,' contains some notes on her reading in George Eliot and Mrs. Humphry Ward; but the chances are that she had returned to America by this time. Miss Dabney had also

[1] Letter to Winifred Bryher, May 28, 1919.
[2] *Ms.* (1916).   [3] Letter to D. H. Lawrence, July 6, 1921.

given her the copy of Alice Meynell's poems which eventually inspired that bitter poem published posthumously in *Ballads for Sale*.

In June, 1900, her father died at Sevenels. On the 19th he underwent an operation, from which he seemed at first to rally; but his strength failed him on the night of the 21st, and he died the next morning at 10:30. On the 25th, the funeral was held in the parlor of Sevenels — that room which later became the front half of Miss Lowell's famous library; the event made such a deep impression on her that she used to say if any room could be haunted, her library would be that room.

Now that both her parents were dead, it was necessary for her to plan her own life. Her brothers and sisters had their separate homes; but she could not bear to part with Sevenels. She tried living there a season, to see if she could afford it; and in order not to be secluded from the world, she also bought a town-house and an automobile. But an automobile made it so easy to live in Brookline, that within a week she sold the Boston house; and as her income proved ample to cope with Sevenels, she bought it. But she did not move downstairs: all her life she lived in her childhood room, Sky Parlour, on the top floor.

She also rented a sixty-acre place in Dublin, New Hampshire, from the Crowninshields; after trying it for a summer, she found it to be just what she wanted, and bought it.[1] She named it 'Broomley Lacey' — 'Broomley,' after Broomley Vale, her great-grandfather's place in Roxbury, and 'Lacey,' meaning 'woods.' It was on a hillside, with vistas of Dublin Lake and Mt. Monadnock beyond; these vistas she had to keep cutting out through the trees, as the pines were constantly growing up. There were innumerable roads ideal for buggy-riding, and many pretty walks;

[1] On May 18, 1901, she bought the Dublin property of the late Caspar Crowninshield which belonged to Elizabeth C. Peabody (*Cheshire Registry Books*, in the court house at Keene, N.H., Book 328, p. 121). On January 22, 1902, and June 20, 1906, she extended her property (Book 329, p. 90; Book 342, p. 9).

The Library at Sevenels

and best of all, plenty of intelligent friends who knew how to enjoy themselves.

In the fall she assumed duties such as were expected of a prominent Boston woman.

> At first, after settling in Brookline for good, I identified myself very largely with the Town's interests, becoming a member of the Executive Committee of the 'Brookline Education Society,' and the 'Chairman of the Library Board' of the same society. I also became a member of the Library Committee of the 'Women's Education Association' and was made one of the State visitors of libraries, the library under my charge being the tiny one of Blackstone, a manufacturing town very near the Rhode Island border. Pursuing these avocations, I made one or two trips to country towns, lecturing on books, etc. I also joined the Women's Municipal League and became Chairman of the Committee for the Suppression of Unnecessary Noise.[1]

Her first speech in public was made perhaps earlier. To appreciate the situation, one must remember that her father's opinion of the place of women was conservative, even for his generation. As the tale is recalled, she attended some meeting at which there was a general pre-arrangement to get rid of a school official whose age had clearly incapacitated him. But nobody could bring himself to utter the first word against the old man; consequently so many kindly and laudatory things were said in his behalf that he was about to be reappointed. Then Miss Lowell, sensing the situation, and determined that the children should not be sacrificed to sentiment, ascended the platform, to state all the reasons against the reappointment. She did it so uncompromisingly that she was hissed; but as she thought she was being applauded, she continued unabashed. When she descended from the platform, the other Lowell women flocked round her, horrified; then she learned that not only was it her own first speech

[1] Ms., 1916.

in public, but also that no woman of the Lowell family had ever spoken in public before. However, as a new school official was appointed, she felt that her act was thoroughly justified.

An undated manuscript of one of her speeches shows clearly enough what her educational ideals were.

Is the Present System of High School Education Prejudicial to Individual Development?

Perhaps I ought to have inquired when I was asked to open this subject whether the word Individual was used in its political sense, as the reverse to Social, or Socialism; or in its everyday sense of personality. I was given no direction as to this, and I have preferred to use this latter meaning. I am not therefore dealing with the political unit but with the personal unit. Perhaps the two qualities which more than any others go to the making of a strong personality are character and imagination. Character means courage, and there is a great difference between the collective courage of a mass of people all thinking the same way, and the courage of one man who cares not at all for public opinion, but goes on his way unswervingly. Our national ideal as to the moral attitude is high. What the people understand, and what they all agree about, that they will do; but it is not so easy to find men who are willing to think and act at variance with the opinions of their neighbors. Strangely enough, with all our horror of state interference, with all our talk of developing the individual, we are really less individual than other nations. The era of machine-made articles has swept over the land, and nowhere has its product been more deteriorating than in the machine-made types which our public schools turn out.

Do not misunderstand me; I do not mean that the types are poor or bad types; on the contrary, machines work with a wonderful precision, but these types are run in a mold or rather several molds. The result is a high state of mediocrity; like democracy itself it is incapable of sinking to the lowest depths or alas! of rising to the most sublime heights.

The difficulty with American civilization is that it is essentially vulgar in tone, not so much in manner as in essence. The theatres, the newspapers, the popular amusements all show this. The few people with refined ideas and cultivated tastes can make no impression against this mass of Vulgarism. The tendency is not so much directly vicious as it is undermining and deteriorating. The cheap and tawdry exert their fatal influence throughout the whole national life.

And how is this the effect of our public schools? These schools are here for the very purpose of making citizens, and when the result is as we have seen, it is natural to suppose that the training has some radical defect. Of course it is very difficult to tell how much the apparent loss of individuality in America is due to a false system of education, and how much to the great mass of immigration which has changed the characteristics of the people who form the populace. Anglo-Saxon blood, with its inheritance, is in the minority. But certainly the education got at the public schools seems to have a great effect on our alien races, so it is fair to assume that some of our national characteristics are much the result of this education.

No national trait strikes such horror into our European neighbors, and none does us so much harm, as our constant sense of hurry. 'Evolution, not revolution, is the order of development,' says Mr. Hughes in his book on comparative education, and evolution is a process requiring much time. Nature cannot be hurried, there is no such thing as cramming. What is not digested is simply forgotten. A congested curriculum results in the proper assimilation of no one subject. And what can we think of a primary school taught by one teacher, in which the children were taught seventeen subjects, with fifteen minutes given to each subject, as was the case in one school in Brookline!

The deep sympathy between Percival, now the oldest member of the family, and his nineteen-year younger sister, is perhaps best exhibited in a letter he wrote her after she had criticized the manuscript of his Memoir of

their father, which was to be published in the *Proceedings
of the American Academy of Arts and Sciences* a year later.

DEAR AMY: Aug. 30, 01

  Thank you for your appreciative letter on the memoir of
Father. I am very much pleased that you like it, and are so
kind to its virtues and blind to its faults. To the points to
which you object I have given my attention and hope the
result may meet with your approval. I quite agree with
what I conceive to form the basis of your distaste to the
dream ¹ — the impression that Father was idle in college
and regretted it afterwards. Such an idea I did not intend
to convey and I have accordingly modified the story with
that point in view. Properly presented I think the dream
decidedly worth preservation and should be very sorry to
throw it overboard. For it is a distinctly interesting and
valuable bit of psychology. Think over my explanation of
what a dream is and see if you do not come to the same
conclusion. I am naturally fond of my own child but I do
not think myself blind to it nevertheless. It is the presentation at which you shy, unconsciously, for almost anything
can be put commendingly if discreetly put. Furthermore
you will tame it to insipidity if you cut out the stories. I
only wish I had more not less. Read Darwin's or Huxley's
autobiography and mark, as you will, that it is the very
things which as a relation you would suppress which most
interest the reader. Darwin's questionable morality as a
boy for instance. Because such incidents are human and
so appeal to man. A faultless statue stirs no one who is
not superlatively gifted with imagination. At all events
read the pages I send herewith and see if your aversion be
not a little mitigated. Your 'fundamental' was an excellent
criticism and I have substituted 'deep-seated' to the great
improvement of the sound. Lastly your suggestion of a
paragraph added to touch on Father's thought and kindness
for others was most judicious and I have instantly followed
it.

¹ [Paraphrased on p. 26.]

... In conclusion let me add how well 'Miss Postscript' writes and how much her appreciation is appreciated by her 'Stepbrother'

alias

PERCIVAL.

In October, 1902, Duse came again to Boston. Miss Lowell had seen her on her comparatively unsuccessful first American tour of 1893, and again on her second successful tour of 1896. The third tour was triumphant. Duse was acting nothing but the plays of d'Annunzio, the poet who (it was more than rumored) had brutally exposed their love-affair in his *Il Fuoco* (1900), a decadent novel made glorious by her personality; the Lenbach portrait, used as a poster, depicted rather a madonna and child; but the audiences paid their religious devotion to the Tragic Muse incarnate.

Duse's ten Boston performances were given in the new Tremont Theater: *La Gioconda* and *La Città Morta* the week of October 20, and the next week *Francesca da Rimini*. Miss Lowell undoubtedly attended the opening performance, on October 21; [1] the date marks the beginning of her career as poet; for that evening, when she returned to Sevenels, she found herself compelled 'with infinite agitation' to write a poem.

> I have had rather a curious writing life. I used to write poems as a little girl, but I was no Hilda Conkling — they were the ordinary verse of little girls, and of no value whatever. From the time I was about fifteen or sixteen, I had a pause; I wrote nothing until I was twenty-eight, which is sufficiently strange, I think....
>
> ... I had always felt that I could write, and I longed to write. I tried my hand at novels, short stories, and plays, but it did not dawn upon me that I could write poetry. Then Eleanora Duse came to America on one of her peri-

---

[1] As we have seen, Duse had been an artistic ideal since Miss Lowell first saw her in 1896; it would not have been like her, therefore, to have missed Duse's opening performance.

odical trips; that was the year she was acting in the d'Annunzio plays. I went to see her, as I always went to see everything that was good in the theatre. The effect on me was something tremendous. What really happened was that it revealed me to myself, but I hardly knew that at the time. I just knew that I had got to express the sensations that Duse's acting gave me, somehow. I knew nothing whatever about the technique of poetry, I had never heard of *vers libre*, I had never analyzed blank verse — I was as ignorant as anyone could be. I sat down, and with infinite agitation wrote this poem. It has, I think, every *cliché* and every technical error which a poem can have, but it loosed a bolt in my brain and I found out where my true function lay.[1]

The poem, seventy-one lines of bad blank verse, was published in *Poetry* for August 1923, in a series of childhood poems by various poets. Its sincerity and its perception, however, are clear enough in the description of Duse herself.

> For she whom we have come to see tonight
> Is more to be divined and felt than seen,
> And when she comes one yields one's heart perforce,
> As one might yield some noble instrument
> For her to draw its latent music forth.
>
> For she herself vibrates to every thought,
> And shades of feeling cross her face like clouds
> That trail their shadows over distant hills.
> Her being is like an aeolian harp
> Clasped in a casement on some summer night
> Whence every breeze that passes draws a sound,
> Now harsh and wild, now sweet, now quaintly gay,
> But always musical, and always true.
>
> Her voice is vibrant with a thousand things;
> Is sharp with pain, or choked with tears,
> Or rich with love and longing.

[1] Letter to Eunice Tietjens, June 5, 1923.

Her little inarticulate sounds are sprung
From depths of inner meaning which embrace
A life's chaotic, vast experience....

And as the evening lengthens, bit by bit,
Little by little, we discern the real.
'Tis that which holds us spellbound far, far more
Than even her most consummate art can do,
Through all the passion of a simulated grief
And through the studied anguish learnt by rote
We feel the throbbing of a human soul,
A woman's heart that cries to God and fears!

Naturally, she went to see Duse 'many times'[1] after that; and when Duse left Boston, Miss Lowell followed her to Philadelphia. There a Dublin friend, Katie Dunham that was, now Mrs. John Bennett, was able to introduce her to the great actress. Duse was in bed, resting; but their conference was so inspiring that Miss Lowell came away 'almost on air'; and twenty-two years later, she believed that Duse might remember her.

The vision of Duse revealed to Miss Lowell that art is an expression of the deep truths of human reality, that her hitherto unguessed vocation was poetry, and that in herself she should find the material.

Her period of incubation had been long. She was now twenty-eight, and had just discovered her calling. But she always felt that the delayed beginning had its advantage. 'The child who remains a child longest is apt to develop into a more mature man than the child who develops very young,' she wrote a correspondent in later years. 'I am convinced that the longer a child can remain comparatively fallow, the better it will be for him. Again we must never forget to allow the greatest possible development to the subconscious.'[2]

[1] Letter to Ellery Sedgwick, March 3, 1924.
[2] Letter to Mrs. C. H. Goddard, November 27, 1917.

'I began to write, not specifically about Madame Duse, but simply out of the fullness of the vision of poetry which she had given me.' [1] Yet filled though her subconscious was with the wisdom learned from her own bitter experiences and with the riches of her travels and her books, and although she was born into a literary family in a literary city, she had the profound disadvantage of being a young lady in society. Her father had taken the conservative view that her writing, like Bessie's painting, was excellent as a private accomplishment but was unthinkable as a public career; and his attitude was generally to be found in Boston society. Of course the Lowells, particularly the Lowell men, were never susceptible to the sterilizing power of conformity; but the insidious assumption that a young lady could not and should not take a place before the eyes of the world as a serious artist was a subtle enervation that had to be realized and faced before it could be neutralized.

However, Bessie Ward (now Mrs. Charles Bruen Perkins) was also interested in writing poetry; and the two young ladies determined to master the art together. They studied Leigh Hunt's book and analyzed Keats and criticized each other's poems freely on their rides over the countryside. Wisely they decided to publish nothing until they were convinced they had produced genuine literature, which they knew would be many years off.

One brother was not unsympathetic, however.

> I remember, when I started to write, that my brother said something to me that has since struck me as perhaps the most profound piece of instruction which could ever be given to a young writer. What he said to me was: 'Amy, do not forget that, no matter what you write about, a book is a failure if it is not interesting.' [2]

On November 24, 1902, Miss Lowell's older sister, Katherine (Mrs. Alfred Roosevelt), married Thomas James

[1] Letter to Ellery Sedgwick, March 3, 1924.
[2] Letter to Winifred Bryher, July 28, 1919.

Bowlker, formerly assistant master at Haileybury College, Hertfordshire, England, and an ordained priest of the Anglican church.

In 1903, a controversy, which had begun two years earlier, over the question of moving the crowded Athenaeum from its Beacon Street building to a new site across the Public Garden, came to a climax. The shareholders (i.e., the members) were now thinking that they had agreed too hastily; one of the ardent defenders of the old building, who had brought them to that attitude, was Miss Lowell. Her great-grandfather and grandfather had both been presidents; other Lowells had held other offices; the old building was full of Lowell memories; and here she had spent many an hour of her life.

In 1901 she had acquired her father's share, which had also been her grandfather's; now, in 1903, for the sake of the extra vote, she bought another share, which she sold the next year, after the matter had been settled. At the monthly meeting of March 16, 1903,

> Misses Loring & Lowell presented, through Mr. Alfred Bowditch, further estimates as to alteration of the present building and the draft of a circular which they proposed to have sent to the Proprietors, either by themselves or by the Trustees, as the Trustees preferred.[1]

Undoubtedly at this time she also wrote her poem 'The Boston Athenaeum,' later included in *A Dome of Many-Coloured Glass*, which contains the line 'And must they take away this treasure house?' It is her first poem written for propaganda.

Sentiment triumphed by a very narrow margin of votes; on February 10, the *Transcript* featured the resolve to preserve the old building; and the triumphant Miss Lowell

[1] *Boston Athenaeum Records*, pp. 325–26 (*ms.*). This is the only mention of Miss Lowell in the official records at the time of the campaign. It is sometimes said that Miss Lowell's first speech in public occurred at this event; if so, it was not recorded, and Mr. C. K. Bolton has informed me that he has no memory of any such speech.

informed her brother Percival, who was out in his Arizona observatory, what she had accomplished. He replied on March 1:

> DEAR AMY:
>
> Bravo! bravo! I know you did it well. And to think that it should have been necessary speaks for the vandalism of the eye and of our own friends and neighbors. I am so with you heart and soul that I have just written a piece for the Transcript on the subject, and send it to them cheek by 'jowl' with this line to you.
>
> Macte virtute, virgine! and continue to be a dear girl to
>
> Your aff^{ate} brother
>
> PERCIVAL.

His 'piece for the Transcript' appeared March 7; it says chiefly what she herself said later, in describing the row:

> Personally, I think that association is a most important factor in municipal life and in the life of the country. Unless the site of a library has become utterly useless as being too far removed from that part of the city where it is convenient to the users of the library, I think it is always better to keep the building on the site where it stands and not move, no matter what the price which might be gained for it might be. We are learning very slowly, but we are learning, the value of association and historical sentiment in this country, and it is a pity to throw it away unless it is absolutely necessary.[1]

Another beloved building, however, the Boston Museum, went this year; when it was razed, Miss Lowell bought two of the double doors, which she put in between the reception room and the music room at Sevenels.

Her thirtieth birthday came on February 9, 1904. On February 23, the Whistler Memorial Exhibition opened at Copley Hall; she went, and saved her catalogue. That summer, Mrs. Whitman died; Miss Lowell went to the Me-

[1] Letter to Henry G. Brengle, January 31, 1925.

morial Exhibition of her works at the Society of Arts and
Crafts, and preserved the clippings from the newspapers.

In December, 1904, she was making some attempt to
get in touch with other literary persons, as she filed, in her
collection of manuscripts, notes from two poet novelists:
one from Margaret Deland (a friend of Bessie's) regretting
that she could not lunch with Miss Lowell on the third, and
one from Arlo Bates, accepting an invitation to dinner on
the sixth.

In 1905, at the Rowfant Sale, she bought the complete
Keats collection of Frederick Locker-Lampson; this was
the beginning of her own Keats collection. Her activities
of this year also included an interest in Radcliffe; on June
13, she went over the new dormitories with Caroline
Hazard, the president of Wellesley. She also gave books to
the Radcliffe library. As she was still not wholly recovered from her nervous prostration, that summer she went
to Europe again, with a companion nurse and letters of introduction to persons in England from William Everett.
In Europe she joined her sister, Mrs. Putnam, and her family. Perhaps she returned in time to spend a month or so at
Broomley Lacey.

> I don't remember when she bought the Dublin house, but
> I know that I saw her in it once, some years after my mar-
> riage, when Frank and I were stopping with Mary Hutchin-
> son, who by that time had become Mary Sumner, and again
> I remember a picnic to Black Top, when I drove with Amy
> in her buggy. The view from the Dublin house was *wonder-
> ful*. Amy was not very well then. The year was *about* 1905.
> She and Mary had come to know each other very well.
> That was a friendship which grew stronger and stronger as
> time went on, and when Mary died in 1915 it was Amy
> who sent a cable telling me the news.[1]

In 1906, Miss Lowell remodelled the main rooms on the
ground floor of Sevenels, to go more appropriately with

[1] Florence Ayscough: 'Reminiscences' (*ms.*).

her gardens; 'it was a work of love for one so wholly en-
amoured of the eighteenth century as I have always been.'
Her architect was Henry Forbes Bigelow; she owed much
of the carrying out of the designs to 'that excellent artist
and wood-carver, Mr. I. Kirchmayer.' The hall she left
just as it was, for love of the old wooden animal heads.
The reception room was wainscotted below, in the Adam
style, and hung with yellow striped satin — a perfect
background for her Egyptian paintings by Joseph Lindon
Smith. There was a large carved eagle over the mantel;
she discarded that, and hung in its place her blue Monet of
Battersea Bridge. The glass doors from the Boston Museum led into the music room (formerly the billiard room),
where she put in a new fireplace.

> The mantelpiece was carved in Cambridgeport from a
> photograph, but the centre panel could not be clearly
> enough seen to be copied, so we took the Marlborough
> Cameo in the Boston Art Museum and copied that. The
> Chinese-Chippendale mirror was adapted from details of
> two original mirrors, both of which I liked and wanted
> combined.[1]

The lighting fixtures in the various rooms were exquisite
— in fact, those in the reception room were so delicate that
they could not be wired. The chandelier in the music
room was a copy of the only glass one Robert Adam was
known to have made. The ceilings, cornices, and other
mouldings, were all done over after Adam designs. Above
the dining-room doors she had set the painted panels of
fruits which had stimulated her imagination so when she
was a child. Her greatest care, however, went into the
making of a library by removing the wall between the two
rooms on the left side of the hall. It was paneled with oak
brought over in the log from England. The two fireplaces
were framed in huge swags of fruits and flowers carved
after the manner of Grinling Gibbons. Above the front

[1] Amy Lowell: 'Sevenels,' *Touchstone* (VII, 210–18), June, 1920.

mantel, before which she customarily worked, she hung
her two Constables and her Whistler; above the one at the
end of the room, the blue 'Kiss of Amon Ra' which she had
commissioned Joseph Lindon Smith to paint for her in
1904. The two high doors opening into the hallway were
crowned with carved festoons. Built-in bookcases, with
invisible shutters that could be pulled down and locked, to
prevent pilfering when the house was closed, ran the length
of the inner wall; above them was hung a series of *ramis*,
or horizontal Japanese woodcarvings. There were bookcases also at the far end of the library; but one section of
these — to the left of the second fireplace — was filled with
false backs, which concealed the door to her room-sized,
airtight safe, in which she kept her manuscript collection.
Three lustres hung from the ceiling, for use when she
turned the library into a ballroom or theater.

In the second quarter of 1906 she paid a visit to Charleston, South Carolina, and found it entrancing.

> ... Charleston has more poetic appeal than almost any city
> in America. Some fifteen years ago, I passed a few weeks
> there, and those weeks have left an indelible impression
> upon me. It was in the Spring, with the azaleas in the
> Middleton Place in full bloom, with the sea a cool, stretched
> blue, with the houses as lovely and fresh as their own gar-
> dens. It is a place for poets, indeed. History touches legend
> in Charleston; art has harnessed nature, and nature has
> ramped away and transcended art. The town is beautiful
> with the past, and glorious with the present; its wealth of
> folklore has been very little touched upon in poetry.[1]

She went out to the Middleton Place, then an all-day excursion, and found the eighteenth-century gardens a
dream that remained with her always. She was taken as a
great favor to visit the last Miss Pringle in the beautiful
Pringle house. She saw the two old sisters who had vowed
never to go beyond their porch while the Yankees re-

[1] Letter to Hervey Allen, September 29, 1921.

mained in possession of their city; and she saw also the jouncing-board on which they had exercised for forty years. She copied the epitaph of a young Englishman who had died there suddenly of 'stranger's fever'; and worked it into a sonnet. And everywhere she revelled in the flowers and the exquisite ironwork and the trees hung with Spanish moss and the neglected side streets.

There are no definite records for any events in her life during the rest of this year, or during the next year. She had recovered from her nervous prostration, however, and was doing a great deal of entertaining in Sevenels. 'I've never been let have a good time,' she confided to a friend; 'I'm going to, now.'

From December 26, 1907, to January 1, 1908, she was on a houseparty at the Gardiners', in Gardiner, Maine. As the whole party was enthusiastic over Kipling's dream-tale, 'The Brushwood Boy,' the group called itself 'The Brushwood Club,' the only article in its constitution being that the story should be read out loud at least once at every meeting. Besides reading, they played bridge, went tobogganing, acted charades, and flirted so effectively that one couple got engaged. Miss Lowell, however, was unprovided with a beau, wherefore she dubbed herself 'The Fifth Wheel' in a fourteen-page 'Report of the First Annual Meeting of the Brushwood Club,' which she drew up and distributed in manuscript.

She then went abroad again, this time with Barbara Higginson and Minna Lyman; going from her beloved Naples to Greece and Constantinople, and back again to Naples, then motoring from Rome to London by way of the Riviera and Biarritz.[1] But it was Greece that she remembered particularly.

> Those trains in Greece and the hours at which they run! We took a four-thirty or five o'clock train somewhere —

---

[1] Her *ms.* (1916) gives the date as 1905; but it is obvious that she confused two trips, as her passport to Turkey was dated January 22, 1908.

God knows where — and landed in the middle of a plain about eleven o'clock in the morning, from whence we drove in a carriage for twelve mortal hours along a lovely road cut into the side of a hill to Delphi, and in the middle, one of our horses fell down, and the carriage turned over, and it was the sheerest luck in the world that we were not pitched right down the side of the mountain. We all fell out safely, however, with our luggage on top of us and our fingers gripping the edge of the cliff. The next day at Delphi is almost a blank to me, as I had a perfectly ghastly headache, and I remember climbing up and down those steep ruins trying to see something out of my eyes almost without success, and then driving again to a horrid little seashore place, only to be told that the steamer that was going to Patras at five o'clock in the afternoon would not arrive until eleven o'clock at night, then getting on board the steamer, the smells of which were indescribable and finding the cabin hopeless and trying to snatch a little sleep on deck in a steamer chair. We got to bed in Patras at two to get up again at four and take a train to Olympia. At Olympia I remember going sound asleep in the midst of red poppies and grey stones and under the most delicious sunlight in the world; then waking up to perfect quiet and the gentle blowing of the poppies and walking into the little house where the Praxiteles Hermes is and his striking on my tired eyes a good deal as the real god might have done had I met him unexpectedly in a grove of olives. I do not know how the statue will affect you, but I have never got over the almost breathless effect its beauty had on me....

What you say about Athens being like America is most amusing, because I remember when we were there saying to my friend, 'Now this is just like Boston.' It is not a bit like the America of the West, but it is exactly like this little town where I live, a certain clean, cozy, provincial friendliness was all over it.... I liked the Grande Britain; it was so old-fashioned, and the staircases were so wide. I used to sit on my balcony and see the little petticoated troops parading in the palace grounds. It was all such a funny jumble of the old and the new. Mounet-Sully was there when I was, and he was to give a performance of Œdipus outdoors in the Stadion. The poor old soul decided that it was too cold, that he would have rheumatism, and it was given up. But he did give an unabridged performance of 'Hamlet' in the theatre which began at nine and ended at two, I remember.

I have seen some beautiful things by moonlight in my life, and I have had two lucky experiences: my first sight of the Parthenon was by moonlight, and my first sight of the temple at Karnak was by moonlight.

Yes, there is something very cozy and nice about Greece. One can understand the ancient Greeks much better after one has been there, but I do think one misses trees in the country round Athens. If you go to Delphi, you will find them again. Do not fail to go to Sunium. That white temple rising almost out of the sea is superb.[1]

She came home for the summer, probably for Percival's wedding on June 10, 1908, to Constance Savage Keith.

At the end of August, the *Merry Widow* came to the Tremont Theater, and on the twenty-eighth, the vivacious Lina Abarbanell took over the part of Sonia. Miss Lowell was enraptured with the operetta, at once so sentimental, sophisticated, and spirited. She gave a party for the leading lady, which caused much talk in Boston society. At Sevenels, Madame Abarbanell played in a melodrama concerning the miseries of courtezans (which shocked the parents whose daughters were present); then to Mrs. Langdon Frothingham's accompaniment, she sang some Bavarian songs, which were doubtless very *risqué* (though nobody knew); and finally she was so exhausted that she had to sit while the indignant guests were presented. Several of the guests on departing told their hostess that they would not have come had they guessed what the entertainment was to be. 'And on a Sunday, too!' was the unanimous chorus in all accounts of what happened.

But there was one happy result of this event: Madame

[1] Letter to Winifred Bryher, April 12, 1920.

Abarbanell introduced Carl Engel to Miss Lowell. This young composer, then associated with the Boston Music Company, became one of her most valued friends. He would always come at her call, to fill in at a dinner, or accompany her to a concert or a play, or simply talk when she was in the dumps. He was very fond of the modern French composers, whom he played brilliantly; he also put her on the track of French poetry, which hitherto had eluded her. Until he became Chief of the Music Division in the Library of Congress, he was a regular member of her circle.

Her poetry was demanding more and more of her time. Convinced that she was accomplishing something, she now resigned from all the library and educational committees on which she had served for several years, to devote herself to writing. She did not abandon her entertaining, however. On January 20–23, 1909, especially elaborate theatricals were given at Sevenels. Upon a stage erected in the library, the 'Amateur Professionals' presented Wilde's *Ideal Husband*, Miss Lowell playing the leading role of Lady Markby. The programs were designed by Berkeley Updike. After the performances, her guests danced in the hall and the music room.

Two months later, she had a horrible experience. Shortly after midnight, in the early hours of March 25, her stables were discovered to be on fire. The conflagration had already made such headway that the horses (including her mare Aura) could not be rescued, and were burned to death. The shock to her was augmented by some ugly and exultant letters, sent her by some illiterate who preferred to remain anonymous. She could not bear even to rebuild the stables.

That autumn, on October 6, her brother Lawrence was inaugurated as the twenty-fourth President of Harvard University. The ceremony was held outdoors for the first time, in front of University Hall.

A month later, on November 9, the new Boston Opera
House opened with a performance of *La Gioconda*; Miss
Lowell attended, dressed in 'black satin covered with net
pailletted in jet, silver, and gold,' according to the society
reporter of the *Boston Herald*.

Meanwhile she had decided to replace her horses by Old
English Sheepdogs. With Barbara Higginson (who later
became Mrs. Barrett Wendell) she started a kennel which
they christened 'Hylowe,' combining the first syllables of
their family names; in the *American Kennel Club Stud
Book*, however, from 1910 on, when the name was first
listed, Miss Lowell was given sole credit. They began with
a pedigreed pair, Ringlow's Sultan (a 'champion of record')
and Flo. On November 28, 1909, were whelped Hylowe
Sir John and Hylowe Prue; and when Prue died in December, 1918, Miss Lowell was to mourn her as the last of her
dogs.

Immediately these dogs became very important members of the household. Highly bred and exceedingly sensitive, they required a great deal of attention, and Miss
Lowell gave it. She lost remarkably few out of each litter;
and if one was sick she would sit up all night with it. Every
day, when the pack was complete, they devoured nine
pounds of the top of the round, with fresh vegetables
mashed. The park was theirs; they never sought to go
roving, though it would have been simple enough to leap
the low stone wall that surrounded the estate. Visitors always found a man waiting at the gate, to escort them to
the front door. At dinner, they appeared with Miss Lowell
herself, but charged in the doorway, never presuming to
enter the dining-room; and after dinner they accompanied
the guests into the library, where each person was furnished with a large towel, to protect his clothing against
their liberal affections. In the summer, they went to
Dublin grandly in a haycart, barking the whole way.
They were Miss Lowell's delight until the war-rationing

killed them in 1918, when they were replaced by her famous black cat, Winky.

She had been working at her poetry now for nearly eight years; it was time to get some of it in print. Her literary acquaintances and connections were so scanty that she had no idea how to go about it, until she remembered that her old friend Mabel Cabot had married Ellery Sedgwick, the editor of the *Atlantic Monthly*. To him she sent four sonnets, which he accepted immediately. One of them, 'Fixed Idea,' appeared in the issue for August, 1910; her first serious poem to be published thus came out in the famous magazine which Cousin James had once edited.

That summer she visited Florence Ayscough in St. Andrews, and was delighted with the quaint old town and its grass-grown streets. She also thoroughly enjoyed sailing on the blue, hill-encircled bay. That autumn, Florence Ayscough visited her in turn; Miss Lowell gave her a dinner.

It was now clear that Boston had worked itself up to a productive state in drama. The city had long been known as theater-loving; and not content to remain mere audience, many persons had organized groups of amateur actors. William Vaughn Moody's *Great Divide* (1906) had been hailed as the beginning of a new era of play-writing. Professor George Pierce Baker in 1907–08 gave English 47 at Harvard for the first time; this course in playwriting immediately proved its practicality in Edward Sheldon's *Salvation Nell*, which triumphed in New York the following autumn. Moody's friend, the exquisite Josephine Preston Peabody (now Mrs. Lionel Marks) had then scored an international triumph by winning the Stratford Prize for a poetic play with her *Piper* (1909), which had been produced in Shakspere's own town (1910), then in New York (1911). Next, Edward Gustavus Knoblauch (who became Edward Knoblock), having written the '96 Pudding Show, scored two successes in 1911 with his *Faun* and *Kismet*.

The Castle Square Stock Company, headed by John Craig and Mary Young, caught the enthusiasm: Mr. Craig offered a $500.00 prize for the best play written by a Harvard or Radcliffe student, which he would then produce; and the very first of these, Florence Lincoln's *End of the Bridge*, packed the house for nine weeks on its first run, and was followed by other successes.[1]

Meanwhile, in the spring of 1911, Mrs. Lyman Gale, inspired by the 'little theaters' abroad, called together a group to consider the possibility of building a private 'Toy Theater' in Boston, where they could stage original and imported plays which had not been produced in the professional American theaters. Miss Lowell was invited, also her friends Joseph Lindon Smith and Mrs. Charles Bruen Perkins, also Professor Baker and Professor Allard of Harvard, also Beatrice Herford and Marie Beulah Dix and Josephine Preston Peabody, amongst others. The executive committee which they appointed consisted of Mrs. Gale, Miss Lowell, and Mr. William C. Willson.

In October, 1911, carpenters started converting an old stable at 16 Lime Street on Beacon Hill into a theater with thirteen rows of seats for 129 auditors. The Boston papers were full of the project: nothing like it existed the length and breadth of America.[2] Then the reporters got wind of a quarrel among the members — perhaps the quarrel over

[1] In February, 1913, Professor Baker limited his pupils to twelve (known as 'Baker's Dozen') and started the internationally famous '47 Workshop.' The pupils, amongst whom was Eugene O'Neill for a time, did everything: wrote and directed their own plays, designed and painted scenery, procured costumes, *etc.* For a theater they had a small auditorium at Radcliffe, the use of which was not exclusively theirs. The audience was admitted by invitation only; each member was required to send in an elaborate criticism within a week. After each performance, there was a reception. In 1925, Professor Baker removed to Yale, where an adequate theater was placed at his disposal.

[2] Maurice Browne's 'Little Theater' in Chicago did not give its first performance until November, 1912, eleven months after the Toy Theater had opened. Mr. Browne, an Englishman, was less interested in native playwrights. The 'Little Theater' of Winthrop Ames in New York had nothing to do with the 'little theater movement' proper.

the question of producing Strindberg's *Countess Julie* —
and proceeded to ridicule the project, stating that the
Boston ladies wanted a private theater because the plays
to be produced were too scabrous for public performance.
On November 1, 1911, H.T.P. of the *Transcript* defended
the 'much discussed and grossly misrepresented "little
theater" here.'

Then on December 19, 1911, a new story burst. Miss
Lowell had resigned from the executive committee, on the
grounds that 'she did not agree with the rest of the committee upon the division of labor in play reading and play
producing.' The real reason was that there had been a
serious disagreement between her and Mrs. Gale, who felt
that she should be the final authority in the theater which
she had planned, founded, and named. The reporters,
playing up the theme of immorality, misquoted the persons they managed to interview (Miss Lowell, however,
was 'not at home' when called on the telephone), until the
executive committee appointed Edwin F. Edgett to give
out a statement:

> Owing to the interest that people in general have taken
> in the organization of the Toy Theater, it has been con-
> sidered advisable to increase its scope and bring it more in
> touch with the public.
> Miss Amy Lowell, under these circumstances, and in view
> of the increased duties she would be called upon to fulfil,
> feels that she would be more useful if not assigned to any
> particular task. She has therefore resigned from the
> executive committee.

Miss Lowell replied on December 27:

> There isn't a word of truth in it. I didn't know they had
> a press agent. I don't know what need they have of one.
> Don't you understand that this isn't a public theater?
> It's simply a case of private theatricals. Just because they
> have a little building in which to give the plays is no reason

why people should bother so much about it any more than
if the plays were given in my house.

No tickets are for sale and I cannot see why the public
should be interested. You may say that I was not the
manager. There has been no manager. The executive committee has managed the theater and, I suppose, manages
it still. I regret receiving any publicity on account of my
connection with the theater.

Horace Stanton and Joseph Lindon Smith replaced her.
Meanwhile she went ahead preparing her translation of
Musset's *Caprice*, which had been announced for perform-
ance on one of the early bills.

On January 1, 1912, at 9 P.M., the Toy Theater opened
with a bill of three small plays: George Middleton's *In His
House*, Shaw's *Press-Cuttings*, and Oliver Herford's *Two
Out of Time*.

Decidedly, Miss Lowell had not made herself popular in
the Toy Theater. One of the young ladies went about almost in tears, spreading the tale that 'She's rehearsing
Henry Higginson with a horse whip.' The whip, however,
was merely a riding crop.

On January 29, 30, and February 1, 1912, the Toy Theater presented *The Cuckoo* by Jeannette Marks and *Caprice*.
Miss Marks's contribution to the American drama had
won a first prize the year before in the Welsh National
Theater competition for the best plays on Welsh subjects.
Caprice, the Toy Theater program announced, had been
'translated, not Englished, by Amy Lowell' — her way of
saying that she had tried to preserve the flavor of the original French. The costumes were modern; the scenery was
by Livingston Platt, one of the foremost scene-designers
in America. She herself took the part of Madame de
Léry; Monsieur le Comte and Mathilde were played by
Mr. and Mrs. A. Henry Higginson, with Mr. M. C. Sturgis
as the servant. Persons who attended the performance
testified that Miss Lowell acted so brilliantly that one

quite forgot her figure. Mrs. Higginson, however, who had had professional experience,[1] was sufficiently exasperated to give out an interview on February 4, in which she was quoted as saying, among other things:

> Boston's Toy Theater is not exactly a great idea. To me it appears as a medium for amusing oneself at the expense of one's friends...
>
> Without practice, it is impossible to make players out of raw material. To use a silly expression, three professionals would have made our cast in 'A Caprice' 'look sick'...
>
> Personally I will not appear at the theater again this season....[2]

Neither did Miss Lowell appear again. Once the performance was over and out of the way, she set about organizing the manuscript of her first book of poems, *A Dome of Many-Coloured Glass*.

A Caprice was counted a success, none the less. Mrs. Gale the following year asked Miss Lowell to put on another play; but by that time Miss Lowell had given up acting in anything but informal charades, as she was too occupied with her literary career.[3]

[1] Seven years before, when she was Jean Calducci, she had appeared in Boston in *Fantana*, and the following year in *The Student King*; she also had been an understudy in *A Chinese Honeymoon*.

[2] This account is based on clippings in the Harvard Theater Collection, and amplified from information furnished by various persons who were concerned with the Toy Theater. Constance D'Arcy Mackay's *Little Theatre in the United States*, New York, 1917, contains only a few vague references to the Toy Theater, not even mentioning the fact that it was the first of its kind in America.

[3] In 1921, Samuel A. Eliot, who had seen the play, asked for the text, to publish it in volume IV of his *Little Theatre Classics*; but the volume was already so large that he reserved it for volume V, which never appeared. Her translation consequently is still unpublished. In 1923, Katharine Metcalf Roof, who had also seen it, wrote Miss Lowell, as she wanted a group of amateurs under her direction to produce it.

' This is the real decadence; to see through the eyes of dead men.'

LITTLE is really known of American poetry during that period between Miss Lowell's birth and her first book of poems. It is too close to us; we still lack historical perspective to see what the main tendencies were, and who really achieved anything. Nothing is more remote than the poets of yesteryear. But fortunately, two events occurred in 1874 which give us some idea of the supposed heights and the real extent of American poetic accomplishments up to that date. One was the copyrighting of Emerson's *Parnassus* (issued the following year), and the other was the printing of an Index to Caleb Fiske Harris's collection of American poetry and plays.

Emerson's anthology was a selection of all that he held worthiest in the poetry of a big continent and a great island; and as Emerson's taste was representative, his choices are of at least historical interest to us. Naturally the English poets predominated vastly. Among the Americans, Bryant and W. E. Channing led with eight titles each; Holmes, Longfellow, Lowell, and Whittier followed with seven; next came Bret Harte, Helen Hunt, and Thoreau with five apiece. Emerson modestly omitted himself; he also omitted Poe, Whitman, and Boker. Channing, we must confess, was favored; Boker was known chiefly as a dramatist (his sonnets were not published until after the World War); as for Poe and Whitman, Emerson was of his times in considering them deviations from the poetic norm — he could not foresee that they were to be the wellsprings of modern poetry the world over within another half century.

Unintentionally, *Parnassus* marked the end of a poetic

period. Poe and Thoreau were dead; Bryant, Melville, and Boker had virtually ceased to publish; Whitman, who had issued his best work, had broken down at Camden; and the New England group, though still hearty, were not to equal their former work. E. C. Stedman, in an interview of 1874, allowed himself to state that 'The New England school of literature centering in Boston has been a brilliant one, marked by originality and power, but it has been a feature of a single generation, not destined to be succeeded by another of equal importance. Just as the literary center shifted from Edinburgh to London, the true metropolis, so now it is shifting from Boston to New York.' The replies from Massachusetts were vigorous. 'Gad,' remarked Aldrich, 'these Bostonians are not thin-skinned on the subject — they haven't any skin at all!' [1]

One can understand their indignation. As Howells said, 'Literature in Boston, indeed, was so respectable, and often of so high a lineage, that to be a poet was not only to be good society, but almost to be good family.' [2] And Boston was overrun with poets old and new.

Unfortunately, the younger generation, whether of New York or Boston, could not keep up the poetic pace. It soon became obvious that something was wrong with their ideals. Whitman cried out, in his *Democratic Vistas* (1871): 'Do you call those genteel little creatures American poets? Do you term that perpetual, pistareen, paste-pot work, American art, American drama, taste, verse? I think I hear, echoed as from some mountain-top afar in the west, the scornful laugh of the Genius of these States.' [3] And a decade later, in his *Poetry Today in America* (1881):

> The prevailing flow of poetry for the last fifty or eighty years, and now at its height, has been and is (like the

[1] Laura Stedman and George M. Gould: *Life and Letters of Edmund Clarence Stedman*, New York, 1910, vol. I, p. 507.

[2] William Dean Howells: *Literary Friends and Acquaintance*, New York, 1900, p. 146.

[3] *Complete Prose Works*, Boston, 1907, p. 219.

music) an expression of mere surface melody, within narrow limits, and yet, to give it its due, perfectly satisfying to the demands of the ear, of wondrous charm, of smooth and easy delivery, and the triumph of technical art. Above all things it is fractional and select. It shrinks with aversion from the sturdy, the universal, and the democratic.... The accepted notion of a poet would appear to be a sort of male odalisque, singing or piano-playing a kind of spiced ideas, second-hand reminiscences, or toying late hours at entertainments, in rooms stifling with fashionable scent. I think I haven't seen a new-publish'd, healthy, bracing, simple lyric in ten years.[1]

Later critics echoed Whitman. The London *Quarterly Review* for October, 1886, commenting favorably on Stedman's *Poets of America* declared: 'Like all modern versifiers, American poets of the cultured school are characterized by scholarly refinement of thought, command of dainty fancies, and mastery of the technicalities of their art.... There is little that is grand-hearted, tumultuous, and self-forgetful.' [2] Henry A. Beers, in 1895, after remarking that 'New England has lost its long monopoly' on literature, added: 'At all events, there are no new poets who rank with Whittier, Longfellow, Lowell, and others of the older generation, although George H. Boker, in Philadelphia, R. H. Stoddard and E. C. Stedman, in New York, and T. B. Aldrich, first in New York and afterwards in Boston, have written creditable verse; not to speak of younger writers, whose work, however, for the most part, has been more distinguished by delicacy of execution than by native impulse.' [3] So, too, Henry Adams, in 1911: 'The twenty-five years between 1873 and 1898... were marked by a steady decline of literary and artistic inten-

---

[1] *Complete Prose Works*, Boston, 1907, pp. 286–88.

[2] *Life and Letters of Stedman*, II, 97–98.

[3] Henry A. Beers: *Initial Studies in American Letters*, Cleveland (1895), pp. 204–05.

sity and especially of the feeling for poetry.'[1] And finally
Miss Lowell herself: 'After the days of Walt Whitman and
Edgar Allan Poe, there was a decided slump in the quality
of poetry written in this country. The main tendency
seemed to be toward a diluted Tennysonism, and it was not
until the year 1912 that a new vigour became visible.'[2]

It was Miss Lowell who put her finger on the real
source of the trouble: Tennyson. These poets, instead of
looking to their own environment and their own past,
sought transatlantic models for feeling, thought, and form.
Had they investigated their inheritance, they should have
learned that the best American poets had all been American in their inspiration.[3] Their roots had been in the soil;
they were not cut flowers. Even the New England poets,
though not giants, had grown to considerable stature by
laboring in their own fields. Thus, and thus alone, they
had attained that perfect clarity, that subtle and seemingly artless art, which kept them clean of copying. Their
verse is more austere and less decorated than that of
Keats, Shelley, and Tennyson. They breathed a purer air;
there is a perfume about them of hay and pine, a sound of
brook and breeze. The landscape that permeates their
poems was one enriched by legend and history — it had
dimensions in time as well as space; and this native material they collected and preserved. Landscape by itself
was not enough, however; and owing to a fortunate historical accident, the soul-searching of German Transcendentalism reached Puritan Massachusetts just at the
moment when Unitarianism had freed it of dogma and
didacticism. Consequently there was a liberal expression
of the native mysticism, so curiously brother to the ancient Hindu philosophers. Abolitionism then strung their

---

[1] [Henry Adams:] *Life of George Cabot Lodge*, Boston, 1911, p. 6.

[2] Letter to M. André Fontainas, March 6, 1919.

[3] This is so obviously true of them all except Poe that the point need not be
labored. As for Poe's essential Americanism, I have treated that question in
my book on Thomas Holley Chivers.

spiritual sinews. Therefore the poets of Concord and Cambridge rose far higher in the poetic world than if they had expended the same effort upon merely imported material.

The younger parlor poets did not understand this. More cosmopolitan, they believed that a steamship ticket was a ticket to culture. But one must be national before one can become international, as the greatest of the world poets have invariably proved. The way to escape provinciality is to discover universality in one's province; to dash overseas is merely to become superficial and insular. Unable to create the language and forms necessary to express the new civilization that was theirs, unable even to build on the foundations already laid, they abandoned the attempt, and tried to be English poets. And who was the great English poet but Tennyson?

Tennyson was the last English poet to be widely mistaken for poetry itself. His position in the nineteenth century was broadly like that of Pope's in the eighteenth. Each interpreted fully the orthodoxy of his age, but never rose above it; and so well did each do his job that nothing thereafter seemed possible but imitation, — imitation which inevitably was decadent. As Pope had pointed back to a false Rome, so Tennyson pointed back to a false Greece and imaginary Camelot, which were also mistaken for Nature. Moreover, each poet was an aesthetic snob, who recognized the poetic existence of only a certain few objects in the universe, and denied the poetic existence of everything else — although, of course, there was a narrow fringe of doubtful climbers which a master might introduce to Parnassus. Roses and violets, for example, were ancient aristocrats of the floral family in the world of taste; but who dare notice coreopsis and squills?

The shadow of genius is always a blight when it cuts off sunlight. It was Tennyson's shadow that bleached the young Americans of the seventies and eighties.

But this blight fell chiefly on the salons, and the whole

continent was versifying. We have mentioned Emerson's *Parnassus* as indicating the heights, and have scanned the foothills that followed, but we have not yet considered the *extent* of American verse. This is indicated by Caleb Fiske Harris's *Index* (1874) to his collection of American poetry and plays, the largest in existence. Harris listed 4219 titles, to the amazement of the various authors and librarians interested in the subject; and the number was growing rapidly.[1]

As one examines the volumes which have accumulated there since the *Index* was printed, an increasing dislocation between the *littérateurs* and the ordinary versifiers becomes more and more evident. The top stratum, or quality, was attempting to become English, while the lower strata, or quantity, were moving ignorantly and irresistibly in quite another direction. The gentlemen, who knew their technique, lacked the enterprise born of conviction; the classes below them had something to say, but did not know how. Or, to change the metaphor, the cultured were content to be cisterns, drawing off Tennysonian waters according to their capacities, and preserving it until it became somewhat stagnant. (Oh, the disease of Beauty-seeking! the sterility of the proprieties!) Meanwhile the would-be poets all over the continent were sinking their pathetic little wells in the deserts, scooping up thirstily the muddy tricklings (yet living waters none the less), and prophesying of oases. Anybody who has dug a well (or read Stockton's 'My Well and What Came Out of It') knows that almost every well seems a failure at first;

---

[1] This collection (which still remains the biggest collection of its kind in the world) was started by Judge Albert G. Greene, author of 'Old Grimes is Dead'; it was greatly enlarged by that inveterate collector, Caleb Fiske Harris; and was enlarged still more by Senator Henry B. Anthony, who left it to Brown University. A second catalogue was issued in 1886. Walt Whitman contributed to the *Critic* for April 16, 1887, an article, 'Five Thousand Poems,' which again expressed amazement that Americans had written so much. At present it contains between seventy and eighty thousand items, and grows at a rate of over three thousand a year.

but as the seasons pass, the underground channels turn
their courses in its direction, and presently it is functioning
perfectly.

What are these books and pamphlets printed in cities
and towns all over the continent? They include hundreds
of volumes of verses scribbled at odd moments, now collected by the author, with his photograph for frontispiece;
or papa's verses gathered by his dutiful children; or tributes to great-aunt Susan. (Oh, the pathos of these claims
on immortality!) They are versified reminiscences of some
battle by a Civil War veteran; or a pioneer's jog-trot account of buffalo hunts and Indian massacres; clerical attempts to make the Bible Miltonic; heart-songs between
pansied covers; optimistic epigrams; cosmic urges and occult systems; rhymes for children about animals, flowers,
or fairies; college verses; verses by colored boys, by the
blind, by invalids; celebrations of mountain or plain or
magnolia tree; town histories and local myths; songsters;
anthologies of regional poets; experiments in free-verse
(uninfluenced by Whitman); inspirational verses dictated
by the discarnate spirits in Summerland; — a heavy growth
of weeds, proving the fertility of the soil.

In short, America had now expanded away from England and beyond New England; but still, in spite of
Whitman, the prairies were uncultivated, unfenced. The
first striking outbreak of democracy in poetry occurred
in 1871, when Bret Harte's 'Heathen Chinee' opened the
way for the dialect school of verse. John Hay in a few
nights promptly tossed off his *Pike County Ballads*, which
added gift-book sentimentality to western humor and local
dialect — poems which in the popular memory have outlasted his distinguished career as a diplomat. It is extraordinary how far those verses permeated.[1] Presently the

[1] Mr. Bloom probably never heard of John Hay's name; yet at Mrs. Bella
Cohen's, he could remark with quiet feeling: 'Jim Bludso. Hold her nozzle
again[st] the bank.' (J. Joyce: *Ulysses*, Paris, 1922, p. 434.)

presses were giving birth to innumerable quizzical home-spun heroes, all rough in manner but warm at heart and soft in the head.[1]

The cognoscenti were promptly horrified. Stedman, writing to Bayard Taylor on September 16, 1873, concerning the latter's 'Lars,' called it —

> a poem that will *last*, though not in the wretched, immediate *fashion* of this demoralized American period. Cultured as are Hay and Harte, they are almost equally responsible with 'Josh Billings' and the 'Danbury News' man [James M. Bailey] for the present *horrible* degeneracy of the public taste — that is, the taste of the newest generation of book-buyers. The whole country, owing to the *contagion* of our American newspaper 'exchange' system, is flooded, deluged, swamped, beneath a muddy tide of slang, vulgarity, in-artistic bathers [*sic*], impertinence and buffoonery that is not wit.
>
> I feel that this is not the complaint of a superannuated Roger de Coverley nor Colonel Newcome, for I am in the prime and vigor of active, noonday life, and at work right here in the metropolis. It is a clear-headed, wide-awake statement of a disgraceful fact. With it all, I acknowledge, the demand for good books also increases — and such works as Taine's *Septembre*, etc., have a large standard sale. But in poetry, readers have tired of the past, and don't see clearly how to shape a future; and so content themselves with going to some 'Cave' or 'Hole in the Wall' and ap-plauding slang and nonsense, spiced with smut and pro-fanity. It is trying, but will all come out right in the end.
>
> ... Am glad you mean to write more poetry, and strongly advise you to get hold of a dramatic, American theme, merely for policy's sake....[2]

Stedman wrote in vain. When the *Old Swimmin' Hole* appeared in 1883 (the year after Longfellow's death), James Whitcomb Riley was promptly hailed as the

[1] A lively account of this school is to be found in Bruce Weirick's *From Whit-man to Sandburg*, New York, 1924.

[2] *Life and Letters of Stedman*, I, 477.

laureate of the people; and in the nineties, Eugene Field (who was to fly a pitch above the others) first became known.

But in the seventies and the eighties, the times were not yet ripe for the successors to Poe, Whitman, and the New England poets. The soil was lying fallow, was steadily being enriched by the slow-dropping leaves of legend and history, of the songs of the people, of the experiments of local bards. Indians were chanting their ancient rituals; cowboys were singing as they guarded their herds at night; college boys were dancing snake-dances to new tunes on the football fields; the negroes of the South were improvising their heart-searching spirituals; in the hills of Maine and Vermont or the mountains of Kentucky, folk-ballads of forgotten origin were being wailed to the fiddle, banjo, or strummed dulcimer.[1] The whalers of Nantucket and New Bedford, the pioneers on the plains or the Irish immigrants on the wharves, the lumber-jacks and railroad makers, even the prisoners in the jails, all had their melodies of triumph and despair and laughter — all the stuff of poetry, leaves dropping steadily, enriching the soil, falling unnoticed.

The times were not yet ripe; but all over the United States, the poets of the future were being born: Robinson and Masters in 1869, one in Maine, the other in Kansas; Amy Lowell in Brookline, Massachusetts, in 1874; Frost in 1875 at San Francisco; Grace Hazard Conkling and Sandburg in 1878, the one at New York and the other in Illinois; Lindsay, the next year, also in Illinois; Sara Teasdale in 1884 at St. Louis, Missouri; Ezra Pound in

---

[1] Usually these ballads have been identified as of British origin, although quite a number seem to be native. Mellinger E. Henry recently discovered in the South a ballad which originally celebrated Henry V's exploits in France (*New Jersey Journal of Education*, XX, 3-4 — November–December, 1930 — pp. 6-7). Perhaps in no other civilized land has native balladry flourished so persistently. Ancient as many of these songs are, others memorialize the fate of the *Titanic*, of Floyd Collins, of the *Shenandoah*, while others recount murders and railroad wrecks no longer identifiable.

1885 at Hailey, Idaho; the next year Hilda Doolittle and Fletcher, respectively at Bethlehem, Pennsylvania, and Little Rock, Arkansas; Elinor Wylie in 1887 at Rosemont, Pennsylvania; Eliot in 1888 at St. Louis; and Aiken in 1889 at Savannah, Georgia. Certainly New England had expanded beyond the Housatonic, and America beyond New England.

With the eighteen-nineties came the first signs that a new century was approaching, and also that some persons were not so much concerned with Being Poets as with writing poetry. In the very first year of the decade appeared a little posthumous volume of verse, issued to preserve the memory of one Miss Emily Dickinson of Amherst. Nobody had heard of her; the surprise was complete; the delighted public devoured edition after edition, regardless of some critics who were disturbed by the free rhythms and false rhymes. Two more volumes of selections were published, as well as her letters; they also went into later editions very soon. A new American poet was discovered and established. And with the name of Emily Dickinson, a history of modern American verse may well begin, for she, a belated daughter of the Transcendentalists, was also the great precursor of the Imagists.

One of those who read Emily Dickinson's poems was the half-starved bohemian, Stephen Crane. As he read these authentic verses, something stirred within his own brain; and almost automatically, before the astounded Hamlin Garland, he wrote out his *Black Riders* in 1893,[1] which was issued very exotically (printed in green on vellum, with a black orchid adorning the cover) by Copeland and Day in Boston, 1895. The bitter cynicism of these free-verse epigrams and lyrics so shocked the critics that Crane enjoyed a small *succès de scandale*; not until his war-story, the *Red Badge of Courage*, appeared in the next

[1] See Garland's accounts in *The Booklover*, (II, 6–9), Autumn, 1900, and the *Yale Review* (n.s., III: 494–506), April, 1914.

year did he wake to find himself famous. In 1899, the year
before his premature death, he issued a second volume of
poems, *War is Kind*. In her 'Introduction' (September,
1924) to his poems, for volume VI of his *Work* (1926), Miss
Lowell wrote:

> ... Emily Dickinson and Stephen Crane had, as a trait
> shared in common, only audacity.... When he suddenly
> started writing poetry, he had in himself a full reservoir of
> intimate, personal experiences to tap. And he tapped them
> until he found that his spring had run dry. Thereafter it
> was necessary to wait until the energy of living had filled
> him up again, and this precisely because his was not a nature
> of inexhaustible subjective reactions. Youth is prone to
> express itself in verse, and, Crane being a youth of genius,
> and of a highly original genius, his verses were sure to be
> eminently worth while.... What baffled [his contemporaries]
> was his use of suggestion. And here possibly lies his chief
> technical debt to Emily Dickinson, for she was past mis-
> tress of suggestion. This and, to a lesser degree, irony were
> what Crane derived from her, but his was no such light
> gossamer touch. Crane's irony clanks by heavily-clad in
> steel and brandishing a molesting spear, Crane is conscious
> of an enemy with whom he is to do battle — most adolescent
> of attitudes! Emily Dickinson's irony brushes as inconse-
> quentially as a butterfly's wing; she is unconscious of any
> audience. The world exists for her solely as she sees it, and
> her carelessness in the matter of whether she exists for her
> readers or not is wholly admirable. This is maturity....
> Crane was so steeped in the religion in which he was brought
> up that he could not get it out of his head. He disbelieved
> it and he hated it, but he could not free himself from it.
> A loathed and vengeful God broods over *The Black Riders*.
> ... Crane handed the world the acrid fumes of his heart,
> and they howled at him for an obscene blasphemer, or
> patted him on the back as a 'cracker-jack' on whom they
> 'doted,' a cranky and unexpected star beaming above the
> amateur magazines and proud to shed its light upon East
> Aurora. Reading the book now, thirty years afterwards,

one is tempted to neither reaction. What chiefly impresses is the volume's sincerity.... He died too soon. He did much, but the temperature of the world he lived in was unsuitable. He ranks in America somewhat as Chatterton ranks in England. A boy, spiritually killed by neglect. A marvelous boy, potentially a genius, historically an important link in the chain of American poetry.

Besides the *Black Riders*, two other gloomy first books by young men put in their modest claims for immortality — claims quite unrecognized for the time being, however: *The Torrent and the Night Before* (1896) by Edwin Arlington Robinson, and *A Book of Verses* (1898) by Edgar Lee Masters. But such autumnal lines had little chance in the fresh breezes that blew through the Hovey-Carman revolt into vagabondia.

Always in poetry there are two parties: the Conservatives, who try for the gist of poetry by shearing away the individualities of the poets they admire, thus reducing the matter to its common denominator; and the Radicals, who try for the gist of poetry by copying and combining the individualities of the poets they admire, and thus keeping up with the latest literary fashions.

At the beginning of the twentieth century, this tendency became geographically manifest in the contrasting groups which sprang up on the Atlantic and Pacific seaboards: the Cantabrigians and the Californians. Both groups were endeavoring to sum up the cosmos, and both were striving for free forms.

The Californians were the Radicals. Free Verse, in the Whitman manner (hitherto little attempted), became quite common. The great open spaces inspired cosmic, optimistic yearnings — belated Transcendentalism, reanimated by western weather, and often tinctured by Point Loma theosophy. Generally, this verse was oratorical rather than poetic; and like the landscape which inspired it, it lacked foreground and cultivation.

The Cantabrigians were the Conservatives. Their leader was George Santayana (whose *Lucifer* had appeared in 1889); they included William Vaughn Moody, George Cabot Lodge, and Trumbull Stickney. Henry Adams was of their company. Aware of the difficulties of their art, they schooled themselves on the Petrarchan sonnet; aware also, however, of the danger of limiting themselves to the restricted models then popular in England,[1] they specialized in the freedom of the irregular ode and the poetic drama, where the form could fit the thought as exactly as the skin fits the hand. Aware also of the disease of pretty verbiage, they eliminated poeticism after poeticism from their vocabulary. But their great feat was the rediscovery of the literary value of thought — thought, which had been divorced so long from verse. Privately they were dubbed the 'Conservative Christian Anarchists.'[2] The scope of their conception was truly cosmic, in contradistinction to the Californians, who rarely rose above thunderstorms and mountains and Sin. The Cambridge anarchists all celebrated the great rebels against the tyrant Nobodaddy: Satan, Cain, Herakles, Prometheus. Santayana's *Lucifer* depicts the strife between Catholicism and Paganism; Moody's *Masque of Judgement* is an analysis of God's failure and suicide in the Last Judgment; Lodge's *Cain* represents the martyrdom of the man who attempts to advance civilization; and so do Stickney's *Prometheus Pyrphoros* and Moody's *Fire-Bringer*.

What these young men might have accomplished, had they been born into a fresher literary atmosphere, or had they lived longer,[3] we can only conjecture. Born about the same time as Miss Lowell — indeed, two of them

---

[1] [Henry Adams]: *Life of George Cabot Lodge*, Boston, 1911, p. 27.

[2] Henry Adams: *Education*, Boston, 1927, p. 405.

[3] Stickney died in 1904, aged thirty; Lodge in 1909, aged thirty-five; Moody in 1910, aged forty-one.

within four months of her — they were all dead when she published her first poem, except Moody, who had but a couple more months of life, and Santayana, who had abandoned poetry and was soon to abandon America. They had the stuff, however, which the country needed. They were sensitive, intelligent, ambitious; they worked hard, aimed high, struggled valiantly against convention of all sorts. True, they looked back to Shelley for form and to ancient myth for symbol. Yet their new thought demanded new and freer forms and fresh symbols, toward which they were working when death cut them down on the very threshold of modern poetry. Moody, who wrote longest, went farthest: such things as his 'Menagerie' are but hints of what he probably would have achieved.

'I wonder,' murmured Miss Lowell, years later in the hearing of Robert Morss Lovett, 'I wonder if he could have kept us back.' [1]

A fresh start requires maturity; the creators of the new poetry were mature men and women when they really began. We look back and are surprised to learn what volumes preceded that beginning: Robinson's *Torrent and the Night Before* (1896), *Children of the Night* (1897), *Captain Craig* (1902) — Roosevelt's *Outlook* appreciation appeared on August 12, 1905 — and *The Town Down the River* (1910); Sandburg's *In Reckless Ecstasy* (1904) and *Incidentals* (1907?) — both, apparently, prose pamphlets issued privately; Lindsay's *Tramp's Excuse* (1909), besides numerous leaflets dating back to 1905; Masters's *A Book of Verses* (1898), which was followed by some half dozen plays; Sara Teasdale's *Sonnets to Duse* (1907) and *Helen of Troy* (1911); and Pound's *A Lume Spento* (Venice, 1908), *A Quinzain for This Yule* (London, 1908), *Personae* and *Exultations* (1909), his prose *Provença* (1910), and

---

[1] William Vaughn Moody: *Selected Poems*, ed. R. M. Lovett, Boston, 1931, p. lxxxviii.

Canzoni (1911). Eliot, at Harvard, had written his 'Love Song of J. Alfred Prufrock,' and had gone abroad; Aiken was running — and virtually writing — the *Harvard Advocate*. The poetic Renaissance was ready to break forth. Yet the public at large did not care for poetry. Magazines used it only as filler at the end of some short story. One commonly argued that poetry was written out; all the forms had been exhausted; there was nothing new to be said; as no more wars were possible, romance was over forever; and of course, all the great poets were dead.

But actually, for a third of a century, American poetry had merely been lying fallow. Then in 1912, the first blossoms of a new period began to flower. The following list of books (which is selective, not all-inclusive) proves that the coincidence of date was no accident.

> Akins, Zoë: *Interpretations* (the first of a series of monthly publications of poetry volumes, announced by Mitchell Kennerley)
> Bates, Katharine Lee: *America the Beautiful and Other Poems*
> Evans, Donald: *Discords*
> Hagedorn, Hermann: *Poems and Ballads*
> Holley, Horace: *Post Impressionistic Poems*
> Jeffers, Robinson: *Flagons and Apples*
> Kilmer, Joyce: *Summer of Love*
> Leonard, William Ellery: *Vaunt of Man and Other Poems*
> Lindsay, Vachel: *Rhymes to be Traded for Bread*
> Lodge, George Cabot: *Poems and Dramas*
> Lowell, Amy: *A Dome of Many-Coloured Glass*
> MacKaye, Percy: *Uriel and Other Poems*
> [Masters, Edgar Lee]: [*untraced volume*] [1]
> Millay, Edna St. Vincent: 'Renascence' (in *A Lyric Year*)
> Neihardt, John G.: *The Stranger at the Gate*
> Peabody, Josephine Preston: *Singing Man*
> Pound, Ezra: *Cavalcanti*

[1] Issued under a pseudonym; mentioned in Amy Lowell's *Tendencies*, p. 157.

Pound, Ezra: *Ripostes* (London)
Riley, James Whitcomb: *Lockerbie Rock*
Schauffler, Robert Haven: *Scum o' the Earth*
Teasdale, Sara: *Helen of Troy*
Viereck, George Sylvester: *Candle and the Flame*
Wheelock, John Hall: *The Beloved Adventure*
Wheelock, John Hall: *The Human Fantasy*
[Wylie, Elinor]: *Incidental Numbers* (London)

There were also a number of anthologies in this year. *American Lyrics*, edited by Edith Ricket and Jessie Paton, collected the best of the shorter poems; Walter Bronson's *American Poems* was a historical survey; Stevenson's *Home Book of Verse* represented the popular taste; John Avery Lomax's *Cowboy Lyrics* was fruits of specialized research; and F. Earle Mitchell's *Lyric Year* was strictly contemporary. Two little magazines devoted to poetry, especially American poetry, started this year: the famous *Poetry: A Magazine of Verse* in Chicago, and the *Poetry Journal* in Boston.

But Amy Lowell, secluded from the literary world in Brookline, was like many another American poet in being quite unaware of the *Zeitgeist* that moved her to publish a book in this milestone year.

CHAPTER IX

A DOME OF MANY-COLOURED GLASS

IF SHE was to be recognized as a poet, it was time to issue a book. Miss Lowell was thirty-eight; she had been working at her poems for ten years; and they had been appearing in periodicals for two. So as soon as she was free of the performances of *Caprice* at the Toy Theater, she organized her manuscript.

The arrangement of a book of poems is always difficult. She kept of course the five poems which had already appeared in magazines; but it was sometimes hard to choose among the others. As she later admitted: 'I very carefully weeded my manuscripts before making up that volume. Even as it was, my inexperience left in a great many poems which should have been rigorously rejected.' [1] The first of them all, the poem to Duse, was set aside, also a sonnet to Matthew Arnold; what others, we do not know. She chose 'Apples of Hesperides' to go first.

The manuscript had been assembled and arranged when on March 12, 1912, she went to a meeting of an informal lunch club of Boston ladies, all of whom were distinguished by some leading interest. Miss Annie Endicott Nourse, the founder, was a pianist; Mrs. Charles Bruen Perkins (who had started writing poetry with Miss Lowell) was a poet and a teacher of art; Mrs. Edward Burlingame Hill was the wife of the composer and Harvard professor; Mrs. John Gorham Palfrey was the mother of the famous tennis players; Mrs. James A. Parker, of a musical family, had studied to be a doctor; Mrs. Joseph Lindon Smith was the wife of the painter; Miss Rose Nichols was the author of books on landscape gardening and her world travels; and Miss Eugenia Frothingham,

[1] Letter to Eunice Tietjens, *Poetry* (XXII, 234–35), August, 1923.

the author, used to sing her repertoire of songs over and over to Miss Lowell when they were girls. For this March meeting, Mrs. Perkins was hostess; she invited Mrs. Harold Russell, the actress, known on the stage by her maiden name, Ada Dwyer.

Ada Dwyer was born in Salt Lake City, February 8, 1863; she married Harold Russell, February 26, 1893; and had a daughter Lorna, born September 5, 1894. Her father, James Dwyer, had opened the first bookstore in the West; he sent his daughter Ada to school in Boston. From the school plays and dramatic clubs to the professional stage proved a very small step. Early engagements in various plays meant training and technique. She was first starred in Robert Buchanan's *Alone in London*. By the 1890's she had won her place. Her favorite rôle in this decade was Roxy in *Puddenhead Wilson* (the play which caused the New York police to start identifying criminals by fingerprints); this play ran for three seasons, one in New York and two on the road. She then had a short season with Mansfield in his dramatization of *Don Juan*. From the production of *Children of the Ghetto*, she was under George C. Tyler's management. This play was produced in England with the original cast. A play entitled *Lost River* followed; then a season with Kyrle Bellew in *Gentleman of France*. Mr. Tyler then starred Eleanor Robson in *Audrey*, a dramatization of Mary Johnston's novel; and for eight years Mrs. Russell was a member of Miss Robson's company. Zangwill's *Merely Mary Ann*, which followed, was so successful that it ran two years in America and a season in London. Their next production was Zangwill's *Nurse Marjory*; after this, Paul Armstrong's dramatization of Bret Harte's *Salomy Jane* ran for two years. Mrs. Russell then went over for a London season to play with William Gillette in trial performances of his new play, *Clarice*, and finished the season with William Collier in Richard

Harding Davis's *Dictator*. In May, 1908, she sailed for
Australia and New Zealand, to play *Mrs. Wiggs of the
Cabbage Patch*; but Miss Robson wanted her for Slum
Bet in Frances Hodgson Burnett's *Dawn of a Tomorrow*;
and the tale of the hurried trip back, round the world,
covering 15,672 miles, and the arrival just in time for the
last rehearsals before the New York opening, reads like
a Jules Verne story. The play was another great success.
After Miss Robson's marriage to Mr. August Belmont in
1910, Mrs. Russell went to England, to play in the *Dawn
of a Tomorrow* with Gertrude Forbes-Robertson.

She opened the season of 1910–11 in Paul Armstrong's
The Deep Purple, which ran for one season in Chicago
and New York, and was on the road for the next season.
That summer she went to England again, where her
daughter was in school; on the boat home she met Mr.
and Mrs. Thomas Ward, and promised Mrs. Ward that
she would send a card to her daughter, Mrs. Charles
Bruen Perkins, when she was playing in Boston for the
month of February 25–March 23, 1912.

The ladies of the lunch club were delighted with Mrs.
Perkins's guest — so delighted, that in her honor they
gave their group a name at last: 'The Purple Lunch Club.'
It is still in existence, holding an annual dinner on Miss
Lowell's birthday.

Miss Lowell and Mrs. Russell at once became friends.
They had much in common: both loved the stage and
books, especially poetry. Miss Lowell read the manuscript of the *Dome of Many-Coloured Glass* to Mrs. Russell,
who tried in vain to get her to exclude 'Petals': things
had gone too far to make any changes now. Mrs. Russell's
professional duties called her away at the end of March,
but the friendship which had started so pleasantly was
to deepen as time went on. At last Miss Lowell had found
the friend who understood her thoroughly and whom she
could trust utterly.

Where to send her manuscript she was uncertain. But one day at the end of 1911 or the beginning of 1912, she ran into Josephine Peabody at a florist's.

I remember consulting her about taking my first book to Houghton and Mifflin, which she advised me by all means to do. I remember being a little dampened by her saying that they 'did not care much for poetry which had no human interest, but why should they?' I wondered if she had read any of my poems in magazines (there were precious few in print anywhere at the time), and if she was giving me a kindly warning.[1]

Houghton Mifflin Company was the most venerable of the Boston publishing houses. It had started in 1828 as Carter Hendee and Company; after various changes, it became Ticknor and Fields, famous for its editions of the great New England poets; in 1878, as James R. Osgood and Company, it had amalgamated with Henry O. Houghton's Riverside Press; and after still more changes had become Houghton Mifflin Company, of Park Street, Boston. It was the obvious press to select.

In April, Miss Lowell took her manuscript to the editor, Ferris Greenslet; but before the formal agreement for publication could be signed (it was sent her on May 21), another important event happened: she began to discover new and freer possibilities of versification. A friend had sent her Samain's *Chariot d'Or*, which had led her to investigate the post-Symboliste French poets, whom she had not read hitherto. Their *vers libre* interested her particularly; stimulated by their example, she wrote 'Before the Altar.' And knowing that it was the best poem she had written, she mailed it to her publishers, with the request that it be placed first in the book, replacing 'Apples of Hesperides.'[2]

[1] *Ms.* concerning Josephine Preston Peabody.

[2] A letter from Houghton Mifflin Company, making this arrangement, was dated May 21, the same day that the contract was sent her. The point is of importance because of the statement one frequently meets, that Miss Lowell knew nothing of the modern French poets and *vers libre* until she met the London

She took particular pains with the format of the book, which she directed be modelled as closely as possible on the first edition of Keats's *Lamia*. The resultant effect was so successful that all her books of poetry had the same format, differing externally only in the color and the label. This label was designed by Berkeley Updike, whom she always called on for that sort of work. On library shelves, consequently, the books belonged obviously together, without the formal appearance of a set. They were unpretentious, yet distinguished, and in perfect taste. Separately, they were of a size that slipped neatly into pockets, were light in the hand, and opened well (the leaves were all cut beforehand). The type was small enough so that a line of verse could be seen in one glance as a unit, while the wide spacing between words made them easy to read. Miss Lowell always fought hard to get everything exactly right, and had especial difficulty in making the printer drop those stanzas which began at the top of the page.

When these main difficulties were arranged, she went to Dublin for the summer, where she entertained Mrs. Russell. Here she received a prospectus from Harriet Monroe, announcing a new magazine, *Poetry: A Magazine of Verse*, to be published in Chicago. Miss Monroe had seen and admired Miss Lowell's sonnets in the *Atlantic Monthly*, and invited her to contribute. Miss Lowell, on September 7, sent her a cheque for twenty-five dollars, and promised to submit some poems later. On September 23, the first number of the magazine was mailed.

group in 1913. She always claimed this poem as her first experiment in Free Verse, and she always insisted that she began these experiments before her trip to London, as in a letter to Miss Harriet France, May 28, 1917: 'I suppose free verse is in the air at the present day, but my attention was turned to it first by studying some of the French Symbolistes. It was some time after I had begun writing it myself that I went abroad and made the acquaintance of the other poets who have been associated with me in the Imagist movement. In London I met a group of poets, who, like myself, had been experimenting with free verse, and, also like myself, had made a study of French poets.' Taupin, who can hardly be said to have favored Miss Lowell's work, states that in this first book he has traced the influences of Samain, Regnier, and Jammes. (*L'Influence du Symbolisme Français sur la Poésie Américaine*, Paris, 1929, pp. 69–70.)

A Dome of Many-Coloured Glass was published October
12, 1912. The title is from a well-known line in Shelley's
'Adonais': the 'dome' is there used to symbolize life itself, in all its brilliant variety and fragility, a construction
in the empty light of eternity. Yet the life recorded in
the book is not that of humanity, but of one shut out from
humanity. This exclusion itself becomes the theme of the
book: it is the veiled record of frustration; a dedication of
an otherwise useless life to poetry; a blind, almost hopeless, determination to succeed.

On the surface there is little promise of success. The
book is sincere but restrained, dignified but conventional.
There are poems about the seasons, about one's longings,
about things. There are sonnets, building up to the predestinate last line; there is syllabic blank verse, with every
urge of cadence ironed out; there are unrhymed hex-
ameters and some rhymed stanza-patterns, original yet
not seeming so. The book might tell the story and the
tastes of a thousand women; yet only one woman could
have written it, as we now can see in light touches here
and there. As with the Italian primitives, the attitudes
are the stock ones, but the landscape behind is fresh —
the flowers are real flowers and the weather real weather.

It is this honesty which constitutes the greatest promise
of the book. It was built of what she knew. There are
memories of childhood — of her grandfather's house at
Roxbury, of the fruit-garden at Brookline, of the field of
blue gentians at Medford, of climbing in trees or watching brook-trout. The most personal poem in the book
is 'The Fairy Tale,' which records the curse upon her
earliest years. There is the long poem to the Athenaeum,
written during the controversy in 1903. There are moments of travel — a European market day,[1] the epitaph

---

[1] '... probably written somewhere about 1910, but of that I cannot be sure,
the poems in my first volume stretched over a number of years and it is very
difficult to tell.' (Letter to Norman Foerster, November 25, 1924.)

seen in 1906 at Charleston, South Carolina. At least half a dozen poems were inspired by Dublin: Mt. Monadnock in early spring, the country roads in autumn, Loon Point (Joseph Lindon Smith's place), and the Teatro Bambino (his private theater there). Other poems were suggested by things she owned: a piece of Venetian glass, a green bowl made for her by her nephew Roger Putnam, a Japanese wood-carving in her library, a print by Shokei, a first edition of Keats.

The influence of Keats, of course, is strong in the book, yet not after the customary manner. There are no imitations of his poems or mannerisms, no borrowings, no seeing things through his eyes or describing them with his pen. But the format of the book is his; the title comes from Shelley's elegy written to him; two poems offer him direct homage; and the first, and best, poem in the book, 'Before the Altar' uses the basic symbol of his 'Endymion.'

This altar is pagan; the deity is the moon. A man stands worshipping; he has nothing to offer, except his life, his heart, to a moon which gives no sign of answer. No Indian Maid offers a perplexed comfort, no choruses celebrate a coming marriage in the skies; there is nothing but a despairing, unassuageable desire.

Although this poem is iambic and rhymed, the irregular line-lengths and rhyme-pattern show the influence of French *vers libre*. Miss Lowell later was to claim it as her first experiment in free verse. It was the last poem in this book to be written; another late one was 'Behind a Wall.'

Besides the poems to Keats, there are two or three others suggested by her reading, but always they are about men, not books. 'J.-K. Huysmans' is perhaps the most interesting of these. Miss Lowell owned a complete set of his works in first editions. She represents him stumbling through a rainy night, repelled by the drunken

The Green Bowl

This little bowl is like a mossy pool
In a Spring wood where dogtooth violets grow,
Nodding in chequered sunshine of the trees;
A quiet place; still, with the sound of birds,
Where, though unseen, is heard the endless song
And murmur of the never resting sea.
'Twas winter, Roger, when you made this cup,
But coming Spring guided your eager hand
And round the edge you fashioned young green leaves,
A proper chalice made to hold the shy
And little flowers of the woods. And here
They will forget their sad uprooting, Lost
In pleasure that this circle of bright leaves
Should be their setting; once more they will dream
They hear winds wandering through tufty trees
And see the sun smiling between the leaves.

'THE GREEN BOWL'

obscenity of a tavern, and finding a haven in a cathedral.

> He could not think, for heavy in his ears
> An organ boomed majestic harmonies;
> He only knew that what he saw was light!
> He bowed himself before a cross of flame
> And shut his eyes in fear lest it should fade.

The meaning of these lines is not obvious at first glance. Huysmans's *En Route* she thought the best of his books; as psychology she found it exceedingly interesting. She was particularly struck — even amused — by that incident when he is practising contemplation, and suddenly remembers that he forgot to tell his housekeeper he would not be home for lunch, then dismisses this unselfish thought as a distraction from the Devil. Miss Lowell accepted his conversion as genuine, but could not do as much for his or any other religion. In her poem, he is deafened and dazzled, then deliberately shuts his eyes in fear that the vision might not prove true.

Her Christmas poem, 'To Elizabeth Ward Perkins,' is on the same theme: although the church is warm and bright, and though she is chilled by the bitter winter wind of doubt, she will not enter. The charming sonnet on Carpaccio's 'Dream of St. Ursula' (which her brother Lawrence in 1896 had particularly recommended to her attention) is more subtly sceptical: the saint's vision of an angel is an immature girl's morning dream, inspired by the song of a lark outside.

'J—K. Huysmans' is one of two or three poems in which she conveys her ideas by the method of extended metaphor. Another is the self-flagellating 'Fool Errant,' the tale of a nameless Parsifal who successively asks a maid (love), an abbot (religion,) and a group of knights (the world of men) for a lift to the city; they all rebuff him, and so he learns at last he is a fool. 'The Way' describes the path across a frail bridge to the same city. These poems

mark the beginning of a symbolic method which Miss
Lowell used much in her later books.

She wrote honestly of what she knew, but she did not
know herself as yet. *A Dome of Many-Coloured Glass*
contains few hints of the real Amy Lowell, with her gustoes
and wit and daring and drama and ideas and colors and
sounds: it represents rather Miss Lowell as she then underestimated herself, blighted by proprieties, and almost
paralyzed by despair. Furthermore, although her material
was genuine as far as it went, the conventionality of the
expression made it unconvincing. Night, Time, Fancy,
Nature, Eternity appear and reappear. 'Life is a stream'
and poetry is 'sheafs of rainbows fraught with storied
meaning for religion's sake.' 'Oh! to be a flower!' she
cries, and 'Who shall declare the joy of the running?'
and 'Leisure, thou goddess of a bygone age.' Yet there
were also indications of true writing:

> ... the moon
> Swings slow across the sky,
> Athwart a waving pine tree,
> And soon
> Tips all the needles there
> With silver sparkles...

When her later success brought the book into prominence, she expressed her own opinion about it.

> But I must protect the poor 'Dome' from your scathing
> remarks. I admit that it is not nearly as good as the other
> two volumes, but it contains certain poems which are quite
> as satisfactory as any I have done. For instance, one of my
> very best *vers libre* poems opens the volume — 'Before the
> Altar.' And I have a weakness for 'Behind a Wall,' and
> 'The Road to Avignon.' The latter is derivative, of course,
> but I think it is well done. I also have a partiality for cer-
> tain of the sonnets, and my later interest in colours and
> movements are prefigured in 'Roads' and 'J—K Huys-
> mans.' And for the sonnets, what is the matter with 'Saint

Ursula,' or 'A Fixed Idea,' or 'The Starling'? Your strictures on the sonnet on John Keats are excellent in essence,
but I think wrong in detail. The sonnet, to put it mildly,
is bad. Not bad as a sonnet, but bad as a poem. It is weak
and poor, and full of the old poetic jargon. But the picture of the man I maintain to be true, and I do not believe
that there is a person in the world who knows John Keats
better than I do, even Sir Sidney Colvin.[1]

And to a more sympathetic critic:

What you say about the 'Dome' is just, but too kind.
The first book is certainly immature, as I now realize only
too well. First books are apt to be so, and I suppose authors
have to get them out of their systems before they are capable of doing better work. You remember that Keats said
of 'Endymion' that he knew it was not good, but that it
was as good as he could make it, and that he wanted to
publish it and get rid of it. That remark is never understood by the layman, but I think every poet echoes it in his
own heart. When they are as good as you can make them,
they must be printed before you can pass on to something
else. If they are left, they fester, as it were; and no more
growth is possible.

I am rather astonished at your picking out 'A Fairy Tale'
for quotation, but I see perfectly why you did it. It hardly
deserves such a marked position, but I suppose in a way it
is autobiographical, if that is what you are searching for.
But what you say about the century of difference between
'New York at Night' and 'Towns in Colour' is perfectly
true. I am glad you like the sonnets in that book; I rather
like them myself. But you say nothing about three of the
poems which I like best in the volume: 'Before the Altar,'
'Behind a Wall,' and 'The Road to Avignon.' The last, I
admit, is old-fashioned, but I think it rather good of its
kind.[2]

A Dome of Many-Coloured Glass was, briefly, the traditional 'first book' in which the author had gone as far

[1] Letter to Professor William Lyon Phelps, June 6, 1918.
[2] Letter to Winifred Bryher, June 29, 1918.

as she could by herself, and had succeeded in saying a few things of her own, though not in her own way. It is to be respected for the persistence, almost the heroism, of working ten years without any instruction or aid from outsiders; and for the boldness in supposing that alone and unaided one could produce great poetry. But in those days, few people knew that there was anything to *learn* about writing poetry: one read, one wrote, and that was all.

For the time being, the book proved a failure. Only eighty copies were sold the first year.[1] The critics, generally speaking, were not interested, though some were vaguely annoyed. The earliest review appeared in the *Boston Advertiser*, October 26, 1912; a dozen others trickled in during the ensuing twelve months. The severest appeared in the *Minneapolis Journal* on December 1: 'The volume is, on the whole, slightly over the average, and the average is very low. Never do we feel that behind the lines lurks a dynamic personality.' The most favorable review was published in the *Springfield Republican*, July 27, 1913; but it was chiefly an essay on why poetry is read. Louis Untermeyer, in his column ' — and Other Poems' (*Chicago Evening Post*, February 14, 1913), wrote the only review that could be called signed; he discussed her book with Cawein's *The Poet, the Fool, and the Faeries* and Hagedorn's *Poems and Ballads* as the work of three minor poets, concluding that Miss Lowell's book, 'to be brief, in spite of its lifeless classicism, can never rouse one's anger. But, to be briefer still, it cannot rouse one at all.'

Nor did the critics unintentionally coincide in selecting one or two poems as the most worthy of reprinting; their choice proved unexpectedly scattering. Miss Lowell's own favorites, with the exception of 'Behind a Wall,' which was reprinted just once, were completely ignored;

[1] It reached a second edition in February, 1915, however.

so were the poems previously accepted by magazines; so also was 'March Evening,' which was probably too March-like in rhyme, rhythm, and image to be pleasingly correct. 'Fragment' (a Petrarchan octave, beginning 'What is poetry?') was the most popular, reappearing nine times; 'A Fairy Tale' was a poor second; followed by 'Petals' and bits of 'The Boston Athenaeum.' 'A Winter Ride' was reprinted in an anthology, *Fifty Best Poems of America*, although she tried to make the editors choose another.

The winter passed on without any great event. Miss Lowell had a long illness, culminating in an attack of gastric neuralgia which kept her in bed over Christmas week. Her doctor scolded her for insisting on writing poetry and getting worn out. On December 27, she was allowed to go to the Symphony Concert; whereupon she wrote Josephine Peabody of her release, asking when they could see each other. 'My children,' she said, referring to the latest litter of puppies, 'are well, & I hear their eyes are open, but alas! it is a week since I have seen any but the older members of my family.'

It was probably in the next month that she went to Chicago, where at a dinner she met Harriet Monroe, who had accepted, but not yet published, some poems for *Poetry*.

At that time Miss Lowell's name was merely a name to me, and Boston genealogies had not impressed their proud authority on my imagination. But during [this] winter I was enlightened. The president of Harvard was being dined by alumni in Chicago, and at the same moment his wife was the guest of honor at a feminine banquet where I occupied an inconspicuous place. As we were beginning the dessert, an imposing figure appeared in the remote distance at the top of a half-flight of steps, and 'Oh, there's Amy!' said Mrs. Lowell, in a voice which accepted resignedly anything which Amy might do. Even then I did not connect this 'Amy' with my correspondent, two of whose poems

we had by that time accepted; absorbed, I listened to her
melodious words of greeting and watched the ponderous
and regal figure slowly descend the steps.

   She took possession of the occasion and the company —
no one else was of any account. Our hostess presented her
to each of the dozen or so women at the table as we all made
room, and my mind was still wool-gathering when, on hearing my name, the newcomer turned a powerfully reproach-
ful eye upon me with the query, 'Well, since you've taken
'em, why don't you print 'em?' [1]

   Back home, life went on much as usual. On February
21, 1913, she went to a reception given for the English
actors, Sir Charles Wyndham and Miss Mary Moore.
On March 25, she gave a concert at Sevenels, the artists
being Edmond Clement (the very popular French tenor
who had joined the Metropolitan) and Heinrich Gebhard
(the composer and pianist). The programs were designed
by Berkeley Updike of the Merrymount Press. Clement
sang the modern songs of Fauré, Debussy, and Chausson;
also four songs by Carl Engel, one of which was a setting
of Miss Lowell's 'Sea Shell'; and finally some French
songs from the seventeenth and eighteenth centuries.
Gebhard played Debussy, Fauré, Loeffler, and Albeniz
on the piano, and various eighteenth century composers
on the harpsichord. The entire program had been approved by Miss Lowell beforehand.

   That spring, the 'International Exhibition of Modern
Art,' which had been on exhibition at Armory Hall in
New York, came to the Copley Gallery in Boston. It
was America's introduction to Post-Impressionism and
Cubism and Futurism and half a dozen other schools;
the public crowded in bewilderment, trying to see something in Duchamp's 'Nude Descending a Staircase' and
Brancousi's sculptures and Matisse's patterns. Miss Lowell
went, and 'came away puzzled and frowning. I had a

---

[1] Harriet Monroe: 'Memories of Amy Lowell,' *Poetry* (xxvi, 209), July, 1925.

faint idea of what the idiom of Cubism must be, but I could get no clue to the other schools.' [1]

But she was getting genuinely excited over some strange poems appearing in *Poetry*. It was becoming more and more evident that Harriet Monroe was making a literary center for the continent. She was herself a poet, with a taste both sensitive and generous towards other poets. Guessing the need for such a magazine, she had travelled abroad in 1911 to feel out possibilities and to gain scope. In London she had fallen under the spell of Ezra Pound, who gave her poems and promised support. Then, sure that the moment had come, she returned to Chicago, persuaded friends to contribute the necessary capital, and started her magazine.

Its astonishing success was due, first of all, to her timeliness. The coming poets were already writing; now they found a place prepared for their work. They needed no longer jockey for position as page filler in the regular magazines. The second cause was Miss Monroe's attitude towards America. The earlier 'little magazines' (now chiefly of antiquarian interest) had relied chiefly, and often wholly, on the work of Europeans already famous, or else on the writings of the editor and his local friends. But Miss Monroe was interested in all good poetry being written: while she took the best she could from European writers, her interest lay mainly with her compatriots. *Poetry* was American, though with international scope. The third cause for her success was the fact that she insisted on paying for the poems she published. Out of the capital furnished her, she set aside a heroically small sum for her own support, and all the rest went to her contributors. Poets immediately felt a new dignity in their profession, and sent her their best work. Her literary taste and editorial instinct took full advantage of the sit-

[1] Amy Lowell: 'Modern Metres and the Poets who Write Them' (lecture at the New York Poetry Society, November 30, 1915).

uation; and poet after poet who later became well-known if not famous, was introduced to the public through her magazine.

Miss Lowell became particularly interested in certain poems emanating from an active if somewhat mysterious group of poets in London who called themselves '*Imagistes*.' Their work seemed odd at first glance; but the feeling behind them was fresh and direct, while the form, though strange, was provocative. Hardly a number of *Poetry* appeared without some specimen of their work, or editorial comment, or tantalizing hint. Then, in the issue for January, 1913, she read some poems signed '*H.D., Imagiste*'; and suddenly it came over her: 'Why, I, too, am an *Imagiste*!'[1] It was the kind of thing she had been wanting to do, without quite knowing how. Then in the March issue, Ezra Pound published some of their principles, which were the soundest comments on technique she had read since Hunt's *Imagination and Fancy*; but annoyingly enough, he said that the most important doctrine of all was not for the public. Evidently he was of their circle.

Challenged by the indifference which had greeted her own book, and stimulated by this new, mysterious school, she determined to go to London, find them, and absorb all she could from them. That summer she sailed for London with her nephew's wife, Mrs. James Roosevelt. Among her papers was a letter of introduction from Harriet Monroe to Ezra Pound.

[1] Advance statement for *Some Imagist Poets*, 1917.

CHAPTER X
FROM *IMAGISTE* TO IMAGIST
'And this is an alien city.'

THE group to which Miss Lowell found entry was a small group very much aware of the sterile conventionality into which English and American verse had degenerated. Determined to escape from this literary paralysis, they were searching for new means and modes derived from the practices of other nations. Their immediate inspiration was the contemporary French poetry, but they were also influenced by the ancient poetry of the Greeks and Romans and (through translations) of the Chinese and Japanese.

The originator of the movement was Thomas Ernest Hulme (1883–1917). This searching and impatient philosopher was particularly interested in aesthetics; his ideas, expressed vividly in his conversations, stimulated sculptors, painters, and architects, as well as poets. In 1908 he founded a 'Poets' Club' which met on Wednesday evenings to dine and read verses; at the end of the year it published a plaquette *For Christmas MDCCCCVIII*, to which Hulme contributed his seven-line 'Autumn,' often quoted by the later Imagists as the first of their school.

Hulme wrote his five poems as blackboard demonstrations, to illustrate his theories. 'Autumn' is the only one without rhyme; 'Conversion' the only one that escapes the iamb. But they have a freshness and contrast of metaphor, a directness of presentation, and an easy use of irregular line-lengths, which mark the new spirit unmistakably.

Besides these five poems,[1] as well as a sixth in the 'Notes

[1] 'The Complete Poetical Works of T. E. Hulme' constitute pp. 58–64 of Pound's *Ripostes*, London, 1912.

on Language and Style,' we have further evidence about
Hulme's theories in the numerous notes which he was constantly jotting down. His death in the trenches prevented
his organizing these ideas into the book he was planning;
his manuscripts, however, are a brilliant chaos which
his convictions were vehemently creating into a universe.[1]
He believed that the Romantic period, with its morbid
egotism and idealism, and its continuous appeal to the
infinite, was written out; and he prophesied an advance
into a modern classicism. It would deal with man as a
being of earthly limitations, living a contemporary life.
This fresh poetic attitude would require a new technique.
By rearranging a selection of sentences from Hulme's
writings we can reconstruct his theory of this new poetry.

Always seek the hard, definite, personal word.

Each *word* must be an image *seen*, not a counter [or
cliché].

A man cannot write without seeing at the same time a
visual signification before his eyes. It is this image which
precedes the writing and makes it firm.

Creative effort makes *new* images.

The great aim is accurate, precise and definite description.

It is only by new metaphors... that it can be made precise.

Never, never, never a simple statement. It has no effect.
One must always have analogies, which make another
world.

Visual meanings can only be transferred by the new bowl
of metaphor.... Images in verse are not mere decoration,
but the very essence of an intuitive language.

By a subtle combination of allusions we have artificially
built up in us an idea which, apart from these, cannot be
got at.... Thought is prior to language and consists in the

[1] These manuscripts were sorted and edited by Herbert Read, who published
them under the title *Speculations*, London and New York, 1924, the year before
Miss Lowell's death. A further selection, 'Notes on Language and Style,' was
published in Eliot's *Criterion*, July, 1925, and was reprinted as the twenty-fifth
University of Washington Chapbooks, Seattle, 1929. The quotations from Hulme
which follow were made from these 'Notes' and from 'Romanticism and Classicism,' a section of *Speculations*.

simultaneous presentation to the mind of two different images.

Style is short, being forced by the coming together of many different thoughts, and generated by their contact. Fire struck between stones.

The art of literature consists exactly in this *passage from the Eye to the Voice*.

The form of a poem is shaped by the intention.

These epigrams indicate the general outline of his theory, but constitute little more than a lifeless skeleton. Hulme must have said much that he never wrote down, and probably implied still more. The important point is that while this theory is not exactly the straight Imagist credo of 1912 or of 1915, all the essentials are present, stated or implied. For example, Hulme did not — in these printed documents — specify that the language of common speech was to be the basis of the new poetry; but if one followed his advice and rejected the old poetic diction in the search for the exact word, it would be difficult to fall back on anything else. Again: although Hulme wrote free verse, there is nothing in his printed prose that preaches it — no mention of cadence — and only one dubious sentence hints at the limitations of meter ('Poetasters write in meter because poets have done so, and poets because singing, not talking, is the obvious way of expressing ecstasy'). On the other hand, the Imagists did not preach 'Classicism' (although Aldington and H. D. practised it), neither were they consciously interested in evoking intuitive thoughts by the combination of opposed analogies. Often their poems bore out these principles, to be sure; but that is another matter.

The search for sources is of academic interest only. Hulme and the Imagists were not straining for originality, but for the discovery of the basic principles of all poetry. Besides mentioning the practice of Athens, Rome, China, and Japan, one might quote Dryden ('Imaging is, in

itself, the very height and life of Poetry' [1]) and Words-
worth ('a selection of the real language of men in a state
of vivid sensation' [2]) and Leigh Hunt's *Imagination and
Fancy*; while the influence of Poe, through the French
writers, was unsuspectedly strong, as we shall see. But
whatever the sources, Hulme made them his own by the
sheer drive of his personality, and they contained everything essential for the doctrines of the school to come.

Another contributor to *For Christmas MDCCCCVIII*
was Edward Storer (b. 1882), a temporary convert whose
Mirrors of Illusion had appeared the previous month.
The opening poem was —

Image

Forsaken lovers,
Burning to a white chaste moon
Upon strange pyres of loneliness and drought.

Storer was thus the first to publish a book of Imagistic
verse; later, however, he renounced the entire movement
and changed his manner completely. In fact, none of the
original members of the Poets' Club ever became official
Imagists.

In the first months of 1909, Hulme met Frank Stewart
Flint (b. 1885). At the age of seventeen, Flint had discovered Keats and begun writing poetry; he was now
twenty-four, about to marry, and also to publish his first
book, *In the Net of the Stars*, a volume of love poems,
which advocated, and once or twice demonstrated, freer
forms, although he had not yet really escaped from the
iamb. As Flint is the authority for this stage of the history
of Imagism, we shall quote his own words:

> At that time I had been advocating in the course of a
> series of articles on recent books of verse a poetry in *vers
> libre*, akin in spirit to the Japanese. An attack on the Poets'

---

[1] 'The Author's Apology... prefixed to *The State of Innocence*'; *Essays of
John Dryden*, ed. W. P. Ker, Oxford, 1926, vol. I, p. 186.

[2] Preface to *Lyrical Ballads; Complete Poetical Works*, Boston, 1919, vol. X,
p. 4.

Club brought me into correspondence and acquaintance with T. E. Hulme; and later, after Hulme had violently disagreed with the Poets' Club and had left it, he proposed that he should get together a few congenial spirits, and that we should have weekly meetings in a Soho restaurant.[1]

This club, which was never named, held the first of its Thursday meetings on March 25, 1909; among those present were Edward Storer, F. W. Tancred,[2] Joseph Campbell,[3] and Miss Florence Farr.[4] They agreed in condemning contemporary poetry; they experimented to improve it. Again quoting Flint:

> We proposed at various times to replace it by pure *vers libre*; by the Japanese *tanka* and *haikai*; we all wrote dozens of the latter as an amusement; by poems in a sacred Hebrew form, of which 'This is the House that Jack Built' is a perfect model; Joseph Campbell produced two good specimens of this, one of which, 'The Dark,' is printed in *The Mountainy Singer*; by rimeless poems like Hulme's 'Autumn,' and so on. He insisted too on absolutely accurate presentation and no verbiage; and he and F. W. Tancred, a poet too little known, perhaps because his production is precious and small, used to spend hours each day in the search for the right phrase. Tancred does it still; while Hulme reads German philosophy in the trenches, waiting for the general advance. There was also a lot of talk and practice among us, Storer leading it chiefly, of what we called the Image. We were very much influenced by modern French symbolist poetry.[5]

[1] F. S. Flint: 'The History of Imagism,' *Egoist* (II, 70), May 1, 1915.

[2] Tancred's 'To T. E. Hulme,' an eight-line poem, appeared in the *Poetry Review*, London (I, 537) December, 1912.

[3] Joseph Campbell was the author of *Songs of Vladh*, Belfast, 1904; *The Garden of the Bees* [Belfast, 1905]; *The Rushlight*, Dublin, 1906; *The Man-Child* and *The Gilly of Christ*, both Dublin, 1907; *The Mountainy Singer*, Dublin, 1909 and Boston, Mass., 1919; *Mearing Stones*, Dublin, 1911; *Judgment*, Dublin and London, 1912; *Irishry*, Dublin and London [1913]; *Earth of Cualann*, Dublin, 1917.

[4] Miss Florence Farr was the 'S.S.D.D.' who in 1896 reprinted Thomas Vaughan's *Euphrates* as vol. VII of the *Collectanea Hermetica* (see Thomas Vaughan: *Works*, ed. A. E. Waite, London, 1919, p. xxiii). Her commentary on the text is theosophical rather than alchemical.

[5] Flint: *op. cit.*, pp. 70–71.

On April 22, 1909, Flint's friends, Miss Farr and T. D. Fitzgerald, introduced Ezra Loomis Pound. In 1905 Pound had graduated from Hamilton College, where he had already established his poetic manner.[1] He studied for two years at the University of Pennsylvania, then sailed for Italy early in 1908. That June his *A Lume Spento* (one hundred copies only) was printed at 'the city of Aldus,' or Venice. It was originally called *La Fraisne*, after the second poem of the book, but was renamed in memory of William Brooke Smith, 'painter, dreamer of dreams.' Most of the poems had been written before he sailed. Travelling northward, he proceeded to London, to meet and study with Yeats, whom he believed the greatest living poet. Here he also met Ernest Rhys [2] and Ford Madox Hueffer (now Ford Madox Ford), the latter of whom was concerned with the *English Review*, which began December, 1908. In the same month Pound's second book was issued at London: *A Quinzaine for this Yule. Being selected from a Venetian sketchbook 'San Trovaso'*; there were two printings, of one hundred copies each. His third book, and the first which was really available to the public, was *Personae*; the initial twelve poems and some others were taken from *A Lume Spento*; it was published at London on April 16, 1909 — just six days before his introduction to Hulme's group at the Soho restaurant. There, in clarion tones, he read a new poem, which was soon to appear in the *English Review*: his 'Sestina: Altaforte' — undoubtedly the most vigorous sestina in English — 'whereupon the entire café trembled,' states Glenn Hughes.[3]

[1] His 'Belangal Alba, ex. Manuscript of Tenth Century, Translated' appeared in the *Hamilton Literary Magazine* (xxxix, 324), May, 1905. This completely typical poem was called to my attention by Mr. N. L. Kilpatrick.

[2] 'Mr. Ernest Rhys is of Welsh descent. In 1888–89 he lectured in America, and afterwards returned to London, where he has published *A London Rose*, Arthurian plays and poems, and Welsh ballads, and edited *Everyman's Library*.' *Poetry* (i, 134), January, 1913.

[3] Glenn Hughes: *Imagism and the Imagists*, Stamford University, 1931, p. 12.

Pound had been searching for inspiration in other fields, and was not soon converted, according to Flint.

> Ezra Pound used to boast in those days that he was
>
> *Nil praeter 'Villon' et doctus cantare Catullum,*
>
> and he could not be made to believe that there was any French poetry after Ronsard. He was very full of his *troubadours*; but I do not remember that he did more than attempt to illustrate (or refute) our theories occasionally with their example.[1]

His literary ideal, as made manifest in the *Personae* and *Exultations* of 1909 and the *Canzoni* of 1911, was to continue the Dobson-Lang cult of intricate and forgotten Romance forms, but to infuse into them the virility of Browning and the melody of Yeats. Always stimulated by forgotten literatures, Pound leaned on his discoveries so heavily that these three books are actually the beginning of 'the modern vogue of erudite poetry.'[2] At the same time, his virtuosity, never content with mere imitation, became virtually creative; while his metrical sensitivity was both so subtle and so daring that it is not easy to say on just which page he first achieves free verse. The best poems in *Personae* transcend meter, though without escaping it. But in 'Night Litany,' the first poem of *Exultations*, the paeons are so thick that metrical scansion seems meaningless and even perverse. Such things as 'Au Salon' in *Canzoni* are completely modern, although in general this volume is the most conservative of the three.

1910 and 1911 were dead years, except for the publication of three of Pound's volumes. The *English Review* passed into other hands with the number for March, 1910, and closed its columns to all experimentalists. Hulme was spending months on the continent; his unnamed Club died of inanition. But presently Hilda Doolittle turned up

---

[1] Flint: *op. cit.*, p. 71. In a letter to Aldington, January 12, 1915, he stated firmly that Pound added *nothing* to their meetings — absolutely nothing.

[2] Hughes, *op. cit.*, p. 226.

from Philadelphia. She was the daughter of the director of the Flower Astronomical Observatory at the University of Pennsylvania; she had studied for a while at Bryn Mawr, where she was 'flunked quite frankly in English,' to quote her own words; and now had gone to Italy for the summer. But instead of heading for home when autumn came, she turned northward to London. She had known Pound in Philadelphia; he was glad to renew acquaintance with a person so entirely devoted to literature. Another newcomer was Richard Aldington, a youngster of eighteen or nineteen, who in the early part of 1911 had already begun to write *vers libre*, inspired by a chorus in the *Hippolytus* of Euripides. He had met Harold Monro already when, early in 1912, through Mrs. Deighton Patmore he met Ezra Pound. Over a beefsteak in Kensington, Pound approved his *vers libre*, remarking that Aldington needed no help from him.[1] Aldington felt that his spiritual isolation was over; the two became great friends. Presently at Mrs. Patmore's he also met Miss Doolittle and F. S. Flint.

Doubtless through Flint's influence (who could read ten languages, and wrote French as easily as English) the group explored Henri de Régnier, Rémy de Gourmont, then other contemporary French poets.[2] Here the three found practised what they had been groping towards in theory. The coincidence is perhaps not surprising when one remembers that Hulme, with Flint and Storer, had first derived that theory from the contemporary French. But to Pound, Aldington, and Miss Doolittle, those writers had been scarcely names. The way was roundabout, but the discovery was genuine and the results were creative. A new mode had been achieved.

---

[1] Letter from Aldington to Amy Lowell, November 20, 1917.

[2] René Taupin: *L'Influence du Symbolisme Français sur la Poésie Americaine*, Paris, 1929, p. 90. Taupin, whose statements sometimes are contradicted by the documents, says that these meetings at Mrs. Patmore's began in the autumn of 1911; Aldington in his letter, however, states that he first met Pound early the next year, and that presently he went to Paris and Italy.

They disagreed about details, of course; but they agreed on three principles: (1) to treat the 'thing' directly, whether it were subjective or objective; (2) to use absolutely no word that did not contribute to the presentation; (3) as regarded rhythm, to compose in the sequence of the musical phrase, not in sequence of a metronome. And they felt that they were as much entitled to a group-name as a number of the French schools which Flint has proclaimed in the *Poetry Review*, August, 1912.[1]

That October, Pound's volume in the new manner (*Ripostes*, London, 1912; Boston, 1913) contained as an appendix 'The Complete Poetical Works of T. E. Hulme' — the five poems, totalling thirty-three lines, with an introductory squib. The restless Hulme long since had let his leadership lapse; Pound's collecting his verse was Pound's assumption of that leadership. Being aware that the poetic principles determined upon were not new, in his 'Prefatory Note' he asserted a continuity with the past. He mentioned a 'School of Images,' which he said might or might not have existed; and asserted that as for the future, *Les Imagistes*, the descendants of the forgotten school of 1909, had that in their keeping. Pound had baptized his new school '*Imagisme*'; this was the first appearance of its name in print.

Americans were supposed to read only that verse which England had acclaimed already; but the *Imagistes* determined to reverse traditional procedure and get a reputation in England by conquering America first. Possibly they foresaw the huge market for poetry that was just beginning to be opened there;[2] more probably they thought

[1] Ezra Pound: *Pavanes and Divisions*, New York, 1918, p. 95. Pound says his group was formed in the spring or early summer of 1912, but his reference to Flint's article (which he misdates August, 1911) places it later. The three principles were first printed in *Poetry* (i, 198–200), March, 1913; it also contains hints about a mysterious 'Doctrine of the Image' which was not for publication.

[2] Stephen Phillips, in the *Poetry Review* (iv, 269), May, 1914, insisted with William Watson that America 'has become far more than England both the market and the assize of modern Anglo-Saxon poetry.... The writer of modern verse must for the future look to America both for audience and criticism.'

America was receptive to literary experiment. For the fact seems to have been that they could get published in Chicago but not in London. Harold Monro had included the work of Pound and his group liberally in the *Poetry Review* during 1912; but his taste proved far too generous for the Poetry Society which had appointed him editor. He seceded, and opened his Poetry Bookshop; in January, 1913, Stephen Phillips replaced him as editor of the *Poetry Review*, which published no more contributions from the Pound group.[1]

Meanwhile Harriet Monroe had started *Poetry* in Chicago; its first issue (October, 1912) published two of Pound's poems (the first of which, 'To Whistler, American,' oddly enough was an arraignment of this country for its inhospitality to the arts) with the following note:

> Mr. Ezra Pound, the young Philadelphia poet whose recent distinguished success in London led to wide recognition in his own country, authorizes the statement that at present such of his poetic work as receives magazine publication in America will appear exclusively in *Poetry*. That discriminating London publisher, Mr. Elkin Mathews, 'discovered' this young poet from over seas....

The campaign proper began in the next issue, which published three of Aldington's poems, and described him as 'a young English poet, one of the "*Imagistes*," a group of ardent Hellenists who are pursuing interesting experiments in *vers libre*; trying to attain in English certain subtleties of cadence of the kind which Mallarmé and his followers have studied in France.' Pound was named as foreign correspondent. In the next issue (December) was an editorial stating that the influence of the neglected Poe was returning to America as *vers libre*, by the roundabout way of Baudelaire, Verlaine, and Mallarmé, through the

---

[1] By the time Monro had organized his quarterly *Poetry and the Drama*, (March 15, 1913–December, 1914), the *Imagiste* movement was already well under way in Chicago.

younger poets in England. The issue for January, 1913, included Miss Doolittle's first published poems, signed 'H.
D., *Imagiste*,' as well as an editorial by Pound, on literature
in London, which contained the following sentences:

> ... The youngest school here that has the nerve to call itself
> a school is that of the *Imagistes*.... Space forbids me to set
> forth the program of the *Imagistes* at length, but one of
> their watchwords is precision.... Among the very young
> men there seems to be a gleam of hope in the work of Rich-
> ard Aldington....

The February issue had nothing to the point, except an
editorial note which showed that Pound's reference to
'that mass of dolts' in his 'To Whistler, American' had
roused resentment.

There had been enough preliminaries; the March issue
unfurled the new banner to the Chicago breeze. '*Imagisme*'
was an article signed by Flint (but obviously written by
Pound), in which he stated that unable to find anything
definite in print about the mysterious school, he had sought
out an *Imagiste*, who proclaimed amongst other things the
three principles which we have given earlier. Miss Monroe
explained this interview by saying that Mr. Flint's note
was published in response to many requests for information. Pound's 'A Few Don'ts by an *Imagiste*' followed —
a brilliant, stimulating article which is among his best contributions to criticism. Twelve of his poems were in the
April number. The May number contained an article by
A. C. H. (Alice Corbin Henderson) insisting that poetic
prose and *vers libre* were two separate things. The June
number added a note of controversy in the form of 'A
Word to Mr. Pound,' by John Reed the radical, who protested that some of his lines had been misused in one of
the April poems.

Amy Lowell had two conventional poems in the July
issue — 'Apology' and the sonnet 'A Blockhead'; these
were followed by Flint's 'Four Poems in Unrhymed

Cadence'; and further on was Pound's review of D. H. Lawrence's *Love Poems*. But probably before the issue appeared, Miss Lowell had reached London, with her letter of introduction to Ezra Pound.

After one has worked ten years by oneself, with no special instruction in technique, with no friend who has mastered the art already, expert criticism is inspiration itself. Fresh eyes put sure fingers on weak spots. And the *Imagistes* were just ahead on the path Miss Lowell had already chosen. Like Flint, she had started under the stimulus of Keats; like the whole group, she was reading the contemporary French poets and was trying out the more irregular forms. The *Imagiste* criticism consequently was opening the gates of creation. The mild melancholy of *Domes* melted away instantly as the gusto of reality came within her hand. She always had good eyes: why had nobody ever told her to use them, to rely on them? The *Imagistes* actually proceeded to do what they had boasted they could do: they rewrote her old poems before her eyes, underscoring *clichés* (Ezra's word) and heaving them out; compressing; making more visible; brooming away Victorian cobwebs; reducing morals to implications; breaking up stiff lines, then reassembling them in any number of different ways, to choose the one with the best cadence; in general, cleaning up 'literature' and concentrating on reality.

In spite of the subsequent feud, she always insisted on Pound's ability to stimulate. 'He could *make* you write,' she would say. But there were times when her own conception of poetry stood up against his criticism. 'He got everything out of books; I never knew him to call your attention to a tree or a sunset or the roofs of the city or anything like that.' Yet even so, the group merely as a group was an incitement: nowhere in uncentralized America could one find such a gathering of young and intelligent persons, all believing profoundly in the importance of poetry, all experimenting, all producing. It confirmed one's faith, made one put forth one's best energies to prove oneself worthy of fellowship.

But there were other poets in London besides the *Imagistes*. Pound introduced John Gould Fletcher to Miss Lowell. Fletcher had absorbed Poe in high school; at Harvard had refused to continue his work for a degree; and finding no literary stimulus in Boston, had sailed for Venice in August, 1908; spent the winter in Rome; and in May, 1909, removed to London. Here he made literary friends who persuaded him to read Whitman, which he did thoroughly and for the first time. In 1910 he met Hulme, who invited him to the Poets' Club, but Fletcher could not bring himself to go. In the same year he made his first visit to Paris, and discovered, through a poem by Verhaeren, the great body of contemporary French literature. When he returned to London, it was reported of him that he read a new French book every day. The Post-Impressionist Exhibition of 1911 and the Russian Ballet persuaded him that poetry, even as music and painting, must employ a new idiom. In 1913 he met Pound in Paris. He refused, however, to be drawn into Pound's circle: jealous of the dignity of letters, he despised all groups of what he considered log-rollers; an individualist, he preferred to make his way alone.

At the time when the *Imagistes* were unable to get published in London, Fletcher was planning to found a Review of his own. Pound, however, approached him with another scheme. A suffragist paper, the *New Freewoman*, had been started in June, 1913; and Pound, with Fletcher's financial backing, was able to persuade the two editors (Dora Marsden and Harriet Shaw Weaver) that Miss Marsden's monthly leading article was sufficient for the cause, and that the rest of the paper should be devoted to advanced literature. Fletcher stipulated that none of his own work was to be published or reviewed in its pages: there was to be no suspicious return of favors.

Meanwhile he had sought publishers, and learned to his disgust that in this center of civilization, 'friends' and 'backing' were prime objects in issuing volumes of poetry. Finally he himself paid for five books, all published in 1913, under four different imprints. Later he said that this gesture was the sowing of his literary wild oats.

It was in the June of that year that he met Miss Lowell. A friend of his, in the office of Constable's, came to him one day with a tale about an extraordinary woman, an American poetess, who had dropped in to demand what had become of her book, *A Dome of Many-Coloured Glass.* Unfortunately no copies could be traced anywhere, and there was something of a scene: she insisted on remaining there until they found them. At last they were discovered, still unpacked, and of course not distributed to the booksellers. Fletcher's friend wanted to know if all Americans were like that.

When Fletcher repeated the tale a few days later to Pound, Pound was annoyed, said that he had just met her, and that she was both generous and interested in modern poetry. A few nights following, he brought Fletcher to the Berkeley Hotel. The evening was memorable. Pound did most of the talking and read his 'Seafarer.' Miss Lowell read from her book, said she had written only one *Imagiste* poem 'In a Garden,' and talked of modern French poetry. Fletcher, who had also given his allegiance to the modern French poets, was enchanted, and asked permission to call again.

At their next meeting, he read her a batch of poems, all written that May; they were much better than anything else he had ever done, and he hoped to get them published under the title of *Irradiations.* She was greatly impressed with them.

They met often after that, talking literary matters and reading their poems. Miss Lowell discovered one of Fletcher's ambitions: that of writing a poem about a great modern city; and she asked how he would set about it. He told her that above all one should sit and look at things; one should not think about them in relation to oneself, but should grasp them as detached objects. She fired with enthusiasm at the possibilities: evidently Fletcher had put into words the thing she was groping towards; and he believed afterwards that she got her theory of 'externality' from their talks. He was impressed with her extraordinary receptiveness to suggestion; it was as though her poetic development had been arrested, but that now it was finding its chance to develop. He told her that he did not think much of the *Dome of Many-Coloured Glass*, and recommended that she read his favorite, Verhaeren, also Rimbaud. She accepted his criticism and recommendation.

Another transfusing experience was the Russian Ballet, just over from Paris. Later generations can scarcely understand how exciting, how liberating that constellation of geniuses was before the War: the weird, rich music of the modernists conducted perfectly by Monteux; the wild and gorgeous colors of Bakst splashed across the stage; the incredibly expressive dancing of Nijinsky that burst through all the mechanical French conventions. The ballets they presented were not the usual gymnastics, for which the slight plot was only an excuse; they were vivid expressions of the human imagination.

In July Miss Lowell made her first visit to Monro's Poetry Bookshop. As the taxi drove down Devonshire Street, she identified the place by the swinging sign of three torches on a blue field. She stood so long on the pavement, fascinated by the books and photographs and periodicals and broadsides displayed in the window, that street-urchins gathered round her. Then she went in and examined the interior of this unique store. Harold Monro was not there that day, but she encountered him frequently afterwards.[1]

[1] A. Lowell: 'The Poetry Bookshop,' *The Little Review* (II, 19–22), May, 1915.

It was probably also in 1913 that Miss Lowell visited Henry James at Rye. When he heard that she hoped to be a writer, he took her away from the group round the tea-table, out into the garden, where he strolled up and down with her, astonishing her with the frankness of his advice.

He was seventy years old, and on his birthday, April 15, a group of some three hundred admirers had presented him with his portrait by Sargent. But James was undoubtedly in that autumnal depression when one's best things are done, and nobody appreciates them — when one is so familiar with them that they seem merely stale. A writer's deepest being is involved in his works: he cannot judge them, and knows that he cannot. Now James had come to feel that all his works were futile: a tangle of temporal and local differences that revealed, after all, nothing of the depths; references as fleeting as O. Henry's slang; flavors mistaken for essences; split hairs, not dissected anatomies. He had severed himself from the culture that had produced him, while the culture that he had tried to acquire was unattained.

He determined to expiate his error; and Miss Lowell listened amazed to a fierce and bitter monologue, in which he confessed a complete failure, and warned her against expatriation. 'I have cut myself off from America, where I belonged,' he said, 'and in England I am not really accepted. Don't make my mistake.' Before she left, she gathered a sprig of lavender from his garden, which she preserved in her collection of manuscripts.

On a sunny afternoon in August she examined the Sir Charles Dilke collection of Keats material, which was kept in the basement of the Hampstead Public Library, as a precaution against possible damage by suffragettes. In order to obtain admission, she had been obliged to arm herself with many letters of introduction testifying to her harmlessness. She had now seen all the Keats collections, except Lord Crewe's.

In the late summer she sailed for Boston. Her natural exuberance was heightened by her new experiences. Surrounded by friends who encouraged her, she ran the boat to suit herself. One time she walked up to the orchestra and told them it was making an outrageous noise, and please stop. It did. She protested against the holystoning of the deck outside her stateroom in the early morning, but that sacred ceremony was continued. She invited one literary young man, known at Harvard as Barrett Wendell's understudy, to hear a poem in her stateroom. He went, no doubt expecting the conventional cosmics or misty moonlight; instead, she treated him to a murder — her 'After Hearing a Waltz by Bartók.' [1] Her declamation in fact was so vivid that he feared it might be misunderstood; and the story has it that by the time she had reached the last stanza —

> One! Two! Three! Give me air! Oh! My God!
> One! Two! Three! I am drowning in slime! —

there actually was knocking on the stateroom door.

When all passengers were supposed to be asleep in their berths, she walked the decks, for this was her only chance to smoke her cigars unobserved. Observed she was, none the less; for when she refused to be interviewed on landing, the indignant reporter rooted out one of the shocked observers; and the next morning the news that the sister of President Lowell of Harvard smoked cigars was screamed in headlines, from coast to coast.

It is said that about this time an American poet went dressed as a cowboy to a London dinner, where he ate nothing but roses, petal by petal. The story cannot be verified — fame is too perverse to recognize such a blatant bid for her favor — and perhaps the whole thing is nothing but blended memories of Joaquin Miller and the

[1] This waltz was 'Ma Mie qui Danse,' the last of the *14 Bagatellen* (opus 6) by Bela Bartók. Miss Lowell was very fond of this electric, bitter composition.

Green Carnation. But the moral is, that Miss Lowell, who always shrank from that kind of publicity, was always having it thrust upon her.

But now that the secret was out, she felt it undignified to be surreptitious about her cigars any longer, even though the prejudice against smoking women was still very strong in America. Not till 1900 (three centuries after Mary Frith — Middleton's 'Roaring Girl' — had gloried in being the first woman to smoke) had women begun to puff cigarettes publicly in London; the American women lagged fifteen years behind. The moral and aesthetic objections urged by clergymen and newspaper editors all over the country resulted in various laws, such as the New York 'Sullivan Ordinance,' making it illegal for women to smoke. On February 20, 1908, 'Women Smoke On Way to Opera' was sufficiently startling news to warrant headlines in the New York *Herald*; in July, 1910, the subject was reopened by the report that the president's daughter, 'Princess Alice,' enjoyed her cigarettes.[1] Only three years later, therefore, the Lowell cigar story proved so good that the 'big black' cigar became virtually Miss Lowell's attribute.

'Big black' was false, however: her cigars were a very light Manila brand, usually too light for the after-dinner smoke of her male guests. They were elaborately wrapped. One evening, in an impish mood, she told a bashful young poet that unwrapping one was like undressing a lady: first one removed the belt (the first of the two cigar-bands), then the ball-gown (the wrapping of silver paper), then the shift (a square of tissue paper), and finally the girdle (the second band). When later the War threatened to stop her supply, she ordered ten thousand of them; the boxes, stacked high against the wall of an upper store-room, outlasted the War and her lifetime.

The public never knew that before she discovered this

[1] Mark Sullivan: *Our Times*, New York, 1930, vol. III, pp. 529, 532.

brand, she experimented with anything that would not inter-
rupt her concentration on her writing. Cigarettes were impossible: they were too brief and too untidy. For a time she
had a set of pipes, which her secretary took in town every
week to be cleaned; but she soon gave these up entirely.

In September, 1913, she began to preserve her correspondence in files. One of the first she put in was an undated note from Pound, asking permission to use her 'In
the Garden' in a brief anthology, *Des Imagistes*, which he
was cogitating, unless she had something she thought more
appropriate.

Then on September 7, Fletcher wrote her a long letter
warning her against appearing in *Des Imagistes*. He told
her of his whole relationship with Pound, which he had
ended: Pound had been puffing him in the *New Freewoman*,
consequently Fletcher had withdrawn his financial support. He said that of all things on earth, the most abominable was the London literary clique with its external
politeness and internal jealousies and underground tactics.
He was not one of those who took favors from others and
then slipped knives into their backs. Miss Lowell had
been kind to him; he was returning the favor by telling the
truth of the whole matter; besides, he sincerely believed
she was trying to create great art, and had a quality in
some of her work which he rated above all the others.
Therefore he did not want her to enter the ranks of the
Imagistes under a misconception.

He said that *Des Imagistes* was really being edited by
Aldington and not Pound; the unavowed purpose was to
boom those two in the United States. Others were to be
admitted merely as satellites, and only specimens of their
weakest work were to be selected. He himself had been
solicited not once but several times to enter, but he would
rather starve in the streets than let his name and work be
used to support a school of which he disapproved.

He advised her either to insist on being allowed more

space, or else to withdraw altogether. If she withdrew, he was willing to put up equal shares and issue another anthology in England; but in that case, he insisted on his right to select or reject anything he wanted, and he granted her the same right with his work.

Miss Lowell's answers to both Pound's note and Fletcher's letter are not in her files. But we know what she wrote to Pound from her letter to him on November 3, 1914: 'You will remember that I wrote you last winter and told you that if yours was to be an *Imagiste* anthology I did not think I belonged in it. You never took the trouble to answer my letter, and the next thing I knew was that I saw my name in the advance advertisement which appeared in the New York Times.'[1] It also seems clear, from Fletcher's reply to her on October 25, 1913, that she did not envisage the situation quite as he did, but that she admired his *Irradiations* immensely.

On October 16, 1913, Aldington and Miss Doolittle were married.

From October 10 to December 20, Miss Lowell was busy translating Rostand's *Pierrot Qui Pleure et Pierrot Qui Rit*, a comedy with music by Jean Hubert. The Boston Music

[1] René Taupin, in his *L'Influence du Symbolisme Français sur la Poésie Américaine*, Paris, 1929, gives quite another account of the event on p. 86. He says that Pound 'avait déjà fait la connaissance d'Amy Lowell dont au dernier moment il avait accepté un poème: *In a garden*. Aldington pensait que ce poème n'était pas digne de figurer dans l'anthologie; Pound avait besoin d'argent et c'était un moyen de s'en procurer.... Ainsi Pound... trouve Amy Lowell pour financer l'affaire,' and even adds in a footnote: 'Son poème fut accepté à la dernière minute. Grâce à la même politique, le soutien d'A. Lowell permit de publier avec les poèmes imagistes de la *Catholic Anthology* quelques poèmes d'écrivains connus comme Yeats.' But these demonstrably erroneous statements give far too little credit to Pound as editor and far too much to Miss Lowell as patron. Neither she nor Pound financed *Des Imagistes*; that was done by the publishers, Albert and Charles Boni. Alfred Kreymborg, in his *Troubadour*, tells how he originally was to publish it, but how his press got broken when it was being unloaded, and how the Bonis later agreed to publish the *Glebe*, a periodical of which *Des Imagistes* constituted one issue. In a letter to Aldington, November 25, 1914, Miss Lowell referred to that financing of *Des Imagistes*. It is still more absurd to imagine that Amy Lowell financed the *Catholic Anthology*, in which she was not represented, and which was issued by Pound, after the schism, perhaps as a kind of counterblast to her *Some Imagist Poets*.

Company was planning to publish it; Carl Engel had
persuaded it that Miss Lowell could do the English text;
Rostand had granted his authorization —'a sufficiently
difficult authorization to obtain,' as Miss Lowell wrote
Mrs. Bradley (December 12, 1914); and her honorarium
was to be $60.

This play was Rostand's first venture, when he was
twenty-one (1889), unless one wishes to count his vaudeville *Le Gant Rouge* of the previous year. It is a French
trifle, nothing without music: a brief act intended to give
three voices a chance to sing prettily. Columbine cannot
choose between her two suitors, who are identical except
that one always laughs and the other always weeps. They
serenade her, woo her, simultaneously. She invites them
to a tiny feast, which consists chiefly of more music. The
mournful Pierrot, at the very moment when he is wishing
he could die, chokes on a fish-bone, and the cheerful one
runs for a doctor. Columbine at last is given a chance to
decide. She tells the mournful one (who has quickly recovered) that she will marry him; whereupon he bursts
again into tears, first from joy, then from dismay at the
thought of marriage. When the cheerful Pierrot returns,
he is told of her decision; first he is angry from disappointment, then he turns his back to hide his tears. Columbine
promptly exercises her woman's privilege of changing her
mind: the laugher who can weep is preferable to the weeper
who cannot laugh; and if the mournful Pierrot still wishes
to die, the fish-bone is still on the table.

As Miss Lowell discovered, translating poetry is excellent practice. The ideas, the images, the verbal effects are
predetermined; these must be preserved in the copy. One
cannot be led astray very far by a rhyme or a cadence,
without gross and obvious infidelity. And of all kinds of
translation, the most difficult is that of something already
set to music. The lightest metrical variations, permissible
enough elsewhere, become monstrous; moreover, there are

special rules about what vowels a voice can sing on a high note. The long *e* and the short *i*, for example, do not marry well with a high *C*. This limitation to open-throated sounds and strict copying of cadence makes translating a libretto into anything resembling literature something very difficult indeed.

Furthermore, French cadence is not English cadence: the fundamental lilt of the language is different. The standard line for French drama (which Rostand used) is the alexandrine, a twelve-syllable line, with a pause occurring strictly in the middle, and with approximately four stresses distributed freely, two in each half-line. These alexandrines are rhymed in couplets. The standard line for English drama is the pentameter, a line approximately ten syllables, with the main pause varied as much as possible, and with five stresses which fall generally on the even-numbered syllables. This line is unrhymed, except for special effect. So at the outset, Miss Lowell was faced with a metrical problem which she solved in her own way. She abandoned the rhyme (which even Dryden could not make popular for long on the English stage), and approximated the French cadence, though without strict counting of syllables (for English is not a syllabic language, like French or Japanese). Her line might be called a variation around the anapestic tetrameter, but the four accents are distributed so freely that the result goes beyond meter without quite being free verse. There is nothing exactly like it in the history of English versification; its nearest relative is the ancient Anglo-Saxon meter, though I doubt if she ever thought of it.

Pierrot II: Oh! I am tired
  Of April and this sweetness in the air which enchants you,
  And these blown perfumes and these breezes which sing:
  The Spring's everlasting and dull repetitions,
  Always the same, always dressing up Nature
  Each year in the same, quite expected, attire.

It is only to scatter its petals at night
That the rose unfolds stupidly, trying to attract
The butterflies of snow which swarm in the sky
To her honied kiss. The sea, always blue,
Very blue, with its distant waves and the same
Undulations, yet always they are the same waves —
None of this has for me any magic. I know
This commonplace scenery by heart, and I hate it!

Pierrot I:

Hé! Spring! For Monsieur, if you please, you must put
New scenery up! Still the hand of a master
Did that! April painted it with a certain smart elegance,
The little white town with red roofs, climbing up
The whole length of the hill, which is green turning bluish,
This scenery pleases me! As in the theatre
(Although to your mind it remains just the same)
It varies... You can see, in the evening, when the sun
Plunges into the ocean, and when a clear star
Shines in the pale azure, how the curtain has changed.
There, in the shadow, blue and soft, which descends,
It seems as though solitude were not quite right,
Under the leaves, which the cool wind is ruffling.
The old, but still always the new, comedy
Of love, and one aspires to play it again...
Feeling this is its hour and this is its scene.

This specimen is to be read only for the ingenious versification and the fresh diction: the sentiments and the *clichés* are Rostand's.

The lyrics were still more of a problem, as the lines were shorter, the rhymes necessary, and the cadences fixed by the melodies. Miss Lowell evidently translated these lyrics with Hubert's music before her; for whenever the cadences of the French and the English seem irreconcilable, one usually finds that her words follow the tune better than Rostand's. The originals are slight enough; Miss Lowell translated them faithfully and competently — even the *tours de force* 'Chanson Triste' and 'Chant Joyeux.'

The whole thing is a trifle, but a trifle well done; and I doubt if there is any other libretto translated into English that approaches it as literature.

She planned to get it performed for charity, with Maggie Teyte as soprano; but Miss Teyte was so busy with engagements in Chicago, San Francisco, and London, that no performance was possible until February, 1915.

On December 21, 1913, the day after Miss Lowell finished her translation, she celebrated by inviting the 'Devils,' a group of friends, to the first of a series of monthly piano concerts at Sevenels. The five 'Devils' were Dr. Herman Adler, Carl Engel (the composer, then employed by the Boston Music Company, later the curator of music at the Library of Congress), Heinrich Gebhard (who furnished the music), Mrs. Russell, and Miss Lowell herself. To this group soon was added Magdelaine Carret, teacher of French at Wellesley, who frequently came to dine and talk French with Miss Lowell; in later years, she assisted her in *Six French Poets* and other work involving that language. The group came to dinner, then Gebhard would play, sometimes well past midnight. Miss Lowell was always fond of modern music: these programs included plenty of Debussy, Ravel, Fauré, Albeniz, and Franck, as well as the German classics.[1]

On January 1, 1914, the *New Freewoman* became the *Egoist*, the editorial staff being Dora Marsden, with Richard Aldington and Leonard A. Compton-Rickett for assistant editors.[2] Some of Miss Lowell's poems had been accepted for this first issue; unfortunately they were delayed until the fourth (February 16).

---

[1] Other Gebhard concerts at Sevenels fell on January 9, 1914, February 17, April 10, May 8, and June 13. There was probably a concert in March as well.

[2] On July 1, 1914, Harriet Shaw Weaver became Editor, Richard Aldington the Assistant Editor, and Dora Marsden the Contributing Editor. On June 1, 1916, H. D.'s initials were added beneath Aldington's name as Assistant Editor: he was shortly to be called for military service. There were only six numbers that year; the December number was the last.

By February, Miss Lowell was gathering together a new book of poems, *Sword Blades and Poppy Seed*; therefore she went to New York to see if she could not make better arrangements with Macmillan than with Houghton Mifflin. True, the *Dome of Many-Coloured Glass* had not been a success; but as Macmillan published both her brothers, it should be willing to make her a liberal contract, if only to keep the other, important Lowells writing for them. The shrewdness by which Miss Lowell pitted the offers against each other, until she finally secured a very liberal contract indeed, was typical of her ability to handle money-matters.

This business started, she turned to selling poems to various periodicals, and having exhausted the possibilities in New York, she went on to Chicago for the same purpose. Harriet Monroe already had on hand some of her poems which she had accepted for *Poetry*, but the publication date was vague, and Miss Lowell had some other poems more worthy of its pages. 'I remember feeling that the star of literary empire was turning westward when this Bostonian daughter of the Lowells brought her poems to a Chicago mart,' Miss Monroe said later.[1] The poems were good; she planned to feature them in her April number.

Mrs. Russell was also in Chicago, acting in *The Deep Purple*; Miss Lowell sought her out, with the proposition that she give up acting and come to live and work with her at Sevenels. But the scheme did not seem feasible, and Miss Lowell returned to Brookline in time to have Edwin Arlington Robinson out to dinner on February 10 — the day after her fortieth birthday.

That same month, *Des Imagistes, an Anthology* appeared as the fifth number of the *Glebe*. This periodical had been started by Alfred Kreymborg at Ridgeway, New Jersey, the previous September; now it was appearing at New York, with the imprint of Albert and Charles Boni.

[1] Harriet Monroe: 'Memories of Amy Lowell,' *Poetry* (xxvi, 210), July, 1925.

Each issue was devoted to a single writer (in this case, a single movement), and the series was supported by subscribers.

The anthology made an attractive little pamphlet in green paper covers. It was not quite what Fletcher had prophesied. True, Aldington opened the book with ten poems, but he was followed by H. D. with seven, and Flint with five. Skipwith Cannéll,[1] Amy Lowell, William Carlos Williams,[2] and James Joyce were allowed one title apiece; then came Pound with six, and a four-page rhymed poem by Hueffer. Allen Upward[3] and John Cournos[4] ended the anthology proper with a title apiece. After this came three 'Documents' by Pound, Aldington, and Hueffer — jocose poems, the first being addressed 'To Hulme (T. E.) and Fitzgerald.'

The April issue of *Poetry* opened with a group of eight of Miss Lowell's poems, the first of which were metered,

[1] Humberston Skipwith Cannéll was born in Philadelphia, December 22, 1886; attended the University of Virginia, 1906–09; studied abroad for two years; and published his first poems in *Poetry*, August, 1913.

[2] William Carlos Williams was born in Rutherford, New Jersey, 1883; got an M.D. from the University of Pennsylvania in 1906; published *Poems* [Rutherford, N.J.], 1909; *The Tempers*, London, 1913; *Al Que Quiere*, Boston, 1917; *Kora in Hell*, Boston, 1920; and *Sour Grapes*, Boston, 1921. He is also an essayist and a novelist. In 1926, he was awarded the *Dial* prize.

[3] 'Mr. Allen Upward, born in Worcester [England] in 1863, has had a varied life. A scholar, a barrister, a volunteer soldier who ran the blockade of Crete and invaded Turkey with the Greek army, he is also the author of plays, romances, poems, and of *The New Word*, that powerful plea for idealism which aroused England six years ago, and for which Mr. Gerald Stanley Lee in *Crowds*, demands the Nobel prize. The *Scented Leaves* are not direct translations, but paraphrases from the Chinese.' (*Poetry*, II, 228, September, 1913.)

Upward stated, in 'The Discarded Imagist' (*Egoist*, II, 98, June 1, 1915), that in 1900 Cranmer Byng brought him Giles's *Chinese Poetry* which inspired him to write poems of his own, which he kept for many years. At last he got them published in *Poetry* and later in the *Egoist*; whereupon Pound included him in *Des Imagistes*. He was equally surprised to discover himself excluded from *Some Imagist Poets*.

[4] John Cournos, a Russian-born American citizen (b. 1881), became art critic of the *Philadelphia Record*, then went abroad in 1911. He has published one book of verse, *In Exile* (1928), two plays, nine novels, and a number of translations from the Russian, including Sologub's *Little Devil*, which he translated with Aldington.

and the last of which was in a new form, later to be called 'polyphonic prose.' This poem, 'The Forsaken,' was the prayer of a girl whose lover had been killed and whose child was soon to be born. The subject of course had been consecrated long since by Goethe's genius; none the less, Ella Wheeler Wilcox, authoress of *Poems of Passion*, was to take Miss Lowell to task for it, perhaps because Miss Lowell had used the word 'whore' as simply as the Bible and Shakspere. Her treatment was frank yet delicate. Consequently her despair was great when she saw that a line of text in the fourth paragraph, where the greatest delicacy was necessary, had been accidentally dropped out, with the result, not that the text made nonsense at that point, but that it made most disagreeable sense. She telephoned Miss Monroe in Chicago at once. 'I shall never forget how the wires hummed because of this error,' Miss Monroe testified. 'The poet's voice over the long-distance telephone was not angry — she kept her temper and did not blame the poor editor — but it was filled with anguish unutterable and not to be consoled.' A correct text was printed and pasted over the remaining numbers of the magazine.[1]

In March, Miss Lowell had been toying with the idea of editing a review. Pound was trying to interest her in the *Egoist*; she wondered if it could not be persuaded to cross the Atlantic; whereupon Pound suggested (March 25) that Hueffer, Joyce, Lawrence, and himself edit the English part of it, while she and her crowd could edit the American part. On April 7 she wrote back: 'I don't know who Joyce is. You say he and Lawrence are the best among the younger men. I quite agreee with you as to Lawrence, but I never heard of Joyce. What did he write, and who is he?' In the same letter, Miss Lowell sent

[1] The censors were still very active in suppressing all references to unpleasant aspects of life. As late as January, 1917, the *Poetry Journal* was forbidden the mails because of Scudder Middleton's 'Interlude,' a poem which also used the word 'whore.'

Pound a wedding present: he was marrying Miss Dorothy
Shakespeare on April 18, 1914.

Mrs. Russell reappeared for two weeks (March 30 –
April 11) in Boston: she was playing Rose Hart in a new
play, *The Dummy*, which was being given its final touches
at the Tremont Theater before the New York opening.
Actually she was marking time till Eugene Walter finished
A Plain Woman, a drama he had been writing for her for
some two years now. Miss Lowell sought her out, entertained her, pleaded with her to join her in a trip to Europe
that summer, wished she could give up the stage entirely
and live at Sevenels. But it seemed impossible, and on
April 13, *The Dummy* opened in New York.

Through all these events, Miss Lowell continued working
on her own poetry. Paul Fort's mixture of forms had been
interesting her particularly. She sent manuscripts (and
possibly the April *Poetry*) to Fletcher; he replied on
April 7 that he disliked Fort's work extremely, but that
he was ready to respect her contrary opinion, and to admit
her right to experiment in any form she chose.

In April, Albert and Charles Boni issued *Des Imagistes* as
a book in blue cloth covers, bearing no sign of the *Glebe*.
Four hundred and eighty copies were ordered in advance
— Pound's propaganda had been effective. It was reviewed everywhere, 'much, but very ignorantly,' as Miss
Lowell said. Established poets and academic critics
bristled; enthusiasm could be heard quite distinctly in
other quarters; and perplexity in still others. Harold
Monro arranged to publish it in London; the unbound
sheets were sent over, and issued with the imprint of the
Poetry Bookshop. But *Imagisme* woke no response in un-
prepared London: only the *Morning Post* gave the book
what could be called a favorable review, several indignant
customers returned their copies, and generally the book
was scorned.[1]

[1] Hughes, *op. cit.*, p. 34.

On May 16, Rupert Brooke wrote her from the Hotel Bellevue. He had a letter of introduction from Harriet Monroe (dated April 5, 1914); he was on his way back to England, and was to be in Boston four days. She gave him a lunch and a dinner, which he overlooked in writing up the customary impressions of America. There can be no doubt that among other things she mentioned her own trip to London the coming month, which he also was to overlook.

By the end of May, the proofs of *Sword Blades and Poppy Seed* were corrected. Her preface raised protest from the publishers; she answered, on May 22:

> In spite of your letter, I have decided to put the preface in exactly as it is.... I really was answering questions that have been asked me... and they have flowed in upon me tremendously since the publication of a few of my poems in the April number of *Poetry*. I find that people are not only interested in the form, they are startled, surprised, by the vividness of the images, upset by the obvious lack of the moral tag.... I think the preface will provoke criticism, possible anger and retort, but I do not know that that is any particular objection to it. If it is sufficiently piquante. I think it will help to sell the book. I have some hopes of the book, now, because the April number of *Poetry* has been sold out three times in the book shop here which carries it, namely, they have sold out their supply of copies three different times, and have had to send for more.... You say in your letter that I do not want to write an essay on poetry, but that is exactly what I do want to do....

Something had to be done about *Pierrot Qui Pleure*, which seemingly had been forgotten. She wrote the Boston Music Company a letter that brought a long indignant reply, but also a promise of the proofs by next Monday (June 8). On the sixteenth came her last Gebhard concert.

Meanwhile Mrs. Russell in New York had learned that the play being written for her, *A Plain Woman*, was not

finished and probably never would be; the news determined her to accept Miss Lowell's invitation.

On the twenty-third they sailed from Boston for Liverpool on the *Laconia*. With them went Miss Lowell's maid,
her maroon automobile, and one of her two chauffeurs
with his maroon livery. A steamer letter from Josephine
Peabody, enclosing a letter of introduction to Thomas
Hardy, added much to the pleasure of sailing. The two
women had become close friends by now.

> We were seeing each other pretty frequently and having
> many long poetry talks. She welcomed my experiments
> in verse with eagerness and sympathy, and I never heard
> her express anything but the warmest approval of poems
> in *vers libre*. It was only the bizarre verse of some of the
> *vers libristes* which she condemned. Her comments on
> poetry were always keen, sympathetic, and extremely
> stimulating.
>
> I got into the habit of reading her my poems as I wrote
> them. Not all, of course, but we passed a good many after-
> noons reading and talking.... I remember very well the
> afternoon by my library fire... [when]... I read her 'The
> Cremona Violin,' which I had just finished, and I remember
> the enthusiasm with which she greeted my attempt to re-
> produce the effect of violin playing by means of free-rhyme
> cadences breaking into the strict stanzaic form of the rest
> of the poem.[1]

Nothing could illustrate their friendship better than this
letter Miss Lowell received bidding her *bon voyage*.

192 Brattle Street, Cambridge
June 22

DEAR MISS LOWELL:

'Fair weather after you,' and going on before! I do hope
you'll have a glorious time, you and Mrs. Russell and all
the good poets and true. (This is not being as inclusive as
you may 'spicion.)

Mrs. Havelock Ellis (have you met her?) goes this day

[1] *Ms.* concerning Josephine Peabody.

to New York, and sails home in a week, with the most
vividly enthusiastic sense of American goodness and Graces
(of character mostly, Imagine!) — you ever prayed for;
and as she is coming back as fast as she can (November)
and may tug along Havelock E. with her, we shall meet
together then and have another kind of lark. I met her in
London, and was altogether astounded to have her drop
in on me most sudden and friendlike day before yesterday.
Anon, anon, madam. —

This empty letter takes the note to Hardy; and you must
forgive the detachable identification coupon this time, because it's for a very shy man, who reads not much of the
newest work, I think, and needs a little coaxing for initial
visits; after that, no. He is simplicity itself. And I hope
he hasn't forgotten me all to pieces. (Here I wink away
my welling childish tears.) I am ever so sorry that Swinburne and his kindly guardian Watts-Dunton have (in C. S.
parlance) taken this untimely notion to be dead. But they
have, like many others that I have had, to speak to, for a
few memorable hours.

So now, Bon Voyage, Amy. — And do drop a word to me,
once in a while, where I perch on a piece of the world, with
my sorely unstrung lyre, like that perfectly detestable Watts
picture that is calculated to destroy the last hope of dis-
pirited creatures! — Oh, but wait till I 'paw the purple
tide, sir' up and down the coast of Maine presently. Then
I shall cheer up. 'All on shore that's going ashore!' (That
doesn't mean me.)

Faithfully yours,

TONY KHAYYÁM.

(Don't forget that Khayyám means Tent-maker — a very
necessary craft for some.)

P.S. It has just occurred to me that you may like to motor
down and see something of the region while this conference
goes on. — Dull as the *title* looks, I found that there is an
altogether exceptional charm about Stratford pilgrims during these festivals.

And the most attractive *English* enthusiasm is here to

be found (if you choose your times wisely). — They used
to scoff very much at American regard for Stratford; but
all that is changed. I wouldn't give up the jolly afternoon
or so when I sat in the balcony beside Ellen Terry, and she
commented (always kindly and shrewdly) in loud whispers
or 'full voice' on the acting of her old parts — worn with
a difference. Try it!

Yours

J. P. M.

P.S. (Probably 3rd or 5th — Records Lost)

It creeps slowly up from my submerged consciousness
that you may find time and inclination to meet Mrs. Havelock Ellis in London (if she's there, after her American
tour!) — And if you do, just send your card and mine to
her at *The Lyceum Club* 128 Piccadilly. I did not think of
her at first, because with her, Radical causes are uppermost and poetry underneather; and yet while I say this, I
feel it isn't true. Whether you love or hate her (she's so
vital and so headstrong, it must be one or the other) 'twill
do you good to know her, if you are thrillable (as I am always) with fearless honesty and pioneer courage. A very
brilliant woman — can't think why I didn't begin with her
address. I am more and more certain you will have a great
deal in common.

Here goes!
Bon Voyage, —
Yours,

J. P. M.

P.S. I'll be after dropping her a line shortly, and I'll speak
of you in that. She doesn't sail home for some few days.

The Archduke of Austria was assassinated while Miss
Lowell was on the Atlantic. The London *Standard* for
July 3 noted her arrival at the Berkeley Hotel. At once
Mrs. Russell and she plunged into things. The Russian
Ballet was there; they saw the entire repertoire, and were
particularly enthusiastic over Rimsky-Korsakov's *Coq
d'Or* and Stravinsky's *Petroushka* and the *Sacre du Prin-*

temps. This last ballet they saw twice; Miss Lowell accepted it instantly as a masterpiece, and eventually came to consider Stravinsky as the greatest living composer. For years afterwards she used to describe with gusto the effect of her first hearing of the *Sacre.*

Pound was very busy organizing a new movement, called 'Vorticism.' Why a man should be running two movements at once requires explanation, but we can offer nothing beyond conjecture. Evidently Pound was in with a new group of friends, and the pleasure of the Vorticist movement was to find oneself at last *inter pares.*[1] Only Aldington and Hueffer of all those in *Des Imagistes,* followed Pound; and Hueffer, who always insisted he was an Impressionist, and not an *Imagiste,* did not sign the manifesto. Perhaps the new group — which included Wyndham Lewis and Gaudier-Brzeska — was unwilling to join a movement already started, especially when its banner was far-flung from Chicago: indeed, *Blast* (the Vorticist periodical) avoids mention of America almost painfully — culture was exclusively English and French. As *Blast* never mentioned *Imagisme,* and as Pound wrote nothing about Vorticism in *Poetry,*[2] it seems obvious that the intention was to keep the Atlantic between the two: *Imagisme* was for America and Vorticism for England. One must confess that the idea (if Pound entertained it) of being the center of two different movements in two different countries, and thus becoming the king-pin of the English-speaking literary worlds, was magnificent — even intoxicating!

But inevitably there was an unavowed connection between the two groups, if only because no writer can honestly subscribe simultaneously to different literary creeds. Could one compare creeds, the task of discovering the

[1] Pound: *Pavannes and Divisions,* New York, 1918, p. 255. It is only fair to add that this statement was written in 1916, after the schism.

[2] In *Poetry* (v, 44–45), October, 1914, there is a brief and unsigned dismissal of *Blast* which was probably written by Miss Monroe.

relationships would be easy; unfortunately, while the *Imagiste* principles were explicit enough, the Vorticist manifestoes though violent were vague. Taupin (p. 86) considers that, in these manifestoes, Pound pushed the *Imagiste* idea to its extreme development; Hughes (pp. 34–35) says that Pound feared stagnation and notes his defection from the *Imagiste* idea. Neither defines Vorticism. Hueffer said that though he was its most loyal champion, he never knew what it was, and could not discern any working creed.[1] The explanation of the difficulty would seem to be that no new literary creed had been evolved.

Yet there were distinctions, and even differences. Vorticism, which included sculptors, painters, and prose-writers, aimed at the formula of all the arts. Every concept, every emotion, Pound said, presented itself in some primary form, which indicated the appropriate art for its expression. The primary form or pigment, of poetry was the IMAGE.[2] In a lecture given that spring, he developed this principle. A vortex, he said, was not an idea but an image, a radiant node or cluster, from which and through which and into which ideas were constantly rushing; wherefore in decency one could only call it a VORTEX. [3]

The 'vortex,' then, was merely a new name for Hulme's 'image,' except that it was supposed to suggest ideas by itself, and not by contrast and analogy with other images. Pound specifically protested against analogies. But he did not object to the super-position of one idea upon another, for thus he explained his two-line 'In a Station of the Metro,' which he quoted as an example of Vorticist poetry. He also quoted H. D.'s 'Oread,' which was doing duty in America as a model of *Imagisme.* So it would

---

[1] *Imagist Anthology 1930*, New York, 1930, p. 16. On the next page he seems to have inverted chronology when he states that Imagism evolved itself as a by-product of Vorticism.

[2] *Blast* (1, 154), June 20, 1914.

[3] *Fortnightly Review* (xcvi, 461–71), September, 1914; collected in Pound's *Gaudier-Brzeska*, London, 1916, p. 106.

seem evident that, at least as regards poetry, Vorticism
really had no new creed.

But Pound omitted the classical title of H. D.'s poem,
probably in deference to another feature of Vorticism,
emphasized particularly by Wyndham Lewis: Vorticism,
plunging to the heart of the present, forgot the existence
of the past.[1]

Now obviously, if only the immediate Present were to
be the direct inspiration, one could not get inspiration
from books, for that at best could only be inspiration at
second-hand. The theory was inconvenient for Pound,
but his troubadours disappeared. Miss Lowell later was
to chuckle: 'Poor Ezra! He sawed off the branch he was
sitting on!'

The first number of *Blast* was dated June 20, 1914,
before she sailed; actually it seems to have been delayed,
for the invitations to the dinner celebrating its appearance
were not issued until July 7, a week before the dinner itself took place. She was among those invited by Pound.
On July 9, she arranged for Macmillan to publish *Sword
Blades and Poppy Seed* in London: they took one hundred
copies, which they agreed to issue with their imprint, and
to sell them for her, turning over all proceeds except a
10 per cent commission. Later George Macmillan gave a
dinner for her at Ranelagh; here she met Sir Sidney Colvin,
the leading English authority on Keats, whose remarks
about that poet made her want to swear a good, round,
agreeable oath. As he was writing a biography of Keats,
she promised to send him copies of all her own original
Keats material, but when the War broke out, she forgot
all about it.

Various Vorticists and new *Imagistes* were presented to
her. She visited Gaudier-Brzeska's studio, in one of the
boarded-in arches of the Putney Railroad Bridge: he was
so extremely poor that he had to make his own tools.
Allen Upward gave her a very jolly picnic luncheon in a

---

[1] *Blast, op. cit.*, p. 147.

park, but as it rained they had to seek cover. She wrote to Cournos that she 'liked Russians,' and had him round. Fletcher's *Irradiations* had not yet found a London publisher; she took the manuscript, promising to try and place it in America.

On July 15, Aldington's review of *Blast* appeared in the *Egoist*; that night the Vorticist dinner was held at the Dieu-donné restaurant. If she had not seen a copy previously, now at last she held in her hands the first issue of *Blast*, outwardly resembling a telephone directory in cerise-pink paper covers, inwardly uttering curses and blessings and manifestoes in enormous black type. Wyndham Lewis, the editor, contributed 'Enemy of the Stars,' the outline of a very modern play; 'Vortices and Notes'; six abstract designs; and an obituary on Frederick Spenser Gore, two of whose paintings were reproduced. Pound contributed twelve poems and a 'Vortex.' Gaudier-Brzeska also had a 'Vortex' besides a photograph of his 'Stags'; Edward Wadsworth reviewed Kandinsky's *Art of Spiritual Harmony*, which he had translated, and contributed five abstract designs; other abstractions came from Epstein, Frederick Etchells, W. Roberts, and Cuthbert Hamilton. There was also a story by May Sinclair and the beginning of another (alas! never finished) by Hueffer (now 'Heuffer') written in the person of an American, and containing the sentence: 'I myself am a Lowell, of Philadelphia, Pa., where, it is historically true, there are more old English families than you would find in any six English counties taken together.' But what the story was about has never been revealed. It is remembered, however, that Hueffer and she disagreed flatly about literary principles; when she returned to her hotel, she was still furious at his attitude.

Two nights later, on the seventeenth, Miss Lowell gave an *Imagiste* dinner at the same restaurant. Her guests were the Aldingtons, Cournos, Fletcher, Flint, Gaudier-

Brzeska, the Hueffers, the Pounds, and Upward. As Mrs. Russell was also there, the number was thirteen, so Fletcher and Mrs. Hueffer sat at a little side table. The dinner was very jolly. Everybody talked a great deal. Allen Upward made a particularly happy speech. Even Gaudier-Brzeska overcame his shyness enough, not only to announce his principles, but also to remain standing while he answered objection after objection — some no doubt from Aldington, who always took occasion to tackle the sculptor for his dislike of Hellenism, and some perhaps from Miss Lowell herself. Pound was sufficiently elated to improvise some kind of juggling with one of the waiters' trays. Only Hueffer seems to have been unhappy.[1]

Meanwhile Rupert Brooke had expressed no awareness whatsoever of the arrival of his former hostess.[2] Perhaps he did not like the company she was keeping (the last reference to Pound in the *Poetry Review* had been Brooke's withering protest against a remark of Pound's about Abercrombie); more likely it was merely the familiar situation which had inspired Henry James's *International Episode* as far back as 1879. The two were to see each other once again, however. Harold Monro had instituted a series of readings at his Bookshop, and Brooke of course was one of the poets invited to read. Though the July afternoon was scorching, the proper atmosphere was created by drawn shades, candles, and dark draperies. Mr. Brooke was at his most expressive when presently he was interrupted by a clear call from the back of the room:

'Louder!'

Perhaps he did not know that this was a Bostonian method of encouraging an inaudible lecturer; perhaps he supposed that the indignant *shsh*ings which immediately

[1] Hueffer's account of the dinner, in his 'Henri Gaudier,' *English Review* (xxix, 297–304), October, 1919, is probably the most violent attack on Amy Lowell in print. He called her a monstrously fat, monstrously moneyed, disagreeably intelligent coward — coward, since he represents her as anxious to leave England because of the War. But of course the War was not even suspected on July 17.

[2] Letter to Aldington, November 1, 1919.

rose round the speaker would intimate her. At any
rate, soon there was another call:

'Louder, please!'

He paused and asked, trying not to break the rhythm of
his reading:

'Can't... you... hear... ?'

'Not one word!' he was told emphatically. Harold
Monro later was to express his annoyance at the interruption.

There was yet another poet in England — Robert Frost.
He had left America in September, 1912, and made his resi-
dence in the town of Beaconsfield, Buckinghamshire, where
he worked on *A Boy's Will*. At intervals he went up to
London, to hear some of the readings at the Poetry Bookshop; he also attended a few meetings of the *Imagistes*,
but felt no inclination to join forces with them. In 1913
A Boy's Will was published, and was 'pleasantly received.'
Meanwhile he was writing *North of Boston*, which he had
started in 1905. He also became a very close friend of
Edward Thomas (killed at Vimy in the spring of 1917),
who encouraged him heartily. When he was putting the
last touches on his manuscript, he met Wilfrid Gibson,
and when the manuscript was in his publisher's hands,
he met Abercrombie. The latter persuaded him to give
up the farm at Leddington, Herefordshire, which he now
was working, and live with him and his family at Ryton,
Gloucestershire; where he stayed from April to September,
1914. *North of Boston* was issued in London that spring.[1]

What ensued can best be told in Miss Lowell's own
words.

> In the Summer of 1914, I was in London, and on one occa-
> sion, when I had strolled into the Poetry Bookshop, I found
> lying on a counter a slim little green cloth volume bearing
> the alluring title *North of Boston*. It is a good title even
> when one discounts any particular bias toward it, but for

[1] Letter from Frost to Miss Lowell, October 22, 1917.

an expatriated New Englander its appeal was nostalgic and completely irresistible. I bought the book then and there, and all that evening, in the impersonal bleakness of a hotel room, I read this most personal book, until I was saturated with the atmosphere of the New Hampshire hills; and when I went to the window and looked out at the moon, it was not Piccadilly that I saw before my windows, but Monadnock and Dublin Lake shining with moonlight. Young poets are the most intolerant of human beings, and the little group with whom I had allied myself were quite certain that blank verse was an outworn medium, and that *le mot juste* was the most important factor of poetry. That night taught me a lesson which I have never forgotten. For here was our vaunted *mot juste* embedded in a blank verse so fresh, living, and original that nothing on the score of vividness and straightforward presentation — our shibboleths — could be brought up against it. Its feeling was undeniable; its reticence equally so. I immediately took off my hat to the unknown poet, and I have been taking it off ever since in a positively wearying repetition.[1]

Surely that memorable night inspired her 'A London Thoroughfare, 2 A.M.,' which ends:

> I know the moon,
> And this is an alien city.

She packed her copy of *North of Boston* with Fletcher's *Irradiations*: here was a second American book that America must know.

There was yet another poet in London: D. H. Lawrence, who had just been married, on July 13. Amy Lowell, who knew and admired his work, was glad to receive the couple, although she was not quite sure what to expect as regards his wife. She was overwhelmed with astonishment and pleasure, however, to meet a lady of exquisite, vital presence. They came frequently to dinner; the friendship which began thus endured until her death.

[1] 'Tribute to Frost,' March 5, 1925.

And of course she saw a great deal of the *Imagistes*. As they had no convenient meeting place, she had them assemble in the drawing room of her suite. Of Aldington she wrote:

> I remember we once took a long motor-ride out into the country, and the afternoon is chiefly memorable to me from the contagion of his enthusiasm. He was always pointing out some bird hiding in the hedge, or hilariously naming some wild flower scarcely possible to be seen as we whirled along. In those days, he wore his hair rather long, and never wore a hat, and he was always turning round to us on the back seat, shaking his hair back as the wind blew it forward when he turned, laughing, gay, just a boy out for a holiday. He was only a boy then, only twenty-two. That was just before the war. It seems very long ago....
>
> What evenings we used to have in London in the old days, before the war! All of us sitting round a big box of candied fruit (our poet has a weakness for candied fruit) glancing lightly over the literature and history of the world, cracking jokes, unmercifully criticising each other's poems, and every now and then stopping to watch the moon cutting through the purple night outside the window.[1]

Meanwhile she sold ten poems to London periodicals.

On July 23, Austria-Hungary issued its forty-eight hour ultimatum to Servia; on the twenty-eighth it declared war. The continent was seething; trains were jammed with Europeans hurrying back to their fatherlands, while most American tourists marvelled at their panic and planned to continue their tours unperturbed by a little trouble off in the Balkans. Russia began to mobilize.

Meanwhile Miss Lowell was delivering a private ultimatum of her own. She was interested in continuing the *Des Imagistes* anthology, but she had no intention of co-operating unless she were accepted as really one of them. The meager page allotted her had classed her, not

[1] Lecture on Aldington, Flint, and Lawrence, at the Brooklyn Institute, March 27, 1918.

with the important *Imagistes*, but as one of the six names used for padding. For her own literary dignity she must be definitely either in or out.

Her scheme was that each of the poets elect should be allowed equal space in the next anthology. But such a scheme would dispossess Pound, in some measure, of his anonymous editorship. She consulted the Aldingtons, then armed with their approval laid the scheme before Pound, when they were alone together. When she had the others in, there was an excited argument, in which the other *Imagistes* were solidly on the side of Miss Lowell. Then she departed, on Friday, July 31, for a quiet week-end at Dorchester and Bath, giving Pound time to think it over.

The fullest account of the break that ensued is to be found in a letter to Miss Monroe, September 15, 1914.

> You ask about the quarrel between Ezra and the rest of us. It is not a quarrel now, it is a schism. It is a very long story, and I do not know quite how to tell you all of it by letter.
>
> Do you remember, Ezra was very anxious to run the *Mercure de France*? He came to me at once as soon as I got to London, and then it transpired that he expected to become editor of said 'Review' with a salary. I was to guarantee all the money, and put in what I pleased, and he was to run the magazine his way. We talked over the cost of expenses, and we both thought that $5,000. a year was the least that such a magazine could be run on. As I have not $5,000. a year that I can afford to put into it, I based my refusal upon that fact, and it was most unfortunate that Ezra apparently did not believe it. Like many people of no incomes, Ezra does not know the difference between thousands and millions, and thinks that any one who knows where to look for next week's dinners, is a millionaire, and therefore lost his temper with me completely, although he never told me why, and he accused me of being unwilling to give any money towards art.
>
> In thinking over what I could do to help the poets less

fortunate than myself, and also to help myself in somewhat
the same manner that a review would do, it seemed to me
that to republish the 'Imagiste Anthology' with the same
group of people, year after year, for a period of five years,
would enable us, by constant iteration, to make some impression upon the reading public. And I thought it would
be interesting for people to see the work of the same group
of poets brought out year after year, and it is a method
which the editors of 'Georgian Poetry' have found most
satisfactory. I mentioned this first to the Aldingtons because I saw them first after I conceived the idea. I suggested that the last little book was too monotonous and too
undemocratic, in that certain poets were allowed much
more space than others, and I suggested that in the 'New
Anthology' we should allow approximately the same space
to each poet, and that we should get a publisher of reputable standing, and I offered, in case we could not get
any publisher to take the risk of the volume itself, to pay
for its publication.

The Aldingtons were exceedingly enthusiastic with the
idea, as have been the other poets we have asked to join us.
Only Ezra was annoyed. He accused me of trying to make
myself editor instead of him, and finally tried a little black-
mail by telling me that he would only join us on condition
that I would obligate myself to give $200. a year to some
indigent poet. I told him that the $200. a year might be
managed should any one in stress of circumstances need
such a sum, but that I absolutely refused to be intimidated
into buying anything, or to buy his poems at the expense of
my self-respect. I also told him that I would not have suggested 'The Anthology' had I known that he would not
like the idea, and that it was intended to benefit him, quite
as much as the rest of us.

He was perfectly furious for some time, and sent for the
Aldingtons, and told them they must choose between him
and me, which was awful for them, as he is a very old
friend, and has done much for them, and I was only a new
friend. They behaved with the utmost honour in the matter. They told Ezra it was not a question of me at all, but

a question of the principle, that they felt it only fair to let the poets choose their own contributions and to give each poet an equal space. He then tried to bribe them, by asking them to get up an Anthology with him, and leave me out. This they absolutely refused to do.

We had many consultations on the subject, in which Flint, Lawrence, and Ford Madox Hueffer joined us, and we all agreed that Ezra could not expect to run us all his own way forever, and that if he chose to separate himself from us, we would be obliged, although most regretfully, to let him. Fletcher is coming in, and a few of the poets in the last volume who have not been producing much in the interval, have been struck out.[1]

'The New Anthology' will consist of seven of us, viz: the Aldingtons, Flint, Fletcher, Ford Madox Hueffer, D. H. Lawrence, and myself, and the harmony and kindly feeling which we have all displayed toward each other has been very marked. In order to save Ezra's feelings as much as possible, we have written a preface, in which we have explained that Ezra has left us from artistic reasons, owing to a slight difference in the interpretation of the word '*Imagistes*.' We have changed the name of the Anthology, in order to let him bring out another of his own under that title, should he so desire. Our Anthology is to be 'Some *Imagiste* Poets.' ...

Ezra has always thought of life as a grand game of bluff. He never has learned the wisdom of Lincoln's famous adage about 'not being able to fool all the people all the time.' Advertising is all very well, but one must have some goods to deliver, and the goods must be up to the advertising of them. Now that Ezra has ceased to be a youthful phenomenon he must take his place in the steady march by which young men of talent gain to a real reputation, and he finds himself falling back at every step, and this naturally makes him exceedingly bitter. He is very brilliant,

[1] These were Cannéll, Cournos, Joyce, Upward, and Williams. According to Aldington, in his review of *Des Imagistes* (*Egoist*, June 1, 1914), the first four, with Hueffer, were not true *Imagistes*, although their poems were admirable. Eventually there was difficulty over Hueffer's contribution ('On Heaven,' which had appeared in *Poetry*, June, 1914), and he withdrew it.

but he does not work enough, and his work lacks the quality of soul, which, I am more and more fain to believe, no great work can ever be without. At any rate, that is the situation about the *Imagistes*. It is not a quarrel, in one sense it never was. I have spared no efforts to keep them all on good terms with each other, even offering to leave 'The Anthology' myself, if it would heal the breach. Ezra and his wife dined with me a few days before I left [England], and we had a very pleasant and perfectly amicable evening, and it would not surprise me if he came into our Anthologies later on, but of course, I have not suggested this possibility to him.

The great thing which my summer has done for me is bringing me the intimacy of the Aldingtons. They are a perfectly charming young couple, and I think Hilda's last work an advance on her other, don't you? I am very glad indeed that you accepted the poems she sent you, with the exception of 'Sea Iris' in returning which I cannot help thinking you made a mistake. I enclose a subscription blank for my old governess in England, who is very much interested in seeing your book.

Don't be discouraged that the subscriptions are not increasing. A magazine devoted to poetry can hardly expect to increase its subscription list hand over fist. Poetry is looking up, but I do not suppose it will ever be really popular, and I think you are doing a great deal to change public opinion and raise the standard in this country....

Such was Miss Lowell's view of the schism. On July 30, she had the Lawrences and the Aldingtons to dinner, and read poetry afterward; on the thirty-first she departed for Dorchester, to have tea with the Hardys. Josephine Peabody had given her a letter of introduction, and she had been trying to present it ever since she reached London. When a severely sprained ankle prevented her appearing on Monday, July 20, the date was postponed to August 1.

The trip began quietly enough.

So little expectation of war was there, so academic the 'conversations' between the powers seemed, that on the

Friday [July 31] preceding the declaration of war, we went down to Dorchester and Bath for a week-end outing. It was rather a shock to find the market-place at Salisbury filled with cannon, and the town echoing with soldiers. The waiter at the inn, however, assured us that it was only manoeuvres. But the next day, our chauffeur, who had been fraternizing with the soldiers, told us that it was not manoeuvres: they had started for manoeuvres, but had been turned round, and were now on their way back to their barracks.[1]

They spent the night at Salisbury. The sister of the author of many studies in European history and government was not deluded: her vivid imagination foresaw the gigantic horror rising on the horizon. To add to the situation, the ride from Salisbury to Dorchester began with an intermittent drizzle and ended with a steady downpour. As Miss Lowell insisted on having the top of her automobile put down whenever it was not raining, and as it took time to put it up again, everybody in the car was drenched and bedraggled by the time they reached the Hardys' home. The bird on Miss Lowell's hat had peeled completely off.

But the hospitality they received was the beginning of an enduring friendship. At first they talked of the European troubles: Miss Lowell was very much afraid that there might be difficulty in getting back to America, and Thomas Hardy had received telephonic messages from London that made him pessimistic as to the outcome. Neither of them knew that Germany had declared war on Russia and flung her troops westward. The conversation turned to literature. Mrs. Hardy and Mrs. Russell sat mute while Mr. Hardy and Miss Lowell talked as though they had been life-long friends.

After tea, Miss Lowell and Mrs. Russell drove on to Bath, where they passed two nights. They spent a quiet

[1] Amy Lowell: 'A Letter from London,' *Little Review* (1, 6–9), October, 1914.

Sunday in the ancient city; then the headlines of August 3 made them start back for London at once, driving through towns suddenly struck dumb and motionless. The long Victorian peace was over.

> As we came from Bath, on Monday, we were told that gasolene was over five shillings a can. That was practically saying that England had gone to war. But she had not, nor did she, until twelve o'clock that night. When we reached our hotel we found a state bordering on panic. There was no money to be got, and all day long, for two days, people (Americans) had been arriving from the Continent. Without their trunks, naturally. There was no one to handle trunks at the stations in Paris. These refugees were all somewhat hysterical; perhaps they exaggerated when they spoke of disorder in Paris; later arrivals seemed to think so....
>
> But that first night in London I shall never forget. A great crowd of people with flags marched down Piccadilly, shouting: 'We want war! We want war!' They sang the Marseillaise, and it sounded savage, abominable. The blood-lust was coming back, which we had hoped was gone forever from civilized races.[1]

Immediately, with remarkable foresight, she had her automobile crated and sent home on the very next boat, so that it would not be commandeered; then she set about trying to get passage for herself. But though she applied to James Bryce himself, it was impossible to find passage on any of the crowded ships. Her brother Percival, who had been in London (she had dined with him once or twice), with typical Lowell independence had already sailed. Something like hysteria came over her. There is always a touch of panic in being trapped on an island (even if only by a storm that must abate); and she had not been trained in childhood to any imperturbable belief in the invincibility of the English navy. Nevertheless, in spite of all her efforts, she was unable to get passage

[1] A. Lowell: A Letter from London, *Little Review* (1, 6–9), October, 1914.

for a month. Automatically, therefore, she gave her energy to public service.

When, that first week of the war, bank holiday was extended to four days instead of one; when the moratorium was declared, which exempted the banks from paying on travellers' cheques and letters-of-credit; and when, to add to that, so many boats were taken off, and there were no sailings to be got for love or money, something closely approaching a panic broke out among the Americans. And what wonder! They felt caught like rats in a trap, with the impassable sea on one side and the advancing Germans on the other. For Americans have not been brought up with the tradition of England's invincibility at sea. They have heard of John Paul Jones and the 'Bonhomme Richard.' And they have imagination. I was told that one woman had killed herself in an access of fear, and I have heard of another who has had to be put in an asylum, her mind given way under the strain. Many of these people had no money and they could not get any; they came from the Continent and had to find lodgings, and they could offer neither money, nor credit. The Embassy had no way of meeting the strain flung upon it. The Ambassador is not a rich man, and the calls for money were endless. Finally some public-spirited American gentleman started a Committee, with offices at the Hotel Savoy, to help stranded Americans. And the work they have done has been so admirable that it is hard to find words to describe it. The Committee cashes cheques, gets steamship bookings, suggests hotels and lodgings, provides clothes, meets trains. I cannot write the half it does, but it makes one exceedingly proud. I do not believe that there is an American in London who has not helped the Committee with time or money, or been helped by it.[1]

'Some public-spirited American gentleman' was one Herbert C. Hoover, who opened an office of his own in the American Consulate, where he gave out $5000.00 of his own in small loans to compatriots with nothing but paper equivalents of money. How this immediate gener-

[1] A. Lowell: *ibid.*

osity of his was only a beginning, how it grew until he was feeding millions in all the suffering countries of Europe, how eventually he became President, are now familiar facts of history.

Miss Lowell joined his Committee at once. She telegraphed for $10,000.00 to put at its disposal; and wearing a large placard she met trains in the Victoria Station, to direct bewildered arrivals to the proper bureaus of assistance. The masses of soldiers she saw on every train leaving for the South Coast intensified her sense of the vast movements of men concentrating upon the continent. Then, when things had calmed down somewhat, she set about her own affairs again.

The chief thing to be done was the organization of the new *Imagiste* anthology. When she returned to London, she found a letter from Pound awaiting her, dated August 1. He said it was true he might give his sanction to letting her and the Aldingtons bring out such an anthology, provided it were clearly stated at the front of the book that E. P., etc., dissociated himself, wished success, did not mind use of title so long as it was made clear that he was not responsible for contents or view of the contributors; BUT such an agreement would deprive him of his machinery for gathering stray good poems and presenting them to the public in more or less permanent form, and for discovering new talent — a machinery largely or wholly his making. He didn't see the use of being saddled with a dam'd contentious, probably incompetent committee; nor could he accept a certain number of people as his critical and creative equals. He could not trust such a committee to maintain the *Imagiste* standards, he could not waste time arguing with it. If anybody wanted a faction or if anybody wanted to form a separate group, he thought it could be done amicably; and he thought it wiser to split over an aesthetic principle, in which case the new group would find its name automatically, almost.

He understood her proposition as not so much that she would find a publisher, and that she would prefer the stuff to be selected by a committee or by each contributor, as that such an anthology would be published and that he could come in or go hang. He admitted that this impression might have been inexact, and suggested that they both might have rushed at unnecessary conclusions.

As we have shown already, Miss Lowell respected Pound's wishes as far as possible. Of course the group could not invent a new literary creed — that would have been aesthetic treason; besides, the *Imagiste* theory was not originally Pound's at all, even if a literary theory could be one man's exclusive property. He had invented the name '*Imagisme*,' however; but as he had merely derived it from the earlier 'School of Images,' an equally slight change was all that was necessary to prevent any charge of theft. So eventually, not to confuse the public, the new anthology was called *Some Imagist Poets*: 'Imagist' without the French terminal *e*; and 'Some,' so that Pound was not excluded from the school but could issue an anthology of his own, if he chose. A preface was written, explaining his defection as due to growing literary tendencies which had produced differences of taste and judgment; later events, however, caused Miss Lowell to decide that it would be a mistake to mention his name there, so it was struck out and replaced by 'former contributors.' She also wrote a poem, 'Astigmatism,' dedicated to Pound, in which she represented her disagreement with 'The Poet,' whose cane was so beautiful and also so destructive, as caused by differences of taste. It ends: 'Peace be with you, Brother. You have chosen your part.' (Pound read this poem in manuscript, and according to Miss Lowell 'said it was all right.')

On Berkeley Hotel note paper she listed the seven poems she eventually included — a fact of interest as it shows they were all written by August, 1914.

Harold Monro warned her that the withdrawal of Pound's name would mean the collapse of the movement, but she was not to be convinced. The Aldingtons, Flint, and Hueffer were on her side. She invited the Lawrences to dinner again at the Berkeley on Thursday the thirteenth. Lawrence thought that Imagism was merely an advertising scheme; and as he hated French poetry, he supposed her enthusiasm over it must be a pose. But he consented to contribute. She did not see Fletcher again in England: he had taken a trip to the Continent before the war broke out, and did not return until August 12; then he went straight to the country supposing that she had sailed long since. But though he had resisted Hulme, though he had resisted Pound, he could not resist Miss Lowell; and by September 15 at the latest, he had joined also.

The remaining days in London were quieter. Flint, in a review of her *Six French Poets*, has preserved one recollection:

> No one, I suppose, will have listened to Miss Lowell's causerie in so happy a setting as the sitting-room of her hotel, when she talked to us in the August of 1914. Through the long French window open in the corner could be seen the length of Piccadilly, its great electric globes, its shiny roadway, and, on the left, the tops of the trees of Green Park, dark grey in the moonlight; the noise of the motorbuses and of the taxis reached us in a muted murmur, and at the corner of the park opposite, beneath a street-lamp, stood a newsboy whose headlines we strained our eyes from time to time to catch. It was in this tenseness created by the expectation of news that Miss Lowell read Paul Fort or Henri de Régnier to us (she reads French beautifully); and it is the emotion of those evenings more than anything else, that her book brings back to me.[1]

Flint did not say, of course, how much Miss Lowell was indebted to him for information about contemporary

[1] F. S. Flint: 'Six French Poets,' *The Egoist* (III, 9–10), January 1, 1916.

French poetry. Her own reading had been eager and extensive, but it was nothing to his. So from him she learned everything that she could; innumerable titles that he named she bought, and spent all her spare time reading them. Six of the poets appealed to her particularly; she planned to write her appreciation of them in three essays for the *Atlantic Monthly*, and in July had unfolded her plan to Flint. He did not think that Samain and Gourmont should be included; he suggested instead that she include the two Americans, Stuart Merrill and Vielé-Griffin. 'But she only motioned the waiter to fill my glass with champagne; and what can a man do against such argument and such a will?'[1]

On August 14, she wrote a war-poem, 'The Allies,' in her new polyphonic prose; she felt sure it was one of her better productions.

On the twenty-third, she drove down to Portsmouth, to see one of her old friends, Sumner Appleton's sister, now Eleanor Standen, who used to sing Franz songs so entrancingly.

When she returned, a letter from D. H. Lawrence was awaiting her:

> The Triangle Bellingdon Lane
> Chesham, Bucks
> 22 Aug. 1914

DEAR MISS LOWELL,

Here we are settled in our cottage, which is really very nice. I spend my days whitewashing the upper rooms, having a rare old time. Meanwhile I grind over in my soul the war news. Germany is a queer country: one can't regard it dispassionately. I alternate between hating it thoroughly, stick stock & stone, and yearning over it fit to break my heart. I cant help feeling it a young and adorable country — adolescent — with the faults of adolescence. There is no peace during this war. But I must say, my chief grief & misery is for Germany — so far.

[1] F. S. Flint: 'Amy Lowell's New Book,' *Little Review* (II, x, 16), January-February, 1916).

In the poetry book, for my seven, will you please put

1. Ballad of Another Ophelia — beginning 'O the green glimmer of apples in the orchard.' Harriet Monroe has got it, & wants to publish the far end of it & leave out the first half: see her in blazes. But even if you don't like the poem, please put it in an you love me.

2. Illicit — beginning — I've forgotten — something about 'a faint, lost ribbon of rainbow.' It is in 'Poetry.'

3. The Youth Mowing — also in 'Poetry.' [1]

4. Birthday — also in Poetry — 'If I were well to do.' [2]

5. Isar Rose Gems.[3]

6. Tired of the Boat.[4]

7. Scent of Irises.   MS enclosed

This is very roughly my selection. I'm quite amenable to change. Tell me yours, & let us compromise. The MS. poems I send you here have not been published: yes, Tired of the Boat, two years ago in the English Review — in an unrevised version. Don't lose MS. of the Irises poem, will you? — it is the only copy. I can't be bothered to write it out again. You might, if you like, offer these poems to Harriett Monroe: but not unless you like. I only insist on your taking the Ballad of Another Ophelia.

Can't you come & see us! Can't you drive out here in your motor car — about 30 miles. Come to Chesham, through Harrow. In Chesham ask for Elliotts farm at Bellingdon — we are 100 yards from the farm. We should be delighted to see you. Do try to come — any day, at any hour — you will eat eggs if there is nothing else in the house — & cheese & milk & bacon — perfectly rural & idyllic.

... Won't you drive over for the day, with Mrs. Russell or the Aldingtons?

My wife & I send many regards to you & to Mrs. Russell

Yours

D. H. LAWRENCE

---

[1] A pencilled note corrects the place of publication to 'Smart Set.'
[2] Crossed out in pencil, and 'Fireflies in the Corn' substituted.
[3] Crossed out in pencil, and 'A Woman to her Dead Husband' substituted.
[4] Crossed out in pencil, and 'Green' substituted.

On Thursday the twenty-seventh they drove down for the visit.

On the twenty-eighth she dated 'a letter from London,' that letter in the *Little Review* for October from which we have already quoted her experiences during that weekend when the war broke out. Other portions of it read as follows:

> As I sit here, I can see out of my window the Red Cross flag flying over Devonshire House. Only one short month ago I sat at this same window and looked at Devonshire House, glistening with lights, and all its doors wide open, for the duke and the duchess were giving an evening party. Powdered footmen stood under the porte-cochère, and the yard was filled with motors; it was all extremely well-ordered and gay.
>
> I watched the people arriving and leaving, for a long time. It was a very late party, and it was not only broad daylight, but brilliant sunshine, before they went home. They did have such a good time, those boys and girls, and they ended by coming out on the balcony and shouting and hurrahing for fully ten minutes. How many of those young men were among the 'two thousand casualties' at the Battle of Charleroi, of which we have just got news?
>
> Devonshire House is as busy this afternoon, but it is no longer gay. In the yard is a long wooden shed, with a corrugated iron roof; there are two doors on opposite sides, like barn doors, and black against the light of the farther door I can see men sitting at a table, and boy scouts running upon errands. The yard is filled with motors again, and there is a buzz of coming and going. Yesterday a man brought a sort of double-decked portable stretcher, with a place above and below, and a group stood round it and talked about it for a long time. For this is the headquarters of the Red Cross Society. So, in one short month, has life changed, here in London.
>
> A month ago I toiled up the narrow stairs of a little outhouse behind the Poetry Bookshop, and in an atmosphere of overwhelming sentimentality, listened to Mr. Rupert

Brooke whispering his poems. To himself, it seemed as
nobody else could hear him. It was all artificial and precious. One longed to shout, to chuck up one's hat in the
street when one got outside; anything, to show that one
was not quite a mummy, yet.[1]

Now, I could weep for those poor, silly people. After all
they were happy; the world they lived in was secure. Today this horrible thing has fallen upon them, and not for
fifty years, say those who know, can Europe recover herself
and continue her development. Was the world too 'precious,' did it need these violent realities to keep its vitality
alive? History may have something to say about that; we
who are here can only see the pity and waste of it....

The other day I was waiting on a street corner. I was going
to cross over and buy a paper. (The papers bring out new
editions all day long, and in taxis, on 'buses, walking along
the street, every one is reading a paper.) Suddenly I heard
someone shout my name, and there were Richard Aldington and F. S. Flint. They were in excellent spirits: Richard
Aldington had just been down to put his name on the roster
of those willing to enlist. Flint cannot enlist: he is already
serving his country in the Post Office, and sits all day long
in the most important and most dangerous building in the
world next to the Bank of England. It is guarded by soldiers and surrounded by bomb-nets, but London is full of
spies! I thought of the exquisite and delicate work of these
two men in the *Anthologie Des Imagistes*, and it seemed bar-
barous that war should touch them — as cruel and useless
as the shattering of a Greek vase by a cannon ball. I remembered the letters of Henri Régnault I had read, long
ago. I remembered how he gave up his studio in Algiers and
came back to fight for France, and died in the trenches.
We read of these things, but when we find ourselves standing on a street corner talking to two young poets who are
preparing to face the same experiences — Well! It is different!...

---

[1] Harold Monro protested against this paragraph very strongly, in a letter to
Miss Lowell, dated October 22, 1914; to make amends, she wrote an article
about his bookshop for the *Little Review*.

Perhaps one of the saddest evidences of a changed England is Mr. H. G. Wells's letter to Americans in *The Chronicle* of August 24th. For an Englishman to *implore* a foreign country to do or not to do anything, is new. Englishmen have not been used to beg weakly, with tears in their eyes. Whatever one may think of Mr. Wells's contention in this letter, the tone in which it is written is a lamentable evidence of panic. Panic has never been an English trait, and neither has whining servility. And the Americans are the last people in the world to be moved by it. I think Mr. Wells need not have *stooped* to ask us for justice or sympathy.

After all, it purports little to point out the spots on the sun. England is still the mother-country of most Americans, even if that was a good while ago. And we love her. She has given us not only our blood, but our civilization. Since this war broke out she has harbored us and kept her ships running for us. In Paris, one must get a permit from the police to stay or leave. In England, one is free and unmolested. England has always been the refuge of oppressed peoples. Does she need to ask our sympathy now that she is, herself, oppressed? Neutral we must be, and neutral we shall be, but we are not a military nation, and despotism can never attract us.

Every American would rather a bungling democracy than the wisest despot who ever breathed.

Soon after August 28, she sailed for home. By a coincidence, the passage she got at last was the same cabin in the same ship on which she had sailed for England in June. As soon as they arrived, Mrs. Russell left at once for Chicago, to visit her daughter, who was now Mrs. Theodore Amussen.

On September 10, Miss Lowell resumed her correspondence. Among the many things awaiting her, perhaps none pleased her more than newspaper clippings which indicated that her 'Tulip Garden,' which had been published in the August *Atlantic*, was being reprinted extensively; her 'Coal Picker' in the August *Poetry* was also

attracting attention. These were the first of her poems
to win public favor. Published copies of *Pierrot Qui
Pleure*, mailed September 3, were also on the hall table.
There was a letter from Mrs. Gale, asking her to be an
Associate of the Toy Theater for the coming season,
and suggesting that she produce a play in December or
January; Miss Lowell refused because of her operettas to
be given in February. She had the manuscripts of *Irradiations* and *Some Imagist Poets* to place, as well as
North of Boston. On September 22, the advance copies of
the finished *Sword Blades and Poppy Seed* arrived.

It is perhaps not too much to say that with the return
of Miss Lowell in 1914, the poetic scales, tipped so long
in favor of England, now tipped definitely in favor of
America. Europe had little more to offer the American
poet: the best of its culture and literary traditions had been
absorbed and were now to be used in the creation of a
transatlantic poetry. Fidelity to foreign standards no
longer was to be particularly admired. American poets no
longer were to win special acclaim by publishing first in
England. It seems a mysterious law of the universe that a
creative period in one land is counter-balanced by a destructive period elsewhere; and for once, America enjoyed
a few years of immunity while the rest of the world was
locked in a death-grapple. Be that as it may, the movement which began to flower in America of 1912 came to its
first fruits in 1914. And thereafter, the energy of Miss
Lowell dominated the scene, and provided a focus of
intellectual battle from which even those writers most
opposed to her work were to benefit.

CHAPTER XI

SWORD BLADES AND POPPY SEED

AMY LOWELL's career really began with *Sword Blades and Poppy Seed*. She was forty years old. Her ten years of writing virtually unaided had brought her as far as she could go without expert aid; her first volume *A Dome of Many-Coloured Glass*, had as it were cleared her brain; her association with Pound and the Imagists had opened her eyes and sharpened her technique; and finally we might suggest that even the schism had done its bit by making her completely independent.

Forty-four of the fifty-four titles had already appeared in magazines; only ten had been unplaced, and two of these were narratives of a length which made rejection automatic. Miss Lowell's success with the editors prognosticated the success of the book, and also prepared the public for a book which was to make quite a little sensation. But the real cause for its success was the fact that, having got the best out of Imagism, Miss Lowell used it for her own ends. Her book may be regarded as a criticism of the movement.

The Imagists preached Art for Art's Sake. Reacting against bad technique, they made technique an end in itself; reacting against undue reliance on substance, they virtually eliminated substance. Pound was fond of quoting Whistler: 'You are interested in a certain painting because it is an arrangement of lines and colours'; also Pater: 'All arts approach the condition of music.' [1] Now music is the very voice of the human will, but it is so close to the inmost reality that it uses only rhythm, melody, harmony, and timbre. It does not name things; or see, touch, smell, or taste things; tell stories; demonstrate

[1] For example in *Blast* (I, 154), June 20, 1914.

ideas; define morals. It is patterned emotion, pure and profound.

Imagistic poetry approached this state as an ideal, but in so doing, eliminated most of the fields of human endeavor from its work. Afraid of moral tags, 'human interest,' platitudes, the Imagists eliminated ethics, narrative, ideas. Even emotions were not presented directly; they were suggested through the contrast of images and the rhythm of cadence. The result was a highly wrought music, excellent in technique but limited in its effect and consequently narrow in its appeal. Consider Aldington's 'Choricos,' H. D.'s 'Oread,' Pound's 'Return'; they are lyrics, harmonic rather than melodic, rich, restrained, brief, and perfect; but they are only one effect in the whole gamut of the possibilities of poetry.

Amy Lowell, who had taken Shelley's synonym for Life as the title of her first book, and who had proclaimed therein that most of all she loved 'the very human heart of man,' was never content with these limitations. In 'Astigmatism' she had protested against Pound's narrowness of taste; to Miss Monroe she complained that he lacked 'the quality of soul, which, I am more and more fain to believe, no great work can ever be without.' Mere Imagism was literature, but not life; and the recording of life, not the evocation of music, was her purpose.

The Imagist technique she consequently welcomed as a means to an end, but never as an end in itself; and furthermore, she used it in her own way. 'A Lady,' for example, expands the typical Imagist two-line contrast of images into a two-strophe contrast between generations. But she rejected the unformulated restrictions which the Imagists tacitly imposed on themselves.

She believed that poetry was a spoken art — was communicative and not merely self-expressive — that no poem was complete until it had functioned in the mind of its audience. This belief not only saved her from the vitiating preciosity of 'Art for Art's sake,' but caused her to build her poems of genuine human material in an emotional, or dramatic, structure. Thus the Imagist monotone became varied and alive. In 'The Taxi,' the first and third sentences are dully despondent, while the second and fourth are rebellious; the poem pulsates in a rhythm of alternate despair and outcry. This feeling for emotional structure grew from her experience in theatricals, and led her to invent 'polyphonic prose.'

When in her *Tendencies* (p. 246) she boiled down the Imagist manifesto into its ultimate terms, she added 'individualistic freedom of idea' to 'simplicity and directness of speech; subtlety and beauty of rhythms;... clearness and vividness of presentation; and concentration.' Poetry should express ideas, because the poet must have something to say. His ideas, however, should not be mere theories, separable from his emotions: they should be convictions, passionate as well as intelligent.

The very title of *Sword Blades and Poppy Seed* proclaims a reaching out beyond Imagistic ends. 'Sword blades' are fighting truths; 'poppy seed,' lulling dreams. The title-poem is a fantastic tale explaining that these two, truth and beauty, are the twin functions of literature. This idea is presented in narrative form: the poet buys his swords and seeds of a strange old man ('Ephraim Bard, dealer in words'), pays as price his whole existence, and the sun rises.

This is symbolic narrative, of course — a form which Miss Lowell used many times, in this book and later. It is the standard method of presenting ideas in poetry: one needs refer only to Dante, Spenser, Milton, Blake, Keats, and Shelley as examples. Symbolism is native to America: Hawthorne and Melville used it in prose, O'Neill and Cummings in drama, and Poe in both prose and poetry.[1]

[1] I include Poe as a symbolist because it is inconceivable to me that so conscious an artist could have been wholly unconscious of what he was doing. Moreover, the elimination of the last stanza of 'Ulalume' as too revealing shows

As the critics generally have avoided the word 'symbol' in discussing Amy Lowell's work, I must intrude my own testimony that I often discussed her symbolism with her. She spoke casually of it as obvious and natural, endorsed certain interpretations, but was evasive when I could not phrase her meaning exactly and asked her to do so. That charming and seemingly naïve poem 'The Book of Hours of Sister Clothilde' had a meaning she cherished too much to explain. A young nun is illuminating a book; no color seems heavenly enough for the Virgin's robe; at last she finds it in the skin of an adder. The adder bites her, but the old gardener sucks the poison out of the wound, and she finishes her picture. Miss Lowell turned off attempts at explanation with a laugh, but she admitted that the use of a poisonous snake for the Virgin's robe was intentional, and the key to the whole meaning. The snake is, of course, an age-old symbol of sex; I now think that she meant to imply this: the glamour which robes the ideal of virginity is a deadly poison dazzling to the ignorant. But this is not the whole of the meaning: its use in art and religion is involved.

There are three more symbolic tales: 'The Great Adventure of Max Breuck,' 'Clear, with Light Variable Winds,' and 'The Shadow' — three variations on a single theme, the fatal lure of the ideal, which drives man to suicide.

Other tales in the book are pure drama, and five of them are monologues: 'The Foreigner,' which sounds like Miss Lowell's challenge to England; 'The Exeter Road,' concerning an eighteenth-century highwayman; 'After Hearing a Waltz by Bartók'; and two prayers to the Virgin, 'Sancta Maria' and 'The Forsaken.' Miss Lowell's experience in acting prevented her from writing poems for the eye alone. Her instinct in such matters was dramatic,

that he and Mrs. Whitman knew what the poem was about. I suggest also that James's *Bostonians* is a symbolic novel after the method of Hawthorne.

objective, hence perplexing to those critics who assumed that all vivid poetry was autobiography at not more than one or two removes. 'The Forsaken' has proved popular as a dramatic monologue, and is often delivered professionally.

The success of 'The Forsaken' is the more notable as it was one of the three pieces written in 'polyphonic prose,' a form invented by Miss Lowell and named by Fletcher. She described it as —

> a metre which I have taken partly from Paul Fort, partly from my inner consciousness. Paul Fort bases his verse upon the alexandrine; I have based mine upon cadence. His is almost always either perfect verse or perfect prose; mine is never either, and I have called it polyphonic because it permits the use of all the methods: cadence, rhyme, alliteration, and assonance, also perhaps true metre for a few minutes.[1]

It is the most various and supple poetic form ever devised in English. It runs without let or hindrance from one rhythm into another, according to the mood of the moment; it allows the use of any and every device known to versification, the only restriction being that 'the sound should be an echo to the sense.' Nothing quite like it had ever been known in English before.[2] The nearest approach had been the old St. Cecilia Odes, by Dryden and his followers, which, written as librettos for young composers, ran through a variety of meters, in order to bring out as many orchestral effects as possible. Miss Lowell, in her search for a form capable of the greatest versatility and expressiveness, invented polyphonic prose, and later used it for some of her most magnificent work. It is a

---

[1] Letter to Mr. Mason, of the *Yale Review*, March 16, 1915.

[2] Unless we accept as precursors Thomas Everard's *Treatise on the Sanctification of the Lord's Day*, Philadelphia, 1813, end of Part v and most of Parts vi and vii (the introduction speaks of portions as 'poetically written'); John Pennie, Jr.'s, *Orpheus and Eurydice*, Albany, 1901; and Stella George Stern Perry's charming *Go to Sleep*, New York, 1911.

difficult form, however; not many others have been able
to manage it.[1]

The three pieces of polyphonic prose in this book ('The
Basket,' 'In a Castle,' and 'The Forsaken') are three
tragedies of love, with contrasted heroines, one cold, one
adulterous, and one faithfully loving. 'The Basket' is a
symbolic puzzle which Miss Lowell always refused to explain. But again we find a man consumed by a passion
which is inadequately returned; art and religion are elements in the affair; the conflagration is the familiar disaster; and the moon with geranium eyes at the end is
again the sterile, unresponsive, maddening symbol. 'In
a Castle' is a tale of Gothic crime ending in murder and
suicide. 'The Forsaken' is the prayer of a girl who has
been callously abandoned.

As with the narratives, most of the lyrics in the book
are conventional in form — indeed, just about three-
quarters of the book, counting by pages, is metrical. The
best lyrics, however, are those in free verse. 'A Lady'
and 'The Taxi' proved by all odds the most popular of the
volume. 'The Captured Goddess,' which opened the first
section of the book, gives the first evidence of that fresh
delight in pure color which later was to blind so many
critics to the solider qualities of her work. 'The Precinct,
Rochester,' another poem about religion, describes its
peaceful existence on the basis of undisturbed tradition,
although the hungry living, in their discontent, are honey-
combing the foundations. 'A London Thoroughfare' was
surely written on that night in the Piccadilly hotel when
she read *North of Boston* for the first time.

'Astigmatism' is her official statement of the quarrel
with Pound. It says nothing of the immediate causes for

[1] John Gould Fletcher's 'Chicago' (dated December 30, 1914) appeared in
the *Egoist* (II, 5), May 1, 1915; his 'Clipper Ships' is another fine example.
Beyond his work I can name only John Wheelwright's *North Atlantic Passage*,
Florence, 1923, and the opening chapter of William Fitzgerald, Jr.'s, *Gentlemen
All*, New York, 1930.

the break, but deals with the deeper dissension. It reads simply enough: 'the Poet' has made a marvellous cane with which he destroys all flowers that are not roses. But the implications and applications go far beyond August, 1914, for in this poem Miss Lowell defends what Dewey names the 'Naturalistic School' of literature (which takes all life as its substance) against the merely Decorative school; she also attacks whatever poet would set up his own literary ideals as exclusive dogma for other poets. The Poet's cane, though exquisitely perfected, is dead in itself and death to the flowers. It is merely an archaic adjunct to his personality. With it he destroys both wild and cultivated flowers because they are not the roses already consecrated, and aesthetically exhausted, by other poets. Miss Lowell was doubtless botanist enough to know, moreover, that roses are something of a monstrosity: their multiplied petals are aborted anthers, vital organs sterilized. 'Peace be with you, Brother. But behind you is destruction and waste places.'

Of the shorter metrical poems there is comparatively little to say. 'A Tulip Garden,' the last in the book, was frequently reprinted; it was inspired by Mrs. Bayard Thayer's magnificent garden at Lancaster, Massachusetts. 'The Coal Picker,' which proved its runner-up in immediate success, was really a transitional poem. It is based on the conviction that beauty is in all things, and that the artist's problem is to find and record beauty hitherto unrecognized. But the beauty she professes to find in the coal heap is not the authentic, indigenous significance that alone can make it aesthetically significant; it is rather the importation of peacock eyes and topaz urns, after the manner of the *Symbolistes.* As a symbol of the poet's labors, the poem has significance; as a character study of a coal grubber, it is false. Huysmans no doubt is to blame. None the less, it was cleverly fashionable; and her smart contrast between dingy reality and the beauty of dreams was to become the literary method of Eliot's *Waste-Lands*. 'A Blockhead' and 'Stupidity' are early poems, interesting only because the first drafts still exist, on the end-papers of a copy of Knoblauch's *Kismet* (1911). 'Cyclists' was written when she was in England in 1913. Automobiles had already made bicycles so scarce in America that their universal use abroad impressed Americans as characteristically foreign. England had depressed her somewhat; her poem is a record of what she took to be its decadence. Later she was to express a regret that she had included it.

The brief preface to the volume answered the questions which people were already beginning to ask. Miss Lowell never was an obscurantist, at least as regards technique: she always told the public what she was trying to do, and thus gave it a chance to judge her by her own standards. After attacking the two vulgar errors that poets need no training and that poems must end with moral tags, she acknowledged her indebtedness to France. She then said that the poet 'must constantly find new and striking images'; defined *vers libre*, or 'unrhymed cadence,' as she preferred to call it; spoke of her polyphonic prose as 'a fluid and changing form, now prose, now verse, and permitting a great variety of treatment'; mentioned her attempts in meter; then wrote this memorable sentence: 'Schools are for those who can confine themselves within them.' The poems were then left to speak for themselves.

And they spoke; the book made quite a stir; everywhere critics responded to the vitality of the rhythms and the colors. Josephine Preston Peabody, with her signed review in the *Boston Sunday Herald*, October 11, 1914, was the first in the field; among others that followed were Ella Wheeler Wilcox (*Boston American*, November 2), Richard Aldington (*Egoist*, November 16), William Stanley Braithwaite (*Boston Transcript*, November 28), Harriet Monroe (*Poetry*, December), Margaret Anderson

(*Little Review*, December), Arthur Davidson Ficke (*Dial*, January 1, 1915), Richard Le Gallienne (*New York Times*, January 10), Magdelaine Carret (*Little Review*, February), Zoë Akins (*Reedy's Mirror*, March 12, 19), William Aspinwall Bradley (*Bookman*, April), H. L. Mencken (*Smart Set*, May), Richard M. Hunt (*Poetry Journal*, June), Herbert S. Gorham (*Springfield Morning Union*, August 15), and William Dean Howells (*Harpers*, September). There were, of course, many unsigned reviews as well. But most gratifying of all was a letter from Thomas Hardy.

> Max Gate,
> Dorchester
> 6 Dec. 1914

My dear Miss Lowell:

We were so glad to hear that you & Mrs. Russell got back home so smoothly & comfortably. We talked of you frequently before you wrote, & wondered if you grew more uncomfortable as the noise of war waxed louder. It is evident now that you did not. The car, too: I hope its adventures were as mild as your own.

I fear I am late in thanking you for your kind gift of 'Sword Blades & Poppy Seed' my correspondence having become fitful by the incidence upon all our lives here of this hideous European tragedy, the sinister feature of which is the barbarousness of the German methods, which seem to put the clock of civilization centuries back. It does not express the German nation at all, as I have imagined that people, who seem to be the victims of an unscrupulous military oligarchy. The whole thing is a mystery to thoughtful Englishmen.

However: of the poems I like those called 'Music' & 'A Lady.' The Browningesque tragedies 'The Foreigner' & 'After hearing a Waltz' are arresting: the latter holds one from the first syllable to the last, & the metre & rhythm keep up the beat of the waltz admirably. This piece reminds me to say that, but for the difference of sex, critics might be asking you when you committed the murder —

that is, if they are such geese as some of them are here, who in my case devoutly believe that everything written in the first person has been done personally.

I also like 'The Captured Goddess,' 'The Tree of Scarlet Berries,' & 'Clear with Light.' Whether I should have liked them still better rhymed, I do not know.

The subject of 'The Book of Hours' seems to me (I may not be right) somewhat too slight to support a poem of that length — charming fancy as it is — & would have had increased beauty if shorter.

But you will not require any criticism from me, even if I could make it real & well-balanced, which I cannot.

We trust that you feel by this time no sort of inconvenience from the accident at the hotel. My wife sends her kindest regards, & unites with me in wishing you & Mrs. Russell a happy Christmas.

Sincerely yours
Thomas Hardy

The publishers had been so sure of the book's success that they printed fifteen hundred copies instead of a thousand for the first edition. Five hundred were sold in America before Christmas; but by spring, only four had sold in England.

CHAPTER XII

THE OPENING OF THE POETIC WAR

'... *proof of the re-creative energy of the poetic impulse...*'

THE success of *Sword Blades and Poppy Seed* determined the rest of Miss Lowell's life. At last she had found her career; henceforth she was free to do as she pleased and make her own friends. Boston might now go hang — and not until the poetry of Amy Lowell was being taught in the colleges did Boston society come to understand that she was really something to boast of, not to blush for. But in the fall of 1914, 'poor Amy Lowell' had merely taken up another freak, and was going about it with her characteristic over-emphasis. She had just got out another book; there were some quite peculiar things in it, including love-poetry; and they were very sorry for her.

And presently the city was afloat with tales of how Miss Lowell still lived in her old room on the top floor of Sevenels, where she made her own enormous bed with sixteen pillows, because no servant would pull the sheets taut enough; how she wrote all night and slept till three in the afternoon; how the mirrors and all other bright things in the bedroom were shrouded with black; how one afternoon she had been seen in bed smoking a hookah and writing under an umbrella to keep the sun off; how she kept two secretaries busy typing the manuscripts they found awaiting them in the morning.

These tales, of the many, were true. Sevenels was as silent and motionless as an enchanted castle until her bell rang; then it magically came to life — the gardener began to garden, the cook to cook, the typewriters to click, and the servants to scurry. Mrs. Russell made it possible for Miss Lowell to devote her entire time to writing. It was Mrs. Russell who preserved the morning silence, quelled kitchen quarrels, got books from libraries, did bits of research, read proofs, and even informed guests they must leave when they were intruding on a creative period. In the evenings she criticized the latest poems; she listened to every composition before it was pronounced finished, standing proxy for the public; and so well did she act as comrade in art that Miss Lowell once suggested they put out a sign: 'Lowell & Russell, Makers of Fine Poems.'

While the rumors about her strange life were being relayed outward through the city, from the confidences of a few old friends, into the absurdities demanded by a public whose appetite had already been whetted by the gossip about Mrs. Jack Gardner, Miss Lowell was quietly cultivating the acquaintance of most of the intelligence of America. Ability to write, or even a hearty interest in modern poetry, was good for at least one meal. Her guests, if they did not command an automobile, took the blue Chestnut Hill car, and got off past the reservoir at Heath Street, then walked up the curving road to the left, till they reached the third entrance, where a sign uttered its warning: 'Motors be careful not to run over the dogs.' There they found a man waiting, who walked behind them and spoke to the sheepdogs, who came bounding ferociously through the trees of the park. Presently they saw the house, with the Genoese statue of Flora above the doorway. When they were admitted, they were shown into the stiff yellow reception-room on the right, where they admired the Monet over the mantel, or Joseph Lindon Smith's Egyptian watercolors, until the maid handed them the *Transcript*. There were no ashtrays. They were invited for seven (later, for seven-thirty), but not until eight o'clock did Mrs. Russell enter and lead the guests into the dining-room. Only people who had never

THE WAY TO SEVENELS

A card enclosed with invitations

been there before suggested: 'Shan't we wait for Miss Lowell?'

The dinner was an old-fashioned one, with oysters, soup, fish, meat, salad, dessert, and fruit, accompanied (until Prohibition) with the appropriate wines. At some point in the meal (usually after the roast had been removed) footsteps and a voice were heard; the seven sheepdogs began barking; and while all the men rose, Miss Lowell made her hearty entrance. The dogs obediently charged in the doorway, never venturing beyond the sill; hands were shaken; then the meal continued, while the vanished courses reappeared, miraculously fresh, for Miss Lowell's consumption. Although she usually had two plates of soup and was always the center of the conversation, the dessert was served to all simultaneously. Then, after peppermints and ginger were passed, the party proceeded into the geniality of the library.

Before all were settled, a certain ritual was gone through. On the lamp shades Miss Lowell hung, in a particular order, the light-shields (silhouettes of children playing in enormous flowers and twigs, by Lucy Morse). Then with pitch-pine splinters, Miss Lowell lighted the fire of four-foot logs, split to four-inch diameter (split thus so that during the night she could replenish the fire without aid). Cigars and cigarettes were produced; coffee and liqueurs were passed. Presently she was settled with her cigar in the corner of the sofa to the right of the fireplace, with feet tucked up under her. A maid furnished each guest with a huge towel for his lap, as the sheepdogs, who had sounded so vicious in the park, were now very affectionate. Glasses of water were set round. And the conversation was resumed.

The flavor of those conversations can never be communicated. Carl Sandburg had them in mind when he called Miss Lowell 'a bright blue wave.' She could talk brilliantly on any subject. Her tale might be nothing at all — how a bird was building a nest in her portico; or how she would direct traffic if she were a traffic cop; or how the police discovered that the mysterious footfalls in her park before dawn were made by the milkman called in because her cow was out of sorts — but whatever it was, the company was kept in gales of helpless laughter. Yet nobody ever felt that she monopolized the conversation, for she made an excellent listener. Whatever a person's chief interest, she was eager to learn all about it; whether bayonet-drill, or the construction of light-houses, or aviation, she asked questions and ventured opinions until she was satisfied she had mastered the essentials for herself. Meanwhile her informant heard himself talking more brilliantly than he had ever talked before. If her opinions were on matters within her own ken, she retained them stubbornly at times, and enjoyed a hot skirmish. But the heat always vanished immediately when the subject was changed; she could not possibly resent honest difference of opinion. On one occasion, after her 'Memorandum Confided by a Yucca to a Passion Vine' had just appeared in the *Bookman*, a guest suggested that guinea-pigs had no tails to waggle, as her text demanded. Since no guinea-pig was at hand to settle the matter, the dispute went on for half an hour or so, neither side yielding. But a couple of weeks later, she told the same guest with great amusement of her mistake, which she had caught just before the book went to press. She had forgotten completely that it was he, and not she, who had discovered it.

Extremely kind-hearted though she was, there was one thing she really disliked: insincerity or affectation of any sort. Poets often acquire poses in self-defence; and it was miraculous how she could pierce through those falsities to whatever was genuine underneath. She talked with such sympathy and intelligence about their work, or about poetry in general, that they forgot their attitudinizing completely. They read their poems to her, quarrelled maybe with her criticisms (she felt her efforts were wasted if they acquiesced politely), and went away with a strange feeling of exhilaration.

If, however, there was nothing underneath — if the person were merely playing at being a poet, without any real instinct for writing; or if he had not even that pretension, but was interested only in the customary trifles of conversation — then Miss Lowell might make a bitter enemy. People without personality hate big personalities. The literary pretender felt as though his very existence were threatened by a blast furnace or a steam roller. The society person simply heard a loud voice talking very fast about things beyond his range, and felt as though he were snubbed. And these people, whether men or women, after being silenced by her presence, became loudly hostile behind her back.

I must insert here the testimony of two women, not writers, concerning the effect of Miss Lowell's presence. The first was a southern lady who had met Miss Lowell at her Richmond lecture; a year or so later, very tired nervously, and on her way to Maine to recuperate, she had hesitatingly called her on the telephone, was invited to dinner, and talked till past three in the morning. 'Her conversation was a tonic for a year,' she said later; 'a tonic — not a stimulant. She put me right; she readjusted everything to its normal relationships.' The relief of the nervous tension was remarkable. 'Her conversation was a personal interest expressed in an impersonal method,' for she always kept her friendships on an intellectual basis. She was genuinely interested in everything, had 'a prodigal generosity of intellect,' was 'greedy for life.' 'She never missed a trick or nuance in conversation; under the exhilaration one found oneself being brilliant.' 'She never descended to you; she always lifted you up to her level.' She had 'a constant supply of gaiety and gusto,' which broke forth in 'her flashing smile.'

The other testimony came from a married lady from Rhode Island, who during a pregnancy had gone out to Sevenels one hot afternoon to call on Mrs. Ayscough. Mrs. Ayscough was not in, and her friend was turning away from the door when Miss Lowell, who had been listening in the library, appeared. 'You can't go away like this; come in and rest for awhile.' She made her comfortable on a sofa, got her a cooling drink, created no fuss, said something about 'what you are doing is far more important than anything I do,' and let her rest. 'She really did and said very little, but somehow I have seldom been impressed with such thorough thoughtfulness and sympathy.'

But at Sevenels in the evenings, conversation never lagged. Sparks sprang from the fireplace upon the rugs; men sprang from their chairs to kick the embers back. The maid might appear to explain that something was wrong with the furnace or the icechest, and Miss Lowell would disappear to fix it herself. When she returned, she would ask for another cigar, direct that three logs be put on the fire, and then make a marvellous tale out of her struggles behind the scenes. At eleven, Mrs. Russell would slip away unobtrusively, usually while the maid was putting a cold supper on a table nearby, to sustain the poet later in the night. The last car for Boston reached Heath Street at 12:15; nobody was ever allowed to rise until the Cromwell clock on the mantel pointed to 12:05. Then Miss Lowell accompanied the guests to the front door, continuing the conversation to the last minute, though without protracting the departure; and as they walked down the drive, they could hear her putting the chain latch on the front door. Dinner calls were ruled out.

Now the hostess became the poet, settling down to work in the deep leather arm-chair before the fire. She braced her footstool with a long piece of firewood that rested against an andiron. She wrote on a blotting-pad propped against a long narrow table made especially for her; she used pencils which she had sharpened herself to remarkably fine points; her favorite paper was called 'cameo sepia block.' The floor was the waste-basket; whatever was found there in the morning was burned. When she retired, she left the involved manuscripts on a table in the hall, for the secretaries to decipher and type before the next evening; then she worked on these second drafts. All drafts of each poem were always destroyed, although once a group of second drafts was rescued by a daring secretary — they are now in the Harvard library. Miss Lowell worked till dawn, and often later; sometimes she prolonged the work just to get a nip of the coffee and toast prepared for the breakfast of other members of the household. Then she was as leisurely about going to bed as she was about rising, or dressing for a dinner-party. There was no hurrying her; she would pick up a shoe, and be found still holding it a quarter of an hour later, although the automobile was waiting and they would be late.

Miss Lowell was not the first writer to find the night held better working-hours. With no dance of sunny leaves at the window, with none of the noises of the household or the world outside, no ringing telephones, no distractions or interruptions, in complete silence and darkness, except for the circle of lamplight, a perfect concentration was possible. And in going direct from the desk to the bed, the creative thoughts were free to continue; one need not dream to wake with the next page written, the next chapter already planned.

But there were other things to be done besides writing poems. Among the letters from the European literati was one from Lawrence.

The Triangle
Bellingdon Lane
Chesham
Bucks
18 Sept. 1914

DEAR MISS LOWELL,

I suppose by now you are at home with your dogs & your manuscripts. Here it is raining, & the apples blown down lie almost like green lights in the grass. Kennst du das Land, wo die Citronen blühen? Yes, so do I. But now I hear the rain-water trickling animatedly into the green and rotten water-butt.

Will you send me the poems of mine that you think of including in the anthology, so that I can go over them and make any improvements I am capable of.

You won't forget to go to Mitchell Kennerley for me, will you?... Tell him how the hollow of his silence gets bigger & bigger, till he becomes almost a myth. Ask him if he received the MS. of my novel.[1] And I kiss your hand, dear Miss Lowell, for being so good to me.

We are likely to stay in this cottage till I am a silvery haired old gentleman going round patting the curly polls of the cottage toddlers. Nobody will pay me any money, and nobody is good to me, and already the robins are brightening to sing, and the holly berries on the hedges are getting redder. Ahimé — ahimé! It's winter, and the wooden gate is black and sodden in the rain above the raw, cold puddles. Ahimé once more. Im dunklen Laub die Gold Orangen Glühn. Give our very warm regards to your friend, & to you

tante belle cose
D. H. LAWRENCE.

My wife sends her love to you.

We've made some first rate blackberry jelly. That's my nearest approach to poetry here.

Miss Lowell wrote at once to Harriet Monroe, on September 26:

[1] [*The Rainbow*.]

. . .

By the way, I am going to say something which must be quite 'entre nous.' I had a letter from D. H. Lawrence this morning. The poor fellow is unable to get back to his little house in Italy, on account of the war, and they are living in a little workman's cottage out in the country. You can imagine the kind when I tell you that the rent is six shillings a month. I understand that Lawrence has consumption, the cottage is very damp, and must be horribly cold.... The letter that I had this morning was a very sad one. It was simply asking me to return him the poems that had been accepted for the anthology, so that he could go over them again, but he could not keep his depression from creeping into the letter. The amount of it is, he is horribly poor, and of course he would not accept charity, but he happened to tell me in the course of conversation that you had accepted another batch of his poems, and it occurred to me that you could publish those poems very soon and send him the money. It may enable him to leave his damp cottage now that the winter is coming on, and go to London, where at least he can keep warm, and his health will be safe-guarded. I have racked my brains to think what I can do for him that he would take, and the only thing I can think of is to send him a typewriter which I am discarding, as I can make this appear that it is of no use to me, and he might just as well have it. He has not even been able to afford to buy a typewriter, which handicaps him very much in his work, as it is expensive to have typewriting done....

The typewriter reached him duly, by means of the chief steward of the Laconia, who was bidden call and get it, then ship it from Liverpool. She also tried (in vain) to persuade the *Atlantic Monthly* to publish something of Lawrence's. On October 16, he wrote her of his delight over the coming typewriter. He had just got a cheque of £50 from the Royal Literary Fund.

We have had a beautiful dim autumn, of pale blue atmosphere & white stubble and hedges hesitating to change. But I've been seedy, and I've grown a red beard, behind which I shall take as much cover henceforth as I can, like a creature under a bush. My dear God, I've been miserable this autumn, enough to turn into wood, and be a graven image of myself.

I wish myself we could come in and drink wine and laugh with you, and hear some of other people's music. When I'm rich I shall come to America....

Meanwhile, on the morning of October 5, she saw an advertisement of *Sword Blades and Poppy Seed*, which startled her so much that she cabled Aldington at once, and then wrote a letter of protest to Macmillan's. The text had described her as 'the foremost member of the Imagists, a group of poets that includes William Butler Yeats, Ezra Pound, Ford Madox Hueffer.' The omissions were as sweeping as the inclusions. Pound's letters to her and to her publisher were vivid.

On the sixteenth, she got off a review of Robinson's new book, *Van Zorn*, to the *Boston Herald*, and that evening had the first Gebhard concert of the season.

On the twentieth, she went to New York, putting up at the Hotel St. Regis. It was a business trip: her particular objects were to try and arrange for the publication of the *Some Imagist Poets*, and to see Mitchell Kennerley about D. H. Lawrence's affairs. She probably took Fletcher's *Irradiations* and Frost's *North of Boston* with her. Her only success was her effort in behalf of Lawrence, and that proved only apparent.

When she returned, not only Pound's letters were awaiting her, but there was an attack by Ella Wheeler Wilcox in the *Boston American* to be answered, and a very indignant letter from Harold Monro, protesting against her description of Rupert Brooke's reading at the Poetry Book Shop, also a letter from Aldington telling her that Rémy de Gourmont was virtually ruined by the war.

And all the while, besides trying to sell poems of her friends as well as her own, and get the presentation and review copies of her book sent off to the proper people, and correcting proof, she was kept very busy arranging for the production in February of *Pierrot Qui Pleure.* But though she was tired, and furthermore suffering from ptomaine poisoning, she continued her correspondence.

Nov. 2, 1914

MY DEAR MR. MUNRO:

I am exceedingly sorry that that paragraph in my 'London Letter' in 'The Little Review' should have so seriously hurt your feelings, but indeed I am guiltless of feeling any of the severe and unpleasant things which you seemed to think in your letter. The paragraph was more poking fun at the reading than intended as a serious judgment.... I am deeply in sympathy with the Poetry Book Shop. I know that you are honest, absolutely sincere, hard working, faithful, and of an idealism which takes a practical form which all idealism should [take] to be valuable.... I am more than anxious to repair my blunder over my own signature and I am writing to Miss Anderson, the editor of 'The Little Review,' by this mail to ask permission to put in an article entirely upon the Poetry Book Shop. If you will send me whatever data or any notes on its history and beginnings which you would like included I assure you you will have as handsome a tribute from my pen as my admiration and sympathy for your work deserves....

I think it a mistake to object to criticism.... You criticized me very severely in an article upon American poetry last year, but I did not write and upbraid you; I did not even resent the criticism. I ask only for honesty and unprejudiced treatment, but I do ask for that.

I sincerely regret the rift which exists between England and America. I do not know why it is so hard for us to take each other simply and justly. I do not know why England is as a rule so anxious to welcome expatriated Americans and so down upon those of us who feel that it is our duty to our country to remain at home. The Englishman is a very patriotic person. Many of us over here are only Englishmen a few degrees removed. I love my country, Mr. Munro, I love yours as one might a grandmother, but I feel it my duty to stay at home and it is because I am at home that I have met with such unjust treatment. This I am not saying in public but personally to you because I think that your magazine might be big enough to heal something of the perpetual misunderstanding which exists between our two countries....

November 3rd, 1914

MY DEAR MR. POUND:

I am exceedingly sorry for this advertisement. It is, of course, quite ridiculous and the fact that I am put down as 'foremost member' was undoubtedly due to an underling's error in the office. I told Macmillan last spring that the inclusion of these two names was foolish, as neither Yeats nor Hueffer were Imagistes, and I supposed that the matter was settled. Imagine my feelings when I came home and found these names printed on the jackets. But indeed you have lived so long out of America that you seem to have forgotten American methods of advertising. The names were simply put in to boom the book, a thing which is constantly done over here and would not in any way surprise anyone in this country. The ludicrous thing is that in my preface I have carefully said that I do not belong to any school....

As to my being put down as an Imagiste, you yourself are responsible for that. If you publish an 'Anthology des Imagistes' and include a person's work in it, naturally the publishers consider that that person belongs to that group. You will remember that I wrote you last winter and told you that if yours was to be an Imagiste anthology I did not think I belonged in it. You never took the trouble to answer my letter, and the next thing I knew was that I saw my name in the advance advertisement which appeared in the New York Times. Having been given the name of Imagiste I shall certainly not repudiate it. One of the foremost members I certainly am, for the amount that I have published and the attention it has attracted I think warrants my being considered in that category. You have only yourself to thank for including me in this group, and it is not agreeable to feel that you only wished the inclusion as long as I could be kept obscure and insignificant....

As to your suggestion that the publishers be sued for libel, you have of course no suit, as even in cement and soap you would have to get out a patent in order to sue anyone. So far as I know you have not copyrighted the name 'Imagiste,' I never heard of a school of poetry being copyrighted, I doubt if it could be done. But if you should feel inclined to sue, I should be exceedingly delighted as then they would put new jackets on the book which I should greatly prefer. Also, it would be a good advertisement. And, in the third place, you would be obliged to prove my inclusion in your group as a libel, and it would be interesting to see whether that could be done.

I do think it is a mistake to take such an unimportant thing so seriously, and I think it is a wrong attitude to take towards me when I have already expressed my regret and have been doing all in my power to suppress the advertisement which I object to as much as you do.

Very sincerely yours

She next tried to do something for Rémy de Gourmont. Aldington had sent him some money as payment for translations he had made from Gourmont's French, was hoping to sell more translations in America, and was trying to get a poem to be submitted to *Poetry*. He had suggested that Miss Lowell back him up with Harriet, get Gourmont some newspaper job as Parisian correspondent, and advance him say two hundred dollars on some shares in the Anglo-Egyptian Land Bank.

Miss Lowell admired Gourmont, though not with Aldington's devotion; on November 6 she sent him $200 anonymously, as a gift.

I do not want his Anglo-Indian Land Bank shares. I do not suppose they are of any particular value and even if they were I do not want to deprive him of them. This seems a very little sum to pay for all the inspiration and knowledge

I have derived from his writings. Through him I can pay
for a little of my immense debt to his nation. Will you therefore transmit it to him with any sort of message which you
think will make it easy for him to accept it.

On November 11, she wrote, announcing that she had
got him the job.

MY DEAR RICHARD:

I have got an offer for Remy de Gourmont. I do not think
it a very brilliant one, but it seems probably the best that
can be done. It is from a new weekly, 'The New Republic,'
which Ezra pitched into so under a pseudonym in the last
'Egoist' I received....

They would like Monsieur de Gourmont to write them
six articles on present conditions in France of fifteen hundred words each at two cents a word. This only makes
thirty dollars an article which he may very probably scorn,
but that is the offer. They also think that they may want
more than six articles but they only guarantee him six to
start with.

I think I told you in my last letter that 'The Atlantic'
did not want them. The illustrated magazines are of course
quite out of the question.... If you do not hear by cable
before this letter reaches you, it will mean that this is the
best I could do.

Now take hold of a table or grasp the arms of your chair
firmly or something, for I know what I am going to tell you
will make you boil with rage. 'The New Republic' is not
'The Egoist,' and I think their 'no taboos' refers to political articles, for they have their way to make in the world,
and they stipulate that these articles shall contain nothing
too French for their American readers. I do not think that
they mean this in the very narrow sense of the word, but
rather that somebody has told the editor that Monsieur de
Gourmont's books are 'very French,' and he has got cold
feet a little on the subject. I have told him that on the subject upon which Monsieur de Gourmont was to write for
them I doubted if there could be anything which they would
consider unadvisable to publish, but have also agreed that

if any such thing does appear it should be deleted in the translation. This may strike you as backsliding on my part. It is my earnest desire to get Monsieur de Gourmont the money for the articles and what you and I both feel is that art should be unshackled, but in a matter of such small importance I doubt whether it is wise to consider it an artistic God. Rather let us consider that Monsieur de Gourmont will gain a wider audience and a few more dollars by submitting to their terms, and also I do not think that the terms need be considered to exclude anything except the most extreme Gallicisms.

I have also promised them that the articles shall reach them translated without extra charge to them.... Now if you are too busy to make these translations for nothing I shall be very glad to do it myself.... If you prefer to take part of this sum and pay yourself for the translation, that would certainly be quite legitimate, and I will leave the matter in your hands. My offer to make the translation myself is merely a suggestion in case you are too overworked to do it, as I am up to my eyes in work now. These French lectures are almost killing me,[1] and I have got another long poem on the stocks, but I should be delighted to do that or anything else to help Monsieur de Gourmont in any way possible....

Presently the *Egoist* was feeling the pinch, and offered to let her edit the literary part of the paper (i.e., the whole thing, except the leading article) for £300 a year; but Miss Lowell refused. She wanted a magazine, but it would have to be within reach of the telephone at least.

Then another letter from Lawrence arrived:

18 Nov. 1914

DEAR AMY LOWELL:

The type-writer has come, and is splendid. Why did you give it away? I am sure you must have wanted to keep it. But it goes like a bubbling pot, frightfully jolly. My wife

[1] The 'French lectures' were to be delivered in Lent, 1915; they were later revised and published as *Six French Poets*.

sits at it fascinated, patiently spelling out, at this moment, my war poem.

Oh — the War Number of 'Poetry' came — I thought it pretty bad. The war-atmosphere has blackened here — it is soaking in, and getting more like part of our daily life, and therefore much grimmer. So I was quite cross with you for writing about bohemian glass and stalks of flame, when the thing is so ugly and bitter to the soul.

I like *you* in your poetry. I don't believe in affecting France. I like you when you are straight out. I really liked very much the Precinct, Rochester. There you had a sunny, vivid, intensely still atmosphere that was very true. I don't like your first long poem a bit. I think 'A Taxi' is very clever and futuristic — and good. I like the one about the dog looking [in] the window — good.

Why don't you always be yourself. Why go to France or anywhere else for your inspiration. If it doesn't come out of your own heart, real Amy Lowell, it is no good, however many colours it may have. I wish one saw more of your genuine strong, sound self in this book, full of common sense & kindness and the restrained, almost bitter, Puritan passion. Why do you deny the bitterness in your nature, when you write poetry? Why do you take a pose? It causes you always to shirk your issues, and find a banal resolution at the end. So your romances are spoiled. When you are full of your own strong gusto of things, real old English strong gusto it is, like those tulips, then I like you very much. But you shouldn't compare the sun to the yolk of an egg, except playfully. And you shouldn't spoil your story-poems with a sort of vulgar, artificial 'flourish of ink.' If you had followed the real tragedy of your man, or woman, it had been something.

I suppose you think me damned impertinent. But I hate to see you posturing, when there is thereby a real person betrayed in you.

Please don't be angry with what I say. Perhaps it really is impertinence.

At any rate, thank you very much for your book of poems, which I like because after all they have a lot of you in them

— but how much nicer, finer, bigger you are, intrinsically, than your poetry is. Thank you also very much for the beautiful typewriter, with which both myself and my wife are for the present bewitched.

We are still staying on here — scarcely find it possible to move. It is cold, as you predict, but I think quite healthy. I am well, and Frieda is well. I am just finishing a book, supposed to be on Thomas Hardy, but in reality a sort of Confessions of my Heart. I wonder if ever it will come out — & what you'd say to it.

I wonder if you saw Mitchell Kennerley. Pinker, the agent, is always worrying me about what he is to do with the American publishing of the novel Kennerley holds at present, in MS. Tell me if you saw him, will you.

We are not so sad any more: it was perhaps a mood, brought on by the War, and the English autumn. Now the days are brief but very beautiful: a big red sun rising and setting upon a pale, bluish, hoar-frost world. It is very beautiful. The robin comes on to the door-step now, and watches me as I write. Soon he will come indoors. Then it will be mid-winter.

I wish the War were over and gone. I will not give in to it. We who shall live after it are more important than those who fall.

Give our very warm regards to Mrs. Russell

Saluti di cuore

D. H. LAWRENCE

Tante belle cose from my wife to you and to Mrs. Russell.

Meanwhile she not only had converted Houghton Mifflin Company to faith in the poetic Renaissance; she persuaded them to issue a 'New Poetry Series.' The difficulty to be overcome lay in the cost; she proposed getting the books out in the French fashion, with paper covers to save the expense of binding; they compromised on cardboard. Her Imagist anthology and Fletcher's *Irradiations* were accepted at once.[1]

[1] Eight volumes of the 'New Poetry Series' were published in 1915; nine in 1916; and one (the last Imagist anthology) in 1917.

That accomplished, on November 30, she went to New York for the Brevoort House dinner given to Jessie Rittenhouse. Fletcher was passing through the city; she dined with him on December 1, and returned to Boston the next day, after persuading him to visit her for a week.

In December, she gave her first public reading. Her poetry was addressed to the ear, and nobody could read it so well as herself. The time had come to make the world listen.

She allowed herself, therefore, to be persuaded by Josephine Peabody to join her in a recital at Steinert Hall, for the relief of the Belgians, on December 17, with Hans Ebell, a young Russian, as pianist. Miss Lowell was placed first on the program; she read fourteen of her poems, grouped as 'Narratives and Adventures,' 'Lyrics,' 'Images,' and 'War Poems.' Her final effort was 'The Bombardment.' As she feared her voice was not strong enough to carry the 'booms,' Carl Engel reproduced the cannon on a bass drum behind the scenes at the proper points. The audience of some four hundred applauded warmly, and Josephine Peabody, although it must have been difficult for her to read her delicate lyrics after what Miss Lowell termed 'this holocaust of noise and terror,' gave her unstinted praise.

Her next appearance in public followed soon after. At a luncheon of the Twentieth Century Club, on December 26, Robert Haven Schauffler and she discussed 'The Failure of American Poetry and its Remedy.' Schauffler (who had recently scored quite a hit with his 'Scum o' the Earth,' a poem which claimed that the immigration of foreign bloods was rejuvenating the American stock) declared that our poetry was being ruined by the drudgery of money-making, and suggested that our poets be subsidized. Miss Lowell, however, denied that American poetry had failed, and was dubious about his remedy. She admitted the economic difficulty; on the other hand, she thought that some work was good for poets. 'There is more danger of pampering weaklings than of breaking great men,' was one ringing sentence caught by a reporter. However, she agreed with him that the attitude of the public was 'simply abominable.' When the discussion was over, English folk songs were sung.

While the last arrangements for publishing *Some Imagist Poets* were being made, trouble loomed again. Pound, who did not know that Macmillan (perhaps because of his letter, Miss Lowell thought) had rejected the anthology, had written an article attacking that publishing house for the *Egoist*, which Aldington stopped only by threatening to resign. Hueffer (now out of it) thought that the best way to prevent future trouble was to drop the name 'Imagist'; Flint agreed; Aldington suggested 'Some Twentieth Century Poets,' and H. D., 'The Six.' Miss Lowell was uncertain what to do.

While that matter was still unsettled, the Gourmont articles for the *New Republic* began to cause a commotion. Gourmont had gratefully offered to send the rich Bostonian an inscribed book; Aldington suggested that he might like to present something to the collection of manuscripts she was making for posterity; and Gourmont planned to send her the only complete manuscript he had — that of the *Nuit au Luxembourg*, with an inscription. But as he was too ill to leave his room, he could not get it off. Meanwhile the six articles had to be written, and the poor man, ill and exhausted, forced himself to pen weary page upon page. As soon as Aldington received them, he translated them (his honorarium being fifteen shillings) and sent them to Miss Lowell.

The first article reached her shortly before Christmas. Gourmont's boredom was all too apparent. On the twenty-second she wrote Mr. Herbert Croly:

> I enclose the first of Remy de Gourmont's articles for the 'New Republic.' I confess that I am disappointed in it.

Richard Aldington told him that we didn't want anything
particularly Gallic; and all Frenchmen, when this restriction is made, are incapable of writing upon anything, no
matter how remote, with ease.

If this article does not meet with your desires, you can
send it back to me, and I will forward it, telling them that
it is a little too simple and childish for our needs. I fear
he regards Americans as in the kindergarten class, and is
writing down to his supposed idea of them, for anything less
like his usual form I have never read....

Mr. Aldington encloses a paper on de Gourmont which
he thought you might like to publish with the first of these
articles, explaining to the American public something about
Remy de Gourmont. I enclose it for your consideration,
thinking that you probably will wish to use it. In printing
the article by de Gourmont, would you please add that it is
translated by Richard Aldington?...

On the twenty-fourth she wrote to Aldington:

Now let me thank you very much for the two letters of
Remy de Gourmont which you sent me. I shall be delighted
to have one of his volumes with a dedication, and even more
delighted if I might have some of his manuscripts, as you
suggest.[1] What would please me more than anything else,
but what I feel would now be impossible, would be to have
you send him a copy of my book and get him to honestly
tell me what he thinks of it. But I am afraid that is un-
feasible: In the first place, because he might not be willing
to be brutally honest to me under the circumstances, and
also because I fear he is too ill to turn his mind to such a

---

[1] Aldington stated, in the Introduction to his *Remy de Gourmont: Selections
from All His Works*, Chicago, 1928 (1, 7): 'I cannot think that two hundred
dollars was a high price to pay for the complete manuscript of *Une Nuit au
Luxembourg*.' But this is doubly inexact, as Miss Lowell bought no manuscripts
from Remy de Gourmont, and never owned the manuscript of the *Nuit*. She
sent the money as an anonymous gift on November 6; on December 4, Aldington wrote that he had suggested to Gourmont that he give her some autograph
manuscript for her collection; on the same day, Gourmont thanked Aldington
for this suggestion, and on December 22, asked if she would be pleased with the
manuscript of the *Nuit*, as it was the only complete one he had left. The manuscript he finally sent, however, was merely that of three chapters of Part I of his
Promenades Littéraires, Series IV.

task at present, and thirdly because I fear it might look as though I had some such idea in my head when I sent him the money. Therefore, it is quite out of the question, although his criticism would have been of the utmost value to me.

Now I am bound to tell you that I was awfully disappointed in that first article of his. Richard, let us be honest — there really wasn't a damned thing in it that any tyro could not have written. I am sorry you told him what I said about Gallicisms, for Frenchmen are so strangely constructed that, if they are told to be careful what they write, they never can write anything at all of interest.... It is either this or because M. de Gourmont regards Americans as in the kindergarten class that he writes such a singularly elementary paper. Now 'The New Republic' is not an elementary paper, certainly has no intention of being one, and I don't think that a mere statement of facts which can be got out of any newspaper will seem to them worth the price they are paying. It would not, therefore, surprise me very much if Mr. Croly returned this article, with a request for something a little more thoughtful....

In December she finished and copyrighted a translation of *La Latière de Trianon*, Wekerlin's well-known operetta with text by Galoppe d'Onquaire, which was to be performed the same evening as *Pierrot Qui Pleure*. She was also arranging for the rehearsals. Hearing that *North of Boston* was to be published by Henry Holt, she got the *New Republic* to let her review it for them. She also suggested to the *New Republic* that she become poetry editor; when her offer was turned down, she wrote to Margaret Anderson, of the *Little Review*, that she was coming to Chicago and wanted to talk over the possibility of her becoming the poetry editor for that periodical. In her Christmas mail was a long and lively letter from D. H. Lawrence and Frieda.

On January 4, 1915, she departed on the Twentieth Century for Chicago, where Harriet Monroe gave her a poets' party. She also called on Margaret Anderson. The *Little Review* differed from *Poetry* in that it specialized in the experimental. It advertised itself as 'making no compromise with the public taste.' Every new number seemed more startling and impossible than the last; but today, on looking over the files, one finds that the lists of contributors included many of the best writers on both sides of the Atlantic: Aldington, Brooke, Cowley, Crane, Cummings, H. D., Eliot, Fletcher, Flint, Ford, Frost, Galsworthy, Gourmont, Hudson, Joyce, Lewis, Lindsay, Lowell, Masters, Morand, Marianne Moore, Pound, Dorothy Richardson, Robinson, Russell, Sandburg, Sinclair, Gertrude Stein, Wallace Stevens, Symons, Turbyfill, Waley, Wheelwright, Williams, and Yeats. Its great achievement was the serializing of Joyce's *Ulysses*, at Pound's suggestion — a feat which kept it constantly in trouble with the postal authorities. Depending chiefly on the generosity of friends, it was constantly in debt; but between March, 1914, and May, 1929, it brought out eighty numbers, all of them stimulating. Miss Lowell's visit is described in Miss Anderson's sprightly autobiography.[1]

Miss Anderson, who always felt that Miss Lowell was one of the most charming persons she had ever met, was instantly delighted with her opening words, about the fight with Pound. But when she offered $150 a month to run the poetry end of the *Little Review*, Miss Anderson sensed a dictatorship, and refused at once. Miss Lowell argued and implored until she was finally convinced of the refusal, whereupon she dropped the subject forever, and invited Miss Anderson to lunch the next day.

The scheme for becoming poetry editor of the *Little Review* having failed, Miss Lowell went on to New York, where she dined with Mr. and Mrs. Croly on the eighth. For

[1] Margaret Anderson: *My Thirty Years' War, an Autobiography*, New York, 1930, pp. 60–62. Miss Anderson is vague as to the date of the visit, but the internal evidence, plus the evidence of the correspondence, makes it positive that the visit occurred in January, 1915.

four days she rehearsed the singers in her operettas, then returned to Brookline. Here she was still bothered with *Some Imagist Poets*, which was already in press. Fletcher also thought that the word 'Imagist' should be dropped, suggested 'The Allies' instead, and advised strongly that a fighting preface be written. Ferris Greenslet, of Houghton Mifflin Company, recommended 'Quintessentialists,' which rather pleased Miss Lowell. There were cables and letters. But the matter was finally settled by letters from Flint to Aldington and Miss Lowell to the effect that Pound had no more invented Imagism than he had the moon; at the most he had merely given a name to a thing which had already existed, in form and spirit, and the substance of which had been the main theme of their discussions at those old Thursday evening meetings arranged by Hulme, where they talked of nothing but the *image*. Pound was a late comer to those meetings, and added *nothing* to them — absolutely nothing. And it seems that Pound had been loth to let Flint into the secret of the doctrine of the image, although Flint had been one of the inventors, or furbishers, of that doctrine! So Flint suggested a historical preface that would put Pound in his place. With this information, Aldington bade Miss Lowell go ahead in the name of God and St. George. The publishers advised her to keep the name as it was; and from the Preface she expunged all mention of Pound, writing Aldington on January 19 what she had done.

On the twentieth she began rehearsing the operettas for six hours a day.

Pierrot Qui Pleure et Pierrot Qui Rit and *La Latière de Trianon* were performed in English on February 2, 3, and 4, 1915, for the benefit of the Women's Municipal League, of which Miss Lowell's sister, Katherine Bowlker, was president. Miss Lowell, besides having made both translations, was the chairman of the Artistic Committee, and the guarantor of the finances. Maggie Teyte was the soprano, with the two tenors John Campbell and George Mitchell. The orchestra of thirty-five pieces, drawn largely from members of the Boston Opera Orchestra, was directed by Arthur Shepherd, Professor of Counterpoint and Harmony in the New England Conservatory of Music, who gave his services. Costumes and scenery were by Livingston Platt, among the best of American scene painters. Berkeley Updike, of the Merrymount Press, designed the tickets and invitations.

Unfortunately, the worst blizzard — a four-day snowstorm — of the season hit Boston; the street cars stopped running; and the performance was a financial failure. The League made no money; Miss Lowell lost 'some thousands,' her only consolation being that everybody told her it was 'the greatest artistic success that Boston ever had.' There were various requests for permission to repeat the performances elsewhere.

It was this loss which made her turn down tentatively an offer of Aldington's. He had met George Wolfe Plank, an American artist who had once run a quarto magazine, *The Butterfly*, in Philadelphia (1907–1909), on $100 a number; he now was making designs for *Vogue*. Aldington was toying with the idea of collaborating on a magazine, if he could get together a little money — say £100 to £150. Miss Lowell was to be the American representative, and of course Fletcher would be in on it. But Miss Lowell was not sure she could afford it now. Furthermore, she had to scold him for a violent letter he had written to the *New Republic* about Gourmont. Gourmont at last had sent her a manuscript — not that of his famous *Nuit au Luxembourg*, but a small *Souvenirs du Symbolisme* (three chapters from Part I of the fourth Series of his *Promenades Littéraires*), inscribed 'A Miss Amy Lowell, en souvenir. Rémy de Gourmont.' Preceding it came a letter in French (January 21, 1915), in which he begged her to accept the three little manuscripts which he had mentioned to Aldington, apologizing for their small value, which would be so great if it equalled his gratitude. 'In brief, I am shipwrecked, and I shall never forget that you came nobly to my rescue, you who know me only through my writings.'

Meanwhile the *New Republic* would not print the two articles Gourmont had sent them through Miss Lowell. Aldington was furious. Croly mailed his letter on to Miss Lowell, with the request that it be returned; somehow she lost it at once. But we can guess at the tone, from Aldington's letter to Miss Lowell of February 1, in which he said he was still sufficiently a goddam Englishman to do & say exactly as he pleased & to have a profound contempt for all things American! By Jove, he slanged that New Republic man — such damned cheek — why, if Rémy wrote 'Fiddle, fiddle, diddle, diddle, dum' a hundred times, he ought to be glad to take it as an article. Not up to his standard? — why, the man was mad! Did he expect Gourmont to write his sort of piffle? And so on.

On February 10, Miss Lowell wrote to Herbert Croly:

I deprecate the tone of Mr. Aldington's letter very much. All that can be said about it is that he is only twenty-two, exceedingly prejudiced, and as far as America is concerned exceedingly ignorant. He is very fond of M. de Gourmont, and so anxious in his behalf that he is evidently quite incapable of seeing your side. Of course, I had no idea that M. de Gourmont was so ill and so incapacitated, when I offered you his articles. He is fifty-seven years old; but that does not necessarily mean an impaired power of writing. I was horrified at the first article, as you remember my writing, and hoped that the others would be better. I think the last two I sent were somewhat better; but that they are not what you want I am very well aware.

Now, as to the question of paying — certainly the order I received was that you would take six articles and pay for them at $30.00 an article. There was no sort of stipulation made that they should suit you when they arrived, other than that any particularly risqué remarks should be re-

moved in translation. It does seem to me that in view of
your having ordered the articles, you are obliged to pay
for them in full, whether they suit you or not. M. de Gourmont was given a commission without qualification, and he
has spent considerable time and, I imagine, spent it painfully enough, in the composing of these articles, and it will
be a terrible disappointment to him not to receive the
money for them.... I am afraid that you are morally bound
to pay him....

Not until her French lectures were in full swing did she
find time to write to Aldington, which she finally did on
February 27:

What you must think of me for not having written for
so long I cannot imagine; but the truth is, I have been working so hard that I have not had time to do anything, and
hardly to get my work finished....

I am sorry that you wrote quite such a violent letter to
Mr. Croly. You see, they do not need to be commercial as
[you] insinuated, and they are not.... Croly is an idealist
in politics, and the magazine was got up to boom that
side.... I am forced to agree with him that those articles
of M. de Gourmont were not as good as they ought to have
been. I wrote him a strong letter, urging him to pay the
full amount, telling him that I considered him morally and
I thought legally bound to do so....

... I think it is foolish, perhaps a little ungentlemanly
if you will pardon the term, I know it is very youthful, to
let one's self go on in the manner of your letter. It does not
impress the editors; it does not even depress them. It only
leaves them feeling that they will never take your judgment
again. And really your scorn of America is a little insular,
and no nationality likes to be told that it belongs to a silly
nation....

The rest of the story may be told here. The *New Republic* selected one of the four articles it had received, and
planned to publish it, but did not as the whole series was
accepted by the *Boston Transcript*, through Ferris Greens-

let's influence. The *New Republic* cheque for all six articles was naturally returned by Aldington, as the *Transcript* was now paying for them. Remy de Gourmont died September 17, 1915.

On February 20, 1915, Miss Lowell's review of *North of Boston* started Frost's reputation in his own country. Miss Lowell's own account was as follows:

> When I returned to America, I brought the volume with me, and at once (unauthorized ambassador that I was) suggested its publication to various publishers with whom I was in relation. But I was a mere struggler, as we all were in those days, and none of these publishers had the prescience to feel the advent of a new dawn in poetry. They would not listen to me, and bitterly have they regretted it since.[1] With the publication of the book by Messrs. Henry Holt and Company I had nothing to do. However, when I saw it announced here, I at once wrote to 'The New Republic,' then in its infancy, and asked — nay, demanded — to review the volume in the columns of that paper. My request was granted, and I believe I was the first to proclaim the book's amazing quality on this side of the water. But the pleasantest part of this tale was its sequel. For Mr. Frost happened to land in New York during the week when my review was published, and walking up from the wharf he bought a copy of 'The New Republic' at a news-stand and read the review. He told me later that it seemed like a welcome to his native land. Not long afterwards, I was called to the telephone and a voice said: 'I am Robert Frost, I want to see you, I have read your review.' He came out to see me, and at once began a friendship, which, on my part, has been an ever-increasing admiration of his work, and a profound attachment to the man.[2]

Her six lectures on the French poets were given at Mrs. George Putnam's, 191 Commonwealth Avenue, on the

---

[1] None the less, Mr. Greenslet, just too late, had been considering the book for inclusion in the 'New Poetry Series.'

[2] 'Tribute to Frost,' March 5, 1925.

Thursday afternoons in Lent, from February 18 through March 25. Admission was by invitation only, although a charge was made. The strain was considerable; she apologized to the quondam 'devil,' Magdelaine Carret, for her silence on March 26:

> It was simply that I have been dead to the world, slaving at my lectures in a way that I had not believed possible: nine, ten, eleven, sometimes fifteen hours a day. To talk an hour it was necessary to write forty pages of ordinary type-writing paper, and to write forty pages it was necessary to know something; and that, as you know, is a difficult thing for me. I got so tired over them that it seemed once or twice as though the price for the course would be a thorough nervous breakdown, but by dint of eliminating all pleasures and all duties while the course was going on, I have come out alive and I believe not so tired that I shall not recover after a few days of rest.
>
> You people who are students by nature have no idea of the strain and unnaturalness of real systematic study on a temperament like mine. Since I began to do these lectures I understand why I was so rotten in school. My natural way of working is to follow my inclination; read what appeals to me and then sit still and let it mature itself in my subconscious mind until it is ripe for use, ripe to be presented, that is, in a poem or otherwise. But these lectures have had to be done by an entirely different method. I had to bother with silly dates in chronological order. It has not been enough to feel: I have had to explain why I feel. Magdelaine, it has been perfectly awful, but it has taught me what I only half realized before, and that is what enormous difference of function, almost difference of construction, there is between a poet's mind and that of a student.

So desperate was her struggle to write these first lectures that her secretary would hand her the last typed pages just as she was stepping into the automobile. But she felt rewarded for her labors when her rendering of Paul Fort's 'Chant des Anglais' at her last reading moved most of her audience to tears; and after it was all over, she had the first draft of a book ready to be rewritten for publication.

Various events sandwiched themselves in between the lectures. Fletcher visited her again for a week at the end of February; Frost came to dinner one night, and thus the two men met. A letter arrived from Paul Fort; in her answer, she sent a copy of her 'Bombardment,' which the *Weekly Despatch* of London had reprinted from the *November Poetry*, with the staring caption: 'How War Comes to the Home, Picture of Bombardment that has Tragic Interest Today.' Edgar Lee Masters sent her an unexpected letter congratulating her on *Sword Blades*. The *Dome* was out of print at last; she arranged for a second edition of five hundred copies. Proofs of *Some Imagist Poets* demanded correction. News came from England that so far, only four copies of *Sword Blades* had been sold, whereas over five hundred had sold in America before Christmas, and it was still selling. *Collier's*, on March 6, reprinted 'A London Thoroughfare,' omitting the last two lines and inverting the order of the rest, in a contemptuous editorial entitled 'Futurist Poetry,' to such great delight of the far-flung line of colyumists that she wished she could sue the magazine for libel. The *Egoist* was planning an 'Imagist Number' for May 1, day dear to rebels; she sent over some poems and began a criticism of Fletcher's work, which later she abandoned, as he wrote the article on her. She was also writing her long-promised article on Harold Monro's Poetry Book Shop (cabling twice for fresh material), to be published in the May *Little Review*. Fletcher's *Irradiations* was scheduled for April 17; she reviewed it for the *New Republic*, signing a pseudonym by special agreement, as the book was dedicated 'To Amy Lowell, Best of Friends and Poets'; but later complications in the office of the *New Republic* made the editors insist that it be signed with her real name, whereupon she was forced to telegraph certain changes in her text, which were not properly carried out. She offered Aldington $500 towards his new magazine (which was abandoned later) and sent £10 to the *Egoist*. On March 21, Gebhard gave his customary concert at her house. Her last lecture fell on the twenty-fifth.

As *Some Imagist Poets* was to appear in April, she determined to say a few words about the book at the March meeting of the Poetry Society of America — 'the New York Poetry Society,' as it was instinctively called in Boston. She telephoned down to Jessie Rittenhouse, the secretary, to say that she would come if allowed five minutes in which to read; that much, or little, being granted, she took the train for New York on March 30.

The five minutes were tacked on to the end of a rather full program. First Cale Young Rice read selections from his own work. Then Edgar Lee Masters's well-heralded *Spoon River Anthology*, to appear in April, was introduced to the Society by Hamlin Garland, who spoke of a visit to Mr. Masters, and by Richard Burton, who discussed the book, reading from the proof-sheets. So skilfully did these two men speak, that the readers of *Reedy's Mirror* applauded their enthusiasm for this daring book, while the more conservative were hardly made aware that it was free in form and freer in content.

Amy Lowell's skill, however, ran to contrary means. Her initial discussion of the principles of Imagism 'bristled,' said Miss Rittenhouse,[1] 'with so much provocative dicta that the right wing was stirred to action and primed for reply.' She then read 'Venus Transiens,' 'Spring Day,' and samples from the other Imagists. The moment her five minutes were up and she had stopped, various persons leapt to their feet, demanding if that were poetry.

She had deliberately provoked, on behalf of *Some Imagist Poets*, the very situation which Hamlin Garland and

[1] Jessie B. Rittenhouse: *My House of Life*, Boston, 1934, p. 257.

Richard Burton had so carefully avoided, on behalf of the *Spoon River Anthology*. Of course the contrast was mere coincidence, as she had known nothing beforehand about the rest of the program. Moreover it was hardly her fault if the conservatives, forgetting the Society's rule that poems by guests are not to be discussed, and forgetting also their endorsement, by silence, of the free verse and free love in the *Spoon River Anthology*, rose in clamorous unity to attack Imagism, and Amy Lowell's poetry in particular, far beyond the allotted five minutes.

This was Miss Lowell's first public row over the new poetry, and it was of such vehemence that the combatants on both sides and the spectators as well were astonished afterwards when they remembered it. The fundamental cause was the tone of the Imagist verse: it was not the roses and nightingales of the pallid pseudoclassic tradition, or the buttercups and bobolinks of the New England tradition, or yet the cosmic aspirings of the Californian neo-Whitmanites. Therefore it did not sound like poetry. As Whitman had said: 'The first sight of any work really new and first-rate in beauty and originality always arouses something disagreeable and repulsive.... People resent anything new as a personal insult.' [1] The little Chams who felt their prestiges endangered rose and thundered against this power that surprised and shocked them. And there were those who could not dissociate the poem from the poetess, especially when she read 'Bath,' the opening episode of 'Spring Day,' where she described the effect of sunlight falling through water and reflected upon the ceiling. It must be remembered that hitherto Miss Lowell had never read away from home; and the New Yorkers, who had expected a fragile, nerve-wracked, intense creature, were taken absolutely by surprise. Person after person sprang to his feet, roaring denunciations seemingly without point; and seemingly without any suspicion of the

[1] 'Old Poets,' *Complete Prose*, p. 486.

cause, Amy Lowell defended her poetry single-handed. But her bathtub, for a couple of years, was a stock newspaper smirk.

She had brought with her to New York the manuscript of *Six French Poets*, which she went over with Magdelaine Carret, to catch typographical errors and the like; then she showed it to her publishers, with a view to revising it from lecture form for publication. On April 3, she returned to Brookline.

Five days later she lectured on 'The New Manner in Modern Poetry' at the Round Table Club.[1] This lecture, which ended by pointing neatly to the forthcoming *Some Imagist Poets*, was also an unconscious anticipation of her later book, *Tendencies in Modern American Poetry*, although its field was wider, as it included the contemporary Irish and English as well, with an introductory glance at the French. A few of her sentences will indicate the course well enough.

> France has been having one of the great poetic eras of the world.... But there are signs... that already decay had set in. The steady, healthy stream of poetic inspiration was giving place to a number of idiotic fads, such as Futurism, headed by Marinetti, with its pronunciamento that verbs should only be used in the infinitive, and its algebraic signs of 'plus' and 'minus,' etc., to eke out a language it had intentionally impoverished; or 'Fantaisism' with Guillaume Apollinaire as chief priest, who wrote 'idiographic poetry,' or poems printed so as to represent a picture of a railroad train with puffing smoke, or some other thing of the sort.
>
> ... I believe that this insincere poetry is dead....
>
> While France, especially, has been having an unbroken period of poetry for eighty years, England and America have had several seasons of bloom and disappearance.... It was Symbolism which dominated English poetry in the nineties.

[1] The opening pages, with some modifications, appeared in the *New Republic* (VI, 124–25), March 4, 1916.

Symbolism died in France with the appearance of Francis Jammes and Paul Fort, but it died because something new came to push it aside; in England it faded away little by little, growing more and more tenuous until it disappeared in a vacuum. The vacuum held sway until very recently. But now a younger generation has started its work, and a new manner unites the members of it and divorces them entirely from the poets of the nineties.

... This manner... is 'externality' — 'externality' versus 'internality.' The Symbolistes were extraordinarily subjective.... Each man's Ego was swollen to a quite abnormal size, and he was worshipped by his other self, the author, with every conceivable literary device and subtlety.

Egoism may be a crime in the world of morals, but in the world of the arts it is perfectly permissible. It makes very good and very interesting poetry. In mentioning it, I am not condemning it, I am only labelling it. It was the manner of the nineties, it is not the manner of today.

... Bryant, Lowell, Holmes, Longfellow, Whittier... were all... rather English provincial poets than American poets. Indeed America was, in those days, a province of England in everything except government. America as a nation, with characteristics unlike those of any other nation, had not begun to exist.

Two great geniuses she has had, Poe and Walt Whitman. But the former was too far ahead of his time to have done more than create a rather hostile wonder, and Whitman, only now, fifty years afterwards, is beginning to be followed, and that is via France. We have had our vacuum too, like England; but... we were forced into it by the pressure of a great national upheaval. The Civil War spent not only men, but money, but energy. At its close, energy recruited herself first, and perforce set about making money to save the resources of the country. Railroads were built, the West was settled. Poetry alone was inert. Inert, that is, save for one still, small voice. One little voice which was the precursor of the modern day. A voice considered only as bizarre and not at all important, by its contemporaries. I refer to Emily Dickinson, who is so modern that if she were living today I know just the group of poets with whom she would inevitably belong.

But while the vacuum was going on, immigrants were coming, and coming, and coming.... Anglo-Saxon characteristics were being modified by contact with all the nations of the globe. The British middle class attitude (the typical American attitude of those days) which forced Whistler, and Sargent, and Henry James abroad, was becoming less and less dominant. It is no longer necessary, imperative, for the American artist, poet or other, to live abroad. On the contrary, as between America and England, America gives the most welcome to change and earnest endeavor after new mediums. Every author knows that American book sales far outnumber British.... The cry that American artists must live abroad is ridiculously old-fashioned....

So, quietly, imperceptibly, and with very few little flutters to show the way the wind was blowing, the new manner, 'externality,' came into being. By 'externality' I mean the attitude of being interested in things for themselves and not because of the effect they have upon oneself....

... The greater includes the less, and 'externality' includes the universe and everything in it. But Milton and Dante were universal, it may be said; were they therefore modern? Certainly not. They were universal, I grant you, but they were not 'external.' Man stuck out in high relief all over their work. Man and his Destiny, man completely out of focus in short, was their theme. The 'new manner' attempts to put man in his proper place in the picture, that is why it is so at variance with the method of the so-called 'cosmic' poet....

Now 'externality' shows itself in two ways: in choice of subject matter, and in treatment; and this last again may be subdivided into general arrangement and ordering of particulars, and style. Perhaps nothing illustrates this better than the case of W. B. Yeats, and J. M. Synge. All the world knows the story of how Yeats encountered Synge at a loose end in Paris, studying his art, and with nothing to write about when he got it studied. Yeats very wisely suggested that Synge come back to his native Ireland, and Synge came, with what magnificent result belongs to the history of literature. For years the Symbolist Yeats had been grinding out Irish poems, all compounded of Deirdres and Cuchullains (far be it from me to pronounce them) and built upon the theory that one must return to the Gaelic; and upon the theories that one must never have descriptions in poems (for Yeats now repudiated the 'nine bean-rows' of his own exquisite 'Inisfree'); that an *s* at the end of a word should never be followed by an *s* at the beginning of the next one; that five lines of poetry were a good day's work, etc., etc. Precious hair-splitting nothings highly fitted to suit a poet with very little to say and a great deal of time to say it in. The Symboliste doctrine exactly: sound, sound, sound! Who cared a snap for the Deirdres and Cuchullains? Nobody at all, really. They were just so many bill-boards for the Irish poets to hang their advertising posters upon. No, I am afraid that the poor old Irish gods were exploited for thoroughly egotistic reasons.

But with Synge came the 'new manner.' He saw things in their relations to other factors than himself. He saw them externally. He wrote of them as he saw them, with the clean edges which are so integral a part of modern verse. He wrote simply, directly, without inversions, and with a sparing use of adjectives....

... Let me repeat in succinct form some of the tenets which go to the making of the 'new manner.' 'Externality' is its main trend, but of course that does not mean that no poet ever writes subjective verses. He could hardly be universal if he excluded himself. It is a fact, however, that modern poetry of the new kind does not concern itself primarily with introspection. Another characteristic of the 'new manner' is humour. Pensive melancholy is no longer inevitably to be worn, like a badge of office. It has gone, with many other obvious fripperies, such as leonine hair and visioning eyes....

Another striking tendency of the 'new manner' is its insistence upon the poetry in unpoetic things. The new poet is never tired of finding colours in a dust-heap, and shouting about them....

The poets of the 'New manner' have another distinguishing mark. They endeavour to write poetry in the syntax
of prose.... How difficult this is, only those who have tried
to do it know....

There is another bug-bear, more insinuating than the
old, evident 'poetic diction.' That is the *cliché*. The
stamped work or phrase, good at first, but so used and worn
that it has lost all force.... If a poet is not too scrupulous,
and can swallow the *cliché*, he can write very good poetry,
all out of other men's brains. Our popular contemporary,
Alfred Noyes, is a remarkable case in point.

Now as to form. It is the belief of most people that interest in metrical experiments is a distinguishing feature of
the 'new manner.' But do you suppose that there has ever
been a time when real poets were not interested in metrical
experiments?...

As we pointed the moral with Synge, let us take the Irish
poets first. Of this younger generation there are three whom
I shall mention tonight: James Stephens, Joseph Campbell,
and Padraic Colum. Of these Stephens is the most expert and
lyrical, Colum the most thoughtful....

[*Here she read Colum's 'The Drivers in the Sunset Race'
and Stephens's 'Blue Stars and Gold.'*]

... It is a curious thing that none of the Irish poets is
in the least impelled to experiment in metre. Even the
English poets who do so are practically all confined to one
group. It is the Americans who are hewing new pathways
for themselves....

... In England, although we have the realistic, it seems to
be chiefly concerned with cities.

Of course, Masefield is the most distinguished realist.
A realist making use of an impressionist palette, as, for instance, when he describes the flying fish in 'Dauber.' But
Masefield is hardly a poet of the 'new manner.' Rather is
he a sort of glorified Crabbe, writing in the old-fashioned
rhymed couplet, and permitting himself carelessnesses quite
unworthy of a man of his talents. He tells a story almost as
Dickens might have done had he been a poet, and there is
nothing in the least 'new' about his point of view.

Next among the realists, I should put Wilfred Wilson Gibson. He never rises to the splendid imaginative pictures of Masefield, but he has an irony which Masefield has not....

> [*Here she read his 'The Ice'; also Douglas Goldring's 'Mare Street — N. S.,' Rupert Brooke's 'Heaven,' Hueffer's 'The Little, Old Market Place.'*]

... In spite of the great charm of Mr. Hueffer's rhythm, it is a fact that present day poets are seeking very different ones. They prefer a less jigging beat. Mr. D. H. Lawrence, for instance, has evolved a very interesting and very odd sort of form. It looks like ordinary metre, but is uneven to an extraordinary degree....

... This care not to point a moral is one of the most distinguishing features of the 'New Manner.' It is this very thing which leads so many poetry lovers of the older generation to find it cold. An old-fashioned editor once said to me that what he missed in modern poetry was its lack of noble thoughts. The poetry which is a pepsin to weak intellects to whom crude life is indigestible, has nothing in common with the 'new manner.' 'Noble thoughts,' neat little uplift labels wrapped in the tin-foil of pretty verses, has its place in the scheme of existence, no doubt, but to the modern poet it is anathema.... But there! We shall never agree, and for people who like to be drugged with fine, conventional sentiments, there is no cure in Heaven or Earth that I am aware of.

But to return to Lawrence. Here you must not expect to find a tract, but an artistic presentation of a tragedy.

> [*Lawrence's 'Ballad of Another Ophelia.'*]

...

When we cross the Atlantic we find ourselves at once in a different atmosphere. American poets have a far more exuberant imagination than their British cousins, but they are much less well grounded in technique....

... First let me take Josephine Preston Peabody, a poet of unusual delicacy of feeling, and with the utmost mastery of her technique.... Modelling herself upon the Elizabethans, she has produced poetry worthy to have been read aloud at the Mermaid Tavern. But Mrs. Marks is too genuinely a poet not to feel the stirring of new impulses, new desires....

[*Josephine Peabody's 'Birdmen.'*]

The next poet I would give as writing indubitably in the 'new manner' is Edwin Arlington Robinson. Mr. Robinson is very little concerned with technique, he has abundance to say and he says it, very straightly and firmly. He belongs to that race of sincere, almost austere, Americans to whom art is not pattern but truth. It is the stuff of which the greatest poets are made. This soil, fertilized to richness by a keen perception of beauty, is capable of any growth....

[*Robinson's 'Doctor of Billiards.'*]

Akin to Robinson in some ways, but with a simpler, even more external outlook, is Robert Frost. In Robinson, you feel a questioning spirit, seeking, prying. In Robert Frost is more of the lyric poet. His feeling for the beauty of nature is greater, his observation is less tinged by his personality. He lacks some of Mr. Robinson's 'high seriousness' (indeed I know of no American poet who has this quality in so strong a degree as Mr. Robinson) but he has a greater vividness of presentation.

[*Frost's 'After Apple Picking.'*]

In Edgar Lee Masters, author of 'The Spoon River Anthology,' we have an attempt at the 'new manner' in form. Mr. Masters writes in 'vers libre.' I am bound to say that I do not consider it a very skillful or musical 'vers libre.' It stumbles dangerously near prose. But if Mr. Masters is at fault in his technique, it is for want of practice, probably. His aim is clear. He is seeking for hard edges, clear presentation, and no hindering ornament....

[*Masters's 'Doc Hill.'*]

We must now leave the realists... for quite a different growth of 'newness'... Nicholas Vachel Lindsay... cares more to make music than to paint pictures, although some of his pictures are very striking. He has a rhythm no less virile than in Mr. Hueffer's poem I read you a little while ago. If the tune is distinctly more vulgar, that is no drawback in Mr. Lindsay's eyes. He frankly says that he wishes to be the Bryan of literature.

He bases himself upon rag-time as being the natural rhythm of the great American people.... This is the poem which first brought him fame.

[*Lindsay's 'The Kalliope Yell.'*]

Will the great American people, in its kindly enthusiasm for a novelty which it can understand, spoil this talented young man? The question will answer itself in time.

Now I am come to that international group, the Imagists. ... It would take too long to go into their theories here at any length. Suffice it to say that they believe to the nth degree in all those qualities which I have included in the 'new manner.'...

[*The lecture ended with her reading a couple of translations from the Japanese by Lafcadio Hearn, Ezra Pound's 'Fan-Piece' and 'Liu Ch'e,' Aldington's 'The Faun Sees Snow for the First Time' and 'The Poplar,' H. D.'s 'Sea Iris' and 'The Garden,' Fletcher's 'Over the Roof-tops, V' and 'The Trees, X'; and finally, after a few remarks defining polyphonic prose, she ended with her own 'Red Slippers.'*]

Some other appointments followed this lecture, which she had to cancel because of illness; but on April 15, she went to New York, to arrange for the publication of *Six French Poets*. On the seventeenth, *Some Imagist Poets* was published in an edition of 750 copies, of which 481 were sold in advance. Fletcher's *Irradiations* appeared on the same day.

At last the troublous anthology was out. The three Americans and the three English poets were arranged alphabetically; each had seven titles, except Fletcher, who contributed two long poems; each was allowed from ten to fifteen pages of verse which had not yet been included in a book, verse of his own choice, although the others had the privilege of veto. Miss Lowell, who stood last, contributed 'Venus Transiens,' 'The Travelling Bear,' 'The Letter,'

'Grotesque,' 'Bullion,' 'Solitaire,' and 'The Bombardment.' *Des Imagistes* had lacked the challenge of an explanatory preface; *Some Imagist Poets* included one, written by Aldington and tinkered by all the others. It explained that the poets were not a clique — some were
personally unknown to others — but that in spite of individual differences they were grouped together as a school
because they endorsed certain common principles, arrived
at independently, which were not new, but rather the essentials of all great poetry. The famous 1915 Imagist credo
followed:

1. To use the language of common speech, but to employ
always the *exact* word, not the nearly-exact, nor the merely
decorative word.

2. To create new rhythms — as the expression of new
moods — and not to copy old rhythms, which merely echo
old moods. We do not insist upon 'free-verse' as the only
method of writing poetry. We fight for it as a principle of
liberty. We believe that the individuality of a poet may
often be better expressed in free-verse than in conventional
forms. In poetry, a new cadence means a new idea.

3. To allow absolute freedom in the choice of subject.
It is not good art to write badly about aeroplanes and automobiles; nor is it necessarily bad art to write well about the
past. We believe passionately in the artistic value of
modern life, but we wish to point out that there is nothing
so uninspiring nor so old-fashioned as an aeroplane of the
year 1911.

4. To present an image (hence the name: 'Imagist'). We
are not a school of painters, but we believe that poetry
should render particulars exactly and not deal in vague
generalities, however magnificent and sonorous. It is for
this reason that we oppose the cosmic poet, who seems to
us to shirk the real difficulties of his art.

5. To produce poetry that is hard and clear, never
blurred nor indefinite.

6. Finally, most of us believe that concentration is of
the very essence of poetry.

Free verse, too complicated a subject for extended discussion in that place, was briefly defined as 'all that increasing amount of writing whose cadence is more marked, more definite, and closer knit than that of prose, but which is not so violently nor so obviously accented as the so-called "regular verse."'

The derivation from Hulme is obvious: many of these things he actually wrote or said; all he would have endorsed. The difference from the epigrams of *Speculations* is chiefly the result of the arguments and experiments of many persons over a number of years. The Imagist credo of 1915 is the sifting out of his theories and the reduction to essentials.

Just what figure Miss Lowell thought *Some Imagist Poets* would cut between the sensational successes of Frost's *North of Boston* and Masters' *Spoon River Anthology* which had just appeared, we cannot say. She probably hoped it would be noticed, and was determined to push it all she could; but she also supposed that at least three yearly installments would be necessary to impress the name 'Imagism' on the public consciousness. As for her own work, her attitude at this time was defined in a humble letter to Macmillan's in London, dated April 27, concerning the sad fact that while seven hundred copies of *Sword Blades* had sold in America, only seven had sold in England: 'If I can once gain a position of prominence among people who care for poetry, the sale will follow as a matter of course, although I do not believe that I can ever be popular in the sense that Masefield and Tagore are popular.' At the same time, she was so profoundly convinced of the validity of her work that she could not quite understand why others did not appreciate it instantly. Consequently, she was always bullying editors, and feeling adverse criticism almost as a personal attack.

It seems evident from Miss Lowell's letters that she expected *Some Imagist Poets* to have a mild success with the periodical critics, and to evoke a calm admiration in a small circle of the truly appreciative. She had not felt how electric the poetic atmosphere of America was at that hour; she never suspected the thunder-storms of controversy over the Imagist credo that were to recur and reverberate for several years. Had she really expected the success she hoped for, had she foreseen the intellectual warfare, she would have girded on her armor with gleaming eyes. Instead, the preliminary shafts caught her unarmed; she was bewildered and hurt.

The first few days prognosticated nothing. On April 20, she read 'Fireworks' and other poems before a meeting of the Writers' Equal Suffrage League at the home of Mrs. Robert Gould Shaw. On May 3, she wrote Harriet Monroe:

> By the way, I have read 'Spoon River' from cover to cover. I quite agree with you, it is one of the most remarkable books ever published in this country. As a novel, it is, as far as I know, unsurpassed. I shall be very much interested to see what Mr. Masters will attempt next. His knowledge of humanity is extraordinarily wide and clear, and these little, headed-up poems give an impression of reality which I do not remember ever having felt so vividly before.

On May 11, a meeting to organize the New England Poetry Club met in the rooms of the Boston Authors' Club.

> The little rooms were crowded. Some Harvard undergraduates who attended have since entered the Club. Sylvester Baxter (of the Metropolitan Park Commission, authority on Mexican baroque) presided, while many persons outlined their ideas for a Poetry Club. Some had hoped for a poetic forum; others, apparently, for poetic teas. For an hour or more, the main discussion was divided between two individuals, one of whom was a stickler for Parliamentary procedure, and the other obsessed with

doubts concerning the advisability of having any Poetry Club. The untoward discussion was brought to an end by the apparently irrelevant query of Denis McCarthy: 'But don't forget the childher.' Those present felt like denizens of Wonderland and most keenly so at the close of the meeting when a man, whose hair was filled with hay, admitted that he was in the right pew but the wrong church as he had intended to go to a meeting of the Poultry Association.[1]

Miss Lowell came, but left very early. She was elected a member of the enlarged committee which met at the Chilton Club on May 18. Before that meeting, however, she had dashed down to New York for the wedding of Miss Carret and Arthur Hutchinson on the fourteenth. On the fifteenth, her review of *Irradiations* appeared in the *New Republic*. The New England Poetry Club committee determined to appoint her its first president (Robert Frost sent her a note of congratulation dated May 21), whereupon she got Mr. Braithwaite to draw up the Constitution. At 4:15 P.M. on May 18, at Wellesley she repeated her Round Table talk, slightly expanded, on 'The New Manner in Modern Poetry,' before the seniors. The news of Rupert Brooke's death had just arrived; in tribute to his memory, she read his last sonnet. She was very much pleased with her reception, was assured that she would have made an excellent teacher, and was invited to lecture again.

Then, about the middle of the month, the long-awaited 'Special Imagist Number' of the *Egoist* arrived.

How Aldington had slaved over that issue; how he gathered together poems by H. D., Fletcher, Flint, Lawrence, Miss Lowell, Marianne Moore, May Sinclair, and himself; how he wrote Pound asking for poems by Pound and Bill Williams, but got no answer; how he persuaded Flint to write a history of Imagism, and Harold Monro to write a

[1] [John B. Wheelwright:] *A History of the New England Poetry Club*, Boston, 1932, pp. 5-6.

criticism of it; how he wrote on Pound's and Flint's work and got articles on H. D. by Flint, on Fletcher by Ferris Greenslet, on Lawrence by O. Shakspear, and on Amy Lowell by Fletcher; how he fought time and the confusion of the war in order to get the number out according to schedule — all this is a small epic in itself. It was hoped that copies would reach America immediately after *Some Imagist Poets* appeared, and that the book would reach England immediately after the magazine appeared; but owing to various delays, that could not be done. Ferris Greenslet and Miss Lowell had made arrangements to distribute one hundred and fifty copies of the magazine here and there in different bookstores. But now that it arrived, they quickly drew the conclusion that it would be bad advertising.

May 19, 1915

DEAR RICHARD:

I am afraid you are going to be awfully disappointed but, after careful consideration, Ferris Greenslet, Fletcher, and I thought it would be a mistake for us to distribute this number of 'The Egoist' over here. There are three reasons for this.

In the first place, Dora Marsden's being on the front page makes it extremely doubtful whether anyone seeing the paper would care to buy it. To advertise it and attempt to sell it as an Imagist number when the most prominent thing in the paper is Dora Marsden's [1] is almost certain to wreck it on the American market.

The next reason is that Harold Monro's article is distinctly unfavorable, and pitches into us all and the movement in general with the most delightful impartiality. I think much that he says is good; but clearly for anyone who does not know our work to read it will go far towards prejudicing them against the book at the start. Now for us to take pains to distribute a hostile criticism is excessively poor business. We shall get hostile enough criticism as it is

[1] Dora Marsden's 'Truth and Reality,' Part III, with her 'Views and Comments' occupied the first five and a half pages.

— hostile, futile, and silly — as you must have seen by the clippings I am sending you. We need someone to tell the world what we are trying to do, even if they cannot say we have already done it. And for us to take special pains to distribute an article to tell the world of what little value we are would certainly be a silly thing. Ferris Greenslet, who knows the book buying condition over here from A to Z, is firm that it would be a mistake to distribute this number. I think, Richard, that sometimes in your anxiety to be quite fair, you stand up so straight that you fall over backwards. One may not do anything to force pleasant criticism, nor to prevent hostile; but in our own paper, our own organ, if I may call it so, to publish a distinctly hostile article in a number which was presumably got up to make our work better known, is hardly necessary, and you can see yourself that it is a distinctly bad business proposition.

The third reason, and to my mind the most cogent of the lot, is Lawrence's poem,[1] which I think for pure, farfetched indecency beats anything I have ever seen. Unfortunately these things are very quickly remarked on over here. Two years ago 'The International' had a cover which I considered perfectly harmless, but they were sued for sending indecent matter through the mails. Now I do not believe there will be prominence enough given to this poem of Lawrence's for us to be sued, although there might be: the Watch and Ward Society is very active; but it would do us immeasurable, incalculable harm to be associated with such an outpouring.... He loses his eye about things; sometimes I think his condition is almost pathological, and that he has a sort of erotic mania.

Now I know how hard you worked over this Imagist number, and I know that you will go round cussing the stupidity of Americans at not being able to see the value of our book through a hostile criticism, or make allowances for Lawrence's poem, or brush away Dora Marsden as if she were an intruding fly. But you must not forget, Richard, that in working with people we have to take them as they

[1] 'Eloi, Eloi, Lama Sabachthani?' the first line of which is 'How I hate myself, this body which is me,' is not in his *Collected Poems*, London, 1928.

are, not as they should be. It is not fair to the publishers
to injure the sale of the book because, although I have paid
for the printing, they have a part interest in the receipts
as they are handling it. The publication of 'Spoon River'
and Frost's books at the same time as our Anthology has
rather injured our sale, and we must not be a party to
anything that will injure it more....

'Spoon River'... is one of the greatest novels ever written and is worthy to rank with Dostoyevsky. Whether or
not it is poetry is another matter....

This is plain business, Richard, and you must not object
if it clashes with your principles of fairness.... I think perhaps you put the importance of criticism higher than I do.
I have personally never received the slightest hint which
was of any value to me in a printed article. Reviews seem
to me much more in the nature of advertisements than anything else....

... I think time and our own efforts will land us where
we wish to be. But we must be awfully careful to persuade
the public that we are serious, high-minded, and hard-work-
ing people, and not cranks. The most important thing
for us is to have a strong 'esprit de corps,' so that the success of one member is an honour to all....

What annoyed me especially about Monro's article was
speaking about 'The Bombardment' as flat prose. He
knows perfectly well it is not prose....

Perhaps another cause for discontent was the fact that
Aldington had toned down Fletcher's article on Miss
Lowell, removing various superlatives. She wrote to
Miss Weaver, sending her the $15 which she would have
made from commissions on the exported one hundred and
fifty Imagist *Egoists*, explaining that the prominence of
Miss Marsden's articles was the trouble. She also wrote
sternly to Harold Monro.

On May 22, the *New Republic* published 'The Place of
Imagism,' an attack by Conrad Aiken, who had already
favored the *Transcript* with his satirical 'Ballade of the

Worshippers of the Image.' Mr. Littell suggested that Miss Lowell reply; she persuaded William Stanley Braithwaite of the *Transcript* to do so; his reply appeared June 12. Meanwhile on May 26, she wrote Mr. Croly what a 'surprise and blow' that 'hostile and ignorant attack' had been, and how she began to question their loyalty to her on three grounds: (1) although she had asked them if they wanted a review of the spring poetry from her, they had not answered her letter, but without warning had issued a Literary Supplement containing two poetry reviews by a single man; (2) the editors had insisted on her signing her review of Fletcher's book, although the original arrangement had been otherwise; furthermore they had placed conspicuously at the end the paragraph explaining the situation, which she had marked for insertion in the middle; (3) although arrangements had been made for a review of *Some Imagist Poets*, this attack by Mr. Aiken, 'who has been in direct communication with Mr. Pound since our split,' was published first. She then wanted to know if she had any secret enemies on the staff.

But the 'New Poetry' was spreading too fast not to produce its own periodicals. Presently Miss Lowell received a letter from Alfred Kreymborg, erstwhile editor of the *Glebe*, asking her for poems for a new magazine, *Others*, to begin in July. *Others* was to achieve distinction in the army of little magazines 'that died to make verse free' all over the continent. A literary colony was forming in New York; besides Miss Lowell's friends, W. C. Williams, Skipwith Cannéll, Horace Holley, and Orrick Johns had gathered round. She sent poems, a cheque, and her book.

Free Verse suddenly had taken! From ocean to ocean, persons reversed the discovery of M. Jourdain, and found that all their lives they had been talking poetry. Fresh cadences fitted fresh subjects: in Free Verse one could write of shoes and automobiles and skyscrapers and oneself, whereas in meter and rhyme one could mention only

sandals and winged horses and Greek deities. The colyumists found Free Verse an excellent way to fill their columns:
they printed their epigrams vertically instead of horizon-
tally, thus gaining more space and more readers, who
found the epigrams much more pungent. Advertisements
followed suit: a slim column of words was read where the
solid paragraph had been passed over. Most curious of all,
Free Verse invaded the spirit world, which hitherto had
been most orthodox (however careless) in matters of
rhyme and meter. Patience Worth, though from the seventeenth century, used the new form;[1] so did the 'Vagrom
Angel' who dictated forty-nine poems through the hand of
Elsa Barker in twenty-two hours.[2]

Why Free Verse succeeded in America but not in
England is a puzzle yet unsolved. The roots lay deep in
the past, and drew nourishment from almost every great
civilization, especially Hebrew and Greek; and already it
had a considerable history. In England, Free Verse had
been written by Milton, Traherne, and Richard Langhorn
in the seventeenth century; by 'Ossian,' Blake, and
Coleridge in the eighteenth; by Scott, Tupper, Matthew
Arnold, Samuel Warren, George Eliot, Henley, Stevenson,
Gerard Manley Hopkins, William Sharp, and the Whit-
manites headed by Edward Carpenter in the nineteenth.
On the wider soil of America, Free Verse, though it started
later, had spread farther and sunk deeper. The first
American Free Verse of any note was written in the 1830's
by Emerson, Thoreau, and the Transcendental translators
from the German. Whitman, Melville, and Longfellow fol-
lowed, each experimenting after his own fashion. Adah
Isaacs Menken's *Infelicia* (1868) became internationally fa-

---

[1] I have no desire to mock at the mediumship of Mrs. Curran; for an excellent
exposition of the problems involved, I recommend the reader to Dr. Walter
Franklin Prince's *Case of Patience Worth*, Boston, 1929. None the less, spirits
of whatever past are surprisingly influenced by the *Zeitgeist* of the present to
which they manifest.

[2] *Songs of a Vagrom Angel*, written down by Elsa Barker, New York, 1916.

mous, or notorious. In 1888, James Wood Davidson's remarkable *Poetry of the Future* prophesied the development of a rhythmic sense which would wholly transcend academic meter; his book anticipated and perhaps inspired the theories of Gerard Manley Hopkins. Not till the death of Whitman did his imitators appear in considerable numbers; but the outstanding Free Verse of the 1890's was some poems of Emily Dickinson's and all of Stephen Crane's. By 1900, the form was commonplace throughout America. There are many other names which could be listed; but it is enough to say here that possibly every year of Amy Lowell's life — certainly every year after she started writing — somewhere in this country somebody published a volume containing Free Verse. But so little was American poetry known to Americans, that she got her inspiration in a round-about way from Poe's irregular stanzas through France to England. Yet with such a tradition saturating the soil, the American cult of Free Verse that now ensued was obviously the development of an innate national disposition.

Miss Lowell was disturbed at it, not only because much of this new poetry showed no ear for cadence, but also because of its content — Free Verse and Free Love were associated all too frequently, and by persons who gladly called themselves Imagists. 'Apparently all the questionable and pornographic poets are trying to sail under the name just now,' she wrote Aldington on June 4. She consulted her brother-in-law lawyer, to try and stop it; she was driven to consider copyrighting the name — the very thing she had told Pound could not be done! It was possible, she learned, to form a business association under that name, and to admit only preferred persons; of course, Pound would have to be admitted, '— it would be frightfully sharp practice to leave him out.' But the whole idea was too absurd, and was abandoned.

Meanwhile she worked away on the manuscript of

Six French Poets, which had been promised the publishers by July 1, except for the appendix of translations due a month later.

On June 11 she wrote Miss Monroe:

> By the way, Ezra's new book 'Cathay' is full of the most beautiful things. I have seldom read anything finer. What a pity the boy does not confine himself to working and leave strictures on other people's work alone. I would rather like to review it, but I am a little afraid that, if I do, he will think I am trying to curry favour with him. What do you think?

Presently the stir over Imagism began to seem more favorable. May Sinclair's 'Two Notes' in the *Egoist*, June 1; a pleasant paragraph by J. B. Kerfoot in the 'Book Number' of *Life*, June 10; and Braithwaite's reply to Aiken in the *New Republic*, June 12, put matters in a much happier light. The very universities were affected! At the Harvard Commencement, June 24, E. E. Cummings spoke on 'The New Art.'[1] After discussing modern painting and music, he opened his discussion of literature by quoting 'Grotesque,' which afforded 'a clear development from the ordinary to the abnormal.' Sanders Theater shuddered in sibilant horror as he recited: 'Why do the lilies goggle their tongues at me....' One aged lady (peace be to her bones!) was heard to remark aloud: 'Is that our president's sister's poetry he is quoting?... Well, *I* think it is an *insult* to our president!' Meanwhile the president's face, on which all eyes were fixed, was absolutely unperturbed. But one of the Boston newspapers, which did not truckle to the Brahmins, came out with the headlines recalled as 'Harvard Orator Calls President Lowell's Sister Abnormal.'

She got off the manuscript of *Six French Poets* on time; then she wrote a poem, 'Patterns,' which pleased her so much that when Mrs. Russell returned from a brief visit,

[1] Published in the *Harvard Advocate* (xcix, 154–56), June 24, 1915.

Miss Lowell read it to her almost at the door. They agreed that it was a trifle risqué for the American public, so it was sent to the *Little Review*. Miss Anderson accepted it at once for the August number. Meanwhile, to everybody's surprise, William Rose Benét accepted the polyphonic 'Windmill' for the *Century*, and the *New Republic* asked her to boil down her Round Table talk on 'The New Manner in Modern Poetry' for its pages. She arranged for a group of her poems in the September *Poetry*; placed Fletcher's polyphonic 'Clipper Ships' with the *New Republic*; and got the Four Seas Publishing Company to accept Aldington's book, *Images*. For some months she had been trying to persuade him and H. D. to come to America; he now replied that he would be only too glad to if he could, but he could never get a passport, as he expected to be drafted at any moment.

On July 6, she was preparing to leave for Dublin; but Mrs. Russell came down with something very like typhoid, and she spent her days looking after her, while working five hours each night on the translation of the poems in *Six French Poets*.

And now the poets began in earnest their attack on Imagism. Every poet writes according to the best principles he can discover; therefore it follows that when a poet turns to criticism, other poets are wrong insofar as they differ from him. He cannot think otherwise, unless he has the background of a scholar and the disinterestedness of a Christian. Hueffer celebrated his twenty-fifth year as book-reviewer by reviewing *Some Imagist Poets* under the title 'A Jubilee,' in the London *Outlook*, July 10. He supposed that he had led the Imagist movement, but he also supposed that they would repudiate him: 'the world is like that.' Only H. D. and Flint ('one of the greatest men and one of the most beautiful spirits of the country') he found worthy Imagists; the others were too preoccupied with themselves and their emotions. The

London *Times* was anonymously disgusted; Edward Storer raged in the *British Review*; Padraic Colum raged elsewhere; Conrad Aiken re-expressed his views in the *Poetry Journal*. *Blast*, of course, ignored them utterly. The July or 'War Number' was its second and last. It announced the death in action of Gaudier-Brzeska. Aldington, Epstein, and Rebecca West were out; T. S. Eliot and four others replaced them. 'American Art' was spoken of briefly on page 82 as yet to come; its best products so far were Red Indian, Poe, Whistler, James, Whitman, and Pound, all but the last of whom were characterized rather patronizingly. But to offset all these discouragements, it was said that favorable articles on Imagism had appeared in two Russian magazines, *Apollon* and *Strelitz*.

By July 29, Mrs. Russell was sufficiently recovered to leave for Salt Lake City; on the next day, Miss Lowell left for Dublin. She had not been there since 1912, and she found her avenues almost impassable because of terrible rains earlier in the year. She described her difficulties in a letter to Eleanor Belmont, dated August 7.

> Then I moved up here, and my waitress, overcome by the isolation of the place, left the next morning. An accomodator arrived upon the scene, and chopped her hand open on a fingerbowl. So, although I still have her as an ornament, she is of no other use.
>
> Then the elements took a hand, and — it rained!!! The local carpenter assures me that he saw to it that the roof was in excellent order and that there were no leaks anywhere, before I got here. The house evidently opened itself to me, for it acted like a sieve. The rain came through plaster ceilings at such a rate that we had to put bath-tubs under them, and I expected, at any moment, to see the ceilings themselves descend with a crash to the floor. But this was not all; my old friend, the neuralgia, came on me with fine vigor (possibly living over a pond, for there is one in my cellar, is not good for neuralgia) and I have been in

a good deal of pain and eating phenacetine all the time. Surely Ada's vacation is not proving exactly a joy-ride for me. Not that she could have stopped the leaks, or staunched the brook in the cellar, had she been here, but all these things are worse when our only human propinquity is a group of startled and unhappy servants. I knew the summer would be a trial, but I never bargained to pass it between the upper and the under waters, suspended in a damp middle space, as it were.

Her arrival that August is still remembered vividly in the village. She telephoned down for every available man to come at once and bail out the cellar. When they arrived, a furnace-fire was drying the house out; and as her refusal to let it be extinguished seemed to baffle the bailing, she ordered them to break up the concrete cellar-floor, to let the water drain out that way.

Many similar tales are still told in Dublin. She *was* a character; when she arrived with her dogs, the whole town knew it at once. Nobody was allowed on her drive before eleven; her light burned till three; she used to smoke a calabash on her veranda; and her monthly telephone bill was vast beyond credibility.

In spite of her neuralgia, she continued to work at the French translations until an attack of acute indigestion made her notify the publishers that they would be delayed a month and a half. On August 10, the proofs of the rest of the book began arriving. On the next day, Randolph Bourne came to dinner, armed with a letter of introduction from Greenslet. He had made a stir with his *Youth and Life*, had become a leading contributor to the *New Republic*, and was spending the summer in Dublin. The meal was not a success. James Oppenheim wrote of it:

> ... An heroic woman, surrounded by great dogs.... Which was one reason why Randolph Bourne, a hunchback and physically weak, took a dislike to her. For he visited her, and the dogs set on him, and he was terrified until rescued.

She loathed Bourne in turn. After the *Seven Arts* days, and during the A.E.F. days, she came to see me down in Ninth Street. She spoke of her loathing of Bourne. She said:

'His writing shows he is a cripple.'

I answered, I am ashamed to say, in these noble words: 'Aren't we all cripples?'

And instead of flaying me alive, she surveyed her monstrous girth and said simply: 'Yes, I'm as much of a cripple as he. Look at this. I'm a disease.' [1]

On August 14, she addressed some two hundred Dublinites on Imagism. A couple of admiring letters from Louis Untermeyer marked the beginning of a long friendship. Frost wrote her that though he was a best seller, he really admired her work; but the great thing was that she and some others had landed with both feet on all the little chipping poetry of awhile ago. They had busted 'em up as with cavalry; they had, they had, they had! She wrote to Mr. Krans of Harper's, explaining the new meters for an encyclopedia he was editing. 'Patterns' appeared in the *Little Review*; she also had a group of poems in the August *Others*, at the sight of which she wrote Kreymborg:

I think your second number is so much better than your first that I am perfectly delighted with it. Who is Mr. Stevens? His things have an extraordinarily imaginative tang. That 'Silver Plough-Boy' is quite delightful, though no better than 'Peter Quince at the Clavier.' William Carlos Williams' numbers I like; and I think Skipwith Cannéll's 'Coming of Night' is one of the best things of his I have seen. Number 4 of Robert Carlton Brown's is very good. Mr. Hartpence's I am not so crazy about. But the whole number is extremely interesting, and I congratulate you upon it.

Who is Mr. Stevens? Tell me something about him.

[1] James Oppenheim: 'The Story of the *Seven Arts*,' *American Mercury* (xx, 161), June, 1920.

On the twenty-sixth she dashed back to Brookline, to see about paperhangers and other matters of renovation, then immediately returned to Dublin.

On September 2, she sent her translation of the 'Milk-maid' to Schirmers; but though they paid her $125 for it, it was never published. On the tenth, she entertained Edwin Arlington Robinson (from the MacDowell Colony at Peterborough), Randolph Bourne, and her old friend Eugenia Frothingham. On another occasion, she had a friendly tilt with Percy MacKaye at the Clubhouse. A little round of letters from the English Imagists arrived, thanking her for their share of royalties. Meanwhile, she alternated her French translations with detective stories from the Old Corner Book Store, occasionally writing a poem in the New Hampshire dialect. About the twentieth she returned to Brookline for the winter, her translations still unfinished. Not till October 9, were the last of the 132 of them sent off; meanwhile, proof-sheets marked 'Rush!' accumulated so fast that her automobile dashed back and forth twice a day to the press in Norwood. Her unwritten poems were also accumulating: she determined, as soon as the last proof was corrected, to take a full month's vacation, in which to do nothing but write poetry. But just now it was time to start the others planning their contributions to the next Imagist anthology. As the public would be awaiting their next (was not Professor William Ellery Leonard thundering in the *Chicago Evening Post*, in a whole series of anathematic articles?), she felt they should exert their fullest powers (now O. W. Firkins was thundering in the New York *Nation*), for by this book they might stand or fall. Between times, she was selling her New England poems written at Dublin.

On October 21, Fletcher arrived again in Boston, and dined with Miss Lowell on the twenty-fourth; about this time, Mr. and Mrs. A. Edward Newton had an evening with her; and at the end of the month there was a committee meeting of the New England Poetry Club.

Meanwhile, appreciative letters about her poems, especially 'Patterns,' began to multiply. Edgar Lee Masters wrote her twice of his enthusiasm for her 'The Reaping' (*New Republic*, October 30). One of the letters which she cherished most came from a person she had never met, Sara Teasdale, who wrote from St. John's Hospital, St. Louis, on October 13:

DEAR MISS LOWELL:

'Sword Blades and Poppy Seed' is lying on my bed. It has been read and reread so much that the cover is beginning to look dull — but the poems inside are always burning with brilliant colors, and the oftener I read them, the more they flame and the more keenly they interest me. I made the acquaintance of your book last spring, tho I had known your work in 'Poetry' and other places for some time. It has always baffled and fascinated me, and I like it all the more because I can not quite analyse what I feel about it. Just when I am beginning to say of a certain passage, 'I don't like this,' I find out that you are creating a happy surprise for me out of the very thing that I didn't like — that you are turning it somehow into a strange vivid bit of beauty. I think that the wonderful 'Patterns' in 'The Little Review' has given me the most delight. It reminds me of an exquisitely enamelled old French snuff-box — so fresh and undaunted in the clear color, and the design so firm and so delicate. You see that I have a great deal to thank you for, and you must try to pardon my informality in doing it. Besides, you aren't quite a stranger, for Harriet Monroe, whom I have visited several times, has often spoken of you.

Once more, let me thank you for your 'Visions for those too tired to sleep.' — They have come to me many a time here where your 'Convalescence' is so real a thing.

Very sincerely,

SARA TEASDALE (*Mrs.* E. B. FILSINGER)

And this appreciative letter from one poet to another was the beginning of another lifelong friendship.

CHAPTER XIII

SIX FRENCH POETS AND MANY AMERICANS

'... my immense debt...'

THE great event of November, 1915, was the publication of *Six French Poets*. On the tenth she left for the Hotel St. Regis, New York, to consult her publishers and to entertain the leading poets and critics. It was often her custom to appear in New York just before the release of a book, to call up the editors of the leading periodicals that ran book reviews, and ask who was to review her book. She then invited the reviewer round for tea; explained that she did not want to prejudice him in any way; she merely wanted him to understand clearly what she was trying to accomplish; and then he was perfectly free to be absolutely frank in his review. Whether he went away glowing with delight or glowering with resentment, his article was sure to be prominent and readable.

How long ago she had started this volume! Carl Engel had introduced her to the *Symboliste* poets in 1908; in 1912, before the *Dome of Many-Coloured Glass* was all written, she had discovered their successors. After her return from Europe in 1913 she had planned a series of essays on these poets unknown to America, and in her first contribution to the *Little Review*, 'Miss Columbia: An Old-Fashioned Girl' (June, 1914), she said:

> An American writer, who had lived in Europe long enough to forget the peculiar American temper, was sufficiently ingenuous as to propose to the editor of one of our best-known magazines a series of three articles on six contemporary French poets. They were refused, because his clientèle did not care to read of things of which they knew nothing. 'They will know less than I,' said the editor, 'and I have only heard of two of these names.'

Undeterred by this rebuff, she had gone ahead with her plan, which in July, 1914, she had unfolded to Flint. Having delivered the papers as lectures the following spring, she then prepared to rewrite them in a less informal style. But it could not be done. On June 16, she wrote to Frederick Marsh:

> In re-writing this book, I have come across an unexpected difficulty: namely, that the essays are still spoken; no matter what I do with them, they presuppose a speaker and a listener; I can almost hear a voice going out of the pages. You and Mr. Brett both begged me, and various other people have begged me, not to lose the colloquial character of the essays; and short of making them dull and inorganic, I cannot lose the speaking quality I have mentioned. Finally I have given up any hope of it, and have simply changed 'last Thursday' to 'the last essay,' and things of that sort; and I shall put in the preface that I have assumed them to be conversations, or something of that kind. I hope this will suit you. Lawrence, my brother, advised me to leave in all the allusions, and say they were reprinted lectures; but I think the method I have adopted is better than that. Lawrence also told me that lectures can never be written over, because a thing conceived in one way can never again be conceived in any other. I have come to the conclusion that this is the difference between literature and journalism; anything worthy to be called literature has an organic life of its own after its birth, whereas journalism is always dead and can be chucked round with impunity.

The publishers insisted that all the poems she quoted be translated in an appendix; and she found that suggesting the different tones of the six poets in English prose required unusual care. On October 22, she wrote of her difficulties to Magdelaine Hutchinson, who had criticized this part of her manuscript:

> The thing, you understand, which makes French poetry so difficult to translate is the French taste for parenthetical

writing. You people do not mind several sentences, one after another, all qualifying the same subject; but it is absolutely against English usage. The English reader becomes tangled up and confused, and the poem is to him an undecipherable conglomeration. It is this fact which has made the poems of Henri de Régnier a heart-breaking job to translate. Of these poets I have found Jammes and De Gourmont the easiest to do; De Régnier and Verhaeren the most difficult.

The book was a success, of course: Miss Lowell had done with failures. The public was ready for another of her stimulating books; and although it did not suspect it, it was ready for this particular book. Verhaeren was known of, but most Americans had never heard so much as the names of the five others. Vance Thompson's *French Portraits* was fifteen years old; Gosse's *French Profiles* was incomplete and otherwise inadequate; Jethro Bithell's *Contemporary French Poetry*, 1912, had scarcely reached America. With the founders of *Symbolisme*, Americans had long been familiar; and the enormous popularity of Debussy and Ravel had continued their vogue over this continent. It scarcely needed the enthusiasm for French culture raised by the War to persuade the public that Mallarmé, Verlaine, Laforgue, and Rimbaud had successors. Miss Lowell's book provided the information.

'Style is not manner but personality,' she had once written; [1] to Flint this book revived the vivid memory of her presence. [2] The general public, which had no idea of her intelligence, but supposed that she was some overwrought, intensely aesthetic creature, was most agreeably surprised when her book about these obscure and difficult French poets turned out to be clear, sincere, direct, and absolutely intelligible. It was not freakish and

[1] A. Lowell: 'Miss Columbia,' *Little Review* (i, 36), June, 1914.

[2] F. S. Flint: 'Six French Poets,' *Egoist* (iii, 9–10), January 1, 1916; also *Little Review* (ii, No. 10, pp. 16–17), Jan.–Feb., 1916.

uneven, a series of unconvincing enthusiasms, larded
with purple patches of bohemian anecdotage; neither was
it exhaustively academic, with the traditional separation
of 'life' from 'works,' and all the difficult apparatus of
footnotes. She did not treat poetry as some Pentecostal
descent or Platonic seizure, nor yet as finger-counting and
source-tracing. Instead, she spoke of it familiarly, as something sane people do, taking its great importance for
granted. She explained things squarely, confiding in her
audience while she shared with it her intelligent and
honest enthusiasms. It was the method of Leigh Hunt,
in his *Imagination and Fancy*: he had introduced her to
English poetry; in the same way she would introduce
America to French poetry. She too was a writer, talking
about her art, as manifest in the works of six different
poets, whose limitations she recognized as well as their
achievements. They were not models for Americans to
copy; they merely indicated certain new literary possibilities. And to many a reader, this book was a liberation,
a refreshing experience, a spiritual trip abroad.

Seven hundred copies were sold by Christmas; a second
edition was expected early in the new year. Macmillan,
of London, ordered one hundred copies, which number was
soon raised to two hundred and fifty; and as this English
consignment sold out immediately, another consignment
was ordered. The English reviews, as might be expected,
were not so generally enthusiastic as the American. Some
(especially Flint's) were frankly pleased; others were disturbed. J. Middleton Murry was positively withering in
the London *Daily News*; and the anonymous review in
the London *Times* was so similar in style and approach
that Aldington and Miss Lowell independently guessed
that Murry had written that article too. Another anonymous review was Lytton Strachey's, in the *New Statesman*.[1]

---

[1] Reprinted in his *Characters and Commentaries*, New York, 1933, pp. 187-91.

Meanwhile, she was in New York for the day on November 30. In the afternoon she gave her lecture on 'The New Manner in Modern Poetry' at the Cosmopolitan Club, and in the evening delivered a new lecture, 'Modern Metres and the Poets Who Write Them,' to the Poetry Society of America. It was a technical discussion, with plentiful illustrations from contemporary poets.

... There is something in the verse of today which sets it apart from the verse of any other period whatsoever.

All poetry is made up of two ingredients in varying proportions. These are: Vision, and Words. When the vision is slight, and not of preponderating intensity, we call it — Fancy. When it usurps a larger place and flavours the mixture to a marked degree, we call it — Imagination. When it is the dominating factor, we call it — Inspiration. The innumerable ways in which Vision and Words may be mingled, make the enormous variations of which poetry is capable.

Poetry might be likened to the human face, which admits of an untold number of subtle differences, while always remaining a human face; so poetry remains poetry under a thousand aspects. But just as it is difficult to see beauty in racial types to which we are unaccustomed, so it is difficult to recognize its presence in new and alien types of poetry. (Alien in the beginning, that is, for poetry and persons become familiar by habit.)

The change which has been going on in poetry has its counterpart in all the arts. I am old enough to remember the howl with which Wagner's music was received. There was an old joke which went the rounds, from 'Punch,' I believe, in which a man says: 'Songs without words are bad enough, but songs without music are too much for me.' The author of the joke was looking for tune, tune with a beginning, and a middle, and an end, and he naturally did not find it. Wagner, one of the greatest masters of tune who ever lived, was deliberately subordinating that faculty to a theory in which he believed — the leitmotif. He could not be understood without first learning his idiom, and in the beginning people were too accustomed to another idiom to realize that he had invented a new one, and that his works must be judged by it.

With Wagner, we have gone through the necessary stages. We have misconceived him and laughed at him, we have admired, wondered, and believed that all music was destined to be written by his canons in the future, and, with the growth of a newer school, we have put him where he belongs, among the greatest masters of the past. For Wagner is a great fact, a great fact among other great facts, and as such he has found his niche, and there we are content to leave him while we crack our jokes on younger men. Debussy is already climbing into his rightful place, but we still chuckle at Stravinsky, and Albeniz, and Bartók, and Schoenberg. Some of these men will attain their pedestals, some fall and disappear. I only point to them here to prove the perpetual struggle on the road of Art. It repeats itself with amusing regularity, and no generation ever learns to wait a little before judging.

After this introduction, she mentioned the parallel difficulties of modernistic painting, and read explanatory passages from Van Gogh's letters. The analogies of modern poetry to painting and music were illustrated by poems of Flint's and Fletcher's; then she discussed and analyzed the freer meters of Frost and Lawrence, continuing with definitions of *vers libre* and cadence. To demonstrate the different tempos possible in free verse, she read poems by Flint, Fletcher, Masters, herself, H. D., Aldington and Sandburg; to demonstrate the power of free verse to move from one tempo to another, she read the description of the concert in her 'Cremona Violin'; and finally, to illustrate polyphonic prose, she read her 'In the Castle.'

Again there was a row, which she described briefly to Aldington on December 15:

We had a most lively time. The Society is extremely reactionary, and the evening turned into a sort of gladiator fight and wild beast show with thumbs turned down and I impersonating the part of the early Christians. Untermeyer was the only person who dared to defend us, and he defended us so splendidly that some members of the Society would not speak to him afterwards.

As before, hardly had she taken her seat when the conservatives began springing to their feet with protests. A German professor from Vassar claimed free verse as a German invention; the audience visibly cooled at the theory that this new form, which they detested, was a product of *Kultur*; and Miss Lowell fervently insisted that, while the Germans might have written free verse, it was certainly not Imagistic. At midnight the discussion was cut short, for her final rebuttal.

She wrote Padraic Colum (who had tried to pigeon-hole her writings as oratory, not poetry) that her reply was on strictly literary, not personal, grounds; won by her attitude, he sought her out; and the two had a pleasant meeting. Other members of the society, who had remained silent, took pains to write her of their enthusiastic approval of her attitude, and their disgust at various of the controversialists. Nathan Haskell Dole gave an amused but sympathetic account of the evening for his column in the *Bellman*.[1]

Immediately after this reading she returned to Brookline, to preside as president over the first meeting of the New England Poetry Club the next day (December 1). Aiken and Fletcher were there, also Josephine Peabody, Katherine Lee Bates, Grace Hazard Conkling, and Margaret Münsterberg. The Boston society proved a restful contrast to the New York one: although Miss Lowell read 'Spring Day' and even smoked a cigar, all was most decorous. Some weeks later, at a reception, Miss Lowell ran into Miss Münsterberg again, and announced in her

[1] Nathan Haskell Dole: 'The Bellman's Notebook,' *Bellman* (xx, 210–11), February 19, 1916.

clear voice: 'Miss Münsterberg and I were together at a funeral, and we were the only alive people there.'

On the evening of December 2, she went to hear the Flonzaley Quartet at Jordan Hall. The special number on the program was Stravinsky's 'Three Pieces for Quartet,' which was played from manuscript. The composer had written a little Pierrot plot, to explain the music; the head of the Harvard Musical Department was persuaded to read it from the platform; but once the music started, he turned his back to the stage and hid his head. Such sounds had never issued from strings before: there were bagpipes and drums and horns and rattling carts, and at the end a very dismal organ. The vitality and poignancy of the music, however, appealed instantly to Miss Lowell; by December 11, she was informing everybody that she had written one of her best poems about the 'Three Pieces,' or 'Grotesques,' and that no editor could ever understand the poem unless he also understood Stravinsky.

On the afternoon of the thirteenth, she read her poems, with some talk of modern meters, at the Hotel Vendôme, in a series for the benefit of the International Institute for Girls in Spain; Miss Bates had arranged for her to read, and Josephine Peabody introduced her. 'Lead Soldiers' and 'Bombardment' were particularly successful. Meanwhile the news of the latest New York row brought in a small shower of requests to speak at various women's clubs.

She had been planning a full month off, for straight poetry; but there were always other things to be done. She had been so dead-beat when she corrected the proofs of *Six French Poets* that a number of errors had been let stand; now she had to prepare an errata sheet for the rest of the edition. Fletcher was in town; she had him out on the sixth, the nineteenth, and January 2, principally to discuss the next Imagist anthology. He had a battling preface to be moderated. Should they include other poets? Eliot,

Stevens, Clara Shanafelt, Marianne Moore, and Mary Aldis were suggested variously by Aldington and Fletcher; Miss Lowell thought that the group should remain as it was, unless somebody very great turned up; then she relented somewhat, in consideration of Jean Untermeyer, though her admission was never arranged. Lawrence's increasing eroticism made her dubious of keeping him; but she had changed her mind already when Aldington wrote her (November 29) about the suppression of the *Rainbow* in England; thereafter his exclusion was not to be considered. One of the poems she had chosen for her own section was 'Off the Turnpike,' but it was voted out by the English group, and out it stayed. She was catching up with her correspondence. The money for a magazine seemed to be a possibility now; she wrote Aldington he would have to come to America to edit it; and he replied, telling the best ways to get him out of England — it was complicated and dubious, but he was eager to try; perhaps he could make it if it was announced he was to edit a pro-Ally paper. To this, she would never consent; moreover, people did not offer to subscribe as generously as she had hoped, and she had to write discouraging him.

On January 3, 1916, she read her poems at the Middlesex Women's Club, Lowell. The next day she gave a new lecture, 'American Poets of Today,' before the Roxburghe Club at Masonic Hall, Roxbury. It was really a reading of modern poets, with some explanation of their works; but the introductory remarks constituted perhaps her best outline of American poetry and its causes.

> One of the strangest things about art is its never-dying quality. No great art which ever existed goes down to posterity as a single phenomenon. For some years after the time which produced it, other styles and methods may seem to have pushed it definitely aside, but years pass, centuries, it may be, and there springs up a generation which turns

back to this old mode for its inspiration. So it goes. Art is a wheel, and the different schools its spokes; they keep revolving. I shall show you today that many of the most 'modern' poets derive their manner from schools of poetry long past. Some derive from the Greek models, some from the Latin poetry of the Decadence, some seek to learn their methods of Chinese and Japanese artists. But, and this is important to notice, almost none of them follow the style of the immediately preceding decades....

People speak of anything new in art as though it were a freakish and hypocritical pose, done to astonish the public and conceived in much the same spirit as the action of a man who should choose to walk down Tremont Street arrayed in pink trousers and with a green parasol over his head.

Now it is a regrettable fact that there are charlatans in art as in other things, and these charlatans do much to bring down ridicule upon honest and sincere workers.... The beauty of old silver is not diminished because unscrupulous jewelers flood the market with poor imitations. It is not very difficult to imitate the exterior manner of a work of art; what is difficult to imitate is its informing spirit. It is just this informing spirit which determines the manner; and a good way to distinguish the sincerity of artistic productions is to see if the informing spirit be sincere and worthy.

The chief disadvantage under which an artist labours is that he feels the changing influences of evolution more quickly than other people. This is why, in old days, an artist was always spoken of as a prophet. He saw the trend of the future sooner than the rest of the world. Today, we do not speak of the artist as a prophet, we are much more likely to consider him a fool; whether the artist or the public suffers most by this attitude I am not prepared to say. But there is a good deal of truth in the remark of the man who said, in reply to the old adage: 'No man is a hero to his valet,' 'So much the worse for the valet.'

I want to show you this afternoon why the poet of today is as he is, why the work that he is doing differs from that of the great period of American poetry, the period which gave us Lowell, and Longfellow, and Emerson, and Whittier, and Bryant.

Everything has a hand in making a poet. The place he lives in — its climate, soil, and geological formation; the people by whom he is surrounded — their social customs, religious ideas, artistic impulses, warmth or coldness of heart; the books he reads — the breadth or narrowness of their outlook, their insistence upon certain phases of life, the dignity or looseness of their style. An artist feels these influences more keenly than other people by the very fact of being an artist, which presupposes a greater sensibility.

Now the great artists I have named were, without exception, New Englanders. They all inherited the English tradition by right of birth, and they were also, by right of birth, puritans at heart, only a few decades [*sic*] removed from the men who settled this country for reasons of faith. In many ways there was less change in New England between the times of Cotton Mather and Emerson than has been the case between Emerson's time and our own.

England was the great Protestant country, and the Puritans who came over here were the most extreme example of that Protestantism. Is it any wonder that their descendants should have produced an art which is at once the quintessentialism of the Anglo-Saxon and the Protestant point of view?...

Now the mainstay of Puritanism was morals. The distinct right and wrong to every conceivable thing. Broadly, they believed that they were right and everyone else wrong; but individually they were always searching their consciences to find out if they were living according to its dictates. This preoccupation with the moral side of life determined the whole of New England civilization....

The modern poet is often accused of being, not immoral (Heaven forfend the term!) but non-moral, and non-moral they certainly are, considered from the Puritan standpoint. The modern artist no longer points an obvious moral, and he is preoccupied with other subjects than the ethical ones of Puritan tradition. Perhaps I should go farther, and say that the Puritan morality was a special kind. It was not a

general interest in the ethical side of life, it was a particular
interest in one sort of ethics. Walt Whitman, great poet
and moralist though he was, was an innovator in form and a
pagan moralist in substance, for which reason it took many
years for his greatness to be generally recognized. Another
poet who stood apart from the Puritan tradition was Edgar
Allan Poe. And he was offering, and many times vainly
offering, his works at [*blank*] a page to magazines and killing himself with drink and despair, at the time when Longfellow was receiving highest honours for what must be acknowledged was only sentimental versifying. We have
learnt to be prouder of Whitman and Poe than of any of
our other poets, but a great change of feeling was necessary
to bring this about. When this change of feeling was accomplished, the 'poetry of today' was born.

I do not wish to be misunderstood. I am by no means be-
littling the work of the early New England poets. They
have written beautiful poems, but I hardly think they rank
with the Englishmen of the same epoch. And they invite
comparison with them as they spring from the same tradition. For English Protestantism is also an affair of morals,
even if the morals be not quite so rigid and uncompromising
as those of our New England forefathers. When Englishmen lose their moral background they seem also to lose their
sense of proportion, and plunge into license. What could
better illustrate the reverse of the medal of English morality
than the eroticism of a Swinburne or an Oscar Wilde? One
of the diverging differences between the English and American poets of today is here. You have only to compare the
poems of the English poet Rupert Brooke with those of any
one of the prominent poets in this country. Rupert Brooke's
poems exhibit all the best and all the worst results of the
English Protestant ideal. Here is the high-minded, religious attitude, and side by side with it a decadent sensuality all the more unpleasant because veiled. In Brooke's
case the sensuality preceded the high-mindedness, and one
feels that, at the time of his death, he was struggling toward
a saner outlook, even if possibly at the expense of much of
his originality. In no modern American poet that I know

will you find either the religious or the sensual aspect of life presented in quite such a way.

We might consider this extreme abandonment of the moral attitude to be a peculiarity of the English poets of our time, had we not the poets of the Restoration to prove their ancestry. The only English poet I can think of who was quite without moral preoccupation of any sort, and yet who never fell into licentiousness, is Keats; and he is a phenomenon hard to explain. Essays and books without end have been written on the subject, but no one, so far, has been able to say why he was as he was. We can only be thankful for him as an inexplicable fact.

All this dissertation is merely to prove that Emerson, Holmes, Whittier, and the others, were merely following the long stream of English literature in writing as they did, and as such should be considered rather as English provincial poets than as American poets proper. Poe and Whitman may therefore be considered not only as our greatest poets, but as our first; and one was [1] born and lived out of New England where the English tradition was certainly strongest. That they could have developed in the New England of that day seems extremely unlikely; as it was, the dominance of New England culture over the whole country, at that time kept them from being understood for many years.

Strangely enough, there started up in New England a rare (if it had not really existed I should have said an 'impossible') anomaly. A true pagan poet shut up in the cage of a narrow provincial Puritanism. But the odd part of this poet was that the cage was not merely the exterior one of family and surroundings, it was the cage of her own soul. I refer, of course, to Emily Dickinson. She was a pagan if ever there was one, but she was also a sincerely religious woman. This led her to address poems to the Deity in so joyous and familiar a strain that her first biographer wrote many pages to explain her seeming irreverence. But really there was no explanation except the one I have given. But one cannot help feeling that sincere though her religious

---

[1] 'one was' read originally 'both were'; evidently Miss Lowell forgot at first that Poe was born in Boston.

attitude certainly was, it was due partly to early education, and partly to atavism (her father was a minister), while her own peculiar, personal characteristic was the pagan one. I have often wondered whether this duality of temperament was not responsible for the shyness and elusive quality which she is said to have had in a marked degree. In wider surroundings might she not have developed into a greater poet and a more tranquil woman? It is significant that those of her poems most prized by her contemporaries are the ones we care least for today.

After the great epoch for American literature of which we have spoken so often this afternoon, there followed what I can only describe as a 'slump.' I have pointed out elsewhere the causes of this. They were the Civil War and the effects it brought with it, a train of events unsympathetic to the growth of poetry. One man, however, who enlisted in the Confederate army in 1861, at the age of nineteen, ranks as an exception to this fact. He was Sidney Lanier. Writing constantly, both during the war, and after, Mr. Lanier's first volume of poems (and the only one issued during his life) did not appear until 1877. Lanier is hardly the great poet his friends claim him to be. His work shows strongly the influence of Keats, dashed over with tinctures of Tennyson and Swinburne. They were not happily chosen teachers for a man of Lanier's temperament. He needed a more astringent training, and oddly enough, his studies in earlier English literature, which his biographer assures us were exhaustive, failed to give it to him. His poetry remained to the end overloaded with ornament, and cloying in its sweetness. Nor is it any more separated from the main current of English literature than the work of the ante-bellum New England poets. He too is an English provincial poet, but a less considerable one than the men who preceded him.... He attempted no new effects in his verse, although in it he certainly achieved a high degree of lilting grace; it remained for the moderns to essay a form somewhat akin to real music.

Coming down to our own time, although contemporary with Lanier, Bret Harte wrote attractive verses, and so,

later, did Eugene Field, and Celia Thaxter, and various
other people, but none of them possess any particular qualities of distinction. They were mostly side issues with their
authors, who were usually far more seriously inclined to
prose. But in the first years of the present century three
young poets appeared who considered themselves as first
and primarily poets. They were: William Vaughn Moody,
George Cabot Lodge, and Joseph Trumbull Stickney.
Sadly enough, although they were all in their twenties when
they began to publish, not one of them is alive today.

The least important of these men, and the last to die,
was Mr. Lodge, he was an earnest worker, but with very
little originality, and encumbered with a weight of outworn tradition. Trumbull Stickney's work is full of a delicate and subtle charm, but it had not attained anything
like artistic maturity at the time of his death. William
Vaughn Moody, on the other hand, had done most important work before death came, he is best known by his play,
'The Great Divide,' but his real work, what he felt to be his
real work, were his poems.

These three men were intimate friends, and undoubtedly
influenced each other to some extent. But contemporary
with them, and also, it is sad to realize, no longer living was
Arthur Upson, a graduate of the University of Minnesota.
Upson, like Stickney, had not perhaps reached his poetic
maturity at the time of his death. But one feels, in reading
him, the pathos of a talent wasted for want of training.
Whoever were Upson's critics, they certainly allowed him
to perpetrate a vast number of indiscretions, so that his
verse, as it is, amounts to very little. And yet here was a
man with real poetic feeling, and his work gone for nothing
because of glaring defects of taste and technique. Perhaps
he felt that something was wrong, and did not know what it
was, nor how to remedy it; at any rate, whatever the reason,
he drowned himself in his thirty-third year.

Although neither Upson nor Moody are alive today, they
really belong to the generation of poets now living. They
are very much akin to the more conservative of these. They
died before the present revival of interest in poetry, and,

also, before much of the freshing influence of change had blown across the literary sky. Still we can by no means refuse them a place in modern American art. Therefore I shall include them among my 'poets of today,' and read you one or two selections from their work.

This is a sonnet of Arthur Upson's, one of a series called 'Octaves in an Oxford Garden':

> The day is like a Sabbath in a swoon.
>   Slow in September's blue go fair cloud-things
>   Poising aslant upon their charmèd wings,
> Stilled to the last faint backward smiles of June.
> Softly I tread, and with repentant shoon,
>   Half fearfully in sweet imaginings,
>   Where broods, like courtyards of departed kings,
> The old Quadrangle paved with afternoon.

It is unnecessary to point out the bad taste, and lack of adequate technique, which caused Mr. Upson to pass an antiquated word like 'shoon' in a modern poem merely because he needed a rhyme. We must forgive him for the sake of the beautiful last line.

No such kindly allowances need ever be made for Moody. He knew his medium well, had thoroughly studied it, and his sense of the dramatic, so well exemplified in 'The Great Divide,' kept his poems clear and all of a piece.

[*Here she read Moody's 'Gloucester Moors.'*]

You will see here the old, fine, moral preoccupation giving place to something not less fine, and, one could almost say, 'emancipated.' Beautiful too are the nature bits which seem as setting and refrain.

The rest of the lecture consisted chiefly in readings from living poets: Josephine Preston Peabody, Robinson, Frost, Fanny Stearns Davis, Grace Fallow Norton, Sara Teasdale, Grace Hazard Conkling, Louis Untermeyer, Edgar Lee Masters, William Rose Benét, Vachel Lindsay; and then, just as Miss Lowell reached the Imagists, the manuscript ends with the pencilled note: 'Finished extemporaneously.'

On January 10, Miss Lowell went to the Athenaeum for some books about New England. As she came in person, instead of sending Mrs. Russell as usual, and as she arrived just before closing time and insisted on keeping the place open half an hour, her visit caused enough of a commotion to be recorded at some length in the Librarian's diary. On the eighteenth, she dined at her brother Lawrence's, to welcome home Katherine, who had just returned from England with her grandchildren, where she had taken them to bid goodbye to their father before he left for the front. On the twenty-first, she heard Masefield read at Wellesley.

Just as she was correcting the second set of proofs for Aldington's *Images*, she got a letter from him, bidding her take the whole book away from the publisher, because he had heard nothing from him in a long while; she wrote back that the book would be out in a few days, that such a remove would be unfair and moreover expensive, as then Aldington should pay for the press-work. She also took occasion to scold Aldington, as Flint's review of *Six French Poets* had appeared in the *Egoist* for January 1, after it had been accepted by the *Little Review* for its January–February number; and the *Egoist* printing had been somewhat abbreviated; but it was actually Flint himself who had done this, thinking she would be better pleased. She heard that the review of her book in *Poetry* had also been bluepencilled; she scolded Miss Monroe, but took it back when the manuscript was sent her.

Meanwhile, there was more excitement in the press. Joyce Kilmer interviewed Josephine Peabody for the *New York Times* of January 23, 1916. Apparently Mrs. Marks (who was coming to resent the success of a kind of poetry so different from her own, and yet wanted to be broad-minded) said more than she intended; while Kilmer ('I have never met him,' Miss Lowell wrote Frederick Marsh; 'but he hates me as much as if we had been friends from childhood') understood more than Mrs. Marks actually said. The headlines ran: 'Free Verse Hampers Poets And Is Undemocratic. Josephine Preston Peabody Says That, Nevertheless, War Is Making Poetry Less Exclusive And The Imagiste Cult Will Be Swept Away.' Miss Lowell's account, to Mr. Marsh, was —

... Although my name was not mentioned, it was practically an attack upon me. Mrs. Marks felt terribly about it, when she read it in the paper. She wrote to me immediately, saying that she had been misquoted; and indeed it did look a little foolish, considering that she had written that splendid review of 'Sword Blades' in the 'Herald' last year. She felt so badly that, with infinite courage, she made a speech at the Poetry Society dinner,[1] explaining how much she admired my work, and that none of the remarks she was quoted as saying applied to me. Her speech, as I have heard it repeated, seems to have been a pretty clear denial of the opinions attributed to her in the 'Times' interview. Joyce Kilmer was present at the dinner, and it cannot have been pleasant for him to hear her denying the things he reported her as having said. Certain it is that in the next Sunday's paper appeared this unskillfully veiled attack.[2] By way of making their position more clear, it seems that Mr. Oppenheim asked Mr. Kilmer to interview him on the other side of the question, that Mr. Kilmer replied that his chief said that he had given all the space he wished to 'free verse.' Mr. Oppenheim, however, had written a letter on the subject, which he insisted that they publish, and this they consented to do, though at the same time making it as little conspicuous as possible by publishing it in the Automobile Section!!!

You advertise so much in the 'Times,' it seems to me that you ought to be able to force them into a somewhat

[1] The annual dinner of the Poetry Society of America was held on January 25; as Miss Lowell was not present, two or three people wrote her about it, stating that Mrs. Marks's speech was a denial of most of the interview and a public apology to Miss Lowell.

[2] In the Book Review section of the *New York Times*, January 30, appeared an unsigned and very contemptuous review of *Six French Poets*.

less hostile attitude to one of your authors, that even if they wished hostility, they might also give the opposite side. But perhaps this is not done in the first publishing circles; in which case forgive my indiscretion. 'Reedy's Mirror' has also published an attack on me, this time for my poem, 'Patterns.' But Mr. Fletcher has answered it in the 'Mirror,' if only they will publish it; and Mr. Untermeyer is to answer it in the 'Chicago Evening Post.' You always said you wanted me to be a storm-centre, and I hope you are satisfied. I can see that private life was very pleasant, as I look back upon it.

On February 1, the Russian Ballet, war-ousted from Europe, began a two-weeks' run in Boston. Some loud protests in New York, particularly against the dark-skinned lovers in *Scheherazade*, caused the Boston police to be ostentatiously present at the opening in the American Athens. But the slaves of Scheherazade had faded to the faintest coffee-tinge; and although the Moor-doll in *Petroushka* was as black as a shoe, the police saw nothing to prohibit — perhaps because their attention had not been called to *L'Après-Midi d'un Faune*, which was performed in the original version that had shocked Paris. Miss Lowell was present that first night, and went again as often as she could.

The next night, the New England Poetry Club met at her house. The Untermeyers were present, also Stark Young. Josephine Peabody, Fletcher, and Grace Hazard Conkling read poems, and Miss Lowell gave selections from her next book, *Men, Women and Ghosts*, a title she had just chosen. This was the last of her engagements for a couple of weeks; possibly during this interval she had a slight operation on her nose, which had been delayed all through January because of the great grippe epidemic.

During this period, she also prepared the manuscript of *Some Imagist Poets, 1916*, which she got off on February 21; worked like mad correcting errors for the second edition of *Six French Poets*, which was selling out in three months; and wrote her next lectures. On February 15, she had her first Gebhard concert of 1916; on the twenty-first, she left for New York, well prepared for another fray.

The next afternoon, James Oppenheim came to tea, and left the manuscript of his *Creation* for her criticism. That evening she addressed the MacDowell Club on 'Poetry and Polemics,' having refused the milder subject of 'Poetry and Religion.'

> ... I realized that under the guise of poetry, you were all asked here to witness a cockfight, with the odds running high against the imported bird. And yet how you have worked to make these odds secure! Here are nine poets lined up along the bottom of your postal-card, of which one, possibly two, may fight on my side. That leaves seven. Seven lusty natives to down one alien woman. Thank you for the compliment...

> One reason that you fight in vain is that you fight with prejudice as your principal weapon. Now to fight with prejudice is about as moral as to fight with a sword tipped with poison. Only, and this is a queer thing about prejudice, when the sword comes to be examined, the poison is always found to have evaporated. The moral obliquity remains, but the weapon is harmless.

> Personally, I believe in the motto: Live and let live. Also, personally, I can admire work done in many styles, and from many points of view. But it has been made evident to me that the large majority of people do not share my tolerance. That the adherents of 'The New Poetry' write in *vers libre* or 'polyphonic prose,' that they point out the beautiful effects of light striking the water in a bathtub, or write a story with its inevitable ending thus denying the 'glad book' principle so dear to the heart of the average American, is taken as a personal affront. Instantly the whole horde of objectors runs yapping into the newspapers, and the poet, who only asks to be let alone to work out his experiments in peace, who only asks that his integrity be respected, finds himself obliged

to waste valuable energy in defending his position lest his enemies create so hostile a public opinion that he cannot work at all.

The public, she went on to say, had lost interest in the old poetry; now the excitement alone was sufficient to prove that its attitude had changed. The cause lay in the desperate sincerity of the new poets. Hitherto, except for Poe and Whitman, there had been no true American poetry: our poets, even when they chose American subjects, wrote in the English fashion. But today, one could not find English prototypes of Masters or Lindsay or Fletcher or even Frost.

> What these men had to say was different from what any English poet has ever had to say. Our environment is no longer exclusively English. Our immense immigration is at last beginning to be felt. We of the pure Anglo-Saxon stock are constantly coming into contact with people of other nationalities, and consciously or unconsciously are being modified by them. We may not realize it, but slowly. before our eyes, the American race is being born. And one of the evidences of it is that we are beginning to hew new pathways for ourselves in this most intimate thing — Poetry, and to free ourselves from the tutelage of another nation....

She defined the new 'externality' of the modern poet as —

> a passionate desire for truth, and a dispassionate attitude toward whatever his search for truth may bring him. He records; he does not moralize. He holds no brief for or against, he merely portrays.
> 'This art is cold,' cry the older generation, 'it is immoral.' It is neither the one nor the other. Because the artist speaks no moral, it does not mean that none exists. Lives carry their own moral with them. The world of 'The New Poetry' is like the world of reality: the morals are there, but it is for us to pronounce them.
> Another desire of the modern poet is to record his truth,

not someone else's. To express what he feels, not... what Alfred, Lord Tennyson, would have felt. Now it is very difficult to know when one is thinking one's own thoughts; we have all of us read so much, and imbibed so many thoughts belonging to other men, that one has to go on through the phase of imitation (often unconscious imitation) to reach a clear, personal outlook again.... So it is safer to hunt for directness among those poets who have earnestly studied their art....

Every young writer begins by imitating his predecessors, as is quite right and proper. For an individual reproduces in himself the gradual evolution of the race. As the writer develops, he gradually sloughs off this subserviency to other men, and produces an art in which he can express himself unhampered. Now, originality is not very well understood by the world at large. In nine cases out of ten, it is distinctly antipathetic and disturbing. The man of original mind is called every kind of thing: idiot, hypocrite, charlatan... When the truth of the matter is that those thoughts are his everyday companions.

It never seems to occur to anybody that the greater the poet, the less he is like the run of ordinary men....

Poetic movements go through regular stages. First is the era of change, of stepping out to conquer new territory; then is the era of accomplishment, when the ground conquered is developed to the utmost extent of its resources; last comes the era of decay. Those poets born to the first era are always treated to contempt and hilarity. But never does the contempt and hilarity stop the march of events. 'The New Poetry' in America today is in the era of change...

She then took up the objection that the New Poetry was not democratic, that it did not appeal to the populace at large. She replied that the majority of a moment was only political democracy; art, however, appealed to the best people over long periods of time.

... No art can be democratic. Is it possible that there is anybody so blinded by a beloved theory as to think for a moment that the great mass of people has any artistic

desire, any real artistic taste? If our painters really wished
to follow the majority of public taste, their pictures would
be endless variations of the smart American girl.... Few
things require more education than taste.

... That there are men in every walk of life with real
poetic feeling in their hearts I do not for a moment deny,
and it is to these men that poets with the welfare of the
people at heart should address themselves. For poetry
should try to lift men to its level, not sink itself to theirs.

And does this new and widespread interest in poetry tell
the objectors nothing? Do they not see that this 'New
Poetry' is reaching a large class of people who were numb
to the older types of poetry, because in them they found
nothing which made them feel at home?

... The conventional minded do not like originality, but
there are many people who are only conventional because
they have not the mental vigour to find a way out. These
are not the creators, they are the appreciators. They find
in 'The New Poetry' the freedom they have longed for.
They find that beauty is not chained upon the other side
of the Atlantic, that it is here at their own doors. That the
Singer Building is an achievement to be proud of and one
need not sigh because we are not evolving Parthenons;
that the Yankee farmer is as interesting as the Wessex
yokel; and that sun, and rain, and cloud are as lyric here
as over the orchards of Normandy.

It is a great deal to have discovered that. And the New
Poetry, the New Painting, the New Music are making such
discoveries every day.... Our artists are only just beginning
to dare to be themselves. And the New Poetry is blazing
a trail toward Nationality far more subtle and intense
than any settlement houses and waving the American flag
in schools can ever achieve. I might say with perfect truth
that the most national things we have are skyscrapers,
ice water, and the New Poetry, and each of these means
more than appears on the surface.

... A poet is a man with a vision in his soul, and for want
of a better word, we call that vision 'art.' Art is a thing,
an organic entity. The artist is concerned only in tran-

scribing the vision, or, if you prefer, in creating art. But, as the greater includes the less, all art stirs the emotions. The greatest art is more emotional than any life save the greatest. Life is transient, art is perennial; and great art bears its emotion down the ages untarnished for our solace and inspiration....

She then read poems by Untermeyer, Masters, Fletcher, and Aldington. Lindsay she omitted, as he was in the audience; and Frost's 'A Servant to Servants' would have overstepped her time. As a finale she read her own 'Cross-Roads,' then sat down, saying 'Now I am ready for the onslaught. Pray begin.' Helen Gray Cone promptly challenged her.

The next day, the twenty-third, she spent conferring with her publishers, dining that evening with the Untermeyers. The twenty-fourth she lectured on 'The New Poetry: with a Particular Inquiry into Imagism' at the Colony Club, of which she was a member. As a dog auction was going on in the ballroom, she had to read in the gymnasium amidst 'a constant *va et vient* of the entire audience'; eight years later she recalled the event as being 'altogether the most unfortunate in my experience.' [1]

The lecture was another approach to the subject nearest her heart. To meet a popular objection, she started by tracing the ancestry of the New Poetry.

> ... To begin with its progenitors (and you will remember that one of the slurs cast upon it is that it has none), let me remind you that once upon a time there lived in England a poet who wrote many unimportant poems, three superb masterpieces, and all done in his youth, that he was for some time a lay preacher, that he spent most of his long life talking, and eating opium, and that his name was Samuel Taylor Coleridge. Coleridge is one of the most immediate progenitors of 'The New Poetry.' Another ancestor is the homely poet of village happenings, George

[1] Letter to Mrs. James A. Burden, December 2, 1922.

Crabbe. But perhaps Crabbe is rather more a friend than an ancestor.... Its other two indubitable ancestors are Edgar Allan Poe and Walt Whitman. It seems a little strange that the poets immediately following Coleridge in point of time should have been the austere and astringent Matthew Arnold, the saccharine, sentimental Tennyson, and later, the Swinburne of confused and redundant imagery, the mystic pre-Raphaelite Rossetti, and the weakly-audacious, artistically-insincere Oscar Wilde. What had become of Coleridge's virility, of his fertile, robust imagination, of his broad strength of phrase, of his unerring instinct... ?

Browning has the robustness, to be sure; but he has no such vivid bold imagination as Coleridge. And the fantastic note, which Coleridge struck in all three of his great poems, 'Christabel,' 'The Ancient Mariner,' and 'Kubla Khan,' is totally lacking in Browning. Coleridge had descendants, however, and it is through them that we derive from him, rather than directly. But we must cross the channel, or the ocean, to find them. The truth is that Coleridge's literary sons were here, and in France, rather than in England. And the greatest of them was Poe.

From Poe is but a step to Baudelaire and Mallarmé. It was the influence of Coleridge and Poe which brought something into French poetry which had never been there before. The precise formal pattern of French verse was broken. It is not the rococo romanticism of Victor Hugo; it is a fundamental awakening of the personal imagination. A daring of imagination for its own sake; for the joy of its functioning, without the slightest heed as to where the imagination might lead. The influence of Baudelaire and Mallarmé on the younger poets of their day is well-known. It not only changed the whole form and content of French poetry, it changed music as well. For Debussy also derives from Mallarmé....

Now we have traced the fathers and grandfathers of 'The New Poetry' on one side; on the other there is Whitman. His is not so important an influence as that of Poe, but it is a very strong influence, nevertheless. Not because he wrote 'free verse,' whatever that may be. But because he wrote about things that had not hitherto been considered stuff for poetry; and wrote about them simply and roughly as he thought.

Imagism, she said, did not spring from the two main currents of nineteenth-century poetry: the romanticism of Byron (which died out, leaving him unappreciated as a satirist, where his true genius lay) and the cult of Words-worth, which in England produced Tennyson and in America almost everything.

> To a more artistic people, to a people who believe in sug-gestion rather than statement, the poetry of the so-called 'great American period' is well-nigh unreadable, because of the constant presence of the poet as showman, perpetu-ally ticketing his characters or his scenes, and telling us how they fit into the Ethical Scheme. And it was only one ethics, with never a hint that there could be any other.

Then times changed, the race itself began to change, new forces were abroad; and Miss Lowell accepted the date of the first number of Miss Monroe's *Poetry* as the official date for the beginning of the New Poetry. Its leading exponents were Frost, Masters, Pound, Lindsay, Fletcher, Aldington, H. D., Flint, Lawrence, Untermeyer, Sandburg, and herself. She spoke of their work as characterized by externality, humor ('I mean the deep fundamental humor which underlies all sane life'), the finding of poetry in unpoetic things, the use of prose syntax, the avoidance of the old poetic diction, the cult of freer rhythms, and the exact picture, the omitting of specific moralizings, and freedom of choice of subject. After a brief history of Imagism, she read selections from some of the poets she had named, ending with her own 'Cross-Roads.'

On the next day, February 25, she attended the luncheon given by the Poetry Society of America for Masefield, and left for Brookline immediately afterwards. On the next day, she attended the dinner for Masefield at the Women's City Club in Boston.

Two evenings later, on the twenty-eighth, she addressed the newly founded Harvard Poetry Society in the *Monthly* sanctum, on the top floor of the Union. Fletcher, who had already addressed the society, probably arranged for the invitation; and in order that a number of undergraduates who were not *Monthly* members might hear her, the meeting was officially called a candidates' meeting. After Miss Lowell arrived and was seated at the big table, there was a pause of embarrassed silence, which she broke by saying:

'Well, I suppose you boys want to know about *vers libre*, and I suppose you think that Whitman wrote it; well, he didn't.'

Her talk continued informally, coming to a climax when she read 'Patterns' and 'The Cross-Roads' from the manuscript of her forthcoming *Men, Women and Ghosts*. The discussion that followed was perhaps memorable chiefly for John Wheelwright's earnest query: 'What do you do when you want to write a poem and haven't anything to write about?' As she was leaving, with a regretful glance at the centerpiece of beer and pretzels, which nobody offered to disturb, E. E. Cummings asked her what she thought of Gertrude Stein.

'Do *you* like her work?' Miss Lowell replied, Yankee-wise.

'Why — yes ——'

'I don't.'

On March 1, the New England Poetry Club met at the studio of Lilla Cabot Perry. Edwin Arlington Robinson and Stark Young were guests. As Robinson never read his own work in public, Miss Lowell read 'Ben Jonson Entertains a Man from Stratford,' from his forthcoming *Man Against the Sky*, a volume which she reviewed for the *New Republic*, May 27. Louis Untermeyer's — *And Other Poets* appeared early in March; she was terribly pleased with his parody of her polyphonics. The first half of this month she spent writing poetry (the Yankee vein had cropped out again), correcting the last errors in *Six French Poets* (finished March 9), and preparing the manuscript of her next book of verse, *Men, Women and Ghosts*.

On March 15, she left on the one o'clock for New York, to attend the Civic Forum Dinner for poets at the Hotel Astor. She was one of the guests of honor; the others were Alfred Noyes, Cale Young Rice, Laurence Housman, Jessie B. Rittenhouse, Edwin Markham, Percy MacKaye, Louis Untermeyer, Josephine Dodge Daskam, Meredith Nicholson, and John Masefield. Each guest was allowed exactly ten minutes in which to speak; and Miss Lowell made the most of her time. She stopped the applause which politely greeted her name by asking for hisses, 'just to make me feel comfortable and at home'; and the audience courteously obliged her, only to renew the hissing more earnestly when she berated some of the poets of the past.

Besides drawing up a contract for her next book with her publishers, she also got hold of Joyce Kilmer, made him interview her on the subject of the New Poetry, then read and approved his manuscript, which was published in the *New York Times* for March 26.[1] She also spent an hour and a half with Theodore Stanton, who wrote the 'American Rubric' for the *Mercure de France*; saw quite a little of Kreymborg, who agreed (politely) that there was very little future for most of the *Others* crowd; and dined with Robert Bridges of *Scribner's*, at Mrs. Charles MacVeagh's.

On the eighteenth she took the Twentieth Century from New York for Chicago, arriving there the next day in time to lunch at Mrs. Arthur Aldis's, with Arthur Davison Ficke

---

[1] Republished in Joyce Kilmer's *Literature in the Making*, New York, 1917, pp. 253–62.

and Mr. and Mrs. Edgar Lee Masters. Mary Aldis was planning to give 'Off the Turnpike' and 'The Grocery' or 'Number 3 on the Docket' as plays in her amateur theater — a scheme long planned but never completed. Mrs. Russell was to play the rôles in a setting devised to show her single figure. After resting and dining at the Hotel Congress, Miss Lowell went as guest of honor to the customary Little Theater Sunday evening reception, then repeated her Colony Club lecture, 'The New Poetry, with Special Reference to Imagism,' in the Fine Arts Building under the auspices of Maurice Browne's Little Theater. It was a surprising success. She wrote to Untermeyer:

> My lecture in Chicago was exceedingly well attended. I was told that they turned a hundred people away from the doors for lack of room, and certainly every seat in the house was filled. There were people standing in the aisles, so that they were afraid of a raid by the police. Even tickets in the adjoining tea-room, where they couldn't possibly see me, were sold, and a sort of overflow meeting, at which I read my poems on Tuesday afternoon — and which was got up on the spur of the moment without any advertising — was very well attended, too. They are very enthusiastic in Chicago, both for and against — everything; hence these wild diatribes on one side, and the extreme of interest on the other.

She spent a week in Chicago, during which time she met and made a firm friend of Carl Sandburg. When she reached Brookline, she was exhausted, and the complete proof for *Some Imagist Poets, 1916,* was awaiting her, also a number of urgent requests for her to lecture in various places. An attack of jaundice and indigestion, resulting from general exhaustion, put her to bed, but did not interfere with her correspondence.

To Miss Pease, of the Chicago Little Theater, she wrote on April 1, accepting the suggestion that she give four

lectures on contemporary American poets some time in
February or March, 1917.

> I am not at all sure that I care to go to any other cities
> in the West. At any rate, I will think that over. I do not
> want to be advertised as a regular lecturer, or bookings
> solicited. I am a poet — not a lecturer — and I only lec-
> ture occasionally as a rest from other work and to help
> along the cause which I have so much at heart. If you
> receive any particularly tempting offers for anywhere
> beside Chicago, you might submit them to me....

To Margaret Anderson, she wrote on April 10:

> I enclose my check for $150.00, as I agreed to do, but
> there is a string attached to it: I want you to get out one
> number, as I told you in Chicago, which will not advocate
> violence. Also, I want you to get out one number in which
> your real principles appear more perfectly than they some-
> times do.
>
> You remember our conversation on the difference between
> love and lust, when I was in Chicago; and you remember
> how well we agreed on the subject? Now, you see, love on
> the purely mental side is apt to be as dry and brittle as a
> withered leaf; but love on the purely physical side is as
> unpleasant as raw beef steak. It is the combination of
> the two which is perfection.
>
> Now your contributors, in their fear of not speaking out
> plainly enough and representing facts as they are, always
> err on one side — the love in most of the stories you publish
> being merely a question of brute animal appetite. This is
> doing your own point of view as much injustice as if you
> were to write the goody-goody stories of the ordinary
> magazines.
>
> Is it not possible to find authors with a sufficiently all-
> around sense of the views of life to portray the combination
> which makes human life what it is, in which neither mani-
> festation is obscured to bring out the other? I would give
> anything to see it in some number, and why not this one?
> I have tried to do it myself in my own work, but a poet can
> do so little. Story-telling is so much more direct.

The next day, she spoke at the Authors' League Banquet in New York, on the position of the poet in the practical world:

> ... Of all poorly paid work, poetry is surely the worst paid.... One moment I regret that poetry is underpaid; the next I desire that it be not paid at all.... Other arts eventually become self-supporting, poetry practically never does. To this failure of the golden lure I believe we owe it that poetry is so single-minded, so prone to follow out its dreams unhindered by public opinion.
>
> [Also,]... I am not aware that I have said anything against the poet earning his living by some other work than that of poetry. History has shown us many examples of poets of the first rank filling practical positions at the same time.... It is only minor poets who are too unpractical to do anything else well, I am convinced....
>
> ... I can hardly urge upon you too insistently the great need that America has for trained criticism. The so-called 'reviews' in our newspapers doubtless serve some good purpose, but it is the purpose of the publishers and the booksellers, not of the poet or of literature. The poet seeking to learn his art finds not one hint in the various discussions of contemporary verse to help him on his way. He is treated as a news item, or he is not treated at all....
>
> It used to be said that no artist could live in America. I do not believe that is true today....
>
> We, in America, are prone to fads, and fads are always transitory. Anything that can be construed as freakish, or odd, or strange, is sure of immediate attention. And often that attention, no matter how clamorous, does scant justice to the work which arouses it....
>
> Another of our American characteristics is that we are inclined to dig artistic movements up by the roots to see how they are getting on. Now it is a melancholy truth that although America produces a great many young artists of unusual promise, she has difficulty in bringing them to a satisfactory maturity. Our literary history is strewn

with clever first books.... Once a man has written a book of promise, the whole force of American life is upon him to urge him to the quick production of another. With us, reputations are made and lost overnight. The habit of the older countries, where it takes ten years to make a reputation, which, once made, is unassailable... is certainly more conducive to the growth of a great art.

Another difficulty against which the American poet has to struggle is the extraordinarily little aesthetic knowledge which the American public possesses. With the breakdown of classical education, there has crept into our schools a strange amorphous system of many subjects, and none pursued to mastery. There could be no better method devised to puzzle and blunt the taste of a people.... There is no playing truant to the schooling one gives oneself.

The last generation — too many of them — fled from these conditions. It is our proud belief that we can be artists and still live in America. And yet many of us realize, since Europe has been closed to us on account of the war, how much comfort and stimulus we derived from occasionally sojourning there.

It is the conditions I have been enumerating which make the advent of the highly trained critic so important. These critics will do more than any other body of men to temper our American atmosphere to the degree in which art can most happily flourish. Again, the critics can do more to raise the taste of the public than we, the artists, can do. We speak, perforce, in terms of art.... It is not the artist's business to explain: it is enough that he create. But his future depends upon explanation.... The work of a great man is re-created in every generation by those few men who study and love him, and who proclaim this love aloud for their contemporaries. If the artist is the heart and brain of art, the critic is its arms and legs — its motive power, in short.

After pointing out that Rupert Brooke and Gaudier-Brzeska were properly appreciated only after their tragic deaths, she continued:

Are not these cases pathetic? And the more so that they are not isolated in the history of art. A little intelligent criticism accorded these men in their lifetimes would have given them what is more valuable than life itself: content, the feeling that at least one has not lived in vain.

Brooke and Brzeska, and others like them on both sides of the Atlantic, are dead. You can do nothing more for them. But there are struggling poets among us today. In spite of newspaper *reclame*, we of 'The New Poetry' have not found our path strewn with roses....

'The New Poetry' is a tree of many branches.... There are the realists, with Edgar Lee Masters and Robert Frost, at their head; the folk singers, chief among them Vachel Lindsay; the romanticists, of which William Rose Benét is a good example; the Imagists, to which group I belong, and the 'vers libristes,' some of whom are Imagists, and some are not. For the followers of 'vers libre' derive from two distinct sources, one being Walt Whitman, and the other, the French Symbolistes.

Roughly speaking, however, all these groups have certain traits which they hold in common, and which separate them from the poets immediately preceding them. Chief among these is 'externality,' the regarding of the world as having an existence apart from one-self. Introspection is not the besetting sin of the new poets, as it was of the poets of the nineties. Again, all these groups seek life and vividness. They are all desperately sincere, and to portray the world about them in its truth and its beauty is their only aim. To this end, they frequently discard metre for the free rhythm of emotional thought. They endeavor to write with the syntax of prose, an artificial arrangement of sentences detracting, in their opinion, from simplicity and directness of presentation.

Only those poets with a natural sense of rhythm can write 'vers libre' well. Had I time, I think I could prove to you by reading two or three examples aloud, that it is among the most musical verse in the English language. It is written to be read aloud. Poetry is a spoken, not a written art....

On the seventeenth she wrote to Aldington:

It was awfully sweet of you to mind Middleton Murry's articles in the Daily News and the Times, against 'Six French Poëts.' I had already gathered that they were by the same man, from the similarity of the remarks and style. Some of the English criticisms have been good, like the 'Observer' and the 'New Witness'; others have been bad. But one and all have accorded me really a great deal of space, and the English consignment of 250 copies was sold out almost immediately and another consignment sent for. The entire first edition has gone, the book has been out of print for a month, and we are rushing ahead a second edition as fast as possible....

I am through my lectures for this year, and am about to settle down and write steadily, as my new book is coming out next Autumn....

I get so homesick for you and Hilda sometimes that I really don't know what to do. It seems a thousand years since I have been in London, and Fletcher and I have often said what we would not give to see you both. If it were not for Fletcher I should go crazy. He is the only person here with whose work I am in sympathy. With the others it is always making allowance in speech, trying to put oneself into their point of view for a moment. But Fletcher and I keep each other going. We have had some rather nice experiences lately; among others, one of the Harvard boys has written a long thesis on 'Imagism' as his candidate's essay for the Bowdoin English Prize — and that's something. Fletcher has seen a copy of it, which Aiken had, and says it was excellent. We do not know who the boy is, as the theses are submitted anonymously, but I am going to find out through my brother. He quoted a lot of my ideas, which I gave in my address to the boys out there this Winter, so I suppose he was in the audience.[1] But it

[1] This essay, written by myself, proved my introduction to Miss Lowell. Her brother evidently proved unable to pierce my pseudonym, for Fletcher inserted a note in the manuscript, asking the author to communicate with him, since publication might be arranged. But as the essay did not get the prize, and as I had kept a copy, I neglected to call for the original. Miss Lowell then seems to have inquired of the editors of the *Advocate*, *Monthly*, *Illustrated*, *Lampoon*, and

all proves we are getting ahead. Sometimes I get awfully discouraged, but I don't suppose that is really necessary....

Arthur Davison Ficke had asked her opinion of a forthcoming article, 'Modern Tendencies in Poetry,' in which he took an attitude of cautious interest. On April 20, she returned his manuscript, with her comments:

> I have kept your paper an unconscionable time, because when it arrived I was having jaundice, and no sooner did I get over that than I went to New York to speak at the Authors' League Dinner, and I have only just come back.
>
> Your paper interested me very much; and, you know, I quite agree with you that there are certain effects which can only be got in regular metre. But, of course, I think that I like the other effects, to be got in *vers libre*, a little better than you do. It is, as I am constantly saying, merely a matter of taste, and when an opponent is so fair and liberal as you are, I personally have no quarrel with him....
>
> I cannot agree with you that the poems of Allen Norton and Donald Evans are anything but 'pastiche'; and to give so much space to them under the head of 'New Poetry' — when, in fact, they are merely 1890 gone a little mad — seems to me to confuse your readers. In fact, on occasions I think your desire to make a telling rhetorical point has run away with your discretion, particularly in your enumeration of the schools of poetry. 'Others' is a magazine. I have never heard Mr. Kreymborg or any of the contributors pretend that they held any tenets which would weld them into a school; and I have already told you what I think of the Patagonians. I never heard of the Spectric School. Is it not a little hard to mix the serious-minded with the merely bizarre in this way? Should not one endeavor to be strictly fair even in politics? [1]

Crimson if they knew who wrote it; but I was not connected with any of those papers, and they did not know. Eventually (with some astonishment that the famous Amy Lowell could have heard of an essay which existed so obscurely) I learned of her interest; telephoned her; and was invited to dinner. My paper was never published, except for such parts of it as she used in her 'Consideration of Modern Poetry,' *North American Review*, January, 1917.

[1] The sentences to which she was taking exception read in the published article (*North American Review*, cciv, 445, September, 1916): 'In future years it will

Let me thank you very much for what you say about the fact that the New Poetry has shattered the illusion that all the poets are dead, and let me again thank you for what you say about form being necessary to art. Raw emotion is not poetry, as I am always preaching, although sometimes like a voice crying in the wilderness, as the conservatives cannot see that we have any form, and those more radical than we say we have too much.

Once more let me thank you for your 'Chats on Japanese Prints.' I have read it again since I came home from Chicago, and always with renewed pleasure. It has even inspired me to write a number of little 'Hokku' poems — for no reason whatever except that you put me so in the mood. I have even taken the liberty of making a poem from one of your translations of one of the Japanese poets, moving it round a bit and changing parts of it for my own benefit, and called it an adaptation from the poet in question. I trust this is a liberty which you will permit.

If you ever come East, do let me know; and let me thank you once again for your interesting and very able paper. I wish we had more discussions of this sort from those who disagree with us. It is a pleasure to argue and to disagree with a worthy opponent, and it is more of a pleasure to find, as I did so often through your paper, passages with which I agreed so fully that I wish I had written them myself.

In his reply, Mr. Ficke denied that he had ever translated from the Japanese; he had a vague hope that one of his own poems had been translated into Imagism, which would be an everlasting joy to him!

doubtless not be possible for the dispassionate critic to take the new poetry quite as seriously as, today, it takes itself. Such an observer may grow a little bewildered and even amused as he surveys our Schools and Movements — the Imagists and Vorticists and Spectricists and Patagonians and a Choric School and Heaven only knows how many others.' Miss Lowell had never heard of the 'Spectricists' in April, because the first printed account of them did not appear till June in the *Forum*. The Patagonians were Donald Evans and Allen Norton, lumped together as a school and named for the former's *Sonnets from the Patagonian* (1914). Ficke evidently struck out 'Others,' substituting 'a Choric School,' which Pound had announced in *Others*, October, 1915.

On April 27, she motored out to Wellesley, where she read from her own poems in Billings Hall.

For the last couple of months she had been one of several active persons who had been raising money to found a magazine devoted to poetry, with William Stanley Braithwaite for editor. Miss Lowell was somewhat dismayed when she learned that his policy was to be eclectic, for she distrusted his enthusiasms; however, she got Aldington a small corner as London correspondent, and submitted poems. The first number appeared in May.

Some Imagist Poets, 1916, which at first had been expected in mid-April, was formally published on Saturday, May 6, but did not actually appear in the bookstores until Monday. The reviews were wide-spread and heated. 'Bath' continued to distress or amuse the feeble-minded. In a letter to Burton Kline, of the *Transcript,* Miss Lowell wrote on the seventeenth:

> I do not mind any serious criticism, no matter how severe; but I do object to all this nonsense about the bath-tub which has been appearing in various papers. 'Spring Day,' of which it is a part, I consider one of the best poems that I have ever done. My treatment of the bath-tub was a purely pictorial matter — a question of the play of light, etc. — not at all the kind of thing they represented, and, also, the bath-tub was the shortest section of a long poem. It is hard for any artist to do serious work when so many of the newspapers persist in this ridiculous attitude.

None the less, five hundred of the thousand copies were sold in a month.

A rival to *Some Imagist Poets, 1916,* as a best-seller was Sandburg's *Chicago Poems,* which appeared in the same month. Ever since she met Sandburg in Chicago, they had been corresponding; on May 8, she wrote:

> I am perfectly delighted with your book! I do not know when I have read anything that gives me so much pleasure. Your 'Omaha' is a wonderful poem, and I feel about

'Billy Sunday' as I did the first time I read it. I think it
is one of the things which ought to have been said, and
which I think you said in exactly the right way. Certain
it is that no book that I have read for a long time has given
me anything like the thrill and delight of this one. I am
reviewing it for Mr. Braithwaite's 'Poetry Review,' and
you will see then just what I think of it.

This review appeared in the July number.

On the same day that she wrote to Sandburg, she wrote
to Harriet Monroe, but in a very different mood. *Some
Imagist Poets* had not contained any reference to Miss
Monroe's encouragement of Imagism, beyond the customary thanks to periodicals for permission to reprint; and
she had felt sufficiently hurt to write to Ferris Greenslet.
Actually, every one of the Imagists felt that she was
dubious and indifferent about their work, and had privately complained about her rejections of their best poems
and her delays in publishing what she accepted. Miss
Lowell in particular had once written her a strong letter,
pointing out that while Miss Monroe gave constant
editorial notices about such poets as Pound and Lindsay,
she never made any such references to Amy Lowell.
However, on Greenslet's advice, she had inserted a handsome sentence of acknowledgment in *Some Imagist Poets,
1916*. Meanwhile on April 4, Miss Monroe had come to
visit Miss Lowell for a week or so, and had gone to the
meeting of the New England Poetry Club on the fifth,
at which the Harvard Poetry Society was present for the
first time. Miss Monroe wrote up this meeting for *Poetry*,
without mentioning Miss Lowell, whose illness had prevented her attending. Miss Lowell thereupon wrote her
frankly:

> I have told you several times that I was deeply injured
> by your neglect of me in your editorial articles. Hitherto
> I had supposed that your neglect was mostly an oversight.
> Of course, I could not disguise from myself the fact that

one does not overlook things in which one is interested, but I did not suppose that there was any studied desire to neglect me in the eyes of your readers. Now, however, I am forced to a different point of view, for in your article, 'Down East,' you do not so much as mention my name, and yet, the very meeting of the Poetry Club which you praise was thought of, planned, and engineered by me, as I told you several times. Also, I am the president of that club, and it seems to me it would have been well to have mentioned me in that connection. As your hostess at the Club that evening (although I was prevented from being actually present by ill health), it seems to me some acknowledgement was due me. You always wish 'Poetry' to be recognized and complimented on its achievements, and proper due given to you as its editor — I do not see why proper due should not be given to me as president of the Poetry Club, even if it was impossible for you to say anything about my work, or my position among the poets of this section of the country; in fact, in the country at large...

I can only take this as a studied insult, which I hope you can explain and devise some method to do me a little more justice in the future. I cannot deny that I am exceedingly hurt. I had not thought it of you. I had supposed we were real friends, and I still sign myself

Affectionately yours,

The May meeting of the New England Poetry Club, to which the Harvard Poetry Society was again invited, was held on the eleventh at Josephine Peabody's house in Lowell Park, Cambridge. Miss Lowell was present.

A letter from Aldington told her that the Conscription Act meant he would be called to the front in about five weeks; that Flint and Lawrence would also be called; and that his father was trying to get him into an officers' training camp. Hilda would take over his job on the *Egoist*. Miss Lowell answered on the twenty-third:

I have not recovered yet from your letter which came yesterday. I cannot bear to have you go to the war! But,

of course, it must be, and I can only hope from the bottom
of my heart that you, and Flint, and Lawrence all come back
unscathed, and feeling that you have gained something by
what is, after all, a great experience.

How can they take Lawrence? I thought he was very
ill with consumption. What will they do with him when
they get him? I should not think he could last long in the
trenches!

Fletcher sent me out Hilda's letter to him to read, and
I must say I think she is awfully plucky. Perhaps she is
right to stay in England. I am sure I should do the same
if I were in her place. But, of course, I wish she were here....

You must not forget, dear Richard, that even in the
trenches one is not dead. Plenty of books are being published from the trenches all the time. They have a kind of
vicarious and romantic interest through being written by
men on active duty....

I want you to feel that although the ocean separates us,
nothing else ever does or can, and that Hilda can always
turn to me for anything at any time. I wish I could come
over and see you before you start for the front. It hurts me
very much to feel that this cannot be. But I am not in
Fletcher's position. If I go abroad I am obliged to take
other people with me, and I do not think it right to endanger
other lives on the high seas at present unless absolutely
necessary; and of course it is not.

I suppose it will take you some months to be trained before you can leave England. So I am sure that the Anthology
will reach you some time, as I sent it two weeks ago. I
do hope you will like it.

If you want to send some poems to me, I have no doubt
that I can get Braithwaite to take them.

Do write to me often and keep me posted as to all that
goes on with you, and how Flint and Lawrence are. If you
go into an officer's corps I do not suppose that you will see
much of them; but I hope you will know something about
them. I shall write to Hilda constantly about myself and
everything, and try to make her feel a little bit as though
I were dropping in. And if she ever decides to come to

America, please let her consider that she can come directly
to me while she is deciding what to do. I wish she would
come from the bottom of my heart.

Good luck, dear Richard. I cannot help feeling that the
war is nearing its conclusion, and I only pray that it will
be over before you get there. I shall write constantly, if
you will give me an address. With a great deal of love,

Sincerely yours,

On the twenty-ninth, Lawrence wrote her from Cornwall:

MY DEAR AMY,

I got the two copies of the new Imagists on Saturday.
It looks very nice, as usual, the book. And I think it is
quite up to the mark, don't you? It should make a considerable impression. Tell me what the reviewers say, if
you have time, will you?

. . .

For news, we have always the same: we are gaily ringing
our last shilling, for the empty heavens to hear it. We have
just got a very lovely little cottage *of our own* here, rent £5
a year, looking down on the sea. There are sea-pinks, like
little throngs of pink bees hovering on the edge of the land,
over a sea that is blue and hard like a jewel. There are
myriad primroses spread out so large and cool and riskily,
under the shadows, and bluebells trailing under the great
granite boulders, and foxgloves rearing up to look. It is
rather a wild, rocky country, of magpies and hawks and
foxes. I love it.

The 'Compulsion' comes into force June 24th. I suppose
they will leave me alone, because of my health. If only
the War would end! It is so bitterly meaningless now.

Have you any news? It is time now that the miracle
should happen — the Lord suddenly shouting out of the
thunder 'Fous-moi la paix, là-bas,' like a man just waked up.

Many greetings from my wife & me.

Yours

D. H. LAWRENCE

On May 29, Richard Hunt interviewed her for an article
in the September *National Magazine*; they talked a great

deal concerning birds. About this time, Fletcher sailed for England, to get married; he reached England just as the news of Kitchener's death was reported. Albert Mordell had discovered the *Dome of Many-Coloured Glass* and was so impressed that he initiated a correspondence, and now was writing an article about her for the August *Poetry Review*. Her letters of June 2, and 15, contained some excellent ideas on aesthetics; but the two never really saw eye to eye.

> ... Apparently poetry is chiefly valuable to you on the ethical side. To me it is chiefly valuable on the aesthetic side. It seems to me that perhaps that is just where the fallacy of your theories about older artists occurs, in that you take them as teachers of life instead of creators of art....
>
> I think we must admit, however, that there is a something which we call art which is as undefinable as love or patriotism or any of the moving forces of the world, and which has an inspiring and civilizing effect and is one of the most worthy projects to which a man can devote himself. This thing called art is primarily important because of being an organic entity — a thing in itself, for itself, and by itself — as important to us as the universe in which we live, and as detached. At the same time it contains many minor importances for us. Among other things, the teaching of life, which you rate so highly; the solace of beauty; the inspiration of knowledge. A thousand things; and the more of these things any given poem can contain, the more overtones it has, the greater will be its appeal; though not necessarily the greater it is in itself....
>
> Your tracing the parentage of my work back to Keats and Poe is very interesting, and it is one which I should make myself, substituting Poe, however, for Poe's master, Coleridge, and adding another ancestor in the shape of the French *Symbolistes*.... Certainly Browning — although I have consciously studied him less than any of the other poets — has a very marked cousinship with some of my poems....

... You seem to me to belittle the style of Fielding and Sterne, who are perhaps two of the greatest stylists in the world. And when you say that there are best sellers that keep up the interest more than the works of these men, I confess I cannot agree with you.

... You say that the conversations of Goethe, Johnson, Napoleon, Northcote, and Coleridge are chiefly interesting because of what is said and not how it is said. May I suggest, however, that four of these men, Goethe, Johnson, Napoleon, and Coleridge are stylists of the first class. Napoleon's conversations, letters, and orders, as translated into English, I admit do not impress, but you must put this down to the stupidity of the translators; in the original French, I think I have seldom read such virile, terse, and eminently beautiful presentations of any subject. To my mind, the value of these older literatures is entirely an aesthetic one — aesthetic and, as you are so often at pains to point out, historical. It makes no difference whatever to me whether I differ with a man's religious views; I can still take an interest in the form in which these views are couched; I can still find the psychology of one who could so believe of great importance to my knowledge of humanity....

Of course, it is true that 'books have done much to hinder the world's progress,' and that 'in the cases of half-educated and ignorant minds admiration for the classics hinders the march of ideas,' but it is not true that we have an 'increased nervous sensitiveness'; on the contrary, those very specimens of morbid religious hysteria so prevalent in convents and monasteries are well recognized nowadays as belonging to the pathology of nervous diseases. And when you say that men have copied great authors and written equally great works in so doing, it seems to me that you forget that to copy something already done requires a much lower mental function than to create something originally; and that the copies are good, is no criterion of the powers of their authors.

It is now generally recognized that Ruskin's art teaching was about as bad as it could be; but I suppose no one will deny that he wrote a beautiful English, and that his descriptions have scarcely ever been surpassed. Here, close to our own time, is a case in point. Carlyle's 'French Revolution' is inaccurate in many points. No thoroughgoing historian would recommend it for a moment, but as a great epic poem it must always hold its own. These are merely modern analogies to Dante, Thomas à Kempis, and St. Augustine. They do not deal with religious phenomena, it is true, but they do deal with things which we have learned to view differently; their worth in one sense is diminished thereby, but in another sense it is still supreme.

I believe that the great value of literature is not in the direct ideas it teaches, but in the mellowing effect it has upon the mind and character; and this mellowing is done by educating and strengthening the aesthetic perceptions. Therefore, I think that perhaps you have not sufficiently pointed out, in your two books, wherein the real value of literature lies. Of course, personally, I am as much a free thinker as yourself, as you will have long since discovered in studying my works, but I am so much of a free thinker that superstition no longer even makes me angry. I pity a man who turns monk and shuts himself off from the world, but he annoys me no more than the primitive savage who puts totems outside the door of his hut.

... That is a splendid sentence of yours: 'A really great critic is always a poet, whether he writes in verse or not.' I believe it to be true, and we need constructive critics very badly in America....

Another bit of literary opinion is to be found in a letter to John Livingston Lowes, June 12. Professor Lowes, then of Washington University, St. Louis, had written asking her to lecture before their Association; in her acceptance she recalled his 'Unacknowledged Imagist,' in which he formularized the Imagist credo and then proved that Meredith was of the school.

I have just thought that it must be you who wrote that extremely interesting paper entitled 'An Unacknowledged Imagist' in 'The Nation' of February 24th. May I take this opportunity to thank you for so excellent an understanding of our works and methods, and also for picking out of Meredith's works these beautiful pieces and putting a frame round them, as it were....

Had Meredith lived today, I cannot help thinking he would have written this kind of poetry. Certainly, if ever a man was hampered by existing forms, it was Meredith in his verse. Is there such a difference between poetry and prose after all, when both are really poetry?

E. E. Cummings, now an A.M., was starting forth on his career; Miss Lowell gave him letters to the editors of the *Century, Scribner's,* and the *Craftsman,* one of which read:

> I am taking the liberty of giving a letter of introduction to you to a young Harvard graduate, named Erstline [*sic*] Cummings. He has been specializing in English I believe, and had one of the Commencement parts last year, in which I hear he was very brilliant. He is extremely interested in all forms of the New Poetry, but I do not think confines himself to that branch of literature. He is very anxious to get something to do on a magazine, and although I have very little hope that you will have anything to give him, perhaps you would be so kind as to see him for a few minutes and give him some excellent advice. At any rate, I hope that I am not trespassing upon a very slight acquaintance; if I am, pray ignore both this note and the letter he will bring you.

In the early part of the month, Maxwell Bodenheim telephoned that he was in Boston, whereat she invited him to dinner. Over a year before he had written her of his liking for her poetry; and the correspondence that ensued had been, on his part, as sensitive and exotic as his verse, which she admired.

But the dinner was a comic failure. Bodenheim arrived two hours early, and thus found nobody at the gate to guide him through the sheepdogs, who instantly disliked him. He fled, trying to hide behind a tree from the seven of them, yelling 'Help!' A maid dashed out with a large whip, but could not rescue him before 'Mary' had damaged his somewhat already damaged coat. After he was jocularly pinned together, and the customary hour had arrived, the meal passed pleasantly enough, except for the ladies, who were astonished that in manner he was so unlike his verse. The post-prandial poetics were highly satisfactory, however; Miss Lowell directed him to read certain poems to Braithwaite the next day. His frankness concerning his difficulties was such that Miss Lowell gave him a cheque, and over his polite protest remarked firmly that that was all she ever paid for torn coats. When he left, she telephoned Braithwaite to be sure and take some of his verse for the *Poetry Review*. A partial account of Bodenheim's adventure got into the *Chicago Illustrated News*, September 12, 1917.

On June 15, *Sword Blades* was exhausted and a second edition was ordered.

All this while she was preparing the manuscript of *Men, Women and Ghosts*. She had also made arrangements to lecture on four American poets in Chicago and Brooklyn; her price she raised from $50 to $100; and she planned to write these lectures in the summer. In a letter to Fletcher on the twenty-eighth she remarked:

Mrs. Jack Gardner has just caught on to us. I read her some of my things the other day at Bessie Perkins's, and she has been raving about those Napoleonic pieces ever since. Now she is all agog — evidently thinks she has got hold of a new thing which it is very well worth while for her to know. You know she always likes to be in the swim. I am sending her your two books today. She will make an excellent advertising agent for us; nothing could be better.

To H. D. she wrote on July 7:

It is extraordinary how the movement is progressing. Margaret Wilkinson of the Los Angeles 'Graphic' was here yesterday. She is tremendously enthusiastic, and I think she will write up some more about us in the 'Graphic.' One can hardly take up a paper that does not mention some of us; in fact, it is becoming a country-wide movement this side of the Atlantic, and it is astonishing to think that a little handful of perfectly unknown poets have done this thing, for as Ferris Greenslet said to me yesterday, we have put cosmic poetry 'absolutely on the blink.' And it just proves what perfect sincerity and earnest endeavor will do.

On July 4, was held the last Sevenels concert of the season. On the fourteenth she sent off the finished manuscript of *Men, Women and Ghosts*, then celebrated by having the Untermeyers to dinner, where they talked over the latest magazine project, the *Seven Arts*. James Oppenheim was to be the editor; Frost and Untermeyer were two of the associate editors; and Miss Lowell, one of the first to be asked to contribute, promised manuscripts aplenty. About the eighteenth or the twentieth, she left for Dublin, where she planned to stay until October.

The summer in Dublin was occupied chiefly with correcting the proofs of *Men, Women and Ghosts* and writing her lectures on the American poets. On July 22, she sent her car over to the MacDowell Colony to fetch the young composer and conductor, Chalmers Clifton, and a poet friend, to dinner. James Whitcomb Riley had just died: when a reporter telephoned her the news and asked for a comment, she said she was very sorry. On July 29, Carl Engel was married; she went down to Brookline for the wedding. He was another of her young men to get married (Fletcher had taken the same step not two months before); it meant the end of those informal long talks that filled evenings absolutely without regard for time. She never was wholly reconciled to the fact. In early August, she had Robinson over from the Colony, to discuss her forthcoming lecture on him. On the nineteenth she read from her poems at the Dublin Lake Club, and though depressed by their reception, was cheered by having Dorothy Foster Gilman, a new admirer, to dinner on the twentieth. On the twenty-sixth she addressed 'The Out-Door Players' (Marie Ware Laughton's pupils) at Peterborough on 'Poetry as a Spoken Art.' [1] Braithwaite, who came up to hear it, reported it in the *Transcript* (September 2, 1916); and Martyn Johnson, who had just bought the *Dial*, and had come to Dublin to talk things over, asked her to boil the speech down for his paper. On Labor Day her house was full in consequence of a Bazaar for the Allies.

The MacDowell Colony invited her to dinner; and when the coffee was served, Robert Haven Schauffler (with whom Miss Lowell had disagreed on aesthetic and sociological principles, during an exchange of letters) made a point of offering her a cigar. She glared, then said with perfect calm:

'Well, you've all paid a nickel to read about me doing this; now you can see it free.'

Later she had the Colony to dinner at Broomley Lacey.

The most momentous event of the summer passed entirely without notice at the time. One afternoon, when Miss Lowell and Mrs. Russell were out driving, a sudden storm came up. It grew so very dark that they had to trust the horse 'Possibly' to find the way home down the mountain road. 'Possibly,' however, in a panicky mood, started up the mountain. Both women had to get out; and Mrs. Russell held the horse's head while Miss Lowell lifted the hind wheels of the wagon back into the road. Though she did not know it at the time, she tore some muscles and started the umbilical hernia that at last was to kill her.

Her correspondence did not lag. Sandburg wrote a poem on the recent death of Adelaide Crapsey, which he sent to Miss Lowell, who replied on August 8:

---

[1] Published, much compressed, in the *Dial* (LXII, 46–49), January 25, 1917; this shortened version is included in *Poetry and Poets*.

Your poem on Adelaide Crapsey is nice, so nice that I am going to be a pig and keep it, if you don't mind. Poor Woman! That is a dreadful book of hers, so poignant and in a way so abortive, so horrible to die with one's work half accomplished in that way — and still, as it is, it is an accomplishment. You have a way of striking a picture in a few words, which gives me great pleasure. I love your 'Among the bumble-bees in red-top hay, a freckled field of brown-eyed Susans dripping yellow leaves in July.' Bully! Bully!

The Van Allison birth-control trial was proving a storm-center, into which she resisted all efforts to drag her. To Untermeyer she wrote on the eleventh:

I have been bombarded with letters about the Van Allison matter, and I am afraid I have hurt all their feelings very much by refusing to take any sides. Granich mourns over me as a 'lost leader.' I did not explain to him that the very excellent reason of my non-committal reply was that I was afraid of having some of the sentences of my letter taken out of the context and printed in the papers, but simply said I was not interested in public questions. Semi-demi true; for I believe that an artist should place art above all other considerations. I know you do not quite feel this way, but I most firmly do. As a matter of fact, I think the whole Van Allison business was abominable. The trial was a disgrace, the remarks of the presiding judge were to my mind more objectionable than the theories he was combatting, and they showed a perfect, and I think an intentional, non-understanding of the point of view of the radicals. However, I really am in an awkward position, because I agree with neither radicals nor conservatives entirely. If I were heart and soul in sympathy with the methods of these advocates of birth control, it would be simple to come out and say so; but I am not. Their theory, as regards the ignorant proletariat, is open to question; they seem to me to defeat their own object by pursuing it in a hectic and tasteless manner.

Of course, I believe, like everyone else, that a sane kind

of birth control is often necessary, and more often expedient, but I think I also have a distinct feeling that there is too much 'prevention,' not only of births but of other things in our modern life, and that a certain luxuriance, profusion, waste, and self-sacrifice are necessary to civilization. If I were asked, I should say that we really need large families more than we need birth control. Under these circumstances you will see why it is impossible for me to take sides. I clearly do not believe in the attitudes of Mayor Curley and the presiding judge; but again I do not believe enough in Van Allison's methods to identify myself with his propaganda.

On the nineteenth she sent off three poems to the *Seven Arts*: 'Flotsam,' which was accepted for their opening number; 'William Blake,' of which they were dubious; and a lost poem, 'A Conversation.' She described it as ——

an answer to Robinson's 'The Man Against the Sky.' It may not appeal either to you or to Oppenheim, as it is distinctly an agnostic poem; but it is all my creed in a nutshell....

Oppenheim replied, approving her healthy and invigorating attitude; but the editors felt that the middle portion did not quite come off. She accepted their objection as just, said she would have another go at it, but evidently could not get it to suit herself, for it was never published, and the manuscript does not exist.

The first *Some Imagist Poets* sold 1301 copies in a year; the second anthology was virtually keeping up with it; and whenever royalties came in, Miss Lowell divided the cheque in six and sent each contributor his share of the gross receipts. D. H. Lawrence's thank-you letter contained his dreams of America.

> Higher Tregerthen, Zennor, St. Ives, Cornwall
> 23 August 1916

MY DEAR AMY

Thank you so much for the cheque for £8, which came today. Those Imagiste books seem to blossom into gold like a monthly rose. I am very glad, too, to hear of the good things the papers are deigning to say. You should see my English critics walking round me in every sort of trepidation, like dogs round a mongoose.

I will ask Duckworths to send you the poems & the Italian Sketches. You know we may only send books abroad, through the publisher or a bookseller. Otherwise, of course, I should gladly autograph them for you.

Thank God they did not make me a soldier. I had to join up, & spend a night in barracks, and then they gave me a total exemption. If they hadn't, I should have been a stretched corpse in a fortnight: that I knew, at four o'clock in the morning, on that fatal night in barracks at Bodmin. There is something in military life that would kill me off, as if I were in an asphyxiating chamber. The whole thing is abhorrent to me — even the camaraderie, that is so glamorous — the Achilles & Patroclus business. The spirit, the pure spirit of militarism is sheer death to a nature that is at all constructive or social-creative. And it is not that I am afraid or shy: I can get on with the men like a house on fire. It is simply that the spirit of militarism is essentially destructive, destroying the individual and the constructive social being. It is *bad*. How Aldington will stand it I don't know. But I can tell that the glamour is getting hold of him: the 'now we're all men together' business, the kind of love that was between Achilles & Patroclus. And if once that lays hold of a man, then farewell to that man forever, as an independent or constructive soul.

I am glad you think the war is virtually over. Official London seems to be saying, with much confidence, two more years of it. But nobody knows. God help us if this is going on for two years more. These last two years have made one at least two centuries older. In two years more, we shall have ceased to be human beings at all. Certainly England has spit on her hands and taken hold at last. The whole nation is hanging on tense and taut, throwing all her weight on the rope at last, in the tug of war. It is our tradition — to get our blood up at the eleventh hour. Well, the English blood is up now, the bull-dog is hanging on —

alas that it ever need have come to pass. What will be
the end, when the war *is* at last over, the mind refuses to
consider: but it will be nothing good.

So one's soul knows misfortune and terror. But there is
a limit to grief for one's fellow man: one becomes callous,
since nothing can be done.

Here we live very quietly indeed, being far from the
world. Here we live as if on one of the blessed Isles, the
moors are so still behind us, the sea so big in front. I am
very much better, much stronger, now. All the winter I
was so ill. I hope it won't be so again this year. But I
think not. I am busy typing out a new novel, to be called
'Women in Love.' Every day I bless you for the gift of
the typewriter. It runs so glibly, & has at last become a
true confrère. I take so unkindly to any sort of machinery.
But now I & the typewriter have sworn a Blutbruderschaft.

We go down & bathe among the rocks — not the typewriter, but Frieda & I. Today there were great rollers
coming from the west. It is so frightening, when one is
naked among the rocks, to see the high water rising to a
threatening wall, the pale green fire shooting along, then
bursting into a furious wild incandescence of foam. But it
is great fun. It is so lovely to recognise the non-human elements: to hear the rain like a song, to feel the wind going by
one, to be thrown against the rocks by the wonderful water.
I cannot bear to see or to know humanity any more.

Your remoter America must be splendid. One day, I
hope to come to see it, when there is peace and I am not
poor. We are living on credit as usual. But what does it
matter, in a world like this. Hilda Aldington says to me,
why don't I write hymns to fire, why am I not in love with
a tree. But my fire is a pyre, & the tree is the tree of
Knowledge.

I wonder if I have said anything censurous in my letter —
I think not. The honeysuckle smells so sweet tonight —
what are the flowers in New Hampshire? Often I have
longed to go to a country which has new, quite unknown
flowers & birds. It would be such a joy to make their
acquaintance. Have you still got humming birds, as in

Crèvecoeur? I liked Crèvecoeur's 'Letters of an American Farmer,' *so* much. And how splendid Hermann Melville's 'Moby Dick' is, & Dana's 'Two Years before the Mast.' But your classic American literature, I find to my surprise, is *older* than our English. The tree did not become new, which was transplanted. It only ran more swiftly into age, impersonal, non-human almost. But how good these books are! Is the *English* tree in America almost dead? By the literature, I think it is.

Remember me warmly to Mrs. Russell. Many greetings to you from my wife & me. You will never come back to the England you knew before. But at any rate, when you do come, you must come here.

D. H. LAWRENCE

Doran is to publish both the books of mine in America.

At the end of the month she sent a hot letter to William Rose Benét: he always wrote he liked her poems, yet had accepted none for the *Century* these eleven months, so she wanted an explanation. His reply was attuned to hers: though he always recommended her poems, they were rejected by his chief. Her next letter to him began: 'Look here, William Rose Benét, let's make up! I got mad, and made you mad, but I cannot altogether regret it, for I think it is just as well to know how things are.' Thus that little episode was closed.

On September 13, she wrote a long letter to Fletcher, in the course of which she urged him to return to America.

> I feel very strongly that, if you want to get ahead at this juncture, you should return to America. I cannot urge this upon you too strongly, as the more I see of the way things are going, the more I realize that one must be on the spot to keep abreast of the march of events.... Kissing goes by favour, and so do contributors. They are not picked out for the intrinsic merit, although editors may fool themselves into thinking so — they are picked out because they are friends of the editors, or they are Johnnies on the spot, or

something of that kind. Now your being in England at this moment is sufficient to make a rift which cannot be got over... England and America are far more separated than they were before the war; the mails are slower; and as far as poetry is concerned, the American poets are rising and overwhelming in popularity and power their English confreres. If you choose to live over there, you will become in the public mind that strange thing, an expatriate American, which again, in the public mind, is all against interest, being neither the home product nor native English. One has to be very great to keep on impressing oneself from a foreign country. You went away just at the moment when your reputation was being made; if you do not come back soon, you will lose what you have gained; and at this juncture you can gain nothing in England to counterbalance what you lose here.... It is a slow, up-hill job at best, and we are all of us merely on the first rungs of the ladder; but one has got to keep pegging up it; and you must not fool yourself into supposing that it is the excellence of the work which will help you. It is the excellence of the work which will keep you in a permanent place, if you once gain it by your own efforts otherwise; but if you wait for the excellence of the work alone to put you where you want to be, it will be a posthumous putting.

Meanwhile the Comstock Society was campaigning to suppress Theodore Dreiser's novel, *The Genius*. Henry L. Mencken asked her to sign the petition against their activity, and she replied on the eighteenth:

I am very glad indeed to sign this petition, and should have regretted not being able to throw what weight I have in the scale of liberty and freedom for the arts to develop themselves as they think fit. Nothing could be more pernicious to the future of literature in America than to have it in the hands of bigoted and fanatical people, who judge it for reasons quite other than its artistic merit. No country can hope to develop itself, unless its authors are permitted to educate it. I wish every success to the cause.

Unfortunately, the petition proved of no practical effect; but the American tendency towards a franker literature continued unhindered.

We may insert here an undatable anecdote, which illustrates the impish side of Miss Lowell's nature, and which was part of her own dinner-table repertoire. After acting very successfully the rôle of a cook in some play or charade got up by the Joseph Lindon Smiths, she went to a reception for some very important English people, who had expressed an especial desire to meet her. When she arrived — late, of course — the hostess dashed down, grasped her by the wrist, and dragged her at once the length of the room, to the guests. The hostess's gown had a long train that switched from side to side as she ran; Miss Lowell swore that to avoid it, she had to hop over it with each step. When they arrived in front of the fireplace, the hostess presented her: '*This* is the cook!' — and went away.

Miss Lowell was out of breath; her face was covered with beads of sweat. 'They looked me over,' she said, 'and saw nothing to make them suspect that I was not the cook.'

'Do you like to work in Dublin?' they asked very politely.

'Yes; but I think the work I do in the city is more satisfactory.'

'Do you like this house?'

'Yes, I am always glad to come here.'

The conversation continued on this basis; but finding it stiff and not very rewarding, she left early.

Later the hostess asked her guests how they enjoyed meeting Miss Lowell; they replied that they were sorry, but they had not met her yet.

'Why, yes you have: she was the person who played the cook!'...

On October 5, Miss Lowell moved down from Dublin. Not only was she glad to be back near a city, but she needed a rest. Overwork had produced its familiar results — neuralgia and gastritis, followed by a severe attack of jaundice. But any possible gloom was swept away by the news that, of the 1250 copies of the still unpublished *Men, Women and Ghosts*, only 300 remained. The book appeared on October 18, 1916.

CHAPTER XIV

MEN, WOMEN AND GHOSTS

Men, Women and Ghosts was originally dedicated to Mrs. Russell (to whom Miss Lowell eventually dedicated all her books, as token of Mrs. Russell's part in them); but at her request, the dedication was removed. The volume is a collection of the narrative poems which Amy Lowell had written since she sent off the manuscript of *Sword Blades and Poppy Seed*. The earliest was probably 'The Allies,' which is dated August 14, 1914; the last were written while she was assembling the book. All lyrics were purposely excluded, as being out of key. Already there were enough of them for a volume by themselves, but Miss Lowell was more interested in acquainting the public with the larger forms she was developing. A half of her new book was in free verse; a third was in rhymed meter; and the rest was polyphonic prose.

Of the thirty titles, twelve deal with war, including the four 'Bronze Tablets' about Napoleon and the five contemporary 'War Pictures.' Three of these, and five others, are studies of love and passion. Except for the ghost-story, 'Cross-Roads,' love is treated exclusively from the woman's point of view.

'Patterns,' the first poem in the book, and the first of her poems to become very popular, remains as great as it seemed on first reading. A dramatic monologue expressing the tragedy of woman in wartime, it transcends both war and love, and is ultimately an expression of the repressed rebellion against the conventions and laws of life that bind the heart of every living soul. As though aware of this universal application, Miss Lowell translated it from the present time back into the Queen Anne period, the 'stiff brocaded gown' of those years being a symbol at once handsomer and more expressive. The dextrous use of the paeonic meter (which usually is light and tripping) to convey the despair of a ruined life, and the balancing of irregular lines to produce a sense of regularity, could have been done only by an expert craftsman. The emotional structure of the poem, including the drop of the voice almost a minor third at the beginning of the third strophe, and the brief interruption of the prose (the letter), culminating in the strangled explosion, half oath, half prayer, 'Christ! What are patterns for?' at the end, is sheer genius. This dramatic appeal of a universal subject, with the honesty of the treatment and the glamour of the setting, triumphed completely over what in 1916 seemed like daring frankness. It has always been a favorite with readers, and once, in a western convent, it was even acted, a little girl being cast as 'Pink and Silver.'

'Pickthorn Manor' also deals with woman's love in a period also vaguely Queen Anne. The heroine of 'Patterns' loses her betrothed in Flanders; the Lady Eunice is a bride who falls helplessly in love while her husband is fighting in the same fatal place. He returns, and in a scuffle drowns with his bride. The central meaning of the poem, however, 'pertains entirely to the realm of psychology'; it is that of ——

> a person allowing his mind to dwell for so long upon a thing that he becomes as it were hypnotized into believing his dream actual. This is the meaning of Eunice taking Gervais for her husband. It is as it were an *idée fixe* which blinds her to reality, and around that obsession, grown horrible by its result, the poem is woven.[1]

'The Cremona Violin,' the third poem in the book, is another study of the neglected woman who falls into adultery. Her husband, however, is not a soldier: he is a concert-master, wholly devoted to his music.

[1] Letter to Winifred Bryher, June 29, 1918.

In 'The Cremona Violin,' my idea was not so much that Herr Altgelt's music absorbed him away from his wife, as it was that she was held in subjection to him by this same music. I think my sympathies were not entirely with Charlotta, for, if a person marries an artist, it is quite clear that they must admit the position of art in the other's life to be paramount; and this does not at all mean that the artist does not give all of himself to the person he loves, but simply that he is dedicated to an ideal which includes the person he loves, and carries him, and the object of his love, beyond. I think Herr Altgelt was extremely fond of his wife; I think, in fact, that he adored her; but it was also a condition of his being that he was forced to give himself to his music. This she failed to understand, and put down as neglect. It was merely a necessity of the situation, and which in marrying him she should have firmly recognized and agreed to. In other words, she was too selfish to be the wife of an artist, although she had enough artistic feeling to be attracted and held by this very art, which, in the final count, she was so terribly jealous of. She broke the violin, not in a rage at him, but in a rage at its being the reason that kept her from following her own purely selfish inclinations.[1]

The concert-master's profession allowed Amy Lowell to experiment in extending the effects of free verse. As she explained in her Preface, Debussy's piano-pieces had suggested using the movement of poetry much as the composer uses the movement of music. This was not the Imagist method of approximating the' sister art: it was more directly imitative; but it brought into her work the ever-changing motility which the Imagists had overlooked. The Imagist lyrics are static in mood from the first line to the last; Amy Lowell's experiments were deliberately dynamic. In 'The Cremona Violin,' the story proper is told in rime royal, while the passages describing the concert run through all meters and rhythms into free verse.

[1] Letter to Winifred Bryher, June 29, 1918.

In the poem on Stravinsky's 'Grotesques,' she set herself to translating a real piece of music into free verse, with such remarkable success that those who have read the poem have no difficulty with the quartet. In 'A Roxbury Garden,' Amy Lowell tried a cognate experiment: that of reproducing the rhythm of hoops and of battledore and shuttlecock in free verse.

'The Cross-Roads' is a tale of a suicide's ghost which waits with its rotting body in its cross-roads grave until the funeral of the woman passes; the poem ends as his avenging ghost pursues her out of sight. Miss Lowell was all but a complete sceptic about the supernatural. She had a famous story about her reading with Evangeline Adams, the astrologer, who told her that she was very soothing to insane persons, and that all the other members of her family were mad. Another time, the daughter of her scrub-woman developed such mediumistic powers that the police was called in; but Miss Lowell walked with the girl in the garden until she confessed the fraud and never attempted it again. Yet the subject fascinated Miss Lowell, none the less: she knew and could discuss all the theories. While she ridiculed the ordinary evidence which such authorities as Sir Oliver Lodge and Sir Arthur Conan Doyle offered as proof of an after-life, she insisted that there were some things which had not yet been explained. She believed in the secret room at Glamis Castle: her parents had been visiting there at a time when the age-old mystery was told the heir, and they had watched his light-heartedness vanish and his disposition sadden. Within a few months she was to visit Patience Worth. *An Adventure*, by C. A. E. Moberly and E. F. Jourdain, which had been published anonymously in 1911, interested her strongly, though she declared that if psychic auras could really saturate physical surroundings, she would have seen her father, whose coffin once stood in the very room where she worked night after night. Her own nerves were capable of affecting her imagination (she knew that Blake was speaking truth when he said he could stare at a knot-hole until he became terrified); but she was too interested in such tendencies not to enjoy them. In 'The Cross-Roads,' for the first time in her poetry, she expressed this side of her nature; while in 'Nightmare,' inspired by the letter N of George Cruikshank's *Comic Alphabet*, she expressed her delight in a playful supernaturalism which always pleased and never disturbed her.

The poems about the World War speak for themselves. 'The Allies' represents a serpent of men marching to destroy the red eagle of militarism. In the long column are a teacher, poet, mill-owner, and others, all determined to make the world safe again. 'The Bombardment' depicts the destructiveness of war: the inspiration of the poet, the life-work of the scientist, the arts (represented by the cathedral), and the crafts (the bohemian glass) are all destroyed, while the lives of women and children are threatened, in a conflagration under a heavy rain shot through with shells. The childishness of the whole thing is symbolized in 'Lead Soldiers,' where the problem is reduced to the microcosm of a nursery.[1] Tommy playing with his soldiers is the spirit of militarism; the nursery fire is patriotism; the china mandarin on the bookcase is the inherited wisdom of mankind; the rose he holds represents the arts. In the manoeuvres against an imaginary enemy, Tommy slips and upsets the pitcher on the wash-stand; but it is blood, not water, that flows. Meanwhile the mandarin bleeds helplessly to death, his rose broken.

'Bronze Tablets' is a series of poems written around one of Miss Lowell's great heroes, Napoleon, whom she admired, not so much as general or emperor as liberator and personality. He appears in only one of the poems — 'Malmaison'; and in that he hardly speaks, for the real subject

---

[1] In her reading at the Middlesex Women's Club, Lowell, on January 3, 1916, she called it 'a war-poem slightly disguised' (*Lowell Sun*, January 4, 1916).

is the tragedy of the Empress Josephine. (When Miss Lowell saw 'Malmaison' featured in the *Little Review*, she thought it the best poem she had ever written; and indeed it drew quite a little sheaf of congratulatory letters from strangers.) In 'The Fruit Shop,' an impoverished aristocrat, spending her last coins for fruit, just catches a glimpse of Napoleon's chaise as he departs for the war. 'The Hammers' is a sequence of sound-pictures of events connected with his fall: the building of the British ships; the destruction of his emblems on the Paris shop-signs; the eradication of the names of his victories from the arch in the Place du Carrousel; the flight after Waterloo; the making of his coffin. But in the last of the 'Bronze Tablets,' his statue on the Place Vendôme column dizzies the travellers. 'Malmaison' and 'The Hammers' are in polyphonic prose, from the changing rhythms of which Amy Lowell developed a new way of telling her story; she evoked it through a series of dissolving views, which imply the history without stating it.

'1777,' another historial poem, contrasts revolutionary Boston with decadent Venice — a contrast of two republics, two kinds of women, two seasons, two sets of color. The garden in '1777' was her own garden at Sevenels, which also inspired 'A Roxbury Garden' with its little girls at play. Besides this poem, and 'Lead Soldiers,' there are two other poems about children. 'The Paper Wind Mill' recounts a child's tragedy that actually happened to August Belmont at the Hague, while his father was Minister there; in Miss Lowell's poem, it becomes the tragedy of grasping the ideal and finding it dead. 'The Red Lacquer Music Stand' is the episode which terminates the first book of Goethe's autobiography, retold in an American setting. It becomes a symbol of the destructive effect of even the most spontaneous religion upon the joys of childhood.

'The Overgrown Pasture' is a group of four dramatic

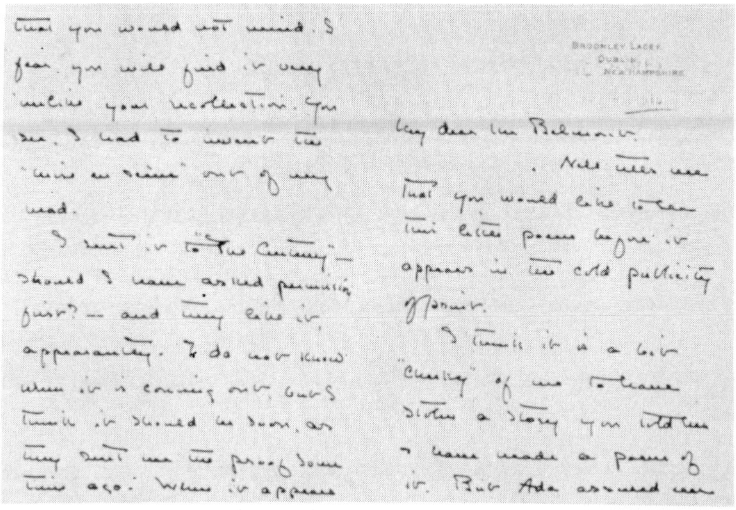

BROOMLEY LACEY
DUBLIN
NEW HAMPSHIRE

My dear Mr. Belmont,

Nell tells me that you would like to see this little poem before it appears in the cold publicity of print.

I think it is a bit "cheeky" of me to have stolen a story you told me & have made a poem of it. But Ada assured me that you would not mind. I fear you will find it very unlike your recollection. You see, I had to invent the "mise en scène" out of my head.

I sent it to "The Century"—should I have asked permission first?—and they like it, apparently. I do not know when it is coming out, but I think it should be soon, as they sent me the proof some time ago. When it appears

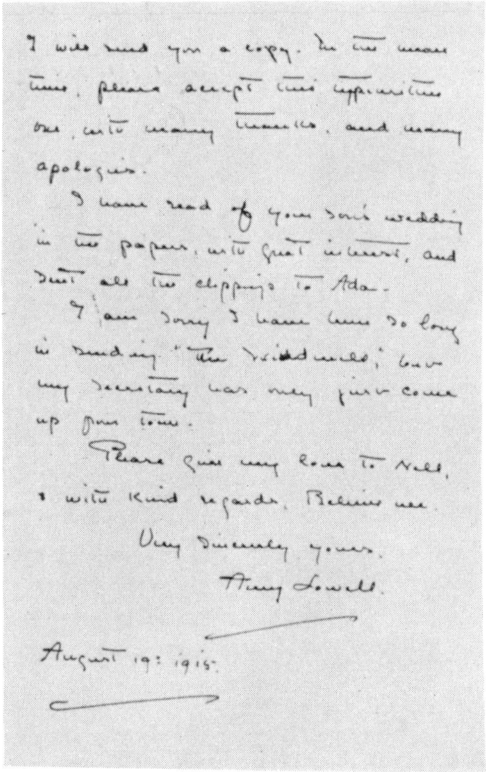

I will send you a copy. In the mean time, please accept this typewritten one, with many thanks, and many apologies.

I have read of your son's wedding in the papers, with great interest, and sent all the clippings to Ada.

I am sorry I have been so long in sending "The Windmill," but my secretary has only just come up from town.

Please give my love to Nell, & with kind regards, Believe me,

Very sincerely yours,

Amy Lowell.

August 19th 1915.

LETTER TO MR. AUGUST BELMONT CONCERNING 'THE PAPER WIND MILL'

monologues in Yankee settings. Miss Lowell believed that
the New England countryside had been drained twice of its
best blood (by the westward emigration and the Civil
War), and that this draining accounted for its decadence.
Frost once asked her what was wrong with the place; she
replied, 'Read your own poems and find out.' When
Ellery Sedgwick, of the *Atlantic Monthly*, was dubious
about the dialect of 'Off the Turnpike,' she wrote him
(October 26, 1915):

> But I must defend myself against your strictures about
> New England dialect. As a matter of fact, there is not a
> single expression in that poem that I did not find precedent
> for in Alice Brown's 'Meadow Grass.' After I had written
> it, I carefully took out her books and went through them
> with a view to correcting my own expressions, and I was
> astonished to find how very accurate I had been. I think
> it must be atavism, for although you yourself may have
> been brought up nearer the pumpkin fields than I, do not
> forget that my grandfather Lawrence was a farmer boy;
> and also I have been living cheek by jowl with the natives
> every summer for fifteen years.

Mary Aldis planned to present the first three of these
pieces in her experimental theater with Mrs. Russell acting at least one of them; unfortunately, the scheme was
never carried through, because of Miss Lowell's inability
to arrange a date. On August 22, 1916, Miss Lowell wrote
Mrs. Aldis:

> In regard to the place in 'Off the Turnpike' where the
> woman sits down hard on pulling the hand, which you and
> Mr. Brown are afraid may bring a laugh, I can only say
> that it depends entirely upon the actress. A good actress
> ought to be able to command laughs or prevent them, as she
> chooses. I have never had anybody laugh in that place
> when I have read the poem, and it seems to me that if you
> take the part of the woman, there will be no difficulty there;
> and if anyone else takes the part, perhaps I could coach her

so as to prevent the thing from appearing humorous. The peculiar quality of the Yankee mind is this constant darting from humor to tragedy, what one might almost call humor in tragedy; and without it, one does not have quite the proper psychology. But if we find in rehearsal that the thing does not get over in the right way, it will be quite easy to delete that line or substitute another. I am not at all pigheaded about such things....

You do not say anything about 'Number 3 on the Docket' in this letter. But I trust you are going to give that too, as it is far and away the most popular of that Yankee series. I have received quite a number of letters from people, speaking of its absolute truth.

Only one poem in the book can really be called personal; that is 'The Dinner-Party,' where Miss Lowell expresses the helpless rage of all original thinkers amongst the polite sceptics 'mildly protesting against my coarseness in being alive.' It was inspired by a dinner she had attended that spring in New York. 'Spring Day' (which begins with the famous bathtub) really belongs to the group 'Towns in Colour,' a series which is primarily visual, and thus allied to and yet contrasted with her experiments in music. The Preface acknowledges the influence of Fletcher's unrelated method, especially in his 'London Excursion.'

'Red Slippers,' the first of this group, contrasts the conventional ideal of beauty with its reality. One sleety December dusk, waiting in her automobile on Washington Street for Mrs. Russell, who was Christmas-shopping, Miss Lowell saw a window display of red slippers. The handsome colors and forms stirred her well-stored memory to its depths, raising momentarily to the threshold glints and gleams of many beautiful 'unrelated' things — stalactites of blood, crimson Japanese bridges, scarlet tanagers, firecrackers. It was the first stage of the creative process, which she caught as part of the poem itself. But past her vision the crowd hurried, to stare in an adjoining window, where an artificial lotus opened to reveal a doll, then shut again. This contraption was awkward, sentimental, tawdry, and meaningless; but it fitted the crowd's idea of what beauty ought to be, so they accepted it as such, never perceiving its real ugliness. 'One has often seen shoes, but whoever saw a cardboard lotus bud before?' Amy Lowell asked ironically.

'Afternoon Rain in State Street' is another color-study of Boston; so is 'The Aquarium,' which was written 'after many visits to City Point.'[1] 'An Opera House' and 'Thompson's Lunch Room' are similar studies of New York subjects.

Sometimes travellers from a rise look back to their starting point, and are surprised to see how far they have gone already; and if Miss Lowell looked back from 'Towns in Colour, to 'New York at Night' in her first book (a conventional protest against a city more like nineteenth-century London than twentieth-century New York), she was entitled to congratulate herself on her amazing progress; for then she was behind the times, now she was ahead of it. But more likely, she was merely distressed that she had ever let herself print that insincere thing.

So rapidly did *Men, Women and Ghosts* sell that on October 26, the eighth day after publication, a second edition of six hundred copies was ordered.

[1] 'Some Musical Analogies,' lecture at Harvard, March 3, 1919 (*ms.*, p. 19).

CHAPTER XV

THE SECOND GREAT OFFENSIVE IN THE POETIC WAR

'The life of a poet is by no means the dreamy aesthetic one people are led to suppose. A mixture of that of a day-laborer, a travelling salesman, and an itinerant actress, is about what it amounts to.'

NEURALGIA and gastritis, followed by jaundice — the result of overwork — obliged her to telegraph Washington University that she must postpone her November lecture; then she collapsed into bed. Everything seemed to be going to pieces around her. Her last two bachelors in the arts, Engel and Fletcher, were now married, a fact she did not like at all; and to make it worse, Fletcher had settled in England, perhaps permanently. She made him offers of indefinite loans if he would return to America. Aldington was in camp; she promised him she would stand behind H. D., if the pinch came; and indeed once it had come so close already that H. D. had been forced to ask for a loan, which, however, proved unnecessary. The Lawrences were living on credit; and Miss Lowell was conspiring with H. D. to help them ('... about augmenting the amount of his royalties. As a matter of fact, I should not have done that anyway, for I do not like deception, and it would have angered me to have it practiced upon me. But I will send him some money, with a note which I trust will enable him to accept it without scruple'),[1] when Frieda was driven to appeal for assistance. Flint she heard little from; he was overwhelmed with endless hours at the post-office. Fletcher informed her that he hoped there would be no more Imagist anthologies because the War had ruined the poetry of the other four.

[1] Letter to Aldington, September 5, 1916.

Lawrence wrote her on October 12, 1916:

> I am still typing away at my new novel: it takes a tremendous time: and the novel itself is one of the labours of Hercules. I shall be glad when it is done. Then I must really set to and write short stories such as the magazines may be prevailed upon to publish. Alas, I am afraid I was not born to popularity.
>
> The winter seems already to have come. The heather on the hills is dead, the bracken is dry and brown, and blowing away to nothingness. Already the fowls stand bunched-up motionless and disconsolate under the stacks, out of the wind, the sky is all grey and moving. One feels like a fowl oneself, hulking under the lee of the past, to escape the destructive wind of the present. The atmosphere all over the country is black and painful to breathe, one dare hardly move. Heaven send us happier days.

Instead of getting better, she got worse. On November 1, she rose and drove in town, to see the window display of her books at the Old Corner Book Store; but the trip proved a mistake, and she returned to her bed, to remain there for the rest of the month and most of the next, during which five weeks she was forbidden to do any work. She could dictate only the most necessary letters; and presently even that became impossible.

In the second week of November, her condition grew so bad that for four days she was kept under morphine. Ordinary doses had no effect on her; they had to be doubled. One evening she woke suddenly to see fire shooting through her room, then discovered that the fantastic flames were only a drug-distortion of the thin crack of light round her door. For an hour or so she enjoyed these amazing fireworks.

On the thirteenth, her brother Percival died suddenly of a stroke; she was so ill that she could not be told for some days.

Not until the twenty-first did she begin dictating a few

letters. H. D. had written that she was sailing for America on November 11: Richard had been privately informed that he would be called to the front any time now. Miss Lowell cabled that she would look out for H. D.; but the alarm proved false, Richard was not called, and H. D. remained in England. Proofs of a poem, 'Ballads for Sale,' which a new bookshop in New York, the Sunwise Turn, was issuing in broadside form for the Christmas trade, had to be corrected. Her books were going well; in fact, both *Six French Poets* and *Men, Women and Ghosts* promised a third edition soon. Miss Lowell was enraptured; 'I do wish I could beat Frost on a book!' she wrote Frederick Marsh, who replied that of all their poetry, only *Spoon River* and Tagore's books sold better than hers.

There was a pile of letters congratulating her on *Men, Women and Ghosts.* Josephine Peabody, in a note which Miss Lowell called 'feline,' said that she found more beauty and as much cleverness in *Sword Blades*; but that she liked the polyphonic things best, in spite of their form. Fletcher, on the other hand, wrote so rapturously that she burst into tears. Sara Teasdale and Jean Untermeyer preferred the Yankee poems; H. D., the garden poems; Sandburg, the 'Allies' and 'Red Slippers'; while Masters in his enthusiasm expressed no preference. D. H. Lawrence's letter was the longest.

Do write a book called Fire Rockets.

Higher Tregerthen, Zennor, St. Ives, Cornwall
14 Novem. 1916

MY DEAR AMY:

I was infinitely touched when there came this morning a cheque for £60, sent by you through the bankers. One is so moved by the kindness: the money, after all, is necessity, but the kindness is given. This I shall always treasure up, the kindness, even if I can pay you back the money. Because, after all, there is not much real generosity in the world.

I was rather sorry Frieda wrote and asked you for money: how do we know what you have to do with your money. But it is wearying, to be so much unwell, and penniless. I shall begin at once to move towards Italy: though heaven knows when we shall really get away. And I hope, from Italy, to come on to America, next year, when I am better and the winter has gone.

Why don't you come to Rome for a while? Think how jolly that would be, if we were all in Rome at the same time. Perhaps you would like it better, in these times, than London.

You[r] book, Men, Women and Ghosts, came two days ago. We have both read all the poems. I like this book better than 'Sword Blades.' I think The Cremona Violin is both a lovely story and lovely verse: an exquisite picture into the bargain. Then I like The Fruit Shop, the sense of youngness and all the gorgeous fruitfulness in store, then the sudden destructiveness of Bonaparte, a smash of irony. I like that. Some of the movements of the Hammers really startle one's heart — one listens, and hears, and lives, it is almost frightening. Only I don't care for the Ship. 'Reaping' seems to me one of the very best — a real straight jet of a story — but of course there isn't the newness of sensation one gets in Hoops — it belongs to the old knowledge — but it is *very* good. I always liked 'Spring Day' — sometimes the prose is best of all, better than any verse-form. — And then, after all, I like Towns in Colour more than anything in the book: and of these Opera and Aquarium most.

It is very surprising to me, now I have come to understand you Americans a little, to realise how much older you are than us, how much further you and your art are really developed, outstripping us by far in decadence and non-emotional aestheticism, how much beyond us you are in the last stages of human apprehension of the physico-sensational world, apprehension of things non-human, not conceptual. We still see with concepts. But you, in the last stages of return, have gone beyond tragedy and emotion, even beyond irony, and have come to the pure mechan-

ical stage of physical apprehension, the *human* unit almost
lost, the primary elemental forces, kinetic, dynamic — pris-
matic, tonic, the great, massive, active, *inorganic* world,
elemental, never softened by life, that hard universe of
Matter and Force where life is not yet known, come to pass
again. It is strange and wonderful. I find it only in you
and H. D., in English: in your 'Bath,' and the fire of the
lacquer music-stand, & Acquarium, [*sic*] & some Stravinsky,
and here & there in Roxbury Garden — which, to my mind,
is not quite chemical and crystallographical *enough*. Of
course, it seems to me this is a real *cul de sac* of art. You
can't get any further than

> 'Streaks of green & yellow iridescence
> Silver shiftings
> Rings veering out of rings
> Silver — gold —
> Grey-green opaqueness sliding down'

You see it is uttering pure sensation *without concepts*, which
is what this futuristic art tries to do. One step further and
it passes into *mere noises*, as the Italian futurismo poems
have done, or mere jags and zig-zags, as the futuristic paintings. There it ceases to be art, and is pure accident, mind-
less. — But there is this to fulfil, this last and most primary
state of our being, where we are shocked into form like
crystals that take place from the fluid chaos. And it is this
primary state of being which you carry into art, in

> 'Gold clusters
> Flash in soft explosions
> On the blue darkness
> Suck back to a point
> And disappear...' — for example. You

might have called your book 'Rockets and Sighs.' It would
have been better than Men, Women & Ghosts.

If ever I come to America I will write about these things.
But won't you try to come to Rome. Think of the Naples
aquarium, and the Naples museum — and Rome itself. We
might enjoy it so much.

Thank you once more, dear Amy. Remember me to Mrs.

Russell. My wife is writing to you. — I have just finished a novel, of which I am proud. — Did you get my 'Amores' and 'Twilight in Italy'? Do let us have a letter.

Yours ever

D. H. LAWRENCE

These things are your best, by far, I think: Spring Day, Towns in Colour, Hammers, p. 344, some p. 346, & p. 347 of the Stravinsky. The shock and clipping of the physico-mechanical world are your finest expression.

Hardly had she got out of bed when Ferris Greenslet brought her the manuscript of *Love's Tragedy*, a new book on which Fletcher had spent three years, and now offered for publication in the 'New Poetry Series.' In spite of the very successful Imagist anthologies, the series had lost money; yet when Miss Lowell reported that while she did not find Fletcher's new book as good as his old ones, she thought it would sell better, it was refused. Fletcher, hearing of her part in the rejection, and knowing that his book was much better than others in the series, wrote her with great bitterness. She replied, reiterating her judgment, but offering to pay for the publication. Fletcher reconsidered, did not accept her offer, but issued the book two years later under the title, *The Tree of Life*.

Imperative business demanded she come to New York; on December 6, she took the Knickerbocker from Boston, putting up at the Hotel Belmont, as she had been unable to engage her usual rooms at the St. Regis. It was apparently on this trip that she invaded the office of the *Seven Arts* in the manner which Oppenheim described so blithely.[1] He always had a tremendous admiration for her — called her 'one of the best of them' — and paid tribute to her terrific energy, her will to experiment, her help to obscure poets, and her fighting for poetry all over the United States, by which she helped to make an era. But he had

[1] James Oppenheim: 'The Story of the *Seven Arts*,' *American Mercury* (xx, 160–61), June, 1930.

also been forewarned of her ways with editors, and therefore flatly refused to let her read her work to him. She glowered a little, then succumbed; the poem was eventually rejected; but she took it sportingly and sent others, which the staff liked immensely.[1]

After a few days in New York, she was back at Brookline again. Although she was not really to regain her full strength until summer came, by the middle of the month she was catching up with her correspondence; buying rare books for her library; arranging for lectures (requests had accumulated); selling poems of her own, of the Imagists, of Cournos (but she could place only one of his); collecting the manuscript for the third Anthology; boiling down her Verhaeren lecture for inclusion in a new edition of Warner's *Library of the World's Best Literature*; and refusing to edit a poetry journal, to be issued by some New York publisher who as yet preferred to remain anonymous. Most immediate of all were her lectures on the American poets, to be delivered in January, but as yet unwritten, though long planned. She had also finished 'Sea Blue and Blood Red,' a companion piece, as it were, to 'Malmaison'; 'I am sending you the best poem I have written,' she informed editors. Both *Poetry* and the *Seven Arts* refused it because of its length. In reply to Oppenheim's objection that her 'Landlady' did not read as well as she read it, she wrote:

> May I point out that a poem is good in itself, and is as good as it is capable of being read, not as good as any particular person or persons can read it. It seems to me to say that a thing reads better when I read it, but does not read as well when somebody else reads it, is a good deal like saying that Kreisler, playing the Bach 'Chaconne,' makes a different thing of it from what some other violinist may do. I cannot for the life of me see that that in any way militates against

[1] It is possible that Mr. Oppenheim's refusal to let her read was not entirely successful; for on December 14, 1916, in a letter accepting her 'Orange of Midsummer,' he returned 'The Landlady,' remarking that 'it doesn't read as well as you read it.'

the value of the 'Chaconne.' However, that is your affair,
and I am only explaining, not criticizing.

Among other letters she received this month was one
containing Christmas greetings from D. H. Lawrence, and
another from Lance-Corporal R. Aldington, at last off to
'somewhere in France' in a day or two, and bidding her
Goodbye.

Between Christmas and her departure for New York, all
was a scramble of lecture-typing and letter-answering.
Besides personal letters, she was trying to sell poems by
Aldington, Bodenheim, Fletcher, and herself, and making
dates for future lectures. On Wednesday, January 3, 1917,
she left Boston on the five-o'clock, telegraphing the St.
Regis to put two electric stoves in her room.

Lecture trips always proved exhausting; to avoid
fatigue, Miss Lowell's plans became more and more exacting. The departure from Sevenels was always a desperate
gathering together of impedimenta to the tumult of typewriters ticking off the last pages of Miss Lowell's lectures.
Helpless as a child in all such matters — everything had
to be handed to her — she always travelled with her 'en-
tourage': Mrs. Russell, Elizabeth Henry (her devoted and
loyal maid for twenty-two years), and sometimes a second
maid. On trains to New York, they had to sit in a particular pattern, so that Miss Lowell (who had blood-pressure)
could be next an open window without its annoying some
stranger. On longer trips she took a stateroom; and on
tours she chose afternoon and night trains ('the worst
trains there are,' she admitted), which interfered as little
as possible with her peculiar hours of sleep. She always refused to stay at private houses, but put up at the best
possible hotel, where she required a suite of five rooms (a
bedroom with a vacant room on either side, a sitting-room,
and a room for Mrs. Russell) besides a room for the maid
somewhere else in the building. All electric clocks had to
be stopped; all mirrors and other shining objects were

sheathed in black; and all telephone messages were sent to Mrs. Russell's room, for it was she who entertained friends, poets, and reporters while Miss Lowell was preparing her appearance — and that preparation might occupy a couple of hours. Meals had to be brought up at strange times. If, after all her precautions, Miss Lowell could not sleep, she would try to remedy matters by moving her bed, or re-making it. Once, when the pillows were flabby, at some dark hour she ripped two of them open, and transferred the feathers from one into the other.

As she made a point of reaching the city in which she was to speak on the previous day, she usually arrived at the lecture hall on time. But the reading did not begin at once: there were always arrangements to be made which furnished a comic prologue and put her expectant public into excellent humor. The slanting lectern invariably provided by the authorities had to be replaced by a table, usually carried in over the heads of the audience: pages of her manuscript then never drifted to the floor out of her reach. Her own reading lamp had to be plugged in: the customary lights were usually too dim for her over-worked eyes. When her eyesight was so severely strained that she needed glasses, she would carry in a small basket of them, explaining 'These are my eyes!' Perhaps other things had to be done. Miss Lowell directed these arrangements in a low voice, with an occasional side remark that kept the audience amused. It was disarmed and won before it knew.

After this, the only danger lay in her introducer, who might be blundering or even hostile; and such persons, in their self-consciousness, often were surprisingly tactless. But she, once a little girl adept at answering back, in-variably made opportunities of these awkwardnesses to put the audience right as to her sanity, sincerity, literary theory, or whatever else had been misrepresented. The gales of laughter ceased at once when she said a few words about the New Poetry, explaining what she was trying to do. These remarks were just enough to give those present an intellectual basis for appreciation; and the first poem was listened to in absolute silence.

When this poem was finished, audiences often seemed perplexed whether to applaud now, and after each poem, or save it all for the end. Miss Lowell solved their problem for them; with mock tartness she would say: 'Well? — Clap or hiss, I don't care which; but do something!' The result, of course, was a double burst of laughter and applause.

It was a commonplace remark in Boston that if Amy Lowell had been beautiful, she would have been a great actress. Her public readings were her substitute for that career. On the lecture platform, without scenery, costumes, or even gestures, she could make the public forget her size, and follow the drama solely from her voice. Her poems were largely dramatic monologues; and at this point in her career she often disclaimed being a real lyrist.

The essentials of her reading were perfect clarity, perfect intelligence, dramatic fire, and an exquisite yet unmistakable rhythm. She did not chant her poems, or read them in a monotone of painful ecstasy; her clear soprano blurred no word but varied continually according to the content. People sat up to hear, and listened with open eyes. Scoffers who came out of curiosity were converted right and left by the relief of hearing verse they could enjoy without getting into any special and suspect state of mind.

There were also those who were outraged to find that her poetry was other than their own; and positive that two kinds of poetry could not exist simultaneously (as though there were not a separate mansion in the poetic heaven for each true poet), they rose unexpectedly after the encores, to reaffirm their truth and wither her with their scorn. She was never withered; she always had a reply sparkling with wit and scholarship, which rose to a cold fire if the battle were prolonged. Scenes like these sometimes made newspaper headlines.

When all was over, Miss Lowell descended from the platform to receive the enthusiasts pressing forward with demands for autographs and for criticism of their manuscripts. The latter were always refused, according to her necessary rule. Soon the reception was cut short: her train was leaving, and she had to go at once.

Her prices for her readings and lectures rose steadily from $50 to $100, $150, $200, with the customary deductions for educational institutions and the like. During the war it sank for a few months, only to rise again.

On January 4, 1917, at 4 P.M., she delivered her lecture on Edwin Arlington Robinson, the first of her series of four on American poets, given at the Brooklyn Institute of Arts and Sciences. Robinson preferred not to come; the two met afterwards, however, to discuss possible changes before it appeared in book form. The other lectures were given on the following Thursdays: 'Frost' on the eleventh; 'Masters and Sandburg' on the eighteenth; and 'The Imagists' on the twenty-fifth. The audiences of three to four hundred increased steadily.

At a party given by Jessie Rittenhouse, Miss Lowell met Witter Bynner, who had published much against Imagism from the first. He proved very friendly, however; wanted to discuss the New Poetry; and asked her opinion of the 'Spectrist School.' He had reviewed *Spectra* in the *New Republic*, November 18, 1916, where he contrasted them favorably against the Imagists. The January *Others* was a special Spectrist number, in which one Elijah Hay joined Anne Knish and Emanuel Morgan. But Amy Lowell could not be broad-minded about any of them. 'Bynner, I think they are charlatans,' she said. He looked at her strangely; and Miss Lowell always claimed that his respect for her began at that moment.

On January 16, 1917, the two English poets, Wilfrid

Wilson Gibson and Walter de la Mare, were guests of honor at a dinner given by the Poetry Society of America, and of course Miss Lowell was present. Gibson began his speech by professing to be at a loss in America, where poetry was divided up into schools: he himself was just plain poet and no '-ist.' This attitude was far too gratifying to the conservatives; Miss Lowell determined to puncture the pose, genially though it was intended, and to defend the New Poetry in the very teeth of the English. Accordingly she informed Mr. Gibson that indeed he *was* an '-ist' — a realist, to be exact; and having pigeon-holed him (and thus subtly destroyed his implication that there was only one kind of poetry), she continued her sallies, punctuating them by tossing and catching a gold-meshed vanity bag, to the delight of the diners.[1]

After her Brooklyn lecture on the eighteenth, she was approached by young Alter Brody who, although outraged by her protests against the class hatred which Sandburg allowed to enter some of his early poems, admired her own poetry enormously. Brody had a scheme for starting a poetry theater, and wanted her opinion. She gave it: it would be impossible, there were no audiences large enough and constant enough, only three or four poets knew how to read their own poems, and no program could ever hope to have a long run, and thus make money. Brody later wrote her a letter protesting against being thus 'squashed.'

On the next afternoon she left on the 4:20 to dine with Katherine Fullerton Gerould and then address a Princeton club of fifty undergraduates, not yet named the 'Fresno Club.' Princeton had the reputation of being the most conservative of the 'Big Three' American universities. But although it was the night of the basket-ball game with the University of Pennsylvania, about ninety undergraduates appeared, as well as various members of the faculty. The students seemed bewildered, but really had

[1] Jessie B. Rittenhouse: *My House of Life*, Boston, 1934, p. 259.

little chance to express themselves, as the professors instantly took the debate out of their hands. They fought hard, but were silenced and demolished to a man, as John Peale Bishop, the president, wrote her afterwards; and certainly with a consciousness of triumph she took the 10:04 back to New York.

The evening of the twenty-second, she read her poems without honorarium at the 'Sunwise Turn,' the enlightened bookshop which had issued her broadside 'Ballads for Sale.' There was an unfortunate delay in the introduction; then presently Miss Lowell was opposed by Miss Landseer Mackenzie, a British musician with theories of her own about rhythm. The debate continued for three hours; [1] the room got colder and colder, but everybody stayed. Miss Mackenzie's attitude was so insulting that Miss Jenison wrote a letter of apology afterwards; to which Miss Lowell replied that, as she was speaking out of pure friendship, she should have been allowed the evening to herself; but since things had turned out so, it would be a long time before she broke her rule again, and spoke without payment.

On the afternoon of the twenty-fourth she went to her publishers, chiefly concerning the contract for *Tendencies*, which she had sent them two days before, but also to arrange for the third edition of *Men, Women and Ghosts*.

Her last Brooklyn lecture came the next day; when she had finished, the audience applauded her for fully seven minutes without stopping. That evening she spoke at the dinner of the Poetry Society of America; the other speakers were Reedy, Masters, Wilfrid Gibson, and Don Marquis. Her speech admitted our cultural indebtedness to England, but proclaimed henceforth a literary independence. As before, the Society was frankly hostile to Miss Lowell; but Mrs. Sylvester Viereck championed her, and Witter Bynner defended her 'Sea Blue and Blood Red,' which she had placed at last with the *North American Review* — it

[1] Madge Jenison: *Sunwise Turn*, New York [c. 1923], p. 100.

was the longest poem they had ever published in their hundred and two years of existence.

One other occurrence in New York, she described in a letter to Fletcher dated February 6:

> I wish you had been with me in New York for I made some interesting experiments with a Mr. Patterson, who is in the English Department at Columbia University and has just written a book on Prose Rhythms in which he affirmed that vers libre came under the head of prose. I met him at [Gertrude] Atherton's and after some discussion he said that he would be delighted to change all of his opinions if I could prove to him that he was wrong. I passed a whole afternoon with him, working with his sound photographic machine and leaving records for him to work on when I was not there with the result that he announced what I believe to be true: that cadence in vers libre is somewhat analogous to phrasing in music. I also discovered in preparing myself beforehand for this seance that cadences are made up of time limits, but the time limits do not have to be exactly the same to each cadence. In other words, they are each of the same portion [proportion?] but there may be uneven numbers of them to a cadence.

On January 26, she returned to Brookline. In her correspondence were several letters from Fletcher. He was suppressing his first five books, his juvenilia of 1913; eventually he was to contribute all the remainders to the paper shortage. Distressed though he was about *Love's Tragedy*, he had sent her another manuscript, this time his volume of war poems, *Under the Guns*.

The February *Bookman* contained the first installment of Edward J. O'Brien's 'Masque of Poets.' His scheme was to publish a series of poems without indication of authorship, so that they could be enjoyed simply for their own literary merit, without any initial preference or prejudice. Miss Lowell saw in his scheme a chance to prove to the public that she was not exclusively a *vers librist*; she therefore contributed to this first installment two poems. The first, 'Shore Grass,' was one of her less important pieces of free verse; the second, which was printed immediately after, was 'The Ring and the Castle,' one of her most powerful rhymed narratives.

But the public was not much stirred by the guessing contest. Nobody denounced 'Shore Grass' as hers, then praised rapturously the unknown poet whose magnificent ballad followed. And for a full year (until the 'Masque' was ended, and the authors named) she was unable to claim one of her best poems as hers. She never published anonymously again.

The annual elections of the New England Poetry Club were held February 7; the evening was so terrible that none of the ladies present would ever do more than hint what happened after all the appalled gentlemen withdrew. Amy Lowell and Josephine Peabody were the opposing candidates for the presidency; and the battle was fundamentally one between the New Poetry and the Old, although it descended lamentably into personalities at the end. Miss Lowell believed that under her leadership the Club eventually would amount to something; and that if she were not re-elected, all modernism would be repudiated; in which event it were better that the Club cease to exist. Josephine Peabody, however, felt that the poetry of the conservatives was being either ignored or torn to pieces in the discussions; the chief plank in her platform was 'No More Criticism'; furthermore she felt, quite rightly, that it was her turn at the presidency if the members wanted to elect her. Miss Lowell took her for an automobile ride beforehand, explaining the situation as she saw it, and extracting from Josephine the statement that she would not mind not being president. But Lilla Cabot Perry, more kin than kind to Miss Lowell, organized Josephine's support.

One grave historian remembers that a flustered little lady, obsessed with the name of her adversary, absentmindedly recorded on her ballot the candidate she most earnestly desired to defeat. When the votes were counted, Amy Lowell was proclaimed President, whereupon the absent-minded voter, knowing that her ballot had been decisive and realizing her slip, insisted upon having her vote changed. The succeeding pandemonium was not a fisticuff. Abbie Brown proved more than the Abraham Lincoln of the situation, as she prevented secession by both sides and stopped the civil war.[1]

When in the succeeding days Miss Lowell tried to get in touch with Josephine Peabody, either to give or demand explanations, Josephine was too ill to see her.

Professor William Morrison Patterson's preliminary report on her reading of poetry into his machine that measured sounds in tenths of seconds was sent her on the twelfth; he said that she had an unusually accurate time-sense, that her reading of H. D.'s 'Oread' indicated an exact time-interval, which however might be increased or retarded, whereas her own 'Thompson's Lunch Room' was still more subtle, following a pattern which he drew something like a flat horizontal S. He concluded that some free verse was not prose, and would lose its cadence if printed as prose.

On St. Valentine's day, Miss Lowell and various other prominent poets received an anonymous and scurrilous valentine attacking her for interrupting, contradicting, and using bad grammar. The authorship was never claimed and never traced.

On the sixteenth she was busy sending out the royalties of the anthologies to the Imagists. The first anthology was now in its third edition; the second was in its second; and the proofs of the third were under her hand. As she had sold Aldington's 'On the March' and 'Leave-Taking' to the *Seven Arts*, which could not publish them

[1] [John Wheelwright:] *History of the New England Poetry Club*, Boston, 1932, pp. 13-14.

before the publication of the new anthology, she substituted 'Dawn' and 'Images.'

The next day, she left on her second lecture tour of the year. Her first stop was at St. Louis, where she delivered her 'New Poetry, with Special Reference to Imagism' under the auspices of the Washington University Alumni Association. She dined beforehand at the Florissant Valley Club with Professor and Mrs. John Livingston Lowes, whom she then met for the first time, and who proved devoted friends from that evening on. Professor Lowes introduced her in a most sympathetic and enthusiastic manner. The hall was so jammed that they had to put in seventy-five extra chairs, although Count Tolstoy was lecturing in a hall nearby, and several other things, including an automobile show, were going on. Both the students and the members of the English Department showed an interest she had not expected. Among other people she met Zoë Akins, with whom she had been in sympathetic correspondence for two or three years, and the poet Orrick Johns.

On Washington's Birthday, she took a brief excursion into the occult. St. Louis was telling marvellous tales of a remarkable medium, Mrs. John H. Curran, through whom a three-century-old spirit, named Patience Worth, gave messages. None of the suspicious hocus-pocus necessary to most mediums was involved in any way. Patience Worth's vocabulary had been analyzed, and pronounced to contain an astonishing number of obsolete words used correctly in their seventeenth-century meanings, although from no particular locality or decade. Miss Lowell held in high esteem the scholar who had made this discovery;[1] she was attracted by the reports of Mrs. Curran's straightforwardness; and when Mrs.

---

[1] Quoted, perhaps overenthusiastically, by William Marion Reedy in *Reedy's Mirror*; see Walter Franklin Prince's *Case of Patience Worth*, Boston, 1929, p. 60.

Thomas McKittrick, one of her Dublin friends, offered to make an appointment, Miss Lowell accepted gladly.

The session was held the evening of February 22, 1917. Miss Lowell sat with Mrs. Curran at a ouija board, which circled vaguely while Mrs. Curran spelled aloud the words of the spirit. Miss Lowell instantly remarked that the dictated letters were not those indicated by the ouija board, an observation at once endorsed by the Currans, who explained that the board was used merely as a means for getting Patience Worth started. (Indeed, a few months later, the board was abandoned.) Patience Worth dictated poems and part of her *Merry Tale*, besides giving brief character studies of the sitters. There was nothing of any 'evidential' value. If Mrs. Curran had not been told in advance who her sitters were to be, she could easily have identified Amy Lowell from her picture in the papers. On the other hand, there was a certain shrewdness in the characterization, which is copied here from the record:

> *Patience*: Ye see ye, dame, I ha'e nothing for to offer ye save a whit o' pappin' like unto a babe's sup. How then shall thy handmaid set her a pace afore thee, when thou mayst take thee e'en up the bellows and tongs and make o' it a beauteous song?
>
> *Miss Lowell*: It must be much easier over there, Patience.
>
> *Patience*: Yea, yea, but look ye, thou mayst plunge thee athin the seas o' the naughts wherein be the shadows' shapes, the wroughtin' o' thy in-man's makin'. Yea, thou mayst pluck out this the stuffs that build up whole things. Behold, I know o' thee, dame, for thou dost set a thing and leave thyself hangin' 'pon it. Then thou settest o' a word and lo, thou leavest thee then arest 'pon it, thereby thou dost weave cloths that ha'e o' little woop [*sic*] and warps, but that be wove 'pon thee. Within thy words thou dost send thyself living. Yea, and this seemeth unto the earth such an babe's task. And they do the

thing and lo, their words mean naught. Thereby thy
word be thee.

Miss Lowell: Yes, and your words are you.

Patience: Yea, and thine and mine be Him. Ye see ye, I be
nay fashioner o' beauteous stuffs. Nay, I but sing a
mighty singin' o' Him, dame, and I crave me not that
they hold me up before the face of man as a weaver of
cloths.

The rest of the session has no importance here. It is
obvious that Patience Worth summed up Miss Lowell as
a true poet, who put her life into her works, and who had
followers whose imitations of her seemingly easy poems
were meaningless. Miss Lowell, on the other hand, was
much impressed by the problem that Patience Worth
presented. She drew no conclusions, but said that such
spellings-out of long messages would be almost impossible for the average person; and the philological puzzle of
the vocabulary deepened the mystery.

She left for two weeks in Chicago, arriving the twenty-
fourth. Maurice Browne had engaged her to repeat her
four lectures on the American poets at his Little Theater;
unfortunately he went bankrupt on the twenty-third, and
as she did not wish to hire the hall herself without other
guarantee, and as the preliminary advertising had been
insufficient, she preferred to cancel the series. On the
twenty-fifth she spoke in Harriet Monroe's series of 'Talks'
for *Poetry*; her speech proved a great success, and was made
to an overflowing crowd. On March 2, the Chicago College
Club gave her a reception, at which she spoke briefly;
again the attendance was tremendous. But the 'abominable' western food brought back her digestive trouble;
she hurried home, cancelling an engagement to speak at
Cincinnati before the newly founded Ohio Valley Poetry
Society.

The success of Imagism was just beginning to reach
England: several long and favorable reviews had appeared

recently over there; but at this moment, as she was finishing the last proofs of the third anthology, the news came that the English were putting an embargo on books bound and unbound. This meant the exclusion of the anthologies and her own books from England, unless the London publishers saw fit to cast duplicate plates, which of course was hardly reasonable, as the English sales had been very small so far. In America, all her books were now in their third printing, except *Six French Poets*, which was still in its second.

On March 28, she took the night train to Buffalo, reaching there the next morning. After lunching with Mrs. Francis Wolcott, she read from her poems at 3:30 to the Garret Club ——

> a private club, somewhat analogous to the Colony Club in New York, so that the meeting was not open to the general public, only to members; therefore the audience was somewhat limited, I think not more than seventy-five people or so. But I have seldom met with such enthusiasm; and what gave me more pleasure than all, was that after I had read an hour, and had naturally stopped, they began to call out for special poems they wanted, showing that they knew my work well, and they kept me reading for another hour beyond my scheduled time. One lady told me afterwards she should go and buy all my books on the spot. Let us hope she did.[1]

After the reading, she took the night train back.

Fletcher had written her that, now Aldington was in the trenches, the vampire Pound was persuading Miss Weaver to let him run the *Egoist*, while H. D. and Aldington remained the nominal editors; in his distress over the situation, he suggested that Miss Lowell invest some money in the paper, on condition that Pound be excluded. She refused, in a letter dated March 29 [*sic*]:

> You see the point is this: — As you say, possibly Miss Weaver would not sell her paper, particularly as you

[1] Letter to Frederick Marsh, March 30, 1917.

planned to leave her as editor. In that case she would go around and tell everybody that she had been approached — she might even call it 'bribed' — to run her paper in a certain way, and she could make a very nasty story about that. Also, suppose she did consent to leave Ezra out of the paper for a consideration, it would give Ezra a splendid handle to beat us with, because he would know perfectly well where the money came from, and he would not only be able to enlist the sympathy of the outside world and pose as a martyr to capital, and I think he might be able to hurt us very seriously by leaving the impression with the public at large that our success was largely due to methods of this kind. I do not believe that any good is to be gained by trying to muzzle one's enemies. That is the action of weakness, and is sure to come back on the perpetrator like a boomerang. The only thing for us to do is to write more and better until Ezra is acknowledged by the world at large to be out of the running with us. I think it only needs time for that to be a fact....

I do not know whether we are wise to discontinue the Imagist Anthology, just at this point, or not. England seems to be waking up to us. The English are a queer people. If you hammer, hammer, hammer, by and by they will pay attention. It always takes years before they realize that anything has anything in it. Now they have just begun to see that we amount to something, and whether or not it is wise to discontinue our collective publication at the very moment that it is beginning to be noticed over there, I cannot quite make up my mind....

As far as America is concerned, I do not think there is any advantage in keeping on the Anthology. It has done its business with the American public....

You will be amused to hear that they have kicked me out of the Presidency of the Poetry Club, and Josephine has practically come out as my avowed enemy. She still tries to hide it under a cloak of friendship, but I am on guard. I shall not go to the Poetry Society again, and I am thankful that I am out of it. It is getting perfectly impossible, and they are asking the Harvard boys for every meeting. Bradley, who went last time, told me that those old women kow-towed to the young men in a perfectly ridiculous way which made him quite sick. He says he shall not go again, either....

Although it was her rule not to read manuscripts sent her for criticism, there were times when the poetry was too good to pass over; and this month she sent encouragements to two different poets: Matthew Josephson and Mark Turbyfill. On March 23, Lawrence wrote her of his dislike for the 'Lacquer Prints' she was using as her contribution to the new anthology:

I don't like them *nearly* so well as your other things, and I do wish you hadn't put them in. *Don't* do Japanese things, Amy, if you love us. I would a million times rather have a fragment of 'Aquarium' than all the Japanese poems put together. I am so disappointed with this batch you have decided to put in, it isn't you at *all*, it has nothing to do with you, and it is not real. Alas and alas, why have you done this thing?

Hilda Aldington seems very sad and suppressed, everything is wrong. I WISH things would get better. I have done a set of little essays called 'The Reality of Peace,' very important to me. I wish they would come out in America. They may appear in the British Review, in which case I shall send them to you. Oh dear, it is a real struggle to get any further, we seem really stuck in a bog of wrongness. I wish above all things the tide would turn in the hearts of people, and make for creation & happiness: for we are almost lost. But we will hope on, & struggle.

Do write from your *real* self, Amy, don't make up things from the outside, it is so saddening.

The April *North American Review* contained 'Sea Blue and Blood Red'; the April *Little Review* announced that Ezra Pound henceforth was to be its foreign editor. Miss Lowell promptly withdrew her support from the second magazine: how wisely, those who have read Pound's letters to Margaret Anderson can appreciate.[1]

[1] Margaret Anderson: *My Thirty Years' War*, New York, 1930, p. 165.

On Good Friday, April 6, the United States declared war on Germany, and the country was transformed overnight. The enthusiasm preceding the declaration was immediately transmuted into a fierce determination to save civilization from the Germans and their fabulous atrocities, to save democracy from the menace of autocracy, to end all war forever, to repay France for 1777 and to demonstrate our forgiveness of England for 1776, 1812, and 1861, and generally to establish the eternal Brotherhood of Man. American armies were to tip the scales at Armageddon and ensure the Millennium. At Cambridge, the Harvard Reserve Officers' Training Corps was organized; Commandant Paul Azan, Lieutenant André Morize, and Lieutenant Jean Giraudoux were sent from France to direct it. Hermann Hagedorn, mobilizing the poets, asked Miss Lowell to join the Vigilantes; she accepted gladly, promising to get published whatever patriotic verse she might write. But the inspiration did not come just yet.

About this time, Miss Lowell was invited to a dinner given by the Edward Burlingame Hills in Cambridge; another guest was a baronet's son, who held a high position in the British submarine service. The conversation ran upon the unwonted sight of uniforms in our streets, and the Britisher agreed that Americans scarcely understood what they were. Why, in the South Station the other day, a woman with a baby actually asked him to direct her to a train. 'Of course I misdirected her,' he concluded.

Amy Lowell rose. Mrs. Russell, her curb, was far away, in Salt Lake City. 'Excuse me for saying so, but you are a cad,' she began. 'Over here, we consider you just the swillmen of the sea.' She continued; it became an oration; the pictures rattled on the walls with her fury.

The rest of the dinner was subdued. When the young man said good night, she thumbed her nose at him. But as soon as she got home, she called up Mrs. Russell on long distance to tell what she had done.

Of course the story spread like mad; and shortly after, the officer was recalled.

She was to read her poems at Bradford Academy on April 11, but that morning she woke up with another attack of indigestion, which kept her in bed all day, and her reading was postponed until May 2. On the twenty-third she read her poems at the Women's City Club; Boston was now so alive to her verse that extra chairs had to be put in. At 4:30 on the twenty-sixth she read her poems to the Radcliffe Poetry Club at Agassiz House.

In the latter half of this month, Amy Lowell, Edgar Lee Masters, and Charles Hanson Towne were judges of an Intercollegiate Literary Competition. She did not believe in poetry prizes, and always refused either to judge or compete; but this once she broke her rule, in order to oblige a friend who had made an unauthorized announcement. Later, when asked to be judge of the Blindman Prize in 1921, she told of her difficulties:

> I had an awful time once acting as a judge. It was for an intercollegiate contest, and I wrote to the persons in charge of the contest telling them that all the poems were so bad that I could hardly see anything to choose and that none of them were worthy of a prize, but that, if a selection must be made, I thought the poems of a certain young gentleman were, on the whole, a trifle better than the others. The next thing I knew, the young gentleman's father had written me a letter of fervent thanks, telling me that I had given his boy a prize which had stimulated him immensely, that he hoped to make poetry his career, and might he bring some of his poems to me. The poor fellow did, and they were awful, as I was obliged to tell him. I never saw him again, nor have I seen any of his poems published. That is what comes of awarding prizes which you know are not deserved.

On April 24, *Some Imagist Poets, 1917*, the last of the three anthologies, was published. Only Amy Lowell's

'Lacquer Prints' were wholly untouched by the war. The first of them, 'Streets,' was an adaptation of a part of a poem by Yakura Sanjin, 1769, which Ficke had already translated from the German; the others were original, inspired by the spirit of the hokku (though without following the Japanese syllabic system) and by various prints she owned. H. D. wrote, not of the war, but in an agony of spirit that reflected her sufferings. Fletcher's contribution included his 'Lincoln' and two which Miss Lowell particularly admired: 'Moonlight' and 'Dawn.' In spite of the success of Fletcher's 'Lincoln,' the most admired poem in the volume, it sold only four hundred copies in six weeks; evidently the work of the series was done; and all the poets agreed that there was no use continuing it.

On the twenty-eighth, the Forbes-Robertsons came to tea; on the next day, Sara Teasdale spent an hour at Sevenels. On May 2, Miss Lowell gave her delayed reading at Bradford Academy.

But though she was finishing 'Guns as Keys,' and though her eyes were now troubling her badly, she kept up her correspondence. Harriet Monroe still would not include her name in the lists of leading poets which appeared casually in *Poetry* now and then; against this exclusion Miss Lowell protested in vain. The fact was that Miss Monroe thought Amy Lowell had 'everything but genius.' [1] Then Fletcher, learning that Miss Lowell preferred his earlier to his later manner, replied with objections to some of her own latest work; she answered on May 8, defending her poems and principles, then continuing:

> What I cannot understand is that you should say that the war has changed your point of view about art and that the individual counts for nothing. If you had thought out any scheme of philosophy before the war, it seems to me it was a funny scheme if it could not stand a cataclysm. Nothing

[1] Harriet Monroe: *Poets and Their Art*, New York, 1926, p. 78.

in my artistic point of view has been affected by the war. I believe in the same forms of art that I did. The great principles you mention — life, love, death, faith, courage, endurance, suffering — have always been the proper subjects for poetry, but I have always felt that they should be represented through images and dramas, rather than definitely spoken about. I thought we called the latter 'cosmic poetry' and all of us preferred to eschew it.

As to the individual counting for nothing, I disagree entirely. The individual is paramount, and the fact that for a brief moment he may have to subordinate himself and throw his energies into combatting an attack of illness, whether the illness of an individual or the illness of a state, or in combatting the illness of a distant state, which threatens the comfort and freedom of his own, as in the present case, is merely an unfortunate interlude. These things are likely to occur in the lives of individuals and of races, and that any philosophic system or religion for the guidance of life can be formed without taking such events into consideration is inconceivable to me. If, therefore, your attitude and faith were properly thought out and considered in the beginning, I fail to see how they can undergo such a radical change because of this war, or any other war. That such a change should take place in the thoughtless of the world, in those people who amuse themselves with sport, and golf, and money getting, and never really think of anything until they are brought face to face with reality, I can understand; but not in a man like you, for a poet must think always and eternally. Without such a formulated basis for existence, his poetry must be nerveless and superficial. Yours was neither, and I cannot understand how you can have undergone such a complete upheaval of mind as you seem to think has been the case.

I wish you were here now. It looks almost like London in some ways — as London did just after the outbreak of the war, that is. The streets are full of soldiers, and there are flags everywhere. Now the French officers are here, teaching the Harvard regiment, and they have brought an atmosphere painfully close to the front with them.

One of my nephews has gone to Plattsburg and will be sent to the front with the first batch of officers. Many other people I know are in training here and almost all the women are mobilized into various departments. Those of us who can do nothing useful in that line are planting every inch of available ground with potatoes and other vegetables to conserve the food. The war is very close to us now, and the country is facing it with a courage and a unanimity which I hardly believed could be possible. One of the most remarkable things about the situation is that only one hundred and twenty-five Germans in the entire country have been interned, and, as our Secret Service has proved itself to be remarkably energetic, this shows that the German-Americans are really American at heart; in fact, I understand that Germany regretfully refers to them as 'absorbed.' The President has praised very highly the loyalty of the hyphenates, and I think that is helping the good will and good feeling all over the country. The internal insurrections, which we feared, have not taken place, and only occasional sporadic outbursts here and there have succeeded the declaration of war. A few munition plants and grain elevators have been blown up, but exceedingly few, considering the numbers of Germans in our midst. Altogether, the declaration of war has proved, and proved gloriously, that America is a nation at last.

Joffre is coming here next week, and I am to have the honour of shaking him by the hand at my brother's. This will be chiefly interesting as an anecdote to tell future generations, I think.

You would not know the country if you were here. There is a serious quiet determination in the temper of the people which I have never seen equalled. There is no 'Hurray, boys!' nor hysterical excitement either of fear or of Mafekingism, merely a quiet gritting of the teeth and determination to see the war through. I sincerely pray it may end soon, for it is a hard time to live, and, as you say, an almost impossible one in which to write.

Keep your courage up, dear boy; I know how hard it is in England just now, and what privations you must undergo.

If you want anything, please do not hesitate to say so. Remember you are my friend, and however we may differ on matters of taste, our friendship will remain undisturbed. I am sincerely fond of you and sincerely admire you as a poet....

On the twelfth, Marshal Joffre reviewed the Harvard Reserve Officers' Training Corps on Soldiers Field. She went, and recorded the event in a poem, 'In the Stadium.'

On May 18, she repeated her Bradford reading at Bryn Mawr, dining afterwards at the Deanery. Late the next afternoon she reached the St. Regis in New York, dining with Professor Patterson of Columbia. After continuing the February experiments on timing poetic cadences in his laboratory, she returned to Boston on Thursday, the twenty-fifth.

As the manuscript of *Tendencies in Modern American Poetry* had been promised the publishers by the first of July, in June Miss Lowell buckled down to putting her lectures into final form. There were photographs and bibliographies to be got from the six poets; the Preface had to be written; then there were problems raised by the dummies and the proofs. June at least she would have to spend in Brookline; the fact seemed to be, however, that Dublin had lost its inspiration for her — she could not write much there. But even in Brookline there were distractions.

On June 9, she was a patroness of the Galli Curci Concert in aid of the N. E. Italian War Relief Fund, at the Boston Opera House. Professor Raymond Weeks of Columbia had been anxious for her to edit the ill-fated Adelaide Crapsey's Ph.D. thesis on metrics. On June 12, Miss Lowell returned it, with the following critique of graduate studies:

Thank you so much for sending me this article of Miss Crapsey's, which I am returning under separate cover by registered mail. It has interested me very much to read it.

It has also depressed me indescribably. I have very little brief to hold for our educational system in America. Sometimes it seems as if its methods were those the farthest removed from common sense. That a young woman of Miss Crapsey's originality and talent should have spent innumerable hours counting the words in 'Paradise Lost' and other poems in order to write a thesis for a doctor's degree, almost makes me weep. When will the new school of critics realize that art cannot be adequately treated without recognizing that its fundamental importance is as art. The pseudo-scientific method in regard to literature fails exactly here. It seldom tells us out of what combination of words, sounds, thoughts, and movements the effect is got; rather, it analyses these things separately by themselves, making no attempt at any synthesis which would teach the layman to appreciate and understand what art is, or teach the artist how more directly to gain his end. I suppose the reason for this is that it is hard to explain an art, and the only people who understand it well enough to explain it are usually those who are themselves artists, and who consider all explanation superfluous and unnecessary.

Miss Crapsey was an artist, and that she should have felt obliged to mould her thought into this unspeakable form, as being the one most sure to gain her admittance in the great 'company of educated men' is a terrible comment on the company. This is, however, beside the mark.

As for the main theme of Miss Crapsey's essay, being an artist myself, I think it superfluous. Certainly, we have always known that the word-accent and the foot were not necessarily coincident, and that awful things occurred when they were too much at variance. It seems to me also that we have always known the different kind of effects given by long words and short words (I purposely refuse to use the more scientific terms). It is just in this matter of long words and Latinized words that Milton seems to so many of us to have made his fatal mistake.

It is to my mind pathetic that Miss Crapsey bolsters up her arguments by reference to the work of so many academic and unintelligent critics. Any one who has read Professor Saintsbury's efforts to reduce the *vers libre* portions of 'Empedocles on Etna' to regular metre, rather, I should say, to scan them as they stand as though they were regular metre, cannot fail to be struck by the fact that there are many things about poetry which the eminent professor had not plumbed. That a person should consider Professor Gilbert Murray — authority though he may be on the original Greek — as possessing any of the requirements by taking over the rhythm of one language into another, is simply astonishing, after one has read his own translations.

Also, I cannot see why Miss Crapsey took the trouble to notice the musical scansionists at all. They have been outmoded for a long time. In fact, they never had much following. The five feet of English metre are simple enough bases for metrical verse. Upon them 'hang all the law and the prophets.' What is adequate is enough. There is no need to confuse by adopting the idiom of another art, nor by changing terms, as Miss Crapsey does in speaking about duple and triple rhythm, when the terms we already have fit all purposes excellently well. The object of criticism should be to clarify and explain, rather than to multiply and confuse. I think Miss Crapsey's article tends to confuse something which is really comparatively simple.

It is strange, also, to find the author apparently following the mistake of Professor Saintsbury in trying to reduce *vers libre* passages to metrical rules. I do not know exactly when this article was written, but, from one of the quotations, it must have been during, or after, 1913. At that time the poetry-reading public had already become much agitated on the subject of *vers libre*. Many French books had been written on the subject, and it was gradually being worked out that *vers libre* was based upon cadence and not upon the feet of metrical verse. I do not think that anything had been written in English on the subject in 1913, but there was a great deal in French. Whether Miss Crapsey made the mistake of supposing that such writings referred only to French prosody, or whether her reading was along purely classical lines and she did not keep up to date at all, I cannot say, but when she speaks of the *vers libre* choruses of Milton's 'Samson Agonistes' as being in 'duple rhythm,' we can only feel that Miss Crapsey allowed her fine ear and intelligence to be smothered under the weight of academic tradition.

The examples she gives of the false accenting of words are very interesting, but, I think, fairly obvious, and I cannot help feeling that had Miss Crapsey lived she would probably have outgrown this youthful and academic hair-splitting.

I am afraid you will have difficulty in getting anybody to print this essay for two reasons. The first is that it is written in a forbidding and difficult manner; the second is that it is not finished, as she herself says. She has, as it were, merely laid down the bare scaffolding of hypothesis, and not had time to erect the building.

I trust you will not mind my having given my opinion of the paper so freely. I imagine that is what you rather wanted me to do, and I do not suppose for a moment that you will agree with me. It will not, I hope, interfere with our goodwill; for what is more healthy than disagreement? I have a great admiration for Miss Crapsey's 'Cinquains,' and I think that American letters lost much in her un-timely death. I do not, however, believe that her reputa-tion would be enhanced by the publication of this thesis.

The June *Egoist* arrived; the names of Aldington and H. D. had been dropped from the editorial staff, and were replaced by that of T. S. Eliot. Because of the British em-bargo on books, duplicate plates of the latest Imagist anthology were shipped to England on the 'Colonian,' but the boat was sunk, and almost immediately England an-nounced an embargo on plates. But if England was un-willing to admit American literature, France seemed anxious to do so. Jean Giraudoux, the author, had been sent over as lieutenant, for the benefit of the Harvard R. O. T. C.; the French government had also sent over the poet Pierre de Lanux, former secretary of *La Nouvelle Re-vue Française,* to tighten the relations between the young

literati of both countries. The two men both spoke ad-
miringly of *Six French Poets*; and after having Lieutenant
Giraudoux to dinner on June 27, to discuss the reasonabil-
ity of getting her *Tendencies in Modern American Poetry*
translated into French — a project over which he was enthusiastic — Miss Lowell asked M. de Lanux to do it, for
an adequate honorarium; a task he gladly undertook.

Meanwhile James Oppenheim exultantly accepted
'Guns as Keys,' her latest long poem, for publication in
Seven Arts.

Five days late, on the night of July 5, she expressed the
finished manuscript of *Tendencies of Modern American
Poetry* to Macmillan's. Her eyes were hurting her badly;
she was obliged to wear glasses; but at least she was free to
write some poems she had been planning. Only first she did
a couple of reviews for *Poetry*, promising also $200 a year
for the next five-year period; re-subscribed to the *Egoist*;
lamented the death of the *Poetry Review*; and wrote letters
to friends English and American, especially one to Fletcher,
on July 16, on the importance of poetry in wartime:

> I have your letters of May 29th and June 15th to answer.
> But the thing I want first of all to say is that you must not
> let yourself get discouraged because of the war, and you
> must not think that the world is going to be all brutal be-
> cause it is undergoing a change which, for the moment,
> seems to count more than art. Nor must you think that you
> are not useful merely because you are a poet and not a sol-
> dier. As a matter of fact, I believe that the world needs
> poetry more than it ever needed it. It is absolutely neces-
> sary to keep the beautiful going, and because most people
> are lost in the maelstrom which the war brings, makes the
> poets of more value because to them is entrusted the duty
> of keeping poetry alive in a world which for the moment has
> little sympathy in it. We poets have the hardest row to hoe
> of any other people in this war, I am sure, in that we are
> naturally aside from it; and unless we are able to absolutely
> come out and fight against that feeling and realize that

'They also serve who only stand and wait.' Perhaps in the future, communities will understand what the artists are doing and how useful they are to humanity, how necessary, in fact, and will not feel that they can only be of value when they are in the firing line. Because most people do not feel this and do not understand, makes it all the harder to keep one's point of view, but it is all the more necessary to do so and to realize that difficult though the task may be, we have the task and it is up to us to be true to it without flinching. Therefore do not lose heart, dear boy, and do not feel that the war is the end of everything, and realize how extremely important you are in the world. Brute force never lasts long, although at times it seems to be let loose in the world, and we feel as if we were living, not on the earth we have known, but in a sort of ghastly chaos. It is not so really, and I am firmly convinced that it is we who are the people who make it not so, who keep alive that spark of civilization to which the others will return.

Poetry is not a thing outside of man; it is absolutely in- herent. It is one of the distinct needs of humanity, and it is as important to administer to that need as it is to grow wheat or raise cattle. Nothing has ever been able to crush poetry out of the world, and it will not be crushed now, be- cause there are people like you in it. So you must not let yourself feel, as you say in this letter: 'Of what use is your brain — your feeling — your strength — before this?' It is of infinite use, of such far-reaching use that that use cannot now be analysed. Keep that faith always before you, no matter what any one says or what any one feels, for it is the truth.

I have sent all the clippings in regard to the 'Anthology' to Hilda Aldington and have asked her to send them to you and the others. You will see that your 'Lincoln' is the poem which carries the volume this year....

It was getting late in the season, so she decided not to go to Dublin for the summer, the more so as the weather had been reasonably cool so far. Besides, the automobiles and the hard roads there were spoiling the pleasure of driving horses. She remained in Brookline, correcting proof, and having people out to dinner. The Untermeyers came, also the Greenslets, the Marshes, and the Loweses, who were passing through on the way to Nantucket. Barrett Wendell sent her some poems by a young lady for criticism; she replied on July 28:

> Thank you very much for your kind letter and the confidence you show in me in asking my opinion of these poems. I do not know just how to tell you what I think of them without seeming to rate them too low. They are quite good verse of a kind that is turned out in immense numbers. They are too unoriginal, and too full of *clichés*, to be in the least important, although I quite agree with you that they contain a real emotion. Unfortunately, real emotion is not enough; one must also be an artist....
>
> Such poetry as this is usually written to relieve an emotion on the part of the writer, and has what you feel in it — the touch of sincerity. It is the kind of poetry which one's friends and relations always consider perfectly beautiful, but — and this is unaccountable to the author — which never leads to any real success. I think the answer is quite clear. It is that the writer belongs to the large class of amateurs, namely, those people who write to relieve a strain of feeling, whereas, to my mind, a professional in art is a person who writes in obedience to the impulse of the creative faculty. The cases overlap somewhat, of course, or rather they overlap on one side, for the true artist sometimes writes to ease an emotion, whereas the amateur never writes for any other reason. The true artist has spent a lifetime in perfecting his instrument; the amateur takes any means at hand, no matter how old and battered, and so unusual is the act of creation that he is delighted with the result, and never realizes that he has only arranged a lot of existing counters into a slightly different pattern....

'Guns as Keys' appeared in the August *Seven Arts*; in thanking Oppenheim she also took opportunity to object to the policy which was to stop its publication unexpectedly in two months' time.

I find myself more and more reading the articles in your paper, and I have only one fault to find with it. I do think it is a pity at this crisis to keep snarling at the war. Whatever you or any one else may think of the advisibility of going to war, we are in it now, and we only weaken the hands of the nation by growling at its existence.

You see I don't believe that we are fighting primarily for the high-minded principles enunciated in high quarters. I think we are fighting for our existence against a country whose idea is military domination. I am sure that if we do not fight now, when we have other nations to help us, we shall be obliged to fight later when we are defenceless and alone. To take any other attitude seems to me to lack both a historical sense and a far-reaching vision, although I do not expect everybody to hold this view, but I do think it is a pity for you, in your paper, never to take it. I think it will weaken your appeal in the long run, and though I realize the necessity for sincerity on your part, still there is also a desire for fair play evinced in every page which you write, and I do wish I could occasionally see an article stating the arguments on the other side; not the side favorable for war, as such, but the side which realizes the extreme danger in which we stand, and the necessity of self-preservation at this juncture.

The article by John Reed was immensely interesting and well written, but it was not true to facts; at least, it was not so in one instance which came under my personal observation.

I was in London when the war broke out. I was able to observe conditions as clearly and with as unbiased a point of view as was Mr. Reed. It would be difficult for any one to find the English people, *en masse*, more unattractive than I do, so that I had no reason whatever, in spite of my Anglo-Saxon blood, to sympathize with them, but I do think that there was much serious endeavour and much self-sacrifice evinced in England at that time. That they resorted to all sorts of silly methods to stimulate interest in enlisting, no one can deny. But that was because again the people are not clear-sighted. I doubt whether they can be quite that in any country. They did not realize the fact that England was fighting for existence.

No matter how much one may believe in the rights of the individual — and I, myself, am a complete individualist, more of an individualist than any of the men who call themselves socialists — still the experience of the world goes to prove that there must be a certain amount of banding together to make life possible. Alone, the individual is too weak to protect himself. This is as true of nations as it is of people. If Germany proves to be the most entirely banded together of any country, if they move more completely with one will and as one man, they will undoubtedly succeed where other countries fail. They will press the military system upon other countries, if not by directly conquering them, by that strong force of will, which any nation which is at the moment dominant can exert over weaker nations.

In other words, the position today is not so very different from the position at the end of the Roman Empire: one civilization stands in the balance in the face of another; but that the other is, to a certain extent, the return of autocracy, I hardly think can be denied. That Germany herself may in time work out of an autocracy is of course possible, but it will not happen so soon should she be the conqueror in the present war. I think all clear-sighted, unsentimental people must believe that this is a turning point — one of the many turning points which happen from time to time in all civilizations. Which way the world will now go depends upon the power of the democratic countries to protect themselves and keep the world free for their ideals. If they are unable to do this when brought face to face with a violent and militant would-be-dominating force, they will fail, and the ideals for which they have striven will fail in them, and the world will not again reach those ideals until several centuries have passed.

When Napoleon was conquered on the field of Waterloo, Emperor though he was, the cause of free thought, free speech and individuality perished out of the world, only to be resumed and to once more reach the plane where he had left them some seventy-five years later than would otherwise have been the case, for although Napoleon was an Emperor, the France of his day was the most advanced intellectually of any country of the time. The England of that time was reactionary, and that reactionarism imposed itself upon all the nations of the world, until it again had been outgrown.

Germany represents the reactionary force in the world at the present day, and it is a reactionary force which is not content to exist for itself, but wishes to impose its ideals upon all the rest of the world.

To my mind, our fighting is a necessity — a necessity which we abhor, and from which we innately shrink. War is foreign to our instincts, completely foreign to our ideals and desires. I regard this war as a social illness, or rather let us call it an inoculation to escape a greater sickness, which we should undoubtedly have to undergo without it.

Of course, you do not believe these things. You will pardon me if I consider that not to see danger is myopic, but that is not what I mean now. Everyone has a right to his opinions, which, of course, are only determined by his natural vision, but I do think that some expression of this sort should appear in your pages, if only in the interest of fair play.

Forgive this lecture, but I feel so much in sympathy with most of your aims that it hurts me to find myself so out of sympathy with you in this important side of your policy....

Oppenheim's reply of August 2 thanked her for her sane, honest letter, and outlined in rebuttal the belief of the *Seven Arts* editors that the issue was not nation against nation, but the people everywhere against autocracy; that internal changes, such as had taken place in Russia, and a League of Nations to prevent conquests, were the remedies.

Letters congratulating her on 'Guns as Keys' came in promptly; she was particularly pleased with one from Paul K. Hisada, a Japanese gentleman, who admired the vivid way in which she described Japanese scenery — which of course she had never seen.

Proofs kept her busy; her automobile rushed to and from the press in Norwood.

The returns from the Imagist anthologies came in, which she divided in six and distributed. The third one had not gone so well: only four hundred and thirty-four copies had been sold. But before the money reached Europe, she got a letter from D. H. Lawrence.

> Higher Tregerthen, Zennor, St. Ives, Cornwall
> 30 Aug. 1917

MY DEAR AMY:

How are you, and what are you doing? It is ages since I have heard of or from you. How is your health, and what are you writing?

I am all right in health. Frieda has been laid low with neuritis in her leg: very bad for a month, but righting now. I think she'll soon be sound.

Here the community seriously thinks of building an ark, for the cataclysmic deluge has certainly set in. It rains and rains, and it blows the sea up on the land, in volleys and masses of wind. We are all being finely and subtly sea-pickled, sea-changed, sure enough, 'into something new and strange.' I shouldn't be a bit surprised to find one morning that fine webs had grown between my toes, and that my legs were slippery with sea-weedy scales. I feel quite spray-blind, like any fish, and my brain is turning nacreous. I verily believe I am metamorphosed — feel as if I daren't look to see.

The corn is cut, and being washed back again to the bowels of the earth. I made a wonderful garden: but the pea-rows are already beaten and smashed and dissolved to nauseous glue, and the leaves are blown to bits from off the marrow vines, leaving the voluptuous smooth-skinned marrows naked like virgins in the hands of the heathen. All's wrong with the world, in contradiction to Browning. But I don't care — why should I!

Nobody will publish my novel 'Women in Love' — my best bit of work. The publishers say 'it is too strong for an English public.' Poor darling English public, when will it go

in for a little spiritual athletics. Are these Tommies, so
tough and brown on the outside, are they really so pappy
and unbaked inside, that they would faint and fall under a
mere dose of 'Women in Love'? — Let me mix my metaphors thoroughly, let me put gravy-salt into the pudding,
and pour vanilla essence over the beef, for the world is
mad, yet won't cry 'Willow, Willow,' and drown itself like
Ophelia.

Chatto & Windus are this autumn bringing out a new
book of verse of mine 'Look, We Have Come Through.'
They are actually going to give me 20 guineas in advance
of royalties. — I will send you a copy as soon as I can.
(not of the guineas) — This is one bright beam in my
publishing sky. — But I shall have to go and look for daylight with a lantern.

That is to say, with an eye to material things as well as
spiritual: at last I am learning to squint: — I am doing a
set of essays on 'The Transcendental Element in American
(Classic) Literature.' It sounds very fine and large, but in
reality is rather a thrilling blood-and-thunder, your-money-
or-your-life kind of thing: hands up, America! — No, but
they are very keen essays in criticism — cut your fingers if
you don't handle them carefully. — Are you going to help
me to hold up the 'Yale Review' or the 'New Republic' or
some such fat old coach, with this ten-barrelled pistol of
essays of mine, held right in the eye of America? Answer
me that, Donna Americana. Will you try to suborn for me
the conductor of one of these coaches? — Never say nay. —
Tis a chef-d'oeuvre of soul-searching criticism. Shall I
inscribe it to you? Say the word!

To
Amy Lowell
Who buttered my bread
these few fair words
For she can butter her own parsnips.
Being well-to-do
She gave to the thankless
Because she thought it was worth it.

Frieda says you will be offended. Jamais de la Vie! cry I. — But please yourself.

Ah me — it's a long way to Tipperary, if Tipperary means a place of peacefulness. — I shall come to America directly the war is over. No doubt you don't want me — but it will be one of the moments of my life when I can say 'Farewell and Adieu' to Europe; the 'It is finished' of my Golgotha. As for Uncle Sam, I put my fingers to my nose, at him.

D. H. LAWRENCE

Another letter, written on the same day, came from Ezra Pound, who now dominated both the *Egoist* and the *Little Review*; consequently, though she subscribed to both magazines, she would publish in neither. In July, when Margaret Anderson had asked for a manuscript, Miss Lowell refused:

> I am awfully sorry to disappoint you, but I am going to tell you the truth. I do not want to put anything in your magazine while you are running those men [Pound and Lewis] so hard. Much as I admire some of Ezra Pound's work, I do not like his attitude, and I feel the same about the other contributors, only in most cases without the admiration.
>
> I have always had a strong feeling of friendship for you, and an interest in 'The Little Review,' and I wanted to do all I could for it, but when you went over bodily to my bitterest enemies, although it in no sense disturbs the feeling of friendship nor my relations to you, it does disturb my relations to the magazine, and so long as you continue to give such prominence to these men, I do not feel like appearing in it.
>
> Should you ever change your policy, I should, of course, reconsider my point of view. In fact, I do not think any one can tell exactly how they are going to feel about things in a little while. Circumstances alter cases. There might be reasons which might induce me to change my attitude....

On the strength of this, Miss Anderson evidently dropped a hint to Pound, as in his note of August 30, he asked Miss

Lowell if she was going to get onto the Band Wagon? —
said that she had tried to stampede him into accepting as
artistic equals various people whom it would have been
hypocrisy for him to accept in any such — and now what
was this nonsense about bitterest enmities? Miss Lowell
did not get round to replying until October 2.

> DEAR EZRA:
> Your letter has come.
> I accept your *amende honorable*, and I am very glad there
> is no hostile feeling.
>   Sincerely yours,

He replied on the twenty-sixth that her use of the word
amende was just a little peculiar; it was, however, quite impossible to dislike her. Pleased as she was with this change
of attitude, nonetheless she did not send another manuscript to the *Little Review* until the following May, when
Miss Anderson was collecting material for an All-American
number. On September 5, she sent off the last proofs; on the
eleventh she went to New York on business. Besides her
publishers, she saw the Untermeyers, Elizabeth Cutting,
and Zoë Akins; scolded Professor Patterson for calling her
poetry 'spaced prose' in the preface to the second edition of
his *Rhythm of Prose* (worse: he had compared her work to
Theodore Roosevelt's!); made the final arrangements with
Pierre de Lanux for the translation of her new book into
French; and sold a series of poems, some of her 'Phantasms
of War,' to the *Independent*. The backer of the *Seven
Arts* had removed her support suddenly, because of that
magazine's pacifism; Miss Lowell saw Oppenheim, and
agreed to give $200, on condition that politics be omitted
from what she considered an essentially aesthetic organ.
But all the necessary sum could not be raised, and the
magazine ceased publication. On the fifteenth she returned to Boston, where she plunged into a semilong poem

so earnestly that she neglected even her correspondence. But the great event was the approaching appearance of *Tendencies*, the advertisements for which still had to be arranged for, and other details, such as the sixty complimentary copies she sent out. The advance sales were satisfactory, and the book appeared on October 10, 1917.

CHAPTER XVI

TENDENCIES IN MODERN AMERICAN POETRY AND THE FIRST OPERATION

'We are no longer colonies of this or that other land, but ourselves, different from all other peoples whatsoever.'

Tendencies in Modern American Poetry was the most important critical work produced in the United States for many years. It gave a structure and a meaning to our modern poetry, which hitherto had been aimless and confused in the minds of the public. To discover the order, the movement, the dynamics, in the seeming chaos of contemporary work is a feat requiring an intellect above the times; and I may remark that the apparent aimlessness of our literature (however vigorous) since the death of Amy Lowell is due to our lack of just such critical work. Matthew Arnold's dictum that the function of the critic is to discover ideas and give them to the poets is not unreasonable — although it is more often true that the critic extracts the ideas first from the leading poets and passes them on to the rest of the literary world. Amy Lowell's book was a fixed point in the fluid realm of creation. Whether or not one agreed with her did not matter: even a flat disagreement clarified and thus strengthened one's individual bent. Thus *Tendencies in Modern American Poetry* had a historical importance that went far beyond her own judgments.

The Preface proclaimed the international importance of our recently awakened national sense, in life as well as in art. Before the war gave us a single purpose, even when materialism seemed triumphant, the new idealism, as expressed in a native poetry, was being born. Now that it is manifest, we receive an understanding sympathy from other nations such as had been inconceivable earlier.

Literature, she continued, is rooted in life; if the roots be not strong and the soil rich, it will perish soon. But the new movement is no frivolous experiment in form: it is the expression of a new point of view. Modern poets are concerned with truth, not dogma; man and nature are no longer divided; the universe is one huge symbol, so real that the poets need not dwell contentedly on its symbolic meaning. This entirely different outlook marks us off from the Victorians.

Her book demonstrates the three stages of this change from the Victorian to the modern. She selected six contemporary poets, and grouped them in Plutarchian pairs, as literary Evolutionists, Revolutionists, and Imagists, thus illustrating the time-spirit as expressed through six contrasting individualities. Robinson and Frost, the Evolutionists, represent the beginning of the New Poetry in their return to the reality of life and speech. In them the literary conventions have broken down, but the race is retained and the environment accepted. Masters and Sandburg, the Revolutionists, represent the breakdown of racial traits and the attack on environment, including the liberation from meter. H. D. and Fletcher, the Imagists, represent the full achievement of the modern point of view, with its completed creed.

But she was careful not to imply that Imagism was the goal, which its predecessors had stopped short of. Genius is genius, at whatever stage of change it appears, and is to be judged solely by its flowering. Unable to separate life and art, Amy Lowell treated each poet as man and artist, with a running appreciation of his works, after the method she had learned from Leigh Hunt. She praised the flowers, and also traced the hidden running root from which these six stems sprang. She preserved admirably the just proportion between man and works and epoch. Their writings she judged as expressions of reality, without recourse to any external tests of special sociological, sexual, or economic shibboleths, and without geographical propaganda. She even strove to keep unprejudiced by friendship; for though she had sought out five of these poets as friends primarily because they were poets, yet as critic she felt she ought to recognize their limitations and lapses, if only to make their best work appreciated the better.

Her book did not pretend to be a comprehensive study of all contemporary American poetry; 'Tendencies' was frankly a selective title. Besides herself (and many were the complaints that she had not included some account of her own works), perhaps the most striking omission would seem today to be that of Ezra Pound, whom she named in her Preface among those whom she regretted passing over. In view of the feud, her attitude was human enough, the more so as Imagism was adequately represented by H. D. and Fletcher. But beneath any personal animosity lay the fact that, however much superficial resemblance their poems might have, actually they were aimed in totally different directions. Pound was primarily a stylist, who carried the old warfare against moralizing to the exclusion of meaning itself; his poems exist entirely in their marvellous textures, except when they curiously reverse towards their sources. Miss Lowell's poems, however, live originally in meaning, which the words express and the images symbolize. The full power of Pound's work did not manifest until after her death, when Hart Crane and others did brilliant work in what we may name the 'Decorative School.'

Eliot was omitted; his *Waste Land* was still in the future, nor did she like it when it appeared. Aiken was omitted; she did not consider him a permanent poet until *Punch* was published, when she made amends with an enthusiastic review. Lindsay, as she often said later, might well have been included; and though in her Preface she tried to force him into the revolutionary company of Masters and Sandburg, she really regarded him as a climax in folk-poetry, notable for introducing democratic subjects and rhythms, but best as an entertainer and worst as a sage.

No conservatives were included, whether Sara Teasdale, whose work she admired, or Josephine Peabody, with whom she was at variance: conservative poetry, however excellent, showed no 'tendency' and thus had nothing to offer to her thesis. The moribund 'cosmic' school, descended from Whitman, was also omitted; and none has missed it.

Seven years later, in her *Critical Fable*, she revised all her judgments merrily, adding to her original Six, Lindsay and herself, Aiken, Sara Teasdale, the Conklings mother and daughter, Kreymborg, the Untermeyers husband and wife, the expatriates Pound and Eliot, ending with William Rose Benét, Bodenheim, Wallace Stevens, and Edna Millay.

A more immediate reaction, however, is to be found in a letter dated October 23, 1917, to Helen Bullis Kizer, on an article (in its first version, chiefly a review of *Tendencies*) to appear in the May *North American*:

> It amused me to have you say that the essay on Edwin Arlington Robinson is more 'rounded and finished than any other in the volume' probably because I have a greater sympathy with my subject and that I have stood where he stands. As a matter of fact, I found myself easily less in sympathy with Mr. Robinson in many ways than with any of the other poets in the volume, and I have never stood where he stands. I have had my own struggles and escapes, but they have not been his struggles, and I have not escaped from his prison. The Robinson essay cost me more pains than any of the others because of the fact that he is, in a way, antipathetic. I have written a long poem in answer to his 'Man Against the Sky,' which I have not yet published. I am afraid I have small sympathy with his inability to shake himself free from tradition and with his constant melancholy. You see I evoluted, not revoluted, I do not

know why: it just came. I remember my brother's telling me what an awful time he had to free himself from his inhibitions. Possibly his freedom helped mine, as he was nineteen years older than I, and a constant influence in my childhood; but I sloughed off many of my swaddling bands in the early twenties, and they seem so remote as hardly to be realized as having existed. Still, I would not have you change your sentence at all. I am rather glad that it appears that way, for it shows what one can do if one sets out really to put oneself into a sympathetic attitude.

The things that I agree with less are your criticisms of my prose style and your belief that my humor is cultivated and not native. Ah, dear lady, if you knew me!... My objection to Frost's 'Hundred Collars' was not on the score of its horseplay, however, but because it was a kind of humor which I think imported into New England, not an original growth.... 'A Hundred Collars' seemed to me Frost for once not writing down himself, but endeavoring to do something on a theory. I think it was forced. I think he consciously forced it. Perhaps I am led to this opinion because I know the man, but that is the way I feel about it. I should add, that he has no doubt of its genuine humor himself, we have argued often about it.

Now let me take up my only real point of difference with your paper, which is the criticism of my style as careless. It may have all sorts of faults, this style of mine, but careless it most emphatically is not. My prose writing is subjected to the same test which I use in my poetry, the test of oral rendering. To me all writing, whether poetry or prose, is merely a symbol for the spoken word. I am quite aware that this is a point of view which is not subscribed to by the academes, but I have 'escaped' the New England superstition of subservience to Academia. I have had too intimate an acquaintance with it from my childhood to see it with a halo and a harp. Every one of my sentences is considered again and again, and even small connecting words are altered and altered until I get the effect I want. That this effect should have the light ease of conversation — elisions, and suggestions, and half-spoken expressions — is exactly what I am aiming at. When you say that I sometimes have a sentence without a predicate, I fear this refers to a habit of mine of punctuating with periods in order to gain a greater emphasis, fully expecting the subject of the thought, if not of the sentence, to carry over in the reader's mind and justify my method. It is, of course, a highly personal style, but one which came without effort, and this is not a contradiction to what I said about thinking it out. It means merely that I write as I feel, but I try to give that feeling its complete expression. However, I think you will find, in reading the book, that I have changed the punctuation somewhat so as to obviate misunderstanding on the reader's part.

I smiled a little at your supposing me startled at the 'Spoon River' pieces. I would be willing to bet a good deal that nothing can 'startle' me, and you will remember that I said that none of these stories was false in itself: it was only that there were too many of one type to remain true in the aggregate. I do, however, strongly disagree with your theory that all life is this way if seen under the surface. Is your life like this, or do you suppose yours an exception? On the contrary. There have been few things which have done so much harm to the world as the promiscuous publication of Freud's theories. No one is capable of putting those theories actually in the light in which they belong who is not a trained psychologist; and I think you would find, if you talked to many such, that they rarely subscribe to his opinions *en bloc.* You know that it is commonly said that Freud being an unmarried man and an Austrian has gained most of his knowledge of women through prostitutes and that he is by no means to be taken as a criterion on the psychology of women of a different type. If you will read his book on 'Dreams,' you will see how dangerous a theory can be when ridden too hard. To suppose that all life under the surface consists of violent sexual desires crushed out or sublimated, that all personal relation is a war of sexual antagonisms is to see life through a perfectly distorted medium. We have run mad on the subject in this country, as a few years ago we ran mad over Christian Science. That the Victorians refused to give sex its proper

weight is of course true, but that we are now over-emphasiz-
ing it, and particularly its perversions, is equally true. It
is only this that I meant to insinuate in regard to 'Spoon
River.' I thought I had explained myself in the text,
but I am beginning to realize that to explain is one of the
most difficult things in the world....

Five of the poets she treated in her volume were pleased,
and wrote her to that effect; the one exception was Masters.
Furious at being linked with Sandburg, he never wrote her
another line. The only hostile critics were those poets not
included, as she wrote to William Aspinwall Bradley on
January 3, 1918.

The rest of October was spent in sending out her sixty
presentation copies, jogging reviewers, and catching up on
her long neglected correspondence.

On November 3, Pierre de Lanux arrived, with the
manuscript of his translation of the first two chapters of
Tendencies. The next day they sat down for a siege, and it
speedily became apparent that the manuscript was un-
satisfactory. Much of it was not typed; the state of her
eyes made reading handwriting difficult; so a secretary was
called in. After five hours, her eyes gave out nevertheless;
and after another four hours, only fifty pages were in
proper form. The collaboration was obviously not a success, and the two agreed to give it up.

Letters of congratulations over the book meanwhile
were pouring in from friends and strangers. One, from the
distinguished author of the *Literary History of America,*
expressed the attitude of a friendly conservative:

358, Marlborough Street,
7 November, 1917

DEAR AMY,

Your book is not a question of an hour or two. It seems
to me a remarkable piece of interpretative criticism, which
must be read slowly but which rewards without ever
straining the attention it demands. So I have been long
in sending this word of the pleasure it gives me.

Though in many aspects like that on the French poets, it is somehow even firmer in grasp and texture, more assured in its clear adequacy of style, at once colloquial and literary. Its individuality is certain but never obtrusive. Its amenity saves it from the obvious danger in such work of exciting reactionary protest.

Yet I do not feel in agreement with you about a good many phases of it. To begin with, your view of Puritanism and of witchcraft — risk[y] matters, to be sure — is by no means what a good deal of study overcoming both has made mine. Do you happen to have an old book of mine called 'Stelligeri'? If not, may I send it to you? There, as long ago as '93, I set forth opinions of both which have lasted; and there is a paper on Whittier, too, which they are about to translate into Italian, after all these years. Your New England, in brief, seems to me rather traditional than sympathetically historic.

But, Lord, I've done worse myself; I once almost printed the statement that Mahomet, like Luther, was an Xian heretic!

What seems to me more essential is my doubt whether the poets you touch on will prove, in perspective, so positively important as you seem to think now. Robinson I have known all along; Frost and Masters I have glanced at. I agree that Spoon River is the most important work of all the three; but I do not find, even with your interpretation, in any of them quite such advance, as distinguished from courageous independence, as you do, nor any such distinct nationality. 'H. D.' is mere Greek, to my mind, that, you quite appreciate — both in feeling and in form: she is new to me.

Well, the question is whether you have done a 'Literati' more thoughtful than Poe's — whom incidentally I value less than you do — or have cast the first light on ways to be. I shan't live to know — for the answer will take years to define itself. That you have done work one would be glad to have done oneself is true.

Always affectionately yours

BARRETT WENDELL

Mistakes in the first edition of her book had to be corrected at once for the second edition; Frost, for example, had informed her wrongly of certain names in England, and she had carelessly believed and repeated the familiar myth that the Salem witches were burned. The reviews were prompt, long, and vigorous. Each reviewer seemed to think that her judgment on five of the poets was sound but that the sixth had been badly treated; and as they differed constantly about the identity of the sixth, she felt sure that she had been just all round.

On November 7, she gave a reading for the benefit of the Surgical Dressings Branch of Needham, at Mrs. F. L. W. Richardson's house in Dover, which netted $325. The next week she planned to go to New York, among other things to speak at a dinner of the Joint Committee of the Literary Arts; but she came down with a cold and had to cancel all engagements. Then on the nineteenth, Florence Ayscough arrived from China. A large sum of money had been embezzled; to help straighten out the situation, she had come to America:

> I wrote Amy telling her about the whole thing, and she instantly cabled asking me to come to her at Sevenels to begin with.
>
> It is quite impossible for me to express what an *immense* difference that cable made for me. The matter in hand was certainly difficult, and my heart sank very low at the prospect before me, but the thought of Amy and her help was a very 'present comfort in time of trouble.' She came to the train to meet me, and as she came towards me down the platform that dark November night, the grimy North Station seemed to be illuminated with a warm and friendly glow.[1]

During her two weeks' visit (Miss Lowell's New York trip was put off again), Mrs. Ayscough naturally showed her hostess the large collection of Chinese paintings which she had brought over for exhibition.

[1] Florence Ayscough: 'Reminiscences' (*ms.*).

SEVENÊLS

Among these paintings were a number of examples of the 'Written Pictures.' Of these, she had made some rough translations which she intended to use to illustrate her lectures. She brought them to me with the request that I put them into poetic shape. I was fascinated by the poems, and, as we talked them over, we realized that here was a field in which we should like to work. When she returned to China, it was agreed that we should make a volume of translations from the classic Chinese writers. Such translations were in the line of her usual work, and I was anxious to read the Chinese poets as nearly in the original as it was possible for me to do. At first, we hardly considered publication.[1]

In four years these translations were to be published as *Fir-Flower Tablets*.

On December 5, Grace Hazard Conkling read poems at the New England Poetry Club, which met at Josephine Peabody's in Cambridge. For the first time since her ousting, Miss Lowell attended a meeting, to hear Mrs. Conkling's poems.

Winter weather set in early: it was unusually cold, and to add to the national difficulties there was a famine of coal, sugar (which Miss Lowell kept locked up in her letter file), and meat. 'Hooverizing' became a necessary fashion. The book market fell off, except for books about war. But if the public at home wanted to read about war, the soldiers markedly preferred poetry.[2] As Miss Lowell wrote Aldington on December 7:

Here we have had a most curious experience. Each of the training camps has a library, and they tell me that the demand for poetry in these libraries is phenomenal. Of course, the kind of poetry is not always what you and I

---

[1] Amy Lowell: 'Preface,' *Fir-Flower Tablets*, Boston, 1921, pp. vi–vii.

[2] This unexpected proof how far the poetry movement had saturated the country is almost incredible; but the fact squares with another fact: that in 1916, 663 volumes of poetry and drama were published — a number exceeding all other classifications except fiction, which had only seventy-three more titles.

would choose, for they like Kipling and Robert Service as well as a lot of other things; but that a lot of private soldiers that come from every walk in life should loudly demand poetry is such an extraordinary thing that I cannot explain it except by thinking that this country is at last seeking for beauty and an expression of the other side of life. I do not think there has ever been a time when common soldiers have requested poetry, and the thing seems to me highly significant of the whole attitude which this country has towards the war.

And it was Amy Lowell who met the demand.

Shortly after America entered the war, I read in our little local paper, 'The Brookline Chronicle,' an appeal for books for the training camps; and what seemed to me as at once odd and profoundly significant, a special request was made for books of poetry. Cut off by health and aptitude from most of the war activities, this struck me as my opportunity. Here was something I could do for my country without deserting the even more intimate preoccupation of poetry. For, I must admit that, like all artists throughout the ages, I am a poet first and a patriot second. I immediately wrote to the librarian of the Brookline Public Library with whose name the appeal had been signed, and offered to give poetry libraries to the camps of this state. I seem to remember that at the time there were six of them. I submitted a list to Miss Hooper, and by her advice, only a few classics were included, as she thought that the classics would naturally be provided and that what was needed was distinctly modern work. I do not remember that Miss Hooper made any changes in the list as finally sent, but I do remember her cordial co-operation and the willing help she and her staff accorded me.[1]

These six libraries were only a beginning; they were to prove so successful that in a couple of months she was to duplicate her gifts for all the camps in the United States,

[1] Amy Lowell: 'Modern Poetry: Its Differences, Its Aims, Its Achievements' (lecture, June 6, 1919).

and then continue to meet the requests from the hospitals.

On December 11, Miss Lowell read from her poems to the Lawrence Women's Club at 3 P.M. in the new Unitarian chapel at Lawrence, Massachusetts. From the twelfth to the nineteenth, she was in New York, seeing her publishers, bringing another 'Phantasm' to the *Independent*, consulting Professor Patterson, dining with Elizabeth Cutting of the *North American Review*, and attending the theaters with other friends. Then she returned home for Christmas.

One of the letters which reached her about this time came from D. H. Lawrence. As part of a general clearing up, he and Frieda had been expelled from their Cornwall cottage in October, and had gone to live with H. D. in London. But they could not afford living in a big city; Lawrence's health was miserable; and they didn't know what to do. H. D. had written Miss Lowell on November fourteenth, suggesting that anything she could do for them would be welcome; and Miss Lowell replied that she would send H. D. some money for them in a little while. Lawrence's letter was as follows:

> 44 Mecklenburgh Square, W.C. 1.
> 13 Dec. 1917

MY DEAR AMY,

Your letter reached me yesterday: your book came a little earlier. This latter I had not acknowledged. But I had thanked you for the cheque for the Anthology, which I received some weeks back. — My publishers have sent you my new book of poems. I hope you will get it all right.

Since writing my last letter, everything has gone wrong with us. The police & military came and searched our house and turned us out of Cornwall — for no reason under the sun, except of course that Frieda is German by birth, and I am not warlike. So here we are cast upon a rather disagreeable world. Hilda like an angel came to the rescue and lent us her room. But now she and Richard are come back, we must yield it up & go down to the country to a cottage that can be lent us by another friend. When one has no money to pay for lodgings, it is no joke to be kicked out of one's house and home at random, & given nowhere to go. However, we shall get over it all.

My book, 'Look, We have Come Through' is out about a fortnight: as usual the critics fall on me: the Times says 'the Muse can only turn away her face in pained distaste.' Poor Muse, I feel as if I had affronted a white-haired old spinster with weak eyes. But I don't really care what critics say, so long as I myself could personally be left in peace. This, it seems, cannot be. People write letters of accusation, because one has a beard and looks not quite the usual thing: and then one has detectives at one's heels like stray dogs, not to be got rid of. It is very hateful and humiliating and degrading. It makes me mad in my blood; so stupid and unnecessary. I want to be in quiet retreat in my own place in Cornwall — but they haul me out and then follow me round: really, [it] is too maddening. One would think they did it to amuse themselves.

I met Fletcher for the first time the other day. It surprised me to find him so nervously hyper-sensitive and fretted. I thought he was a rather hearty American type, from his poems. I was mistaken. But I liked him.

The Aldingtons are in London — Richard has another fortnight or so: and then heavens knows where he will be sent: let us hope, somewhere in England. They seem pretty happy, as far as it is possible under the circumstances. We have had some good hours with them in Mecklenburgh Square — really jolly, notwithstanding everything: remembering that evening at the Berkeley with you, when we all met for the first time, and laughing at ourselves. Oh my dear Amy, I do wish to heaven we could all meet again in peace and freedom, to laugh together and be decent and happy with each other. This is a more wintry winter of discontent than I had ever conceived. — Never mind, the devil won't rampage in triumph for ever.

Frieda sends her love. We both hope that nice things will happen to you for Christmas: and we look forward to a meeting again — soon.

D. H. LAWRENCE

She was planning to leave for New York soon after the holidays, but a 'flurry of influenza,' coupled with bad headaches from eye-strain, kept her in bed for a few days. On January 7, 1918, Professor Lowes (now of Harvard) began his Lowell Institute Lectures on 'Convention and Revolt in Poetry,' which ran Mondays and Thursdays at 5 P.M., in a lecture room of Huntington Hall so cold (because of the coal shortage) that the audience kept its coats on. Miss Lowell sat under the reading desk, in the little space roped off for the use of Lowells. On January 11, she read her poems to the Poetry Society at Springfield, spending the night there. On the fourteenth, she left for New York, to read at the MacDowell Club, for Witter Bynner's 'Anthology Barbecue.' He was introducing a dozen poets, who read their own poems which were to appear in this anthology; she read 'The Breaking Out of the Flags' and 'The Cornucopia of Red and Green Comfits,' from her *Phantasms of War*. The latter poem was 'absolutely drowned in' applause.' After visiting a few friends, she returned to Brookline on the eighteenth. On the twenty-third, Masefield was reading in Boston; she hoped to entertain him, but her ill-health (another cold) prevented. On the twenty-fourth, Grace Hazard Conkling came to spend the week-end. In the midst of these activities, she kept up her correspondence with poets and critics; agreed to let poems of hers be translated into Spanish for a new magazine, *Pan American Poetry*; answered theorists of metrics; got a former gardener, who had contracted tuberculosis, discharged from camp and sent to Colorado; bought books for her library; and of course wrote various poems and articles.

In February, the 'Work or Fight' order went through; Conrad Aiken got poetry classified as a 'useful occupation.' Amy Lowell was working at 'Bronze Horses,' and gathering material for a lecture on the English Imagists. Her gifts of poetry libraries to seven camps (a special request had come in from Alabama) had been so successful that she agreed to duplicate the list for the remaining twenty-seven camps in the United States. To take up her story where it was cut short:

> Shortly after this, the monthly bulletin issued by the Poetry Society of America contained a request from the librarian at Camp Sherman, Ohio, asking the members to send copies of their books to his library as the demand for modern poetry was greater than he was able to supply. I immediately wrote to this gentleman, enclosing my Massachusetts Camp list, and asked him if he would like me to send him one of the libraries; but I was in love with my self-imposed task, and rashly suggested that if he knew of any other camps which would like similar libraries I should be glad to send them.
>
> Of course I had no idea what I was letting myself in for, and I confess I was somewhat staggered when a letter from Dr. Putnam in Washington warmly commended my efforts and as warmly accepted my offer for all the camps in the country to the number of thirty-four. But Dr. Putnam is human, and he intimated that he doubted if I had realized the necessary magnitude of my proffered generosity; if I only felt like sending to a limited number of camps, etc., why, they would be grateful to have what I could give. Naturally, however, I could not take a dare. One must be a sportsman even where poetry is concerned.
>
> I sent those thirty-four libraries; and, since the war, requests have been coming in from army hospitals and have been filled as fast as received. I could never have done this work had not Miss Hooper kindly undertaken to pack and forward the libraries. Between us, however, the dough-boys have had the poetry to their hands, and from the letters that I have received they seem to have made use of it.[1]

Another grateful letter, from Frieda Lawrence, told her that H. D.'s rooms had been bombed in an air-raid, though

[1] 'Modern Poetry: Its Differences, Its Aims, Its Achievements.'

without hurting anyone. On the thirteenth she wrote Professor Lowes:

> My dear Mr. Lowes:
>
> Your letter of February 8th came this morning, and I am very glad indeed that you liked the 'Madonna of the Evening Flowers.' How could so exact a portrait remain unrecognized?
>
> I am also glad to know that you find Dr. Patterson's article interesting. I thought his subject of his return to the Anglo-Saxon tradition was very intriguing. He says that he is going to get awfully jumped on throughout Academia. Perhaps it is his boldness at being so willing to say what he thinks regardless of the powers that be (and which to him must make a great deal of difference) that makes me think so highly of him. Some day, I trust you two will meet. You will find him very pleasant to talk to.
>
> I only hope your lectures will come out in book form. They taught me a lot. They have reduced me to a sad state of pulp as regards the education that I did not have. If you could see me with my nose to the grindstone tracing those dreadful bronze horses through history you would be thoroughly amused. It is hard indeed to gain an education at forty year.

At one of their parties, it seems that a certain young lady started to leave early, in order to write a necessary editorial on the coal shortage. In order to persuade her to stay, Miss Lowell and Professor Lowes wrote it for her, dictating alternate sentences, in which Professor Lowes tried to end his as far as possible from the subject, and Miss Lowell to bring it back. The next paragraph of her letter refers to the consequences of their distinguished collaboration.

> By the way, my sense of honesty was a little outraged by being told that the editorial we composed together was turned in to a teacher, not to a magazine, and was due for a mark. That method of proceeding is not cricket to me, and

I certainly should not have lent myself to the deception had I known of it. I thought, as I think you did, that it was to be an editorial for their little magazine, which anybody might write. However, it will amuse you to know that we got an 'A' although the teacher qualified her approbation by saying that the arguments did not seem to be very clearly carried out. I can imagine the lady's consternation if she knew who wrote that article and how it was written....

Mrs. Russell joins me in love to Mrs. Lowes. As to you — well, did I not toil in town twice a week and up a most ungodly flight of stairs into the bargain, and are not actions stronger than words?

Sincerely yours,

AMY LOWELL

For February 20, she read war-poems of the allied nations at the Copley Plaza for the benefit of 'The Special Aid Societies.' On the twenty-second, Carl Sandburg sent her a poem, 'Good Night' (collected in *Smoke and Steel*), in lieu of a letter.

The end of February was tragic for her: 'Hooverizing' was proving a slow, sure death to her highly bred sheep-dogs. Accustomed to nine pounds of the top of the round every day, they sickened on the horse-meat, which was all that the government would allow them. By February 23, five of them were down with ptomaine poisoning, and one of the oldest — her special pet — had died. She sat up all night with them, to make sure that everything possible was done to relieve their sufferings. She paced the floor till dawn, wrestling with the situation. There was only one merciful thing to be done. 'I can't stand this any longer,' she finally told Mrs. Russell. 'Have them all chloroformed, but don't tell me when it is to happen — don't tell me anything whatsoever.' It was the end of the Hylowe Kennels. Only one dog still remained: the ten-year-old Prue, who belonged to Josephine Engel in New York; and Prue died in December.

For a week Miss Lowell was unable to work. Already, however, she had acquired her famous black tomcat Winky, who henceforth was her solace.

On March 12, she sent off the Imagist receipts, plus $200 for the Lawrences. The next day, Robert Frost dined with her; two days later, she entertained Mr. and Mrs. Padraic Colum.

From the sixteenth to the twenty-eighth she was in New York. On Monday the eighteenth she read from her poems at the Brooklyn Heights Seminary. On Saturday she read briefly from her poems at a dinner in her honor given by 'The Coffee House,' a professional club, to which she had been invited by Charles Hanson Towne, of *McClure's*. Frank Crowninshield, of *Vanity Fair*, inadvertently announced that Miss Lowell would read some poems, then the entertainment would begin. Needless to say, the entertainment started from that very moment. But the real reason for her trip was a series of two lectures on 'Imagism Past and Present,' delivered at the Brooklyn Institute on the afternoons of March 20 and 27.

The first of these lectures began with a condensed statement of the Imagist principles, which were then illustrated with examples from the works of Theocritus, Blake, Coleridge, and Emily Dickinson, all four of whom were born at the end of some literary era, and who revivified poetry by a return to reality.

Theocritus, in Alexandria of the fourth century before Christ, lived in a city surprisingly like modern New York. Reacting against the deadening cult of the classics, he wrote brief poems of a country as real as Frost's, of cities as teeming as Sandburg's, and of nature as sharp and beautiful as Aldington's. His diction was that of the contemporary speech of peasants and burgers; his images are clear, hard, exact and as real today as they were twenty-four centuries ago — too real for Andrew Lang, whose translation Miss Lowell modified for her own use.

Blake reacted against formal eighteenth century London with an imagination so vivid that he confused pictures in his brain with those before his eyes; had he lived today, he might have recognized them as projections of his subconscious mind. Yet it was Blake, not Wordsworth, who first returned to nature. Also a painter, he wrote as pictorially as Theocritus, but with the addition of a modern power of fantasy and suggestion. His rhythms advanced steadily, till at last he achieved free verse, the first and best analysis of which is in the preface to his *Jerusalem*.

Coleridge, who apparently founded no school, was the real grandfather of Imagism. His profound influence on Poe had a determining effect on Mallarmé, from whom sprang the French *Symbolistes*, from whom in turn were descended the Imagists. In his few real poems ('The Ancient Mariner,' 'Christabel,' 'Kubla Khan,' 'Frost at Midnight,' and 'The Nightingale') he presented details perfectly and directly seen, without the aid of metaphors, processions of adjectives, or charming conceits. It is the very essence of poetry. His valuable pioneering, to release rhythm from the tight bands of meter, stopped just before he actually attained full freedom for himself.

Though Emily Dickinson's life was restricted, she was racy and forthright in her verse. Besides her refreshing whimsy, there are other poems that reveal brutally the tragic truth of her life. Though unaware of any non-metrical verse, she experimented with new rhythms and false rhymes until she achieved pure cadence (as in 'Victory comes late'). She also anticipated the Imagists in her use of the 'unrelated method' (as in 'The Humming Bird').[1]

The second lecture, on Aldington, Flint, and Lawrence, began with a statement of Amy Lowell's belief that the fullest criticism must consider the artist's work as the product of his life; thus it traces the flowers of literature to

[1] The section on Emily Dickinson is published in *Poetry and Poets*.

their roots. She felt free, therefore, to stress the lives of these comparatively unknown poets (although Lawrence's promised letter of biography had never reached her).

Aldington, pure English, is particularly stimulated by the Greek and the Elizabethan traditions, yet his poems are as sincere as any in our language, being written from his own life. Essentially a lyrist, he wrote of his three great preoccupations (books, nature, and love) until the war ended his first period as poet, and began another, bitterer one.

Flint's sensitive poetry is entirely subjective, and is drawn from his own experience. In his work we see the struggle of sentiment and fact; and while the quiet melancholy of each poem seems gentle, the cumulative effect is tragic. At least two of his lyrics ('Swan' and 'London') have achieved immortality.

About Lawrence she found more to say, and more need to say it.

> He has no prototype that I can find. He is a poet of sensation, but of sensation as the bodily efflorescence of a spiritual growth. Other poets have given us sensuous images; other poets have spoken of love as chiefly desire; but in no other poet does desire seem so surely the 'outward and visible form of an inward and spiritual grace.' Mr. Lawrence does not do this by obscuring passion in a poetical subterfuge: he gives the naked desire as it is; but so tuned is his mind that it is always the soul made visible in a supreme moment....
>
> Mr. Lawrence has been spoken of as an erotic poet, and that is true, but it is only one half of the truth. For his eroticism leans always to the mystic something of which it is an evidence. Not to understand this is to fail completely to comprehend the whole meaning of his work.
>
> ... I do not hesitate to declare Mr. Lawrence to be a man of genius. He does not quite get his genius into harness; the cart of his work frequently overturns or goes

awry; but it is no less Pegasus who draws it, even if Mr. Lawrence is not yet an entirely proficient charioteer....

Mr. Lawrence's last volume of poems, *Look! We Have Come Through!* is an amazing book. It is to my mind a greater novel even than *Sons and Lovers*, for all that it is written in a rather disconnected series of poems....

Beautiful as the individual poems are, it is only when one reads the book from the first page to the last that one realizes the extraordinary truth, the naked simplicity and vigour, of it. I dislike the expression 'human document,' it is so often employed to designate vulgar outpourings of no real merit, but if we forget its abuse for a moment, this is the only term to apply to Mr. Lawrence's book. It is terrible in its intensity. It is sorrow made flesh. It is courage 'coming through.' It is illusion, disillusion, mounting at last to vision, to a humble, even a grateful, acceptance of life....

It is difficult to analyse dispassionately the poetry in a volume so full of travail. The bitterness, the anguish, the hard clarity of the revelation, all disarm us. The poems are born in a rush of passionate eloquence, and they are poetry because the man who wrote them is a poet, not because he has been at pains to make them so.

As a book, the volume is a masterpiece; as poetry, perhaps it is not quite that. Art is not raw fact. Poetry cannot rise into its rightful being as the highest of all arts if it be tied down to the coarse material of bald, even if impassioned, truth. Truth has its own beauty, but it is not the beauty of poetry. In the greatest poets, the two go, or seem to go, hand in hand, for the highest poetry is also the most simple. Sappho's 'I loved you once, Atthis' gives us this shock of poetry and truth in one. Dante, Shakespeare, have no fear of losing passion by transmuting it into poetry. In Mr. Lawrence's case, the God-given spark of poetry in the man often saves him; and yet, as poetry, the volume fails by a too loud insistence upon one thing, by an almost neurotic beating, beating, upon the same tortured note. It is not because the effect of the volume is over-sensual, for we have seen how Mr. Lawrence regards the sensual:

it is because of the way in which it is done. *Look! We Have Come Through!* is all the more a 'human document,' perhaps because it is unbalanced; but on that very account it falls short of being the immortal poetry it might have been.

The most momentous event of the New York trip, however, was the moving of a bed at midnight. Miss Lowell, unable to sleep, tried to remedy matters by pushing her large brass bed to a new position. Suddenly she felt something give and break in her body. The abdominal muscles, strained by lifting the buggy in the summer of 1916, had separated, although she did not learn that it was a genuine rupture (an umbilical hernia) for two months to come.

The outstanding events of April were various war charities: on the fifth, she read at Jacob Sleeper Hall, under the auspices of the Boston University Women's Graduate Club; on the eighteenth, she read two poems by Rollinat at Mrs. Henry Forbes Bigelow's entertainment to raise funds for musicians in France; on the twenty-third, she read 'Guns as Keys' at Mrs. Frederick P. Bagley's, under the auspices of the Writers' League Equal Suffrage Association; she was also a patroness of the entertainment given by the Friends of Poland Dramatic Club for starving children on April 3, and on the tenth she was patroness of a concert at Mrs. Bigelow's, again for the relief of French musicians. It was perhaps about this time that Boston learned of Stravinsky's plight; Miss Lowell was one of those who contributed to Mrs. Edward Burlingame Hill's fund for his support; in 1930 he expressed his gratitude by dedicating the *Symphonie de Psaumes* to the Boston Symphony Orchestra.

Presently Aldington sent her the manuscript of a new book, *War and Love*, which he wanted her to place, and also sell some of the poems first, if possible. There were complications, because the Reverend Charles C. Bubb had printed some of them in a private edition of fifty copies, under the title *Reverie*, at his Clerk's Press, Cleveland, Ohio.[1]

But before Miss Lowell accomplished anything, she learned that Aldington had already signed a contract with the Four Seas, his former publisher. On April 11, commenting on his manuscript, she wrote of the love poems:

> If I had a criticism it would be, not that your poems are too physical in their expression, but that for the first time in your work you have entirely obliterated the other side of love — the spiritual. Of course, they are both true, and they must both exist together in any real love, and possibly, after the trenches, the more physical side seems the most important....
>
> I do not believe that it is what one says in a poem that matters, it is the kind of light that plays over it; and I do think you played the physical rather more than most people can appreciate. I have a theory that you have been somewhat influenced in this by Lawrence, and do you mind my urging you to be careful not to let his influence go too far? He has ruined his own public by his attitude, and I am dreadfully afraid of its effect on you, particularly as it is not in the least your natural mode of speech. By this time you are sighing and saying, 'Oh Lord, Puritan New England!' but you know it is not that. I suppose the real crux of the situation lies in the extreme difficulty of touching anything so sacred as the relation between man and woman without vulgarizing it. A prurient world reads vulgarity into certain expressions which do not in the least connote vulgarity. But, after all, words are a means of communication, and if one communicates something other than what one intended, I think the result might be termed 'bad writing.' That is the blunder which Lawrence makes, I think. To you and me and a few people like us, he expresses exactly what he means; but those people are a hand-

---

[1] Apparently in the summer of 1917. He also issued Aldington's *Love Poems of Myrrhine and Konallis* (July, 1917), which had already been published in the *Little Review*; and H. D.'s *Tribute* (August, 1917).

ful, and it has always been so. To most people, he says something entirely different. Now you may say that you do not write for the ignorant masses, but for the cultivated few, but I do not believe you do. Only the minor poets do that. Great poetry is and must be universal, above the customs of cliques or the delight of the initiated.

On the fifteenth, Frieda Lawrence thanked her for the money, and also sent (far too late) a brief biography of her husband, which was mostly an appreciation.

On the twenty-sixth, Miss Lowell attended a special matinee performance of the Metropolitan Opera Company at the Boston Opera House; her favorite *Coq d'Or* was being given, for the first time in Boston, by general demand. It was followed by Henry Gilbert's ballet, *Dance in the Place Congo*, which was also new to Boston.

The May *North American Review* contained Mrs. Kizer's long article on her; the May *Bookman* had another by Professor Phelps of Yale; the *Pan American Poetry* was running a series of her poems translated magnificently into Spanish; and presently a whole pamphlet about her work, signed 'Winifred Bryher,' arrived from London. This shy young lady had run across *Six French Poets* early in 1916; it had opened a new world to her. 'Red Slippers' then came her way. Overwhelmed to learn that someone else shared her tastes and enthusiasms, she had written Miss Lowell in September, 1917, telling of her loneliness and asking for a reading list; meanwhile, with infinite trouble, she had got copies of Miss Lowell's books. The result was her pamphlet, a handsome tribute to her friend.

On May 2, Amy Lowell was invited to a smoker given by the *Harvard Advocate*. 'I was, as usual, smuggled into an upper chamber, and kept quiet with cigars while they heckled me in true undergraduate fashion. I think I held my own; I tried to.'[1] Of her own poems, the most successful was 'Castles in Spain,' which was to appear in the

[1] Letter to Richard Hunt, May 27, 1918.

August *Atlantic*. Donald Clarke was her chief challenger;
but she managed various counter-attacks. 'Masefield
hasn't got organic rhythm, and I told him so,' is one of her
sentences recollected by Ben C. Clough. Joseph Auslander read his 'Whither?' which had just won the Lloyd
McKim Garrison prize; and it was perhaps on this evening that he also rendered a poem about a skylark, which
prompted her to ask if he had ever heard one; for, she explained, conventional subjects unillumined by actual experience do not produce literature. She had him out to
dinner once, but their literary ideals pointed too diversely
for her to keep up the acquaintance. Malcolm Cowley and
Royall Snow, later of her circle, were at the smoker; she
invited the latter to dinner on the twenty-seventh, to discuss his projected poetry magazine, *Youth*.[1]

On May 7, Amy Lowell finished 'Bronze Horses,' thus
completing the poems for her new book, *Can Grande's
Castle*, for which she had already been laboring over the
dummy and the label. On the next day, she read four of
her 'Phantasms' at Tufts, as the Phi Beta Kappa poet.
Judge Moorfield Storey was the orator of the occasion; they
drove up together.

> It amused me considerably to march up the chapel aisle
> in company with Reverend Doctors in caps and gowns and
> hoods, I in ordinary clothes, never having had any educa-
> tion and consequently no degree. The Dean of the Women's
> Chapter wished me to wear her gown, but as she was a
> little reed of a woman I explained to her that the only
> way in which I could do it would be to hang it over one
> shoulder and keep that side constantly turned to the
> audience. She looked grieved but recognized the impossi-
> bility, and the matter dropped.[2]

On the ninth, she went to Mount Holyoke College, at
Northampton, to read her poems on the invitation of

[1] It ran six numbers, October, 1918, to August, 1919.
[2] Letter to Richard Hunt, May 27, 1918.

Jeannette Marks, then spent Friday with Mrs. Conkling, dining that night at the Hampshire Book Shop, and returning home Saturday.

The rupture started in New York was giving trouble; on the twenty-fifth Miss Lowell, awaiting a final examination, wrote to a former nurse, Miss Grace Parker, to disengage her if possible from her war work and get her back from France to Sevenels.

DEAR PORKY:

. . .

Oh, Porky, what do you think is going to happen! I have got to have a really, truly operation, no shirking this time, and you are not here to look after me! There is a great deal more of a tragedy than you realize — not the operation, but your not being here. I really do not think that I should mind it very much if I were to have you, for the truth is I have an awful weakness for my Porky, not only as a caretaker and severe governor but as a person and a very dear friend.

The operation is not much, though kind of nasty. It is a ridiculous little umbilical hernia. Did you ever know of anything so silly? Apparently I started the business lifting the hind wheels of a carriage the last Summer I was in Dublin and finished it moving a bed in New York this Spring. Anyhow, here it is, and Dr. Washburn says I must be operated on. I cannot tell you how unfortunate I think this is. I suppose you are more needed over there, but I do not know. There are a lot of them over there, and there's only one Porky for me. Do hurry up and come home because we want you terribly.

... And then, Porky, we have got another job for you, for here is Sonny [Mrs. Russell's grandson], and they are going to spend most of the Summer with us, and his grandmother is growing thin and pale racing after him, for he is a big boy now, and his hair is cut short just like a little man. He is in trousers, and he prefers the men in the garage to anybody else on the place. He drives every day with Jerry and goes up to the stable and sits on the Shetland

pony, and his interest in flowers seems for the moment
to be in abeyance and more masculine joys have taken its
place. We have a large sand box, six feet long and four and
a half feet wide, under the trees on the front lawn, and Mr.
Man is out there now, surrounded by an admiring audience
of his mother and grandmother, making sand pies and
having a beautiful time. And his digestion is not quite
right, and I do not believe anybody can fix it but you.

Mrs. Amussen is going to have another baby in the
Autumn, and if you were here I think maybe they could
persuade you to go back to Washington with them and
hold Sonny's hand while his mother produces Mehitable.
(You understand Mehitable is my name for the new
arrival. I think it is a charming appellation, but I am awfully afraid that Mrs. Amussen will not adopt it as a
permanency.)

You cannot think what a happy family we should be if
you were with us. Mrs. Russell spends a great deal of her
time going around saying, 'Oh, if we only had Porky!'

Miss Burris tells me that she has heard from you more
recently than I have, and that you are having a terrible
time coping with the wounded from the big drive. Ah,
Porky, I suppose you are more useful there, but we love you
in the jungle, and there is only you for us.

...

You will be glad to know that whatever else is the matter with me, my eyes have entirely recovered. We shall not
go to Dublin this year as we expect Mrs. Amussen and Sonny
back again for July and August, and the house in Dublin
is too small, but I am more than reconciled to have an
excuse for not going, and I think Mrs. Russell feels the
same way.

You would hardly know the place, such terrible damage
was done by the severe Winter. Almost all the rhododendrons in front of the house were killed, and the big laurel
bush which has been there since I was a child. Miss Putnam tells me that they have lost two box hedges on their
place in Manchester, one sixty years old and the other
twenty-five. The coal situation here is more acute than

the food, and they say it will be worse this Winter, so of course we are praying for milder weather this year.

...

The doctor that afternoon told her that the operation could be put off till September, and that it meant merely two weeks in bed, and perfect health in a month. (And Miss Parker remained in France).

On May 29, she finished the last revisions of her manuscript and expressed it to Macmillan's, then turned to her accumulated correspondence.

One of the first letters she sent off was to Witter Bynner, who she had just learned was the 'Emanuel Morgan' of the erstwhile Spectrist School. Back in 1916, when 'Imagists and Vorticists and Whatnotists' were threatening to blossom on every side, Bynner was arguing about them with Laird Bell, a former editor of the *Harvard Monthly*, during a performance of the Russian Ballet. Bell told him not to be annoyed with the Gists and the Cists because, after all, it was something to found a school; to which Bynner replied that he could do as much himself, and what was more, would! His program lay open at 'La Spectre de la Rose'; thus the school was named.

Arthur Davison Ficke proved an eager collaborator in this scheme to show up modernism. For three weeks the two men improvised poems at a great rate, shrieking with laughter. Mitchell Kennerley agreed to publish their volume. The introduction was a parody of Vorticism; the poems had opus numbers for titles; and the volume professed to be the work of two Pittsburg radicals in art.

Amy Lowell, of course, was the biggest game they were gunning for; apparently they really expected her to welcome their exhilarating nonsense on the grounds of its exhilaration alone. As early as March, 1916, Ficke had sent her the manuscript of his 'Modern Tendencies in Poetry' (published later, in the September *North American Review*); in it, he mentioned the Spectrists casually in a list of contemporary 'schools.' She replied (April 20) that she had never heard of them; nor did she inquire further.

The next move was an article in the *Forum* for June: 'The Spectric School of Poetry,' by Anne Knish [Ficke] and Emanuel Morgan [Bynner], which announced that Vorticism had died before it went far enough; sneered at Imagism; and announced their forthcoming book, with two specimen poems. Miss Lowell sent the article to Fletcher, who replied (June 28) that he had never read worse rubbish.

Spectra appeared so unobtrusively that, except for Ficke, with his mere mention of the school's name, the first person to discover the book was Witter Bynner, who reviewed it very gravely in the *New Republic* for November 18. He wrote that he approved of experimentation; and that while he did not actually endorse the Spectrists, he found them far preferable to the Imagists. A presentation copy was sent to Miss Lowell 'from the authors,' but she did not acknowledge it.

Others gave the newcomers their customary chance in their January, 1917 number, which Miss Knish and Mr. Morgan filled, with a supposed convert Elijah Hay (Marjory Allen Seiffert). Three months later, the April *Current Opinion* reprinted three of these poems, in its customary column for that purpose. The July *Little Review* was persuaded to publish one of Morgan's 'spectra'; but four pages later one reads this editorial comment:

> Banish
> Anne Knish
> Set the dog on
> Emanuel Morgan.

Then, after nearly a year of waiting, the secret was let out by Martyn Johnson in the *Dial* for April 25, 1918. Of course the hoax was represented as a great success; but the only specific success mentioned was 'a Harvard undergraduate, for instance, [who] forswore Imagism for Spectrism, and had his apostacy roundly rebuked by the high priestess of his earlier faith.' An interview with Bynner appeared in the *New York Sunday Times*, June 2, wherein he said that a favorable review had appeared in *Reedy's Mirror*, which now claimed that *Spectra* contained the best work of both poets. The tale of the Harvard undergraduate reappeared, slightly varied; this time he approached Bynner, told of his great admiration of the Spectrists, and at Bynner's suggestion sent some of his poems to Emanuel Morgan with the plea: 'Dear Mr. Morgan, please tell me — am I a Spectrist?' (For the honor of Harvard and the peace of mind of Royall Snow, I must give his version: he swears that Bynner tried to persuade him he was a Spectrist, and when he denied it vigorously, was persuaded to write, which he did, saying: 'Bynner thinks I am a Spectrist; I don't; am I?')

Amy Lowell had overlooked the *Dial* exposé; but when she saw the *Times* interview, strange thoughts came over her, of hostile poets suddenly turned friends, meanwhile spreading these nets in her path. Bynner's review (which he said had been asked for by one of her own chosen Six) now revealed itself for what it undoubtedly was — an attack on Imagism pure and simple. Her letter to Bynner ran:

June 5, 1918

Dear Emanuel:

You certainly did well with 'Spectra'! And how glad I am that I always said it was charlatanism! I verily believe that you began to respect me from the very moment that you asked me what I thought of it, and I told you that I thought the authors were insincere. Of course I had no idea it was a genial hoax. I simply thought that Miss Knish and Mr. Morgan were trying to gain notoriety out of a singularity in which they themselves did not in the least believe, and perhaps you will remember that I never acknowledged the presentation copy which you so kindly sent me.

But I must say that I think you sailed a bit close to the wind in your review in 'The New Republic' where you said:

'It may be that the spectrists are offering us a means toward the creation or understanding of the essential magic of poetry. Their attempt, at any rate, goes deeper than the attempts of any of the latter-day school in that it cuts under mere technique. Not that we fail to welcome dusters of technique or to realize that the imagists' insistence on natural cadence and clear-driven expression is a salutary insistence. But we are always looking for something inside technique, something to hold and keep. And, though the imagists seem to be surviving the chorists and vorticists, yet I feel sure that they will not count so much in themselves as in their jacking-up of the technique of poets through whom vibrate richer matters than the tickling of a leaf on a window-pane or the flickering of water in a bath-tub. The imagists note with admirable accuracy all sorts of small adventures of the nerves, but very seldom for me relate those adventures to heart, head, and — or even stomach. They don't connect. They give the heightened localized nervous sensations of a sick-bed, as though all the faculties were paralyzed except a finger-tip or one eye or one ear. Perhaps, without them, we should not have had the group of poets represented in "Others" who, to me, show more interesting vigor, even though most of their experiments are in gayer vein than those of the imagists. The spectrists, true to their expressed plea for humor, often share this gayer mood with the Kreymborg poets.... But on the whole these later comers bring to the "new poetry" a quality it rather lacked. They have more than fancifulness to add to discernment: they penetrate the surface with a curious vibrancy of imagination... Perhaps a wider experience of life and of media has made the spectrists' ability in English verse more flexible and more potent than that of the other poets we may compare with them. Certainly theory demands an art not stopping short with direct notation by the senses, but reaching connotation of all kinds. And they are ambitious, without being too solemn!

'If I have over-estimated the importance of "Spectra,"
it is because of my constant hope that out of these various succeeding "schools" something better may develop
than an aesthetic dalliance of eyeglass and blue stocking.'

Was this quite 'cricket'?

Perhaps you thought you had a right to treat us in that
way, believing us to be insincere also. But, dear me,
that is all past, isn't it! And now I understand the reason
for Mr. Ficke's sending me one of his beautiful Japanese
prints after my first lecture in Chicago, inscribed, 'With
the admiration of the enemy.' This was his *amende
honorable*, and yours, I take it, was your defence of 'Guns
as Keys' at the Poetry Society last year, for which I am
most grateful. In what terms should a lady acknowledge
a gentleman's admission that perhaps he made a mistake
in trying to cut her throat?

Still, your stiletto has not quite lost its keenness, since
in this interview in 'The Times,' I notice that you again
refer to us as a part of the dubious company of 'Gists'
and 'Cists.' 'Ah, Saul, Saul, it is hard for thee to kick
against the pricks!'

It is very 'sporting' of you to attempt the dual personality plea; but how will it affect the dear public, so ignorant,
and so fearful of being made a fool of? And how will it
affect your serious lectures? But that is for you to decide,
and please believe that although the specific instance of
your early hostility is news to me, the general attitude
certainly is not; and that, barring this return on your
track which your present remarks seem to indicate, I freely
forgive you, even to the extent of sending you my new book
as soon as it comes out, and I trust you will like it.

The hoax was a bit of fun, but the way you pushed the
hoax — ah, well, permit me to quote from the immortal
Emanuel:

'Asparagus is feathery and tall
And the hose lies rotting by the garden wall.'

The only question is whose hose.

Sincerely yours,

He replied without rancour on July 11; she wrote him again on July 22; and a friendly correspondence ensued.

A far pleasanter event was the receipt of a letter from Donald Evans, the poet, who was also 'Claire Marie,' publisher of Gertrude Stein's *Tender Buttons*. A year ago January, he had requested an autograph poem to be sold for charity; she had sent 'White and Green.' Now, on May 31, 1918, he wrote her from Camp Crane, Allentown, Pa., as an enlisted man. He had been sent four of her books for a birthday present; they had been his sole reading matter for two months; they had started him writing again; and as a token of thanks he was sending her the second edition of his *Sonnets from the Patagonian*, with a new preface concerning poetry and war. Her reply was typical in its kindly frankness.

7 June, 1918

My dear Mr. Evans:

I cannot tell you how much pleasure your letter gave me. It is most satisfactory to know that, after living exclusively with four of my books, you still find them interesting. You could not have given me a higher compliment than to say that you found you could work under their influence. To fecundate other poets seems to me the highest function of poetry, and that my work should have that effect upon you is an infinite source of satisfaction to me. I shall be very anxious to see your new book, and I hope you will not forget to send it to me when it comes out.

Your 'Sonnets from the Patagonian' arrived yesterday, and I am very glad indeed to have this sumptuous new edition of the book. I suppose I must admit that I am not particularly in sympathy with the key in which this earlier volume of yours is written. You see I am such an elderly person that I lived during the 1890's. My twenty years saw the annual reappearance of 'The Yellow Book,' and these 'mauve joys' and 'purple sins' were the very 'latest thing' during my adolescent period so that I must be pardoned for finding their manner somewhat dusty and, indeed, a good deal like a cotillion favor resurrected from a bureau drawer. I understand exactly how that sort of thing intrigued you. I agree with you that it is a part of the search for beauty, but somehow, personally, I find so much beauty in the world, so much lurking in my imagination (getting it out is another matter) that I do not seem to have to hunt for it down back alleys.

Sometimes I wonder why you like my work. You glory in your pose, as you say yourself; I detest pose, and have never found the need of being other than straightforwardly what I am. I confess I think you are better than your pose. Do not tell me that anybody ever enlisted as a private soldier for the sake of a pose. You remind me a little of a man who has stuck a monocle in his eye for effect, and afterward is afraid to take it out because of a kind of *mauvaise honte,* a dread lest the change be commented upon. *Courage, mon enfant! En avant!* Break the monocle, and go ahead! Of course we need more beauty in the world; of course that is what we are all fighting for; and, of course, that is what we must make the world safe for. But do not let us lisp this creed in a kind of dying languor; let us shout it lustily — and dare be happy — and dare be robust — and dare be a thousand things which mean poetry just the same.

Some time I trust that you and I may meet and talk over all these things, and in the meantime you have my very best wishes both for the new volume and for the soldiering. I think you are a plucky fellow. I am sorry you feel obliged to deny it in pursuit of a pose, and I think, if I were you, I should believe enough in beauty and brains to become an officer if I had the chance. I have a curious feeling that if a poet is any sort of a poet, he ought to be able to do the other things of the world better than the people who can do nothing else. Therefore, being a soldier, I should wish to be a general; being a cook, nothing but the chefdome would satisfy me. I am afraid I put the poet on a higher level than you do. I think he should be an inclusive kind of creature, not side-tracked, but universal, not preferring his own line because he cannot do others, or even if not 'because,' just because he can. This is a little cryptic, but I trust you will understand.

Very sincerely yours,

His reply was prompt, and as it was largely autobiographical, it should be preserved.

Camp Infirmary,
Camp Crane, Allentown, Pa.
10 June, 1918

MY DEAR MISS LOWELL:

I am glad I wrote my preface, since it moved you to send me a letter which has touched me deeply. It was indeed graceful and gracious of you to go to so much trouble, at such length, for a stranger, even a poet, and for the very enheartening advice you give me I am sincerely grateful. I find I entirely agree with all you say, and I fancy if I had the privilege of your friendship you might not find me conspicuous for posing. My Patagonians, you must remember, are eight years old, and America, despite The Yellow Book, rather needed something of the sort to break down the entrance doors for the young men.

Because I have always been an honest citizen, making a decent living in straight-forward newspaperwork, 10–12 hrs. daily for 13 years, I have perhaps in my poetry been a little too conscious of the poet, and in an imagined need provided him with a shield of artificiality which he never requires. When among intelligent people I think I pass for simple, unaffected, modest, but there are so many pretentious bores and unworthy bigwigs one must meet and live with when one cannot freely choose one's company that to keep alive it has sometimes seemed necessary to me to be a shock distributor. Nothing else makes any impression.

As for soldiering, I too am of your opinion that a poet ought to want to make a good general. That is why I started in as a private; I shall know enough to be a general if I am ever needed. When we entered the War I was just 33, 122 lbs in weight, and rather exacting and self-indulgent in my manner of life. I wished to give my body and my brain to the Republic, and I feared of course that it would not stand much strain nor for long. I did not wish a non-fighting nor a training camp commission, for the very simple reason that had I broken down a bit I should have been allowed to resign. As an enlisted man I was bound for the War, and I wanted to be bound beyond my power of freeing myself, for I am human and I don't like rubbing elbows. Successively, I tried Army, Marines, Navy, but was rejected. Then I stuffed for a week, and found an accomplice examiner, and made the Army Medical Field Service. It has all worked out, with God's help, better than I could have dreamed. I weigh 140 lbs, and I am 15 years younger (and it is not Muldoon forcing, either). I was made a sergeant here, and put in charge of the Camp Infirmary last summer. I worked pretty hard. I personally oversaw the inoculation of as high as 2700 men a day, without one case of infection. Often my hours were from 5:30 A.M. till 9:30 P.M. I had much unnecessary responsibility because the officers, fresh from small community practice, lacked executive experience. I was too busy then, literally too busy to take an afternoon off, to stand examination for a commission. It seemed to me probable it would come of itself when the time was ripe, and besides I was terribly proud of being an efficient sergeant, and a trifle disgusted at the wild scramble for commissions when the bars were let down to non-medical men in the Ambulance and Sanitary Corps. It really impressed me that everyone was thinking more of what he could do for himself than of doing his best toward winning the War. And I was ashamed of being ashamed of being a common soldier. For a fortnight drilling almost stopped while those who hadn't the stamina to remain in the ranks scurried to cover. It was too easy. And so I waited. I am thought an exceptionally trustworthy soldier (which gives me infinite satisfaction — and amusement). The war is for a long time. The opportunity for me will doubtless come. I shall be ready. In the meantime, because my mind is fresher, younger, freer, and because, my dear lady, I had your four books I am writing, I truly believe, better than I ever have before.

Faithfully,

DONALD EVANS

In his next book, *Ironica*, was a long poem, 'Before the Curtain,' dedicated to Amy Lowell.[1]

Another letter she received this month came from D. H. Lawrence.

> Mountain Cottage
> Middleton by Wirksworth
> Derby, England
> 18 June 1918

MY DEAR AMY

I have just read your lectures — the one on me — which I got from Hilda; thanks for the nice things you say about me. I don't mind what people think of my work, so long as their attitude is *passionately* honest — which I believe yours is. As for intellectual honesty, I care nothing for it, for it may rest on the most utterly false *a priori*.

I never thanked you for the dollars, either: not because I was not grateful, but because sometimes one's soul is a dumb rock, and won't be either coaxed or struck into utterance. We were very glad of the help — it is always a case of touch and go, with us, financially.

I have just heard also that Huebsch is bringing out an edition of 'Look We Have Come Through,' in New York. I am glad of that. Perhaps America will like it better than England does. Nothing but shams go down here, just now. I suppose it is inevitable.

I have not seen Hilda for some time — but believe she is happy in Cornwall — as far as it is possible to be happy, with the world as it is.

I have just gathered a new MS. of a book of poems — 'Coming Awake' — so named after the first poems. I have worked at some of them for a long time — many years — but many are new, made this spring. I have just inscribed the MS. to you: simply put 'to Amy Lowell.' You must let me know if you would like this to stand. I finished the book, and made its list of contents, this very day — and I shall send it off today to Pinker. It is all different kinds of poems — nothing for anybody to take exception to, I believe. I hope you will like it.

---

[1] This volume was his last; he died in New York on May 27, 1921.

We are here in Derbyshire, just near my native place — come home, in these last wretched days — not to die, I hope. Life is very wretched, really, in the outer world — and in the immediate world too, such a ghastly stress, a horrid pressure on one, all the time — and gnawing anxiety. The future seems utterly impenetrable, and as fathomless as the Bottomless Pit, and about as desperate. — But no doubt the world will sail out again, out of the Maelström. Perhaps even now it is moving clear from the Vortex.

I still want to come to America, to see you and the New World, when everything quiets down.

Frieda sends her love. Just let me know about the inscription.

Yours very sincerely

D. H. LAWRENCE

She accepted the offer of the inscription gratefully.

From England also came the London *Sphere* for June 15, with a full-page illustrated article by Clement K. Shorter: 'A Literary Letter: the Art of Amy Lowell,' in which he had 'no hesitation in proclaiming' her 'as one of the most remarkable figures in... the literature of the English-speaking countries.' This article, with the Bryher pamphlet, both written without Miss Lowell's fore-knowledge, made her feel that her prestige had crossed the Atlantic by its own virtue.

Some time in the first half of June, Mrs. Ayscough, with her scrolls of Chinese poetry, spent several days at Seven-els, to work over the translations which she and Miss Lowell were projecting. It was during this visit that Miss Lowell made her important discovery that the components of an ideograph furnish the poetic overtones. As Mrs. Ayscough described the event:

> I translated and she made careful notes, and while so work-ing Miss Lowell made a discovery which I believe will be far-reaching in its result. She found that frequently an analysis of an ideogram, rendered by a phrase instead of a single word, made the meaning of a line far more vivid.

The way the discovery came about was this: We were at work upon a poem, and I read aloud the character *Mo*; 'it means "sunset,"' I said, and then added casually, 'the character shows the sun disappearing in the long grass at the edge of the horizon.' 'How do you mean?' asked Miss Lowell. 'Why, what I say,' I replied, and forthwith showed her the character or pictogram in its ancient form, which shows plainly the sun sinking behind tufts of grass on the far-off horizon. She was more enthralled than ever, and insisted that I give her a long dissertation on the composition of characters, a subject that has always been of intense interest to me, but which I had *never thought of applying in translation*.[1]

July passed uneventfully. Among other things, Malcolm Cowley returned from his ambulance work in France, and showed her some poems which she liked so much that she undertook to sell them for him: he could not do so, as he was soon to enter a camp. Salomon de la Selva enlisted in the Canadian service; she spent a hot hour in the South Station, trying to catch him as he passed through on his way to Fort Edward, but missed him. August also went by, while she struggled over dummies and proofs, divided and sent off the Imagist proceeds, worked on the Chinese lyrics, dictated letters.

In mid-August she went up to Dublin 'for a few minutes.' The cause is forgotten, but the visit is still remembered in the town, as a motor-cop chased her car for miles. When she started to turn off the main road, he stopped her. She wanted to know why he had let her break the speed-limit for such a long distance; he replied: Because you was headed straight for the court-house, ma'am.' Determined not to be outdone in smartness by a mere man, she summoned up her best dramatic powers, and persuaded him that her three men (the two chauffeurs and the groom) ought not to have to enter the service of

[1] Florence Ayscough: 'Amy Lowell and the Far East,' London *Bookman* (LXX, 107–09), May, 1926. Miss Lowell communicated the discovery, as just made, to Harriet Monroe, June 19, 1918.

their country (they were all joining the aviation service the next day, she said) with the disgrace of an arrest for speeding tarnishing their reputations. By gorry, the cop nearly cried, and let them go.

She had been planning to visit New York at the end of August, but her digestion was poor, and she preferred to save up strength for the coming operation. Miss Parker, the nurse she had hoped for, wrote from France; of course there was no possibility of her return. 'Appuldurcombe Park' appeared in *Poetry*, rousing the customary ripples of reaction; among them being a letter from William Carlos Williams, saying that no one had ever handled the Revolutionary Period so well, yet making certain apposite strictures. She replied:

August 7, 1918

MY DEAR DOCTOR WILLIAMS:

Your letter came this morning, and I am very glad indeed to know that you like 'Appuldurcombe Park.' Your criticism is an excellent one. You are entirely right; I wish one could get more of such sensible criticisms.

I liked your Orchid thing in the last 'Egoist.' That stanza about the 'falling spray of snow-flakes' is good, and also the 'blue butterflies,' though I regret the repetition of the word 'spray.' It is so fine each time that it is a pity to spoil the shock of it by having it repeated; but it is an excellent thing, and full of color.

I like your work, but if I tell you so, you will instantly think that I have some ulterior motive. Therefore, let me hastily say that you used 'would' and 'should' wrong in your letter. Seriously, I wish you were not such a pesky, touchy creature. There are not too many of us, and some time one might like to talk to you. Still, I think it might be something like smelling at a thistle.

Have you heard that Sandburg is going to Sweden, in perpetuity, I am afraid.

Sincerely yours

Her operation was originally scheduled for the sixth of September, but her doctor was suddenly called to Washington, so that it had to be put off till the twelfth. Apparently up to the last minute she was still dictating letters; one to Margaret Widdemer [1] thanked her for a volume of poems just received, the more gratefully as her favorite 'St. Jeanne Rides Out' had been dedicated to her.

> I think that 'The Old Road to Paradise' itself is the next most beautiful to my poem. I know but one poem in all literature which has anything like the feeling that you have got into these two pieces, and that is Joyce Kilmer's 'Blue Valentine.' But Mr. Kilmer never did it but once, whereas you have done it again and again. By the way, I know how fond you were of him, and will you permit me to say that my sympathy has been with you and with Mrs. Kilmer and with all his friends ever since I heard of his death. We did not get on, as you know; in fact, as you will probably have observed in 'The Sun,' he criticised me with his dying breath, but nevertheless his 'Blue Valentine' will always be to me a very beautiful thing and one which I should be extremely sorry to lose from my memory.

The operation (the first of four in the next two years) went off successfully. As a patient, Miss Lowell was difficult; she herself said that when she was suffering, she was just an animal raging for a comfort not to be had. She insisted on large beef sandwiches as soon as she came out of ether. Early the next morning, she woke and rang for the nurse; but the current was accidentally off for four hours, and she had to get up from bed to summon the nurse (as she took pains to let the Selectmen of Brookline know when she was writing letters again). On the eighteenth, she renewed her correspondence, though she was to remain in bed a week more; on the thirtieth she got down stairs for the first time, but was so exhausted that after an hour she had to go back to bed again.

Her solace was *Can Grande's Castle*, published on September 24; two days earlier she was sending out the advance copies.

[1] Dated September 13, the day it was copied, not the day it was dictated.

CHAPTER XVII

CAN GRANDE'S CASTLE

EVERY poet who is seriously interested in literature as an art, sooner or later gets tired of the constant implication that he must have experienced personally everything of which he writes; therefore, to offset this vulgar error (that his works are fragments of a veiled autobiography) he attempts something that he could not possibly have experienced. Amy Lowell had been particularly plagued by this attitude. Friends and foes, too often overlooking the essentially dramatic (or objective) nature of her work, identified poet and poem 'so much, that the person of the one obscured the sincerity of the other. The columnists, for example, were still filling their daily inches with mechanical guffaws over the thought of Amy Lowell shingling a roof, Amy Lowell taking a bath, and so on. Perhaps this was one reason why she chose subjects so remote from Brookline. The castle of Can Grande was the refuge of Dante; in her title it represents the poet's refuge from the world, and the high point from which he can view it. (But it is a tower of stone, not of ivory.) The motto of her book she took from Aldington's 'At the British Museum.' 'That simply means, as you will observe,' she wrote Untermeyer on May 14, 1918, 'that I could not possibly have experienced these things: I must have read about them; but that the reading becomes real.'

And any poet who is not content to remain definitely minor must progress beyond the brief poems which are all he can manage at first. The lyric points toward the character sketch, the character sketch toward the drama. And in those tragic years 1914–18, every headline in every newspaper pointed daily toward the Titanic drama of the

nations. Dante began with Hell and attained Heaven;
Amy Lowell began with War and attained Art. As she
explained in her Preface, the four poems —

> all owe their existence to the war, for I suppose that, had
> there been no war, I should never have thought of them.
> They are scarcely war poems, in the strict sense of that
> word, nor are they allegories in which the present is made
> to masquerade as the past. Rather, they are the result of
> a vision thrown suddenly back upon remote events to
> explain a strange and terrible reality. 'Explain' is hardly
> the word, for to explain the subtle causes which force men,
> once in so often, to attempt to break the civilization they
> have been at pains to rear, and so oblige other, saner, men
> to oppose them, is scarcely the province of poetry. Poetry
> works more deviously, but perhaps not less conclusively.
> ... For an artist to shut himself up in the proverbial
> 'ivory tower' and never look out of the window is merely
> a tacit admission that it is his ancestors, not he, who possess
> the faculty of creation. This is the real decadence: to see
> through the eyes of dead men. Yet today can never be ade-
> quately expressed, largely because we are a part of it and
> only a part. For that reason one is flung backwards to a
> time which is not thrown out of proportion by any personal
> experience, and which on that very account lies extended
> in something like its proper perspective.
> Circumstances beget an interest in like circumstances,
> and a poet, suddenly finding himself in the midst of war,
> turns naturally to the experiences of other men in other
> wars. He discovers something which has always hitherto
> struck him as preposterous, that life goes on in spite of
> war. That war itself is an expression of life, a barbaric
> expression on one side calling for an heroic expression on
> the other. It is as if a door in his brain crashed open and
> he looked into a distance of which he had heard but never
> before seen. History has become life, and he stands aghast
> and exhilarated before it.

The subject of her book, then, is war — not the World
War, nor war in the abstract, but a study of various wars

in the past. Inevitably, Amy Lowell's conceptions were affected by the Boston historians. Parkman, Prescott, and Motley had viewed history as a series of picturesque scenes, which they re-created in a highly literary form. John Fiske was transitional to the Adams brothers, Henry and Brooks, who philosophized on the hidden laws of history. The earlier group treated it artistically, the latter reduced it to a science; and Amy Lowell combined the brilliant presentation of the one with the analytic intelligence of the other. In *Can Grande's Castle* — particularly in 'The Bronze Horses' — she accepts Brooks Adams's theory that civilizations arise cyclically upon economic success, then decay as the racial energy runs out; she also accepts Henry Adams's theory that international crises recur more and more frequently as the speed of history accelerates. But Amy Lowell, in organizing and completing her theory, won a place of her own amongst the historical philosophers. To her, art was not only the expression of a civilization: it was life's highest achievement and its only permanence — it was almost civilization itself. The economic system is the root, the popular pleasures are the transient flower, and the arts are the seed-bearing fruit. In giving art this importance, she was unknowingly reviving, secularizing, and extending the old Puritan theory that man was created for the purpose of being happy, and that individual happiness was proof of a life in accord with the will of God.

Her method of presenting her material was predetermined by this philosophy of history. The surface of these poems is a brilliant series of magic-lantern dissolving views of the past. They depict various civilizations at those critical points when one is hurled against another, to the subjugation and even the destruction of the physically weaker. But the real subject is not historical: it is rather the survival of civilization in the eternal struggle against war. The superficial pictures are splendid with the colors of life; they represent the arts and amusements which constitute a civilization; but behind these pictures are at work the acquisitive and destructive forces which give meaning to the poems — a meaning anything but splendid. The surface is life, the depths are death; combined, the result is history.

In reading *Can Grande's Castle*, then, one must watch the flow of seemingly unrelated pictures of carnivals and triumphs and love-affairs and horse-races with an eye to what they signify in human society, for they were selected to illustrate and explain the civilization under discussion. The flow is life itself; war is the death-force that destroys them. The splendor of the surface sheds no glamour upon the meaning; Amy Lowell was not glorifying war.

Carlyle's *French Revolution* (which she had called 'a great epic poem'), Hardy's *Dynasts* (which so curiously anticipated the moving eye of the cinema), and Griffith's mammoth films (*Intolerance* had been released in 1916) may be considered as precursors of her method of presentation. Nevertheless, springing as it did from her own conception of history, it was entirely original, and so completely expressive of her meaning and appropriate to her poems as to be inevitable. Its validity is amply proved by the many later writers, in both prose and verse, who have used it for their own historical writings.

Her metrical form was equally her own: it was her 'polyphonic prose,' now developed so far beyond Paul Fort's alternation of alexandrines and prose, that the fundamental conception was entirely different. In a later lecture she described her search for a measure that would be epical:

> For years, I had been pondering this difficulty. How to get the breadth, the serious scope and grandeur, into the new work that the old had. We could do much with our medium that the older poets could not do; but they could do things with theirs which we could not touch...

It was this very pattern-weaving I was seeking when I hit upon what has most misleadingly come to be called 'polyphonic prose.'...

...The work of the French poet, Paul Fort, gave me my first inkling of a new form. Working from his advance, I gradually evolved a system of verse which should make use of the old as well as the new, and so, employing all the voices proper to poetry, should at once fuse them to its purpose and create a new medium out of the result. I wanted an orchestral effect, and the delicate flute-notes of *vers libre* must be augmented by other instruments, no matter where I got them.

...The object was to find a new form for epic poetry... The modern epic, as I conceived it, should be based rather upon drama than upon narrative. This came partly from the greater speed and vividness demanded today of all the arts; and partly from the realization that, without the formality of metre, a sustained narrative of considerable length tends to become prose... Epic poems on the old pattern did not seem to fit in with the workings of the modern 'poet's mind. At least it would appear so, since he was not moved to write them. But I was moved; I had conceived some subjects which could come under no other head. I believed that the musicians had got hold of the right idea, and in 'polyphonic prose' it seemed to me that I had stumbled upon a form which could sustain the grandeur of a large conception, and treat it at once musically, dramatically, lyrically, and pictorially.... [1]

Amy Lowell's narrative structures also were original; but as each poem has an architecture of its own, and as that architecture is the final expression of her meaning, each must be discussed separately.

'Sea-Blue and Blood-Red,' the first of these poems, is a tale of the love of Lord Nelson and Lady Hamilton, ad-

[1] Amy Lowell: 'Some Musical Analogies in Modern Poetry,' lecture at Harvard, March 3, 1919 (quotation from *ms.*). A revision was published in the *Musical Quarterly* (vi, 127–57), January, 1920.

miral and actress, from the Battle of the Nile and their first meeting, to his death at Trafalgar and her miserable grave in the lumber-yard at Calais, with its wooden marker slowly being chipped away by souvenir-hunters. It is a poem color-saturated and choral, a series of glowing historical frescoes. Nelson's triumphs are those of reactionary England crushing French liberalism: he is the 'Savior of banks'; his victories 'stamp out liberty'; or, as he sees it, 'It is Duty and Kings. Caste versus riff-raff.' Amy Lowell's enthusiasm for Napoleon (who does not appear in this poem) was that of Beethoven's when he dedicated the Heroic Symphony to the Liberator — a dedication he blotted out when Napoleon was crowned.

The lovers are the other side of the two makers of history; and their tale is a queer mixture of coarseness and idealism. Amy Lowell's attitude towards 'quivering, blood-swept, vivid Lady Hamilton' is best summed up in 'The woman is undoubtedly mad, but it is a madness which kindles.' The whole poem is kindled by her; yet Miss Lowell also felt her to be somewhat of a fool. 'A fig for good taste!' — and the exuberance of her frocks and deeds cancels their vulgarity; but there is sure misery at the end. 'Wife in the sight of Heaven' — but the rest of Nelson's letter (which Miss Lowell owned) has never been printed, is perhaps unprintable; and Parliament was not to see with Heaven's eyes.

'I have been very accurate in these historical poems,' Miss Lowell wrote Barrett Wendell, 'perhaps more accurate than a poet has any business to be. In fact, fearing in some way to travesty my originals, every remark that Lord Nelson and Lady Hamilton make in the first poem has been copied from their letters. My facts are correct throughout; my fancies — do they equal them?'

Only a scholar could have been so accurate and so thorough; yet the scholarship is always subordinate to the poetry, and never intrudes; wherefore Miss Lowell was hardly of the 'Erudite School of Poetry.'

The structure of the poem is comparatively simple, being the tale of this single love affair at the focus of imperial conflicts. But the ordinary way of telling a story would not do; instead, we are given a series of pictures, through which one guesses at the amour, much as persons in Neapolitan society doubtless did. The admiral's ships anchor under the flaming mountain ('the red thread to the blue thread cleaves'); he presents the Ambassadress with a satinwood table; they are seen much together; they are missed from a reception, and glimpsed disappearing through a postern; there is gossip.... So the tale continues. Realism merges into symbolism, then re-emerges; for Nelson himself is the blue of the sea, Emma the blood-red Vesuvian flame. They are two threads, red and blue, whose interweaving and unravelling is the *leitmotif* marking the beginning and end of episodes, and binding the whole poem together. In fact, the significance of each event becomes so intense as to make that event a symbol, which is in turn a stage in the story. Thus the admiral's ship coming to anchor beneath the volcano is no mere preparation for the meeting of the lovers: it is Nelson himself as lover — the warrior, after his great achievements, returning to haven for rest, restoration, happiness, which he finds through a woman. Only by following the series of symbols can the plot be followed; but such was Amy Lowell's skill, that no audience ever was baffled by the meaning of the poems in *Can Grande's Castle*.

'Guns as Keys: and the Great Gate Swings' takes us from Europe to the other side of the world, in 1853-54, when Occident and Orient — America and Japan — meet. It is the first momentous confronting of the white and yellow races in modern times. The United States sees the chance to acquire another market, and sends Perry to obtain a treaty by means of a show of warships, which he does, thus ending the seclusion behind which Japan has lived its idyllic life.

The theme is Commercialism versus Art. 'I wanted to place in juxtaposition the delicacy and artistic clarity of Japan and the artistic ignorance and gallant self-confidence of America.... Which of them has gained most by this meeting, it would be difficult to say.' The poem leaves no doubt. America gained its market, but at what cost!

> Commerce-raiding a nation; pulling apart the curtains of a temple and calling it trade. Magnificent mission!... Romance and heroism; and all to make one dollar two. For centuries men have pursued the will-o'-the-wisp — trade. And what have they got?

What indeed but an exchange? While Japanese art inspired a Whistler in America, American guns inspired a Japanese army and navy.

> The sands of centuries run fast, one slides, and another, each falling into a smother of dust.
> A locomotive in pay for a Whistler; telegraph wires buying a revolution; weights and measures and Audubon's birds in exchange for fear. Yellow monkey-men leaping out of Pandora's box, shaking the rocks of the Western coastline. Golden California bartering panic for prints. The dressing-gowns of a continent won at the cost of security. Artists and philosophers lost in the hour-glass sand pouring through an open Gate.

'You have blown off the locks of the East, and what is coming will come.' The war which inspired this poem is still in the future.

It is divided into two parts. Part I alternates polyphonic prose (the voyage of the dynamic, aggressive, commercial Americans) with free verse lyrics (the life of the static, pacific, aesthetic Japanese). As there was no communication between the two countries, there was the more reason for not relating the stages of the sea-voyage to events in Japan. The print-like lyrics, therefore, summarize Japanese civilization in its respective attitudes towards nature, sex, popular and aristocratic entertain-

ments, the state, the church, the stage, politics, and death.
Part II is a pictorial narrative of the negotiations. The
Postlude, dated 1903, partially answers the questions:
'Then wait — wait for fifty years — and see who has conquered.' In Japan, a disillusioned student commits suicide; in America, crowds throng the memorial exhibition
of Whistler's paintings. These two episodes 'are facts, but
they hardly epitomize the whole truth. Still they are
striking, occurring as they did in the same year.'

> What I meant to give in both those postludes was the effect
> that each country had upon the other. In the Japanese
> section, how difficult it was for the Oriental to assimilate
> the Occidental habits of thought, how he broke in the
> effort; in the American part, how, in conquering Japan for
> our commerce, as we thought, we had ourselves been con-
> quered on the aesthetic plane, and our habits of thought
> insensibly modified by contact with the Japanese.[1]

'Hedge Island, a Retrospect and a Prophecy,' the third
and shortest of the four poems, is a paean over the vitality of England in the Napoleonic days — the England of
hedges (which always impress the New Englander used to
rambling stone walls) and of coaches, which had been her
love ever since as a young girl she had persuaded her
mother to give her W. Outram Tristram's anecdotal
Coaching Days and Coaching Ways.

The hedgerows, starring out from London, are the setting; between them roll the coaches to the compass-points.
We ride in the Glasgow mail through its first night as far
as Derby. Then follows a series of pictures, hearty as
Rowlandson, lively as Cruikshank, quaint as Hugh Thom-
son, summarizing English civilization: romance, in an
elopement to Gretna Green; literature, agriculture, religion, and fashion, as travellers; eating, in a dinner at the
George; drinking; Christmas, a fog, a gibbet, snow, as they
affect the coaches; royalism, in a procession of the mails

[1] Letter to Linda Hawley Brigham, November 4, 1919.

to celebrate the King's birthday; and physical courage, in all England driving to a prize-fight.

But everything changes; a warning tone is heard, repeated:

> Ah, hedges of England, have you led to this? Do you always conduct to galleried inns, snug bars, beds hung with flowered chintz, sheets smelling of lavender?
> What of the target practice off Spithead?...

It is the navy. Some pages on, the army appears:

> 'Damn the soldiers! Drive through them, Watson.' A fine, manly business; are we slaves? 'Britons never — never —' Waves lap the shore of England, waves like watchdogs growling; and long hedges bind her like a bundle. Sit safe, England, trussed and knotted; while your strings hold, all will be well.

A puff of steam — Industrialism — and the coaches disappear. Soldiers marching — to the World War. But the Prophecy is a cheer, a triumphant 'England forever!' gathering volume as the poem ends.

'The Bronze Horses' is the last poem of the book, and the longest.

In 'Guns as Keys' Amy Lowell had stated her belief: 'Your gains are not in silver, mariners, but in the songs of violins, and the thin voices whispering through printed books.' In 'The Bronze Horses' we behold Art, the climax of civilization, triumphing across centuries, surviving the wreck of empires; the one thing permanent in the course of war and greed.

The conception is enormous. Four civilizations are represented, four different ideals of happiness; they are contrasted with opposing civilizations; the more vigorous triumphs; and the conquered collapses under stress of war, evades it, or endures it. The four wars are respectively wars of conquest, of religion, of liberation, of mere madness; but all are destructive and glut the greed of the conquerors. Yet the bronze horses, always the spoil, survive unharmed.

The poem begins at the center of civilization, Rome under Vespasian, in 71 A.D. Patrician (the languid lady in her bath) and plebeian (the bored workman) are alike spoiled, stale, enervate, for the armies ravage the rest of the world to provide them with luxuries. These wars are the Roman economic system. Now the city is regaled with a triumph: Titus has conquered Judea, whose most sacred treasures are paraded through the streets. Jehovah has fallen before Jupiter; but that overthrow reminds us that Jupiter also will fall to another god, under the onslaught of other armies. And the bronze horses, who placidly watch the procession, have also been spoils of war — a glance backward, showing that the beginning of the poem is hardly the beginning of the subject.

In the second section, the poem leaps forward to the Eastern Empire, Constantinople of A.D. 1204. It is a city made enormously rich by commerce; its chief amusement is betting on the races. But the Fourth Crusade is launched; the Roman Church conquers the Greek Church, and the city of gold is destroyed for its gold by the pious crusaders.

The third section describes Venice of A.D. 1797, with its carnivals and frivolous love-making, under the tyranny of a corrupt oligarchy, aided by the Inquisition. General Bonaparte's armies try to liberate the Venetians, but they bewail the loss of their beautiful horses more than they rejoice over freedom; and 'tomorrow come the Austrians.'

The last section leaps forward only a comparatively few years (so fast has history speeded up) to Venice again in 1915, at the time of Italy's break with Austria and her entry into the World War. Venice is bombed.[1] Her

---

[1] 'And, by the way, the poem is done, and Ada thinks the air raid is good. It will amuse you to know that I read aeroplane books for a week, but in none of them did I find anything like the vividness of description or the poetical perception which characterized your account.' — Letter to Eleanor Belmont, May 22, 1918.

churches are banked with sandbags, and the bronze horses are sent to Rome for safe-keeping. The poem ends as they glide down the canals, completing a cycle, as it seems, by returning to the city where they stood nearly two thousand years before.

But the ending is no ending, as the beginning was no beginning. The horses are not to remain there; and the poem stops with a glance forward. 'For how long? Ask the guns...'

Framing the poem, so to speak, are four preludes on elemental themes: fire, the life-giver and transmuter, in which the metals, rising from the other three elements, take forms which endure until the fire comes again. It would seem as if each section were dominated by an element; for clearly Rome is of the earth, Constantinople perishes in a conflagration, Venice is built upon the waters, and her last trial comes from the air. But Miss Lowell, while she admitted the fact, denied that it was intentional. Yet how far unconscious intent builds a structure is yet to be determined.

Can Grande's Castle was Amy Lowell's first completely original book — original in meter, method, structure, and meaning. It has a glory and exultation to it that reminds one of Blake's *America*: turning the pages is like an increase of light on the retina. Never did she produce anything more purely splendid, though some of her later work was richer.

The reviewers were all but uniformly dazzled by the brilliance of the coloring, the sonorities of the orchestration, and the scope of the panorama; indeed, in their enthusiasm they could see little else. The New York *Sun* called it the biggest thing since Whitman; the *Boston Transcript* said that Amy Lowell had replaced Poe. Only three reviewers, in trying to keep their heads, ran foul of the book: Aiken, Harriet Monroe, and Ben Hecht, according to Miss Lowell; and even they dropped some reluctant sentences which she extracted and sent on to her publishers, for possible use on new jackets. In three weeks it looked as though they must get out a second edition before Christmas; but the sales continued at such a rate that the second edition actually came out in October. Her friends wrote congratulatory letters of many kinds. The composer Loeffler was one of the promptest: he had not been so moved since he had read the best pages of *The Ring and the Book*, he thanked God that she was alive, and asserted that History, being made only by those that have great vision and imagination, could only be understood by Poets. Barrett Wendell, interested in the meter, suggested the hexameter or elegiac couplet as a basis for polyphonic prose, and warned her against too precise detail and too staccato rhythm. Sara Teasdale was ill with the influenza when the book arrived; her husband read it to her; and they became so enthusiastic that at first she forgot her illness, then had to rest awhile. Fletcher was sure that future time would consider this book her most important achievement; at first he preferred 'Guns as Keys,' but in a week preferred 'Bronze Horses.' Only Thomas Hardy was baffled by the book; nonetheless, in his kindly letter he called her 'Cousin Amy.'

Max Gate, Dorchester
26th January 1919

DEAR MISS LOWELL:

I am truly glad to hear from you again, not only for personal reasons but because you are so staunchly zealous in the cause of poetry. The kind gift of your new book is most welcome to me, and I send warm thanks for your thought of me in presenting it.

I have not yet mastered your argument for 'polyphonic prose' — (Qy: polyphonic prosody?), but I daresay I shall discover it as I go on. I don't suppose it is what, 40 years ago, we used to call 'word-painting.' Curiously enough, at that time, prose having the rhythm of verse concealed in it, so to speak (e.g. in the novels of R. D. Blackmore and others) was considered a fantastic affectation. Earlier still, when used by Lytton, it was nicknamed 'the ever and anon style' — I suppose because of the rhythm in those words.

This however may be quite a different thing from what you mean, and if so you must consider my mention of it an irrelevent reminiscence. I am, naturally at my age, what they call old-fashioned, and having written rhymes and metred numbers nearly fifty years ago — before you were born! — you must forgive a pedagogic tone if you find it in me.

Though of course in divine poesy there is no such thing as old fashion or new. What made poetry 2000 years ago makes poetry now.

My wife has read some of your book aloud to me, and sends her kindest regards. By the way, in taking up your book I say, 'Let's read some more of "Cousin Amy"' (after the lady in Locksley Hall). 'A great liberty!' you will say, especially as she was of a faithless nature. But you must excuse it, remembering under what strange conditions we met when you were here — when the whole world seemed to be in incipient combustion.

With best wishes and hope of seeing you again, believe me

Yours most sincerely,

THOMAS HARDY

P.S. Kind regards also to Mrs. Russell. T. H.

CHAPTER XVIII
THE CAMPAIGN CONTINUES

'... *What you forget is that I come from a family of orators, that public speaking is natural to me, that it is no more effort for me to give a lecture than it is to talk in a drawing-room, that I enjoy reading poetry to an audience as I should enjoy acting a play to an audience, because it is one side of my genius.*'

THE operation proved more serious than the doctor had expected. She did not get downstairs till the last day of September, and then was so exhausted that she had to go back to bed in an hour. A terrible pandemic of influenza was sweeping the world, and was to kill half a million persons; on October 1, 1918, two hundred and two persons died in Boston alone. Mrs. Russell's daughter in Washington came down with it; it turned into pneumonia; and the chances were that even if she should survive, at least she would lose the child she was expecting in December. Mrs. Russell left Brookline, with a nurse (none was available in Washington), and found that she had to do the cooking, as no servant could be got. The danger-point was completely passed by October 24, but Miss Lowell had worried so much that her own recovery was postponed. The doctor would not let her work, so she spent her time catching up with her correspondence; considering the feasibility of changing her English publishers (Bryher had written of her as a poet absolutely unknown!); selling Bryher's and Cowley's poems; writing letters of introduction for Stella Benson, who was going to San Francisco; thanking Eugene Saxton for a box of books; trying to place a review of Sandburg's *Cornhuskers* (he had sailed for Sweden the day before it appeared); and looking for someone to translate *Tendencies* into French. The letters of congratulation for *Can Grande's Castle* poured in; they had to be answered. H. D. wrote that she had met Winifred Bryher, and had stumbled upon the fact that the name was a pseudonym; and Miss Bryher confessed in a long letter that her real name was Ellerman, but that she was determined to make her way under a pseudonym because her friends always attributed what success she achieved to her father's wealth. She was planning to come to America as soon as passports could be obtained, which would probably be soon, as the war seemed near an end. D. H. Lawrence wrote on September 11, thanking her for favors; he said that the *New Poems* dedicated to her would be out in about six weeks, and that his friend Robert Nichols was coming to America on a poetry lecture tour — he hoped she would see him.

> Frieda and I are here trying to be patient. I am slowly working at another novel: though I feel it's not much use. No publisher will risk my last, and none will risk this, I expect. I can't do anything in the world today — am just choked. — I don't know how on earth we shall get through another winter — how we shall ever find a future. Humanity as it stands, and myself as I stand, we just seem mutally impossible to one another. The ground dwindles under one's feet — what next, heaven knows.
> I wish we could see you.
> Warm greeting
> D. H. LAWRENCE

On the twenty-third he sent her the proofs of his book, which would be out in a month; he wished Harriet Monroe would publish some of the poems first. 'Let me know how you like them. Write to us.' Her answer was as follows:

October 4, 1918

DEAR LAWRENCE:

I shall be delighted to see your book of poems, and as I told you in my last letter, I shall be extremely proud to see my name in the dedication. I am sorry you are so blue. I know how hard it is, and I know there is no use in counselling you to make any concessions to public opinions in your books and, although I regret sincerely that you cut yourself off from being published by an outspokenness which the English public does not understand, I regret it not in itself, as I think I said in my remarks about you in that lecture, but simply because it keeps the world from knowing what a great novelist you are. I think that you could top them all if you would be a little more reticent on this one subject. You need not change your attitude a particle, you can simply use an India rubber in certain places, and then you can come into your own as it ought to be. But what is the use? You will turn from these remarks with a shrug of disgust and say, 'Another, another, they are all against me!' Of course that is not true, and of course you must know that I do not mean it that way, but when one is surrounded by prejudice and blindness, it seems to me that the only thing to do is to get over in spite of it and not constantly run foul of these same prejudices which, after all, hurts oneself and the spreading of one's work, and does not do a thing to right the prejudice. Few people are pure enough minded to take your books as you mean them, which I tried to point out in my essay. I wish that I could have made that essay on you longer, but you remember that you never sent me any biographical material, and when Frieda finally wrote me the thing had already been written and delivered.

I am sending you my new book. I do not know whether you will like it or not. Sometimes I think you will not. You see, this poetry is entirely objective, and you rather like the subjective kind. However, such as it is it has gone to you, and I do hope that you and Frieda will like some of it. At any rate, tell me just what you think of it, please.

I will write again before long. In the meantime, with kindest regards to Frieda from Mrs. Russell and myself,

Very sincerely yours

P.S. I think the war looks better, and some day we may all meet again.

From November 6 to the 15th, Miss Lowell was in New York, ostensibly on business, but really to get a necessary vacation. The waiters at the St. Regis struck, so she took her meals at the Colony Club, to which she had belonged for eleven years, though hardly ever entering it. She went to the theater with Miss Cutting; she dined with Sara Teasdale and her husband on the 10th; the next day the city went mad over the announcement of the Armistice. When she returned to Brookline, she felt much better, and started to work again, not going to bed till 8 o'clock in the morning.

A letter from D. H. Lawrence arrived.

Chapel Farm Cottage
Hermitage
nr. Newbury
Berks
5 Nov. 1918

My dear Amy,

I have received Can Grande's Castle. You are wrong when you say I only like subjective poetry — I love visions, & visionary panorama. I love 'thunderheads marching along the sky-line' — and 'beautiful, faded city' — and 'fifty vessels blowing up the Bosphorus' — and English Coaches — all those things. I love the pomp and richness of the past — the full, resplendent gesture. The sordidness of the present sends me mad — such meagre souls, all excusing themselves. — But why don't you write a *play*? I'm sure you could write a handsome drama. Pity we can't do it together. I do wish we could have some rich, laughing, sumptuous kind of days, insouciant, indifferent to everything but a little good laughter and splendeur de vivre which costs nothing. — Why not, one day. — Meanwhile as it happens to be a very sunny day, and the war will soon end, I feel already like a holiday.

No, Amy, again you are not right when you say the india-rubber eraser would let me through into a paradise of popularity. Without the india-rubber I am damned along with the evil, with the india-rubber I am damned among the disappointing. You see what it is to have a reputation. I give it up, and put my trust in heaven. One needn't trust a great deal in anything, & in humanity not at all.

I too have written a play: not wicked but too good is probably the sigil of its doom. Que m'importe! I go my own way, regardless. By good I mean 'sage': one of my unspotted 'sagesses.'

We went to London, Frieda & I — got the Flu. — fled here — have recovered — shall probably return soon to Middleton. I have one really passionate desire — to have wings, only wings, and to fly away — far away. I suppose one would be sniped by anti-aircraft guns. But one could fly by night. Then those indecent searchlights fingering the sky.

Frieda sends her love. Remember us warmly to Mrs. Russell.

D. H. Lawrence

The next weeks passed uneventfully. She tried to place a book of Royall Snow's poetry; on request she gave yet another of her poetry libraries, to the hospital at Camp Dix, New Jersey; she joined the MacDowell Club of New York, by special invitation, and was appointed to its Committee on Literature; she arranged to read 'The Bronze Horses' there in January, when she was also to lecture and read at Columbia. Prue, the last of her dogs, which she had given to Carl Engel's sister, died: 'The thing is too close to me to write about. I can only thank you for having been so good to her.' Then, just before Christmas, she 'caught a bug,' and was confined to her bed, so that her presents got off late. D. H. Lawrence wrote on December 28, asking why he had not heard from her since October. Aldington asked her to hurry up his *War and Love*; and the proofs came, for her to correct. She sold a poem, 'Der Tag,' on the surrender of the German fleet, to the *New York Tribune*. The editor was so pleased with it that he not only paid her $50 — more than she had asked — but devoted an entire page to it on

December 22, with humorous marginal sketches by Gropper. The season and her illness combined to prevent her outburst of indignation until the 28th:

> You see your and my attitude start from an entirely different point of view. You think a poet wants to touch 'the great mass of the people who never read a poem at all,' but that is not so. A poet — or at least this poet — wants to touch the people with a spark of poetry in them, be they blacksmiths or millionaires, but she has not the slightest interest in the rest of the world nor their opinion. Also, I detest the idea of poems as propaganda. If they are not enjoyed as poetry, I do not care whether they are enjoyed or not.
>
> I have no desire to live in an ivory tower, but, on the other hand, I must be presented with dignity. I have no objection to boldness; I have objection to vulgarity. I think those pictures were vulgar and utterly out of key with my poem. You say that the 'Tribune' has never published a more successful 'stroke.' I am very glad to know that, but that some of the public are of my opinion, not of yours, is evident from the following letter from unknown admirer....
>
> As to putting myself in your hands, that is what I have never been willing to do to any editor or any publisher. Now look here, I started in the world with one of the greatest handicaps that any one could possibly have. I belonged to the class which is not supposed to be able to produce good creative work. I was writing in an idiom which was entirely new and to most people extremely disagreeable. I knew not a single editor and had entrance to no magazine nor paper. Will you say that I have engineered myself badly in five short years? Is it not possible that you can trust me to know my own business and the way to advance it? I do need you, and you can help me a great deal, but only if you will be somewhat guided by me in the presentation of my work; otherwise, I am as bad as Napoleon, I believe in my star, and I have not a doubt that in following it I shall reach the goal, although I confess I personally may be dead before that happy day arrives....

On January 4, 1919, she had planned to leave for New
York, to keep engagements at Columbia and the Mac-
Dowell Club; but a second wave of the influenza epidemic
broke over Sevenels, and she was confined with a com-
bination of headaches, indigestion, and violent coughing.
Postponing her dates, she spent her leisure in writing
reviews of Jean Untermeyer's *Growing Pains*, Edward
Waldo Emerson's *Early Years of the Saturday Club*, and
Dorothy Richardson's novels. Then on the 14th she had a
severe relapse, which made travelling and even speaking
impossible for some weeks. She cancelled the New York
dates, and postponed a reading in Richmond, Virginia.
Only by a narrow margin did she escape pneumonia.
By the 27th, however, she was recovered enough to read
at a musicale of Miss Terry's, arranged by Mrs. Jack
Gardner, at the Copley Theater; but she had no voice or
vigor, and although she sat throughout was exhausted
afterwards. She and Alfred Noyes were to address the
Contemporary Club of Philadelphia on February 10;
but the epidemic made both of them cancel the engagement, and Robert Nichols replaced them. James Russell
Lowell's centennial was celebrated in New York, but she
did not go on for it. She remained at home with a trained
nurse, trying to recover her digestion; when a new com-
plication arose: the high blood pressure, which never left
her thereafter, and made her observe special precautions.
Vachel Lindsay dined with her on February 7, and she had
a few others in for dinner, but she spent most of her time
quietly, selling poems and composing an article on the
younger English novelists. D. H. Lawrence wrote her
on the 5th, saying that another copy of his *New Poems*
was being sent her, in place of the one which never arrived;
Thomas Hardy's letter about *Can Grande's Castle* reached
her; Aldington wished she could get him a correspondence
job on some American periodical; Sandburg, apparently
much disillusioned with his trip to Sweden, wrote her that
he had returned to America.

At the end of the month, she was working hard on her lecture, 'Some Musical Analogies in Modern Poetry,' which the Music Department at Harvard had invited her to deliver for the benefit of the American Friends of Musicians in France. On Sunday, March 2, she had a musical evening with the Edward Burlingame Hills and Gebhard, going over the compositions she was to mention in her paper. The lecture was delivered the next day, at Paine Hall — it was the first lecture ever delivered by a woman under the auspices of Harvard University.

It began with a discussion of the relationship between music and poetry as separate arts. Even as her brother had learned to write prose by studying the old Italian masters of painting, so her chief guide in learning to write had been the composers of music. She was not speaking of songs, where the music requires and over-shadows a text: a real poem exists completely in itself, and needs no music.

> It is quite true that both music and poetry are arts in time; but music is chiefly an art of tone, poetry an art of ideas, and if both also have emotion, why that is merely a *sine qua non* of all and every art whatsoever. When music endeavors to do away with tone and substitute the actuali-ties of noise,... its perpetrators overstep the boundaries of their particular art. When poetry seeks to suppress thought and substitute sound,... the same sharp defeat occurs...

All such poetry should be chanted; but the poet has really abandoned poetry and tried to write music.

Primitive peoples have a fine sense of strong and subtle rhythms, which gets lost when their art becomes civilized, but is recovered still later. The Gregorian chants gave way to Bach; *Beowulf*, to Alexander Pope. But in Blake's free verse and such manifestations as Keats's displaced accents, we find a return to the fundamental and subtler rhythms.

Even before the war, Germany had ceased to lead the arts; and now the young composers look to France and Russia, the young poets to France and the Orient. The great French traits of clarity, precision, and lightness are paralleled in the new poetry's clearness of picture, suggestion, and rhythmic *finesse*. Debussy's 'Preludes' parallel various *vers libre* poems in their impressionism, objectivity, and hatred of the *cliché*, as she demonstrated by poems of Aldington's, Fletcher's, Sandburg's, and her own 'Aquarium.' After an explanation of free verse, with reference to Professor Patterson's laboratory tests, she read examples of her own experiments in conveying movement: 'Dolphins in Blue Water,' 'After Hearing a Waltz by Bartók'; 'Marching Hessians'; and Stravinsky's 'Grotesques.' She also read part of Lindsay's 'Congo' as genuine ragtime.

As dissonance enriches music, so poetry must also have its contrasts. Mere cameos can never be ultimately satisfying; and in attempting to discover an epic form to fit the new spirit, she developed polyphonic prose from the experiments of Paul Fort. She wanted an orchestral effect, in which the delicate flute tones of *vers libre* could be augmented by all the other instruments at the command of the poet; thus her subject could be treated musically, dramatically, lyrically, and pictorially, all at once. As an example, she ended her lecture by reading the Venetian carnival from 'The Bronze Horses.'[1]

Inquiries from France made her feel that her fame was spreading. Paul Fort wrote, asking for a contribution to his new magazine, *Le Monde Nouveau;* André Fontainas, doing a series of articles on American poets, sent for information; meanwhile Magdelaine Hutchinson was busy translating *Tendencies.* Miss Lowell was sure that she could conquer England, if only she could get there; but

[1] This lecture, in revised form, was published in the *Musical Quarterly* (VI, 127–57), January, 1920.

her sister Katherine warned her from England that while rationing continued, it was very unwise to come.

On March 17, she read to the Woman's Club at Richmond, Virginia. Her illnesses had obliged her to break several dates, but at last she arrived, was met at the station, and taken about to see the Confederate Museum and the other sights. She was tired, and showed it; but when the reading came, all fatigue seemed to vanish. She was so superb that, according to one witness, the younger writers of Richmond were permanently liberated from the literary conventions which had been paralyzing their work.

After the reading there was a dinner. Miss Lowell was seated between the hostess Ellen Glasgow and Miss Julia Sully. Turning to the latter, Miss Lowell said: 'I hear that you were asked to introduce me, but refused: why?' Miss Sully had the presence of mind to reply: 'Why, I have always felt that the only perfect introduction was "Alice, mutton! Mutton, Alice!" — and that would never have done here.' Miss Lowell burst into a hearty laugh; a permanent friendship was instantly established. She asked Miss Sully what unofficial sight she ought to see, and was told of the old, overgrown garden behind the Valentine Museum, with its iron fountain and box. Later, Miss Sully got a letter thanking her for the suggestion, concluding: 'Don't be surprised if you see a poem about that garden some day.' But the poem was never written.

On her way back, Miss Lowell stopped off at the Hotel Belmont, in New York, to read 'The Bronze Horses' at the MacDowell Club on the 20th. She sold seventeen poems, met Percy MacKaye at a tea, arranged for the contract of her next book, *Pictures of the Floating World*, had Sara Teasdale to dinner, and (also apparently on this visit) dined at Mrs. Simeon Ford's, where she sat next to C. Lewis Hind, an Englishman who had the inspiration to identify her well through the meal. 'Who did you think I was?' she glared; and a few minutes later made an unpreserved retort to his ingenuous question, 'Why were you not at the James Russell Lowell centenary celebration?'[1] But all social engagements were cancelled by the sudden news that her nephew, Major James A. Roosevelt, who had fought in the Argonne, and who was to land in New York that week, had died suddenly of spinal meningitis on the transport, the night before it docked. 'I practically brought him up,' she wrote Winifred Bryher two months later, 'as my sister was an invalid, and he was almost like my son. The result of this, coming immediately after the influenza, was to diminish my vitality and nervous force

[1] Mr. Hind, who admired her as conversationalist and literary theorist, published his account of this dinner, signed 'Q.R.,' in the *Christian Science Monitor* December 20, 1921; it will also be found in his *More Authors and I*, New York, 1922, pp. 193-98. Miss Lowell's comment on his article, which included her own version of the event, is in a letter to Miss Edith Standen, January 5, 1922:

Who is the writer for the 'Christian Science Monitor' to whom you seem to have written some time ago asking him to write a paper on me? This the gentleman has done in the issue for December 20th. He mentioned your having written to him, but gave no name, in a number of the paper which came out last Summer, I think. In this second article he refers to an occasion which, if not entirely apocryphal, is certainly extremely altered from the original. It has taken me some time to recall any meeting or any hostess who has symposia of literati such as the gentleman said his hostess was in the habit of giving. I think, however, that I have at last tracked the story to its source. It was not a supper-party, but a dinner-party. I think it took place at the house of Mrs. Simeon Ford in New York. I was late, but they had not sat down to dinner. I did not recline on a sofa, à la Mme. Récamier or otherwise, but sat bolt upright on one. I remember there was an Englishman there who was in America on some theatrical mission, and from what I remember of him I should not suppose him to be the sort of person who could understand my poetry, and the fact that he does not makes me quite sure that I have got the right person in mind; but I should be very glad if you would tell me his name, as that has gone completely out of my head. There was no large gathering on the evening I refer to. I think there were ten people at dinner — and nobody came in during the evening — of which ten, one was Mrs. Ford herself, two were her brother and sister-in-law, three others were Mrs. Russell, the gentleman 'Q.R.' and myself, and two more were two poets, Percy MacKaye and Kahlil Gibran. I admire the way in which he has worked up a simple little evening into a large and flourishing party. He is evidently a kindly and sympathetic soul, but inexperienced in modern poetry. I should like to know his name and how he comes to be writing for the 'Christian Science Monitor.' The curious part is that he writes just like a woman.

I foresee that I shall have the same difficulty in being understood by the English as I used to have in the case of the Americans....

again.' Her letters for the past two years had been full of his achievements; now she cancelled all dates, and remained in New York for the funeral on the 29th.

On the thirty-first, she read from her poems at the Desmond Fitzgerald Art Gallery in Brookline, under auspices of the Relief and Reconstruction Committee, the proceeds to be devoted to the restoration of devastated France. The other speakers were Basil King, Judge Robert Grant, Josephine Peabody, Miss Eleanor Potter, and George Arliss.

Meanwhile her *Times* review of Edward Waldo Emerson's *Early Years of the Saturday Club* (at a meeting of which club Longfellow had once carried her in a wastebasket round the table) had drawn some replies; the mild controversy thus aroused simmered for a couple of months. This review was only the first of many she wrote for the *New York Times*. But April was spent chiefly in preparing the manuscript of her new book. 'I wish I felt any of that spring restlessness which you describe,' she wrote Jean Untermeyer on the 11th; 'I feel only an immense languor — partly the remains of the "flu," I think, and partly the results of fatigue and emotion.' A sympathetic letter from D. H. Lawrence arrived.

Mountain Cottage,
Middleton-by-Wirksworth,
Derby, England.
5 April 1919

MY DEAR AMY

I am sorry you have been so seedy — one gets so pulled down. I had Flu. also — nearly shuffled off the mortal coil — am well on in convalescence. It was a vile sick winter for us all. — Hilda also had pneumonia some weeks ago, & it left her weak. I hear her baby, a girl, was born last Sunday, and that both are doing well. We shall be going to London soon, & may see her.

I am sure you are wise to defer your lectures on poetry — but I wish you were coming over to Europe. One feels a great longing for a bit of a gathering of friends in some sunny, careless, genial place. But the world is all at cross purposes, and gets worse: everything seems tangled in everything by a million bits of string. I want to go to Switzerland or Germany, and then come on to America this summer. But I can see we shall never manage it. I want awfully to come to America — first to the north, then later to go south, perhaps to Central America. It is what I intend to do when the world becomes sane again, and oneself free.   •

Here in England nobody cares about anything, literature least of all: all bent on scrambling uneasily from day to day, as if we were all perched on a land-slide, and the days were stones that might start sliding under one's feet. I don't know why it all seems so uncertain, so irritable, such a sequence of pinpricking moments, with no past to stay one, and no future to wonder over. But it is so. And it is hateful to have life chopped up into disagreeable moments, all gritty.

We hear from Frieda's people: terrible distress there seems to be. F. worries — we all worry. I suppose it will soon end. My brother-in-law is Minister of Finance to the new Bavarian republic. He seems to weather the storms. But it is a perpetual question of what next. — We want to go to Munich when we can. Frieda wants to see her mother and her sisters: I too want to see them all again.

When you write will you address me at — Chapel Farm Cottage, *Hermitage*, nr. *Newbury*, Berks. We are going down there at the end of the month, and I suppose we shall stay there till we leave England. I have not written anything these last few months — not since I have been ill. I feel I don't want to write — still less do I want to publish anything. It is like throwing one's treasures in a bog.

I agree with you, that the poetry of the future, and the poetry that *now* has the germs of futurity in it, is rhymeless, naked, spontaneous rhythm. But one has an old self as well as a new. — I hope you got the copy of New Poems. It was much better received than 'Look We have Come Through.' The press only spat on that. — What is Huebsch publishing of mine in New York, do you know? I never hear anything. I do hope you are well & happy. I would love to see your garden, particularly to get the scents at evening. I would love the gorgeous, living lavishness that America is capable of, naturally — and Europe isn't. Remember us to Mrs. Russell. Frieda and I send warmest greetings.

D. H. LAWRENCE

On April 16, Carl Kjersmeier, Danish poet, sent her a postcard telling her how he had come to love her poems while guarding the Danish frontier. On the next day, one of her orchids (a Cattleya Thayeriana, with eighteen blooms on a single stalk) won a prize at the exhibition of the Gardeners' and Florists' Association.

By May, her blood-pressure was still up to 240, and her eyes were giving her trouble; she was not supposed to work: but on the 3d, she sent off the manuscript of *Pictures of the Floating World*. On the 5th she took the night train to Cincinnati, arriving in the morning. She lunched with Miss Mary Macmillan and her friends, then was driven round to see the city and its environs. The next day she read her poems to the Ohio Valley Poetry Society, and found the members unsympathetic. When her first poem was received in silence, she remarked with dangerous sweetness: 'I will read it to you again.' But that did not help matters. 'Ada said I lost my temper and gave them a scolding, which I am afraid is true, but it is little to be wondered at, for I had so bad a headache that I had to take thirty-six grains of phenastine to get me there at all,' she wrote Grace Conkling afterwards. She took the train home on the morning of the 7th. On the 15th, she spoke for ten minutes at the dinner of the Booksellers' Convention at the Copley Plaza. One of the several consequences of that brief talk was that the head of a big book-buying concern asked her to make out 'A Bookshelf of Modern Poets' for libraries; which she did. It was neither a list calculated to please all tastes, good and bad, such as she had made out for the camp libraries; nor was it a critical list for students. It was a bookseller's list, of the best contemporary poetry published in America, and still in print, to attract those people who buy in department stores and railway terminals. Naturally the list aroused another controversy. Some poets who were omitted thundered in the newspapers, either in person or through friends; others meekly sent her their volumes, which they assumed she had overlooked.

The subsiding blood-pressure (which never went wholly) had left a weakness of the muscles of the retina; consequently, whenever she used her eyes, she got a headache. The doctor forbade her working for two weeks. Unwilling to be idle, she devised a scheme for circumventing the eyestrain. She had a set of glasses made, in a scale of increasing strength, identified by colored strings; as the night wore on, she changed her glasses according to the hour, beginning with the weakest, and going through the rainbow, until dawn came. The scheme was not perfect, but there were consolations. A. Edward Newton, who had been corresponding with her very pleasantly for some years, as fellow author and collector, insisted on presenting her with a letter from Lord Nelson to Lady Hamilton, as a reward for writing 'Sea-Blue and Blood-Red'; her New England conscience protested in vain against accepting such a magnificent present; but Mr. Newton was unable to acquire the letter after all. On May 23, she gave a dinner for Clement Shorter, who had come to America. After reading her *Tendencies*, he had been writing articles on the American poets for London periodicals; now she hoped to tell him more of the subject, but he preferred European gossip. At the end of the month, she learned that the famous letter from Shelley inviting Keats to stay with him in Italy was to be sold at auction; she cabled a bid, but the censor stopped the message, as she had also bid for some letters written by those suspicious-sounding Huns, Schumann and Brahms. She frantically repeated her cables; then, in desperation, appealed to the State Department, so that her bids reached England in time; and she got the letter, though it 'broke' her temporarily.

On June 6, she gave a new lecture, 'Modern Poetry: its Differences, its Aims, its Achievements,' at a joint meeting of the Massachusetts and the Bay Path Library Clubs, in The Town Hall at Southborough.[1] It was chiefly a summary of the New Poetry, calculated for the needs of the officials of public libraries. She asserted that we were in the midst of a poetry revival, and cited as proof the demand for poetry in the camp libraries.

> Wordsworth, Keats, Byron, and Coleridge are the four main influences of Nineteenth Century poetry. Wordsworth represents simplicity, reflection, spirituality; Keats, pure sensuous beauty and wealth of imagery; Byron, verve, humour, and materialism; Coleridge, philosophy, phantasy, romanticism. Each had its followers, but the Byron bent expended itself the most quickly; the Wordsworth stock had the larger influence during the whole Nineteenth Century; the Keats vein ran to exhaustion through a host of followers; while Coleridge as an influence crossed the water and impregnated Poe, and, through him, Mallarmé and the whole *Symboliste* movement in France, to return to us again as one very marked trend in what we call the 'new poetry.'
> What then is the 'new poetry' reacting against, since, like all new movements it is a reaction? Specifically against the work of none of these poets, but distinctly against the trends which they inaugurated. Against the trends of three of them, that is, for I have already shown that I consider Coleridge as the father of one branch of them. The new poetry is a revolt against the didacticism of Wordsworth, against the vulgarity of Byron, against the over-embroidered saccharinities of the followers of Keats. Observe, I say 'followers,' for many they have been, but the widest known, and, in his day, the most admired, is the especial goal of

---

[1] A revised version was published in the *Massachusetts Library Club Bulletin* (ix, 8–10), October, 1919.

departure for the moderns; I refer, of course, to Tennyson. Both for his matter and his manner, the modern poets (to what group soever they belong) unite in cursing Tennyson.

The new forms, she continued, were two: *vers libre* for short poems, and polyphonic prose for long ones. Having defined these, she then indicated Suggestion, Vividness, Concentration, and Externality as the virtues of the reaction; made an abstract of her *Tendencies* as a statement of the New Poetry's achievements; and ended with a catalogue of the other contemporary American poets whom she had not included in her book because they belonged to established schools.

D. H. Lawrence had written her on May 26; he was coming to America at last, and hoped to help make his way by giving lectures — could she perhaps arrange some dates in Boston? She was obliged to reply that New England would not welcome him. In the 'scruple' room of the Athenaeum (where dubious books, indicated in the catalogue by the apothecary's scruple symbol, were locked up) she had recently found Compton Mackenzie's *Sylvia Scarlett*, which she heartily admired, along with novels of Gilbert Cannan's and Beresford's.

I also found there, to my horror, your 'Sons and Lovers.' Now if a superb volume like that is not considered proper to put into the hands of the public, what can you think of the attitude over here? I do not know whether that is true of other parts of the country in the same way at all, but it is perfectly true of this little corner of it.

It will be the greatest pleasure for me to see you personally; I long to have the talks of which you speak, and I long to see you and Frieda again, and Mrs. Russell joins me with the utmost cordiality, but I am afraid you will find America a very different place from what you imagine; and what will be disgusting to you, as it is to me, is that they cannot see the difference between envisaging life whole and complete, physical as well as spiritual, and pure obscenities like those perpetrated by James Joyce.

.... You must not look for El Dorado, because it is anything but that. Personally, I like it better here. I think
that we have a truer feeling for values, and a grander conception of life, and a higher idea of art, even if we do not
always get it on paper. But for people to understand what
your books mean, they will have to see and know you, and
for that reason I think it would be a good thing for you to
come over; but I do not think it would be possible to get
you any large quantity of lectures until you have made
yourself known in other ways....

There is a mistaken and ridiculous prejudice against your
books, and that is the long and short of it; because it is un-
deserved it makes me want to weep. I think you are a big
enough fellow to know that I write you a letter like this
because I want you to know the facts of the case as they
really are. If I cared less for you, I should put you off with
some platitude. No one who knows you can fail to understand you, but it is almost impossible to make the general
public understand, particularly when your books are preju-
dicial to their preconceived notions....

His reply came immediately.

> Chapel Farm Cottage
> Hermitage nr. Newbury
> Berks, England
> 3 July 1919

MY DEAR AMY

This morning comes your long letter. I do understand
& believe perfectly what you say: particularly about lecturing. As for an El Dorado, when I set out to look for one, I
shall find one: for nothing is easier to find than money, if a
man sets out straight for it. I don't want El Dorado: only
life and freedom, a feeling of bigness, and a radical, even if
pre-conscious sympathy. I don't want to lecture — never
did. I only want to be able to live. And I believe that, once
in America, I could soon do that by writing. All I want is
to feel that there is somewhere I could go, if necessary, and
somebody I could appeal to for help if I needed it. That's
why I am afraid of putting a burden on your friendship.

Huebsch said he was coming to England early this month. I am going to London to-day to see about things — a pass-port for Frieda, etc. She will go to Germany to her people quite soon: this month, I hope. I shall come to America, because I mean to come. Probably I shall sail in August. I shall come alone, Frieda will stay in Germany till I am a bit settled, then I shall send for her. — I am not afraid of preju-dices: they are rarely in the very blood, only in the mind, on top.

I want to feel that I may come to you, to stay with you for a week or two, if I can't provide for myself just at the very first. Don't fear, I can soon get on my own feet. It is merely the start.

My articles in the English Review were on *Classic* Ameri-can literature. I hope to do a series on the moderns, next.

Anyhow & anyway, I shall be seeing you soon — quite soon. The wind blows that way. Then we can have a laugh and many a talk.

D. H. LAWRENCE

On August 13, Miss Lowell wrote separately to Lawrence and Frieda, advising them strongly not to come, as she was sure his plans would never work.

Summer passed uneventfully. In May, Mrs. Russell had gone to Salt Lake City, not to return until the middle of July. Meanwhile Miss Lowell became an 'enraged gardener' by day, and by night occasionally dined the passing literati. But all the while she continued her cus-tomary activities; selling the few yet unpublished poems which were included in her next book, prodding editors to be sure the things were published before September, ar-ranging new lecture dates, and writing letters to her friends. The dummy of *Pictures* had to be got just right; meanwhile Florence Ayscough was sending Chinese trans-lations in complicated versions to be worked over. Some of the poems had already been completed and sold; Arthur Waley had published a correction; and Miss Lowell had to confer with her colleague across the Pacific before replying.

Several other minor controversies were simmering vaguely.
And of course she was writing poems — more long ones.
There was no question of going to Dublin this summer.

On the afternoon of June 27, she read her poems before
the Whittier Home Association at Amesbury, where she
viewed his house. On July 7, after finishing Marguerite
Wilkinson's *New Voices*, she wrote the author to congratulate her, and also to state some convictions about
poetry.

> ... I absolutely disagree with your idea that the value of
> poetry consists chiefly in the arousing of people's emotional
> qualities. That is one of the attributes of poetry and a
> necessary adjunct to its existence, but the value of poetry
> is in itself and itself alone. I think it is well to rouse the
> populace to an appreciation of poetry; it is very bad to sug-
> gest to the poet that his ultimate value is in the attitude of
> the populace toward him. The amount of it is that the
> populace will always come round to first class work in the
> end, although it may take some hundreds of years. You
> will say that the two points of view are really the same, and
> with that perhaps I agree, but the approach must be from
> diametrically opposite points of the compass.
>
> I object to all this theory of democratizing poetry, be-
> cause poetry can only be democratic in a highly intellectual
> community. Poetry advances upon its base which is al-
> ways static above the mass of the people, and to suggest
> that it should be otherwise would be to doom it to wander-
> ing in the valleys.
>
> It is not always that folk poetry is the best or the most
> important. That there are certain persons or people (some-
> times several of them in one) who have written poetry
> which may possibly be considered folk poetry, for instance
> the Norse sagas or Homer, is true; but they have become
> folk poetry more with the years and people reading them,
> than that they started as such.
>
> I think it may be fairly stated that there has never been a
> first class poem written by a primitive people, and to insist
> upon the childlike attitude of the poet is to insist upon an

impossibility. The simplicity of the poet is far other than the simplicity of primitive man. If poetry were really democratic it would not be considered so important. It is just because so few can really produce it that it always remains one of the transcendant activities of humanity....

I also think it is a mistake to suppose that people who have a highly developed intellectual faculty are thereby entirely atrophied in their emotional qualities. As a matter of fact, it is probably true that the highly intellectual people are also the most deeply emotional, but that the expression of this emotion is different from the expression of the more elementary, is indubitable.

Personally I disagree entirely with Benét's theory that the poet should learn his poetry by heart. I do not know any of mine by heart; in fact, I detest learning it by heart, for it goes round and round in my head; and all poetry, Shakespeare, Keats, any one you like, is horrible to me when I have it morning, noon, and night....

Through July and the first three weeks of August she was correcting proofs and writing poems. On July 12, she sent the *Bookman* a long legend she had just finished: 'Memorandum Confided by a Yucca to a Passion-Vine'; it was accepted for the Christmas number. Then she began on a Chinese legend; and as the Athenaeum was not so well stocked with books on this subject as was the Harvard Library, she arranged for the privilege of going into the stacks and taking out as many books as she wanted. Margaret Fuller in 1844 had won that privilege for her sex; but they were always turned out of the stacks at 5 P.M. Miss Lowell, though informed of that rule, found it very difficult to get to Cambridge before that hour, and thus was the first of her sex to assume that privilege. She read all the Chinese literature that she could lay her hands on, in English or French; and though in the middle of July she wrote a friend that she was working on her poem, a month later she had not yet put pencil to paper for the actual composition.

There were pleasant interruptions. Elsie Sergeant was back from France. Miss Lowell had met her before she went abroad last autumn, to write up the battlefields for the *New Republic*. On the first battlefield, however, one of the journalists picked up a bomb, which exploded, killing one person, blowing the arm off another, and breaking both Miss Sergeant's ankles. In her long convalescence she wrote *Shadow-Shapes*, and also started a very friendly correspondence with Miss Lowell. Now that she was home again, Miss Lowell naturally had her over to Sevenels, to hear the manuscript. On one occasion, Miss Sergeant brought Lieutenant Hervey Allen out to dinner; he read his 'Blindman' (in which Miss Lowell suggested some improvements); and as he was studying at the Harvard Summer School, he was invited out again. Indeed, this was the beginning of another friendship that lasted as long as Miss Lowell lived. A few days after his first visit, Miss Julia Sully telephoned that she was in Boston, on her way from Richmond to Ogunquit for a rest. She came out to dinner, and although she had been nervously very tired, the two talked almost all night, and she reached her hotel at 4 A.M., feeling much refreshed. Among other things, the conversation ran on the sufferings of the South. Miss Lowell, whose father had been a Southern sympathizer, said: 'I don't see how you ever forgave us; I don't see how you can stand us round, how you can let us cross your thresholds.' Miss Sully was persuaded to come to dinner the next night; the invitation to visit became a standing one. Once they searched the gardens with a flashlight, looking for Winky; another evening they made merry over Chinese symbols ('home' was a woman and broom, 'peace' a man and woman under a roof, 'discord' a man and two women). Another time Miss Sully arrived to find the house in an uproar: Miss Lowell had broken the nose-piece of her glasses, and had summoned an optician from town. She raged audibly through the three hours re-

THE FIREPLACE IN THE LIBRARY

quired to get them precisely adjusted, then appeared late for dinner, as serene as though nothing had happened. From a Boston woman, Miss Sully heard an anecdote she considered authentic: Miss Lowell's car had broken down in the country, and when the local garage man hesitated at accepting her cheque, she told him to telephone her brother, the President of Harvard. The President asked, 'What is she doing now?' 'Well, she is sitting on a stonewall across the way, smoking a cigar.' 'It's my sister.'

On August 21, Miss Lowell wrote to Miss Sergeant:

> I am glad you are enjoying Chocorua, and you make me most anxious to see the beach at Ogunquit where you found so many poems. I did a delightful thing last Sunday. We motored down to Marblehead where the Engels have a place for a month, and went out in a motor boat all along the coast. Then we went round that fascinating little town, and through an old-fashioned house which is owned and kept up by a furniture dealer, and is full of things of the clipper-ship period. The flavour of the crooked streets, and the look of the grey rotting shingles behind great tufts of golden glow is something splendid.
>
> I find Brookline becoming more and more the mart of fashion. People keep coming over, and it is far more exciting than ever Dublin used to be. I am now seized with a desire to hire a motor launch in Boston and cruise among the islands of the harbour, a plan which I think I may carry out one day next month. At any rate, we are going down to Marblehead again next week, and are going to motor-boat clear way over to Magnolia. As I have a perfect passion for the sea, these little trips are delightful, and I come back so sleeping [*sic*] that I cannot do anything at all.

It was useless to think of going to Dublin again, and she offered her house there for sale. On the 27th she ran up to look it over; and two weeks later, without the assistance of any agent, she sold it for $18,000, removing only the Dutch tiles in three fireplaces and some furniture.

The last proofs of *Pictures* were corrected by August 21,

and she turned the more eagerly to the Chinese poems; but her eyestrain returned so severely that the doctor forbade her to use her eyes at all. She did use them a short time each day, however: besides the pages and pages of notes on the poems, to be sent to Florence Ayscough for consideration, there were also pages and pages of corrections of fact and suggestions about style to be sent to Magdelaine Hutchinson, who was translating *Tendencies*.

On September 11, the police force of Boston went on strike; and for three days, before Governor Coolidge could call out the State Guard, hoodlums broke shop windows, stole clothes and sporting goods, and played craps on the Common. Miss Lowell continued to work at night, with a loaded pistol in her library table drawer. On the 14th, Mrs. Conkling came to dinner, with the manuscript of a book of poems by her eight-year-old daughter, Hilda: Miss Lowell was amazed to discover them genuine literature, judged by any standards whatsoever. On September 20, Helen Bullis Kizer, Miss Lowell's devoted admirer and reviewer, was killed instantly by a fall from her horse. Four days later, *Pictures of the Floating World* was published. The first edition was completely sold out before publication; the second edition was delayed by a strike at the press.

CHAPTER XIX

PICTURES OF THE FLOATING WORLD

'I HAVE a volume of lyrics which I have been wanting to bring out for two years,' Amy Lowell wrote Professor Phelps after the appearance of *Can Grande's Castle*, 'but the publishers have insisted on these more timely poems of mine coming first.' And to Aldington she wrote on February 17, 1919: 'I have two [books] on the stocks at present, and I do not know which my publishers will elect to print first. One is a series of war poems called "Phantasms of War," and the other is a collection of short lyrics which I have been writing at odd moments for the last four years, and which have been printed in magazines and newspapers, but, owing to the scheme of my last two books, have not yet seen the light of day in book form.' The World War ended too soon to make the publication of *Phantasms* timely; so *Pictures of the Floating World* was chosen instead.

The title was a translation of the Japanese word *ukiyoye*, a term commonly applied to their eighteenth-century art, which delighted in the passing frivolities of life. It was therefore appropriate for this collection of 174 short poems, collected from thirty-one magazines and the Imagist Anthologies — all those written since the publication of *Sword Blades and Poppy Seed*. Some were five years old; some were very recent. Her longer poems, such as 'Dried Marjoram,' she was saving for another volume, to be called *Legends*.

The first section is a series of fifty-nine 'Lacquer Prints,' written on Japanese subjects, after the method (but not the meter) of the *hokku*. The *hokku* juxtaposes two or three details which coalesce in the reader's mind, there sketching a picture, hinting a thought, conveying a compliment, or indicating some sentimental or dramatic moment. Such a poem must be just right, and the effect instantaneous; otherwise, only a riddle remains. It may be considered an experiment in economy of means. For example:

Outside a Gate

On the floor of the empty palanquin
The plum-petals constantly increase.

The plum-petals indicate that it is spring; the palanquin is the equipage of a noble; its place at the gate shows that he is visiting; the accumulation of petals shows that his visit is a long one — and to whom does one pay long visits in spring but to one's beloved? To take another spring poem:

Passing the Bamboo Fence

What fell upon my open umbrella —
A plum-blossom?

No: the reader is to guess that it is a love-letter. Another example, this time of a non-oriental landscape, is that remarkable poem 'Trees in Winter,' found later on in the volume; one section of it is —

Hemlocks:

Coned green shadows
Through a falling veil.

In these nine syllables she conveys a three dimensional shape, the colors of green and white modified, and the immobility of the trees contrasted with the motion of the snow.

The seven 'Chinoiseries' which follow 'Lacquer Prints' are longer and consequently do not rely on those concentrated instantaneous effects. They are human situations, rather than moments. The last of them, 'Li T'ai Po,' is Amy Lowell's tribute to one she considered amongst the greatest lyrists of all times, and presents the problem of the relationship of dissipation to art.

The rest of the book has a general heading 'Planes of Personality' and is subdivided into six parts. The first of these, 'Two Speak Together,' are chiefly love poems, including the popular 'Vernal Equinox' and the famous 'Madonna of the Evening Flowers.' 'Coq d'Or,' written in the summer of 1918, is all that was saved from a projected novel in verse, which was to be entitled *Lady Waterlease*; the rhythm was based on Browning's 'Householder' (the epilogue to *Fifine at the Fair*). 'The Country House,' 'Nerves,' and 'Haunted,' all written at Dublin, sprang from the nervous state into which she frequently worked herself while writing through the night. The second of the 'Planes of Personality,' entitled 'Eyes, and Ears, and Walking,' consists of those poems which are chiefly sensorial. 'Violin Sonata by Vincent D'Indy' is dedicated to Loeffler, who played that sonata to her in his home at Medfield. 'I meant to give the limits of humanity seeking to spiritualize itself to accord with its conception of Deity, which is d'Indy's very idiom, it seems to me.'[1] 'Eucharis Amazonica' was inspired by some lilies which Mrs. Bayard Thayer sent her. 'Dolphins in Blue Water' was a study in motion suggested by a painting of Charles Woodberry's; 'Motor Lights on a Hill Road' was another such study written at Dublin.

The third part, 'As Towards One Self,' is a group of poems dealing with the position of the poet in the world. The first three describe periods of inability to write; the others are about the process of writing, its purposes, the poet's difficulties in getting understood, and the act of selling his work. 'Fireworks' is addressed to a magazine editor, 'Generations' to a younger poet, 'Entente Cordiale' to a foreign poet. The last, 'Castles in Spain,' is an

---

[1] *Boston Transcript*, May 5, 1919; quoted in an article correcting a misprint in the poem as published May 2.

extended sonnet which proclaims the endurance of art in a destructive world.

The next part, 'Plummets to Circumstance,' is more objective and intellectual in treatment; as every poem presents a thesis, a few of these may be stated here. The majority of them deal with the function of art in the world; the others are chiefly about love and passion. 'Ely Cathedral' contrasts the repulsive decay of formal religion with the beauty of the building which houses it; 'An Incident' (Blake's marriage) shows that religion lives with the living, even though the church be spurious. 'The Bookshop' is Miss Lowell's repudiation of poppy-seed literature: the dreams of the past are tyrannous superstition when they are allowed to dominate the poetry of the present. 'Gargoyles' proved so bewildering to the public that William Marion Reedy, who first published it in his *Mirror*, received forty letters asking what it meant. 'It is supposed to present the utter impossibility of amalgamation between the top and the bottom under the figure of an ordinary merrymaking,' Miss Lowell wrote him. When later he accepted 'Chopin' she wrote him again:

> I am sorry that you think it cryptic. It is not at all, really. It refers to an incident in Niecks's 'Life of Chopin.' You will remember that Chopin went with Madame Sand to Majorca where they lived in an ancient monastery in the hills. One day, when she and her children had been to the coast to do a little shopping and buy some of the necessities which were so few and far between, a very bad thunder storm overtook them on the way home and they were very much delayed in their return, not getting back until quite late in the evening. George Sand, in her autobiography, tells how they came in and found Chopin at the piano composing one of his preludes, that he looked up at them with a wild expression, and for a moment really believed them to be ghosts, and exclaimed excitedly, 'My God! I knew that you were dead.' You will remember that Chopin was taken very ill while at Majorca, and the quotation at the end of the poem is from a letter he wrote his publishers.

The poem simply means that no matter how difficult life seems to be at the moment, or even as it seems to the cat, other more important people have had more unpleasant things to put up with.

'Gargoyles' and 'Chopin' were experiments in applying the 'unrelated' method to ideas rather than images; we might call them a kind of symbolic impressionism; but she did not pursue this method further. 'Appuldurcombe Park,' one of the most successful poems in the book, is the tale of a woman cheated out of her right to physical love by the invalidism of a husband and the treachery of a cousin. When it was accepted for *Poetry* because it was in the vein of 'Patterns,' Miss Lowell explained it to Miss Monroe:

> I am very glad that you like 'Appuldurcombe Park.' Of course it is in the vein of 'Patterns,' but it is so different. One is a bad woman and one is a good woman. In one, the woman goes insane, in the other she does not. One is a liaison, and one real love. In fact, it is just these differences, these slight changes, that put a different phase on everything, which is to me interesting.

'Flotsam' pictures the love rejected by the flirt which is gathered casually by the maidservant. 'Little Ivory Figures Pulled with String' — another splendid poem — is a study of the aging aristocrat's bitter inability to let himself live. 'On the Mantelpiece,' the last in this section of the book, is a symbolic tale in the manner of Hans Christian Andersen: the china shepherdess (any highly bred young lady) flings away her flower at the behest of love, and then leaps disastrously after it, while the cricket (the poet) goes on singing, uninvolved and therefore unharmed.

'As Toward War,' the penultimate section of the book, contains poems symbolic and realistic. 'Misericordia' she explained in a letter to an editor.

Here is a man who has spent all his life in playing with the shows of things without any regard to their true meaning. Things have been to him largely ornament and convention, and when suddenly war breaks upon him he is overwhelmed. He feels as if the world were going to pieces, and in his horror he at first throws away the very things which had meant so much to him. The reality is so terrible that he cannot bear even to be reminded of it, and turns to art for distraction, the art being typified in the poem by the tissue-paper ballet dancer. But as time goes on he realizes the real meaning of life and the necessity of facing it bravely and uncompromisingly, and he sets to work to adjust himself to circumstances and to see meaning in the war, which at first had appeared to him only as a nightmare of terror. He realizes that it is a war of mercy, a war to save the world and to save it for peace. The war is typified by the cavalry sword upon which he carves a Pietà, namely the representation of the Virgin holding the dead Christ upon her lap — the dead Christ who has died to save the world for love.

There is my symbolism, and the title simply means Mercy. As I told you before, I consider it one of the best poems I have ever written.[1]

'Dreams in War Time' symbolize the individual's plight, in a series of weird and vivid flashes. 'In the Stadium' is a realistic record of her attitude at Joffre's review of the Harvard Regiment; 'The Fort' was a fort near Revere, where her nephew George Putnam was stationed. The last poem in this section, 'The Night Before the Parade,' expresses her bitterness over the whole futile question of war. While all Boston was preparing to celebrate the final parade of the New England troops (the 26th division), she was haunted by two lines from Poe about the ruins of an ancient civilization. The grass now crushed by the grandstands will finally conquer all.

The last section of the book, 'As Towards Immortality,' contains but a single poem, the well-known and wholly re-

[1] Letter to Harold Howland, June 3, 1918.

markable 'On a Certain Critic.' The source is a brief passage in one of Keats's letters to Reynolds, dated November 22, 1817:

> I like this place very much. There is Hill and Dale and a
> little River. I went up Box hill this Evening after the
> moon — 'you a' seen the Moon' — came down, and wrote
> some lines.

Keats at this time was working on his first long poem,
Endymion; and by certain indubitable calculations of his
progress, Miss Lowell identified the lines, probably the
loveliest in the whole work (IV, 496–502): [1]

> Full facing their swift flight, from ebon streak,
> The moon put forth a little diamond peak,
> No bigger than an unobserved star,
> Or tiny point of fairy scymetar;
> Bright signal that she only stoop'd to tie
> Her silver sandals, ere deliciously
> She bow'd into the heavens her timid head.

Endymion was that poem of his which had so entranced
her, many years ago; she recalled especially the exquisite
sensuousness of the love-scene in Book II, where the
despairing Endymion in the dark touches the 'naked
waist' of his mysterious mistress and finds solace.

Amy Lowell's poem describes John Keats on Box Hill,
working himself up into an imaginative fury over the
moon, then coming home and placidly working the material into his poem. It is the overflow of powerful emotion
(somewhat deliberately churned, to overflow), then the
tranquil recollection and the complacent, almost shame-
less, satisfaction at the result. A century later, 'a sprig
little gentleman' handles the manuscript and talks know-
ingly but in complete ignorance. He objects to Keats's
moon as a copybook maxim, quite unaware that his own
platitudes will never reach even the copybooks; he trots

[1] See her *John Keats*, 1, 446.

out his formulae about romantic solitude as though they were wisdom itself. Actually, they have absolutely no connection with Keats or *Endymion* or poetry. There is no possible way of explaining to him what it is really about.

The title 'As Towards Immortality' is perhaps to be explained by the fact that *Endymion* opens with two passages (I, 73–79, 371–392) contemptuously describing the vulgar belief in a future life, and that it closes with the hero married to a goddess and himself immortal. But John Keats's immortality, according to Amy Lowell's poem, is in his poetry. And of what does such immortality consist? Of academic lectures? Certainly not! For the 'sprig little gentleman,' essentially nameless, whatever name he might have in the flesh, is a characterization of the academic type. It is he who is doomed to extinction, if we can suppose that one who has never lived the life of the imagination can be said to die. The ironies become complicated.

CHAPTER XX

THREE OPERATIONS

'We cannot stand up with the poets of the world unless we do something that shall be not only beautiful technically or in a scrappy way, but that shall have a large significance.'

As soon as *Pictures of the Floating World* was out, Miss Lowell hurried up to Dublin, to close the sale of Broomley Lacey and get her furniture. She returned, to find herself a best-seller in non-fiction, but with no books to sell. The first edition of *Pictures* had been completely distributed before publication date; now the printers' strikes prevented the issuing of the second edition until November. But this very difficulty of getting her book added to its success, and her morning mail was filled with letters of congratulations from friends and strangers.

Her eyes were not yet adjusted to her glasses; each lens had to be ground three times, and even then she felt the strain for a while. Then she broke her glasses, and paced the floor with a headache instead of sleeping. Yet she wrote a memorial article on Helen Bullis Kizer, which was published in the *Times Book Review*; and also arranged to write an introduction for little Hilda Conkling's book of poems, another introduction for Lucy G. Morse's book of silhouettes (a book she herself had suggested, as she was exceedingly fond of Mrs. Morse's silhouettes in her light-screens), and yet another introduction for three diaries of Japanese court ladies, translated by Elsie Sergeant's aunt, Annie Shepley Omori. She was also writing lectures.

D. H. Lawrence was determined to come to America; now Gilbert Cannan and Waldo Frank approached her, hoping she would make the trip possible. But she was sure it was a mistake, she wrote them. Lawrence had no idea what the place was really like. He could sell almost nothing here, and get no lecture dates at all, on account of the prejudice against his books. He might even be excluded, on account of his tuberculosis; his wife, as a German, certainly could not be admitted for some time yet; and after he got here, who would look after him to the end? She would be glad to contribute to a fund, but could not guarantee all the expenses. He would come here, only to meet a cruel disappointment, and die in a foreign land, separated from his wife.

On October 3, 1919, she entertained Mr. and Mrs. John Drinkwater, whom she found wholly delightful; another permanent friendship was formed. They had come over for the New York production of his *Lincoln*. On the 14th, she spoke before the State Federation of Women's Clubs, at the Copley Plaza. On the 20th, she went to the opening night of Charles Hanson Towne's version of Offenbach's *La Belle Hélène*. On the 25th, she repeated her lecture, 'Modern Poetry; its Differences, its Aims, its Achievements,' at a joint meeting of the Massachusetts Library Club and the Western Massachusetts Library Club at Springfield.

She was not well: she had risen from her bed to keep some of her appointments, while she had been obliged to cancel others. But on November 7, she read at Montclair, New Jersey, prefacing her poems with a modified abridgment of her librarian lecture; on the 9th, she read at Saint Mark's In-the-Bouwerie, New York, to 921 people; and on the next evening to 720 students at Columbia University. On the 11th, she went to Philadelphia, where A. Edward Newton was to give her a dinner, but had to cancel it on account of a heart-attack. On the next evening, she gave a new lecture, 'Walt Whitman and the New Poetry,'[1] at the Contemporary Club of Philadelphia, in

---

[1] Published in the *Yale Review* (XVI, 502-19), April, 1927; included in *Poetry and Poets*.

their celebration of the Whitman Centenary — an event of which they were making much, as theirs was the only club to which Whitman had ever belonged.

This lecture was the occasion of the last public row over the New Poetry in which Miss Lowell was involved; in a letter to Winifred Bryher (February 3, 1920) she characterized it as 'without exception the most stupid and virulent attack to which I have ever been subjected.' For some time now she had felt the futility of public debates; and it had been her custom to try to prevent them in advance. As she wrote to H. D. later (February 3, 1920) about the fracas: 'I had especially stipulated that there should be no discussion. I think that the time for discussing the new poetry has gone by. I am willing to talk about it, explain it, anything, but I will not stand up to be badgered even with the result, as always happens, of my beating my opponents.' She was to be the main speaker; three others were to talk briefly afterwards. Two of these gentlemen, as one learned from the subsequent correspondence, had not been notably successful with their own conventional verses. 'You find some of them in every city,' Miss Lowell told a friend a few days later, 'but in Boston we've put them where they don't dare squeak.' One, who had known Whitman personally, was to talk on 'Whitman the Man'; the other preferred to talk on poetry in general, with reference neither to ancients nor moderns.

The chairman's introduction of Amy Lowell was not auspicious: he read Untermeyer's parody as one of her poems. Then her speech was the very kind to irritate idolaters. It took Whitman's greatness for granted; pointed out his limitations; declared that in general the modern poets were not indebted to him for form and cadence (in fact, he had no ear), but were indebted for his tendencies in nationalism and use of words; read from Sandburg to show the changes sixty years had brought; and concluded:

.... Whitman was — he was several things — a great voice, and a silly, flattered old man; a conceited, ardent young fellow spattered with genius, and a primitive being teased by violent animal reactions. He was a powerful original poet, with a somewhat disconcerting dash of the poseur. Singer, prophet, orator, lover of beauty, sentimentalist and often slovenly workman, his poems are that splendid paradox — himself. Magnificence punctuated with 'the things no fellow can do'; in substance, technique, fact, it is the same. To follow him is merely to imitate the pattern of his cloak. His time is past, we have ours. It is (to use the sort of language affected by his closest imitators) 'up to us.' Let us be thankful for him as we are thankful for Theocritus, and Dante, and Chaucer, and Browning. But our skies are not his, and he would be the first to wish us 'God speed' under them. Has he not written: 'Let me not dare, here or anywhere, for my own purposes, or for any purposes, to attempt the definition of Poetry, nor answer the question what it is. Like Religion, Love, Nature, while those terms are indispensible, and we all give a sufficiently accurate meaning to them, in my opinion no definition that has ever been made sufficiently encloses the name Poetry; nor can any rule or convention ever so absolutely obtain but some great exception may arise and disregard or overturn it.'

Sane and wise words, but indeed the writing of books is dust unless we can also say with him:

> Camerado, this is no book,
> Who touches this touches a man.

Professor Spaeth spoke next; what he said was all but obliterated from the memory of man by the succeeding outburst against Miss Lowell. Hardly had he finished when the attack began.[1] The next person on the program leapt to his feet, denouncing the New Poetry. He said that the world was sick of the creatures who thought they knew

[1] My account is based on the long newspaper versions and the letters to and from Miss Lowell concerning the matter, which thoroughly substantiate my own recollections of what she told me three days later in New York.

how to write; we had had enough of them. Presently he was defending Whitman, and dilated upon his lack of recognition and the consequent suffering he had to go through.

'What do you think I am going through now?' Miss Lowell interjected.

Above the laughter he replied: 'Madam, I hope you are going through a reformation,' and continued. The chairman made no effort to stop him until Miss Lowell, reminding him of her stipulation that there should be no discussion, threatened to leave the platform. But the next speaker merely continued the tirade of abuse. He called her a 'literary hand-grenade thrower' and asserted that she had used classical quotations in one of her poems 'to cover the inadequacy of the rest.' In spite of the hisses now sounding from all parts of the hall, he extended his attack to cover all the modern poets she had named; as for Sandburg in particular, he had not known that anybody took him seriously.

'And then I slammed back good and plenty,' Miss Lowell wrote Sandburg (November 25, 1919). When she rose, she was so angry that she choked, speechless for a moment. 'As there was no way of answering these gentlemen, except by saying "You're another," I refused to answer at all, merely telling the Club that I had made this stipulation about there being no discussion, that it had been agreed to by their secretary, and that I did not think they were keeping faith with me. On the whole I think my silence scored as well as any eloquence would have done,' she informed H. D.

Afterwards, 'quite a number of people came up to me — I should think fully half those present — and registered themselves firmly on my side,' she wrote on November 25, answering a letter of indignant sympathy from Anna Coleman Ladd. But that was not the end of the tale, as it should have been.

The next morning, the *Public Ledger* featured an account of the row, which obviously was written from the point of view of the opposition. The headlines read: 'Tears Punctuate Stormy Spots in Vers Libre Debate,' and the story alleged that finally she was reduced to sobbing out her protests. The reporters called upon her at the Bellevue-Stratford, and were told she was not up yet. They waited, but got no other response all morning; consequently the next editions informed the world that Amy Lowell was suffering from a nervous breakdown as the result of her treatment at the Contemporary Club.

She rose at her customary hour, and was astounded to find herself the center of controversy in an excited city. After reading the newspaper accounts of what had happened, she had the reporters in. 'Well, boys, do I look like a person suffering from a nervous breakdown?' she asked grimly; and they admitted she did not. As for the alleged tears, 'I was plumb mad,' she said; 'I was mad, and I don't weep when I'm mad. Do I look as if I were a weeping woman?' She did not, they agreed. Then she repeated her charges of bad faith in allowing an 'organized opposition,' in spite of her stipulation. The unfortunate club secretary, in self defence, gave their official correspondence to the press, and in his apology assured her that while both he and she knew that these other persons were to speak after her, he never suspected that they would abandon their subjects to attack her.

Every book of hers in Philadelphia had been sold, and the New York bookshops were being drained of their quota to meet the Philadelphia demand.

Letters supporting her poured in upon her from America and England. In answering them, she was particularly anxious to deny that she had burst into tears. 'We did have a jolly row in Philadelphia, but I did not cry,' she wrote Hervey Allen (December 3). 'That was a little malicious touch on the part of the assistant editor of the "Public

Ledger" who was one of my hecklers. They behaved abominably; nothing that you can imagine will equal the reality.' And to Mrs. Ladd: 'My only regret about the matter was that Mr. ***** undertook to invent a little passage about my weeping which had no foundation whatever in truth. I was excited and my voice did shake, but I was never farther from tears in my life.'

Dr. Rosenbach made a point of giving luncheons for visiting personages; but because she never lunched, he gave her a dinner instead, on the 13th, which was one of the most exotic affairs she ever attended. The Pennells and the Newtons were among the guests. After dinner, they wandered through the galleries; Miss Lowell gave a delightful talk as they turned over the treasures in the book department. Breakfast was served at 5 A.M.

That evening, Miss Lowell dined with the students at Bryn Mawr, and read to them afterwards. The girls themselves paid for her reading out of the proceeds of a volume of their own poems; the place was crowded, even to the passage behind the stage. After the reading, Miss Lowell went on to New York, to spend a day or so. Here she saw Lucy Gibbons Morse, and talked over her preface for the book of reproductions of Mrs. Morse's light-screens. She also saw John Drinkwater, who brought a cold with him, which she caught, and therefore was unable to do anything more, even to go to the huge Grolier Club exhibition of Blakes. She was expected to read at Grand Rapids, Michigan, and Nashville, Tennessee; but she cancelled these engagements.

In December, the *Egoist* stopped publication, and the *Dial* was bought by Scofield Thayer, who transformed it into a *Seven Arts* without politics. *Pictures of the Floating World* went into its third edition; Basil Blackwell agreed to publish her books in London, beginning with *Can Grande's Castle* — a choice which seemed to her dubious, as she feared it was too original for a starter. In spite of her bad eyes, she finished another long poem, the 'Legend of Porcelain,' and began casting about for an Indian subject; she wrote a tribute to Edwin Arlington Robinson for Percy MacKaye's collection of tributes, to be published in the *Times* on the 21st to celebrate Robinson's fiftieth birthday; and she spent long hours over the manuscript of Magdelaine Hutchinson's translation of *Tendencies*. On December 9, she thanked Waldo Frank for a copy of his *Our America*, which she enjoyed very much, though differing on certain points.

I think you have misunderstood your Puritans, somewhat. Personally I believe them to have been an extremely high-spirited and vigorous race. Indeed, the fact that they could stand up so many years under such fearfully restricting laws and customs proves them to have had no common amount of energy and vitality. It is the descendants of those people whose energy has petered out under generations of such laws that have been the difficulty, and no one in the world, in spite of his splendid volume, represented so well the inertia of the worn-out race as did Mr. Henry Adams. I wish you had known him as I did. It was a lesson in what not to make of your life, as he recognized himself, poor old fellow, recognized to the extent of pen and paper but never to any farther extent. There is something infinitely pathetic about this old man who had let all life slip by while he lacked the energy to do other than contemplate it. Seeing himself clearly and uncompromisingly, he wrote for his own private instruction and the eyes of a few sympathetic friends the terribly ironic estimate of himself. That he blamed it all on his education shows that he was not above human weaknesses. It was not his education; it never is any one's education. Any one with vigour and energy can educate himself out of almost nothing at all. It was not his education, it may have been his blood. The answer is that he could not transcend his blood, and that again was probably not his fault; but it was not an inspiring spectacle in the life, however it may be in the book.

On the same day, having learned that Harriet Monroe had rejected Grace Hazard Conkling's review of *Pictures of the Floating World*, Miss Lowell wrote to Miss Monroe, reminding her of the attacks (by Kreymborg and Alice Corbin Henderson) which she had published, and accusing her of 'complete suppression of everything in my favour.' She suggested that Sandburg do the review, but Miss Monroe had already given the task to Marjorie Seiffert.

About the middle of the month she noticed a swelling near the wound of her operation. A stitch had broken, probably because of her coughing when she had influenza. The operation would have to be repeated; the indications were that it would be more difficult this time. But as it did not have to be done immediately, she postponed it till after her January lecture tour.

So she enjoyed Christmas thoroughly, and wrote to Mrs. Russell's daughter a full account.

> I wish you had seen me last night at the Christmas party. I behaved really abominably. We had crackers with caps and little toys in them, and the real trouble was that all the people did not have the ones with toys, and some had only caps. Now both my niece and nephew present have families of children, and of course their one desire was to grab these toys and take them home, and my one desire was to save them for your children. Katherine Putnam looked across at me where I was hugging a little figure of Pickwick, and said, 'Do give me that, Aunt Amy. You haven't any children.' Whereupon I secreted it jealously in the folds of my napkin and said, 'Certainly I have, and I am not going to let anybody have any more.' I had a dreadful feeling when I left that I had been rather rude about it, but between your mother and me, we managed to grab five figures, a ten pin set, and a grid-iron, all of which will go to you in due course. I decided that the little figures were absolutely necessary to be customers in Sonny's shop, and although I have no doubt they are undersize for that occupation, nevertheless they may be useful. I think they cannot be sucked,

which is too bad as I suppose Alan would enjoy sucking them, but somehow the paint on them looks as if it would suck off if a tongue were applied real vigorously.

Now, my dear, I must stop, and write to your son, a far harder task than writing to you....

DEAR SONNY BOY:

I hope you had a nice Christmas. Did you play with your grocery shop, and did you go out on your sled? We had a Jack Horner pie, too, for dinner, and I got a funny pipe to play on with a balloon on one end. I am sending it to you. We also had some crackers which snapped when you pulled them, and inside were little men and women. Your Nanna is sending you some of them, and perhaps they would like to buy something out of your grocery shop.

I got your lovely card this morning with your name written on it. What a fine boy you are to be able to write so well. I send love and kisses to you and Allen.

On December 27, an interview, 'What is the "New Poetry"?' was published in the New York *Evening Post*: Miss Lowell ended it with a few firm, contemptuous sentences directed at the 'colyumists' who these many years had found the New Poetry excellent material for lightening the drudgery of the diurnal wise-cracks; and Miss Lowell, of course, had always been particularly good copy. In flippancy rather than malice (all of them affected literary taste, and many of them really admired her personality), they had steadily poured forth a mechanical and vulgar ridicule upon her poetry and her ideals, even her size and her family name. Separately, each item was as harmless as it was tasteless; but the great mass of them, as they accumulated in her scrapbooks, proved a very bad habit which had gone far towards turning her into a national joke. Now she struck back.

One of the hardest battles that the new poetry has waged has been against the pettiness, the stupidity, and the ignorance of the so-called 'free press.' There is an incurable desire prevalent in all American newspapers to make fun of everything in season and out.... If I had my way, there would be no mention of literature at all in the American newspapers.

Look at the 'colyums' in the daily papers. These are not funny, and yet they pass as being so.... They are ghastly and pitiful....

The colyumists, thus denied either literary taste or wit, found themselves for once on the defensive. Surprised and hurt, they replied that she was unfair. Franklin P. Adams, in the *Tribune* for December 30, disagreed vehemently: he said that the newspapers gave the poets publicity, and that Miss Lowell, in her attack, was merely seeking publicity in her own way. Then on February 20, 1920, he with Don Marquis, Christopher Morley, and Baird Leonard felt it necessary to take issue with her again; but thereafter they preserved a dignified silence about all of her doings. Which was exactly what she wanted.

There was a method in my madness; I realized that after a little adverse screaming the columnists would leave me alone, for I personally was more willing to do without the notoriety they conferred for the sake of the dignity their silence would bring. Since then they have let me conspicuously alone, which I suppose they think is paying me back. Not one of them seems to have been bright enough to understand that that was exactly my object in making the remark.[1]

Meanwhile the Christmas cold snap had brought zero weather; Winky insisted on staying out in it for four hours, and was so ill that he had to be sent to the hospital.

January, 1920, was a month of desperate lecturing, made miserable by the impending operation. On the 5th, she talked about the new poetry and read her poems before the Century Club of Springfield. After clearing up her correspondence (and sending $100 to D. H. Lawrence), she set

[1] Letter to Theodore Maynard, March 14, 1922.

out for New York on the 10th. The next day she read her
entire 'Bronze Horses' in the Hall of St. Mark's-in-the-
Bouwerie; when even the window-ledges were crowded
with people, the doors had to be locked against later ar-
rivals. On Monday the 12th, she went to Philadelphia, to
work all night with Magdelaine Hutchinson over the
French translation of *Tendencies*. On Tuesday afternoon,
she read before the Philomusian Club; as she had hurt her
foot, she sat while she read. When she asked a woman in
the front row, 'Does the light from my reading lamp shine
in your eyes?' she was touched with the reply: 'No, something else shines.' Afterwards she dined with Mr. Newton
and Mrs. Pennell, then took the train back to New York.
On Wednesday, she gave a long deferred lecture, 'Some
Musical Analogies,' at Columbia, going to see Drinkwater's *Lincoln* in the evening. The next day she spent
with her publishers; on the next (the 16th) she read her
poems to the Cherry Valley Club in Garden City. On
Sunday the 18th, she was given a reception by the Pen
and Brush Club (and protested later, when a conversation
of hers there was given to the newspapers); then she dined
with the Henry Holts. On the 19th, she read to the undergraduate Short Story Club at Wesleyan University,
Middletown, Connecticut, reaching home the next day.
On the 21st, she addressed the New England Women's
Press Club at a dinner in the Bellevue, Boston, explaining
how the country was turning to the reading and writing of
poetry. On the 23d, she visited the Grolier Club exhibition
of Blake's books and paintings, which had been moved to
the Fogg Art Museum at Cambridge and augmented by
various Boston items. On the 24th, she sent off the revised manuscript of eighteen Chinese poems to Florence
Ayscough. She also thanked Mr. Newton for the gift of
the proof-sheets of Whitman's *Passage to India* — a very
happy recompense for her experience over Whitman in
Philadelphia. She owned the manuscript already. Then

she prepared herself for her operation 'to pick up the dropped stitch,' on January 29th.

But she caught a cold, and the danger of 'ether pneumonia' caused a postponement to February 5th. She took advantage of the respite to hear John Drinkwater lecture in Boston on the 3d. On the 4th, she sent off the scenario of a ballet based on her Peruvian legend to Edward Burlingame Hill, for him to set. Another request for these rights she had to refuse. John Alden Carpenter was anxious to write new music to her translation of Rostand's *Pierrot Qui Pleure*. But none of these projects were realized eventually. Meanwhile, what odd moments she had she spent in gathering material for her next long poem. 'I have been reading Parkman's "Oregon Trail,"' she wrote Sara Teasdale, 'until I feel Indians leaping out from behind the bookcases and pouring down from the chandeliers and get so nervous that I have to go to bed.'

February 5 came, and with it such a terrible blizzard that the doctors could not possibly reach Sevenels. Two days later, snowbound Sevenels was just being dug out. But at last, on the 10th, the operation was performed.

Restless nights with little sleep followed; but apparently it had been successful. As had been prophesied, however, it was much more severe than the first one. Mrs. Russell and the secretaries had to take over her correspondence; not till the 28th was she even dictating notes again. Meanwhile Mrs. Russell had to leave suddenly for Washington: her younger grandson had died, and her daughter was prostrated; and the shock of this to Miss Lowell delayed her recovery considerably. Then, before she was able to leave her room, she was kept there by a severe cold, another wave of a world epidemic which reached even Sevenels. Her surgeon came down with some trouble; another, who was unacquainted with her operation, had to be called in.

She began to resume her correspondence. Lawrence had written her from Capri on February 13:

My dear Amy

Today I have your letter, and cheque for thirteen-hundred Lire. How very nice of you to think of us this New Year. But I wish I needn't take the money: it irks me a bit. Why can't I earn enough, I've done the work. After all, you know, it makes one angry to have to accept a sort of charity. Not from you, really, because you are an artist, and that is always a sort of partnership.... I am a sort of charity-boy of literature, apparently. One is denied one's just rights, and then insulted with charity. Pfui! to them all — But I feel you & I have a sort of odd congenital understanding, so that it hardly irks me to take these Liras from you, only a little it ties me up. However, one must keep one's trust in a few people, & rest in the Lord.

I am extremely sorry you are not well, and must have an operation. Such a thought is most shattering. Pray to heaven it won't hurt much & will make you right....

No, don't go to England now, it is so depressing and uneasy and unpleasant in its temper. Even Italy isn't what it was, a cheerful insouciant land. The insouciance has gone. But still, I like the Italians deeply: and the sun shines, the rocks glimmer, the sea is unfolded like fresh petals. I am better here than in England. — Things are expensive, and not too abundant. But one lives for the same amount, about, as in England: and freer to move in the air and over the water one is, all the while. Southwards the old coast glimmers its rocks, far beyond the Siren Isles. It is very Greek — Ulysses' ship left the last track in the waves. Impossible for Dreadnoughts to tread this unchangeable morning-delicate sea.

Frieda came down to Florence from Germany: a bit thinner & wiser for her visit. Things are wretchedly bad there. I must have food sent all the time to F's mother from England, & for the children — there absolutely isn't enough to eat.

We have got two beautiful rooms here at the top of this old palace, in the very centre of Capri, with the sea on both hands. Compton Mackenzie is here — a man one can trust and like.... — But Capri is a bit small, to live on. Perhaps I shall go to the mainland — perhaps not. Anyway this address will always find me. — I have just begun a new novel.

I feel we shall see you in Italy. I do hope you will be better. Is Mrs. Russell with you always? A thousand greetings from both.

D. H. LAWRENCE

And on March 9, while the Fascist revolution was brewing, he wrote her again from Taormina: there was some trouble about the cheque she had sent, so he asked her to stop it and send another, in dollars.

We have come here, and taken such a lovely house in a garden, for a year. It costs 2000 £. It is really lovely. Only travelling is so trying and so expensive.

There are real good hotels here. If you are well enough, perhaps you will come, during the course of our year.

I do wish you felt well & strong. Tell me if you get the various books I have ordered to be sent to you.

Italy feels shaky — Europe altogether feels most insecure. There'll be another collapse soon. Mais à la guerre comme à la guerre.

Send me a line to say how you are.

On March 15, H. Buxton Forman's library was sold at New York. It included a copy of the rare first edition of Keats's *Lamia*, inscribed 'F. B. from J. K.' — Keats's presentation copy to Fanny Brawne. Miss Lowell felt that she must have it for her collection, and engaged Dr. Rosenbach to bid for her, on the principle (as she explained to somebody else) that 'I have always found that it was necessary to stifle the opposition in auction sales, and the only way to do so is by getting the opposition on your side.' After several letters, she telegraphed him on the crucial day: 'Get it and good luck!' In the evening, he telephoned from New York; it was hers for $4050.00, the top price paid for any single book the opening day of the sale.

She got down to dinner for the first time on March 22. As soon as the meal was over, she opened the safe in her library, to make sure that her collection of manuscripts was all right. When the door swung back, however, she saw a ghastly sight: the whole interior was leprous with mildew, and everything was soaking wet. Someone had left a pail of water inside; and as the safe was air-tight, and the pail of lime left there to absorb any superfluous moisture had of course proved wholly inadequate, the evaporating water had been absorbed by everything that could possibly do so.

Grimly she had the furnace drafts opened, and all the fires in the fireplaces lighted; then she, her guest (S. F. Damon), and Mrs. Russell, who had just returned, set to work drying the things out. On the registers and in front of the fireplaces were ranged all the great dead — Blake and Mme. Pompadour and Jane Austen and Ben Jonson and Charlotte Brontë and Voltaire and Beethoven and all the others. Miss Lowell herself took charge of the 'Eve of St. Agnes' — a tissue-paper manuscript, that every time she passed, fluttered off the back of a chair and curved determinedly toward the roaring blaze. The guest left after midnight, to catch the last car to Boston; but she worked on till the dawn, preserving her collection. When Mrs. Russell rose, she found Miss Lowell not only exhausted but alarmed about her wound. A muscle had slipped; when it returned to place, a strange lump remained. She was told not to lift anything, and to wait.

A consolation arrived: Mr. Newton gave her a lock of Fanny Brawne's hair, which he had bought at the Forman sale.

Professor Allan Abbott of Columbia sent her some pamphlets, 'Exercises in Judging Poetry,' which he used in his experiments to study the nature and extent of poetic appreciation. Each pamphlet contained thirteen poems in four states: one was the original, the other three were rewritten with intent to spoil the meter, imagination, or sentiment. His selections ranged from Mother Goose to Shakspere (the authors were not named, however), and included Miss Lowell's own 'Sea Shell.' She picked all the original versions except a passage from Milton; and when he wrote her that he was rather severely disillusioned by the general results of his experimentation, she replied:

23 March, 1920

MY DEAR PROFESSOR ABBOTT:

Your letter of March 19th is very interesting. I do not wonder that you are discouraged at the result of your questions, but, really, I think that the whole thing springs from a mistaken point of view on your part and on the parts of so many other people. Appreciation of poetry is rather a rare quality, the writing of it rarer still. It is to my mind absolutely quixotic to suppose that most people have any real appreciation of poetry at all; most people have none. It is one of the highest functions of the human brain and appeals only to people who have it instinctively or who have slowly and gradually trained a small faculty to a greater knowledge and appreciation. It does not necessarily exist with other intellectual faculties: it has to be born in one. It appears in the masses as well as in the classes; quite as much in one as in the other. It is rare in every grade of society. I have my doubts whether it can be cultivated at all unless there is a very strong bias there beforehand.

As to your Professor of Literature who chose the 'Tender, tender Sea Shell,' my experience with Professors of Literature is that they have less instinctive knowledge of literature than almost any one else.

I hope that the great fallacy of the democratisation of the arts will sometime give place to a more reasonable outlook on the subject, and we shall no longer be surprised at failures such as you have encountered, but rather place the arts in the unique and elevated position where they should naturally be, and so regard those persons, capable of development in them, as they used to be regarded, namely, as persons apart and, in their own particular region, better equipped than the mass of mankind.

We do not expect school children to understand the higher mathematics. We know perfectly well that when you get into the upper regions of mathematics, the people capable of comprehension are exceedingly few, a mere handful throughout the world. Art is more universal than mathematics, but it requires as distinctive a faculty, both for comprehension and for creation. To a certain extent it can be stimulated and cultivated, but unless there is a spark of original instinct in one, I am convinced that nothing can be done. As I told a girls' school some time ago, there is no necessity for liking poetry. If you do not like it, let it alone. You will lose, but that is all the harm that will be done. I doubt whether anybody can learn to like poetry by trying. It is like adding a cubit to one's stature.

That your tests are admirable for finding out how much or little a person has of this faculty is indubitable. The value of them is the undeniable proof of how few people have it.

You certainly have me on the Milton lines. I fell down badly there. But, really, may I compliment you by saying that, with the exception of the cliché 'rich and rare' and the short foot in the fourth line, I think you have got the very jargon of the Miltonic utterance, and I liked your last two lines very much indeed, although I confess that Milton's 'spher'd and radiant cloud' almost urged me to choose the right stanza. Your excellent 'raindrops' and 'rainbows' threw me off the scent. But then I admit that Milton at his most Miltonic is so antipathetic to me that an imitation sounds a good deal like an original in my ear....

If your endeavour will only prove to you how little most people can understand poetry, and persuade you to realize how rare indeed is the instructed teacher of literature, it will certainly not have been in vain.

Sincerely yours,

A tonsil infection persisted; the tendency to hernia remained; she was generally run down; so she agreed not to
make any more engagements until June 1, when she was
to deliver the Phi Beta Kappa poem at Columbia. She remained in the house, reading up for this poem, the more
gladly as the spring was late (snow and freezing weather
continued well into April). On the 5th, she wrote to Elsie
Sergeant, who was in Santa Fé:

> How I envy you dashing round and seeing these cere-
> monies in Holy Week! It is just what I should like to do
> now above all things, for my Indian legend is crystallising
> in my mind, and it is fearfully hard to get everything out
> of books, and I know if I could see some of their ceremonial
> dances I could do something worth while. What is so fear-
> fully handicapping is that in all the books they say: 'Here
> they sing songs' — and then they do not give the songs or
> only a word or two of them, and when they do they are
> not well translated. There have been a good many songs
> of the Pueblo Indians, done by poets, which have appeared
> in 'Poetry' from time to time, but I do not know how
> authentic they are, although they are very interesting....
> I have got a splendid skeleton for my legend from one
> of the Smithsonian publications which Mr. Lowes lent me.
> This is an Alaskan Indian legend, but it is so arranged that
> I think I can have all the Indians lumped together: Alaskan,
> Plains, and Pueblo. This sounds a bit mixed up, but I
> do not think it will when I tell you the framework. As I
> read them up, by far the most interesting of all to me are
> the Pueblos. I would give anything to see a Hopi snake
> dance or a corn dance or some of those dedications to Spring
> I am reading about. The Hunting and Fishing Indians
> seem to me much more elementary, and the fragments of
> their songs that I have been able to get hold of are nothing
> like as interesting as the little snippets I have seen from the
> Southern tribes. The whole thing is immeasurably diffi-
> cult to do; I think harder than anything I have tackled be-
> cause I have never thought anything about Indians before-
> hand, and it is all new. I am wild to get at the Pueblos, but

I began with the Plains Indians, and am stuck in them now, pushing and hauling to get away. I have only been working a week, but I find that my appetite for work is, if anything, enhanced, and it does not seem to tire me much, which I think is rather surprising as I am not yet able to go out doors. That means two solid months in the house, and most of it in one room, and the greater proportion in bed. I am up and dressed now and downstairs as usual in the evenings....

Please note down everything you can about these Indian dances, particularly colours and things that nobody records, and then stick them on paper and send them to me. I never have forgotten your description in France of the horizon-blue uniforms of the officers against the grey of the villages. That is the kind of thing I want: colour, atmospheric effect, all the queer, outlandish things, the things that only a poet and a painter see, and I know you can give them to me. I can get their symbolism here, and a rough description out of books, but I cannot get the atmosphere, the sounds, and the clash of one colour on another, and the whole under that blue sky. So pass it along, there's a dear, and I will do my best with it.

She allowed herself all of April for the necessary reading, and did not expect to start the actual writing until May.

Among the many requests for permission to set poems of hers to music was a letter from George Antheil, a seventeen-year-old modernist composer, who interested her so much that she replied at some length.

I have but one piece of advice to give you in the matter of setting these poems to music: it is what I should give to a young poet under the same circumstances, which is, do not think that to be different and queer is necessarily to show originality. Do not be afraid of the old any more than you are of the new. Be yourself, and have everything you do justified by your main theme. The bizarre may be enormously original, or it may be simply the weakness of a personality not strong enough to find its own idiom....

I usually charge ten dollars apiece for setting my poems, but I imagine that fifty dollars may be rather a staggerer for you, so supposing we leave the question of payment out of the matter until I hear your settings, and I have no doubt we can come to some terms that will be satisfactory to both of us. I shall not hold you up on money if I like your songs. It is no use setting these things of mine in the old-fashioned modes, and I shall be glad to see somebody with your point of view and energy have a try at them.

Another letter that provoked a long answer came from Professor Waitman Barbe, of West Virginia University, who inquired what in her opinion was the trouble with professors of English. She replied on April 28:

MY DEAR MR. BARBE:

Your letter of April 21st opens up a vast field. I cannot possibly tell you in the space of a correspondence what I consider to be the matter with the teaching of English in our colleges. That there is something very markedly the matter is my firm conviction, and I think I could best sum it up by saying that literature is being more and more taught as a science and less and less as an art. In other words, the imaginations of the pupils are not stimulated by literature per se. They are made to dwell far more upon the history of literature and upon its philological import and its various antiquarian connotations than they are upon the construction of it as an art and its imaginative and dramatic suggestion. I think the so-called variorum method has done a great deal of harm in the teaching of literature; that it may be necessary for advanced students I do not deny, but it has usurped the place of literature treated as one of the humanities. I remember a course of Shakespeare which I took for two years... which I think did me incalculable harm.

Of course one reason that it is so difficult to teach literature as an art is that so few teachers know enough of the art in question to be able to impart their knowledge or their enthusiasm. After all there is nothing which inoculates like the disease itself. If one is genuinely devoted to literature in all its branches one cannot fail to hand on the germ of enthusiasm to one's pupils. If one is not, the pupil will get nothing but bare bones. Let us cultivate a delight in literature before we undertake to force analysis; that would seem to be the wisest plan. Let us try to persuade teachers to regard poetry and fiction from the aesthetic standpoint and to train their own taste and knowledge to the highest point.

She then described Professor Abbott's experiments, with their discouraging results.

It is, however, fair to remember that colleges were never designed to teach geniuses. Genius will always find its own best teacher in itself; for instance, the object of a college is to train the ordinary man to know things which he would not come upon by himself, so perhaps to expect the colleges to turn out creative writers is to ask more of the curriculums than was ever intended by their designers.

Amongst the many foreign literati who were swarming over America,[1] there was occasionally someone who combined decent manners with literary achievement. Drinkwater had been one; Siegfried Sassoon was another. His was the first important voice to protest in English against the sentimental glorification of war; and Miss Lowell, who was now fighting her publisher's recommendation that her popular 'Phantasms of War' be issued in book-form, publicly supported him. The New England Poetry Club and the Harvard Poetry Society joined funds in an effort to get him to read in Cambridge, and as they still could not

---

[1] 'Since 1918 these had descended upon Chicago (and all America) like a plague of locusts, starting usually in New York and sweeping westward, devouring the pleasant verdure of greenbacks and chirping as they came. Returning to Europe, bursting with profits and spleen, they thriftily wrote of what they had seen and the result was more clever than amiable; bearing, too, the taint of bad taste.' Edna Ferber: *So Big*, New York, 1925, pp. 344–45. The Women's Cosmopolitan Club of New York, as a reaction against this invasion and as an affirmation of faith in our own writers, had planned a dinner on February 29, to be given to about ten of America's most distinguished poets. Amy Lowell's inability to attend caused the dinner to be postponed.

afford his fee, Miss Lowell paid the balance. On April 29, the poet arrived; Miss Lowell gave him a dinner; then the party motored to the Harvard Union, where the great hall was jammed. It was her first outing since her operation.

The Phi Beta Kappa poem, 'Many Swans,' was finished about the middle of May. In preparation, Miss Lowell had read sixty-three volumes — all that she could discover concerning Indian poetry and ceremonials.

Just as she was finishing it, she received an appeal from the Mayor of Hampstead, England, to organize the American branch of the committee to raise funds for buying Wentworth Place, the house where Keats wrote the 'Ode to the Nightingale.' The building was to be restored to its condition as it was during the two years that he lived there, and was also to be made into a library for Sir Charles Dilke's collection of the poet's manuscripts and books. It was hoped that all this would be done in time for the centenary of Keats's death next year. Although she had never tried to collect money before, Miss Lowell accepted the post, organizing the Boston branch (which met on May 24) and inviting prominent persons to establish branches in New York, Philadelphia, Providence, and Chicago.

After a medical examination, which proved beyond question that the trouble in her wound was a stretched fascia, which could never be remedied, she left for New York on May 31. On June 1, she dined with the Phi Beta Kappa society at Columbia, afterwards reading her 'Many Swans,' as the poem of the occasion. Elected an honorary member of the New York Delta chapter, she was thereafter entitled to wear the key. On the evening of June 3, she addressed the staff of the Brooklyn Public Library on 'Modern Poetry for Librarians.'

From New York, she went on to Waco, Texas, to receive the degree of Litt. D. in the Jubilee Commencement celebrating the Diamond Anniversary of Baylor University.

President Samuel Palmer Brooks had determined to make the occasion memorable; fifty-six honorary Litt. D's were to be conferred. Miss Lowell reached her suite at the Hotel Raleigh on the 14th, too late to join Edwin Markham, Vachel Lindsay, Judd Mortimer Lewis, and Harriet Monroe (the other poets to be honored), in reading poems on the occasion of the presentation of a bronze cast of the clasped hands of the Brownings, given by Lillian Whiting. That evening, she attended a dinner for the ladies.

The next day, the Department of English gave the 'Diamond Jubilee Luncheon' at the Raleigh, in honor of the five poets. Lindsay read his 'General Booth'; John Avery Lomax sang some of his cowboy songs (and a rhythm started in her brain — sign that a poem was to be written); two of Markham's poems were sung; and a negro double quartette from Paul Quinn College performed their folk melodies. When the lunch was over, Miss Lowell invited Mr. Lomax to her rooms; astonished him by lighting a cigar; and chatted about his ballad collection and Baylor.

At three o'clock she lectured on 'Vers Libre and Imagism,' with selections from her own poems, in the English Lecture Rooms. Later, she went to the President's reception, and in the evening attended the President's dinner at Georgia Burleson Hall.

Commencement was celebrated the next day, June 16, with the thermometer at 106 Fahrenheit. The academic procession formed at 9 o'clock; and she was on the campus in cap and gown, being 'movie-pictured and kodaked.' [1] The ceremonies began at 10, the honorary degrees of course being reserved for the end of the morning. The heat in-

[1] Henry Trantham's *Diamond Jubilee, a Record of the Seventy-fifth Anniversary of the Founding of Baylor University* [Waco], 1921, contains a full account of the occasion. Miss Lowell's official photograph occupies page 47; an outline of her Tuesday lecture is on page 48; while page 49 is filled with 'Madonna of the Evening Flowers.' The President's citation is on page 129; on page 171 is an excellent snapshot of Miss Lowell on the campus while the procession was forming.

creased; Edwin Markham, who sat next her, removed
coat, tie and collar, in spite of her efforts to prevent it, by
sheer strength of arm, with the assistance of Lindsay who
sat on her other side. 'I wish you could have seen us, fifty-
eight strong, lined up on the platform of a Billy Sunday
sort of tabernacle, receiving our degrees with the perspira-
tion rolling in streams off our faces, all wound up in silk
gowns, velvet hoods, and generally rumpled finery!' she
wrote Abbie Brown on July 7. The president's citation
was:

> Amy Lowell, born in New England and proud of the fact;
> educated in private schools and in the library of your
> parents and by your own determination; bearing a name
> honored and dear to the history of this country, noted for
> its scholars, statesmen, poets and preachers — by virtue of
> your versatility as a poet evidenced on our platform here,
> evidenced and reechoed by your fellow scholars, we have
> pleasure in conferring upon you the honorary degree of
> Doctor of Literature and admitting you to all the rights
> and privileges that pertain to this degree.

Edwin Markham was on the same train going north,
and quite won her heart. 'I learned to know his worth and
to appreciate his fine generous, unselfish nature; and with
this knowledge has come appreciation of much that he
says and tolerance when he grows a trifle garrulous,' she
wrote Jessie Rittenhouse in August. She wrote 'Texas' on
the way, and found herself unusually prolific when she
reached home, about the solstice.

On her return, she plunged into the new poems which
the trip had inspired, and also took up the matter of the
Keats fund, which was encountering difficulties. Committees had been formed only in Boston and New York,
and even there the money was coming in too slowly. A
Keats Memorial Volume was being planned to provide additional funds for Wentworth House; she contributed the
'lost Woodhouse letter' from her collection, with an ex-

planatory note, thus making the volume a Keats 'first.' There were many letters to answer. One from D. H. Lawrence sounded like his old self.

Fontana Vecchia
Taormina, Sicily
1st June 1920

MY DEAR AMY

...

I have been very busy here at Taormina, and have finished a novel which I hope may get serialised, and then I shall be quite well off. Secker is to do it in England. He will also do the Rainbow again, and Women in Love, the sequel to The Rainbow. In New York, Thomas Seltzer, of 5 West 50th Street, is doing a limited edition of Women in Love, 2 vols., 15 dollars — he says. I shall tell him to send you a copy, and I hope you'll like it because I consider it my best novel. — Seltzer will also, I suppose, do the new novel *The Lost Girl*; but I want to get this serialised first, perhaps in The Century, which Secker suggests.

We went to Malta, and it was so hot I feel quite stunned. I shouldn't wonder if my skin went black and my eyes went yellow, like a negro's. The south is so different from the north. I believe morality is a purely climatic thing.

The bougainvillia creeper is bright magenta, on the terrace here, and through the magenta the sea is dim blue and magical, summer-white. Nearly all the strangers have gone from Taormina, we are alone with the natives, who lie about the streets with a sort of hopeless indifference. Here the past is so much stronger than the present, that one seems remote like the immortals, looking back at the world from their other world. A great indifference comes over me — I feel the present isn't real.

The corn is already cut, under the olive orchards on the steep, sloping terraces, and the ground is all pale yellow beneath the almonds and the vines. It is strange how it is September among the earth's little plants, the last poppy falling, the last chicory flower withered, stubble and yellow grass and pale, autumn-dry earth: while the vines are green and powerful with spring sap, and the almond trees, with ripe almonds, are summer, and the olives are timeless. Where are we then?

We love our Fontana Vecchia, where we sit on our ledge and look far out, through the green, to the coast of Greece. Why should one travel — why should one fret? Why not enjoy the beautiful indifference. Earnestness seems such bad taste, with this coast in view.

But Frieda is a bit scared of the almighty sun. She.hankers after Germany, after the Schwarzwald — fir-trees, and dewy grass. She makes plans that we shall go north to Baden in August, for a couple of months. But I don't know. It costs so much, to travel, and is such a horrible experience nowadays, particularly in Italy.

We send you two bits of Taormina work. The women sit in the streets all day long, and do it. It is what the loom was to the pagan women, Penelope or Phaedra. Only the pagan women were indoors in some upper room, while these women sit together in the street, week after week, year after year. In the South there is no housework: no one knows what a Hausfrau is. Soup is boiled at evening, when the light fades. While the long day lasts the women sit with their frames in the street, dark, palish, intent, rather like industrious conspirators, working and talking: a wee bit sinister, as pagan women always seem to me sinister.

The brown strip, Frieda says, is for a dress or coat or something: the cushion is amusing. I wonder how many hours of Taormina life they represent. The women are Greek here — not Italian: lean and intense. The coast is all Greek — Naxos buried just below us, Polyphemos' rocks in the sea way down.

Well, I hope your health is good, that's the chief thing. Your garden will be gorgeous now. We both send many good wishes. Remember me to Mrs. Russell.

D. H. Lawrence

I send you a copy of my play. Seltzer will send you another copy, which you can give away.

The first part of this letter had inquired about a cheque already sent; on the 26th he received it, and wrote her again.

So you are a Doctor by now: of Divinity I nearly said.
And shall one address you as Doctor Amy Lowell? — and
'My dear Doctor' — ? Well well — all titles seems to me
comical: even Mr. & Miss & Mrs. I like my stark name
best.

In answering a letter from J. L. French, on June 25,
Amy Lowell summed up in a few lines the whole problem
of nationalism in art:

I have said, and said often in print and elsewhere, that we
need not only the strong feeling of locality, out of which
I think all poetry springs, but the wider vision which makes
us more properly estimate ourselves. I have felt that American subjects were very proper when the poets were inspired
to write them, but that Oriental, European, or other subjects were equally proper, and that no person with strong
American blood in his veins could help being anything but
American, no matter what civilization he attempted to
portray.

There were also two gifts to be acknowledged. One,
from Waldo Frank, was a Jewish translation of the Old
Testament, in which the text was not divided into short,
numbered verses, but was printed normally as prose and
verse. The book came upon her 'with a shock of a new
discovery'; and while it did not change her own beliefs, it
gave her an understanding of the religious impulse in an
ancient civilization that she had not really felt before.
The other gift became one of her famous dinner-table
stories. On a certain hot June day, a horrible odor approached Sevenels; the heart of it was a package borne by
the distressed postman. The maid received it on the fire-
tongs and offered it to Miss Lowell, who would not touch
it.

'Take it outside and open it, and find out what it is; but
for God's sake be careful!'

It was taken outside and actually opened; but the interior was a mess of corruption quite unidentifiable through

the haze. There once had been a letter; but that was so obviously illegible by now that attempts to salvage it were not undertaken. So the mystery was hastily burned, unsolved.

Then a letter arrived from Hervey Allen, telling her that he was sending her a nice treat: some new-laid turtle eggs, in a basket woven specially for the occasion. She wrote back a restrained, courteous, but truthful note:

> Your gift conveyed everything that you would have it convey except itself. Your letter was awfully nice, with the description of the moonlight and the old turtle crawling up to lay her eggs. But alas and alack, the eggs themselves had passed into a different sphere before we received them. Much throwing round had broken them, much heat had changed their substance, and there was nothing to do but rejoice in your consideration, lament a lost delicacy, and burn them and their basket up with the greatest rapidity possible, since unfortunately the basket had got an irrevocable taint. I never eat turtle eggs and I am awfully sorry that these had passed on and could not be eaten, but some day perhaps I shall have a chance again.

July went peacefully and busily, with poems and book reviews and prefaces. The Keats money was trickling in. Guests came and went. 'Many Swans' appeared in the faithful *North American Review* for August. She dared not be very active, for the fascia was stretching badly; yet as she could not go out into the world, the world came to her gladly enough. On August 4, she wrote of her summer to Clara K. Rogers: [1]

> You ask after my report from Dr. Porter. Alas! it was anything but reassuring. Apparently the whole thing is to happen over again, and it looks as if another operation would be imperative. I myself feel that no operation will

---

[1] Clara K. Rogers had been Clara Doria, the opera singer. Her *Musical Memories* was so charming a book that Miss Lowell wrote to tell her how much she had enjoyed it; and thus another long friendship was begun.

be successful, but I am to see a specialist in New York shortly
and get his pronouncement on it.

You make me smile when you speak of the solitude of a
Brookline Summer. It is anything but a solitude. I do not
know how it happens, but there seem to be more people
round lately than for a long time past. You see Brookline
acts as a midway point between New York and all the
various Summer resorts on the coast, and people are constantly dropping in on us going up or coming down.

The other day my friend from China, Mrs. Florence
Ayscough, passed three days here and we did eighteen
Chinese poems during her stay. Then Mrs. Omori, who
translated the 'Diaries of Court Ladies of Old Japan' to
which I am writing a preface, came to have me go over the
poems in the text with her. That took another two days.
I have also accomplished a number of reviews and a couple
of poems in the month that has passed since I have been
at home. And then there are people. There is a nice, young
fellow who has written a book on Blake, who thinks no
chapter complete until he has read it to me; and there are
a couple of others who ask my advice so prettily that I
have not the heart to refuse them. Also, there is my friend,
Elsie Sergeant, who has a splendid book all of which I
have had to read during various evenings. The result has
been that we have hardly passed an evening alone since we
saw you last. I am beginning to think Brookline more full
of movement than other places people go to meet their
kind. This is, of course, nonsense, taken literally, but, as
far as poets are concerned, there are more passing through
here than I could meet in a whole summer at Newport or
Bar Harbor.

I envy you the quiet and calm of Ingonish; it sounds
perfectly delightful. And I envy you that sea bathing for
I love to swim. The other day, we motored down to Cohas-
set to dine with the Lowes. I never saw a more beautiful
place! It is right on a little brook which was the old bound-
ary between Plymouth Colony and Massachusetts Bay.
Long green meadows, with a brook turned river running
between them to the sea, dotted with huge elms. When we

got there at sunset the effect of light was most beautiful. In the evening, we sat in John Lowes' study in a house they call the Brook House right over the brook, looking out on the long line of elm trees and listening to the brook running softly beneath us. It was perfectly beautiful and so soothing!

I wish Ingonish were within motoring distance, and we could drop in and have supper with you and Mr. Rogers. But you will go to such distant parts! Both Ada and I miss you very much and our delightful, inspiring talks. We often speak of you and say how nice it will be when you get back again.

I am as busy as a bee, as you see, and I have foolishly contracted to do so many things that I have not a moment to turn round in and, when I have, I find I want to write poetry, so there is no time for play. My friends, the Untermeyers, motoring through here, passed last Sunday with us. He brought with him the proof of the 'American Miscellany,' a collection of the poems of eleven of us moderns, which is to come out next Autumn and which I think will be a splendid thing. You will have to read it, so I might as well prepare you.

Next week we are going to Chicago for my lecture before the Summer School of the University, and I rather expect to stop in New York on my way home and see the aforesaid specialist.

I wish there were forty-eight hours to a day instead of twenty-four, then you would have a great many letters from me. I always feel like writing letters when my secretaries have gone, but I have a frightful objection to writing with my own hand partly because it is so hard for any one to read it and partly, I suppose, because I write so much that I hate the mere mechanical act of it.

I am so sorry that I cannot send in for you this afternoon and bring you out here. The white clematis which is in bloom in my garden measures three inches across and is as white as a moon. It is perfectly beautiful and I have already spun it into a poem. I shall have a lot of things to show you when you come home and such a welcome to give you!

But you will write again, will you not? And I will answer, if only a little line.

You never told me how you bore the journey, but I presume from your both being well and happy that the journey has faded into a mere incident. We think a little of motoring down to the Streeters one day, but I doubt if we really get there, as we shall not get back until the twentieth of August and then I think Ada's daughter will come back to us for a little, and Autumn will be here. My long trip to the West has made the Summer seem excessively short. I feel perfectly well in spite of my probably painful future.

Ada sends her love, and you know you have mine, and tell Mr. Rogers he is included too.

I shall long to see the new chapters of your book when you come back to town; you will have been able to do a lot, I imagine. Some morning, when you are taking that cool bath in the sea, think of Ada and me sweltering in Chicago. My lectures are arranged a week apart, so that we shall be in that hot, boiling city all that time.

Again a great deal of love.

Miss Lowell's brother Lawrence was abroad, getting degrees from Oxford and Cambridge; she wrote him on August 11, just before entraining for Chicago.

I shall be very curious to hear your accounts of the attitude of France and England in regard to America. I am afraid it is quite as hostile as your letter suggested, from all I know of the matter. I am sorry to say that I was obliged to slang an anthology of the work of some young English poets in the 'Dial' lately,[1] which I am afraid will not help my popularity among my confrères when I get to England; but truth is truth, and art is art, and life is short, and I am fool enough to hope for posterity, probably groundlessly.

I am having rather a difficult time here, and I hope you will get home early enough to advise me what to do. You

[1] 'Weary Verse,' a review of *Georgian Poetry, 1918–1919*, in the *Dial* (LXIX, 424–31), October, 1920.

know I have always owned my own books, and now I am selling so many that Mr. Brett has decided that he wants to own them in the future. He has decided it in no unmeasured terms. I do not want to part with them, but I think he will push them harder if he owns them. I have sold about seven thousand volumes or so of my various books within the last year. I have been through all the burden and heat of the day with these books, and backed them when they had no sale, and now I naturally want to reap the benefit, but Mr. Brett is quite determined that I shall not do so, and in order to bring me round to his point of view, he says he must dock my percentage as his selling expenses have mounted to so high a figure that he loses on our present contracts. I rather think that is true, but I cannot receive less and make any profit over publication expenses, and the wretched old man knows that perfectly well, and he knows that will force me to accept his offer to take the volumes....

My hernia is getting rather painful again. I am to see the New York doctor in September. I know very well that they will all advise another operation, and none of them guarantees a success, and I myself believe that one might have any number of these operations, but I do not think there is any real hope of cure in my case. They all tell me that this is a very difficult thing to cure, and my age and size are against me, but to feel perfectly well and energetic and be tied by a little local thing of that sort is hard. Dr. Porter even says that I ought not to go on a sea voyage without an operation for fear of strangulation, which, of course, although not extremely likely with a hernia of this kind, is quite possible. I do think I have had enough illness in my life, and it is hard to keep up a career and do all you want to do under these difficulties. Of course we manage somehow, meanwhile I try not to think about it any more than I can help.

Excitement over the election is working up hard here. The nomination of Roosevelt for Vice-President has greatly helped the Democratic Party, helped it over the edge, I am afraid. People seem to consider Cox and Harding, and stand off in horror; but there is no doubt about it that Roosevelt is more universally popular than Coolidge. The mere nomination of Harding, a machine politician, has discouraged a good many people with the Republican Party, and the fact that Harding is against the League is doing a great deal of harm. Bessie has thrown herself heart and soul into Harding's election, and has even gone so far as to say that she thinks him not a bad choice. I do not think that so; in fact, I am very blue as to the result....

She arrived in Chicago on August 12, and read from her poems to the students of the Summer School at the University of Chicago. Leon Mandel Hall, though it had a capacity of 1200, was so full that people were standing in the aisles. Among the poems they heard was a new one, just finished, called 'Lilacs.' On the 17th, she gave her lecture, 'Walt Whitman and the New Poetry,' in the same hall, which again was over-full. On the 19th, she dined with the Aldises at Lake Forest, and on the next evening with the Sandburgs at Elmhurst. She took the train home on the 21st.

The evening at Elmhurst remained so pleasant in her mind that she wrote 'To Carl Sandburg,' a poem which she promptly mailed to him. Crossing it in the mails came a poem which he had also written about the evening.[1]

THREE NOTATIONS ON THE VISIT OF A MASSACHUSETTS
WOMAN TO THE HOUSE OF NEIGHBORS IN ILLINOIS

(for Amy Lowell)

She regrets a lost town in Vermont,
the go-by of streets she knew when a girl,
grassroots tugging at the streets and taking Main Street
in her old home town, the town of her girl memories in
    Vermont:
        and each regret is a grassroot
        and a grassroot may be strong and bitter.

[1] Published here by the kind permission of Carl Sandburg.

She regrets a horse chestnut,
a tree with a torso ten people join hands and circle round,
a buckeye dying, a tough and beautiful horse chestnut dying;
she regrets black branches must forget next year or the
    year after to set their white leaf drift of blossoms on the
    summer sky, next year or the year after when the doomed
    buckeye goes:
        and each regret
        is a high thin goose of autumn
        crying south, crying south.

She fixes the millimeters of her eye-glasses herself.
She fixes the curve of her eyesight, wishing to measure
the curve of the arch of the sky of night, the curve of the
    running hours on the level of night,
And the curve of a moon stumble across early morning,
    testimony of dawn across the first light sheets.
She measures the millimeters of her eyesight with regrets
        and each regret is a grassroot
        and each regret is a high thin goose of autumn
        crying south.

The poem was good, even though Vermont was an error.

The second week in September, Miss Lowell went on to New York for several purposes.

H. D. and Winifred Bryher were landing in New York, on their way to California. Miss Lowell met them, dined with them, read poems and gave advice, then saw them off. Next she went to her publishers, where she encountered a situation that provoked her to cancel all her contracts immediately, and to telephone to Houghton Mifflin that she was returning to them. Finally, she consulted a specialist on umbilical hernia, who prescribed a third operation as soon as possible; while he could not guarantee success, he assured her that nine cases out of ten were definitely cured. She agreed to an operation at the end of October, and returned to Brookline.

'I do not fear the operation at all,' she wrote to Miss Bryher on September 23, 'but I do terribly fear and dread the long weeks flat on my back, when I am not myself, but a hysterical maniac feeling that the ceiling is pressing itself down on my throat and I cannot breathe, and all the real world and its interests seem dissolved in a nightmare of pain and discomfort.... There is a certain awful breathlessness about these weeks preceding an operation which makes it difficult to settle down comfortably and work.'

There were poems to sell and reviews to write and Chinese translations to labor over and letters to answer. D. H. Lawrence had sent her a letter from Florence and a postcard from Venice. On the 30th, there was a meeting of the Keats fund committee: money was coming in slowly, but already the Bostonians had collected more than all England, and it was feared that the Americans were being relied on mainly. On the morning of October 12, when she was expecting to lecture on Whitman at Northampton, she woke with such a sick headache that she had to cancel the engagement. The next day she went to New Britain, to give a reading, spending the night in a Connecticut hotel. Sara Teasdale had sent her her new book, *Flame and Shadow*, only a few days before; in thanking her, Miss Lowell praised especially 'Eight O'Clock.'

> The other night I lay awake — an unusual thing for me — in a most uncomfortable hotel in Hartford, and found myself repeating that poem again and again, and it really did me more good than anything else. Is it a compliment to say that I went to sleep repeating it? — it is intended as one.

She signed a contract for *Legends*, which troubled her, as all the legends were not written as yet; but the book would not be published until the spring. On the 19th, she gave a reading at Harvard, and described it to Miss Bryher in a letter dated October 25.

Harvard has a Poetry Club, and the boys asked me to go over and give them a reading before my operation, to sort of start the Winter with. They had the courage to get Paine Hall for me to speak in. I do not know how many people it holds, but I should think not less than seven hundred, possibly more. As luck would have it, the Democratic candidate for President, Cox, suddenly decided to speak in the Harvard Union at exactly the same hour. Both the boys and I were somewhat upset about it, but the boys did not wish me to change the day, so we trusted to luck. I, of course, expected to have a mere scattering of people in the hall, thinking that everybody would go to hear Cox. You can imagine my surprise, therefore, when I reached the place, to find the hall absolutely crammed, both floor and balcony, so full, in fact, that people were standing five rows deep at the back; and when I got through my reading at the end of my hour, my audience simply stayed on, and after reading one encore I had to tell them that was all. It was really a delightful experience, because right here in my own community I hardly expected to receive the greeting that I get in distant cities. I have read here before, and always before good audiences, but never such a cram-jam as that one, although it is by no means an unusual occurrence in other places.

The president of the society, not expecting a large audience, and being of a conservative taste, determined to be broad-minded towards experimentalism. He did his earnest best to explain who the speaker was and what the New Poetry was trying to achieve; then he pleaded for open minds. Miss Lowell gaily thanked the audience for being such good sports as to risk coming in such numbers to hear an unknown freak. The reading was a success from the moment she began to speak.

Ten days later, on October 29, she had her third operation. Five doctors and three nurses were present. The wound was huge, the time of the operation was very long, and as she wrote later to Miss Cutting, the next three weeks were 'the most dubious three weeks I have ever passed.' Large amounts of alcohol were needed to bathe the wound; and as all legal substitutes irritated her skin badly, she had to apply to a bootlegger.[1] Three quarters of an hour were needed to adjust the elaborate bandage; and then if it did not seem right, the whole thing had to be done again. Thereafter Miss Lowell got down to dinner later and later, because of putting off the dreary ceremony as long as possible. But not until November 27 was she able to go down even one flight of stairs.

On November 23, a copy of the English edition of *Can Grande's Castle* arrived; it had been published on September 24, and the flabbergasted reviews were coming in.

Among the many letters of sympathy came one from D. H. Lawrence, who had apparently not heard of the third operation.

> Fontana Vecchia
> Taormina, Sicily
> 30 November 1920

MY DEAR AMY

I wonder how you are. Here we sit in Sicily & it has done nothing but rain masses of rain since we are back. But today a rainbow and tramontana wind & blue sea, & Calabria such a blue morning-jewel I could weep. The colour of Italy is blue, after all. Strange how rare red is. But orange underglow in the soil & rocks here.

The little rose cyclamens are almost over: the little white & yellow narcissus are out among the rocks, scenting the air, and smelling like the world's morning, so far back. Oranges are nearly ripe, yellow and many — and we've already roasted the autumn kids: soon it will be Christmas.

---

[1] The so-called 'Food Production Bill' (war-time prohibition), which was not signed until after the Armistice, went into effect July 1, 1919; the Eighteenth Amendment went into effect January 16, 1920. Miss Lowell, although she cared nothing for cocktails, and had an instinctive dislike of anything that dulled the keenness of the mind, had no respect for Prohibition at all. She expressed freely her thorough contempt for the politicians' lack of moral courage in letting themselves be stampeded by a bit of fanatic propaganda; and she gasped with amazement at the orders that our fleets should be sent out without the proper stimulants.

I had your review notice of *Touch & Go*. Did I thank you? I hope you've got *Women in Love* from Seltzer: I asked him to send it to you. Of all my novels, I like it far best. But other people don't & won't. Tell me *please* what you think. — I've ordered Secker to send you also The Lost Girl, which is just out in London. Perhaps this will sell, & make me some money. I don't think *Women in Love* will sell.

I did a little book of vers libre — *Birds, Beasts, and Flowers*: am awaiting it from the typist. Frieda hates it: I like it. *Songs without Sound* I'd like to call them. When I get the MS. I think I shall send it to you for your opinion, am so curious to know.

Haven't you got a new book?

We keep making plans for the Spring. I think I shall go to Germany for a time. Where are you going.

Greetings from both of us to you for Christmas.

D. H. LAWRENCE

Even if you don't like *Women in Love* very much, have a certain gentle feeling towards it, because I ask you.

On November 27, she was able to descend one flight, to Mrs. Russell's room; by December 16, she was dining downstairs regularly and had even been out of doors; on the 22nd, she motored in town to see her publishers, for she had been working on the format as well as the manuscript of *Legends*. But on Christmas she was unable to go to the annual party at her sister's, so she had the Loweses over. That week she wrote two poems. The doctors were sure the operation was a complete success, and their enthusiasm was overcoming her doubts. January passed quietly. Just as she had finished her last 'Legend,' she was asked to be the Francis Bergen Foundation lecturer at Yale and deliver the Keats Centenary Address. She had unpublished Keats material, she always had worshipped him, and she had never spoken at Yale, so she accepted and set to work on her address. The cold that customarily followed her operations was severe, but she found it a convenient excuse for refusing many requests that she review books and the like. About the end of the month, the Drinkwaters returned to America, for the production of another of his plays, staying with her before they went to New York.

On St. Valentine's Day, she herself went to New York, for another lecture trip. The next afternoon, she gave her Whitman lecture at the Brooklyn Institute; on the 16th, she studied the Keats material in the Morgan Library, then dined with Elsie Sergeant, who had also invited the Berensons. On the following evening, the Authors' Club met at the Morgan Library, to hear her 'chat' (she refused to 'talk') for about twenty minutes on Keats.

Winifred Bryher was also in New York, married — in fact, the license has been issued the very day Miss Lowell left Brookline. Some poems in *Poetry* by Robert Menzies McAlmon had attracted her; when she returned to New York from California, she met him in Greenwich Village; they were married at once. Miss Lowell had the blushing pair up, and with a quaking heart gave them her blessing before they embarked for England. A month later, the news of the marriage leaked into public print, where it was outrageously featured as an international romance between a millionaire's daughter and a penniless poet.

On February 22, Miss Lowell left the Belmont in New York for the Taft in New Haven; that evening she read from her poems at the Elizabethan Club, and then was shown their remarkable collection of Elizabethan books.

The Keats Centenary Address was delivered on February 23. Amy Lowell endeavored to sum him up as a man, and to explain the chivalry of his relations with Fanny Brawne. Of course her own collection was used for material: she had three and a half unpublished letters besides other unknown things. As she wrote her future biographer:

> ... I had something very closely approaching an ovation. The hall held 750 people, but they had chairs in the aisles, all

over the platform and in both dressing rooms, which must
have brought it up to something like 200 more I think, and
even then cordial New Haven continued to come, so they
had to put a sign at the door announcing that no more could
be allowed in. This, as you can imagine, was most flattering
to me. Mrs. Russell says that the applause afterwards was
very long and enthusiastic; I cannot say I realized that
myself as I was busily engaged in trying to prevent President Hadley from dropping my eye-glasses on the floor which
he seemed possessed to do.

And to Ferris Greenslet, of Houghton Mifflin Company:

> It would have amused you if you could have seen the
> boys at Yale running up to the platform with books for
> me to sign. They were, I think, all brand new, which cuts
> both ways as far as one's feelings are concerned, and the
> ones I had a chance to look at bore your stamp in pink on
> the slip cover, so I presume they were bought then and
> there. I do not know how many I signed that night, some-
> where between thirty and fifty, I think: I lost count in the
> middle. I was surprised to see how many copies of the
> 'Dome' were brought up until I reflected that the 'Dome'
> sells for twenty-five cents less than the other books. Then
> I began to wonder if we had not perhaps put the books too
> high at two dollars and should not have to reduce to a
> dollar and seventy-five cents, in which case publishing
> would clearly be at a loss for me on those old books any-
> way. However, that shows what stimulation of interest
> my going to a place will do.

On February 24, she was back and in bed, resting for her
next excursion. Edwin Markham sent her a couple of his
broadside poems inscribed to her, also a carbon copy of his
reply to a question which the *Pittsburgh Dispatch* had sent
out to various librarians: 'Can you understand Amy
Lowell?' The manuscript of *Legends* was finished; and as
she could not go in person to The Riverside Press, she summoned the Press to her bedside. Harvard wanted to exhibit her Keats collection; she sent Mrs. Russell over with

it to Cambridge, to make sure that it was displayed pro, perly. Yale was anxious to publish her lecture; she determined to make a book of it, and write Keats's life properly, using the unpublished material in America. *Can Grande's Castle*, in spite of some excellent reviews, was going slowly in England; she felt that her presence there was essential to its success; but her vitality was still so low that she could not think of leaving until the autumn; but as she was very susceptible to colds, she preferred to wait until the spring of 1922.

On March 3, she lectured on Whitman for the Institute of Arts and Sciences at Columbia in the Horace Mann Auditorium. One of her evenings was spent with the Untermeyers, when for the first time she heard Kreymborg play on his mandolute, chanting his poems. On March 8, she read from her poems to the University Extension Society at Witherspoon Hall, Philadelphia; the reading was followed by a symposium of witticisms about free verse; A. Edward Newton invited her and the Pennells to dinner, however. On March 10, she read her poems at the Brooklyn Institute, and returned home.

She was full of enthusiasm for her projected life of Keats, which she planned to have finished by the autumn. There was more Keats material in America than in England; her own collection was the finest and the biggest in existence; unpublished material was plentifully available; and she planned to take a psychological attitude which would show how Keats appealed to the younger generation. Wentworth Place was bought; and as America had raised more than half the sum, largely because of her own efforts, she hoped to be able to get permission to use English material. But first, there were proofs of *Legends* to be read — a task not finished until the first week of April. And she had agreed on certain lectures and readings: on March 14, the Keats address for the Women's City Club at Ford Hall; a reading with remarks on the new poetry, at the Chilton

Club on the 20th; and on the 28th, the Keats address again
at the Chestnut Hill Study Club.

On April 7, she motored down to Providence, where she
was to be the Marshall Woods Lecturer at Brown University. Unfortunately the chauffeur lost the way, so that she
arrived very late for the dinner given in her honor beforehand. After the fish-course, in spite of her protests, she
was dragged away to Sayles Hall, where a huge audience
had been waiting for an hour; then there was an explosion
and instant darkness when her reading-lamp was plugged
in. But such events always proved favorable to Amy
Lowell; her poems were received with great applause.
Theodore Francis Greene (later the Governor of Rhode
Island) went on the platform to ask her to read more; she
refused; but when he addressed the audience, asking if
their applause did not mean that they wanted more, she
capitulated.

On April 11, she went to New York for two weeks. There
were more readings to be given, on the 12th at the Cooper
Union Forum, and on the 20th at the Brooklyn Institute,
where William Carlos Williams, whom she had invited,
heard her read the Peruvian and Chinese legends. She
also went to the Poetry Society, where William Rose
Benét read. Most of her time, however, was spent over the
Keats material in the Morgan Library and elsewhere,
which she had been given permission to use in her forthcoming biography. But of greatest moment was a visit to
the hernia-specialist, who confirmed her suspicion that a
stitch had loosened, and said that all would be well if it
were fixed immediately. Grimly she agreed to have it done
in May. It would be her fourth operation in two years or
so.

She returned by way of Northampton, where on April
21 she gave her Whitman lecture at the Hampshire Bookshop. She was home on Sunday the 24th, when she entertained the Hills and Eva Gauthier. *Legends* had been de-

layed by a strike; the biography of Keats would be delayed
a year by the operation; so Houghton Mifflin decided to
bring out the volume of Chinese poems, *Fir-Flower Tablets*,
in the autumn. It was just possible to complete the manuscript, as Florence Ayscough arrived about May Day with
the last sixty-seven poems, to be turned into English verse.
Relentlessly they worked on them night and day, although
Miss Lowell got very nervous and tired, but they finished
the job twenty-four hours before the operation. That
evening she went over to her brother's, who began talking
about James Russell Lowell's *Fable for Critics*; and when
she went home, she tried characterizing Frost and Robinson in her cousin's meter and trick rhymes, more to keep
her mind off the operation than anything else. On the next
day, May 17, the operation was performed. It was merely
the closing of a very small hole; as the rest of the wound
was holding, it was expected to be a perfect success.

Three days later, on May 20, 1921, *Legends* was published, in an edition of 2500. The advance sale had been
approximately 1500 copies.

CHAPTER XXI

LEGENDS

The poet who wishes to compete with the great poets of the past must have great subjects. Amy Lowell, after the historical studies which produced *Can Grande's Castle*, delved yet deeper for *Legends*, going into folklore, which is the very tap-root of literature. Her new book contained seven symbolic tales, three tales of superstition, and one dramatic lyric. 'Stories, as such, they emphatically are not,' Amy Lowell stated in her Preface, which so briefly and surely placed the arts in civilization, and the symbolic tale in the arts.

> ... Civilization is the study of man about himself, his powers, limitations, and endurances; it is the slowly acquired knowledge of how he can best exist in company with his fellows on the planet called Earth. As man learns, he becomes conscious, first of an immense curiosity, and then of a measure of understanding, and, immediately after, of a desire to express both; and the simplest form of expression is by means of the tale or (hateful word!) allegory. Hence legends; they are bits of fact, or guesses at fact, pressed into the form of a story and flung out into the world as markers of how much ground has been travelled. If science be proven truth (and I believe it is), legends might be described as speculative or apprehended truth.

Her own legends, then, were emphatically not mere stories, 'since all have that curious substratum of reality, speculative or apprehended, of which I have spoken.' This 'reality' — her own insight into the significance of life — caused her to remould (and not merely repeat) the source-materials, which she indicated at some length. 'I have changed, added, subtracted, jumbled several together at will, left out portions; in short, made them over to suit my particular vision.'

After all, originality (as the great writers have proved) consists not in inventing new material but in using one's material (whether new or old) in such a way as to give it meaning. Truth is always original.

The first poem, 'Memorandum Confided by a Yucca to a Passion-Vine,' (or 'From a Yucca to a Passion Vine,' as the running-title put it — which in her letters she sometimes reduced briefly to 'The Yucca'), is a Peruvian legend suggested by a single sentence in *Purchase His Pilgrimes*: 'The spots in the Moone they fable to have come of a Foxe, which being in love with the Moones beautie, went to heaven, and touching her with his forefeete left those foule memorials.' [1] It is another poem of that moon-worship which had been the theme of the first poem in her first book. There is a close kinship between Mr. Keats on Box Hill watching the 'naked waist' of her he had put into his second canto, and the love-starved fox under the thorny cactus watching the same 'virgin waist.' The symbolism of the poem is sufficiently indicated in the title, for the yucca is the lily of the desert, while the passion-vine names itself. This vine drapes the gates of the sacred city of Cusco, into which the little fox creeps, to assault the virgin moon, who has been drawn down to the earth. The Inca texture of the poem is a triumph, from the opening torrid sunrise and the chattering animals, to that extraordinary reascent of the defiled moon at the end; and of course Amy Lowell would never miss the gold temple of the Sun, the silver temple of the Moon, and the garden of precious metals. The versification swings from rhymed meter to unrhymed free verse and back with such deftness that it is quite unobtrusive. The action is so dramatic and the poem so musical that it is almost a ballet; and, as we have said, at one time she actually turned it into a ballet-scenario for

[1] *Hakluytus Posthumus or Purchas His Pilgrimes*, Glasgow 1906, XVII, 333–34.

Edward Burlingame Hill, to be called 'The Legend of the
Fox and the Moon.' The two acts of the scenario follow the
poem closely. The text ends:

> For a moment the Goddess stands quite still, then she
> unclasps the emerald which holds her girdle and her bright
> garment slips down; as this occurs in a sort of hush of adora-
> tion over everything, the Fox breaks away from the Virgin
> and dashes snarling and yelping up the temple steps. He
> flies straight at the moon and seizes her in his arms.
>
> There is a loud thunder-clap and a great deal of rolling
> thunder with gashes of lightning, and the moonlight dis-
> appears and gives place to a comparative darkness, but
> one in which objects can be faintly seen. As the thunder
> ceases, the Fox half rolls, half stumbles, as though he had
> been violently flung, down the temple steps. He rolls al-
> most down to the footlights and lies still. At the same mo-
> ment, a terrible moon mounts slowly up into the sky behind
> the temple, round it are three rings, the first blood-colour,
> the second black, and the third of blowing smoke.
>
> As the Fox lies, down stage, a little to the right of centre,
> the Virgin comes slowly forward with her face bowed and
> hidden in the sleeve of her left arm, and the other arm
> stretched over the prostrate body of the Fox. The gesture
> must symbolize awe, horror, and submission; she must seem
> to have given up her own desires, and here again to dedicate
> herself to religion, with sorrow, but with strength. The
> moon with its three terrible haloes is in the midmost sky as
> the curtain slowly descends.

Anticipating a performance, Miss Lowell wrote to Adolph
Bolm, the dancer, on April 6, 1920:

> ... The chief character, the fox, is of course an animal
> figure. My idea was that he should be played as part ani-
> mal and part human, somewhat the same kind of beast as
> the faun in Debussy's 'L'Après-Midi d'un Faune.' He
> should be unctuous, lascivious, cunning, and exceedingly
> wheedling and attractive. There seems to me to be scope
> here for your remarkable imaginative symbolisation. I

cannot see the character danced by any one else. His solo
dances should be made most important, and his by-play,
when nominally in repose, significant in every particular.
I know the story to be quite unusual, and I think the stage
effects could be made to be equally original and astonishing,
particularly the undulating rainbow colours, which must
give the effect of moving flowers in the second act....[1]

'A Legend of Porcelain,' the second poem in the book,
combines three Chinese legends into the tale of Chou-
Kiou; her self-sacrifice in art saves her father, who had
been kidnapped by demons, and wins her a husband,
through the intervention of the Goddess of Mercy. The
story proper has little meaning beyond the idea that great
labor and self-sacrifice must go to the creation of genuine
beauty. As she wrote to one critic: [2] 'I cannot feel with
you that the action in "A Legend of Porcelain" has
human significance. The human part of the poem seems
to me very conventional and mild. I was interested primarily in the atmosphere, but I am glad you like the human
side.' It is a poem about 'things'; Amy Lowell's descriptions of the porcelains are some of her most felicitous writing.

But 'Many Swans' she thought the best poem in the
book. It is the tale of a man who attains his ideal (the sun)
and then consumes with fire every town he approaches, so
that he must live alone; and at the end, even his gift is
taken from him.

One line, 'And a poison leaf from Gethsemane,' which
was inserted as a clue to her meaning, made explanations
necessary.

---

[1] After she had written out her scenario, she sent it to Robert Edmond Jones;
and they planned to work on it together, but they never got round to it. In
1923, when Edward Burlingame Hill had given up the idea of setting it, she
sent it to John Alden Carpenter, who had asked for it, but again it proved unsuitable.

[2] Letter to Padraic Colum, September 14, 1921, concerning his review of
Legends in the Freeman.

I must set you right on one point. You accuse me of a lack of taste in bringing in a word with an obviously Christian association in 'a poison leaf from Gethsemane.' Evidently you have not read Mr. Malcolm Cowley's review of 'Legends' in 'The Dial.' In that, he discovered my fundamental intention in 'Many Swans,' which no other reviewer has hit upon; namely that it was a double allegory, the sun myth being one, and the other being the destruction of the Indian races through the all-imposing power and intelligence of the white man. Many Swans typifying both the Indian arrogance and the racial greed and omnipotence of the whites. The whole lyric, of which the Gethsemane line was a part, was intended to give this idea, and the line you refer to was meant to show the fatal and cruel blunder of trying to do away with the religion and ritualistic dances of the Indians. Gethsemane, therefore, was introduced with malice aforethought, meaning that Christianity reached those nations incapable of assimilating it, in a debauched and poisoned form. I stated in my preface that all legends mean more than appears and mean different things to different generations; hence the legends in my book mean their primitive content and whatever else I choose to put into them.[1]

She used, then, the Indian sun-myth to explain the obliteration of the Indian civilizations. The sun is Christianity, essential to humanity, but destructive when imperfectly grasped and controlled by the primitive mind. Many

[1] Letter to Padraic Colum, September 14, 1921. On January 4, 1922, she wrote to Dr. William N. Guthrie:

It is a sun myth of the North American Indians, but I have made it doubly symbolic. I have kept the whole sun myth as it appeared in the original, but have added another symbolism by making it the extinction of the Indian before the march of the white man, the crowding out of the Indian religions through the unwise and non-understanding attitude of some of the Christian missionaries. I wanted to show that all religion was the same in essence and that in suppressing the natural expression peculiar to the Indians, the white man has reduced the Indian nation mentally to ashes, as in many cases the Indian is not yet capable of grasping our peculiar pattern of truth. That is the meaning of a line of the lyric on page 117 where I speak of 'a poison leaf from Gethsemane.' I mean that the leaf has been poisoned by the misrepresentation of those in charge of its dissemination.

Swans abandons his family and the ordinary callings to achieve his ideal; but after he has gained it, and tries to bring it to his people, it destroys successively the native cultures of the North-West, the Plains, and the Pueblos, until at last nothing — not even his ideal — is left.

The 'Funeral Chant' that follows is simply a ceremonial song, without ulterior meaning.

For 'Witch-Woman,' a Yucatan legend, Miss Lowell named no source. It depicts the agony of a man in love with an evil and avaricious woman. He spies on her devotions to the moon, when, seeing beyond her beautiful flesh, he learns that her inmost being is death (the skeleton), which ascends into the heavens, enters the moon, and corrupts it. This poem is related to the 'Yucca' as 'Patterns' was related to 'Appuldurcombe Park' — the one treats of real love, while the other is only of the body.

'The Ring and the Castle' is a ballad which Miss Lowell wrote on the threshold of sleep. She woke from the middle of her slumbers with the first line sounding in her brain: 'Benjamin Bailey, Benjamin Bailey, why do you wake at the stroke of three?' Another line answered it; and thus the entire poem unrolled itself from that first line. The symbol is of a Hawthorne-like simplicity: Benjamin Bailey kills his mistress by trying to remove her wedding-ring. The man's name was that of one of Keats's friends, who offered his heart to Miss Hamilton Gleig when he had just begged Miss Marianne Reynolds to reconsider her refusal. Neither John Keats nor Amy Lowell approved of his act.

'Gavotte in D Minor' is a portrait rather than a tale: the portrait of a woman too proud to marry beneath her, even though the cry of the flesh pursues her with ghostly voices. She is Dictynna, the virgin nymph, incessantly pursued by the subterranean Minos, whom she escapes at last by dying. (Or is she delivered at last into his power?) The poem may be called the feminine counterpart of 'Little Ivory Figures Pulled with String.'

'The Statue in the Garden' is based on a legend which was probably Roman in origin; William of Malmesbury, who died in 1143 A.D., introduced it to English readers;[1] since then, many authors have used it, including Morris and Mérimée. Amy Lowell found it, however, in Burton's *Anatomy of Melancholy*, and made it over to suit her own meaning. It became a study of the struggle between the two worlds of reality and of false dreams, in the brain of Julius, a successful writer, who woos solitude too dangerously, and who adorns his garden with a gaily painted leaden statue of a maiden. To indulge a whim, he slips his ring on her finger, and cannot get it off. Thereafter she pursues him, almost to the point of ruining his marriage with the flesh-and-blood Hildegarde. In vain he buys the male companion statue; he is now pursued by leaden jealousy as well as leaden love. At last, almost mad, he leaps into the lake; they leap after, but sink; and he is restored to normality.

The originals of these two statues were a pair called 'Paul and Virginia' in the old garden on the Francis Brooks estate in West Medford.

Padraic Colum, in his review, compared her tale to Mérimée's; she replied, explaining what new meaning she had given the ancient plot:

> If you think that Prosper Merimée's 'Venus of Ille' is better, then indeed am I humble, for I think that tale of Merimée's of an insupportable dullness. 'The Statue in the Garden' seems to be about divided between its lovers and haters, some people liking it very much, and others detesting it with equal vigour. It may interest you to know that I had never read Merimée's tale until after 'The Statue' was written. I did read the story in Burton's 'Anatomy of Melancholy,' but a student of mediaeval history has just told me that it is a constantly recurring tale during the whole mediaeval period, and is often woven into

[1] George Lyman Kittredge: *Witchcraft in Old and New England*, Cambridge, 1929, p. 111; for bibliography, see p. 440, notes 59, 60.

legends about the Virgin Mary. I departed from the original version which Mérimée gives. My object was to show the lure of the aesthetic, and how inhuman it might make a person, who could only be saved by the return to human love and human desires.[1]

In a letter to Royall Snow, on February 14, 1921, she described her method of creating the proper atmosphere for this near-tragedy of this cerebralist who, born in one world, tries to live in another. She did it by writing the poem itself in two centuries and two techniques.

> You will notice that the new poem, 'The Statue in the Garden,' is not placed in any period unless it be the present, but an undercurrent of the eighteenth century runs through it all, hence the rather tight rhymes of much of it, bursting out in modern freedom every now and then as antithesis, something the same kind of thing which Richard Strauss has done in his music for the 'Bourgeois Gentilhomme' where he has directly imitated Lully, but with just the difference. Strauss has done a good deal the same thing in the 'Rosenkavalier.' I took the idea of the treatment of this poem more or less directly from these two operas of his in the way he has worked seventeenth and eighteenth century feeling into a perfectly modern treatment, if that expresses what I mean.

Apparently the three remaining tales have no deeper significance than the plots for their own sakes. 'Dried Marjoram,' the ancient tale of the mother gathering the bones of her criminal son for burial, as they drop from the gibbet, was told as fact in some English guide-book which Miss Lowell read. After her poem was written, she learned that she was not the first to write it; as she notified Ellery Sedgwick on January 29, 1919:

> I had a funny experience about 'Dried Marjoram.' I came across the incident in an old book about Hampshire

[1] Letter to Padraic Colum, September 14, 1921.

as a true fact, and I promptly wrote a poem. After I had got it written and typed, somebody told me that it was the same subject as Tennyson's 'Rizpah,' which I had never read. It was very funny to read it afterwards and see how differently two generations treat the same idea.

'Before the Storm' is another vision of the New England Flying Dutchman, Peter Rugg, that genuine legend, although now we can name his creator, William Austen. It was a story which had filled her with terrified delight when she was a child. 'Four Sides to a House' is a murder told in ballad manner; she got the idea from one of the Smithsonian Publications, which described a house with the horses' skulls still nailed over the windows, to keep out ghosts.

The format of the book was by no means to the liking of Miss Lowell. Between her operations and the strikes at the Press, it was brought out 'any way.' The binding was not what she wanted; there were other details that were wrong; and then she would have preferred a fall publication — spring had no Christmas shopping to multiply sales; and the whole book market was hopeless that year anyhow.

But market or no market, two thousand copies of *Legends* were sold in three weeks. The critics hailed it with such a chorus of praise that a cautious or grudging note here and there could hardly be distinguished, certainly not heeded. *Can Grande's Castle*, success though it proved, had blinded and confused a public already thrilled; but when *Legends* appeared, there was no question of her triumph. Her readers, now accustomed to her manner, supposed they understood her; and swept along by the powerful music, they accepted her book without debate as authentic poetry.

CHAPTER XXII

FIR-FLOWER TABLETS AND A HOAX FOR DISTRACTION

'For I really don't think there's one person in ten who can tell the first-class from the second-class men.'

NOT until June was she allowed to sit up; then June came in hot, and she, who usually delighted in great heat, suffered under it. *Fir-Flower Tablets* was now chiefly in her mind: she signed the contract on the 9th, arranged and re-arranged the dummy, and worked hard selling the yet unprinted poems to the magazines. On the 15th, she got downstairs for the first time, and was so exhausted that she did not try the trip again for a week. Her wound was hurting much more than the old ones had done. Then she suffered a series of abscesses, caused by non-absorption of the kangaroo sinews used for interior stitching; these abscesses had to be lanced as they rose to the surface, and persisted well into July, although by June 28 she had been out in her garden twice.

In her convalescence, her mind recurred regularly to James Russell Lowell's *Fable for Critics*, which her brother had read her just before the last operation, and to her own attempts at characterizing Frost and Robinson in Cousin James's manner. Why should she not continue, and hit off the leading poets of her day as he had done for his, some sixty-odd years ago? Thus she could correct and supplement her judgments in *Tendencies*, carry on a family tradition, amuse the tedium of convalescence, versify without the labor of research, and perhaps put over a successful hoax. For who would suspect the leading writer of exotic *vers libre* of being a satirist and an expert rhymster? Only Ferris Greenslet was told of the scheme; and to him she wrote —

29 June, 1921

DEAR FERRIS:

Not a word about my modern fable to anybody, even to Mr. Scaife. It may never be good enough to see the light of day, and if it is, the whole fun will be springing it on the unsuspecting public, so don't you dare whisper it. It amuses me, anyway.

Very sincerely yours,

From the mass of correspondence, which kept up undiminished, it is perhaps worth while to preserve the following specimen of her business acumen, — a note answering an offer to sell her a Keats manuscript. The writer evidently had become over-enthusiastic at the Forman sale, and was now endeavoring to mend his mistake.

July 2, 1921

MY DEAR MR. ********:

You paid too much for that Keats manuscript. If I had not thought so, my agents would have secured it for me. As I can hardly suppose you to be willing to sell it for less than you gave for it, I fear I must relinquish the hope of possessing it. Thank you very much for offering it to me.

Sincerely yours,

When D. H. Lawrence heard of the latest operation, he wrote Mrs. Russell, suggesting that his next share of the now rapidly dwindling Imagist royalties be spent on a fuchsia tree for Miss Lowell. She thanked him for the thought on July 6:

6 July, 1921

DEAR LAWRENCE:

Your letter to Mrs. Russell came the other day, and I have at last got far enough to write to you with my own voice, if not my own hand. In spite of your sweetness in wanting me to buy a pot of fuchsias with your share of the Imagist royalties, I cannot feel justifying in not forwarding it to you. There will be another pittance from the same source shortly, I suppose. The bond between us is intensified by your picking fuchsias, as they are one of my favourite flowers. I shall never forget how they used to hang over the walls of the house in Devonshire when I passed a Summer there years ago.

Your reputation is coming on here by leaps and bounds, I am happy to say. I did not place any of the poems in the last batch you sent because your agent in New York, Mr. Mountsier, seemed to think that that was his prerogative, and I thought he probably got a percentage on it and so did not like to butt in. I suggested making a try at it, but he made it so evident that he preferred to do it himself that I let it alone. I did, however, tell the editor of the 'Bookman' that he ought to get your 'Mosquito,' and he did, and it appears in the current number of the magazine, as does also a little criticism of mine of your 'Apostolic Beasts,' which came out shortly before in 'The Dial.' I would send you the number only I have my doubts about its following you about Europe and ever arriving.

I do not know when I was ever so interested in a book as I was in your 'Women in Love.' The scene on the lake, beginning with the wonderful beauty of the lanterns and ending with the horror of the drowning, was superb, I thought. I confess I did not care as much for 'The Lost Girl.' It did not seem to be as truly you. I felt that you were modifying yourself to gain your public, which was undoubtedly a very wise thing to do, but I did not find the result as interesting. I could not review the book, because of these perpetual operations which have made my life such a burden lately....

Your description of Baden Baden sounds charming. Now that Harding has signed the Peace Treaty, I suppose the question of mail will not be so difficult. Do write and keep me in touch with all you are doing. I have seen nothing but my bedroom for weeks. Give both Mrs. Russell's and my love to Frieda, and forgive my long silence; you know it could not be helped.

Affectionately yours,

P.S. I am sending you a copy of my new volume, 'Legends.' I hardly know whether you will like it or not, but I trust, at any rate, that it will reach you.

On July 18, she gave a party for John Lane, of London; it was the first time she had seen anybody since her operation. He begged her to write a bibliographical book, something like A. Edward Newton's *Amenities of Book Collecting*; but she was sick of books about books, and refused. On the 23d, she went out in the motor for the first time, and returned very tired; moreover, the abscesses had reappeared in full force. But by the 28th, her *Critical Fable* was complete, except for polishing here and tinkering there and also except for a titlepage.

> I simply cannot do a title-page in rhyme. Houghton Mifflin seems to rhyme with nothing but 'pifflin.' Is it not unfortunate? I sweated for hours over it last night, and expect to begin again as soon as I finish this letter. I should hate to be stumped by the dear departed.

By this time, however, the Houghton Mifflin Company travellers had gone out with the autumn books, so the *Critical Fable* was delayed a year.

D. H. Lawrence sent her a couple of postcards, and then a letter on the receipt of *Legends*.

> Villa Alpensee
> Thumersbach
> Zell-am-See bei Salzburg, Austria
> 31 July 1921

DEAR AMY

I had your letter and the eight dollars yesterday. I had much rather you had had the fuchsia tree. There are lovely ones here.

Very many thanks for looking after my poems so kindly. Mountsier is over here just now.... I had understood that you had said, of the poems, that The Mosquito was the only one worth printing.

I do hope the operation was successful & final & that you can live your own life freely.

I read Legends last night — and again this morning. I like them the best of all your poems. You have always written of the existence & magic of *things* — porcelain and rain: and of *things* you catch an essence: even cannon & ships. But in this book it is life and death superseding things. So I like this book the best.

I like best *Many Swans* which I have read twice and which I feel really speaks inside my unexplained soul. I should not like to try to explain it, because of the deep fear and danger that is in it. But it isn't a myth of the sun. It is something else. All the better that we can't say offhand what. That means it is true. It rings a note in my soul. Then I like Blackbird & Witch Woman. But I doubt if you quite get her — the Witch Woman.

Those three, for me, are much the best, & the best of all your poems.

The Statue is very amusing & nicely done — only Julius got off too lightly. His *things* should have pinched him a bit more excruciatingly. She should have flung her leaden arms round his neck in the lake, & nothing but bubbles to tell the tale. I must read Yucca & Passion Vine again. I don't quite get it. But it is most *interesting*, after Swans. Porcelain is lovely as things.

I hope you'll have as much pleasure as you wish out of the public reception of the book.

Wonder what you'll do next.

D. H. LAWRENCE

Among the books she read during her convalescence was Conrad Aiken's *Punch, the Immortal Liar*, which impressed her so tremendously that, although she had met Aiken only once, and although he had attacked her work so constantly in print that she looked on him as one of her most steadfast enemies, she wrote him a letter of hearty congratulation.

2 August, 1921

MY DEAR MR. AIKEN:

You will be surprised to get a letter from me, I have no doubt, but I have read your 'Punch' with so much admiration that I feel I must write you a line and tell you so. I am very sorry that I had not read it at the time I wrote that very brief account of your work in the current 'Book-

man.' That account would have been very different had
I seen 'Punch.'

I have for a long time admired a great deal that you do;
but, until 'The House of Dust,' I had not felt that it had
composed very well into a volume. 'The House of Dust'
I read over many times with ever-increasing delight, finding a great deal of it — and especially that dance of the
maenads and satyrs — exceedingly fine, but 'Punch' has
bowled me over completely. It seems to me one of the most
important books of the poetry renaissance. Perhaps you
will realize how strongly I feel about it when I tell you that
I heartily wish I had written it myself. Not only is it
beautiful in passages, as all your poems are, but the thesis
on which it is built is big, as only the older poets are big.
It is as fine a subject as Faust. We cannot stand up with
the poets of the world unless we do something that shall be
not only beautiful technically or in a scrappy way, but that
shall have a large significance, and this book of yours has
that significance. Your characters are splendidly sustained
throughout and your change not only of feeling but of
rhythm between the bombastic passages and the reality is
marvelously done.

The last part, 'Mountebank Feels the Strings at his
Heart,' is technically superb, I think. You have chosen
exactly the right metre. I also particularly like the lyric
of the Fifth Voice. The only part that I did not care for so
much was the Queen of Sheba section, which seemed to
me a little muddled and not so interesting as the rest,
though I can see why you needed it.

The way in which you have arranged the poem, beginning
with the old men remembering Punch and going on to his
bombast and then reality is splendid architectonics, and
your scenery in the churchyard I have read over and over.
It seems so easy and is so immensely difficult.

I have not read a book for years that has given me the
pleasure that yours has. I have been carrying it upstairs
and downstairs with me, and reading in it for the last
month. I wonder where it has been reviewed. I saw an
excellent review by Louis Untermeyer in the current 'Book-

man,' but I have been very ill, as perhaps you know, having
had three operations in fifteen months, and have not been
doing a great deal. I have not seen any one to know what
has been doing and what has not. If you know of any
place where it has not been reviewed — any place where
I am *persona grata* — I shall be very glad indeed to say a
little about it.

With heartiest congratulations, believe me,
Very sincerely yours,

His reply was pleased and prompt; she replied in turn on
August 6:

I was delighted to get your letter and was particularly
interested to know just how you wrote 'Punch.' I do not
think the fact that you were uncertain about it counts for
anything at all. I have never been really thoroughly pleased
with anything I ever wrote, and I frequently do not like
my poems at all until a year or more has elapsed since I
have looked at them, and then they sometimes seem to be
better than I remembered, and sometimes, of course, it is
the other way round.

Following your suggestion, I have written to Ridgely
Torrence, who is supposed to be running the poetry in the
'New Republic,' I believe....

Her review, 'Marionettes of Fate,' appeared in the *New
Republic* for September 28, 1921, one and a half pages
long — a full half-page over the customary limit.

On August 9, Florence Ayscough came to town again,
and the two women put in three weeks of solid work on the
Chinese poetry. The Introduction was finished and sent off
on the 29th; and that evening Hervey Allen and DuBose
Heyward, on their way south from Peterborough, dined at
Miss Lowell's, who had also invited her future biographer.
Jessie Rittenhouse called one afternoon, and found her
busily at work with Mrs. Ayscough. Bubbling with
animation, Miss Lowell explained that, though her
physician had forbidden her to work, she was determined

to get *Fir-Flower Tablets* on the market before Witter Bynner's *Jade Mountain.* She then read Miss Rittenhouse some of the poems; never had she read with more creative fire — it was almost as though she herself had written those antique poems.[1]

On September 7, the day before the first batch of proof came in, she wrote a number of letters. One was to D. H. Lawrence.

> DEAR LAWRENCE:
>
> I wonder if you have the slightest idea of how much pleasure your letter about 'Legends' has given me. I know what you mean by my insistence on *things.* My things are always, to my mind, more than themselves, but I do believe I have laid too much insistence upon them, and obscured the more important issues beneath them for my readers. I am trying not to do this now except in poems that are apparently only things, and that you see what you do in 'Many Swans' makes me very happy, because it was exactly what I tried to put into that poem. Sometimes I wonder whether I shall live long enough, and grow enough, to be able to put into my poetry what I want to have there. I don't know, one can only live and try to go on growing. The technique of poetry is easy, very easy to any one born that way; life is not easy, and it is still less simple to express in words the real throb, and misery, and gusto which it has. That is what you do, and that is what I wish I could learn of you.
>
> I never said that 'The Mosquito' was the only one of the poems of that batch that was worth printing. I do not know who could have so misrepresented me. I thought 'The Turkey-cock' superb. I am enclosing a few remarks I made on 'The Apostolic Beasts,' which may interest you. Your whole 'Tortoise' set was magnificent, but I feared the public would misunderstand them and fall upon you with renewed vigour. The public is a mole, a blind, blundering bat. I have written about you again and again, and tried to get it into people's heads what you are, what you are

[1] Jessie B. Rittenhouse: *My House of Life,* Boston, 1934, p. 263.

striving for, and I do believe things are moving at last. ... The reviews of 'Legends' have been almost uniformly fine and complimentary, but I cannot see that many people have grasped my intention as you have done. A few have, and the papers have accorded me much space, and, after all, one does not write for the public, but for the few people whom one can really speak to. I do not know any one whom I would rather please than you. I do not think I ever write what pleases myself.

I read a few excerpts from an article of yours in an English paper on Walt Whitman. It does not seem to me that you have quite got him. I doubt whether you will quite get America until you see it. It is so different from any other country, but it seems to me the only country left reasonably alive just now. We have all the vigour, and urge, and zest which all the other countries have lost, but we lack the discipline of many generations of writers behind us, therefore the English technique still beats ours. In prose, you are miles ahead of us; in poetry, I am not so sure that, taking it by and large, the American output is not better than the English just now — yours and mine excepted, of course, and watching from the side lines....

The tide was now turning against the moronic sentimentalizing of the world war; one of the first important protests in this country was John Dos Passos's *Three Soldiers*, a copy of which Eugene Saxton, of the *Bookman*, sent Miss Lowell, who wrote him on September 27:

Thank you very much indeed for sending me the 'Three Soldiers.' It is an extremely interesting book. I cannot say it came upon me as a surprise; it seems to me I knew all he says before. Also, like all realistic books, the other side of realism, the side that makes life worth living is left out. Doubtless it felt left out for the men at the front, but I imagine that some of our youth had intelligence and backbone enough to take the horror for what it was worth. They knew that war was hell before they went into it and expected nothing else. My chief quarrel with realism is that it is not real, but this is one of the best books of the type that I have read. I know Mr. Dos Passos as a poet however, and, with his highly romantic imagination and extreme sensitiveness, I can imagine that war must have been torture indeed. The book is a remarkable record of the attitude of a certain kind of soldier, but it should perhaps be remarked that the soldier is but one man throughout the book, in spite of the three different characters taken to portray him.

I think that nothing has been so remarkable to me as the fact of the crumbling of ideals, and belief in things spiritual versus material, evidenced by our young so-called intelligentsia on account of the war. I am afraid that it shows that the intelligent part is a little bit fluid, that these young fellows are smarter than they are deep. I did not go to the war, so perhaps I have no right to speak, but I have read no single volume on the subject which has told me anything I had not realized before. Having but a limited belief in humanity under stress, I have not lost what I had by contemplating the horrors of the last few years. As religion to me has always been a matter of ethics and not of superstition, that has not crumbled either, and I cannot understand why these young men have been so — shall I call it green? — as not to have been able to withstand any circumstances, no matter how desperate, and yet keep themselves and their attitude intact. The advantage of believing next to nothing is that it does not flatten out when exposed to fact. Perhaps I speak foolishly; perhaps not — anyway, here you have it.

A thousand thanks. The whole family are plunged in gloom on account of the book, which they are snatching from one another.

Just about the equinox, the hernia broke through again. It was not serious; there was no need for an immediate operation; but she determined absolutely that there were to be no more operations unless the thing strangulated and threatened her life. She had, in short, wisely given up any hope of a permanent cure; even though it meant that henceforth she could never dare go more than twenty-four hours away from a surgeon.

At once she cancelled a western lecture trip, that was to run from the latter part of October well into November, and take her as far away as Wisconsin; then she settled down to the manuscript of the Keats biography and the proofs of *Fir-Flower Tablets*.

Fontana Vecchia
Taormina Sicilia
9 October 1921

My dear Amy

I had your letter forwarded from Baden Baden yesterday — also the cheque for six dollars. I am so sorry you have had such a summer of illness. Have you really not been able to leave your room? I call that bitter. Can you go out now? Deve Finire, questo guaio.

Yes, do quote anything you like from my letter, about Legends. I said what I felt, for anybody to read or hear.

I agree with you, that American poetry today is better than English. As for me, in direction I am more than half American. I always write really towards America: my listener is there. England has gone all thick and fuzzy in the head, and can't hear, tant pis pour elle!

After all the shifting about, we are both so glad to be back here, in silence and peace and sunshine. It is lovely weather. The sun rises day after day red and unhidden out of the sea, after the morning star, which is very bright before he comes. I watch the dawn every day from my bed: but when the suns rim makes the first bit of fire, we get up — I love the Ionian sea. It is open like a great blue opening in front of us, so delicate and self-contained. The hibiscus flowers are coming again in the garden. I am so thankful to come south. The north just shatters one inside. Even as far as Naples. But south of Naples — from Amalfi — there is the pristine Mediterranean influence, never to be shattered. Such a lovely *morning* world: forever morning. I hate going north and I hate snow grinning on the tops of mountains. Jamais plus.

When I gather myself together I want to get to work.

I only did two poems all the summer — *Fish* & *Bat.* But I did 'Harlequinade of the Unconscious.'

Have you done your Chinese book? I shall be interested to see that.

I am thankful to be at rest for the moment — but feel more than ever come loose from all moorings. I suppose I shall really leave Europe. But feel very mistrustful of the States. Wohin? We shall see.

I do hope you will be better, and able to go about and taste the world. After all, one's writing is only for when there is nothing nicer to be done.

Do you have any feeling about Mexico? I have an idea I should like to go there — and have some little place in the country, with a goat and a bit of a garden. But my compass-needle is a shifty devil.

Greet Mrs. Russell from us both. It must be sad for her too, if you can't go out. Be better — be on your feet, thats the chief.

> Saluti cari
>
> D. H. LAWRENCE

On November 9, the last proofs of *Fir-Flower Tablets* were sent off, and the printing of the book began. She was now free to finish her biography of Keats, which she planned to get done before the spring, when she hoped to go to England. In her correspondence was a query from a movie-company, asking about *Legends*: 'We are not familiar with this work. Do you think it has picture possibilities?' She answered that she thought *Can Grande's Castle* had better material; but nothing came of it. On the 15th, she wrote to Winifred Bryher, now in Berlin, to ask her if she could not get a special kind of bandage for the hernia, and to advise against publishing her books in Germany.

> The truth is, I do not understand the situation in England at present. The Americans all seem to find it hopeless, with the exception of Lindsay, Aiken, and a few others. But the exodus of Americans to Europe is not very good for them

and never has been. I think Whistler and Sargent are the only ones who have come out successfully, and they were painters, for I am one of those who think Henry James would have done far better had he remained at home.

Theodore Maynard (born in India, bred in England, conservative poet, Catholic convert, and now professor of English at the Dominican College, San Rafael, California) sent her the manuscript of his 'Fallacy of Free Verse,' which was to appear in the January *Yale Review*. Though his birth did not predispose him to sympathy with American literature, and though his religious training led him to deplore modernism, he tried to reopen and settle with urbanity and intelligence the now somewhat demoded question.

November 16, 1921

DEAR MR. MAYNARD:

Your letter of the seventh came this morning, and I thank you very much for sending me your article on 'The Fallacy of Free Verse.' You have seen what no other of the antagonists of *vers libre* has seen, that the real objection of the conservatives to modern poetry is not primarily because of its form, but because of its point of view. This is, undoubtedly, an age of scepticism, but not, I think, the bitter and iconoclastic scepticism that you suppose. My title 'Pictures of the Floating World' may typify an attitude, but I never thought of it as such. It is a translation of the Japanese 'Ukioye,' the name of the school of colour printing which dealt with the everyday world. This was its symbolism to me. I imagine that you would consider a creedless religion a contradiction in terms, whereas, to many moderns, it is the breath of life. Philosophically, this may be a matter for discussion; artistically, I do not believe it is. I do not know what 'futurism' is, and I have never seen it defined satisfactorily, but I do know what 'modernism' is, and it is not 'pragmatism.' You will be the first to agree with me that poets do not speak scientifically, but emotionally, and I know none of the better poets today who consider the work of destruction as their chief endeavour. They are trying desperately to build, but this very fact has led to a clearing away, and it is the clearing away that has been most remarked by the opposite camp.

I should take exception to your postulate that the modern poet denies the validity of reason, and if he disbelieve in Absolutes, it is because he feels he knows too little of the universe to rely upon their validity. I should say that this is emphatically not the mark of the 'barbarian,' despite Mr. Santayana. I, for one, am uncertain whether mankind will ever attain to full knowledge of the Absolute in anything, which is, perhaps, the best explanation of the term 'sceptic,' and is not at all the usual one of 'doubter.' If A cannot accept the creed which satisfies B, it is A's misfortune or his glory, but it is out of his power to amend his attitude unless evolution in his own soul amend it for him.

What you mean by 'Absolute Beauty' I do not quite know. But certainly, to the moderns, beauty is to every man what he perceives to be such, and actually, I think this has always been so, for, most certainly, 'what is one man's meat is another man's poison.' And it is not true that modern poets do not pursue beauty. They are forever pursuing it, but the beauty they pursue is sheer ugliness to the conservatives.

Is it a fact that modern poetry is any more egocentric than the older poetry was? Is not Keats's 'Ode to a Nightingale' concerned with the poet's personal reactions to the nightingale's song? There has been, of course, a good deal of striving after originality among the lesser poets of today, but no one strives to be original who is so. After all, are poor poets any worse with this preoccupation than they were when their desire was merely to copy an accepted pattern?

You are quite right in your contention that *vers libre* is anything but formless, but I think you are wrong when you say that it is 'unnatural form.' I am sure that free rhythm is more 'natural' than restricted rhythm. But, really, the term 'natural' is neither here nor there, since art is not nature. You must, however, take into consideration one marked American quality, and that is an acute rhythmic sense. The American is a born dancer, which is merely to say that he is what Dr. Patterson has called 'aggressively rhythmic.' I have been struck many times with the fact that the most conservative have been unable to follow the rhythms of *vers libre* until it has been read aloud to them. I doubt whether you have ever heard *vers libre* read aloud by an expert. I have often had people come up to me, after my lectures, and tell me that they had no idea of the musical effect of this type of verse before. You are quite right when you say in your letter that there is a double rhythm in much metrical verse, the rhythm of the metre and the rhythm of the words. But there are times when this double rhythm jars, and the particular kinds of rhythm of cadenced verse can by no means be arrived at in strict metre.

The poet whom you quote as not knowing when metrical lines had crept into his cadenced verse must have been a very uneducated young man. If you had said that the majority of American poets were quite ungrounded in the technique of their art, you would have made a point which no one could dispute.

To be so expert in a form that it can be forgotten even while composing in it, is a good point, but you seem to forget that the *vers libriste* also may have reached the point where he can forget his form.

Your statement of the Imagistic point of view is correct and sympathetic in the main, but a few misstatements have crept into it. For instance, T. S. Eliot is not, in any sense, an Imagist. I fear you must leave him out, or you will open yourself to the charge that you have not clearly comprehended what Imagism is. I think, to be fair, you must put in, that in their statement of maxims, the Imagists carefully said that their tenets were not new, but that many of them had fallen into desuetude.

You go too far, also, in saying that the Imagists 'will describe sand with words that are as sandy as possible; hair with words that are as hairy as possible.' That is pushing a theory to the point of the ridiculous, and the older poets have sinned (if it be a sin) in this matter far worse than

ever we have done. What about Southey's 'Falls of Lo-
dore,' or the famous

'Quadripedante putrem sonitu quatit ungula campum'

of Virgil? Why, even that arch-conservative, Alexander
Pope, says:

"'Tis not enough no harshness gives offence;
The sound must seem an echo to the sense.'

And he proceeds to do the thing you despise for eight lines,
as illustration.

The essence of Imagism, and indeed of most modern poetry, you have not got. Nature is always 'still elsewhere.'
Yet this feeling for the something beyond we do get when
we look at 'the pine-tree, the river, or the bank of flowers.'
The modern poet believes that when he gives these pictures
of scenes as they appear to him, the something beyond will
be present to the reader as it would be if he actually saw them.

In comparing 'Wakefulness' with 'Westminster Bridge'
you choose one of my poorest poems and one of Words-
worth's best, which is a little hard on me, and I cannot see
any connection between the two except that Wordsworth
has Westminster Bridge in his title, and I have Battersea
Bridge in my text.

You give Masters some hard knocks, which I think are
deserved. His work since 'Spoon River' is lamentable. I
am afraid that you weaken your point by considering him
as a technician at all, but I can scarcely be the one to quarrel with that.

I am a great admirer of Mr. Sandburg's work, but I
think he overdoes his Americanism in his wording, on occasion. The differences in our points of view (yours and mine)
could hardly be better illustrated than in the two poems
you quote, his and Mr. de la Mare's, for I think Sandburg's
is a fine thing, and Mr. de la Mare's a poor example of his
style. To borrow your method for a moment, I should call
this poem excessively weak and dull — will you forgive me?

To come to myself. I quite agree with you that 'A Dome
of Many-Coloured Glass' is a very juvenile first book. I
have long wanted to let it go out of print and only save the

best poems in it, but my publishers will not hear of it. I may shock you by admitting that I should preserve the sonnets. I wonder what you mean by saying that they are not technically correct. I suppose you mean in the arrangement of the sestet, but I think I could cite authority for everything I do in them. I am scarcely the one to defend them on the score of their being bad poetry, am I? But I should be interested to talk to you about them.

You do however make one sad blunder. I have never in my life written a line to sustain a thesis. I wish you knew me. Being both a poet and a critic, I see the reason after I have written the poems. Also, I am neither a pragmatist nor a liar (and these are synonymous terms, are they not?), I should consider it the height of dishonesty to write a book of critical biographies to prove my point of view the only tenable one. If I see in the Imagists an evolutionary change, I must say what I believe. The book was written, not to rank certain poets as 'good, better, best,' but to show why and how a movement came into being and to what it is tending.

You make a mistake in stating that 'Men, Women and Ghosts' appeared immediately after 'A Dome.' It was 'Sword Blades and Poppy Seed' that followed 'A Dome' and that after an interval of two years, in 1914. 'Six French Poets' came out in 1915, and 'Men, Women and Ghosts' not until 1916.

Are you not a bit dogmatic in saying of the art of Japan, 'it is an art remote from us, one alien to the texture of our souls,' since to some of us it is not alien at all. Had you not better qualify this? You do not wish to open yourself to the smile which greeted the remark of that ingenuous member of Commodore Perry's expedition who, in speaking of a colour print by Hokusai, announced that the painter was ignorant of design.

I wonder if I am really growing more metallic. I hope not. You do not prove it by your quotation. Surely you know that the Incas' gardens were really made of gold and silver and precious stones. You are the first person who has discerned signs of 'failing strength' in 'Legends'... But this is your point of view and I am glad to learn it.

I escape you, however, when you say 'she has resigned herself with practical completeness to "polyphonic prose."' How do you make that out? There were eleven poems in 'Legends,' and only three of them were in 'polyphonic prose,' while four were in strict metrical verse, two in *vers libre*, and two in a mixture of *vers libre* and metrical verse. My next book of poems will be entirely devoted to New England scenes and subjects, and so far as the book has progressed, not one of the poems is in 'polyphonic.' Also, I have, in this coming volume, done no searching for my subjects, they lie to my hand. No, dear Mr. Maynard, you cannot pigeonhole me, I am the despair of critics who try to do that. It may be a weakness to be so eclectic in taste, but I cannot help it, I am made that way.

Your definition of poetry is ingenious, but I scarcely think it covers all the ground. Poetry is one of the great fundamentals of life, and fundamentals do not fit neatly into definitions. But no one can be more in sympathy with the point of view that poetry is a high and serious calling, we are at one on that. It is more important to agree than to disagree. I am reaching the years when I care little for argument. The good will last, the bad will perish. Hostile criticism can only affect the moment, the work criticized bears in itself the seeds of continuance or decay. So you must forgive me if I see in your paper more friendliness than severity, in spite of your strictures. You have wisely eschewed argument in favour of opinion, and no one has a right to object to another's opinions. Taste is individual and cannot be quarrelled with. I do not agree with you, of course, but I recognize that you have tried to be fair and your attitude forbids me to be less generous. After all, we are a small company, we seekers of beauty, and we differ more from the rest of the world than we do from one another. And now I have written too long a letter, both for your time and for mine, so I will only thank you once more for your letter and for letting me see this interesting paper.

Sincerely yours,

On Saturday the 19th, after the Yale game, she gave a dinner for Professor Paul Miliukov (former Minister of Affairs in Kerensky's Cabinet), Dr. William B. Coley, the Loweses, the Streeters and the John Palfreys. Miss Lowell argued vehemently about America with Miliukov; later he wrote that she had changed many of his ideas.

A less successful if more dramatic dinner was that given for John Collings Squire, editor of the London *Mercury*, and his friend Alan Patrick Herbert, on the staff of *Punch*. Both wrote conservative verse. Mr. (now Sir John) Squire had early taken a dislike to Amy Lowell's work; and in 1917, when he was editing the *New Statesman*, he had even published this choice morsel of his own, over the pseudonym of 'Solomon Eagle':

> The dominating figure (I am not speaking of the great public, but of the younger literary circles) is Miss Amy Lowell, a terrific Amazon who has headed charges of young and very bad vers-librists into every newspaper office in the States. You cannot open a paper of any standing without finding her name scrawled all over it. Her own verse is very banal. But it is written in lines of unequal lengths, so (it is argued) there must be something more in it than meets the eye.

Needless to say, a clipping bureau provided her with a copy as reprinted in the *Chicago Post* of May 18, 1917; and since his later writings on the New Poetry in America were of a kind, she had no reason to expect much of their meeting. Still, many enemies had become personal friends after meeting her; and many persons insisted that Jack Squire was not a bad sort; so, hearing that he was in America, she wrote him on October 31, inquiring when he was to be in Boston, and inviting him to dinner.

> Vachel Lindsay wrote me a year ago, and asked me to look you up when you came to this country, and this letter is my endeavour to obey his request and my own desire at the same time. On paper, I believe, we are at daggers

drawn, but I see no reason why our controversy should be carried into life. As a matter of fact, there are few modern writers whom I enjoy reading so much as I do you, and although I scarcely imagine you can echo the reverse of that sentiment, yet certainly we must meet.

The meeting, however, was not auspicious. The guests arrived in a blizzard. The conversation at the dinner-table between the two, and over the coffee afterwards, ran chiefly on this model:

'But why did you call me an Amazon?'

'Oh, I assure you, Amazons are very charming.'

'Yes, but why "terrific"?'

Meanwhile Mr. Herbert sat silent behind a fixed smile.

Presently the conversation turned upon Keats, and Mr. Squire insisted that he must see her collection. So the safe was opened, and item after item was handed to him; but nothing seemed quite to satisfy him. There was a mistake in the Latin on Keats's school medal, and so forth. Finally, however, when the manuscript of the 'Eve of St. Agnes' was produced, he assured Miss Lowell that it was not the original manuscript. The original was somewhere else; just where, he could not recollect at the moment; and Professor Lowes remarked firmly:

'If you will look at it, Mr. Squire, I think you will see it *is* the original.'

But Mr. Squire dropped it on the table and sauntered away to join the rest of the guests at the other end of the library, leaving the two gazing at each other across the famous paper, while the blizzard raged outside.

It was no elfin storm from faery-land. Long after the guests had gone out into the storm it raged on, then paused only to return. The snow became sleet, and weighted down the boughs of the trees in her park, until they split from the trunks, snapping like gunshots. All the wires went down: she had no lights and no telephone on the 29th. It was one of the handsomest and most disastrous ice-storms that New England had known for many years.

On the 30th, she left for ten days in New York, beginning with a speech at the National Arts Club (it was an 'author's day' — and perhaps this was the occasion when the club cat interrupted a poem by strolling onto the platform; whereupon Miss Lowell read 'To Winky'), afterwards signing copies of *Legends* for admirers, then dining there, only to rush away at 10:30, to speak on poetry at another dinner, that of the Society of Arts and Sciences, at the Hotel Astor. Most of her hours in New York she spent working over the Keats material.

She returned in time to read from her poems to the Brookline Women's Club, at Whitney Hall, on December 12. On the 14th, she began sending out the complimentary copies of *Fir-Flower Tablets*. The delay had been long; and it appeared too late to get reviews in time for the Christmas trade.

For four years, since Mrs. Ayscough's visit to Miss Lowell in November, 1917, the two women had worked over these poems, chiefly by trans-Pacific mail, though with occasional meetings. It was an unusually happy collaboration. Mrs. Ayscough had lived in her birthplace, Shanghai, practically all her life, although she went to school and came out in Boston, her mother's city. For many years she was the librarian of the North China branch of the Royal Asiatic Society; and so well did she do her job that she became one of the eight honorary members of the society, the first woman to receive that honor. An expert sinologue, she also had the services of Mr. Nung Chu, who, though he knew no English, gladly furnished her with all the apparatus of the scholia as well as the analyses of the written characters, the importance of which Miss Lowell had discovered during Mrs. Ayscough's visit in June, 1918. Mrs. Ayscough would prepare a word-for-word translation of each poem, with expansions, explanations, and references added in red ink, all of which was followed by an analysis of each character into its roots, various meanings, and implications. From this complicated manuscript Miss Lowell would work, writing her poem line for line with the original, then sending her version to Mrs. Ayscough. Some poems would turn out satisfactorily in half an hour; others crossed and recrossed America and the Pacific several times before they were right. When Mrs. Ayscough came to Sevenels, they would go over all the manuscripts that had been completed since they met last.

Fir-Flower Tablets may be looked on as a climax of a literary trend of the times. In 1852, the year before Perry's great expedition, Richard Henry Stoddard included some Chinese subjects in his *Poems*, and Chivers published his 'Chinese Serenade'; from that year on, the Far East appealed more and more to American writers.[1] By the time that the New Poetry began to appear, there were many translations, English and French, which poets were reading and paraphrasing or imitating. To ascribe the source of this interest to any one person or book would be impossible; it was simply in the air.

The older poets had been attracted, after the romantic fashion, by a new *flair* or *décor*; the modern poets, however, recognized in the Chinese poets not something strange but something kindred. As Mrs. Ayscough pointed out in her Introduction, there had lately sprung up in America and England a type of poetry which was so closely allied to the Chinese in method and intention as to be very striking; she was therefore able to illustrate the difficulties of translation by using Amy Lowell's 'Nostalgia' as an example, on the supposition that it was to be translated into Chinese. The modern attitude of mind was closely akin to that

---

[1] For a brief outline, see William Leonard Schwartz's 'L'Appel de l'Extrême-Orient dans la Poésie des États-Unis,' *Revue de littérature comparée* année 1928, fasc. I.

of the ancient Chinese; therefore the kinship was felt, and
therefore so much translation and imitation were in the
air. Pound's *Cathay* (based on the notes of Ernest Fenol-
losa of Salem), which Miss Lowell admired very much,
was one of these volumes; she praised it in a letter to
Miss Monroe, and when she broached her own project to
Fletcher, she wrote him (August 16, 1918): 'I do not claim
that these translations are any better as poems, nor perhaps as good, as Ezra's, but they are much more accurate.' [1] Arthur Waley's translations were already appearing in the periodicals when Miss Lowell and Mrs. Ayscough started; before they finished, Witter Bynner's were
in progress.

Miss Lowell's enthusiasm and her plans for the book appear in a letter to Florence Ayscough, August 16, 1919:

> The great poets of the T'ang Dynasty, particularly Li
> T'ai Po, are without doubt among the finest poets that the
> world has ever had. I am perfectly willing to shriek Li T'ai
> Po's fame to the winds of Heaven. He seems to me to rank
> second to none in any country in lyric poetry, and it seems
> to me as though Tu Fu were equally fine, and a number of
> these T'ang poets, as I keep coming across them, are re-
> markable. But, as a rule, the later people are not so good,
> not nearly so good; and as to those ladies' poetry which
> your teacher is attached to, they simply are not worth
> anything....
>
> The best translation of all is Waley's, and he hardly
> gives anything of Li T'ai Po's, and personally, considering
> how greatly you improved upon all of Waley's translations,
> I do not think it matters if we duplicate some of the things
> he has used. The French translations are on the whole
> better than the English, but even they have not the pe-
> culiar flavour of the originals. Therefore it comes down

[1] The curious might find it amusing to compare 'Gone' on page 18 of Herbert
A. Giles's *Chinese Poetry in English Verse*, London, 1898; 'Liu Ch'e' of Ezra
Pound, in *Des Imagistes*, New York, 1914; and the Lowell-Ayscough version of
the same poem, 'To the Air: "The Fallen Leaves and the Plaintive Cicada"'
on page 139 of *Fir-Flower Tablets*.

to the fact that any one who wants to know anything about Chinese poetry must read Waley or nothing, for in no other way can one get anything at all. Now that is exactly where our position comes in. We are to give other things from those Waley has given, and do those in which we duplicate his choice better than he has done them. We are to keep the Chinese flavour, but it is absolutely imperative that we pick out the best Chinese things to translate and do not spend our time wandering down bypaths, no matter how inveigling the bypaths may be. I think also that we cannot, in this book, go in for narrative things....

I do not think we had better attempt any of the odes in this volume. They are too long and to me not as interesting. It is the lyrics and the human lyrics to which we want to cling, and the lyrics of the best poets that China has produced. Never mind if they have been done before fifty times, they have never been done well except by Waley, and that is all that need concern us.

By the way, I have been reading a most fascinating Chinese novel of the 16th Century. It is called 'Yu Chiao Li' and is translated by Remusat. I can imagine that in the original it must be extremely charming. Even in the translation, with most of the local colour taken out, it is very beautiful. Get hold of it in the original. We might possibly do it in English when we have finished our book of poems, but for God's sake, don't go off on it now. Let's stick to our lyrics until we have translated two hundred of them....

I am absolutely drowned in Chinese literature, all I can get in English and French translations, and I am beginning to understand a good many things that I did not understand before....

At last, however, the four years' labor was over, and their volume of 137 Chinese poems, eighty-three of which were by Li T'ai Po and thirteen by Tu Fu, was on the stands in time for the Christmas sale though not for Christmas reviews.

With the new year, 1922, the reviews began to come in,

at first of a uniform enthusiasm. Mrs. Ayscough sent over the translations of some poems by Tu Fu, who was to be the central figure of their next book, but Miss Lowell objected (January 9):

> Now, my dear, please do not send me any more poems at the moment. You know I cannot do them now; I told you that I should not be able to look at them for a year. I am doing Keats now, and as soon as I see these Chinese poems and read them, I immediately begin doing them in my head; and that is just what I do not want to do, for I must not be taken out of the Keats mood until the book is done. This does not mean that I do not want you to write me about them and tell me all your difficulties; it only means that I must not read even the analyses until the Keats book is finished, and that will not be until I get through the proof next Autumn.

In fact, the more she got into Keats, the more there seemed to do, and she determined to give up the spring trip to England in order to make sure that her manuscript would be finished. (Actually, when autumn came, she was just starting the writing; and when the next autumn came, only half the book was done; and not until July, 1924, was the manuscript complete. So much slower is scholarship than creation.)

In the second week of January, she set out on another tour. From the 11th to the 15th she was in Cleveland; on the evening of the 12th, she read her poems to the Cleveland Women's City Club. On January 16, she was in Pittsburgh, in the afternoon reading to the Twentieth Century Club and in the evening being given a reception by the Fine Arts Department of the Carnegie Technological Institute between two plays 'In Honor of Miss Amy Lowell.' Among those who greeted her were the parents of Malcolm Cowley and of Hervey Allen. On the 19th, she went to New York; on the 20th, she read to the Contemporary Club of Newark, New Jersey; on Sunday afternoon, the

AMY LOWELL IN 1922

22d, she read 'Many Swans' at St. Mark's-in-the-Bouwerie, with two intermissions of Indian music. On the next day, she read at the MacDowell Club, for the benefit of the MacDowell Colonists' Building and Organization Fund; another reader was Elinor Wylie, whose first book, *Nets to Catch the Wind*, had just appeared. Miss Lowell was instantly attracted by the woman and her work, placing her below her adored Emily Dickinson and above Edna St. Vincent Millay, in spite of her great admiration for *Aria da Capo*. On the 24th, she dined with the Cosmopolitan Club; all the guests rose as she entered. Robinson was there, but silent as usual; Sandburg and Untermeyer were among the speakers. On the afternoon of the next day, she read at the Bowling Green Neighborhood Association; the other readers were Anna Hempstead Branch, Bodenheim, Hamlin Garland, Arthur Guiterman, Edwin Markham, and Margaret Widdemer.

That evening, the Poetry Society of America held its annual dinner at the Hotel Astor. Witter Bynner, the president, had announced an 'all-American night,' and had actually got representative poets from forty of the states; the program, consequently, was very long, and (as the published accounts of it complained) not very enlivening. The first speech of real interest was given by Dr. Chang Peng Chun, who contrasted the American and the Chinese attitudes towards poetry. It was after midnight when Sandburg (in gray suit and blue shirt) roused the guests again, with his definitions of poetry and his 'Windy City.' Miss Lowell was saved for the very end; it was nearly one o'clock when she rose — and all the guests rose with her, in tribute to her services to poetry. Her appeal for true criticism became an acid anathema of the trend of the whole evening. The president (she complained to Florence Ayscough on February 15) 'insulted me in his introductory speech. Naturally I got back at him with an awful slam and left him nowhere.' Excepting Dr. Chun and Sandburg, she damned the dinner as 'a phonograph repeating errors,' and called for 'the sharp clash of critical emotional insight.' Finally she read 'Lilacs.' [1]

On January 26, she gave her Whitman lecture at the Free Public Library, at Trenton; on the 27th, she talked at a symposium held under the auspices of Mrs. Edwin Markham at the Waldorf Astoria for the Mary Fisher Home. After this, she was free to return to Brookline.

In February, the sinologues began to publish their reviews of *Fir-Flower Tablets*. Arthur Waley, the one person who they thought knew enough to pronounce seriously on their work, and who would surely be hostile, published his critique in the 'Literary Review' of the New York *Evening Post* for February 4, 1922; although not so violent as had been expected, it nevertheless contained a list of their errors which Miss Lowell was sure were not errors at all; but she needed Mrs. Ayscough's aid to answer authoritatively, and she, alas! was far away in China. Witter Bynner, whose letters signed 'Emanuel' had been so friendly ever since the Spectrist hoax, but whose public utterances sometimes required private reassurances that he had been misquoted, published sixteen Chinese poems in the February *Poetry*, with an article on translating from the Chinese, which contained a sentence about the danger of overemphasizing the component radicals of Chinese characters. Miss Lowell explained his attitude by a natural pique that his own book had been anticipated so effectively. And again (as she wrote Mrs. Ayscough on February 18):

> I am enclosing a nasty slam which came out as a review in the 'Chinese Students' Monthly.' I told Mr. Koo, the editor of the monthly, what would be the result if he handed the review to a pupil of Professor Babbitt's. You can see

[1] Dorothy Dudley: 'Notes from the P.S.A., Annual Dinner,' *Poetry* (xx, 53–56), April, 1922. Jessie Rittenhouse: *My House of Life*, Boston, 1934, p. 261. John Farrar: 'Gossip Shop,' *Bookman* (lv, 87), March, 1922.

Babbitt's gunman's manner in this young whipper-snapper's remarks about 'free verse.' It is such a silly paper that it could not hurt a flea; besides which, the 'Chinese Students' Monthly' goes nowhere except to Chinese students, so far as I know. I have written a somewhat strong letter to Mr. Koo, a copy of which I enclose. I should not take it up with him if I were you, but go ahead with the paper you are writing for him utterly regardless of this review. It is not worth noticing....

I am considerably wrought up over these things and am awfully mad with the 'Chinese Students' reviewer. It gave me a violent headache and a sleepless night, but these things cannot be helped, they are part of the game. All of which proves what I have always known, that scholars are the enemies of literature. They have nearly killed the Greek for us, and up to date they have killed the Chinese.

Now, my dear, I will not write any more now, or my heated feelings will burn up the paper. Please back up my contentions in my letter to Mr. Canby in your article, and above all things pitch into Waley for thinking that Giles's translation of 'Night Thoughts' is nearer the original than mine. I have not taken up his objections to my cadence because they are nonsense.

On February 4, Carl Sandburg came on to give the first of a series of poetry lectures at the Women's City Club in Boston; she entertained him, and two weeks later gave the last of the series herself. Then she went on another brief tour. On Monday the 20th she gave her Keats lecture at Vassar; then, after two days in New York, she read her poems at the Troy Forum, in the Y.M.C.A. hall at Troy, New York, and after spending the night at Albany returned home. Here she found awaiting her a copy of Elinor Wylie's *Nets to Catch the Wind*, which she acknowledged on February 28:

I am very glad indeed to have this book from you, and very glad indeed that I bought the other which I have already given away to some one who did not know your work. My admiration for your poetry is only deepened by reading it again. I have been over many of these poems several times, and the neatness and deftness of your touch is something very remarkable. I think you chose among your best to read that night at the MacDowell Club, but I have also a great weakness for 'Bronze Trumpets and Sea Water' and 'A Proud Lady.' Some of your lines are so striking and inevitable that I feel I shall never lose them, such as 'Silver wasp nests hang like fruit.'

I can see perfectly why you do not care to write in cadenced verse. Your particular kind of effect could not possibly be got in *vers libre*. You must have just the sort of rhythms you use, and you must have the impact of your perfect and delightful rhymes; were you to put any of these poems into cadenced verse they would lose at least half their value. I know no one in this country who can give the scene-pictures in this kind of form that you can. It is a quality I had thought peculiar to English poets until I came across it again in so many of your things; for instance: 'Wild Peaches' and 'Velvet Shoes.' I like you least when you copy a mode as in 'The Eagle and the Mole' and 'The Lion and the Lamb' and 'The Prinkin' Leddy.'

You have set yourself an awful task to live up to your own first book. But what an excellent first book to live up to! Strength to your pen, and believe me, with appreciation and gratitude,

Very sincerely yours,

The answer was written March 9:

DEAR MISS LOWELL —

I must thank you with all my heart for your letter, which contained such kind & unexpected encouragement that I have been quite breathless ever since I read it. Most of all I thank you for bidding me stick to my last of rhymed verse, for only in that medium do I feel at ease & happy. Nevertheless, I owe much to your example, though you might not think it — you have taught me a great deal, & your six Frenchmen have also taught me something. 'Velvet Shoes' would never have been written but for the

Simone poems of de Gourmont — he made me think of stepping softly, like that, without emotion.

Perhaps my five years in rural England gave me my pastoral accent, but I think twenty-five New England summers gave me more.

You have given me new hope for the hard work which is inevitably in front of me, if I'm to be any real good at all. Believe me, with gratitude

Faithfully yours

ELINOR WYLIE

March 9th

As she was not going to Europe in the spring, she planned to visit Charleston, South Carolina, instead. Hervey Allen had been urging her to come, and a poetry society had been started there (to which she sent an encouraging paragraph for its bulletin). But just now, Mr. W. van R. Whitall offered an annual cash prize of $250, which he placed at the Society's disposal. It was to be called 'The Blindman Prize' in honor of Hervey Allen's war-poem, 'The Blindman,' which long ago he had read to Miss Lowell, who persuaded him to revise it, and then sold it for him to the *North American Review*. It was only fitting that she should be asked to judge the first contest; after some hesitation, she accepted, on condition that all the manuscripts be sent her. After the contest was closed, however, she made a second stipulation; that all the manuscripts be typed; which meant that somebody in Charleston did it. Three hundred and sixty poems in an eight-pound bale were shipped north in January. By March 1, she had read through the entire lot; on March 11, she announced to the Society that Grace Hazard Conkling's 'Variations on a Theme' was the winner, with Wallace Stevens's 'From the Journal of Crispin' as the first Honorable Mention.

Besides working up her notes for the life of Keats, she was also selling poems for Malcolm Cowley, who was abroad; reviewing V. Sackville-West's *Dragon in Shallow Water*; contributing to Untermeyer's second *Miscellany of American Poetry*, which was being run on somewhat the scheme of the old Imagist anthologies; and trying to get Fletcher's books reissued, on the grounds that one of her 'Tendencies' ought not to be unavailable. On March 10, she gave her Keats lecture at the Hampshire Bookshop in Northampton; on the evening of the 20th, she read her poems to the Springfield Poetry Society, in the hall of the Technical High School there.

Then she started southward. On the 23d, she was in Philadelphia; in the afternoon she filled the ballroom of the Bellevue-Stratford with a lecture on 'Three Chinese Poets,' the second lecture in a series of four sponsored by the Bryn Mawr Chinese Scholarship Committee. That evening she dined at the college, and spoke informally at the Deanery to a group of students. She spent the week-end in Washington, reaching Charleston on the 28th.

She had anticipated so much glamour from the trip! To Hervey Allen she had written: 'I certainly hope to be able to see the Middleton place again while I am there. I remember it so vividly. It used to be an all day excursion.' And to H. D. (March 20):

> I am just starting off on another lecture trip which will carry me to Charleston. It should be lovely there. I was there once sixteen years ago. There is a beautiful old place there laid out by Michaux, a famous landscape gardener, in the eighteenth century. The place is abandoned, has been, I think, since the Civil War, but the grounds remain all laid out with azaleas, and paths running between them, and the azaleas are as high as small trees, and their blossoms drop on paths, and you walk softly upon the colours of the rainbow. How you would delight in it!

Michaux had given some of these same azaleas to her great-grandfather; they still bloomed at Sevenels.

Charleston was not all as she had remembered it:

modernity had been busy cleaning and paving and improving. 'Commerce, are you worth this?' she inquired in a poem called 'Charleston, South Carolina.' Many of the old families had disappeared, and the beautiful Pringle home was now a boarding house. The two sisters who had taken oath not to leave their house until the city was free of Yankee dominance were dead; to commemorate them and the jouncing-board on which they had exercised, Miss Lowell wrote 'The Vow.' The magnificent Middleton Place, with its formal garden of ogee terraces, had been cleared of its jungle of overgrowth, but was as lovely as ever, and inspired yet another poem. Nearer town was its rival, 'Magnolia-on-the-Ashby,' recently opened to the public; but as the flowers had reverted to a single flare of magenta — the color she detested so strongly that it was never allowed at Sevenels — she recorded her disappointment in another poem.

> Mrs. Ravenel says that there used to be more white and shell-pink and deep crimson and pale yellow in the garden, and that is my recollection of it seventeen years ago.
>
> The truth is, those ancient azaleas have done what many plants do when left to a state of nature: they have reverted to that awful blue-crimson, which, for want of a better word, I have called magenta. We all know the colour, phlox reverts to it constantly.[1]

Josephine Pinckney, DuBose Heyward, and Hervey Allen saw to it that she had a wonderful time. They took her on a ride through a ghostly forest, which again stirred her creative imagination. Her coming was a social event; she was delighted with the surviving old-time ritual of punctiliousness, which reminded her of the Boston of her youth. One thing puzzled her, however: somehow she was never asked to dinner, the meal that she enjoyed best; and not until some months later did she learn that in Charles-

[1] Letter to Harriet Monroe, January 16, 1923.

ton, the dinner hour was 3 P.M., after which the servants always left for the evening.

She met Beatrice Ravenel, with whom she was to correspond at length; and she learned the name of Henry Timrod, the official poet of Charleston.

On March 30, she gave her reading to the Poetry Society of South Carolina; and when the audience rose at her entrance, she was deeply touched.

The first week of April was spent in New York; on the 5th she went out to read at Rosemary Hall, Greenwich, Connecticut, returning to New York for the night. Her room was always waiting for her there, at the Hotel Belmont, with her mattress, lampshade, and so on, just as she preferred them. When she finally got back to Brookline, a great pile of correspondence awaited her; she began answering it on the 12th.

The *Little Review* was in desperate need of assistance. Volume VII (May, 1920 – March, 1921) had dwindled unintentionally into a quarterly. Then the thirteenth episode of *Ulysses* had proved very unlucky: the trial of October, 1920, had forced it to cease publishing what perhaps should never have been serialized in a periodical. One must read all of *Ulysses* before one can understand any single part of it; and even then, some sort of critical introduction is necessary. Consequently, in this series of fragments, published without a word of explanation from the author or editors, and surrounded by dubious material seemingly of the same nature, nothing but the indecency was discernible; and it may even be conjectured that the notoriety which ensued was the chief cause in delaying the American publication of *Ulysses* for thirteen years.

This was the reason why Miss Lowell, who defended Lawrence constantly, could not be persuaded of Joyce's value. As she wrote to Winifred Bryher (March 20):

> ... I think one can say anything, no matter how peculiarly revealing, if one says it in keeping with the setting of the

rest of the poem. For instance, D. H. Lawrence's eroticisms never strike me as otherwise than beautiful because of his point of view in regard to them. On the other hand, James Joyce's attempts in that line are as disagreeable as putrified meat.... It seems to me that realism takes one side of life and throws it on a canvas without its haunting, opposing, and modifying counterpart, with the result that although that side is true to fact, the effect given is not that of real life. Some day I am going to say this in print, for it seems to me the real key to the failure of the realistic school. If you want real realism, and that which is no more squeamish in expression than the moderns are, read Fielding's 'Amelia.'

But it was not a question just of *Ulysses*, it was the whole magazine that Miss Lowell objected to; and she refused any aid.

I feel so strongly that the 'Little Review' has been taking a wrong tack that I cannot see my way to doing anything to help it to continue. If it were possible to give Margaret anything to help her which would not eventually see its way into the 'Little Review,' that would be a different matter; but I know that you and she are so wrapped up in the magazine that it would be quite impossible for either of you to keep to any such condition; therefore I must, most regretfully, say no to your suggestion.

Do you remember that I told you, years ago, when you started on your new tack, that I should have to be counted out as one of the supporters of the magazine, either morally or financially, and I fear I must adhere to that attitude until you and Margaret have a change of heart on the subject. I am awfully sorry, and I know that this letter will grieve you very much, but I cannot see any other direction for me to take.[1]

There was also a cryptic letter from Ezra Pound, dated March 10, which bade her once more to the breach, asked her if she wished to repent and be saved, reminded her that

[1] Letter to Jane Heap, April 15, 1922.

the eye of the needle was narrow, and offered further information if she wanted it. She replied:

24 April, 1922

DEAR EZRA:

Pas de bile, of course, I have never had any. As to what people say about me — bless your heart, do you think that worries me? Because it doesn't, not the least little bit. Of course they say that I pay for my advertising, that's just the sort of thing they would say. It is always a wonder to me why they do not go a step farther and say that I hire somebody to write the poems.

Now how am I going to answer your letter when I do not know what it is about? Of course I should like to know what new scheme you have in view, but I cannot possibly give any assent or dissent to anything until I know what that thing is. Financially, I am a broken reed since the war; aesthetically, I am obstinate; personally, I am friendly, and I consider you an uncommonly fine poet who ought to have an impresario, for your knowledge of how to 'get yourself over,' as we say in this little country, is *nil*.

Good luck, and let us hear from you.

To a poetess who asked whether or not she should publish a book, Miss Lowell replied (April 15):

I do not know how professionally you regard your poetry. (You see I am being quite frank, which I suppose is what you want.) What I mean by 'professionally' is, how much can you count on your creative faculty? Is it going right along, or has it been momentarily galvanized into life by the wave of interest in poetry which is passing over the country? Is it the expression of the experience of your past life only, or do you think that it has energy enough to continue and increase in power? You see, I know nothing at all about the way you started to write, or how long you have been writing and publishing.... I rather imagine that you have been writing off and on all your life, but that in the new poetry movement you have found your true expression — am I right?

To Conrad Aiken, who wrote from England asking permission to use some of her poems in an anthology, she wrote (April 18):

> I think this anthology of yours is an excellent thing, and you have the distinction of being the only American resident in Europe who has lifted his finger to help his countrymen in the eyes of the English. The complete disloyalty of the expatriate Americans is one of the things which keeps America from being as important as it might be in English eyes, for though an Englishman may insist that England is the only country and that all Americans ought to be thankful for the privilege of living there, yet there is no Englishman who does not in his secret heart look down upon a man who denies the worth of his native land. It is because the English so sincerely believe in theirs that they have been able to produce so much in the past and to impose themselves so forcibly upon the world at large.

And to a teacher in a high school who wrote twice asking for a helpful sentiment to inspire a group of eight pupils, she wrote (April 28):

> Your original letter was not answered because I think, as you yourself suggest in this letter of April 26th, the request is presumptuous. In the second place, I do not believe in the silly sentimentalism which supposed that any one's mere words can inspire any one to do anything. If a person cannot be inspired by their sense of duty and their own anxiety and ambition to do good work, no amount of mottoes will help them.
>
> I shall be very glad if you will communicate this as my message to your 'eight.' Tell them from me to learn to rely upon themselves, not to depend upon sentimentalism and false emotionalism, to read all they can of the authors they like, but on no account to bring themselves to the notice of said authors. The authors have done as much for them by writing the books as they have a right to expect, and they have no business to take their time to answer letters. Tell them that there is no difficulty whatever at any

given point in one's life in knowing how one ought to behave or what one ought to do; that the object of life is work
and not amusement; that the way to get ahead is to be
jealous of your hours of work, not jealous of your hours of
leisure; that no man ever succeeds on eight hours a day, and
that I wish them all success.

On April 16, she gave a small dinner for Vachel Lindsay,
after which he developed the written names of the ladies
into fantastic pictures and wrote small poems to accompany them. On the 25th, she took the manuscript of the
Critical Fable to the publishers: it was decided to publish it
as a hoax. The next day she gave a reading for the
Harvard Poetry Society; but as the authorities suddenly
refused to allow an admission charge, the honorarium was
probably the smallest she had ever received. Florence Ayscough arrived on the 26th and stayed until she sailed for
England on May 10; together they arranged for a few corrections in *Fir-Flower Tablets*.

On May 4, Miss Lowell attended a dinner of the American Academy of Arts and Letters at the Somerset Club, to
meet Maurice Donnay and André Chevillon. In the second
week of the month, she went to Michigan; on the 10th, she
spoke and read to the librarians at the Detroit Public
Library, and that evening went to a Faculty dinner at
Ann Arbor, then read afterwards to a crowd of 2500.
Robert Frost introduced her. But before things got
started, the famous reading lamp blew out a fuse, and the
place was plunged in darkness. The janitor could not be
found for half an hour; meanwhile Miss Lowell and Frost
kept the invisible audience in howls of laughter by their
impromptu jests. When at last the lights went on again,
and the audience had sobered down for the poetry, Frost
set them all off again by tripping over the cord, extinguish-
ing the reading lamp once more, and upsetting the pitcher
of water on the speaker's table.

From Ann Arbor, Miss Lowell went to Chicago, where

on the 16th she lectured about Chinese poetry for the
Moody Foundation, in Mandel Hall at the University of
Chicago. The hall was jammed with 1100 people; the
authorities assured her that other would-be auditors had
been turned away 'by the hundreds.' From Chicago, Mrs.
Russell went westward, to Salt Lake City, while Miss
Lowell returned to Brookline. She was to read at Dart-
mouth on the 25th, but the western food had its customary effect on her digestion, and the date was postponed.

On the 27th, she wrote to Florence Ayscough concerning
many matters, but chiefly about the review of *Fir-Flower
Tablets*, and the mean spirit that some people were showing.

I suppose it is inevitable that I should be stressed in reviews here and that you should be stressed in reviews in
China, the reason being, of course, that the magazines
know me and are used to cadenced verse and take the book
as poetry, whereas the sinologues know you and understand
Chinese and know no more about poetry than a flea. Waley
begs me to learn Chinese and do without you, the Chinese
reviewer begs you to let your translations stand as they are
and kick me out. I hope you don't agree with them, for
personally I think our collaboration has been extraordinarily successful and I delight in it.

Mr. ******'s review is negligible to my mind. I do not
know how much Chinese he knows, nor how well qualified
he is to speak on the translations as translations merely,
but he is quite unqualified by temperament and training to
speak on any other side of the book. He is simply a good,
old, narrow-minded, Colonial Englishman, and nothing in
the world is quite as clamped and unintelligent as that.
******'s review was very nice, I thought, in spite of his not
entirely appreciating me. ***** *******'s is really quite
good, but I would not trust too firmly in her if I were you.
I believe that family to be awfully sneaky. I know *****
********** is. They will lick your boots when you are round,
and stick a knife in your back when you are not, with the
greatest joy in the world. The reason she is reserving her

'attack' on me for '*******' is that she knows perfectly well that nobody will care a snap whether she attacks me or not in a Chinese paper, whereas it may make some impression if she attacks me in an English paper. I have written her a letter which I am enclosing to you. Please read it and then pass it on. If she attacks me after that, she will be brazen indeed, for her attack springs from a complete misunderstanding, as I explained to ******* ******* the other day when I was in Chicago. ******'s own review in *** ****** **** is none too nice. You will see how she gets back at me. Now the reason for this is quite simple. ****** told me herself that she had tried to do some of these poems from *** ******'s rough translations, and had given them up as too difficult. Naturally she does not want some one else to do what she could not do.

Ah, my dear, you are an innocent lamb! You have no idea of the rings of intrigue in this poetry business. The more successful I am, the more I am hated. Mr. Brett always told me it would be so and I could scarcely believe it, but I am having greater proof of it every day. The public is more and more for me, the poets — that is, those less successful than I — more and more against me. I meet with no jealousy from men who have arrived, like Frost, Lindsay, and Sandburg, but I meet with nothing else from those of the lower rank. Meanwhile my books increase their sales, and I had twenty-five hundred people to hear me speak at Ann Arbor two weeks ago.

Another vigorous letter was written to an unfortunate candidate for a higher degree at some university where students were allowed to apply academic methods to contemporary subjects.

31 May, 1922

My dear Miss ******:

I wrote to you on November 20th and told you that you did not understand what Imagism was and that I thought you would be wise to abandon your thesis. Your letter of May 8th shows that you have learnt nothing of the matter since I wrote. I told you in my first letter that there were no poets who called themselves Imagists now. Imagism is not a school but an attitude of mind. You ask me if the present school consists of the six poets in my 'Tendencies in Modern American Poetry.' There is no school; a person may write Imagistic verse at one time and not at another just as they may write Impressionistic verse at one time and not at another. The truth of the matter is, dear Madam, that you have not any idea of what you are writing about, and you will do very well to abandon it once and for all. It is quite clear that your type of mind is quite incapable of making the necessary distinctions in manners of verse. I write severely because there is no sense in a person's trying to write upon a subject when they do not know what the subject they are writing about is, and it is just this sort of muddle-headed thinking which should be combatted in our modern educational system.

I have never heard of any Imagistic poets in France, and I do not think there are any or ever were. The three issues of 'Some Imagist Poets' are all equally important, and they are intended to contain only Imagistic verse. Mr. Lawrence's contributions, however, depart from the type. I now beg you once more to give up the idea of writing on the subject.

Sincerely yours,

As yet, not a line of the Keats biography had been written. She had been tracking down great-nieces of the poet in Kentucky and other places; following vague rumors of books annotated by Keats; getting manuscripts copied and collated with the published texts; and even giving one shy and reluctant collector half her lock of Fanny Brawne's hair.

She was delighted to get a letter from Edwin Markham, who addressed the envelope ——

Amy Lowell,
Poet,
Near Boston.

D. H. Lawrence sent her a postcard from Ceylon, and a letter from shipboard:

20 May 1922

MY DEAR AMY:

Here we are rolling gently in the Great Australian Bight, on a sea swelling from the Antartic. It is very nice. Once having started wandering I feel I shall never stop. We stayed two months in Ceylon and two weeks in West Australia. I got your letter two days ago in Perth, an hour before we sailed. Glad everything goes on. — This makes two books you have sent me to Germany, and neither of them have I got. — As for Keats, while there's a human being left on earth the last word will never be said about anything.

I am enjoying the face of the earth and letting my Muse, dear hussy, repent her ways. 'Get thee to a nunnery' I said to her. Heaven knows if we shall ever see her face again, unveiled, uncoiffed.

The earth — & man — is a strange mystery: always *rather* what you expected, and yet oh, so different. So different. One wonders if all books are just so many parish magazines. — The talk is just on top.

Alas for me and my erotic reputation! Tell them I have sent my Muse into a nunnery while I took a look at the world.

I expect we shall come via the South Seas to America.

Greet Mrs. Russell. Not having a secretary to sign my letter I sign it myself.

D. H. LAWRENCE

On May 5, Aldington had written her about the serious illness of a poet he knew, and whose work he valued highly; he wanted her to become privately the American representative of a committee to provide him with an annuity. Though she had never met him, she did not send her refusal until June 24, as she had wanted to think the thing over, and also make certain inquiries. Pound, she learned, had approached Harriet Monroe for the same purpose. Miss Lowell thought it surprising that the man's family had not been appealed to, in the first place; she doubted the value of helping a man that way, unless he was in dire straits; and finally, she had seen nothing yet in his work which led her to suppose that he would ever rank very high.

I do not greatly admire his poetry although I consider it expert and rather captivating. I think he has more cleverness than real poetic feeling, and that is not in the least because his kind of poetry is not the kind I write. His criticisms seem to me a mixture of the pedantic and jejune....

Sometime I hope to meet [him] in the flesh, and, if his prejudices against me will permit, perhaps I may find out what he is really like, and my own prejudice may vanish into the wind, although I scarcely think that my opinion of his literary merit will undergo any alteration. However, it is up to you to bring a meeting about, and under as pleasant auspices as possible, if we should ever find ourselves all three in the same town.

Suddenly Pound announced publicly what Aldington was trying to do privately, and the two men joined forces — though in vain, as far as Miss Lowell was concerned.

Proofs of the *Critical Fable* came in and were corrected in the first half of July; as for Keats, it seemed as though she never would get to the creative part, the actual writing. To Elsie Sergeant she wrote on July 2:

Keats goes forward steadily and extraordinarily slowly. The pure drudgery connected with it is something colossal. At the moment, I am doing a task which bores me so completely that I go to sleep over it every night. It wears out my eyes and my nerves and nearly drives me crazy. Here it is, and you can judge: Mr. Whitall owns the copy of 'Endymion' annotated by Woodhouse. These notes were copied by Buxton Forman, but Mr. Whitall felt confident that Buxton Forman had not used all the notes, so he very kindly lent me his copy, which means that I have to compare everything written by Woodhouse in a nasty crabbed, little handwriting, with the notes in Buxton Forman's five volume edition in somewhat smaller print

than newspaper print, and you can conceive what happens
to my eyes and my temper after a couple of hours of such
work. I have been through more than half the book and
have only found ten things which I felt it necessary to take,
either because Buxton Forman had not got them, or because
he had put them in such cryptic form that it was difficult
to understand them. At the end of twenty pages, I give out
entirely, and there are two hundred in the book. I still
have two cantos left of Keats's annotations in the 'Faerie
Queene' to copy, and the dear boy in his zeal annotated
almost everything. If I could only get to the real constructive work I should be happy, but this sort of thing gets my
goat. I was not made for a scholar.

Miss Lowell actually, however, had reached the second
stage of scholarly work. The first is the enthusiasm at the
choice of a subject, when the completion of the task seems
easy. The second is the drudgery of heavy spade-work,
necessary to break up the ground. The scholar is then
busy in learning all that his predecessors have discovered,
and in gathering whatever new material he can find; and as
yet he does not really know how his own work is going to
shape itself. At the end of the month (July 25) she wrote
to Lowes: 'I have got to the point where I am setting up
my volume, and I have struck a large sized query. Shall I
write it as a biography, or shall I write it as a series of chapters on certain subjects: his poetry, his friends, Fanny
Brawne, etc., etc., etc.?' She had not, in short, yet
reached the third stage, where the work takes form, the
material is pretty much covered, and genuine discoveries
begin to rouse the hunting or detective instinct, which
provides scholars with their ecstasies. But it is notable
that, while she was in this dreary second stage, she never
allotted the work however monotonous or mechanical to
another: she herself had to decipher the crabbed handwriting and read the small type of the printed version, as
she did not trust anybody to do it as accurately as herself,
and furthermore, there was the danger of not getting into

the thing so well. She had, in short, the instinct of the genuine scholar.

On Monday, July 17, she went to see the professional debut of the Braggiotti sisters at Keith's Theater. Everybody in Boston knew them; for one grandmother had been a Boston woman and the other a Polish countess. The family had a villa near Florence, well-known to the W. W. Story group, and a Brookline house with a piano in every room. They combined social position with talent; the glamour of their fashionable, bohemian lives added to their attractiveness; and when difficulties made it necessary for the girls to take the step from the Vincent Club to the professional stage, Boston loyally made an event of the debut. The sisters were indeed charming dancers, and Amy Lowell responded to their charm with a poem, 'To Francesca Braggiotti,' which she wrote when she got home from the performance.

Another poem she wrote this July was 'To a Gentleman who Wanted to See the First Drafts of my Poems in the Interests of Psychological Research into the Workings of the Creative Mind.' This gentleman was Professor Walter V. Bingham, the head of the psychology department of the Carnegie Institute at Pittsburgh, who just then was teaching at the Harvard Summer School. As he had married the daughter of Mabel Loomis Todd, the first editor of Emily Dickinson's poems, he was naturally interested in poetry; and at Harvard, Professor Lowes was struggling to finish his study of the creative processes of Coleridge. Lowes brought him out to Sevenels, where he became enthusiastic over the possibility of studying the creation of poetry with Miss Lowell as his subject. Science had virtually no evidence on this most important phenomenon, in fact had not even any slightest notion of a means of approach. And here was Miss Lowell with seemingly no reticences, with a memory that behaved itself at command, and with an intellectual curiosity that promised the heartiest co-operation.

Yet, when it actually became a question of trying to record all that she could remember about the genesis of a poem, she found herself resisting, baulking. She protested that from first drafts, nothing was to be learned except small points about technique and tinkering; and she could not bring herself to save them, even in the interests of science. In spite of a letter he wrote her on July 23, she could not do it: she felt that too much of her life had actually gone into these poems for her ever to be able to disentangle and make clear even the main elements, and then they would probably be misunderstood; furthermore, she feared the effect of this vivisection upon her future work. At last she solved the situation characteristically — by writing her poem, which was really a reply to his letter.

Princeton was planning a series of monographs, to be called *Men and Ideas*; Miss Lowell signed a contract to write one of the series, on the free forms of verse, with the stipulation that the manuscript was not to be expected until January, 1924. But she was never even to start it.

She had not heard from the Hardys for some time. She had never received a reply to her letter about polyphonic prose, written in answer to his questions which he asked after reading *Can Grande's Castle*; and supposing that he had lost interest, she had not written again. On his eightieth birthday, she was one of the many signers of a long cable of congratulations, from the younger writers of America. But now, in the March *Dial* he had told an interviewer that a family named Keats lived within two or three miles of his place; and Miss Lowell wrote for further information. Mrs. Hardy sent the information on July 29; she also said that her husband often spoke of Miss Lowell's visit, which seemed to end an epoch in their lives. He had followed her work with considerable interest, asked American friends who called if they knew how she was, and wrote her when he heard she was ill. Had that letter failed to reach her?

Neither Miss Lowell nor Mrs. Russell had received such a letter; evidently it had gone down in some boat, or otherwise had been lost in transit. She made what amends she could for her seeming rudeness by sending him an inscribed copy of *Legends* in August.

When the August *North American Review* published Amy Lowell's 'The Sisters,' which contained an appreciation of Emily Dickinson, Mrs. Todd sent an enthusiastic letter to Sevenels. Miss Lowell replied on August 9:

> Your letter has given me more pleasure than I have had for many a day. That you, who know Emily Dickinson's work so intimately, should like my poem is something I never dared to hope. To my mind, Emily Dickinson is one of the greatest women poets who ever lived. I wish I could claim to be a pioneer in this attitude, but really, everybody agrees as to her merit today. She wrote half a century ahead of her time, that was all. There is not, to my mind, a sadder page in history than the picture of good, well-meaning Mr. Higginson trying to guide Emily's marvelous genius. You will find that all the modern poets and critics rate her as I do, and it is owing to you, who have collected her poems and her letters with such care, that we know what she was, and a debt of gratitude do we all owe you.
>
> It has been a dream of mine sometime to write a life of Miss Dickinson, but I fear it will never materialize; in fact, I hardly think Mrs. Bianchi would smile upon any one undertaking such a scheme. I am writing a life of Keats now.... However, I shall still keep the hope of writing a book on Emily Dickinson as a dream for the future....

Miss Lowell really hoped some day to write this life of Emily Dickinson — hoped, that is, without committing herself to any over-definite intention. It was something to speculate about; after she had recovered from the Keats biography and had written enough poetry to feel the need of relaxing into prose again, then indeed she might well do it. But much as she admired Emily Dickinson's genius, she was often out of patience with her eccentricities; sometimes she would get to scolding about her Puritan background, her narrow life, her passive submission. But did one of her guests reply in kind, he was at once firmly and unmistakably put right: Emily Dickinson was one of the great poets. Then of course before any biography could be considered, Miss Lowell would have to reconcile the two factions jealously warring over the dead poet's memory and manuscripts; she would have to get the co-operation of Madame Bianchi as well as Mrs. Todd. 'It's just what happened over Keats,' she said; and from the glint in her eye one could see that she rather looked forward to managing the situation. And if she failed, then she could wait until inevitable Time removed the difficulties.

On the 14th, the advance copies of the *Critical Fable* were sent out; the official date of publication was to be September 15, but for such a book, the guessing should start early. It did. Ferris Greenslet told Vachel Lindsay about it, and illustrated the broadmindedness of the author so effectively by mentioning his attitude *pro* and *con* Amy Lowell, that Lindsay proclaimed fiercely that towards her there was no *con*. Greenslet kept Miss Lowell informed about this and other episodes; and she herself prepared an indignant string of arguments to meet those of some man who suspected her of writing it. Louis Untermeyer also suspected her; she replied on September 9:

> I quite agree with you that 'A Critical Fable' is a good book. Ferris sent me an advance copy just as he did you. But, my dear Louis, you are mad if you think I wrote it; I wish to God I had. And permit me to offer you my congratulations on your excellent bluff. From the first moment I opened the book I said to myself: Louis is the only person I know of who would have been likely to write this book, and now you hastily forestall me by suggesting that I have done it, which is one of the neatest little side-steppings

I have ever seen. Oh, Louis, Louis! So you were not going to do that sort of thing again, weren't you? 'Heavens' was to be your last skit, and all the time you had this up your sleeve. All I can say is I envy you in the way you have got us all off and the neatness of your versification. Oh, but don't I recognize that neatness! I chuckled again when I read 'Roast Leviathan.' How anybody, after reading that poem, can think it was not written by the same man who wrote 'A Critical Fable' I do not see. I think it is a bully book, and you have hit the people off wonderfully. If nothing else gave it away, your remarks about my thunderous quality would have done it. You are so kind as to say you will preserve my anonymity; you need not. Alas, Fate will preserve it! But I will preserve yours with the greatest possible care until you give me permission to announce it.

Thus she embarked upon the necessary career of mendacity to which hoaxers are privileged.

On September 8, she read her poems for twenty minutes, between baseball scores and a contralto recital, in the evening program of Station WGI at Medford. Of the unpleasant event she made a pleasant letter to Francesca Braggiotti (September 11):

... it was about as unsympathetic an experience as can well be imagined. If I had stood on the top of the 350 foot radio aerial and shouted poems at the sky, I could have found a sort of thrill in it. What I actually did do was horrible, if one is used to the response of an audience.

We drove up to a large wire enclosure, kept locked and carefully guarded, where we were inspected and let in to a miserable little jerry-built shed. All these precautions were to safeguard the patents which were being perfected in the laboratory at the back. We were ushered into a stuffy little office where the manager's wife, in a bright red glass necklace and clothes to match, did the honours. Then we were shown the transmitting room, about as big as a good-sized closet, stuffed with apparatus, a grand piano, three chairs and a goodnatured, portly contralto and her equally

goodnatured and portly accompanyist, several men, reporters or other, etc. Our station was still for the moment
and the Shepherd Stores were 'operating.' Operating indeed, and we were the patients. Somebody was playing
a flute solo, and the timbre of that flute as it dripped into
the horn was unspeakable. I escaped to the office where
the singer lady seriously consulted me as to whether to sing
two verses or three of a song where somebody parted with
somebody under what appeared to be distressing circumstances. The lady said she was going to sing twelve songs,
at which I promptly advised her to cut all the verses
possible of each, and seriously considered ending my stunt
by advising the listeners to send for the nearest doctor and
ambulance before the concert began.

By this time, that pleasant excitement which always
precedes going into action, as you very well know, had
entirely evaporated, and I felt a good deal as one feels during one's first night at sea. Then they called me, and Mrs.
Russell and I went back into the little closet and I stuffed
myself up against the grand piano on which stood a small
brass stand from which depended a small barrel-shaped
thing which trembled ominously. Mrs. Russell sat behind
me; the manager, having shut the door, ensconced himself
directly in front of me round the curve of the piano, so
that I felt if I spoke loud it would blow his head off. 'Now,'
said he, 'there must not be a sound.' I stopped breathing —
but it was so stuffy there wasn't any air to breathe anyway.
A man in the corner began twirling wheels on a dial-plate.
The manager nodded, and I began desperately to pretend
that that bobbing barrel was the 'fifty thousand people at
least' I was told were listening.

I finished the poem — the fifty thousand could make no
sign, the wheel-man whispered to the manager and went
out. I began another poem, the wheel-man returned, the
manager went out and came back. The next poem —
silence. Began another, the manager shifted the barrel
stand slightly, and suggested some modifications of tone
to me by writing on a piece of paper, all this while I was
reading. It grew hotter and hotter. Electric cars screeched

in the road below; it seemed to me the fifty thousand must hear them. Eight poems did I read, and the fifty thousand grew dimmer to my consciousness every second. Maybe somebody in Ohio was in a fever of appreciation, but I did not know it. My head was splitting. I read eight poems, I said 'Goodnight', and stumbled out to find a melancholy reporter growling that he, who had been listening through receivers in the office, had been cut off and had not heard the end of the last piece, a dramatic story of which he had forever lost the point. I heard the manager telling the contralto that if her voice was powerful, she had better sing out of the window and not at the barrel. I suppose my voice had been stronger than he expected. So ended that experience, and so nearly ended me. I have seldom been so tired. I wonder if dancing to the movies would be as uninspiring as reading to the radio....

It was the first broadcasting of free verse in this country — and probably in the world.

CHAPTER XXIII

A CRITICAL FABLE, KEATS, AND THE RETURN
OF DUSE

'I am no hero worshipper, yet for your sake...'

A Critical Fable was published September 15, 1922. All possible precautions against the discovery of the author had been taken. In the files of Houghton Mifflin his name was William Williams John, of 76 Peterboro Street, Boston — actually the address of her secretary's husband. But only a prying office-boy could discover that much; the general public would use other means; and Miss Lowell had the excellent idea that the question of authorship should not be left open to vague conjecture: the finger of suspicion should be pointed toward some specific person. And for that person she selected the unwitting Leonard Bacon.

Leonard Bacon was then unknown to the public. A recent graduate of Yale, he was professor of English at the University of California, where he had written 'The Banquet of the Poets' for a Harvard-Yale dinner out there, and then had published it anonymously in a students' monthly. Miss Lowell had seen one of the off-prints, and had recognized it as the best satire in verse written in contemporary America. She had never met him; consequently, the ascription of the work to him would take the question of authorship out of her entire circle. And what would be more natural for the author of that anonymous, dextrous, and amiably critical satire on contemporary poets than to produce another, equally anonymous, dextrous, and amiably critical? As he was little known, the public would have that added excitement, the seductive sensation of discovering a genius. Furthermore, Miss Lowell probably hoped that the Yale group of literary journalists (whose preferences often exasperated her) would be stirred to unquestioning enthusiasm if they thought that the author was a Yale man. And finally, it would not do the foremost exponent of free verse any harm to be mistaken for one of the most expert living rhymesters.

So in the morning mail of September 15, Bacon was astounded to receive three letters, from relatives or friends, congratulating him on his *Critical Fable*. Simultaneously, the *Literary Review* (edited by Henry Seidel Canby, of Yale), announced his authorship; and when he denied it, repeated the assertion in a long review. As he later said, he was so bewildered that he almost thought he must have written it; but clinging to his sanity, he replied in rhyme, denying the authorship and attributing it to Amy Lowell.

> Thereupon Miss Lowell wrote a relative of mine that I must be lying. This was a scabrously immoral act. For I now began to appear as a perjurer who had told his story and meant to stick to it, but none the less I had made a lucky hit. I have before me as I write another letter of Miss Lowell's; in which she goes at length into the motives for her duplicity. All of which seems to me rather delicious. But for a bit of luck, I should have found myself playing a modern version of the role of Isaac Bickerstaff for the next ten years.
>
> Nor can I refrain from a word of admiration for Miss Lowell's mendacity which ran the whole gamut from disingenuous innuendo to naked and shameless perversion of the fact. The humor which enabled her to revel in her sins is something which will be missed. I never knew her or even saw her, but how I wish I had! [1]

A Critical Fable was not an analysis of the line of development in modern poetry, like *Tendencies in Modern*

---

[1] From the Introduction to Leonard Bacon's *Guinea-Fowl*, New York, 1927, which outlines his position in the hoax; 'The Banquet of the Poets' is also in the volume. It is the symbolic adaptation of an episode of 1910; youth, naked and intoxicated, bursts in upon a party of poets — the reality shocking all the guests at the very moment when they were defending and even recommending it.

American Poetry; it was a literary portrait-gallery of all those American poets who in Miss Lowell's opinion were the best of their kind, whether modern or conservative. It was an amplification of her prose book, which revised slightly the judgments pronounced there — for example, Frost now took precedence of Robinson, and Sandburg of Masters. The once doubtfully omitted Lindsay was now included; so was herself; and Aiken forces his way in between H. D. and Fletcher. From that point on, all was new material: Sara Teasdale, the Conklings, Kreymborg, the Untermeyers, Pound and Eliot, William Rose Benét, Bodenheim, Stevens, and Millay. Each was chosen because he seemed of something like permanent importance; and as the inclusion itself was a token of respect, Miss Lowell felt free to carp airily at what she felt was his chief fault, as well as to point out his chief excellence. Jocose in tone, the book was really a most serious estimate of the leading figures of American poetry in 1922.

In scheme, the book was a sequel to James Russell Lowell's *Fable for Critics*. Form and meter, even to the rhymed titlepage, were a copy of her cousin's. The action opens on the banks of the Charles in Cambridge, which have now been 'improved' into a parkway; and as the young ego of the plot is poking at a bottleneck of some German vintage (symbol of the inspiration of the older New England poets), James Russell Lowell joins him and praises the place as it used to be. The two glance at the past; the ego puts Poe and Whitman together, and Emily Dickinson after them; the other standard American poets are dismissed as excellent in prose; then the ego explains the obvious failings of the newspaper critics and the scholars. After a glimpse of James Russell Lowell's old home, Elmwood, through the trees, the youngster characterizes the contemporary poets for the older man. At the end, Lowell suddenly vanishes, and dusk comes on.

In the portrait of herself, Amy Lowell of course started

with the contemporary attitude towards her — 'broncho-busting with rainbows,' as she tersely put it. This sketch was the quintessence of hundreds of newspaper clippings, all of which praised her pyrotechnical colors and her gusto, and virtually never saw beyond that dazzle; the reader today will be surprised that her poems ever seemed so noisy and outrageous. Then she took occasion to correct this impression by pointing out that her poetry was not mere surface.

> Despite her traducers, there's always a heart
> Hid away in her poems for the seeking; impassioned,
> Beneath silver surfaces cunningly fashioned
> To baffle coarse pryings, it waits for the touch
> Of a man who takes surfaces only as such.
> Her work's not, if you will, for the glib amateur,
> But I wonder, would it be improved if it were?
> Must subtlety always be counted a flaw
> And poetry not poetry which puzzles the raw?

It was another index-finger, like her preface to *Legends*; but few critics understood it well enough to think of looking for any meaning.

The poets who knew her well recognized her opinions pretty quickly; even though she brought her marvellous histrionics to bear upon them in a variety of remarkable denials, they seldom believed her after they got home. At one party, Conrad Aiken accused her point-blank of writing it, and for the rest of the evening she referred to the putative author as 'he,' while Aiken referred to him as 'she.' She protested that there was a portrait of herself included, and not too complimentary; 'Oh, I think you did that part very well,' he replied, and she felt the ground cut from under the feet of that argument. At last he remarked: 'Well, since you persist that you didn't write it, I can say what I really think of it. I think it's damn rotten!' At this point, Mrs. Russell intervened. This was one of the few times that Aiken and Amy Lowell saw each

other, and she felt that her skit had made a permanent
enemy of him.

The guesses as to authorship which came in to Houghton
Mifflin as the result of the advance copies were not so
unanimous. Amy Lowell led with six votes, Gamaliel Brad-
ford came next with three, Conrad Aiken and Leonard
Bacon followed with two, while Untermeyer, Masters,
Don Marquis, Nathan Haskell Dole, Grant Code, Chris-
topher Morley, Wallace Irwin, Caroline Ticknor, and
Ferris Greenslet himself had one apiece.

In writing to John Farrar (September 29), who had appointed her the chairman of the *Bookman* poetry committee, which was to make out, or endorse, programs of readings for women's clubs and the like, she asked:

> Have you seen 'A Critical Fable' published by my firm?
> I must say I find it immensely amusing in spite of not
> particularly enjoying the part about myself. But then, I
> imagine that none of the poets in it are going to enjoy the
> parts about themselves. I saw Aiken the other night, and
> he most emphatically did not enjoy his. I wonder who
> wrote it? Louis Untermeyer guessed me, and I guessed him,
> and then we agreed to cry quits on the strength of each
> other's denial and find a third person. It is really funny to
> see everybody begging the authorship. Sara Teasdale
> says it is Gamaliel Bradford; Gamaliel Bradford says it is
> Leonard Bacon; who Leonard Bacon says I do not know as
> he lives in California, so I have not seen him. Between you
> and me and the gatepost, he seems the most likely person,
> judging from a little privately printed skit I saw of his a
> little while ago. I am chiefly interested in it as being in
> the line of tradition from Butler's 'Hudibras' down through
> Byron's 'English Bards and Scotch Reviewers,' 'The Feast
> of the Poets,' James Russell Lowell, of course, and so on.
> Very different from the type of humour we've been having
> lately in this country!

But all these things took time; her eyes were giving out
again under the strain of working on Keats; and in order

to avoid distraction, she determined not to do any more
lecturing until February. Lawrence's *Women in Love* was
being attacked just about the time he landed in San
Francisco, whence he wrote her:

8 Sept. 1922

DEAR AMY

Well here I am under the Star-spangled Banner — though
perhaps the Stripes of persecution are more appropriate.

San Francisco is sunny & pleasant, though noisy & full
of the sound of iron. We leave tonight for Santa Fé. Send
me a line, c/o Mrs. Mabel Sterne, *Taos*, New Mexico —
to tell me how you are: unless of course the new prosecution
of Women in Love makes you feel that least said soonest
mended.

We still feel a bit dazed after the long trip across the
Pacific. Will take me some time in a little quiet place to
myself to gather together the me that is me. Pour tous les
autres, je m'en fiche.

Greet Mrs. Russell. Frieda sends her Wiedersehen.

D. H. LAWRENCE

She replied at once.

16 September 1922

DEAR LAWRENCE:

I was just going to mail this letter when yours came. A
hearty welcome to these United States of America. I am
delighted to know that you are here at last. Please tell me
when you are thinking of coming East, for really in New
Mexico you are almost as far away as in Australia.

If you think there is a noise of iron in San Francisco, I
wonder what you will think when you reach Chicago or
New York. The country takes a good deal of getting used
to, and I am a little afraid you may not like it; but there are
so many different kinds of it that you ought to be able
to be suited somewhere.

If you stay in Santa Fé, you will be right in the nest of
my enemies. Alice Henderson and Witter Bynner — how
they hate me! I do not know whether Witter Bynner is
still in New Mexico, but Alice Henderson lives there all the

time for her health, poor child. By the way, if you search
the seven seas and all the lands impinging on them, you
could not find a better place for your health than New
Mexico. I have not been there for thirty years, not since
Indians on donkeys rode down the streets of Santa Fé
arrayed in gaudily striped blankets and feathers, but they
tell me that it is still lovely and very interesting. While you
are there, you ought to go to some of the pueblos and see
some of the ritualistic dances of the Indians, if it is not
too late in the year.

If you run across my friend, Elsie Sergeant, who is in
Santa Fé a great part of the time, and in contradistinction
to Mrs. Henderson and Mr. Bynner is one of my greatest
friends, just tell her you are a friend of mine, and she will
do everything to make you feel happy.

Are you really such a silly fellow as to suppose that the
suppression of 'Women in Love' can make a difference to
me? I think 'Women in Love' one of your very finest books,
and this suppression business makes me sick. Everybody
knows that I am one of your chief champions in this country,
and, by the way, I enjoyed 'Aaron's Rod' extremely, although I do not think it as fine as 'Women in Love.'

And presently Lorenzo wrote from Taos:

Taos, New Mexico,
19 Oct. 1922

MY DEAR AMY

Well, we have been here for five weeks, and are more or
less getting used to it. We have a gay little adobe house
on the edge of the desert, with the mountains sitting round
under the sun. The Indian pueblo is about two miles off,
& Taos Plaza one mile. We don't see much of the 'world' —
save Mabel Sterne and her visitors.

The land I like exceedingly. You'd laugh to see Frieda
and me trotting on these Indian ponies across the desert,
and scrambling wildly up the slopes among the piñon
bushes, accompanied either by an Indian, John Concha, or
a Mexican, José. It is great fun. Also we go to hot springs
and sit up to our necks in the clear, jumping water.

Of course, humanly, America does to me what I knew it

would do: it just *bumps* me. I say the people charge at you like trucks coming down on you — no awareness. But one tries to dodge aside in time. Bump! bump! go the trucks. And that is human contact. One gets a sore soul, and at time yearns for the understanding mildness of Europe. Only I like the country so much.

I wasn't aware of being in a nest of your enemies: but I must have been, according to you. We slept the very first night in New Mexico at Witter Bynner's house in Santa Fé, and Alice Corbin was there. They talked of you too, but everything quite nice and I should never have suspected enemies. A bit critical of your work, of course, but that goes without saying. When poets talk of my poetry I don't expect them to leave one line hanging on to another — Shreds!

Seltzer won his 'case' all right, and seems mighty pleased. He sold out his *de luxe* Women in Love and now has a two-dollar edition, I hear. He is supposed to bring out Fantasia of the Unconscious this week. I'll send you a copy when he sends some to me: though I don't suppose it is in your line. — He urges me to come east, and has a house for me in Connecticut. But I like this land so much, and shrink from the witches' cauldron of New York. So he must come to [*word blotted out*] Mahomet — can't spell it — for Mahomet isn't budging yet awhile.

I have done two poems here: my first in America. Wonder whom I shall send them to. Harriett Monroe has two from Birds Beasts in November's Poetry.

No, the books you sent me never came on. Probably Germany wouldn't let them out without a license. That's how it is. — I shall look forward to the new one.

You don't say how your health is: I hope it's quite mended. And I really look forward to meeting you again. So does Frieda. We both send many greetings — also to Mrs. Russell.

Af[1]

D. H. Lawrence

---

[1] 'Af' is a conjectural rendering of a series of exuberant circles: in a later letter, the 'f' is unmistakable.

Another interesting letter which she answered in October came from Mrs. Thomas Hardy (September 5), thanking her for *Legends*. 'Dried Marjoram' had pleased Mr. Hardy particularly: he remembered executions for sheep-stealing, and his grandmother, when a girl, had often been driven past just such a gibbet. They were going to read 'Many Swans' that evening. He said he wished Miss Lowell could repeat her visit, because (and Mrs. Hardy asked Miss Lowell to forgive the naïve way in which this was put) he liked her so much. He said that he had told her so.

Miss Lowell spent October 20–25 in New York, going down ostensibly as chairman of the Poetry Committee for Women's Club's Programmes, arranged by the *Bookman*. The Committee met on the 21st at the Untermeyers. On Sunday the 22nd, Robert Edmond Jones called on her to discuss the possibility of putting the 'Bronze Horses' into the movies. She also spoke at the Dutch Treat Club, to which John Farrar introduced her. The remainder of her time she spent on Keats. And when she returned to Brookline, she felt that most of the preliminary work on her book was done, and that now she could begin to write it pretty soon.

The November *Dial* published T. S. Eliot's *Waste Land* complete; but still Miss Lowell did not like his work, as she wrote to Gilbert Seldes (November 1):

> I have read 'Waste Land' with very great interest. It seems to me that Mr. Eliot is following what Ezra calls the 'Sordello form.' In spite of interesting passages, I am afraid the poem leaves me rather cool — cooler even than Ezra's 'Cantos,' for Ezra cannot escape being a poet now and then, and many of his lines are very beautiful in spite of the jumble of the context. I do not think that Eliot was intended by nature for a poet, and, try as he will, I cannot find his philosophies in verse turn into poems, however I look at them. I know this will disappoint you and that

you think I am blind in one eye, and perhaps I am. I am quite willing to be converted to his excellences, but nothing that I have yet seen of his converts me. The man is indubitably clever, but I cannot find him poetical. It is as if he laid a fire with infinite care, but omitted to apply a match to it. Forgive me if you can, for I know that I shall require forgiveness in your eyes. I think you were quite right to print the poem, and time will prove which of us is right.

On the 10th, she gave a reading at Clark University, in Worcester, then returned to work over the Keats material once more.

At the end of November, the news of the death of Alice Meynell made her turn to that volume of her poems which Miss Frances Dabney had given her in 1897, as a possible clue out of her labyrinth of unhappiness. The verses she once loved to quote now merely seemed well-made; but the stirring of those far-off days brought back memories of the old bitterness, which she put into her poem 'On Looking at a Copy of Alice Meynell's Poems.'

In December she took another brief trip to New York. On the 8th, she read her poems at Wanamaker's in the afternoon, and in the evening at the Town Hall to the League for Political Education. The next day she read over the radio at the Newark Broadcasting Station, and received a poem from a man in Lexington, Kentucky, who happened to be reading '1777' from a copy of *Men, Women and Ghosts* 'given by the citizens of Brookline' (actually herself) to an erstwhile war-camp, at the very moment her voice began reading it.

On December 19, she spoke at the Brookline Town Meeting. Various regulations were under consideration; one by-law proposed to forbid children skating, sliding, or pulling their sleds on sidewalks. 'Are we going to make all our children criminals?' she asked. 'Are we to be entirely officialized? Are we to abandon our constitutional rights to the pursuit of happiness?' The by-law was amended to give the children the right 'to drag their sleds over the sidewalks on the return from coasting down designated streets.' If memory serves correctly, women with perambulators were also forbidden the use of sidewalks, but after Miss Lowell's protest, the Council of Thirty agreed not to enforce the regulation, even though they retained it.

By this time, the December *Poetry*, which included Amy Lowell's poems inspired by Charleston, had reached that city, with the result that some indignant citizens were fuming, especially about 'Magnolia Gardens' and its unfortunate magenta. Suspecting that some such sensitiveness might exist, she had read these poems to Josephine Pinckney, DuBose Heyward, and Hervey Allen when they dined with her in August; and they had approved the publication of them. So had Beatrice Ravenel. But now that they were in print, *Poetry* received quite a pack of protesting letters and poems, while others appeared elsewhere. It was unfortunate, but inevitable and without consequence. Miss Lowell was somewhat distressed, none the less, the more so as she was getting very tired. In order to finish the Keats book, she had been going on no more than four hours' sleep; but by the end of December she could hardly keep her eyes open to work, and would sleep for several hours on the sofa downstairs before going to bed. It was nothing but plain overwork.

A blizzard came on December 30, and was followed by a spring-like thaw; on January 2, 1923, she read at the Fall River Women's Club, and got home just before another blizzard. On the 11th, she read at the Boston Art Club. The second edition of the *Critical Fable* was nearly gone, and the *Boston Transcript* announced that the author's name was William Williams John, which many took to be a pseudonym.

At the end of January she went on what proved to be her last extended lecture tour, from which she did not return until March 10. Her honorariums totalled $1825. She took every possible precaution against fatigue — always arrived the day before her lecture; would not speak at dinners given in her honor — but she returned exhausted, none the less.

Her headquarters for the first two weeks were at the Belmont in New York; from there she motored or took trains to the first set of engagements. On January 29, she read to the Monday Afternoon Club at Plainfield, New Jersey; on the 30th, at the Colony Club in New York; on February 2, at the New York Town Hall, for the League for Political Education; on the 4th, at the Greenwich Village Theater. This last reading had been organized by Kreymborg, as one of a series of recitals by writers and composers. People were standing wherever they could, although it was a terribly cold and snowy day. The radiators set up a terrific clanking in the midst of one of her poems; she shouted out jocularly: 'Where's Mr. Kreymborg? I might have known he'd put up a job on me.' That evening, Miss Lowell went to hear *Pierrot Lunaire* with Eva Gauthier. On February 8, she lectured on Chinese poetry at Brooklyn Institute of Arts and Sciences; and on the 9th she read to the Women's Club of Pelham.

She started west on February 12, reading to the Women's Club of Springfield, Ohio, on the 13th, and to the Contemporary Club of Indianapolis on the 15th. She reached Chicago the next night, read to the Arts Club on the 17th, and to 'Les Petits Jeux Floraux' (a forum run by Mrs. William Vaughn Moody) on the 18th. On the way to Milwaukee, the cold increased severely: her watch froze on the train, although all windows were as tightly sealed as was possible. To avoid stifling one night Miss Lowell made the porter bring and hold a ladder while she mounted on it and broke one of the little colored glass panes near the roof. Although she gave the astonished porter her card, with the instructions that she wished to pay for any charge of damage, she never received a bill. On the 20th, she read to the Wisconsin Players in Milwaukee; on the 23d, to the Women's City Club of St. Paul, Minnesota; and on the 28th, to the Omaha Society of Fine Arts. Then she turned eastward again, reading at Northwestern University Evanston, Illinois, on March 3. She was beginning to feel the fatigue, the cold long train rides and the bad cooking combined to make her miserable, and a cold was coming on. But though she felt too ill really to do anything, she determined to put it through without a break.

On March 6, in a heavy blizzard, she motored eighty-four miles out of Chicago to St. Catharine's, Ontario, where she read to the Canadian Women's Club, motoring back again that evening, reaching her hotel at half-past one in the morning.

> Canada can hardly be looked upon in the light of a journey, yet it is extraordinary to see the difference between Canada and America, psychologically. Among other things, directly opposite the bridge facing you as you cross the river from America, flaunting in broad daylight its advertisements of ales and wines, is a saloon. Such sights are no longer part of the landscape in this country — not, of course, that the inhabitants are very much affected, only they do sub rosa what the Canadians are still permitted to do above board.[1]

> It is very curious to see the difference between a Canadian audience and an American one. My country people are smarter, quicker, more lively, but the Canadian audience was more serious and seemed to wish to get to grips with the subject in a way that an American audience never does.[2]

> I count Canada this country, do not you? It was very amusing when I was lecturing at St. Catherine's this year to hear everybody talk about 'your country,' as though I lived a thousand miles away instead of just over the bridge across Niagara.[3]

[1] Letter to Richard Aldington, April 4, 1923.
[2] Letter to Winifred Bryher, April 2, 1923.
[3] Letter to Florence Ayscough, May 8, 1923.

On the evening of March 7, she read to the Junior Class of the Women's College, at the University of Rochester. By now, she was wretchedly ill: her voice was much diminished. Her annoyance when she arrived at the hotel, and learned that she had been provided with two single beds instead of the double one she had ordered, is now part of the city history. In the lobby she informed the clerk that certain people know exactly what they want and that it was his business to distinguish those people. What did he expect her to do with two beds? Put her head on one and her feet on the other? or sleep half the night in one and half in the other? Eventually he summoned up voice enough to say: 'Madam, I have been in the hotel business thirty years ——' But she interrupted: 'Yes, and look where you are!' Which concluded the episode. In Rochester was a presentation copy of *Endymion* from Severn; Miss Lowell was unable to track it down in person, but eventually discovered it.

On the evening of March 8 came her last lecture of the trip: a reading for the English Club of Syracuse University, in the Fine Arts Building. The 'Friends of Reading' had joined with the university men in giving her a dinner beforehand; and although the city was small, a thousand people appeared for the reading.

The next day she reached home, and found that she was stepping back into mid-winter again. Drifts of snow lay many feet high before her house. And of course she was exhausted and ill. As she wrote to Eva Gauthier (March 10):

> I have returned from my trip with the most diabolical cold ever seen. Although I accomplished the trip successfully as far as lectures are concerned, I think I caught all the varieties of grippe rife in the various towns I passed through and I am a victim of them one and all. Add to this the fact that my sister has been desperately ill and that I have been living the last few weeks in great anxiety about her and come home to find her for the moment out of danger, I believe, but that is all that can be said just now.

Her illness hung on for the rest of the month, partly, no doubt, because the cold weather continued — in fact, the thermometer stood at only 9 above zero on the spring equinox.

The accumulation of mail was tremendous. The Keats fund had proved insufficient; Wentworth Place was bought but the £700 remaining was obviously insufficient for repairs and upkeep; would she not renew her labors and see what more money could be got? There were requests for autographs, for autobiographies, for criticisms of the enclosed poems, for free lectures. Elizabeth Cutting had written, and Miss Lowell's answer (March 14) contained some valuable remarks about the place of a knowledge of technique in appreciating poetry:

> ... Technique is only important for the person who likes to do puzzles, to dig into the roots of things and find out why they sprang. It is a scientific mechanism which follows on creation. No artist ever thinks of technique while he is writing a poem; that is all done by his subconscious mind. It is only when he happens to have a critical faculty too, that he is able afterwards to find out what he has done. No lay reader should ever be concerned with technique. He should only know that he is reading something delightful, and enjoy it in that way. The older I get, the more I despise scholarship of the German variety. We need to treat poetry as common sense, as one of the human things. In all of Matthew Arnold's essays, in all of Thoreau's, in all of Pater's, you will find no word of technique, or very little, only so much as any intelligent reader, who is also a sensitive and thinking reader with a real mind, can put in.

Presently a letter arrived from Thomas Hardy:

Max Gate, Dorchester
7th March 1923

DEAR MISS AMY LOWELL:

'I do remember my faults this day.' — Never have I acknowledged receiving that book of American Poetry at the end of last year with your charming inscription, although I read as much as I could of it when it arrived. This 'could,' by the way, has a sinister ambiguity that I did not mean; I merely alluded to spare time. I read all *your* pieces anyhow, and much like 'The Swans.'

Edna Millay seems the most promising of the younger poets, don't you think? As to the free verse which appears so frequently in the volume, I suppose I am too old to do it justice. You manage it best; but do you mind my saying that it too often seems a jumble of notes containing ideas striking, novel, or beautiful, as the case may be, which could be transfused into poetry, but which, as given, are not poetry? I could not undergo an examination on why (to me) they seem not. Perhaps because there is no expectation raised of a response in sound or beat, and the pleasure of its gratification, as in regular poetry; which only ancient poetry, like the English Bible, is able to dispense with because of its other character of antiquity.

As for myself, I am rather perplexed by letters I get on whether readers can have a difficulty in obtaining my books of verse in the United States, particularly 'The Dynasts' complete in one volume (green, published by Macmillans). If you or any friend should be in a book store any day, and would not mind asking if they keep that edition, or if it is readily obtainable, I shall be greatly obliged. It is so difficult to get information through the publishers and booksellers themselves. With best wishes for your poetry and your self,

Believe me, Your affectionate friend,

THOMAS HARDY

Though much pleased with this letter, she did not answer it until May 8, when she had had a chance to inquire at several bookstores about the possibility of buying the *Dynasts*. She enclosed 'The Rosebud Wall Paper,' cut out of the February *North American Review*, and the manuscript of 'Evelyn Ray,' which had not yet appeared in *Poetry*.

On March 21, she was the guest of honor at a dinner given by the Club of Odd Volumes (the Boston equivalent of the Grolier Club); afterwards she talked about her Keats collection. Two nights later, she was the guest of honor at a dinner given by the Japan Society; after dinner she talked; and after the talk, Untermeyer's 'Jade Butterflies' (dedicated to Miss Lowell) was sung. On April 7, she was a guest at the annual banquet of the Boston Proof-Readers' Association.

April was spent mostly in writing on Keats, but she also was catching up on her accumulated correspondence. To Aldington (April 4) she had many things to say, including her impression of Eliot's latest work.

> I read Eliot's 'Waste Land' with great interest, but I am more skeptical than ever. The book is immensely interesting as a record of a state of mind. As such, I think it is quite moving and startling, but I cannot find it poetry and I cannot help thinking that the state of mind itself is a pathological one. I think I should call it war hysteria if I were asked to analyse it; it seems to me the state of mind which a good many of the men of that generation are in. For instance, John Dos Passos, who wrote 'Three Soldiers' — I do not know whether you read it, but it was a very powerful book — has written one of the most enchanting travel books, called 'Rosinante to the Road Again,' being his adventures on a walking trip through Spain. I saw him the other day in New York and thought he was coming out of his bitterness well.

To the Committee for the Keats Memorial House Fund she wrote on April 14, to the effect that she doubted the possibility of raising any more money in this country.

> All the committees have now been disbanded, and I think it quite impossible to start the interest over again, particularly as America gave exactly double the amount that was raised in England. That fact, I see, is not mentioned in your circular, which will not, perhaps, endear the project to American eyes. I lost several subscriptions because of an unfortunate happening in, I think, the collection of the Henry James letters; it was at any rate some book on

Henry James. In this volume, the fact that Americans raised more than half the money for the portrait painted by Sargent and paid for by public subscription, was not mentioned. These things are short-sighted and naturally tend to irritate donors.

She did, however, make some effort towards raising more money for the fund.

By the beginning of May, she knew that she could never finish the Keats biography in time for autumn publication. She was nearly going to pieces over it: she had been working till eight in the morning, wearing her eyes out, and then not sleeping. So she informed her publisher of the necessary delay, and also wrote Florence Ayscough that the Tu Fu book would have to be delayed also (May 8):

> ... I have not yet finished my Life of Keats nor do I believe I shall finish it before the Winter, although I have been working like a perfect Trojan on it; and there is a little volume I have promised to do for the Princeton Press on the modern free forms which must be got out of the way as soon as the Keats book is over.... The result is that I am extremely tired, so that I am afraid, my dear, (bear up if you can) that I shall not be able to start work upon the Tu Fu book before a year from this Autumn, because I must certainly go to Europe next Summer, as Basil Blackwell there, and Ferris Greenslet here, both insist that it is very important, and I think it is. Also I need a rest if any body ever did.

She wrote to her former governess, Miss A. E. Chapman, on the same day:

> The garden is perfectly beautiful at this moment, I wish you could see it. The double cherries are just passing, but the magnolias are in full bloom. It has been a very cold and slow Spring, so that the trees are holding their early green for a long time, which is their prettiest effect I think. The daffodils are passing over and giving place to the tulips. I do not think that the place has gone down at all since

Papa's time except that I do not grow quite so many roses. I still have some in the hot beds and the garden is full of them where they used to grow, but I have done away with the beds in the fruit garden. I did that, I remember, the first year, so you probably remember all about it. There is scarcely any change, except a few clipped trees, but a year ago we had a terrible ice storm and that has certainly made a big change. I have not a deciduous tree which is not topped, and some of the largest and most superb limbs on the oak opposite the parlor window were broken off. Still it is all very pretty and I am very fond of it.

On the 10th, she left for New York, to be initiated formally into the Phi Beta Kappa at Columbia. In full academic regalia, with the Baylor green and gold hood, she read her 'Fool o' the Moon,' 'View of Teignmouth,' and 'Lilacs.' Before returning to Brookline, she examined a book that had just turned up in the library of the Authors' Club — *Guzman d'Alfarache*, with unknown annotations by Keats, which she copied.

Even though *John Keats* was delayed, she did not want to take time off to arrange and put through the press a volume of the poems she had published in periodicals. There were plenty of them, but she did not want to be distracted. (If a poem came through, she would write it, as creation was more important than criticism; but that was another matter.) So in order to keep her name before the public, Houghton Mifflin considered reissuing 'Hedge Island' illustrated with thirteen old coaching prints — a delightful idea, which she approved wholly, but which was abandoned as too expensive.

Caroline Hazard, ex-president of Wellesley, contributed again to the Keats Memorial House Fund; in thanking her, Miss Lowell added (May 24):

How shall I take your reference to the 'Critical Fable,' considering that I have said again and again that I am not

In the Garden at Sevenels

its author, and believe that it was your nephew, Leonard Bacon? His mightily clever rhymed denial in the 'Literary Review' did not change the opinion I had of him. I meant to reply in the same paper in kind, but lacked the energy to jump out of the Keats mood into one appropriate for an answer. I am sure the author, whoever he may be, will be most grateful to you for having bought ten copies, if he ever finds it out. I have enjoyed the book very much indeed and, had I known your nephew, would have written to congratulate him. The publishers have already announced that it is by a gentleman named William Williams John, but whether that is a *nom de plume* or not, who shall say?

June went by, almost without event. She was evidently working hard at Keats, as she wrote only sixteen letters this month: one of these to the Princeton University Press, advising them that the book on free verse would be delayed, and another to Elinor Wylie, inviting her to dinner on her way to Peterboro. July was also eventless. On the 7th, she gave her opinions about the status of the living American poets, to May Lamberton Becker, who was planning a series of lectures.

I still think, and I hope I am not prejudiced, that the old guard — Robinson, Frost, Masters, Lindsay, and Sandburg — are the best living poets we have. I cannot see that the younger poets have touched them in any way. As I pointed out in a paper in the 'Literary Review' last year, the young poets seem to aim at a minor utterance; for instance, Edna Millay enchantingly able though she is in her own line, attempts nothing beyond the personal, which is the hall-mark of minor poetry. Of course, I do not use the word 'minor' to mean inferior, but merely to denote a difference in aim....

Of the younger poets, I think Elinor Wylie and Edna Millay rank the highest for achievement and Hervey Allen for potentialities. With Hervey Allen, the book to be paid attention to is 'Carolina Chansons'.... I am bound to say, between you and me, that the work of the younger *men* is distinctly disappointing. There seems to be nobody to take up the cloak falling from the shoulders of us seasoned old poets.... Hervey Allen seems to be the only man who has a broader vision; I have a belief in his promise, but it is too early yet to say whether my belief is justified or not.

Along with these reactionaries, there is a group of young iconoclasts who verge toward the 'Dada' type of poetry. In confidence, for I should not wish it to go further, I do not think they have the slightest future....

To go back to the better known poets, directly after the five men I have mentioned come Conrad Aiken, whose best book to my mind is 'Punch,' although both 'The Charnel Rose' and 'The House of Dust' are very interesting; John Gould Fletcher, whose best work can all be found in the two books 'Preludes and Symphonies' published by Houghton Mifflin Company and 'Breakers and Granite' published by Macmillan; 'H. D.,' who is the author of two books, 'Sea Garden' and 'Hymen,' of which only 'Hymen' is in print, published by Holt; Sara Teasdale, all of whose books are good and about equal in merit; and that remarkable volume, 'Profiles in China' by Eunice Tietjens.

Maxwell Bodenheim should not be omitted. He is an intellectual pure and simple, with a touch of irony which is very extraordinary. His best book, because it is the most sympathetic, is 'Advice.' Grace Hazard Conkling's two books 'Afternoons in April' and 'Wilderness Songs' do not, strangely enough, do her full justice, but a careful selection should be made in these books of her better work, 'The Whole Duty of Berkshire Brooks,' 'The Mexican Garden,' etc., represent her fairly well. Her best work is still uncollected. Hilda Conkling's two volumes, 'Poems by a Little Girl' and 'Shoes of the Wind,' will have to be treated by themselves. Her work is so uncommonly good, even for a grown-up person, that I think, in spite of her age, you cannot omit her.

Of the younger group, as I have said before, the women rank highest, and of the women Elinor Wylie and Edna St. Vincent Millay. Mrs. Wylie is far and away the more intellectual of the two, but Edna Millay has great charm.

Her finest work is the little known 'Aria da Capo,' but Miss Millay is tending recently to repeating herself and to make verbal tricks carry a certain flimsiness of content. Of the still younger women, Babette Deutsch, Jean Starr Untermeyer, Winifred Wells, etc., all do very good work, within the limitations I have mentioned.

Of the young men, I really cannot choose. I have been struck by none of them, except possibly, as I said before, Hervey Allen. In the 'Eight More Harvard Poets,' both Malcolm Cowley and John Brooks Wheelwright had some good things, particularly the latter, but I do not see enough in their work to warrant them much of a future.

I see I have left out Louis Untermeyer, which is stupid on my part because of the excellence of his new book, 'Roast Leviathan.' I should place him in the same rank as Conrad Aiken and the other poets of the second order I have mentioned. Hitherto Mr. Untermeyer has seemed one of the great parodists of all time and a critic of considerable ability, but his poetry has not equalled either his parodies or his criticism; now with the publication of 'Roast Leviathan,' he has leapt into a poetical rank which none of his earlier work prefigured.... For some reason best known to himself, Mr. Untermeyer did not state in his preface that he took the form of his 'Roast Leviathan' and 'Boy and Tadpoles' from my polyphonic prose. He calls it polyphonic verse, because he writes it in lines and not in a block, and because it has a more marked and less elastic rhythm than polyphonic prose, but the idea of interweaving rhymes came directly from polyphonic prose, as he told me himself....

I have omitted William Rose Benét, which is a mistake. His 'Merchants from Cathay' is very fine and his 'Perpetual Light' is appealing in a very different way. I have also omitted Stephen Benét, because I see nothing but imitation, and a rather feeble imitation, of older poets in his work.

The ignorance of poetry in America is perfectly astounding. I know of no single poetry critic outside of the poets themselves whose judgment is of the slightest value.... As a people we are extremely uncritical, and my experience

of the perfectly unequal poems which are rated as extraordinarily good by most people constantly sets me wondering. In my travels among American colleges, I have found
more intelligence on the subject of poetry among the undergraduates than among the professors, but this you must not
let escape you even in private conversation. In the larger
colleges, the professors are erudite to a remarkable degree,
but lack the touch of instinct; in the smaller colleges, they
lack both the instinct and the training. There is one
marked exception, the English Department at Bryn Mawr....

At the end of July she had a two-week 'poem-burst,'
during which she set *Keats* firmly aside, while she wrote
eight poems. Then she heard the Lawrences were in New
York and tried to get them to come on to Brookline.
Back in April he had written her from Mexico:

> Hotel Monte Carlo.
> Ar. Uruguay 69.
> Mexico D.F.
> 21 April 1923

DEAR AMY

I have your letter, & the ciro postale. Here we are, cir-
cling uneasily round, wondering whether we shall settle for a
time, or not. I would like to sit down and write a novel on
the American continent (I don't mean *about* it: I mean while
I'm here). But it is hard to break through the wall of the
atmosphere. — I didn't really dislike the U.S.A. as much as
I expected. And I don't *mistrust* it half as much as I mistrust the present England, with its false sentimentalism.
So I hesitate here.

Probably I shall come to New York, by sea, before the
autumn passes. Then we should both very much like to
pay you a little visit, if you feel equal to visitors. While the
flowers still last in your garden.

Mexico *is* interesting — but I feel I haven't got the right
hang of it yet.

Remember us to Mrs. Russell — and I do hope you are
feeling well & strong.

> Yrs ever
>
> D. H. LAWRENCE

On July 3, he wrote her that they were in New York — or at least in a Seltzer cottage in New Jersey — and wanted to come up to visit her before they sailed. She really wanted to see them, but was concentrating on Keats and tired out into the bargain; to add to the difficulty, the Lawrences' plans were not yet settled. She waited a month before sending the invitation; there was a small flurry of letters crossing in the mails and long distance telephone calls, which did not end till Frieda had sailed, leaving her husband behind. Lawrence appreciated Miss Lowell's state of mind, as his next letter showed:

> N. Jersey
> Saturday evening
> 18 Aug.
>
> MY DEAR AMY
>
> I have just got back from seeing Frieda off on the steamer, & found your letter. — I'm sorry we are not seeing you. I wasn't very sure if you wanted to be troubled by visitors. I knew of course your health was not good.
>
> *I am leaving this Cottage for good on Monday — expect to leave New York on Tuesday D. H. L.*
>
> But I have always a very warm memory of you in those days in England: the Berkeley, & when you came with Mrs. Russell to that cottage. — Tempi passati! Già troppo passato!
>
> I ought to have gone to England. I wanted to go. But my inside self wouldn't let me. At the moment I just can't face my own country again. It makes me feel unhappy, like a terrible load.
>
> But I don't care for New York. I feel the people one sees want to jeer at us. They come with a sort of pre-determination to jeer. — But that is literary.
>
> I am going West again — to Los Angeles, & then, if I can get a sailing ship of some sort, out to sea. This New York leaves me with one great desire, to get away from people altogether. That is why I can't go to Europe: because of the many people, the many things I shall have to say, when my soul is mute towards almost everybody.

Seltzer is bringing out various books of mine, & I have asked him to send you a copy of each. — The poems, *Birds Beasts & Flowers*, should be done — published I mean — by Sept. 20th. I'll ask Seltzer to send you an advance copy. But don't review it unless you *really* feel like it.

Thank you for the little cheque.[1] Sending these tiny sums is a nuisance to you; don't bother to do it, give the money to somebody who is poor.

Frieda wanted to see England again: it is four years since we were there. And her mother in Baden Baden. My heart goes like lead when I think of England or Germany. — I am thankful we are no longer poor, so that we can take our way across the world.

Either Frieda will come and join me somewhere west — perhaps in Mexico: or I shall go to her in Europe. In which latter case, I'll let you know in plenty of time. And then tell me if you really want me to come: if you feel equal to the effort of visitors. As for me, I never want to be a visitor for longer than two days. That is enough.

But we'll keep a bit of decent kindliness at the bottom of our hearts, as we had ten years ago. I'll never let the world bankrupt me *quite* in this.

Greet Mrs. Russell. I hope you'll feel strong again.

D. H. LAWRENCE

Two other letters particularly pleased her this month. One came from William Ellery Leonard, offering her a copy of his privately printed *Two Lives*, as an *amende honorable* for his series of articles published eight years ago in the Chicago *Evening Post* — that onslaught upon Imagism, which he characterized as nothing more than a frolic. The other letter was a request from the *Encyclopaedia Britannica*, asking her to contribute an article on the new poetry to the next edition.

By the middle of September, the Keats biography was half done. At the end of the month, Florence Ayscough ar-

---

[1] [His share of the royalties from the three Imagist anthologies. Every six months Miss Lowell sent them out, as the books still sold, though in decreasing numbers.]

rived for a couple of weeks, and Miss Lowell took a vacation from her work. Between September 26 and September 30, they did 250 poems by Tu Fu: then on October 1, the three women, with the Streeters, motored down to Providence for the opening of Eleanor Belmont's play, *In the Next Room*. Mrs. Ayscough was away from the 2nd to the 5th; when she returned, they did more Tu Fu poems; and after a party on the 9th, where Mrs. Ayscough showed colored lantern slides of Chinese gardens and the Yangtze in the music room, they went at the poet again, finishing the 500th poem at 4 A.M., October 10. They planned to use not more than two hundred for their book; but as the labor of analyzing characters, tracking down allusions, and so forth was great, it was necessary first to run through these five hundred poems in rough translation, to decide which to eliminate and which to keep.

On October 25, she read her poems under the auspices of the New England Poetry Club at Steinert Hall. It was her first public reading of her own poems in Boston since 1914. The young men who were managing the event were unskilled in business matters; they supposed that her name would so surely fill the hall that prolonged announcements beforehand would be a mere waste of money. At the last minute Abbie Brown and Miss Lowell took matters in hand, and the advertisement telephoned to one of the papers was understood as coming from the 'New England Poultry Club,' whereupon the columnists were free to make merry over 'Plymouth Rocks.' The hall was full, though without being jammed; the audience, however, made up for lack of crowding by an extraordinary intensity. Amy Lowell read 'The Conversion of a Saint' with special success.

On November 8, she read a wholly different program for the Women's Municipal League at the Copley Plaza.

It was now just over a decade since the New Poetry had burst forth, yet already a new poetic generation was beginning to win its place. On the one hand were the lyrists, of whom the public's favorite was easily Edna St. Vincent Millay. Miss Lowell admired her *Aria da Capo* along with Aiken's *Punch* as one of the two things by her contemporaries she wished she had written herself; but the lyrists generally seemed content with quatrains and sonnets done very much after the romantic manner of Louise Imogen Guiney. They showed no desire for great achievement, such as had inspired *Can Grande's Castle* and *Legends*. To Miss Lowell, this reversion seemed pure decadence; it was about this time that she invented the phrase 'the ambition to be a minor poet.'

The younger experimentalists, however, were doing queer, awkward things she did not believe were permanent literature. Eliot's work she distrusted and found cold; Cummings she thought was an Elizabethan lyrist gone eccentric and shocking; then there were those youngsters who were playing with the magazine *Secession*. Malcolm Cowley and John Wheelwright she knew; the latter persuaded her to have Matthew Josephson and Kenneth Burke in for tea when she was in New York, but the meeting was not a success. Never, apparently, had the two young men heard literary dicta promulgated over tea-cups at a first meeting; and instead of standing up to her, they assented politely, then got very indignant as soon as they left.

As a younger generation of poets, both wings were distinctly disappointing; there was no one in sight to drop mantles to. She wrote an article about the 'lyrists' and 'Secessionists' for the *New Republic* autumn literary supplement,[1] but none of the youngsters seemed to have stamina enough to fight back, when the article appeared in December.

But not such events, and not Keats himself, could hold

    [1] 'Two Generations in American Poetry,' *New Republic* (xxxvii, No. 470, Pt. ii, pp. 1–3), December 5, 1923; collected in her *Poetry and Poets*.

her long from New York; for the great Duse, who had inspired her first poem, was there. Emaciated, white-haired, frail, the great tragedienne had returned to America on October 16, when escorted by motor-cycle police she had been driven from her boat, through stilled traffic, to the Hotel Majestic. Her opening performance on the evening of the 29th had jammed the Metropolitan Opera House with $30,000. Though she was sixty-four and physically worn-out, the glamour of her personality and the strength of her art overwhelmed even the most captious of the youngest critics; her greatest and last triumph had begun.

Over twenty years had passed since she had been in America; and those years constituted the whole of Amy Lowell's literary life. Something of that must have been conveyed in a letter (now lost) which Miss Lowell sent to Duse the night before she went to New York; and from hints in other letters, it is reasonable to suppose that she mentioned their former meeting, hoped to meet her again, and offered whatever services she could render during the Boston engagement. It ended by saying that there need be no answer as she really expected none.

This letter was mailed on November 15, the same day that she left for New York. On the 16th and again on the 23d she occupied a front seat at Duse's matinees, *Cosi Sia* and *La Porta Chiusa*. Profoundly moved, she could not return to her drudgery; and hearing that Eleanor Belmont's *In the Next Room* was to open in New York on the 27th, she stayed over for that, not reaching Sevenels till late the night before Thanksgiving.

And there awaiting her she found — not an answer from her letter to Duse, but something far more flattering yet — a letter from England, which said that Madame Duse before sailing had expressed a wish to meet Miss Amy Lowell; also a telegram from Katherine Onslow, who was travelling with Duse, saying exactly the same thing.

Everybody had taken it for granted that Duse's poverty

was the sole cause of her coming; and her statement to the reporters that she wanted to escape from sorrow-laden Europe into the buoyancy of the New World was taken as merely conventional. But it was not wholly so. A woman so sensitive to environment obviously might well share D. H. Lawrence's passionate desire to escape; certainly she had refused the pension which Mussolini had offered, to keep her in Italy; and before she sailed she had inquired about the younger American poets and had learned Amy Lowell's name.

Duse's two performances at the Boston Opera House fell on the afternoons of December 3 (*Spettri* — Ibsen's *Ghosts*) and 6 (*Cosi Sia*); Miss Lowell attended both performances. Florence Ayscough, who was staying at Sevenels that week, had a tale how she and Mrs. Russell reached the theater before Miss Lowell, and how a strange woman insisted on occupying the third seat, until Mrs. Russell said quietly that it was Miss Amy Lowell's; whereupon the woman 'fled like a fleet hare, never to be seen again.'

After the first performance, Miss Lowell had tea with Miss Onslow, who told her, among other things, that Duse ate almost nothing, but required a glass of champagne before any special effort; and none was to be got in prohibition America. Miss Lowell promptly raided the cellars of Sevenels and of her friends, with such effectiveness that she was able to round up thirty-six bottles for the great actress. Furthermore, Mrs. Russell knew so many people scattered across the continent that wherever Duse went, more champagne was placed at her disposal.

On the 7th, the day after the second performance, Duse came out to Sevenels. Twenty-one years had passed since her meeting with Miss Lowell; in that period her inspiration had turned the purposeless girl into a great poet. Surely Miss Lowell tried to tell her something of this; but of their conversation only one sentence remains: Duse's

'The past is dead; the future alone lives.' Duse admired
'The Kiss of Amon-Ra' so much that Miss Lowell later
had it photographed for her, and she admired Sevenels so
much that she accepted an invitation for a long visit there
after her twenty performances were over. Miss Lowell
was thoroughly prepared to be disappointed — she could
hardly believe that Duse really meant to come — yet she
prepared everything for her, even to building a new bath-
room.

The Frosts spent Sunday the 9th at Sevenels; then Miss
Lowell left for a brief lecture tour. On the 12th she delivered her 'John Keats, in the Light of New Discoveries' at
the Brooklyn Institute; on Sunday afternoon of the 16th
she read the 'Yucca' and 'Guns as Keys' at St. Mark's-in-
the-Bouwerie. Then she went on to Washington, where
Duse was opening, and managed to get her some champagne there. On the 19th, after dining at Mrs. Arthur B.
Kinsolving's, she read to the Maryland Poetry Society
in the Emmanuel Parish House, Baltimore.

Duse was also in Baltimore; here she gave the twentieth
and last performance of her contract. Evidently Miss
Lowell invited her to a private reading, possibly hoping
that they might return to Sevenels together. The exhausted actress, however, rather than face Europe again
so soon, was busy signing another twenty-performance
contract that was to take her to New Orleans, Havana,
San Francisco, then back East. She could not go to Miss
Lowell's reading, and refused on December 20, in a note
(written in Italian) addressed to 'Amie.' 'These short
days of December are filled with memories and regrets,'
she wrote. She wished that she could be among those who
that evening were to listen to the 'word of the Spirit'
which her dear friend would bring them; but her absurd
life of labor was driving her still farther. Wishing her
every happiness, she concluded: 'I hope to return to
Boston. Au revoir.'

When this letter was translated to her, Miss Lowell in her disappointment supposed that it was a busy woman's polite evasion of unnecessary attentions. She was, moreover, ill of 'a cheerful little pneumococcus bug' that had set up a violent inflammation in all the passages of her head, so that she was deaf and blind, and would have been dumb if she had not been lecturing. When she got home the doctor discovered some nodes in her vocal cords, which probably dated back to her last long lecture tour; but they were nothing permanent.

The cold did not get better; and after Christmas, Miss Lowell collapsed into bed. In her enforced idleness, she wrote a poem 'To Eleonora Duse, 1923,' expressing her devotion and lamenting her inability to establish a friendship; then she got an Italian dictionary and translated Duse's letter for herself. In her surprise at finding it friendly and even intimate, she wrote a second poem — the answer that she would have sent to the letter if she had understood it properly the first time. Then she wrote six sonnets to Duse. When the batch was finished, she sent copies to Sara Teasdale, who also had been inspired to her first poem by Duse's acting.

22 January, 1924

Dear Sara:

I think the enclosed poems may interest you. They are the result of my weeks in constant contemplation of Madame Duse. They all came in a bundle one after the other after I got home from New York last time. I am rather anxious to know what you think of them. The cadenced ones are better than the sonnets, I think; I do not consider myself a star sonneteer. But I believe they all show feeling, certainly there was plenty of feeling there. They came in the following order: 'Eleanora Duse. 1923,' 'To Eleanora Duse. In Answer to a Letter,' 'Eleanora Duse.' The reason I am so particular about the order is because historically they are better understood that way — by you, I mean.

The first one is simply the result of the realization of the hopelessness of ever getting anywhere near her as an individual; by the time the second was written, my attitude had a good deal changed, because I managed to read with the dictionary the letter she wrote me in Baltimore, with the result that I found it much more intimate and poignant than I had expected. Among others was this sentence, replete with tragic implication: 'These short December days are full of regrets and memories.' I felt that my answer to that letter, written in Baltimore, was anything but adequate, but her letter, as translated to me there, was nothing like the letter as read by the dictionary. I therefore sat down and wrote this poem as another answer. The sonnets have no *raison d'être* except that the well was still full.

I have a feeling that the first poem is altogether too intimate, too psychologically correct, for her to see. Certainly I should not think of sending it to her without consulting Miss Onslow. The second poem and the sonnets I have sent to Miss Onslow asking her to translate the sonnets into straight French prose for her, and seeking her permission to print them. I told Miss Onslow to use her own judgment about whether to show her the poem 'In Answer to a Letter' and she telephoned me a week ago, just before she left Chicago for New Orleans, and said she thought she should read that too. I sincerely hope she will, because I think Madame Duse will prefer it. However, there is not time yet for me to have heard from New Orleans, and I do not know the fate of the poems at all — whether Miss Onslow really ever got round to reading them to her, whether she liked them or anything else. The truth is, she has had so much of this sort of thing that I do not suppose it will make any impression, but the letter, as I read it over, was so curiously close and intimate that I cannot help thinking that with time and opportunity we might have some nice talks. Whether there will ever be such time and opportunity seems to me doubtful, but I saw in the paper today that she was coming back to Boston in April, so I suppose she will be in New York before or after that. At any rate, I thought you might be interested to see these.

I do not want to bother you with my manuscripts, so

just send them back when you are done with them. Of course I shall be charmed to give them to you if you want them, but I cannot conceive that you should. I do not think that they are half as good as your sonnets which I read at intervals and cut myself upon.

Tell me what you think of these, particularly tell me about one line in the 'Letter' poem. The line is 'Shivering, leafless trees,' which I am quite aware is a cliché, but the more I try to change it, the more I feel sure that the line should not be made to stick out of the text as anything particularly unusual, and I am much inclined to leave it, as green grass, or blue sky, or any other usual and unconsidered thing. That poem seems to me rather good as it is, with quite a little feeling, and I hate to change a line of it. I remember our discussing once how often one had to subordinate something one liked for the total effect, making the parts subservient to the whole, and in this case I want to leave my striking epithets for the description of Madame Duse herself and not lay any stress upon the scenery I am looking at when I write. That is my point — how does it strike you?

I ought to apologize for stealing your figure of her body scarcely shadowing her spirit. It is an inevitable thought, I have pondered it myself many times even before I read your superb lines. Mine are so differently expressed that I felt sure you would pardon them. I trust I am right, and that you will not mind....

Sara Teasdale's answer came soon:

Crissey Place
Norfolk, Conn.
Jan. 27, 1924

DEAR AMY:

Outside there is new snow and purplish shadows from many trees. Inside I am alone with your poems to Duse. I have just read them for the first time. They moved me more than I can tell you. This cold New England Sunday hush makes a space in which they can burn with the 'hard gem-like flame.' You have praised the lady as she deserves. That is the highest praise that could be given you, I think.

I know it is the highest praise you would ask. I am glad that I waited to read the poems here. I have been feeling like a sort of fringe around nothing. The country is making me chipper again. The sight of a world uncrowded, unshaken by elevated trains, unharrassed by motor horns — it is the only medicine for me.

'Eleonora (she spells it so, I think) Duse 1923' is the finest of the poems, I believe, and next 'In Answer to a Letter.' I don't know that I have ever read finer praise from one woman to another. Sappho's praise of Anactoria being out of the running, as representing a wholly different sort of thing. It is a shame that Duse can't get them in the English! I am going to keep these poems since you say I may. You know well enough that I want them! They are true pictures of both you and the lady.

It is nearly noon. If I am to get any feeling of morning I must go out while the shadows are still a bit west of south. Good bye, dear Amy. Thank you again!

I had almost forgot to say that Ernest tells me the truth about 'A Critical Fable' is out at last! Congratulations on that too!

All length of years to you, dear Amy.

SARA

On January 14, Miss Lowell wrote the Princeton Press that her book on the free forms of poetry would have to be postponed. This was the first contract she had ever broken. Two days later, she signed the contract for the Keats biography. And presently she received a letter from Thomas Hardy:

Max Gate, Dorchester
January 4, 1924

DEAR MISS AMY LOWELL:

We have received your New Year's cabled message, and that wakes me up to my delinquencies. However we reciprocate your good wishes heartily, and you will remember that our air over here is not so stimulating as yours, which makes us slower in starting things — at least, so I fancy.

I have not gone into the question of free verse lately — to

which you allude in your letter of last summer — and on this side of the Atlantic it seems to have sunk into a calm for a while. I am sure it would make all the difference if I could hear you read it as you do at your lectures.

Those young interviewers who take notes without one's knowledge are a pest: but their conduct is what is called over here 'a fat trouble' — and one is apt to have thrown back in one's face — 'better a fat trouble than a lean one.' Well, I don't know.

I hope the Keat's [*sic*] book is finished. Who would have supposed a little more than a hundred years ago that that young man's private life and affairs would become so interesting to the world. Of course if you do come over this year you will call down and see us.

I read the poems when they came: many thanks for them. I think I liked the Rosebud Wall-paper best. But it is impossible to go appreciating verses in a letter, and I won't attempt it.

My wife sends her best love, and I am

Your affectionate friend,

THOMAS HARDY

One of the letters she wrote this month was to a young lady whose sister was developing a neurosis in the attempt to become a poet.

10 January, 1924

MY DEAR MISS ******:

Your letter is very pathetic, and, to my mind, your sister's poem is even more so. I am sorry to say that I can give you absolutely no encouragement as to her talent. It really would be better, I think, if she would abandon the idea of being an artist, and turn her attention firmly and with an effort of will toward being a sensible, sane, and sober human being.

Art is not, as so many people believe, primarily an outlet for personal emotions. On the contrary, it is the creating of something apart from the artist which, when created, should have a separate existence and justify itself by its power of reproducing an emotion or a thought in the mind of the reader. The amateur writes poetry under great stress of emotion to free himself of an oppressive state of mind. The professional poet (and by professional I do not mean the word in its usual sense, but in the sense of an artist whose life is given up to the creation of poetry) writes, it is true, only when he has something to say, but, at the same time, with the object of making a beautiful poem, not with the object of relieving himself from any particular state of mind.

It is perfectly evident from your sister's poem that she is writing to relieve herself from an oppression. The form her words take proves her to be almost completely ignorant of the laws of poetry and without the necessary knowledge of how to produce an effect. Evidently the idea of the necessity of self expression has taken a strong hold upon her and is ruining her life. If she could only realize that the great artist is not engaged in self expression, but is creating something outside of himself, no matter how closely related it is to himself, she would have gained an important step.

Your sister has not, I think, anything of the artist's temperament except its sensibility, and there is no more dangerous possession for man or woman than artistic sensibility without the curbing and restraining knowledge of the laws of creative activity. If you really have your sister's welfare at heart, and will forget this modern cant of the necessity for everyone to live his own life and express himself, in talking to her, I think you will do her a great service. I am sorry to seem harsh, but I know that what I tell you is the truth.

I thank you very much for the kind things you say about my poetry.

Sincerely yours,

She had agreed to write an introduction to the poems of Stephen Crane, which were to be published as Volume VI of his Complete Works. The publisher then asked her if he should respect Crane's rather modernistic lack of capitals in his verse; Miss Lowell's reply (January 24) was positive.

There is no possible doubt on the matter of having Crane's poems set up as he wrote them in manuscript. You probably know that the non-capitalization of poetry is almost a creed with some people; it would drive 'H. D.' or E. E. Cummings perfectly crazy today if any one presumed to capitalize their poems. Personally I agree with you, I hate no capitals in the printing of verse. But there is no slightest doubt about it that, in Crane's case, if he followed this rule, as I did not know he did, it was part and parcel of his idea of the poems, and it would be as flagrant an error to change it as it would be to change any of the words in the poems themselves. I am surprised that he succeeded in getting the printers of his age to follow his wishes in the matter; that he did, shows that he made a point of it. It is no easy trick now to get printers to follow no capitalization in setting up poetry. If you have followed the new poetry, you have discovered that the actual manner of printing poems is of more importance to it than it was to the older metrical school, because the way the poems are arranged is considered by their authors in the light of musical notation. It interests me considerably, and it will interest everybody, to know that even this early, Crane adopted so idiosyncratic a rule....

In the last week or so of January, the authorship of *A Critical Fable* was discovered. Miss Lowell had included it in the list of her works for the English *Who's Who*; on a hint from Frost it was spotted immediately by Mr. Melcher, who announced his find in the *New York Post*. At once she started writing letters of explanation. One of these, to Sara Teasdale, included further news of the Duse poems.

30 January, 1924

DEAR SARA:

Your letter came this afternoon. Thank you very much indeed for what you say, although you do not give me your opinion on that mooted line in 'In Response to a letter' [*sic*].

You say, in the letter I got the other day, that you will

not be envious. Sure and you need not be, I assure you there is nothing to be envious about, and I doubt whether I shall ever approach any nearer to her with the barrier of language between. Being prepared for a disappointment, I was not surprised to receive a letter from Miss Onslow saying that her attempts at translating the poems into French to Madame Duse were not a success. The way she put it was, 'I doubt if Madame will ever have patience enough to listen, not to you, but to me translating your poems into bad French.'

She went on to say that I had Madame's permission to publish them if I wanted to, but added a footnote to the effect that she, Miss Onslow, thought it would be wiser not to publish 'In Answer to a Letter' as being too intimate. I did not send her '1923,' so that left only the 'Sonnets,' which you and I both think the least good of the bunch. I could not help being amused at her suggestion, as it was so eminently not that of an artist, and I feel quite sure that no such embargo would have issued from Duse herself. However, I am now contemplating translating 'In Answer to a Letter' myself, and having my translation looked over by my quondam French teacher, who is now married and lives in Philadelphia, when I am there speaking at Bryn Mawr next month. Then I think I shall hold it until I see Duse again, and read it to her myself in French, when I hope she will give me permission to publish it. I do not think I shall publish '1923' for a long time — until she is dead, possibly — and I certainly shall not read it to her; you can easily see why.

Now, as to the 'Critical Fable.' Can I ever apologize sufficiently for all the lies I have told you? Ananias was not in it with me, I think. I became so expert at it that I could lie without turning a hair. Ada said it revealed depths of wickedness within me which she had not even suspected before. But what was there to do! The joke had to be kept. It was another little joke of mine to put it into the English 'Who's Who,' but I did not suppose it would come out so quickly....

The wonder to me is that anybody ever had any doubts

as to who wrote the book, it was so obviously me. I made no attempt to disguise my preferences; I put in only the people who I thought deserved to be put in. The one omission I am sorry for is Elinor Wylie, but at the time I wrote it — three years ago — she was not so prominent as she has since become....

The principal difficulty I had was in dealing with myself. My instinct was to leave myself out altogether, but I reflected that my revered ancestor put himself in and probably for the same reason I put myself in, namely for disguise. I felt that to leave myself out would be a dead giveaway, but it was a very difficult thing to do, because I felt that if I blamed myself too much that would lead to detection, and just the same if I praised myself too much....

... In practically every case my opinions were based on the profoundest admiration....

Poor old Braithwaite was the person who sized up my intention in writing the book best. He said that the movement had now received the accolade of satire than which there is nothing more potent to launch anything on the stream of history. A good many people did take it in this way, but there were some fools, notably an old duffer in Rochester, who really believed that the author intended to slang the poets in question.

I learnt a great deal from 'A Critical Fable,' among other things how crude the sense of humour of most Americans is. It cannot understand irony. What seemed as plain as day to me they never saw through, it was funny. F. P. A., who has always hated me since my attack on the columnists years ago, guessed at once that I had written it, and took the opportunity to make a malicious and nasty raid upon me, a thing he does not do with the books which bear my name. Following him, a number of New York reviewers slanged the volume; in contradistinction to which almost everybody in all the other cities in the country praised it. I believe that you did not like it much, but I confess that my heart is very warm toward my little anonymous child; in fact I think that considering its style and the kind of thing it is, it is as good as anything I have done, and I am right behind it with both feet.

Her fiftieth birthday, which fell on February 9, 1924, was celebrated in the newspapers appropriately; at Sevenels, the poet still worked feverishly over the second volume of the Keats biography. Katherine Onslow kept her informed of Duse's progress: they had had a terrible time at Havana, but were starting tomorrow from New Orleans to Los Angeles; the Los Angeles triumph was amazing; and all your friends were so kind; now they were going to San Francisco and then turn east; they would give two performances in Boston before the farewell three in New York... the invitation was indeed kind but she was sure that Madame would never go anywhere except to a hotel ... it was all really only *au revoir*. None the less, Miss Lowell was making no engagements for the latter part of March and the early part of April: 'I have invited her to stay with me, though I doubt very much if she will; at any rate, I had rather you did not mention this because I do not think it will come off. But it is nevertheless a fact that she accepted, although I think in the vague way that people do and which they usually change their minds about.'

On February 19 she set off again, reading to the Washington Society of Fine Arts on the 20th, reading at Bryn Mawr on the 22d with an informal reception afterwards, and speaking briefly if vividly on the 24th at the Lucy Stone League dinner in New York. When its president Ruth Hale (Mrs. Heywood Broun) had asked her to be guest of honor and chief speaker, Miss Lowell had doubted much her sympathy for the League's purpose; Ruth Hale, however, continued to urge her, on the ground that she liked debates; but Miss Lowell refused to debate. She finally agreed to talk on condition that she be the last speaker, with no replies allowed. So she told the League frankly that a happy marriage consisted of two people working together, whereas the desire to retain the maiden name was too often the expression of an exaggerated egotism. The newspapers tried to make out a passage of arms between Ruth Hale and Amy Lowell, but they did not understand the situation, and the two ladies parted more than good friends.[1] By March 6, Miss Lowell was back in Boston to give a reading from the *Critical Fable* at the Women's City Club.

Awaiting her was a letter from Untermeyer in Vienna. She was anxious about the possibility of a third *American Miscellany*, so she wrote a long and chatty letter about the doings of American literature in general, on March 12.

> Elinor Wylie's new prose book, 'Jenifer Lorn,' is having a great *succes d'estime* (I know nothing about sales), as I suppose you have heard. Edna Millay is whirling round the country giving lectures. I hear that she is not a good platform orator, but people are so enamoured of her work, at the moment, that they are ready to fall down and worship her as soon as she appears. There seems to be a general opinion that she cannot continue her reading career, because she is not good on the platform, but speakers learn how to manage audiences after a time. However, her next move is to go to Japan on a walking trip with her husband, after which they expect to go round the world. I hear that Wallace Stevens' book sold practically not at all, which is too bad, because it was a good book.
>
> What you say about Estlin Cummings is absolutely true. I think I told you long ago that what Cummings really was was an Elizabethan lyrist. It is the endeavour not to be what nature meant him to be, which has kept him back. If he would once throw off his wolf's clothing and appear as the Arcadian shepherd of sweet song, a *genre* which he really does uncommonly well, Edna would have a rival in popular favour, I do believe....
>
> Archie MacLeish has a book out this autumn issued by my publishers, Houghton Mifflin. I have not seen it since it was in print, but Archie read it to me one day last Autumn and I thought it had considerable points in various ways, although anything but a finished thing....

[1] *Bookman* (LIX, 252), April, 1924.

The 'Encyclopaedia Britannica' people asked me to contribute an article on modern poetry to the 'History of Our Own Times' which they are getting out. I told them I would do so gladly if they would confine the subject to English and American poetry, but that I had no time to make a study of all the recent poetry of all the other countries, particularly as I could only read French and English. As the editor was particularly anxious that all the countries should be included, I was obliged to forego writing the article which, considering how rushed I am trying to get Keats done, was on the whole what I wanted to do. Instead, I understand that they have asked Fletcher to do the paper....

Frost's book has been a great success, so far as fame is concerned, at least: I know nothing about how it is selling. I have seen him several times this year and got to know both him and Elinor much better than ever before, and I must say they wear well.

Sandburg blew in for a few minutes between lectures in different cities. He was as sweet as ever, and entirely drowned in his Life of Lincoln. It will be very interesting to see what he does with a biography. I had grave doubts of his ability to do such a thing before I talked to him that night, but I must say that after we had conversed on the subject of Lincoln for some hours, both Ada and I felt that he had a great deal to say on the subject. I have heard very little of 'Rootabaga Pigeons,' but I imagine it has not been so successful as the first book. I am to give a lecture on him at the Public Library this afternoon, but I have talked so much about Sandburg and written so much about him that I think I shall devote most of my time to reading some of his works with explanatory remarks such as I make for my own things. I hate to read Sandburg's stuff, because his way of reading it is so unique and so entirely beautiful. However, I shall ramble along as well as I can....

Keats is nearly killing me, and that's a fact; I have completed six hundred and thirty pages of it and have three hundred and seventy left to do, so it is really approaching the stage when one can think of it as a book, particularly

as the illustrations are made and the dummies are ready to
go out. I think I shall never want to undertake so long a
job again....

Her lecture on Sandburg that afternoon was one of a
series of lectures on contemporary poets, given by the New
England Poetry Club at the Boston Public Library. Although the day had turned out to be the worst blizzard of
the season, her lecture was the most successful of the
series. As she wrote to the Untermeyers (April 14):

> [The storm] was so bad that I said to Ada that I did not
> believe there would be anyone in the hall, and I might just
> as well summon her and my secretaries down in the morn-
> ing room and read to them, for I thought the three of them
> would be the only people present in the Public Library
> where I was talking. Imagine my feelings when I got there
> to find the hall, which holds about four hundred and fifty
> people, solidly crammed, with people standing three deep
> in the back, and to be told by one of the assistant librarians
> that five hundred had been turned away. A lady told me
> afterwards that she had inquired of her neighbor in the
> next seat, who looked a lively sort of person, why there
> seemed to be so many youngish women in the audience, and
> the lady replied that delegates had been sent from all the
> Women's Clubs in the state. She also volunteered the fact
> that 'A Critical Fable' was being taken up by all the Wo-
> men's Clubs as a text book. This amused me immensely; I
> think Sandburg and I probably share the honours for the
> very large audience.

And all the while she kept working on the manuscript of
Keats. By now she was arranging for the dummy, specify-
ing exactly what kind of binding, what kind of lettering on
the spine. A photographer had to come to Sevenels to
photograph the treasures which she would hardly trust out
of her own hands, let alone her own house. And steadily
from the west came a small stream of Katherine Onslow's
letters, keeping her informed of Duse's progress: Dear
Amy... San Francisco gave us such a splendid send-off...

the assistant manager sees to your champagne... such dis-
tances... Madame is as lovely as ever and *so gallant*...
your friends have been *most* kind... we shall be in Boston
idle for Holy Week... our plans are uncertain, but *no*
parties... tonight we go to Pittsburgh, 12 hours nearer
N.Y., which gives us a feeling of home... you have smoothed
Madame's path so much for her all these weeks... when
we see you next... Pittsburgh is hell on earth....

On April 5th, Duse played the part of Bianca Querceta
in Marco Praga's *La Porta Chiusa* ('The Closed Door') at
the Syria Mosque, Pittsburgh. It was pouring the night of
the performance; and when she reached the theater, the
stage door by some mischance was locked. For five
minutes she stood there in the rain and the icy wind.
'Sola — sola,' the last words of the play, were her last
words on any stage. The next day, she was stricken down
with a high fever. Though she was obliged to postpone her
Cleveland appearance, yet her illness did not seem particularly serious.

Meanwhile Miss Lowell, anxious to get Keats well advanced before Madame Duse arrived (there were still
three hundred pages to write), was trying to do four
months' work in two. April 8, however, was the date of a
long-deferred recital; for over a year she had been trying to
arrange a time when Eva Gauthier could sing at her house.
It was already evening when she learned that a sudden illness made it impossible for Miss Gauthier to come; no
worthy substitute could be got at the last moment ('I did
not want some second-rate player from the Symphony
Orchestra to come and twaddle some old classic to a bored
audience especially asked to hear novelty'); so Miss Lowell
herself became the entertainer, and with chagrined
apologies for springing this on her fifty guests, read them
her own poems.

That night, her eyes gave out suddenly, with a terrible
pain that returned unexpectedly and overwhelmingly.

She could not sleep, and was kept walking the floor. On the supposition that it was mere fatigue, she was ordered not to use her eyes at all for at least a week; actually some small blood-vessels had broken in both retinas. For the next two days she merely dictated answers to her accumulated correspondence. Among other things, she was arranging to go on to New York for Duse's final performances, and making sure that the *New Republic* would publish her Duse sonnets at that time. On the evening of the 12th, she went to hear Monteux conduct the *Sacre de Printemps*.

Then she read of Duse's breakdown, and at once sent an anxious telegram to Mrs. Walter Bingham at Pittsburgh, asking for news. Mrs. Bingham, who was one of the string of friends across the continent which Mrs. Russell and she had arranged to make Duse's way smooth for her, telegraphed back (April 13) that the doctors reported a decided improvement, and on the 16th wrote further details: it was never more than a bronchial cold. That same day, however, the newspapers ran the story that Duse had caught the influenza; Miss Lowell, still more worried, telegraphed and telephoned, to ask if she could do anything; but Mrs. Bingham replied that Duse's condition was unchanged. On Good Friday, the 18th, Miss Lowell wrote again, offering to do anything in her power, and stating frankly her fear that Duse might die. She arranged to have bulletins sent her twice a day. Before dawn, on Easter Monday, the end came.

The *New Republic* asked immediately if she still wanted her sonnets published; she replied that she did, as soon as possible, as a sort of requiem. She telegraphed money for flowers; then, in response to the message from Katherine Onslow, left for Pittsburgh, where Duse's body lay in state for several days.

On April 27, Duse's body reached New York; on the 30th, Miss Lowell's sonnets appeared in the *New Republic*;

on the next day, May 1, the funeral mass was celebrated. Miss Lowell, who was present, wrote an account of it to Mrs. Bingham (May 5).

... Katherine Onslow told me that their train was quite late, that they stopped in Philadelphia for some little time and a band of Fascisti with black shirts came into the car and saluted Madame's coffin, which was very impressive. They were met at the train by the Consular Committee, and went at once to the church of Saint Vincent Ferrer where some sort of short receiving service was performed. From this point on, the body was in the charge of the Dominican Fathers, and the company seem to have given up their long vigil of watching, which I suppose they will resume on the ship.

I went down to the church the next day and again two days later; it was a most impressive sight. It is a beautiful church, one of Goodhue's.... The windows... are simply diamonds and squares in patterns with an occasional pane of slightly tinted red or blue glass. The colours are very faint, but they do pick out a sort of pattern, which, however, does not tinge the daylight at all, so that the whole inside is full of daylight.

I know very little about Catholic churches and never go into them, but the modern method of votive candles seems to me very pretty and effective. Instead of candles they have little glass lamps called 'vigil lights.' They are made somewhat on the order of a regular night light, and somewhat like the wicks in oil floating in glass cups so much used in Italy, and they are of various colours. In this particular church, they were mostly red, with a few green, and the effect was like parterres of flowers burning on the floor and a few on stands. As they flickered, blew down, and flared up, the colours were wonderfully beautiful, changeable, and glowing.

The chapel, inside of which the coffin lay was filled with flowers, which increased daily until, by the last day, they were not only banked up in the chapel itself, but all along the aisle beside it, and a number of little bouquets from poor people were laid down against the rails in front of the chapel, and a great many of the little lights I have spoken of were burning. All day long, from six in the morning until nine at night, there was a steady stream of people; I cannot imagine how many there must have been in the whole three days, thousands and thousands of them. No one was allowed to stop for more than a moment in front of the chapel itself, but one might sit in the pews near it, and many people did apparently just this for hours at a time... It was all most wonderful and perfectly dignified, and not in the least a jarring tribute.

Mrs. Belmont had got consular tickets for Ada and me, which meant that we could go to the funeral and be in one of the first fifteen rows — as a matter of fact, we were in the fourth row. The church part was rather badly managed, for they did not let in even the stamped ticket holders for a long time, and, by some mistake, there had not been enough unstamped tickets given out, so that the back pews of the church and side far back were empty, while ten thousand people stood outside longing to get in and were refused admittance because they had no tickets. Apart from this everything was done quite fittingly and beautifully.

The solemn high requiem mass was given, which I had never heard before. They had something like seventy-five choir boys, I believe, and the choir was exceedingly fine. Martinelli, of the Metropolitan Opera House, sang the Benedictus. Ten or eleven Dominican Fathers officiated, with superb silver and black velvet copes and some entirely white.... The coffin was covered with an Italian flag, and it seems to me it had some sort of a pall on it too, of silver and black, but of that I am not sure; it was almost entirely obscured by a huge wreath of white roses from the King of Italy. There were some other wreaths leaning up against the side of it, among which was Mussolini's, but the only one I actually saw on it was the King's. I never saw such flowers in my life, not only were they banked round the bier on which the coffin stood, but they stretched in a long line down both transepts, and a mass of them were laid in front of the choir stalls on both sides all the way along the chancel to the altar. It took two automobiles filled chock full to carry the flowers, which preceded the hearse.

... Everything was very beautiful, quite dignified, and extraordinarily solemn and impressive. In the middle, suddenly, the sun shot a beam of light directly down upon the coffin from the high window at the end of the chancel. It was like a symbol taking tangible form. At the end of the service, the coffin was wheeled out of the door of one of the transepts, followed immediately by the Ambassador and Katherine Onslow, and after them the members of the company and the Consular Committee. We went out with the crowd afterwards and had some difficulty in finding our motor, and when we did find it we pursued the funeral, but only reached Central Park after demonstrations by the Fascisti and the Berserglieri and other organizations of the sort had finished, although they were still standing in line. I believe the party had halted for three or four minutes while the coffin was being saluted, and we did not follow the funeral procession to the boat.

The next day they had a long talk with Miss Onslow, then returned to Sevenels. She tried to plunge back into the Keats biography, but for the time she was still distracted; moreover, her eyes were not well yet. But at least she had the satisfaction of receiving a series of telephone calls congratulating her on the Duse sonnets, followed by quite a sheaf of letters from strangers as well as friends.

On May 22 and June 16 she read her poems respectively at Boston University and the Women's Municipal League; otherwise she did little but work at Keats. The first draft was finished on July 22. Some chapters were read to John Lowes; then, after revision and copying, they were rushed to the press. Mrs. Russell corrected all the proof; Miss Lowell verified quotations and checked up the hundred last stray points; and three stenographers were kept busy through the summer. It was planned to get the book out, if not by autumn, at least in time for the Christmas trade; but it was a two-volume work, and could not be rushed unduly. 'If you could see my correspondence basket!' she wrote Magdelaine Hutchinson (August 15):

> It looks like the Eiffel Tower, and as though it were going to fall over and smother me. I shall lose all my friends, because I have not answered a letter for ever so long....
>
> We are really going abroad at last. Some time toward Spring, we are going to England, in the hope of my being able to give a few readings over there. I have two English publishers — one, Basil Blackwell, for poetry books, and the other, Jonathan Cape, who has taken the Keats book — and both of them are most anxious to have me appear on the scene and give some readings, and this I have promised to do. I have not much faith in an English audience for me; I think your country will be the first to appreciate me. I think I told you that M. Feuillerat of the University of Rennes is writing an article on me for the 'Revue de Deux Mondes'; and Jean Catel, who is a professor in the University of Montpellier and has been for a long while the writer of the American rubric in the 'Mercure de France,' has just published a perfectly delightful article on me in the 'Literary Review' of the 'New York Evening Post.'...

She seldom left the house now, even to walk in the garden; her only relaxation was the occasional entertainment of guests at dinner. Dr. Tsunejiro Miyaoka turned up with his wife — she had not seen him since she was nine years old, when he opened to her the fairy-world of the Far East. Another visitor was Professor Bingham, about whom she wrote to Archibald MacLeish (August 29):

> His efforts to understand me are interesting, but I confess do not seem to get very far, as he is no poet. He brought out an English psychologist to converse with me the other day, as he is interested in the psychological processes of artistic creation. I felt as though I were an insect being examined under a microscope. But these scientists have

not the ghost of an idea how to approach anything like creation, and their flounderings amuse me to death.

It was probably on this occasion that he tried a word-association test. She answered with remarkable speed; the results were totally incomprehensible. To 'moon' she answered 'deep'; to 'cow' she answered 'man.' As he could make nothing of these associations, he asked her if she could explain them. 'Why, it is very simple,' she answered. 'Last night I was reading a poem of Keats in which he spoke of the deep moon; therefore when you said "moon" I said "deep." Then I always work all night and go to bed at dawn; the last sight I see out of the window is the man leading the cow out. So when you said "cow" I said "man."'

The revising of Keats was finished in the first week of September. At once she wrote the long promised introduction to the poems of Stephen Crane, for the collected edition of his works, and sent it off on the 13th. The Keats proofs, however, were to come in for a couple of months as yet, and October had hardly started when she learned that the book could not possibly be got out by Christmas. Meanwhile interest was becoming apparent in England as well as America; J. Middleton Murry, for example, had written asking for a copy of the book, so that he could discuss its views in his lectures on 'Keats and Shakspere' at Cambridge University, and also review it at length in the London *Times Literary Supplement*. She was both delighted and surprised at what she took to be a change of attitude on his part, as her reply of October 7 showed:

> Your letter of September the seventeenth was the greatest surprise and pleasure to me. Mr. Cape had written me that you might review the book for the 'Times' and would speak of it in your lectures at Cambridge University; but the genuine interest and cordiality with which you are prepared to receive it is something I could not have expected. You said one of the most amusing things about me once, when

I published that long Keats letter [1] in the Keats Memorial Volume in 1921. You said that Miss Amy Lowell had evidently come to regard herself as the recipient of the letter. I have chuckled over that a great many times since. I do not suppose one can live in such close communication with a man, even if he be dead, for four years without feeling as though one knew him. At any rate, I cannot; but in the book I have tried as far as possible to stand in the wings merely, entirely out of sight of the audience....

There were other letters to write: letters to magazines which had planned to run an article on her Keats book in their Christmas numbers; letters refusing to go anywhere to lecture, as she was saving up her strength for her trip to England; a long autobiographical letter to Archibald MacLeish, who was planning to write an article on her — one poet's estimate of another — for the *North American Review*; a letter to Jean Catel, who was now studying at Princeton, recommending the poems of Emily Dickinson and inviting him to visit her in the Christmas vacation.

On October 4, she read her poems to the Women's City Club of Boston. On the 11th, she gave a dinner for Henry Seidel Canby, who was lecturing in the city. On the 20th she was notified that at last she had won a prize from *Poetry*; the Helen Haire Levinson Prize, which was awarded to her 'Evelyn Ray.' [2] On the 24th, she went to a dinner given by the Edward Burlingame Hills in Cambridge, and the next day, in thanking Miss Monroe for the prize, wrote: 'I have been out of the house exactly four times this summer, one of which times was to go to the

---

[1] [An unpublished letter in her possession, which she contributed to the Keats Memorial Volume, proceeds of the sale of which went to the support of Wentworth House.]

[2] Previous winners of this prize — the largest that *Poetry* offered — were Sandburg, Lindsay, Masters, Cloyd Head, John Curtis Underwood, H. L. Davis, Wallace Stevens, Lew Sarett, Frost, and Robinson. Miss Lowell's pleasure in receiving the prize was perhaps tempered by Miss Monroe's article on her, in the October issue, which began: 'One may as well begin by granting Miss Lowell everything but genius.' The award was not announced publicly till December.

funeral of my brother-in-law [William Lowell Putnam, Bessie's husband]. I have not had even an hour to walk round the place in.' On the 29th, she entertained Dr. A. S. W. Rosenbach, who produced from his pocket Keats's own annotated Shakspere when she remarked that it was the one book she wanted more than anything in the world.[1]

By November, page proofs of volume I and galleys of volume II had been corrected, the appendices were not yet set up, the index was being made. 'The press and I keep about neck and neck on it, neither of us holding the other back at all,' she wrote to one inquirer. In order not to lose any more of the Christmas sale than was necessary, Houghton Mifflin issued a card which prospective donors of the book could send to their friends, to announce their intention; these cards were distributed among the bookstores. But the book itself could not appear until January 31.

Jonathan Cape had been busy with his advance notices in England; requests for lectures began to come in; and Miss Lowell engaged passage on the *Berengaria,* which was to sail on April 15, 1925.

On December 13, the very last proofs were corrected; her part was over; she could rest now, until the book was actually out. She began again on her correspondence, especially letters to those friends who were expecting the Keats for Christmas. During the vacation, Jean Catel came up from Princeton to spend three days with her — it was his introduction to New England. As soon as he had left, she wrote a few letters while preparing for a vacation of her own in New York. One of these letters was to D. H. Lawrence.

31 December, 1924

DEAR LAWRENCE:

I hear you are still at Taos, but, as I do not know for certain, I am going to send this letter care of Thomas Seltzer. I wish I could have reviewed your last book of poems,

[1] A. S. W. Rosenbach: *Books and Bidders,* Boston, 1927, pp. 39–40.

but I was absolutely drowned in my life of Keats and could do nothing outside; I knew you would understand.

Our little Imagist anthologies are gradually giving up the ghost. I am sending you enclosed a cheque for the February and August statements. They are both so small that I thought it better to keep them and send them together.... The first two anthologies went out of print with the August statement, and there are only six copies of the '1917' left, so we shall soon have done with them altogether, and these remittances of two cents a time will disappear.

Some one told me that Frieda had come back and was with you now in New Mexico. I wish we might have met last year, and I hope we shall have a chance of meeting again before long.

Mrs. Russell and I are sailing for England in April. I am to give some lectures and talks there, and we expect to stay about three months, when we shall return to these diggins [sic] and settle down as usual. I expect to have another book of poems out a year from now. I have not read your last book, 'The Boy in the Bush,' because I have read nothing since I have been working on the Keats. Some day I hope to be able to read again; just now I am too tired to do anything but sleep and eat, for Keats was an awful task and I am thankful that it is over.

You are the most indefatigable worker I ever saw; your energy amazes me. My many operations took a great deal of my energy away, but I hope to get it back again some day. I hear rumours that you hated New York, at which I am not in the least surprised, and that you like New Mexico, which does not surprise me either, but I wish you could come on here because I think you might like this place, although not as much as New Mexico I imagine.

I hear from Hilda occasionally and from Richard once in a while, and I hope to pick up the threads of many things when I return to England. I am only sorry that you and Frieda are not going to be there. I would send you the Keats when it comes out, but I doubt very much whether you will care for it; however, you shall have it if the idea seems in the least attractive to you, but beware, it is in two large volumes!

I read your book on American literature with a great deal
of interest, and not a little divergence of view. The Puritans were not so puritanical as they have been represented,
but it takes some time to know that. Neither is any corner
of America America; until you have seen the whole of it you
cannot be said to have seen it at all. But of course, you dear
prejudiced soul, you will never believe that. If you will
come to me without fail the next time you are in this region,
I can show you something you have not yet seen.

Give my love to Frieda, in which Mrs. Russell joins, and
love to you from both of us also.

Affectionately yours,

In New York she was busy with entertaining and interviews anticipating the publication of the Keats, which
kept up for two mad weeks. 'I had to let myself out in
half-hour pieces, and the half hours went on until two
o'clock in the morning,' she wrote Josephine Pinckney on
her return. 'To be sure, they did not begin with the lark,
but they retired to bed with the owl.' Yet her only official
engagement seems to have been a reading for the Writers'
Club of Columbia University on the 12th. She returned
on the 19th, to await the Keats and to start getting ready
for Europe. 'I imagine if we once get ourselves landed
over there, we shall get on splendidly, but to start on the
trip looks awful, merely putting away the books on the
tables before we go looms before me as an intolerable task.'
A letter from Lawrence was awaiting her.

> Av. Pino Suarez #43.
> *Oaxaca* (Oax) Mexico
> 16 Jan. 1925

Dear Amy

Thank you for your letter & the little cheque.

We were the summer in New Mexico — you know Frieda
is the proud possessor of a little ranch there, up in the
mountains, about 17 miles from Taos. But we came down
here end of October, because of the cold. It got my chest a
bit: or the altitude: 8,500 ft. I expect we shall go back there
in the summer: like it very much: come & see us one day.

But about March I think we shall go to England & Germany, for a month or two. Frieda's mother is very old, & keeps wanting her to go home. And my father died, & my sisters keep wanting to see me. — Probably we shall be in London when you are. If so, I hope to see you again: it was 1914, & Richard was not yet a soldier — You can always find me c/o Curtis Brown. 6 Henrietta St. Covent Garden. W.C. 2. He's in the telephone book: is a literary agent.

I should like very much to have Keats. Am as a matter of fact rather fond of fat two-vol books with letters in them and all that. Did my Quetzalcoatl novel down here. It scares me a bit. But it's nearly done.

I wonder where I should ask you to send me the Keats book. Perhaps best c/o Curtis Brown and *to await arrival*. Tell them to mark it that, please. Then perhaps I'll review it in London. A threat! — But I should like to have it. — And if you tell either Thomas Seltzer or Martin Secker to give you the Boy in the Bush from me, they'll do it at once.

It's awful to have such a bad time with your health.

I never said I knew all America: or all about it. God forbid! and keep on forbidding!

One day, perhaps, we may be aimiable [*sic*] to one another for half an hour in your Brooklyn Garden. If pansies are out — jusqu'alors! — or no, till London again.

Af.

D. H. Laurence
Frieda sends saluti e ricordi.
Remember us to Mrs. Russell.

D. H. L.

Sheets of the Keats biography were going out to the prospective reviewers; requests for lecture dates were flowing in from England. Beyond these two matters she wrote only the most necessary letters: one to Arthur Waley, saying that she would be most happy indeed to recommend his translation of the *Genji Monogatari* to her publishers; and another to the *Saturday Review of Literature*, protesting against its review of Grace Hazard Conkling's *Ship's Log*, and suggesting that someone review

Dream Tapestries by Louise Mary Bowman, 'the most important poet now writing in Canada.'

On February 5, the first advance copies of the Keats book arrived. She breakfasted with the unopened package before her; then, just as she was about to look at the completed book, the labor of these many years, she was told of the sudden death of her sister, Katherine Bowlker, who had been killed instantly by a fall from a window of the Hotel Vendôme.

On February 10, *John Keats* was published. The second edition, which was not yet available, was already sold out.

CHAPTER XXIV

JOHN KEATS

Amy Lowell was predestinate to write a biography of John Keats. The history of her book might be traced back to the day when the girl of fifteen, devouring Leigh Hunt's *Imagination and Fancy*, discovered that a poet called Keats had once lived, and was actually in her father's library. But it really begins when the woman of thirty-one bought all the Keats material in the Locker-Lampson sale, including the manuscript of the 'Eve of St. Agnes'; this became the nucleus of her own collection, which grew steadily until it was, as she believed, the largest in the world. She outlined it in a letter to Miss Isabel Boyd, on August 22, 1924:

> I have been a Keats collector for a great many years, and, as far as I can now make out, I have one of the largest, if not the largest, collection of Keats material now in existence. I bought all the Rowfant Library Keats collection on the death of Frederick Locker-Lampson, and I have been adding to it year by year ever since. It will be impossible to give you anything like a detailed account of what I have, but a *resumé* is as follows: I have over forty letters of Keats to various correspondents, including a few hitherto unpublished, which will appear in my forthcoming Life of Keats. I have something like fourteen holograph manuscripts of Keats's poems, many of them first drafts, others copies made by Keats himself. Among these are the first draft of the 'Eve of St. Agnes'; the first draft and first copy of the 'Ode to Autumn'; the first draft of the 'On Looking into Chapman's Homer' sonnet; unknown and cancelled passages from 'Lamia'; some unpublished, or only partly published poems, etc. I have five presentation copies of Keats's three books, including the copy of 'Lamia' given to Fanny Brawne and owned by the late Buxton Forman, and a par-

ticularly interesting copy of the 'Poems' given by Keats to his brother George and annotated throughout. I have five books from Keats's library containing most interesting annotations, and the annotations in these volumes, with others I have found in other collections, are to form one of the appendices of my book.

Besides this direct Keats material, I have various other Keatsiana, notably a small medal which Keats won at school, and a number of letters from his friends, among them fragments from three quite unknown letters from Dr. Clark who took care of him during his last illness in Rome. ... One of the most important of my Keatsiana is the long-vanished Memoir sent by Taylor to Woodhouse, after a conversation with Keats's quondam guardian, Richard Abbey.

This hasty résumé is hardly even an index — it omits such items as the 'lost' Woodhouse letter, which contained the second draft of 'Autumn' and Shelley's letter to Keats, inviting him to stay with him in Italy — but it gives an impression of the scope of her collection, which even then was not complete, as on November 10, 1924, she bought a fragment of the journal-letter of February–May, 1819, which Keats sent to his American brother. As this material arrived too late to be inserted in its proper place, she could only include it as an appendix.

When she began this collection, she had already been writing poetry for a few years, but she always claimed that she learned more about poetic composition from the manuscript of the 'Eve of St. Agnes' than from any book or human being. 'I think the constant studying of his manuscripts with his corrections, and seeing why he made them, has taught me more about writing poetry than anything else in the world.' [1] Only once did she deny this; when she read in the Bryher pamphlet that she admired nobody except Keats, she wrote to correct the statement (June 29, 1918): 'Personally, I have found more instruction in

[1] Letter to Jeannette Marks, April 25, 1917.

Chaucer than in any other English poet.' But it was Keats, of all poets, who was nearest to the Imagist ideals: none other had ever attempted so thoroughly to describe things as they appear to the senses illumined by the imagination, without the intrusion of morals or personalities. It was Keats who had opened Amy Lowell's five senses, and had taught her the meaning of love, physical and spiritual. It is significant, I think, that they both had a cult of the moon.

So strong was his influence that she was thoroughly aware of the danger of imitation. When Miss Marks wanted her to lecture at Mt. Holyoke on the influence of Keats, she refused (January 24, 1918):

> ... I am afraid I cannot talk on the subject which you suggest. I am quite as enthusiastic as you are about Keats. He has been my great inspirer and teacher, but in spite of that I feel that all of us of the younger generation have had to break away from his influence, not that it was not at one time a stimulating influence, but that it has become, through constant iteration, so diluted and nerveless as to almost act like one of those habit-forming drugs... I think the minor poets have been copying Keats for a hundred years now... Wherefore, if I were to lecture on the subject you suggest, it would be principally to show the present-day poets revolting from that influence.

And again, in a letter to Caroline Newton (July 24, 1920):

> I am very fond of Keats; surely you must have guessed that from my collection of him, but I do not think it possible to write like him to-day. He did it once and for all... They are a part of me and I love them; and when he hit it off, how he did hit it. Do you remember the description of the moon as 'swimming into the blue with all her light'? Dear me, dear me, how I wish I had written that line!

But besides admiring his work, she admired the man for himself. Sensitive though he was, he had nothing in common with Shelley's hysterics and radicalism. Instead,

Keats was quiet but liked fun immensely; though only five feet tall, he fought bullies; he was loyal to his family; he could have supported himself as a surgeon, had it been necessary; he was intellectually honest with himself, and rejected a religion meaningless to him without bothering to disturb that of others; and generally speaking, behaved. Only at the end, when his illness made him morbidly jealous, could he be censured, and surely the throes of a despairing death were sufficient explanation and excuse.

It is not surprising, then, that the format of her own first book was copied from the format of Keats's 1820 *Lamia*; the first and best poem in it utilized the moon-symbol of *Endymion*, and two other poems were frankly inspired by Keats. Since then, she had written several more poems about Keats, notably 'To a Certain Critic' and 'View of Teignmouth.' Consequently, when the Yale press urged her to publish her Keats centenary address, she suddenly realized that he was too important to her to be dealt with in a mere pamphlet; and at the end of February or the beginning of March 1921, she determined to make a full book of it.

This book, instead of being the occupation of a single summer, took four years of her life and hastened her death.

The Keats material which she did not own was put readily at her disposal. Lord Crewe's collection was the only important one she had never seen; the Dilke collection she had examined in 1913; and the Keats Memorial House Association assisted her towards getting the use of such English material as she needed. The material in America was not only of great importance, but had never been used: 'It is a fact,' she wrote Jonathan Cape (August 18, 1924), 'that none of the English biographers or commentators on Keats have ever come over here, and examined the collections of Keats in this country.' This material had started coming to America as early as 1818, when the poet's brother George emigrated with the intent of making his fortune. John faithfully sent George long journal-letters and manuscripts of poems, with the result that the *Western Messenger* of Louisville, Kentucky, first published the initial letter of the Scotch tour series, which remained there unknown for ninety years, also the 'Ode to Apollo.' James Freeman Clarke, the editor, valued and preserved the manuscripts; and the first draft of the 'Ode to Autumn' had finally been inherited by Mrs. Charles Bruen Perkins, who left it for years in Miss Lowell's safe, until Miss Lowell acquired it for herself. Then the cult of Keats in America, as against the neglect of Keats in England, gave the lead to the American collectors.

> The most important of these [collections] have been the Morgan Collection of New York and the Day Collection of Boston. The Morgan Library contains, as you probably know, the manuscript of 'Endymion,' the second draft of the 'Chapman's Homer' sonnet, of which I have the first, some letters of Keats, and a number of other contemporary letters pertaining to the poet, some entirely unpublished, which I have been given permission to publish in my book. It has been very interesting to find letters from certain of Keats's friends in the Morgan Library to which I have the answers in my collection. This cross-reading has made possible some interesting new information about Keats and his work.[1]

The collectors of both America and England were most generous in allowing her to use their treasures. Fred Holland Day indeed was almost inaccessible: bed-ridden for years, he lived in seclusion, expressing an open contempt for all modernism and all poetesses. At first he refused to see her, on the grounds of propriety; but after her letters won permission to visit him, her presence proved quite enchanting. He told her he had expected a bob-haired, jazzing giggler; and for months he smilingly tormented her by

[1] Letter to Miss Isabel Boyd, August 22, 1924.

holding up packets of letters, from which he read extracts — especially the precious letters from Fanny Brawne. But at last she got permission to use the best passages, on condition that his name be suppressed. There was only one item she could not use, or even see: the seven-volume Shakspere with Keats's annotations, which the owner, George Armour of Princeton, had already offered to Caroline Spurgeon for her scholarly study.[1]

All this new material was itself a more than sufficient cause for a new book about the poet; but she had another reason. 'A great poet has something to give to every generation,' she said in her Preface; and as yet no authentically modern voice had spoken of Keats's meaning to the twentieth century. To Miss Lowell, he was essentially modern: one read his letters almost as though they were by a contemporary, in a way that one could not read Shelley or Byron. Keats's way of looking at things or entering into them was far ahead of his own times; these excellences had never been pointed out, and it was to the interest of contemporary literature that they should be.

A third cause of her writing the life was a family matter, which she hardly took seriously; but in a letter to Mr. Day (February 11, 1922) she mentioned it: 'It is a curious thing that James Russell Lowell planned to write a life of Keats and never did so. I like to imagine that the task has been deputed to me in his stead.'

The biography which she proposed to write was to be simultaneously a psychological novel, a book of poetic criticism, and a contribution to scholarship. Aldington wanted her to keep the life and the criticism separate, but that went contrary to her basic theory of such work. She had outlined her theory at the beginning of her lecture on Aldington, Flint, and Lawrence several years before:

> I think it was Sainte-Beuve who warned his readers that criticism, to be fundamental, must concern itself with the

[1] Caroline F. E. Spurgeon: *Keats's Shakespeare*, Oxford, 1928.

life of an author as well as with his art. Criticism is not
merely an interpretation of technique: it is a tracing of
mental bias, a tracking of angles of thought to their starting
points, a realization of the roots from which the flowers
spring. There has lately arisen a new school which denies
the virtue of a consideration, in any work of art, of anything
but itself. The contention has a certain *raison d'être*, but
we must not fail to remember that it represents a natural
reaction from the excessive use of anecdote and gossip about
important people by means of which the cheaper sort of
essay writers endeavour to spice their own insipid remarks.
What Sainte-Beuve had in mind was not this sort of after-
dinner talk; in laying stress upon the importance of the life
of an artist in relation to his art, he meant an understanding
of the man: his aims, motives, and desires. A knowledge of
the man illumines his art if we mean by 'knowledge' a
realization of his psychology and its shock against the world
in which he lived. This in no way militates against the
aesthetic consideration of his art *per se*, but leads in the end
more directly towards it.

Profoundly believing this, I have always attempted to
set a poet of whom I was speaking in his frame.[1]

Generally speaking, critics hitherto had tended to
separate life and works, because they could not relate the
two. Poetry was a something all by itself, existing beyond
time and space and even human meaning, a magical pattern of words, quite inexplicable in terms of its temporal,
spatial, and human creator. But Amy Lowell could not
possibly separate the two, and would not. She knew that
poetry springs from the life, that it is born in time and
space, and that much of it is a failure; she knew that
genius is something that develops; she even admitted that
most of Keats's poems were experiments that simply had
not succeeded. Therefore in her Preface she wrote:

Keats and his poetry are so much of a piece, that I have
followed a rather unusual method in dealing with the two

[1] 'Imagism Past and Present,' ii, Brooklyn Institute, March 27, 1918.

aspects of his character, the personal and the poetic. I have given his life as a whole, bringing in the poems at intervals as they occurred to him. My object has been to make the reader feel as though he were living with Keats, subject to the same influences that surrounded him, moving in his circle, watching the advent of poems as from day to day they sprang into being. I have tried to bring back into existence the place, the time, and the society in which Keats moved. A host of commentators have dealt with him solely in his quality of poet functioning in the timeless area of universal literature; my endeavour has been to show him as a particular poet, hindered and assisted by his temperamental bias as a man, writing in a certain *milieu*.

John Keats she saw, not as a Poet, a Being Apart, with dishevelled locks, wild eyes, and a halo, but rather as the kind of pleasant young man who might live next door, with a remarkable gift for writing. His life was short and uneventful; therefore she was able to examine it the more intensively, showing how casual things — a sore throat, lines underscored in some book — were more significant than the person himself knew. Keats himself had said 'A Man's life of any worth is a continual allegory, and very few eyes can see the Mystery of his life — a life like the scriptures, figurative — which such people can no more make out than they can the Hebrew Bible.' Miss Lowell unconsciously took him at his word; but what she discovered was not Allegory and Mystery but a young man struggling to develop a gift and to control a temperament.

Here indeed lies the chief genius of her book, in this sympathetic, unsentimentalized narrative of a thoroughly human young man, as he lived, worked, and died. One does not feel him as belonging essentially to another century and civilization: the differences of costume and custom, which would figure so largely in the picturesque type of biography, are here relegated to their proper unimportance. It is a psychological novel indeed, though without

dabbling in the superficialities of the 'stream of consciousness' or the profundities of psychoanalysis — a psychological novel in which the chief strands of the narrative are
Keats's brain, his heart, his nerves, also his vocation, his
money, and his disease. Particularly, it is a study of the
development of his genius: of how he started to write
poetry, and how bad it was, and how good things began
to come through when he hit his stride, and how he had to
guard it against Leigh Hunt and Shelley, and how he tried
to write a long poem, and how parts of it went well and
other parts were sheer labor, and so forth, until his early
death at the age of twenty-five. Altogether, it is a sane and
intelligent answer to the awed question 'What is a Poet?'

To a lesser degree she made all Keats's friends and acquaintances alive also. A whole series of bright portraits
frames the great portrait of the poet himself, who thus is
given existence in a dynamic world. That Amy Lowell
liked some and disliked others, and said so, adds to the
reality of the whole group: we feel as concerned about
them as though they were our own neighbors. Even when
they were Keats's enemies — as in the case of the reviewers for *Blackwood's* and the *Quarterly Review* — Amy
Lowell's good-hearted, intelligent indignation (and she
herself had had her difficulties with reviewers) refreshes
one even at this late date; while Messrs. Lockhart and
Croker, instead of appearing as incredible Devils warring
against Beauty, are represented for what they surely were:
two smart young cads.

But her best work was done in straightening out Keats's
relations with Fanny Brawne. The mawkish and false
interpretations of that affair had worked to the great dis-
credit both of the young girl and her lover; and it was Amy
Lowell who first applied a sympathetic common sense to
the tragic situation. She had already sized it up when she
first learned of the Fanny Brawne letters she was eventually to use, as is evident from a note she wrote Fred Day

(February 7, 1921), hoping to get permission to use one of them in her Centenary lecture:

> I have never thought Fanny Brawne to be the heartless and frivolous girl which some of Keats's biographers have insisted upon. That his friends thought she was not good enough for him, was inevitable. She was also very young, and Keats was an invalid; but there is nothing derogatory to him in his sufferings, nor to her in his jealous strictures, I think. I understand Keats's character too well, and the circumstances too well, to misconstrue either Keats's or Fanny Brawne's attitude throughout. One of the things I am proposing to do, in this lecture, is to make the simplicity and clarity of their relations a little more evident, and to rescue Keats's memory from the silly animadversions against his love letters made first by Matthew Arnold and continued by almost all his critics ever since. Psychology has made great strides of late — strides with which even Keats's recent biographer, Sir Sidney Colvin, has been unable to keep up — but I do not regard his love letters as either silly or insane. They are merely the expression of a mind tried by illness and temperament beyond endurance; and underneath all the agony of mind, they show his constant chivalrous endeavour to do the right thing.

Fanny Brawne, she thought, was an affectionate and truly devoted young lady, who behaved with remarkable affection and unselfishness when her lover, overshadowed by death, and clinging bitterly to the happiness he was losing, wrote letters that were simply the morbid desperation of a sick man — letters not to be judged as though the author were mature, healthy, and untroubled. And Miss Lowell's view of the situation was entirely and remarkably confirmed after her death, when a certain letter of Fanny Brawne's was recovered and published in the London *News Chronicle.*[1] It was the letter to Charles Brown containing

---

[1] Reprinted in the *Saturday Review of Literature*, July 16, 1932; see also W. T. Scott's 'The Legend of a Dead Poet and his Darkened Memory' in the *Providence Sunday Journal*, July 24, 1932.

that famous sentence, 'I fear the kindest act would be to let him rest forever in the obscurity to which unhappy circumstances have condemned him' — a sentence which sounds like the height of cruel indifference. But Miss Lowell did not need to see the all-important context to know that Fanny Brawne, in allowing Brown to publish their love-letters, had made her 'final sacrifice' for John Keats in this 'crowning act' of her love (II, 136); and it was in this letter that she agreed to make the sacrifice.

Such accuracy in conjecture lends force to Miss Lowell's astute guess when the two first met, and her proof that they became engaged on Christmas, 1818, just before the burst of inspiration in which he wrote the 'Eve of St. Agnes.' But if there remain any doubt on these heads, there can be none on the question of Keats's illness. Amy Lowell's assembling of all the symptoms, with the expert medical interpretation of them which she procured, is final.[1]

The biography as a whole showed remarkable insight into poetic psychology, such as was possible only for one poet writing on another. Amy Lowell traced the emergence and heading up of Keats's inspiration; quoted the best lines and told why they were good; and sprinkled through the book such a profusion of dicta and aphorisms (such as 'The mark of the minor poet is that he can never forget himself; the proof of greatness lies just in the fact that the artist transcends the man.') that one admirer has collected and arranged them into an *ars poetica*.[2]

As a work of scholarship, the book is such a contribution to knowledge that no one henceforth can write on Keats without taking Amy Lowell's book into account. The new material which she collected and expounded was enough to make it a source book; but she added discoveries

[1] See, for example, Dr. Robert L. Pitfield's 'John Keats,' *Annals of Medical History* (n.s. II, 530-46), 1930.

[2] George H. Sargent: *Amy Lowell, A Mosaic*, New York, 1926.

about the old material as well. She nailed down several dates and sources, any one of which was worthy a whole learned article in *PMLA*. For one example, she was able to identify the Box Hill lines in *Endymion*, written about the moon-rise on November 22, 1817, by proving an editorial miscount of lines throughout that poem.[1] She was also able to prove that Keats could have read, and probably used, Drayton's *Endimion and Phoebe*, when writing his own poem on that subject.

But though she kept the proper subordination of scholarship to criticism, and criticism to biography, the scholarship sometimes obtruded, chiefly because she enjoyed it so much. Full of the ardor of the chase after facts, she was sure that the excitement would be communicated; but the unscholarly reader, interested only in the results, was confused when she made up her mind in print.

If she fell short anywhere, it was in not solving the problem of the meaning of *Endymion*, which had also baffled all her predecessors. Keats himself began the trouble with his beginner's mistake of an apologetic preface; thenceforth his commentators looked for immaturity and confusion; and Amy Lowell decided that '*Endymion* is chaotic because Keats was chaotic at the time he wrote it' (I, 457).

Yet the more we examine her analysis, the more we feel that she evaded stating the meaning because the poem was so close to her. It had particularly affected her at the age of fifteen; the moon-symbolism runs through all her own poems; and her 'To a Certain Critic' described the poetic act in terms of Keats writing lines 498–504 of Book IV. The author of the preface of *Legends* might have gone into the significance of *Endymion* more deeply; but she was content to keep her intellectual finger on Keats's poetic pulse, charting his creative rhythms: showing how at times

[1] She never was able, however, to discover the provenance of the early 'Alexander fragment,' and therefore omitted it entirely. It is to be found in Walter Cooper Dendy's *Philosophy of Mystery*.

his inspiration ran strongly and how at other times he struggled desperately to keep it running at all. Beyond that, the poem seemed too much a part of her to allow any revelation beyond '*Endymion* is the spirit of youth rampant. Its adolescence is irresistible; to read it is to touch the dayspring of life' (I, 455–56).

She was more specific about the central idea of *Hyperion*, though it remained only a fragment. Keats, she conjectured (II, 345–46), was questioning where the poet stood in the great scheme of things.

> Of what value are he and his work? It is really much the same idea which he had speculated on to Bailey in his letter from Burford Bridge the Autumn before, and again, under a somewhat changed aspect, to Taylor from Shanklin. The poet can attain to the possibility of great poetry only by scaling the height of the ideal, the far-rising shrine of his personal, dedicated life. He must lose much to gain more, parts of his ego must perish that sublimer parts may rule. This last idea is given in the form of a symbolical dream, in which the older gods are dethroned and overcome by their more human and beautiful counterparts, the hierarchy of Grecian mythology. All this comes precious near to being allegory, but luckily never quite gets there. It does not get there because Keats was working with two entirely separate themes: one, the question of the poet's value to humanity; the other, a mythological narrative, full of grandeur certainly, but vague in outline, and although capable of many implications, explicit in none.[1]

Here she definitely discovered the meaning of the poem, but shied away from the thought that the idea was implicit in the narrative.

Such was the book on which she spent the last four years of her life: a great biography of a poet, a profound book about poetry, and a remarkable feat of scholarship. It was dedicated 'To A. D. R. This, and all my books. A. L.'

[1] *John Keats*, II, 345–46.

CHAPTER XXV
FAREWELL DINNER

'...to be a storm-centre seems undesirable now...'

John Keats went into its fourth edition on February 15, 1925 — five days after publication. In other words, it was entirely out of print: the second edition, which had been bought out before the book appeared, was being hastily bound, the third edition was being hastily printed, while the fourth was ordered. The reviews were heartily enthusiastic; every mail brought envelopes fat with long clippings. The first that read at all dubiously was that of Katharine Lee Bates, in the New York *Sun*. Miss Bates, herself a poet and scholar, had labored hard over a review that should be both enthusiastic and critical; but her manuscript had suffered after it left her hands, as she wrote to Miss Lowell.

> 70 Curve Street
> Wellesley
> Massachusetts
> February 19, 1925

DEAR MISS LOWELL

Your magnanimous letter makes me even more unhappy about that review than I was before. At the outset I told Mr. Nevins, over the telephone, that I was not the one to review your Keats, and I urged Miss Shackford or Miss Sherwood or Miss Scudder, all nineteenth century specialists — whereas my field is the sixteenth — instead; but when he insisted that it was your own desire, I assented. He asked for 2500 words, but just as I was closing the review, less than a week before his date, he wrote that his columns had become over-crowded and he hoped that I would make it 1500. My next few days were full and so I had to send it as it was, only condensing at the end. And even so he has spoiled whatever literary quality it might have had by cutting it down himself by the process of slicing off modifying clauses all through. For instance, half protesting against too intensive source research — you see I have had forty years of the classroom — I added that you and Mr. Lowes were nevertheless 'redoubtable thieves and as virtuous, from the academic point of view, as Robin Hood,' all of which he renders in the two monosyllables 'bold thieves.' I had, of course, asked for a proof, but didn't get one. In fact, I didn't succeed in getting a copy of the paper till Tuesday night.

That condensation at the end accounts for my inaccurate use of Imagist. I didn't want to say Materialist, and I couldn't, in face of the editorial request for brevity, develop what is my fundamental difficulty with your treatment of Keats as well as with some of your own poetry — the sense that it is confined to 'pictures of the floating world.' You may remember how I rejoiced in your closing Duse sonnets where you were using nature as language rather than ultimate, with no less beauty in image but with a new significance and inflooding of spirit.

Please believe that I am sincerely grieved to have added even a passing annoyance to these sorrowful days and that my intentions, at least, were not unfriendly.

Hoping that the English trip will bring refreshment and honor and inspiration

Faithfully yours

KATHARINE LEE BATES

Her mail was enormous, but she was too tired to keep up with it. She wrote letters of thanks to Joseph Auslander, John Farrar, Sara Teasdale, and Robert Morss Lovett for their reviews.

On the 23d, she read her poems at Amherst; on the 27th she read at the Phillips Club, Andover, Massachusetts.

Throughout March the enormous mail continued: letters praising the Keats biography, notes pointing out misprints in it, poems inspired by it; requests for autographs, for photographs, for interviews, for advice on careers, for criticisms of writings, for lecture dates, for permissions to call, to use poems in anthologies, to set poems to music. She was supposed to be resting, building up strength for the trip to England; there was no coping with her mail as a whole. But she wrote tributes to celebrate the fiftieth birthdays of Robert Frost and Percy MacKaye, and got off her contributions to the third *American Miscellany*. Her own fiftieth birthday had passed without a public dinner, as she requested; but now the time had come; and arrangements were being made to give her the dinner on April 4, shortly before she sailed. Inevitably there were some invitations and other arrangements which only she could make. Then she was collecting and correcting misprints in the Keats book, which various readers delighted to catch and send her. A grandson of Fanny Brawne's wrote to thank her for not repeating the conventional charge that Fanny Brawne was heartless and trivial; he said that really she cared more for Keats than Keats did for her, that at his death she cut off her hair and sent it to be buried with him, and that she wore a locket of his hair all through her married life and died wearing it. A great-grandson of the Dr. Lambe who sent Keats to Italy wrote that it was left to her enthusiastic researches to identify him properly. Archibald MacLeish had written an article about her for the *North American Review*; she thanked him in a letter of March 14:

> I have been unable to discover what part I am going to violently disagree with, as you suggested I should. I agree with all you say in the main, with the exception of your suggestion that the coming generation is made up of Eliot and Cummings and their followers. There I cannot see with you. I think they are a passing phase. There is no hope for Cummings unless he stops revolting against Cambridge and his Unitarian minister father and tries to do something, and stops trying not to do anything; and I have no hope at all for Eliot unless he can overcome his mental anaemia, but as it seems to be a real disease with him, I do

not think there is much likelihood of its cure. Louis Unter-meyer, who has been seeing Eliot abroad, tells me that he now repudiates 'The Waste Land' and is writing poetry of an entirely different kind, but Louis did not give me a very clear impression of the kind, so I have nothing to go upon.

As to what you say about me, I am delighted with it. My generation is not that of these very much younger men, of course, but, to tell you the truth, I do not know that I am quite so averse to the comfortable garments of fame as you seem to think. Supposing that this apparel should ever come my way, I feel I could bear it with equanimity. There are always the few in every generation who will dig one out and make one a living poet again, if one be worth it, and the battle ground no longer appeals very much to me. To cre-ate appeals to me immensely, but to be a storm centre seems undesirable now. I never did like it really; I was forced into it because of the inability of my fellow-sufferers to fight their own battles.

I am glad you like 'Legends' so much. I am not sure that it is a better book than 'Can Grande,' but certainly those two rank higher than the others I have written, on the whole. With your contention that my work stands for art and that art is the principal reason for poetry, that it should be regarded as an art and not as a splashing round of emotion, I entirely agree, and I am thankful that you took the attitude you did and left out all the stuff and non-sense about *vers libre* or anything else in the line of form, which is, of course, not the point. And I bless you for not referring to the leadership side, or anything of that sort...

The itinerary of her English trip was filling up rapidly. It was now arranged that she would arrive at Southamp-ton on the *Berengaria* on April 21 and proceed to the Berkeley Hotel, London. Then, according to an incom-plete list, she was to lecture or read as follows:

April 24, English Association, London
April 29, Oxford
May   1,   "
May   5, Birmingham University

May   8, Bedford College
May 12, Forum Club, London
May 14, Keats House, Hampstead
May 16, Cambridge
May 18,   "
May 20, Lyceum Club, London
May 23, English Association, Edinburgh University
May 26, Bournemouth Literature and Arts Society
May 28, Kensington Poetry Society
May 29, Eton
June   4, Poetry Book Shop, London
June   8, Sussex Poetry Society, Brighton.

There were other dates, still tentative. The rest of June and the first part of July were to be kept fairly clear, so that she might assemble her old friends, see her relatives, and make certain calls, especially to the Hardys. Then on July 18, she was to sail home from Liverpool on the *Samaria*.

By March the first English reviews were coming in; their tone was not American, and indeed was such that Miss Lowell wrote to R. N. Linscott, of Houghton Mifflin Company, on March 9:

> ... I am losing my erstwhile admiration for English criticism, or rather, I should say that it seems to me that all the critics are dead, and that the newer men who are taking their places are quite unscholarly and unsympathetic. At best what they do is to write a nice *creative* article and call it criticism.

The traditions of book-reviewing were very different in England and America. American journalists tended to praise, the English to dispraise. What an Englishman considered a favorable review often seemed to the American a series of fault-findings and quibbles over trivialities; whereas the American review seemed to the Englishman an obvious bit of log-rolling and indiscriminate, meaningless enthusiasm. Furthermore, however, it was notorious that serious books by Americans were never reviewed favorably in England, unless they dealt with life among the lower classes. Miss Lowell herself, not long before, had warned a young scholar not to expect any pleasant reviews from England; and though his book was successful there, her warning was thoroughly justified.

But to explain the extraordinary ferocity that vented itself upon the biography of Keats, one must remember that it was published in the great anti-American reaction which followed the end of the World War. It almost appeared as though the English were as incapable of forgiving the American Revolution as Rome of forgiving the Reformation. They seemingly had determined that America must be a cultureless desert (and indeed, for more than a century their travellers had brought back this popular news); and what else could it be, when culture necessarily flowed from England to America, and suffered such a sad sea-change crossing the Atlantic? Throughout all English literature, except for Thackeray's *Virginians*, one may search in vain for a hint of the American gentleman; and when Americans satirized themselves (as in *Babbitt*), their works were hailed as masterpieces of realism. Apparently no English university paid attention to the arts in America; all American paintings in the National Gallery were labelled 'British'; skyscrapers were tacitly discounted as American boasting; and as for the American popular arts, such as jazz and movies, they were synonymous with vulgar immorality. American books were difficult to get in England, largely because the booksellers would not handle books in American spelling; a collection like Palgrave's *Golden Treasury* could claim on the titlepage to be a selection of 'the best songs and lyrical poems in the English language,' and then silently exclude all Americans; but if American authors persisted even after death, then the English claimed to have discovered them first. It was this comfortable superiority myth that Amy Lowell's book threatened.

Add to this the fact that Sir Sidney Colvin's biography, which he had been re-editing these thirty years, had overlooked the rich American material, and that consequently his authority was threatened with an overseas rival; add again an obscure sense of the fact that Keats had been recognized in America long before he was recognized in England,[1] and the causes are clear why several of the more reputable critics cast aside the 'certain condescension,' reentered the Lockhart-Croker tradition, and set upon the book like wasps upon an intruder. It is unfortunate that the shrill scolding of Sir Sidney's partisans (whom Shorter nominated 'the Keats clique') should have drowned out the praise which was liberally given in calmer quarters.

The very first two reviews indicated this opposition of attitudes: Hugh I'Anson Fausset's 'The Definitive Life of Keats' (*Yorkshire Post*, February 19) and Horace Thorogood's, subtitled 'Biography As It Should Not Be Written' (London *Star*, February 19). The reviews that followed seemed to be dominated by the doctrine that Colvin's biography was standard: what need of another? That Amy Lowell's conception of biography was fundamentally different — that she had tried to reconstruct and interpret Keats's life, not merely to arrange and record all known facts — was entirely overlooked. As though England had never known a two-volume biography before, its reviewers complained of its size, even its completeness, and declared that her new facts could have been compressed into a mere pamphlet. They objected to its vivacity on the score of loquacity.

Such was generally the tone of Robert Lynd (*Daily*

---

[1] Two American editions of his collected works (Philadelphia, Grigg, 1831, and Philadelphia, De Silva Thomas & Co., 1836) appeared before the first English edition (London, William Smith, 1841); and two more (New York, Wylie and Putnam, 1846, and the *Poetical Works of Howitt, Milman, and Keats*, Philadelphia, 1846) before the Monckton Milnes edition (London, 1848). Sir Sidney Colvin (page 528) also mentions an edition published at Buffalo in 1834; but the existence of this is dubious.

News, February 20), J. C. Squire (*Observer*, February 22), Edward Shanks (*Evening Standard*, February 24), Leonard Woolfe (*Nation and Athenaeum*, February 28), R. Ellis Roberts (*Guardian*, March 6), and Thomas Moult (*Time and Tide*, March 9). Thomas Hardy saw too well how the wind was blowing; he wrote, affectionately warning her not to take notice.

Max Gate, Dorchester
6 March 1925

MY DEAR COUSIN AMY:

It has been a great pleasure to me to receive this valuable book, your life of John Keats, & I don't know how to thank you enough for it. I have not been reading it straight on — I should say we, for my wife has read it aloud on account of the weakness of my eyes. I am quite amazed at the skill & industry you have shown & to me at any rate, every page is interesting.

Not Shakespeare himself, I should think, has been so meticulously (is that the right use of the word? I never know) examined as it has fallen at last to poor neglected Keats's lot to be. If he could only have known! How you have sifted out the legends for & against him. It was in one respect fortunate for him that his brother went to America, as it rendered accessible to you many papers, &c., that would otherwise have been buried here in England or lost.

By the way, did it never occur to you that the words 'Pure serene' in the Chapman's Homer sonnet may have been an unconscious memory of the line in Gray's Elegy ending 'purest ray serene'? This seems to me more probable than Paget Toynbee's suggestion of it having come from Cary's Dante.

My wife's mother, who grew up at Enfield, Middlesex, knew the Clarke school building of which you give an illustration. Her maiden name was Taylor, & there is every reason to believe that she & the publisher Taylor were of the same family.

Another thing: I may be wrong, but for many years I have fancied that the Grecian urn which inspired the poem

is actually one in the British Museum: at any rate I remember standing before one & concluding that it must have
been the same one Keats looked at. But you have probably
thought all that out.

I am sorry to say I cannot write all I would write about
the book. You must not take any notice of what our funny
men of the newspaper press say about the size of it, &c.
That's how they are; & it never makes any difference.

My wife sends her love, & believe me

Affectionately yours

Thomas Hardy

Not content with this letter to Miss Lowell, he sent a
message to a friend, a well-known critic, telling him it was
a fine book and worthy of a good and careful review.[1]

At this moment there were signs of a reaction against
the monotonous and overdone hostility. George Russell
('Æ.,' in the *Irish Statesman*, March 14) and A. E. Coppard
(*Saturday Review*, March 14) published favorable reviews.
But their tendency was more than offset by Sir Edmund
Gosse (*Sunday Times*, March 15). Hitherto, many of the
hostile reviewers had endorsed Amy Lowell's rehabilitation of Fanny Brawne, and all had admitted at least the
existence of the new material. But Sir Edmund grandly
rejected the new material, especially that on which Fanny
Brawne's rehabilitation was based, by suggesting that
'our ingenuous transatlantic friends are being more and
more generally swindled.'

These letters (now at Hampstead[2]) were owned by Fred
Holland Day. On July 16, 1894, Mr. Day, as representa-
tive of the American literati, had presented to Edmund
Gosse, representing the English literati, a bust of John
Keats, by Anne Whitney of Boston, at the Hampstead

---

[1] Letter from Mrs. Thomas Hardy to Mrs. Harold Russell, June 24, 1925.

[2] The originals of these letters from Fanny Brawne to Fanny Keats have
been deposited in the Keats Museum at Hampstead; the unique printed copy
is similarly deposited at Harvard. They are not to be used for publication
till 1961.

church. It was the first memorial to Keats on English soil. Immediately afterwards, Mr. Day departed for Madrid to acquire these letters. As this event had taken place over thirty years before, and as Miss Lowell was not allowed to name the owner, Sir Edmund's doubts about these particular letters were of course a coincidence. Although Clement K. Shorter (*Sphere*, March 28) bluntly attacked him for these unfounded doubts, his charge was to be reiterated by H. W. Garrod, the Oxford professor of poetry.

Consequently, by April the tone of the English reviews had roused a widespread indignation and contempt in the American press.

Such were the cheerful clippings that reached Miss Lowell daily, as she was wearily closing her house and getting packed for Europe. On April 1, she wrote to Miss Cutting about the farewell dinner: 'I have been completely collapsed lately, but hope to perk up by Saturday. I wish I were — not safely on the steamer — but safely on the other side. I dread that voyage; I hate a ship like poison.'

On April 4, the 'Complimentary Dinner in Honour of Miss Amy Lowell' was held in the ballroom of the Hotel Somerset. The sponsors of the dinner included John Singer Sargent, Professor John Livingston Lowes, Charles Martin Loeffler, Ellery Sedgwick, William James, Mark A. DeWolfe Howe, Mrs. Charles Greeley Loring, Mrs. Edward Burlingame Hill, Mrs. J. Montgomery Sears, Mrs. Bayard Thayer, Mrs. Lorin F. Deland, Mrs. Frederick G. Hall, Mrs. John Gorham Palfrey, and Miss Ada Comstock. The decorations were in charge of Mrs. Bayard Thayer and Mrs. Montgomery Sears; they had the ballroom banked with all sorts of spring flowers culled from their own greenhouses; and Albert C. Burrage furnished particularly marvelous orchids for the speakers' table.

There was a delay of nearly an hour before Miss Lowell arrived.

After the dinner, when the coffee was served, it became obvious that a single question was in many a mind: would she — would she — smoke a cigar? In a dead silence, while every face on the floor, absolutely blank of all expression, was fixed upon her, she opened her cigar-case, drew forth a cigar, and lighted it. At once everybody relaxed, and began talking of other things, until the gavel of the toastmistress, Elizabeth Cutting, Managing Editor of the *North American Review*, called their attention to the speakers.

John Livingston Lowes, Dean of the Graduate School of Arts and Sciences, and Chairman of the English Department, Harvard University, began the speeches with a handsome tribute to the woman, the scholar, and the poet. Then Edward Burlingame Hill, Professor of Music at Harvard, spoke of the unusual variety of rhythms in her poetry. Henry Seidel Canby, Professor of English at Yale and Editor of the *Saturday Review*, stressed the combination of scholarship with literature. Elinor Wylie, author of *Black Armor* and other books, told what Miss Lowell's work had meant to her when she tapped her own poetic vein; and to illustrate her point, lifted up a silver bowl filled with especially fine white orchids; she did not know that later the bowl was to be presented to Miss Lowell. Grace Hazard Conkling, Professor of English at Smith College, and author of *Ship's Log* and other books, made perhaps the best speech of the evening: it was a surprisingly complete appreciation of the poetry, ending gracefully with gratitude for what Miss Lowell had done for her and Hilda. At this point, Glenn Frank, Editor of the *Century Magazine*, asked to speak next, as he had to catch a train; he explained that he could not give a literary estimate of her work, but analyzing the qualities she showed, he believed they were sorely needed in our politics, and thereupon nominated her for President. S. Foster Damon, author of *William Blake: His Philosophy and Symbols,* spoke briefly; after him Hervey Allen, author of *The Blindman and Other Poems,* read a paper on Miss Lowell's significance to the younger generation; and John Farrar, Editor of the *Bookman,* remarked that her life of Keats was so universal that it covered the lives of all poets. Irita Van Doren, Managing Editor of *Books,* was unable to appear. Abbie Farwell Brown, author of *Heart of New England* and other books, spoke of Miss Lowell as a neighbor to be fond of. A. Edward Newton, author of *The Amenities of Book Collecting,* praised her as the greatest book-collector in America. And finally Roger Scaife, of Houghton Mifflin, ended on a note of affectionate humor, in telling of her critical acumen which was always tempered with kindness.

Amy Lowell now rose, remarking whimsically that in all these speeches she hardly recognized herself, but when she got home, her cat Winky would know her. After a few more words, she read 'Lilacs' splendidly, and finally, as thanks for the flowers Mrs. Thayer had procured, 'A Tulip Garden.' Mrs. Edward Burlingame Hill then presented her with the silver bowl, after which everybody flocked round and congratulated her.

The dinner was a huge success; it was one of those affairs well planned and well performed, that swept along to the end. But Miss Lowell went home very tired. The newspaper heading the next morning read 'Many Friends Bid Amy Lowell Adieu.'

In the still enormous mail came a lonely letter from D. H. Lawrence, wondering what she was doing, and hoping to hear from her.

> Del Monte Ranch.
> *Questa*
> New Mexico
> 6 April 1925

DEAR AMY

I have so often wondered if you are sitting in London, in the Berkeley, maybe: & see where we are. I got malaria in

Oaxuca: then grippe: then a typhoid inside: was so sick, I wearied of the day. Struggled to Mexico City, was put to bed again for three weeks — then packed off up here. We had booked our passages to England, but the doctor said I *must* stay in the sun, he wouldn't be answerable for me if I went on the sea, & to England. So we came here. The Emigration Authorities at El Paso treated us as Emigrants, & nearly killed me a second time: this after the consul & the Embassy people in Mexico — the Americans — had been most kind, doing things to make it easier for us. They only made it harder. The Emigration Dept is Dept of Labour, & you taste the Bolshevist method at its crudest.

However — after two days fight we got through — & yesterday got to our little ranch. There is snow behind the house, & sky threatening snow. But usually it's brilliantly sunny. And the log fire is warm. And the Indian Trinidad is chopping wood under the pine tree, & his wife Lufina, in her wide white boots, is shuffling carrying water. I begin to feel better: though still feel I don't care whether it's day or night.

I saw notices of your Keats book. Pity after all I didn't ask you to send the promised copy here: I could have wandered in it now. But I'll write to Curtis Brown. And I'll send you a copy of my little novel *St. Maur.*

I managed to finish my Mexican novel *Quetzalcoatl* in Mexico: the very day I went down, as if shot in the intestines. But I daren't even look at the outside of the MS. It cost me so much: & I wish I could eat all the lotus that ever budded, & drink up Lethe to the source. Talk about dull opiates — one wants something that'll go into the very soul.

Send a line to say where you are and how you are liking it. If you come west, come and see us. I hope to get to Europe in the autumn. Frieda is happy arranging her house. Souvenirs!

D. H. Lawrence

They were leaving for New York on April 11, to lecture there the 13th, then sail on the 15th. On the 9th, Miss

Lowell took up her correspondence again by sending a handful of cables and telegrams thanking various donors of the silver bowl. On Good Friday, the 10th, she dictated a letter to John Drinkwater.

DEAR JOHN:

Your letter of March ninth gave me great pleasure. I should certainly have looked you up when I got to England in any case, but it is particularly nice to have you look me up, as it were, beforehand. It seemed a little awkward writing in the beginning as you had not written to me, and after that I feared it looked like a bid to have you write something about the Keats, so I was waiting to see you when I arrived.

I am delighted to know that you are to review the book for the 'Yale Review.' It has been splendidly treated here, and in your part of the world 'A.E.' (George Russell) in the 'Irish Statesman' and A. E. Coppard in the 'Saturday Review' and Clement Shorter in the 'Sphere' have treated me very kindly. But, oh dear me, the rest of the reviewers! I remember your article on the insincerity and general hostility of English critics to Americans. I think it has never been better illustrated than in their endeavours to down my Keats. No one seems to have realized that the book was not written to delight an audience which greeted Maurois' 'Shelley' so enthusiastically; it was written to put on record many things which I thought should be recorded, but it was written mainly to please myself. I am happy to say it pleased Professor Lowes, whose opinion I value more than that of any one else in a case of this sort.

I shall be at the Berkeley Hotel, and I expect to arrive there on April twenty-first. I shall be very glad indeed to make Mrs. Drinkwater's acquaintance, and it will be a pleasure to see you again.

Very sincerely yours,

This letter was apparently signed and sent; then she dictated a letter to Clement Shorter, thanking him for his review; and another to Albert C. Burrage, thanking him for the orchids at her dinner. These letters eventually were sent unsigned.

A terrible pain struck through her: it was her hernia breaking out again, but she had never had such an attack before. The physicians, summoned at once, watched for two hours, preparing to operate if necessary; then the need for such an emergency measure subsided. Absolute quiet was prescribed, to avoid strangulation; it was even hoped that if she kept quiet long enough, they might avoid the operation. At all events, she was too run down and weak, and had lost too much weight, to risk an operation now. The English trip was absolutely forbidden; a slight attack of seasickness might cause her death.

The next day — the day on which they had planned to leave Sevenels — cables, telegrams, and letters were sent out, cancelling all engagements. The newspapers published the fact of a serious illness, and her mail was swelled still more with letters of condolence from friends and strangers in England and America. The secretary was set to answering the accumulating correspondence, one note after another, thanking people for poems (Miss Lowell had received five addressed to her this month), thanking them for appreciations of the Keats biography, explaining that Miss Lowell was unable to write now but would later, extending the hope that next year perhaps she would be able to lecture again, regretting that she could not disturb Miss Lowell to get the information about the book in her library, apologizing for the fact that during the last months of finishing the Keats book her mail had gone unanswered, reiterating that Miss Lowell had made a strict rule never to accede to requests for autographs or criticisms of poems, and so on, day after day.

Meanwhile the doctors watched, hoping that she would build up some strength and regain some of her lost weight, so that they might operate. But a constant nausea prevented her from doing so; sometimes during a whole day she could retain only a few grains of rice or a few fibers of meat; and the slow agony of starvation reduced her steadily. Nevertheless she insisted on getting up and going down stairs every day, enforcing her routine as though it were proof of life.

On April 23 she wrote to Edgar H. Wells, the New York bookseller, to buy some books which had belonged to her cousin and which were being sold by error; this was the only letter she signed during this month after her seizure. On May 2, she wrote once again, to Ferris Greenslet about typographical errors in the Keats biography.

2 May, 1925

DEAR FERRIS:

I have received your list of corrections. You notice that I did not quote 'love is the principal of all things,' and I meant 'principal' in the sense of the principal of a school, at least I think I did. Some of these, of course, should be changed, perhaps all, but I do not wish anybody to make any changes of any kind except myself. If Mr. Bianchi will send me a set of sheets as he did for the last corrections, I will make my corrections on them. I am surprised that there are so few errors; I had supposed there would be a great many more, but, as I say, no one is to touch a hand to the plates to make any corrections whatever except myself, and if you will just order Mr. Bianchi to send me the sheets I will disobey the doctor and make these corrections on them at once.

I am sorry to say I do not get any better. I have two nurses now and I am no good at all for anything. The nausea persists and I feel as sick as a dog. Whether I am going to escape an operation or not, I do not know.

If Basil Blackwell comes to these parts, please let me know and I will see him if it is possible to do so. I do not want to fly from the poor man as though I were on shipboard every minute or two, and when I know when he is coming, I shall know whether it will be safe for me to see him for a few minutes' talk or not.

The sooner we get through these corrections the better, I

think, so please tell Mr. Bianchi to hurry right along with these sheets. He may send me the particular pages and not the whole set of sheets if you prefer.

Very sincerely yours,

On the 10th, she spoke to Mrs. Edward Hill over the telephone; in a voice that was hardly more than a whisper she said, 'Alison, I feel like hell.' An operation was decided on for the 13th; privately the doctors were very much afraid that she would not pull through; but it was a necessary risk, for she now weighed only 159 pounds, a weight abnormally low for her.

When she woke on the morning of May 12, she expressed complete despair to Mrs. Russell. 'Peter,' she said, using a pet name, 'I'm done. Why can't they let me alone! The operations never have been any good.' After turning over her mail for a long while, she decided to be dressed.

She sat before her mirror, while her maid and the nurse wound the elaborate bandages around her, straightening them at the back. When Miss Lowell reached to pin the bandage herself on the left side, she stopped, puzzled, saying that her hand hurt. Mrs. Russell, who was standing behind, laughed, saying that hers often did. 'It's numb,' Miss Lowell replied. 'I can't use it.'

Then suddenly, as she was gazing at herself in the mirror, she saw the right side of her face drop. She recognized her death.

'Pete,' she said in a low voice, 'a stroke.'

As she sank, the nurse and the maid moved her chair to a sofa, on which they got her, while Mrs. Russell hurried instantly to telephone the doctor. When she came back, she bent over her friend. 'Get Eastman,' Miss Lowell murmured, to the last directing what should be done. 'I have,' Mrs. Russell answered.

Amy Lowell became unconscious immediately, and died an hour and a half later, at 5:30 P.M.

CHAPTER XXVI

WHAT'S O'CLOCK; EAST WIND; BALLADS FOR SALE...

I know the moon.'

THE death of Amy Lowell was an unanticipated shock to the continent. When she had countermanded the English tour, the news of her illness had swelled her huge mail with numberless letters of sympathy; the reporters had been told her condition was 'not dangerous'; after which, for a month, no bulletins were sent out. She was supposed to be improving. Then, without warning of any sort, came the headlines of her death. It was all but incredible that a person of her vitality was gone. The lovers of poetry still remember where they were when they saw the headlines; and in that moment, at least some of her literary enemies felt as though they had lost a valued friend.

Blooms of the lilac, then in full flower, were gathered and laid about her.

On Friday morning, May 15, she was cremated and buried in the family lot at Mount Auburn. As she had wished, there were no religious services. Only the family, Mrs. Russell, Mrs. Belmont, and Elizabeth Henry (Miss Lowell's personal maid) were present.

On the same day, her will was filed. The great collection of books and manuscripts was left to Harvard, with whatever of the furnishings of her famous library seemed desirable — chandeliers, hangings, carvings, pictures, even the ceiling — to fit up a poetry room in which the collection was to be kept. If Harvard did not accept the gift, it was to be offered to the Boston Public Library.

Remembering the poetic stimulus she had once found in London, she also gave Harvard a travelling scholarship for a poet of American birth, the sole conditions being that he live abroad and produce at least three poems.

To Mrs. Russell she left the use of Sevenels and the income from a trust-fund. Some years before, in her 'Penumbra,' she had expressed the hope that Mrs. Russell might go on living there; and she stipulated now that the books were not to be removed until Mrs. Russell saw fit; and the scholarship was not to be offered until after her death.

And now from England came the surprising news that Amy Lowell had been killed by the brutality of the British reviews of her *John Keats*. It had sprung from a couple of sentences in a letter which Miss Lowell had dictated to Clement Shorter on April 10, to thank him for his review and to express the expectation of seeing him soon in England. The two sentences were: 'But, dear me, what a lovely time most of the London reviewers have had! Their feeling for America is anything but pleasant to an American.' She had been taken ill almost immediately after that; the letter was mailed unsigned on the 15th, with an explanatory note from the secretary. Mr. Shorter had replied on the 28th that any bad reviews in England were due to the natural jealousy of the 'Keats clique' (as he called 'Gosse, Colvin, Squire and Co.'); it would have happened just the same if they had been living in America. Then came the news of her death; and in his *Sphere* obituary (May 30) he ventured the statement: 'It is generally believed among her friends that she was killed by the English reviews of that book.'

The parallel — Keats and Amy Lowell, two bards killed by reviewers — was sentimentally seductive to those unaware of the nature of her illness, not to mention the character of the woman. But before the tale had spread too widely, it was scotched by her friends. John Farrar, who was shown the carbon of the letter to Shorter, ridiculed the theory in the August *Bookman*; another vigorous defence was 'On a Certain Condescension' by Merrit Y. Hughes and Hazelton Spencer, in the *New Re-*

public for August 12, which began: 'Not from Brookline but from London comes the incredible story that the stout heart of Amy Lowell was broken by the strictures of the British reviewers on her great life of Keats.'

On August 25, 1925, *What's O'Clock*, her first posthumous volume, was published. She had prepared the manuscript herself, also that of *East Wind*; but as her last book of poetry, *Legends*, had consisted of long poems, the publishers had thought it wiser to publish a book of lyrics next, and therefore chose *What's O'Clock*. Mrs. Russell selected the binding for this and indeed for all the posthumous volumes. The title, taken from *King Richard III*, indicated Amy Lowell's realization that her hour was about to strike. The opening poem, 'East, West, North, and South of a Man' is really a portrait of herself, as knight-errant, story-teller in love with magnificence, pedlar, and book-worm.

There are no poems about war or Yankee-land in this book, and no elaborate historical reconstructions; but all her other types of poetry are handsomely represented. 'Evelyn Ray,' the second poem, was the most popular of her later dramatic narratives. All of this kind read very effectively — 'Orientation,' 'Pantomime in One Act,' the delicious 'In a Powder Closet,' and 'Attitude Under an Elm Tree.' There are two symbolic narratives: 'Which, Being Interpreted, Is as May Be, or Otherwise' and 'The Green Parrakeet.' The first of these was based on a story told by George Barnard at Dublin; he had seen the original statues; in Amy Lowell's brain it became a tale of a man who lived high above the world, despising it, and who was destroyed by the beauty he discovered. The original version of the poem was lost. It probably fell from her writing table to the floor, and was gathered up and burned the next morning. After the whole house had been searched thoroughly, Miss Lowell telephoned to Mrs. Russell, who was on her way to Salt Lake City; she caught her at

Chicago, but in vain. So Miss Lowell had to write the poem a second time; and she always felt that the way the first version opened was much better than her second attempt.

There are also shorter symbolic pieces: 'The Swans,' suggested by a tavern sign in England, 'Once Jericho,' and others, including the impish epigram 'The Sand Altar.' Some deal with the literary world: 'Footing Up a Total' (her honest envy of an imaginary rival poet), 'The Watershed' (addressed to insincere admirers), and 'La Ronde du Diable' (the unseemly struggle amongst poets for reputation). The greatest of these is unquestionably 'Fool o' the Moon,' which represents the psychology of the genius — one might call it the triumph of Endymion. She had been reading this poem with such effect that in March, 1923, the *North American Review* had asked for it; but when that magazine became a quarterly, and thus could not publish it before *What's O'Clock*, Miss Lowell got the manuscript back and offered it to the *Atlantic Monthly*. '"Fool o' the Moon,"' she informed Mr. Sedgwick, in a letter which virtually dared him to print it, 'has been one of my most successful poems in my readings; in fact, I think it has been more successful than almost anything I have written, except "Lilacs," "Patterns," and the "Sonnets to Duse."' Mr. Sedgwick recognized its beauty, but feared its effect upon the schools throughout the country which used his magazine in their discussion of current events; so he accepted the poem, delaying publication until July, when the schools would be closed for the summer vacation. The story goes that a school in the Philippines, which was still running, promptly cancelled all its subscriptions; certain it is, however, that readers of the *Atlantic* were pretty generally shocked by the frankness of the ending: 'I have lain with Mistress Moon.'

Other literary poems are not symbolic. 'The Sisters' is her well-known discussion of the personalities of Sappho,

Elizabeth Barrett Browning, and Emily Dickinson. 'View of Teignmouth' describes a morning in Keats's life, which she expanded from a sentence in one of his letters; and 'On Reading a Line Underscored by Keats' sprang from a still slighter source.

The famous 'Lilacs' and its autumn companion-piece, 'Purple Grackles,' led the group of poems about land-scapes and seasons; they were followed by 'Meeting House Hill' (Dorchester), 'Texas,' those of the Charleston poems that had found favor, and 'The Congressional Library.' 'Lilacs' caused two or three persons to write her that the song of the oriole was not 'little weak soft'; but as she had got her adjectives from listening to orioles busy nesting at Sevenels, she kept them. She described the inspiration of 'Texas' to Professor A. J. Armstrong of Baylor (April 11, 1924):

> I wrote it in the train on leaving Waco. Its genesis was a motor drive which one of the very kind ladies of Waco took us on. When we got far out on the prairie, in the direction of what I believe is your Country Club, I looked back. Waco had disappeared from view and its one skyscraper was hull down on the horizon with all its windows gleaming and twinkling gold in the sunset light. It was a day or so after Mr. Lomax had been reading us his cowboy songs, and you will recognize the cowboy refrain.

'The Congressional Library' she explained to Professor Paul Kaufman (March 29, 1923):

> I am very much amused at this meticulous and unpoetical architectural student of yours who cannot conceive that an elaborate renaissance order can possibly be taken as a sym-bol of America. I was not observing the library from an architectural standpoint, nor was it the reading room that I referred to. It was the main hall with its tiers of balconies and its bright coloured marbles. The confusion and bril-liance of the whole, from floor to roof, is, I think, very typi-cal of America.

I did not intend 'wine-blues' to carry any emotional meaning; I was referring to colour. Have you forgotten the 'wine-dark ocean' of Homer?

With these poems we should include 'Wind and Silver' and 'Night Clouds' — two nocturnes made like Chinese pottery, and 'If I Were Francesco Guardi' — two love-songs made like Guardi's eighteenth-century paintings.

Her more personal poems deal with frustration, love, and Duse. 'The Red Knight' is by all odds the best of the first group. The love-poems open with 'Twenty-Four Hokku on a Modern Theme' and 'The Anniversary,' both in Japanese syllabics. 'White Currants' puzzled one reader, to whom Miss Lowell explained it:

> 'White Currants' is really very simple... Here is what I should call an analysis of the poem. For some reason or other, in this case it was a letter of Keats, the idea of white currants comes into the poet's mind. He realizes what a beautiful thing they are, these little translucent globes, opal-tinted, strangely reticent and clear, with their embedded seeds just faintly discernible underneath the white skin. He thinks of them as separate entities, hardly as currants; being akin to jewels in shape and colour, he imagines them as something valuable, as though they might be a worthy gift to the person he loves. He has no currants; he is, as he says, empty-handed, and, it all being in the realm of the imagination, he might as well have imagined Indian gems and offered them to his beloved, but for some reason inexplicable to himself he finds currants more desirable at the moment, and he thinks to himself that one reason they are more desirable is because it actually happens to be mid-winter, and currants mean not only their own beautiful selves, but the warmth and brightness of midsummer. In offering them, however, he realizes that they may be considered bizarre and inconsiderable. He therefore suggests to the lady that she consider them as a symbol. She may take them either as fruit or as beauty; it makes no difference how she regards them, provided she

takes them as a love gift, the acceptance of which will mean her attitude toward him.[1]

The six sonnets to Duse close the book. When she first sent them to the *New Republic* (March 8, 1924), she wrote: 'The first sonnet refers to those persons who did not see her years ago and could not see her charm and great art in her present visit. The rest of the sonnets speak for themselves and refer only to Madame Duse and a little to me who have been so much affected by her all these years.'

What's O'Clock was one of her best books. It had already outsold all the others when on May 3, 1926, it was awarded the $1000 Pulitzer prize 'for the best volume of verse published during the year by an American author.'

In October, 1925, the inventory of her estate was filed; and Harvard accepted 'The Amy Lowell Collection of Books and Manuscripts,' to be housed in a room designed for the practitioners and lovers of poetry. The collection was sent over immediately. Ten years were allowed for the final housing, and the larger part of that time was consumed in determining upon and opening the 'Poetry Room' on the top floor of Widener Library. The difficulty — that of money — was met by a fund in memory of George W. Woodberry. All the furnishings of the Sevenels library were rejected; and the portrait of Miss Lowell as a debutante was finally presented to Lowell House instead. Although the official inventory valued her estate at slightly more than eight hundred thousand, the collection of books and manuscripts alone might have been calculated as now worth a million.

Some time in 1926, Clement Wood's *Amy Lowell, A Critical Study* was published by Harold Vinal in New York. It was not a book calculated to advance her reputation; and none of the leading periodicals seem to have reviewed

[1] Letter to Miss Clem Irwin Orr, November 2, 1921.

it. The reason is doubtless that expressed by John Farrar in the June *Bookman* (LXIII, 503):

> ... Clement Wood... informed me that he had written a life of Amy Lowell. This is the last word of that project which shall be heard in the pages of this magazine, for Wood was always hostile to Miss Lowell, and it seems unnecessary and ill-conceived for an antagonistic critic to indulge in a biography such as I suspect this one to be. I must say that I honestly hope it may be born to blush unread, although certainly nothing that can be written about Amy Lowell's great memory can in any way dim it.

The following May the *Bookman* also published Robert Hillyer's indignant sonnet, 'On Looking into a Book on the Late Amy Lowell.'

In August, 1926, *East Wind*, Amy Lowell's second posthumous volume, was published from the manuscript which she had been preparing as far back as the summer of 1921. On September 21, 1923, she wrote Winifred Bryher: 'I am in two minds as to whether to begin my "East Wind" book with "Lilacs" and end it with "Purple Grackles," or leave it as it now is with nothing but stories.' The *Critical Fable* and *John Keats* intervened; then the publishers chose *What's O'Clock* as her next book of verse; so that, altogether, *East Wind* was delayed five years.

It is a collection continuing 'The Overgrown Pasture' in *Men, Women and Ghosts* — thirteen monodramas of the decadence of rural New England, in blank or free verse. The original New Englanders, she believed, had been an intense and hardy stock, which had rather run out in the nineteenth century, its countryside having been thrice drained of its best blood: by the western emigration, by the battlefields of the Civil War, and by the trend to the cities. A town-woman, she scarcely felt herself a part of it.

> My bringing-up was very cosmopolitan, and my forebears for several generations have been much travelled

people, and the decaying New England which Frost presents and which, if you remember I also present in 'The Overgrown Pasture,' has been no part of my immediate surroundings. Therefore it is no grief to me to have it disappear. It seems less native to me than the life of London or Paris. I can write about it I think through atavism, for something inside of me seems to come up, and I recollect things I have never experienced, but I think it is approaching the cataleptic state which your Deborah entered into when she prophesied; certainly, it is none of my doing. But then, I imagine that that is one of the gifts which Heaven has dropped upon me.... [1]

Eight years later she wrote in much the same vein:

Our attitudes [hers and Frost's] towards the natives of the New England countryside are rather different: he is much more sympathetic to them than I am and makes excuses for their idiosyncrasies. I pity them, and, in some ways, admire them, but, as far as time goes, I am a complete alien; not until I grew up did I know anything of the native Yankee, and I can only regard my knowledge of his language and his psychology as atavistic, since I never lived in rural New England until I bought a place in New Hampshire some twenty years ago to live in for the three Summer months. But you remember that my cousin, Mr. James Russell Lowell, was one of the authorities on Yankee character of his day, and all I can think is that subconsciously I inherited a sort of general family acquaintance with the country people. [2]

As a matter of fact, however, in Boston itself were plenty of little ivory figures pulled with string — Henry Adams, for one — who exemplified amply, to a woman of her superabundant vigor, the decay of the will to live. And melodramatic though her tales may appear, most of them were inspired by things which actually happened, whether in or out of Boston.

[1] Letter to Helen Bullis Kizer, October 23, 1917.
[2] Letter to Albert Feuillerat, January 24, 1925.

'The Doll,' she wrote Elizabeth Cutting (November 16, 1920) —

> is based in a real incident which was told me by an old lady who had met the originals in a small Maine town some years ago. It is of course subtle, Freudian, and all the horrible undercurrent things I find in New England.

'The House in Main Street' was a real house in Boston. The original note for the poem, found on one of the few scraps of original manuscript of hers remaining, reads:

> An old man has a house in which he does not live. His coachman lives in it, but he only keeps apples on the parlour mantelpiece. There he lets them ripen and once in a while goes in and eats one. Will not sell house.

To Glenn Frank she wrote (October 15, 1921):

> It happens to be true, as I think I told you before, one of those curious human happenings which somebody chanced to mention to me once, but I do not know what it means. I do not think that the old man keeps the apples to coddle, I imagine it is a sort of Freudian complex: apple — forbidden fruit — serpent — anything you like. I was told that it was a family in which there had been much insanity, and I think the particular mania means more than we think. Life is so much stranger than fiction, and I imagine that is why the poem always makes such an impression on audiences. There is some weird truth about it which fiction rarely achieves. Frankly, I do not know what it means, but I believe it means something.

'A Dracula of the Hills' is a tale of vampirism, which she got out of the *American Folk-Lore Journal*. 'The last case of digging up a woman to prevent her dead self from killing the other members of her family occurred in a small village in Vermont in the '80's. Doesn't it seem extraordinary?' [1]

[1] Letter to Glenn Frank, October 15, 1921.

The idea for 'The Note-Book in the Gate-Legged Table' came from England.

> The meeting of the four men was a purely imaginary one, nothing of the sort ever having occurred. The coffin episode I found in an old book of local events, a sort of history of one of the English counties — I forget which — not the ghostly part of it, but merely the man having himself buried in a coffin and swung from the rafters of his own barn.[1]

'The Rosebud Wall-Paper' was built round the inscription on an actual tombstone. Probably she was told of this stone by her physician, Dr. Theodore Eastman, a nephew of Sarah Orne Jewett; he used to amuse her for hours with his tales of Maine Life. 'The Conversion of a Saint' was elaborated out of the bitter quarrel between two persons which involved the reputation of a dead poet. 'The Gravestone' was an actual incident told her by Robert Frost. 'The Real Estate Agent's Tale' was developed very slightly from an episode recounted in a letter from Mary Starbuck of Nantucket (July 30, 1922), congratulating Miss Lowell on her 'Aquatint Framed in Gold.' '"And Pity 'Tis, 'Tis True"' came out of a newspaper. 'The House with the Marble Steps' was a tale told Miss Lowell by a Bryn Mawr girl on the train to St. Louis in 1920. The origins of the other three tales have been lost.

Amongst Miss Lowell's papers were found notes for three other New England tales, which she never wrote:

> A woman aging, starved for love. Witch delusions. Wax figures.
>
> .   .   .   .
>
> Captain Lightfoot, the highwayman. Drake, p. 119.
> .   .   .   .
>
> The Scarlet Letter, used in a totally new way.

And clipped to a sheet of New England names for use in

[1] Letter to Miss Esther Strong, March 8, 1924.

these poems was a scrap containing two anecdotes which apparently she thought she might find a place for:

> Woman. *all* contents of house out in front yard 7.30 A.M. housecleaning. Neighbor passes. 'How are you this morning Abbie?' 'Porely but up.'
>
> Toll gate. Excuse necessary to pass on Sunday. Man demanded to pass. 'What reason?' 'I got a father lyin' dead in Boston' — Excuse O.K. He passes — & in a few rods turns and adds 'and he's been layin' there 20 years.'

On April 1, 1927, the Boston Symphony Orchestra performed '*Lilacs*,' *Poem for Orchestra* (*after Amy Lowell*), by her old friend Edward Burlingame Hill, who inscribed his score 'In Memoriam A. L.,' and eventually presented the manuscript to the Amy Lowell Collection at Harvard.

On September 16, 1927, *Ballads for Sale*, the third posthumous volume, was published. It was edited by Mrs. Russell.

Ever since Amy Lowell's death, many a new burden had fallen upon Mrs. Russell's shoulders. On her devolved the task of closing Miss Lowell's great correspondence, with the added bulk of condolences. (One letter, from Mrs. Thomas Hardy, said that Miss Lowell was the only person her husband ever nominated 'cousin,' that although they had met but once, he entertained a real affection for her, and that for months he had been telling his friends with pride that she was coming to see him again.) In the safe was found a paper written by Miss Lowell in anticipation of her death, directing just what was to be done, with a design for the grave-stone. According to her wish, all manuscripts of unfinished poems were thrown into the furnace.

Obviously, Mrs. Russell could not keep up the estate at Sevenels; but before she could move to a smaller house nearby (which she did in May, 1926), Sevenels had to be closed in preparation for the sale. In the garrets she found great masses of stuff to be disposed of, for Miss Lowell's mother had saved everything systematically — receipted bills, letters, even dance-programs. Miss Lowell's books and manuscripts had to be got over to Harvard, and the poetry room arranged for.

When she was settled again, the scrap-books of clippings had to be brought up to date and continued, and the correspondence files arranged and purged of the hundreds, if not thousands, of mere requests for autographs (which Miss Lowell never granted) or for material to be used in high school themes.

Then came the preparation of the manuscript of *Ballads for Sale*. Mrs. Russell chose the title from Miss Lowell's Sunwise Turn broadside of 1916 (still uncollected), sold over $600 worth of finished but unpublished poems, chose the binding, arranged the text, and saw the book through the press.

Ballads for Sale contained all the remaining poems that Amy Lowell had finished, except for the *Phantasms of War*. It was the last great profusion of her work. It contained poems personal and objective, realistic and symbolic, poems of people and places and other centuries, poems about the agonies of creation and about other authors past and present, poems of love and hate and frustrations.

The book opened with the poem she addressed to Professor Walter Bingham in July, 1923, explaining her inability to let him analyze her creative processes. The next poem was the one written just after the death of Alice Meynell, whose poems Miss Frances Dabney had given her in 1897. Farther on are the two long poems to Duse, withheld from *What's O'Clock* as too intimate. Both are answers to the note Duse sent Miss Lowell in Baltimore: '1923' was written before she understood the note perfectly; it expresses her despair at not being able to mean something to Duse, who had meant so much to her. 'In

Answer to a Letter' was written after she had translated the note herself.

Quite a number of poems in the book are character studies of real people. 'Portrait' is dedicated to its original, Eleanor Robson Belmont; 'The Mirror' was originally dedicated to John Gould Fletcher; 'Portrait of an Orchestra Leader' was Chalmers Clifton. Others of these poems were hardly so complimentary, or indeed so exact; they are studies of types rather than of the personalities who suggested them.[1] But she had hesitated to collect them, none the less. 'The Revenge' and 'Proper Invective' were addressed to two critics; 'The Customer' was a magazine editor; 'Easel Picture' described one of her own servants; 'A Communication' was inspired by a former suitor. There were also originals for 'Correspondence,' 'To a Lady of Undeniable Charm,' 'To Two Unknown Ladies' (Irish authors), 'Aquatint Framed in Gold,' 'The Irony of Death,' and probably others.

'Apotheosis,' one of the few symbolic tales in this book, is a Blakish vision of the curse on love. Its source, however, was —

> a peculiar tale which I was told by a scientist last Winter; namely, that the Argentine ant is multiplying so tremendously, and running over our Southern states so fast, that man can only just keep even with it, and cannot get ahead of it at all. The only thing which checks its advance is the cold of the Northern states, where it cannot live, but there seems every reason to suppose that the ant will survive on the earth after man has perished. I think that the pre-Raphaelite scenery, and the form of the poem, rather added to the horror.[2]

The group called 'Gouache Pictures of Italy' she de-

---

[1] I recollect that when I was laboring over a paragraph which was to explain that Blake's Satan was not so much an analysis of Hayley as an explanation of what Hayley stood for, she declared that she understood perfectly what Blake was doing, as she had often tried to do it herself.

[2] Letter to Gilbert Seldes, October 3, 1923.

scribed as 'little pieces on Italy in the Eighteenth Century, done in the French sonnet form with an extra couplet tacked on at the end.'[1] 'The idea of them came from Henri de Regnier's *Cité de l'Eau*.'[2] The 'Palazzo Contarini,' however, came out of Fanny Burney's diary, and the coat described in 'The Ambassador' is still preserved at Charleston, S.C. It had belonged to one of Josephine Pinckney's ancestors; when he was appointed Minister to Spain, he sent his coat to China to be embroidered.

The 'Songs of the Pueblo Indians,' which close the book, were done as 'side-shows' while Miss Lowell was working on 'Many Swans.'

> They are not translations, nor are they based on any translations except generally, but they are based on known occasions in which the Hopis have songs, but, so far as I know, and I have read 63 volumes on the subject, there have never been any translations of any of these particular songs; in other words, they are my own idea of the ceremonies in question and of the general way in which Hopi songs are constructed, but the songs themselves are perfectly original.[3]

In April, 1928, was published *Selected Poems of Amy Lowell*, edited by John Livingston Lowes. From the more than six hundred and fifty titles in her eleven volumes, Professor Lowes selected seventy-five which he considered the best, that the scope of her work might be more fully appreciated by the general public.

In May, 1930, a selection from her scattered lectures and reviews, chosen by Ferris Greenslet, was published under the title of *Poetry and Poets*. These essays were arranged in three groups: 'On Poetry,' 'On Elder Poets,' and 'Contemporaries.' Two in this last group championed D. H. Lawrence, who had just died, on March 2. Again, a pub-

[1] Letter to Winifred Bryher, September 21, 1923.
[2] Letter to Albert Feuillerat, June 3, 1924.
[3] Letter to Harriet Monroe, May 18, 1920.

lication of Miss Lowell's proved to be timely; this posthumous acclamation of her dead friend was so opportune
as to be the first important voice in the establishment of
his fame.

On February 13, 1931, Robert Hillyer was the first lecturer in the 'Amy Lowell Memorial Poetry Series' conducted by Bertha Mahoney Miller for four years, under
the auspices of the Bookshop for Boys and Girls, at the
Women's Educational and Industrial Union. The Bookshop paid the poets' fees; the audience was composed of
children from the public and private schools in and near
Boston, chosen for their ability in writing verse. Mrs.
Harold Russell opened the series each year; the last meeting was always devoted to the writings of the children
themselves.

One last book of Amy Lowell's poems remains to be considered: the still unpublished *Phantasms of War*. This
manuscript, prepared for publication in 1918, consists of
eleven longish poems about the World War. The first was
written shortly before we joined the Allies; the last, shortly
after the Armistice.

Always a Pro-Ally, Miss Lowell originally believed in
American neutrality; then, when Wilson finally failed to
limit the activity of the German submarines, she became
convinced that it was impossible for her country to remain honorably out of the conflict. 'I never had any
patriotic fervour,' she wrote Aldington (April 4, 1923). 'I
thought it imperative to go out into the back garden and
kill that skunk.'

The 'Vigilantes' in April, 1917, began to organize the
poets for propaganda; she promised Hermann Hagedorn to
write and publish what she could. She had already written
three Phantasms: 'Before War is Declared' in February,
at the news of the sinking of the Lyman W. Law, to express her shame for America, 'sick with words'; 'Bei
Nachtlicher Weile,' on the theft of large quantities of

bronze from the Pocasset Cemetery in Cranston, Rhode Island, allegedly by Germans who stole the metal for ammunition; and 'The Breaking Out of the Flags' on our declaration of war. A Spanish translation of this last poem appeared in the first number of *Pan American Poetry*.

> Gonzales Martinez, who, I am told, is the most considerable poet in Mexico, wrote this translation and published an article in the chief Mexican newspaper in which the following sentence appeared: 'We have had American bullets and they have inclined us to hate the Yankee; we have had American diplomacy and it has tickled us into laughing at the Yankee; we have seen American adventurers and they taught us to despise the Yankee; but now comes "Pan American Poetry": there is at least one poem in it with sufficient convincing power as poetry and as national expression to make for respect, if not for outright sympathy, toward the Yankee, here and in all lands.' [1]

As introduction to the Phantasms that followed, one must remember that ever since 1914, America had been swamped in such a flood of propaganda as the world had never known; and the last vestiges of common sense were swept away when the United States entered the war. Sanity had nothing left to cling to. The populace was believing newspaper incredibilities just because they were incredible, while the more intelligent could not possibly resist the conviction that at the heart of so much smoke there must be some fire. Miss Lowell remained as rational and sceptical as was reasonable; she justified, for example, the execution of Edith Cavell, though she blamed the Germans for not guessing what propaganda would be made of it. But the crazy tales appearing daily in the newspapers appealed so strongly to her creative imagination that perforce she had to turn some of them into poems.

> The idea of them was to take real happenings and make poems of them, showing how much more terrible the real

[1] Letter to Richard Hunt, October 7, 1918.

things were than anything one could imagine. Every one of the events actually occurred, and the poems as originally published in newspapers and weeklies were headed with the newspapers' accounts of the events dealt with.[1]

I call the set 'Phantasms of War,' because they are all built upon the fantastic. I am trying to show the horrible grotesqueness, and the ghoulish hideousness of war, principally as waged by the Germans, although all these poems do not deal with the German atrocity, but with other sides of fighting. They might all be given as a subtitle the motto which Hoffman used before a series of his tales — 'In the manner of Callot'... His war engravings are the most grimly fantastic things you can imagine, and it is on this principle that these poems of mine are written, but I have tried to infuse into them an underlying pity which is absent from Callot's work.[2]

These poems, therefore, were intended as literature, not as propaganda. 'I detest the idea of poems as propaganda,' she informed Burton Klein (December 28, 1918), concerning one of the Phantasms. 'I do not think art should be used as propaganda,' she explained to Michael Sadler (May 25, 1918); 'but the poems insist on being written, and like all things which you honestly feel, they have the effect of moving other people.' For she did not fool herself into thinking that these poems had no propagandistic effect.

I regard these poems... as the best part of my 'bit' for my country. They are the strong reaction which these horrors have produced in me, and I only hope that, feeling so fervently as I did when I wrote them, they may arouse a like feeling in the reader. If any one feels more strongly our necessity for entering this war to put an end to 'frightfulness' in the world after having read these poems, I shall be happy indeed.... I do not hunt for them; I wait until I read something which starts my fighting spirit, and then I write.[3]

[1] Letter to Albert Feuillerat, June 3, 1924.
[2] Letter to Helen Bullis Kizer, December 10, 1917.
[3] Letter to Sara Teasdale, November 7, 1917.

Certainly, when these poems appeared in the *Independent* and other periodicals, and when she read them in her lectures, they roused her public to a most gratifying enthusiasm. 'Twelve Loyal Fishermen' was a ballad of those German sympathizers in American canneries who were supposedly filling the food for the Allied armies with myriads of tiny fish-hooks. 'The Cornucopia of Red and Green Comfits,' one of her most effective, was based on a story that German aviators were dropping poisoned candy for the half-starved children at Bar-le-Duc. Amy Lowell began her poem with the production of the famous jam; went on to the war, the sugar shortage, and the suffering children; then, after ironically invoking the spirit of Christmas with its German fairies, she described the Walpurgis-night brewing of the witch-broth candy, and its distribution on Christmas Eve. 'Business As Usual,' written after a conflagration in Baltimore, told of a German banker who sells the souls of his nation for two generations in exchange for this diabolical gift of fire. 'Sugar,' another of the best, was inspired by the sugar-shortage. Amy Lowell's evocation of all the delectable forms which sugar may take was a welcome compensation to a sugar-hungry nation. Unfortunately, part of her poem involved the supposition that sugar-beets were red; and rather than sacrifice her color-effects and conceits, she tried to argue the point with various objectors. None the less, her poem was republished in the *American Sugar Bulletin* (January 18, 1918). 'Marching Hessians' sprang from a report that German agents were releasing swarms of insects and poisoned pollen to ruin our wheat crop; she contrasted the hated Hessians of the Revolution with the present menace of the Hessian fly. 'The Diamond Shoal Lightship' was a splendid fresco of the Diamond Shoal, treated geologically and historically, with its passing vessels. The lightship there had been sunk by a German submarine; Miss Lowell's contempt for this easy victory was superb. 'Der Tag' exulted over the surrender of the German fleet and the flight of the Hohenzollerns. 'Requiem for a Probable Occasion' laid the blame for the death of a million and a half men squarely and solely on the Kaiser.

It is impossible to read these poems today as one read them in 1917–18. The background of war hysteria is gone; we resist with determination any attempt to rearouse hatred of the Kaiser and his nation. We apply historical tests; and although 'The Diamond Shoal Lightship' and 'The Cornucopia of Red and Green Comfits' are equally fine as literature, the former seems much the better because we refuse to believe the latter.

The national soul is always divided in wartime between love for the fatherland and hatred for the enemy. *Phantasms of War* is a record of this divided state of soul. The description of Diamond Shoal, for example, is in Amy Lowell's best manner; but when the enemy approaches in a submarine, she becomes a satirist, a master of full-blooded contempt. This contrast of poetic modes is disturbing unless one exercises that suspension of disbelief which constitutes poetic faith, and reads with the same disinterested appreciation which we apply to *Absalom and Achitophel*.

So the book will stand, as a record of the American state of mind in 1917–18, as a warning against the power of propaganda, as a protest against the horrors of war, and finally as poetry.

But Miss Lowell suspected the limitations of the book. 'Somehow I cannot divorce art from life; and if Homer made art out of the Trojan war, it seems to me that we ought to be able to do the same with this war. Anyhow, I am trying, and if I fail — well, it is all in the day's work.' [1] *Can Grande's Castle* appeared in September, 1918, and by that time the war seemed to be approaching an end. She wrote to Florence Ayscough (October 4, 1918):

[1] Letter to H. D., December 3, 1917.

The war news is so good, however, that I really think some day the nasty thing may be over. I confess to a sad regret that I cannot pull one trigger before it is over. To make up I am trying to pull lots of triggers of 'Phantasms,' and get the book out before the war ends. My diatribes are so violent that they surely cannot be post mortem.

In a month, however, the war was over; she never had thought it wise to publish poetry in the spring; and the next fall, *Pictures of the Floating World* appeared. She had laid down her poetic guns once and for all.

All these war phantasms of mine will appear some time in book form, when it is long enough after the facts for them to have become general poetry built upon a matter of history. Now I think they are entirely inopportune, as we are neither at war nor so far away from it as to take poems about it as pure literature.[1]

She had no book for the fall of 1920, but she refused to entertain the publishers' suggestion that they bring out *Phantasms of War*.

.... I am more and more convinced that it would be an awful mistake to do so. The war seems to me literarily as dead as a door nail.... I think it would look Jingoish.... It would be better to let this year go by with nothing... Mrs. Russell and I have talked it over exhaustively, and we both feel this way. It is rather a blow to me, for some of my best poetry is locked up in these 'Phantasms,' but I think it can only do me harm now. The war at this moment is neither present nor past; it is not actuality nor history, and anything so alive and bitter as these 'Phantasms' can only fail to make a good impression in the present temper of the world I am sure.[2]

To others in the following years she was to repeat her belief that *Phantasms* contained some of her best poetry; but

[1] Letter to André Fontainas, November 1, 1919.
[2] Letter to Edward C. Marsh, April 8, 1920.

she refused firmly to consider publication until the war had passed from the people's consciousness and become ancient history. The manuscript, ready for the press, with the newspaper clippings attached, is still awaiting that time.

There can be no question but that death cut Amy Lowell's career short. She showed not a sign of having been written out; her work was advancing steadily, interrupted though it had been by the biography of Keats. She should have had at least a decade more. If Milton or Goethe had died at fifty-one, what would be their fame to-day? But such speculations are futile.

And though ten years have passed since her death, the time has not come yet to pronounce upon her place in the poetic firmament. Such a judgement cannot be passed until the poet has sunk into obscurity and then re-emerged. The poetry of Amy Lowell has not been forgotten. Her books sell; the anthologies find it essential to include specimens of her work; the historians of American poetry discuss her achievements lengthily. She remains a living force.

But it is possible to indicate some of her achievements.

First of all, unquestionably she wrote poems — and how many expert versifiers achieve reputations without ever quite achieving a single poem! The test is simple but severe. Look over the anthologies issued in her lifetime, and observe how irretrievably the bulk of verse then thought worth preserving has faded and disintegrated, until scarcely a single adjective is left. What experiments that failed! what promises never fulfilled! But Amy Lowell's poems are as fresh and vital as when they were first written. Their gusto and brilliance and tenderness are untouched. Indeed, if anything, they seem to have matured: future generations will never conceive how perverse and puzzling many of these poems appeared at first printing, which now are so straightforward, unaffected, and inevitable.

In her work, she extended the strait limitations of the poetry of her day, in both method and substance.

Her sense of larger rhythms led her to transcend the metrical foot as the basis of her *vers libre*; she used the line, or cadence, as the fundamental unit, emphasizing also the paragraph or strophe as a larger unit. Her structures were built both according to the thought and the feeling; and her polyphonic prose established the ultimate of the principle of rhythmical (or dramatic) variation.

In substance, she got away completely from her predecessors' doleful egotism, effeminacy, and conventional moralizings, by recording life as one knows it, not as former poets had written of it. Her flowers came from the gardens of Sevenels or the fields of Dublin, not from the limited *hortus siccus* of the literary past. Her five senses ranged freely in her search for sharper and more inclusive perceptions of reality. In 'Lilacs' alone one may study out how she saw shapes and colors, heard sounds, smelled perfumes, touched things, appreciated spatial relationships, then brought her culture to bear upon her subject, invoking its aesthetic significance and its historical past, until the depths of her experience were stirred, to release a variety of seemingly unrelated things; yet at the end, her completed poem was a human unity.

Amy Lowell was the first of our poets to take full advantage of the civilizations across both the Atlantic and Pacific, and yet remain thoroughly American.

She brought back to life the limited and over-conventionalized emotions deemed appropriate to verse, and added others, until the whole range of human feeling was laid open. Her poems express gusto, wit, anger, fun, sensuousness, fear, tenderness, contempt, despair, bitterness, and delight of all kinds. Thus she broke completely with the traditional poetic monotone, which in some quarters had reverted to actual intoning. This suppleness of voice informs all her poems, long and short, and accounts in part for their effectiveness when read in public. But besides being dramatic, her poems are also musical; they inspired hundreds of composers to write for permission to set her lyrics.

Her variety of subject-matter was endless. She told stories of all kinds, realistic, romantic, symbolic, about times past and present; she also wrote lyrics, satires, monodramas, and epics after her own formula. As a result of this profusion, she was the despair of the contemporary pigeon-holers, who were at a loss to place her, in spite of the fact that her personality came out clearly in all she wrote. That she wrote objectively as well as autobiographically added to the difficulty.

But the sensorial and emotional aspects of her writings were usually the expression of her thought. She experienced life intelligently as well as passionately; her convictions about it were the true substance of her poetry. She had various things to say, and she had to say them. Whether studying the course of human history or delving into the dim foundations of the individual soul, she wrote honestly, courageously, and brilliantly. Her poetry thus expresses the complete human being: it includes brain as well as the heart and senses. But the public, used to verse that was intellectually negligible, and even believing that intelligence and poetry were incompatible, usually overlooked her message — which was as well, for that message was often dangerously liberal.

Thinking as well as feeling, she naturally became a critic as well as poet. Criticism in America has so often been confused with book-notices that her importance in this field has been underestimated; but there can be no doubt that she won her place among the few critics of importance whom America has produced.

Her attitude towards the arts was actually a contribution to aesthetic philosophy. Taking for granted that happiness was the test of a successful life or civilization, she placed the higher pleasures — the arts — as the purpose and climax of our existence. This conviction of hers was so complete that she hardly bothered to labor so obvious a point; but it is the implication and trend that lay behind all her aesthetic dicta. These dicta, scattered through her prefaces and other critical writings, could easily be arranged into a complete system. Had she lived longer, she might well have done so herself.

She was far more explicit about her conceptions of poetry. It was the expression of experience, to which nothing human was alien; and to express experience more effectively, she extended the bounds of rhythm and form. She did not seek for originality in her theory, but for fundamentals, which she was content to clarify and reaffirm. Her indebtedness to the Imagists and such other theorists as Hunt and Hulme was obvious and frank; perhaps only her theory of symbolism was wholly her own.

The development of her theory of criticism is demonstrated in her three critical books. *Six French Poets* introduced the chief post-*Symboliste* writers to America, and opened their new realms of experience to her readers. *Tendencies in Modern American Poetry* detected and defined the deep trend of the 'New Poetry' and made its chief personalities vivid in the public mind. Amy Lowell's treatment of their poems as springing on the one hand from their lives and on the other from the time-spirit was precise and convincing. Her *John Keats* went still further. It was scholarly in its accumulation of facts, critical in her explanation of his work, and creative in the telling of his life.

But had Amy Lowell written nothing at all, she still would have earned an important place in American literary history by her crusading for the New Poetry. She, more than any other single person, challenged and defeated the forces of public ignorance, indifference, and contempt, and of aesthetic egotism, snobbery, and envy.

Her rousing of the public was something of a miracle. In 1912, it believed firmly that Beauty was Prettiness plus a Moral, that all poetry was effeminate, and that all the great poets were dead forever. It had no taste, no knowledge; it was disturbed at vitality, fluttered at originality, indignant at significance, and completely baffled by the unfamiliar. But never once compromising with the public lack of taste, she made it listen to the works of our leading poets and buy their books, coerced the dictators of literary fashions to support them, and in spite of parodies and violent personal attacks, broke the belief that America could produce no poetry, and built up a national audience. When a nation supports a great art, a renaissance is in progress.

Of course she did not do this single-handed; she was merely the chief spokesman for a national art. Advertising breaks down after a while, if the goods do not come up to specifications. Her championing of Imagism succeeded, where a hundred imitative movements since have failed, because the principles of Imagism were the results of the lengthy observations and arguments of many persons. The poets were already writing, the poetry magazines were beginning to appear, and the New Poetry was already well rooted when Amy Lowell took charge. But it was the moment for somebody who combined creative ability, critical integrity, and a powerful personality to take the leadership. Amy Lowell was the person who assumed that leadership.

The result was a general rejuvenation of American literature. Even those who despised Free Verse and Imagism found themselves writing with greater clarity and conciseness and intensity and truthfulness.

These were the public accomplishments of Amy Lowell; of the private ones, the full tale will never be told. She constantly was seeking out good poets in the making, talking over their manuscripts, recommending them to editors, even selling their poems for them at times. Literary merit was her sole test here: she discounted personal friendships and enmities as far as possible. Any private charities were chalked up as service to the art, never as personal obligations.

Hampered by constant illness, by a late beginning, by all the forces of bitter egotisms and literary enmities, and an early death, none the less she fought her way to the top. Elsie Sergeant spoke truly when she said: 'Amy Lowell was a dynasty in herself.'

THE END

A LIST OF PUBLICATIONS

THIS list is simply a chronological arrangement of the first printing of poems and prose by Amy Lowell. A complete bibliography would make a small book by itself, especially if it also listed the reprints of her poems, as well as the paragraphs, articles, chapters, pamphlets, and books about her. Frances Kemp has contributed to the *Bulletin of Bibliography* (xv, 8–9, 25–26, 50–53) for May–August, September–December, 1933, and January–April, 1934, a 'Bibliography of Amy Lowell' which answers the ordinary needs of the critic and student.

Other material — the portraits, parodies, interviews, reviews, reprints, poems addressed to Miss Lowell, reports of lectures, etc. — will be found in her scrapbooks, with their exhaustive indices, now at Harvard.

In this list, prose articles have been distinguished from the poems by the use of a star. The bracketed letters following the titles indicate the books in which they were reprinted, according to the following table:

BFS....................................BALLADS FOR SALE
CGC...................................CAN GRANDE'S CASTLE
DMCG.......................DOME OF MANY-COLOURED GLASS
EW..EAST WIND
FFT.................................FIR-FLOWER TABLETS
L...LEGENDS
MWG............................MEN, WOMEN AND GHOSTS
P&P.................................POETRY AND POETS
PFW....................PICTURES OF THE FLOATING WORLD
POW..................................PHANTASMS OF WAR
SBPS.........................SWORD BLADES AND POPPY SEED
WOC...................................WHAT'S O'CLOCK

1887

December 19. DREAM DROPS, OR STORIES FROM FAIRYLAND [written with her mother, Katherine Lawrence Lowell, and her sister, Elizabeth Lowell, as co-authors]

1910

August. Fixed Idea, A [DMCG], *Atlantic Monthly* (CVI, 227)

1911

February. Japanese Wood-Carving, A [DMCG], *Atlantic Monthly* (CVII, 225)

May. Leisure [DMCG], *Hampton's Magazine* (XXVI, 529)

September. On Carpaccio's Picture [DMCG], *Atlantic Monthly* (CVIII, 375)

1912

July.	Starling [DMCG], *Atlantic Monthly* (CX, 91)
October 12.	DOME OF MANY-COLOURED GLASS, A

1913

July. Apology [SBPS] ⎱ *Poetry* (II, 134–35)
       Blockhead [SBPS] ⎰

September. In a Garden [PFW], *New Freewoman* (I, 114)
September. *[Review of Fannie Stearns Davis's *Myself and I*], *Poetry* (II, 225–26)
November. Absence [SBPS], *Atlantic Monthly* (CXII, 609)

1914

February. THE GLEBE [DES IMAGISTES]
February 16. Aubade [PFW]
              Captured Goddess, The [SBPS]
              Pike, The [PFW]   ⎱ *Egoist* (I, 68–69)
              Precinct, Rochester, The [SBPS]
              White and Green [PFW]
March. After Hearing a Waltz by Bartók [PFW], *International* (VIII, 88)
March. Patience [SBPS], *Atlantic Monthly* (CXIII, 383)
March. *Vers Libre and Metrical Prose, *Poetry* (III, 213–20)
April. DES IMAGISTES [Book form]
April. Anticipation [SBPS]
        Bungler, The [SBPS]
        Cyclists, The [SBPS]
        Foreigner, The [SBPS]
        Forsaken, The [PFW]   ⎱ *Poetry* (IV, 1–11)
        Gift, A [SBPS]
        Lady, A [SBPS]
        Music [PFW]
April. Exeter Road, The [PFW], *International* (VIII, 124)
April. *[Review of W. R. Benét's *Merchants From Cathay*], *Poetry* IV, 32–33)
May 3. *Why Should One Read Poetry [P&P], *Boston American*
June. *Miss Columbia: An Old-Fashioned Girl, *Little Review* (I, 36–37)
August. Blue Scarf, The [PFW], *Century* (LXXXVIII, 535)
August. Coal Picker, The [SBPS], *Poetry* (IV, 178–79)
August. Convalescence [SBPS], *Scribner's* (LVI, 223)
August. Tulip Garden, A [PFW], *Atlantic Monthly* (CXIV, 230)
August 1. Epitaph of a Young Poet [SBPS]
           Miscast, I & II [SBPS]
           Obligation [SBPS]   ⎱ *Egoist* (I, 288)
           Taxi, The [SBPS]
           Tree of Scarlet Berries, The [SBPS]
           Vintage [SBPS]

September.   Bullion [PFW]
              Flame Apples [PFW]
              Grotesque [PFW]   *Poetry and Drama*
              Letter, The [PFW]   (II, 291–94)
              On 'The Cutting of an Agate' [uncollected]
              Pine, Beech and Sunlight [PFW]
              Wheel of the Sun, The [PFW]

September 3. PIERROT QUI PLEURE ET PIERROT QUI RIT [French text by
              E. Rostand; music by Jean Hubert; English translation
              by Amy Lowell]

September.   Clear with Light, Variable Winds [PFW]   *Little Review*
              Fool's Moneybags [SBPS]   (I, 20–21)

September 22. SWORD BLADES AND POPPY SEEDS
October.   *Letter from London, A [dated August 28, 1914], *Little Review*
              (I, 6–9)

October.   *Nationalism in Art, *Poetry* (V, 33–38)
October.   *[Review of E. A. Robinson's *Van Zorn*], *Boston Herald*
November.   Bombardment, The [MWG], *Poetry* (V, 60–63)
November.   *Sister of the Wind, The [Review of Grace Fallow Norton's
              Sister of the Wind], *Poetry* (V, 87–88)

December 26. *[Review of Ibsen's *Robert Frank*], *Boston Herald*

1915

January.   Allies, The [MWG], *Little Review* (I, 1–2)
February.   Bright Sunlight [PFW]   *Little Review* (I, 7)
              Ely Cathedral [PFW]

February 20. *North of Boston [Book review], *New Republic* (II, 81–82)
April.   Fireworks [PFW], *Atlantic Monthly* (CXV, 512)
April.   Red Slippers [MWG]
              Solitaire [PFW]   *Poetry* (VI, 9–11)
              Venus Transiens [PFW]

April.   *Miss Lowell Not the Editor [Letter, denying her editorship
              of *Some Imagist Poets*], *Poetry* (VI, 52)
April.   Travelling Bear, The [PFW] [with six other poems previously
              published], SOME IMAGIST POETS

April 24.   Ballad of Footmen, A [MWG], *Boston Transcript*
May.   *Poetry Bookshop, The, *Little Review* (II, 19–22)
May.   *Some Imagist Poets by 'George Lane' [Amy Lowell and
              John Gould Fletcher], *Little Review* (II, 27–35)

May 1.   Spring Day [MWG], *Egoist* (II, 76–77)
May 15.   *Mr. Fletcher's Verse [Review of *Irradiations*], *New Republic*
              (III, 48–49)

July.   Fruit Shop [MWG], *Yale Review* (IV, 723–27, n.s.)
July 1.   Haunted [PFW]
              Maladie de l'Après-Midi [PFW]   *Egoist* (II, 113)
              Middle Age [PFW]
              Rainy Night, A [uncollected]
              Comparison, A [uncollected]
August.   Peddler of Flowers, The [PFW]   *Others* (I, 19–20)
              Trees [PFW]
August.   Patterns [MWG], *Little Review* (II, 6–8)

August   7.   After a Storm [PFW] ⎫ *New Republic* (IV, 21)
                 Sea Coal [PFW]   ⎭
September.   Aliens [PFW]
                 Fenway Park ['Back Bay Fens, The,' PFW] ⎫
                 Lead Soldiers [MWG]   ⎪
                 May Evening in Central Park [uncollected] ⎬ *Poetry*
                 Painter on Silk, The [MWG]   ⎪ (VI, 269–79)
                 Strain [PFW]   ⎪
                 Vernal Equinox [PFW]   ⎭
September.   La Vie de Bohême [PFW], *Poetry Journal* (IV, 14–15)
September.   *Richard Aldington's Poetry, *Little Review* (II, 11–16)
October   30.   Reaping [MWG], *New Republic* (IV, 338)
November.   SIX FRENCH POETS
December.   Paper Windmill [MWG], *Century* (XCI, 232–35)
December 13.   *French Patriot, A [Letter to editor, dated Brookline, Dec. 11,
                 defending patriotism of Gourmont], *Boston Transcript*
December 18.   *Imagist [Reply to Padraic Colum], *New Republic* (V, 174)

1916

January.   *Prizes and Anthologies Again [Article replying to Conrad
                 Aiken in *Poetry Journal* (IV, 95–100), November, 1915],
                 Poetry Journal (IV, 194–203)
January   8.   *Do People Read Poetry, [Anon. review of Braithwaite's
                 Anthology, 1915], *Bellman* (XX, 35)
February.   Paper Garden, The ['Planning the Garden,' PFW], *House and
                 Garden* (XXIX, 50)
March.   Stravinsky's 'Grotesques' [Stravinsky's Three Pieces, MWG],
                 Little Review (III, 7–9)
March   1.   August: Late Afternoon [PFW] ⎫
                 Dog-Days [PFW]   ⎬ *Egoist* (III, 37)
                 Pond, The [PFW]   ⎭
March   4.   *New Manner in Modern Poetry, The, *New Republic* (VI,
                 124–25)
April.   Impressionist Picture of a Garden [PFW], *Trimmed Lamp*
                 (V, 181)
April.   Poem, The [PFW], *Masses* (p. 21)
April.   Summer Rain [DMCG], *Smart Set* (XLVIII, 124)
May.   Country House, The [PFW] ⎫
                 Decade [PFW]   ⎬ *Chimaera* (I, 6–7)
                 Mirror, The [BFS]   ⎭
May.   Number 3 on the Docket [MWG], *Poetry Review* (I, 4–5)
May.   Off the Turnpike [MWG], *Little Review* (III, 19–25)
May.   Pyrotechnics [PFW], *Poetry* (VIII, 76–77)
May   6.   SOME IMAGIST POETS, 1916 [Contains three poems all previ-
                 ously published]
May   27.   *E. A. Robinson's Verse [Review of *Man Against the Sky*],
                 New Republic (VII, 96–97)
June.   Grocery, The [MWG], *Masses* (VIII, 17)
June.   *Two Imagist Poets [i.e. Aldington and Flint], *Poetry Review*
                 (I, 11–13)
June–July.   Malmaison [MWG], *Little Review* (III, 1)
July.   *Is There a National Spirit in the New Poetry of America,
                 Craftsman (XXX, 339–49)

July.   Merchandise [PFW], *Atlantic Monthly* (CXVIII, 55)
July.   *Poems of Democracy [Review of Carl Sandburg's *Chicago Poems*], *Poetry Review* (I, 46-47)
July   7. Aquarium, An [MWG], *Reedy's Mirror* (XXV, 453)
August.   Battledore and Shuttlecock ['Roxbury Garden, A,' MWG], *Scribner's* (LX, 192-93)
August.   1777 [MWG], *Poetry* (VIII, 219-26)
August.   Wakefulness [PFW], *Little Review* (III, 3)
August   28. Charm, The [PFW]
                Mise en Scène [PFW]   *Independent*
                Opal [PFW]   (LXXXVIII, 307)
                Opera House, An [MWG]
                Thompson's Lunch Room [MWG]
September.   Cross Roads, The, *Poetry Review* (I, 72)
September.   In a Time of Dearth [PFW], *Century* (XCII, 766-67)
September.   *Modern Monologues [Review of Mary Aldis's *Flashlights*], *Poetry* (VIII, 318-21)
September 7.   *In Defence of Vers Libre [Letter to editor], *Dial* (LXI, 133)
October   18. MEN, WOMEN AND GHOSTS
November.   Flotsam [PFW], *Seven Arts* (I, 30-31)
December.   Ballads for Sale [BFS] [Sunwise Turn Broadside]

1917

January.   *Consideration of Modern Poetry, *North American Review* (CCV, 103-17)
January.   Ombre Chinoise [PFW]
                Trades [PFW]   } *Yale Review* (VI, 396-97)
                William Blake [PFW]
January   25. *Poetry as a Spoken Art [P&P], *Dial* (LXII, 46-49)
                                              Bookman (XLIV, 624-27)
February.   Shore Grass [PFW]   Edward J. O'Brien, *The
                Ring and the Castle, The [L] Masque of Poets*, N.Y., 1918,
                                              [pp. 73-81]
February   28. Before War is Declared [POW], *Boston Transcript*
March.   Autumn [PFW]
                Camellia Tree of Matsu, The [PFW]
                Desolation [PFW]
                Disillusion [PFW]
                Document [PFW]
                Emperor's Garden, The [PFW]
                Ephemera [PFW]
                From China [PFW]
                Illusion [PFW]   *Poetry*, (IX, 302-07)
                Lover, A [PFW]
                Meditation [PFW]
                One of the Hundred Views [PFW]
                Paper Fishes [PFW]
                Streets [PFW]
                Sunshine [PFW]
                To a Husband [PFW]
                Year Passes, A [PFW]

July.	Sprig of Rosemary, A [PFW], *Scribner's* (LXIV, 79)
August.	Appuldurcombe Park [PFW], *Poetry* (XII, 260–63)
August.	Castles in Spain [PFW], *Atlantic Monthly* (CXXII, 212)
August.	Hedge Island [CGC], *North American Review* (CCVIII, 261–68)
September.	Garden by Moonlight, The [PFW], *Bookman* (XLVIII, 57)
September.	Misericordia [PFW], *La Revista de Indias* (Ano I, 60)
September 24.	CAN GRANDE'S CASTLE
October.	In Time of War [PFW] Lady to Her Lover, A [PFW] } *Youth* (I, 4) Poetry [PFW] Vicarious [PFW]
November.	Diamond Shoal Lightship [POW], *North American Review* (CCVIII, 754–61)
November 16.	Camouflaged Troop-Ship, Boston Harbor [PFW], *Dial* (LXV, 403)
November 17.	Fort, The [PFW], *N.Y. Herald-Tribune*
December.	Flute [PFW], *Century* (XCVII, 272)
December.	Interlude [PFW], *Bookman* (XLVIII, 434)
December.	One Winter Night [EW], *Touchstone* (IV, 222–26)
December 14.	Bei Nächtlicher Weile [POW], *Independent* (XCVI, 372–73)
December 22.	Der Tag [POW], *N.Y. Tribune*

1919

January.	*Case of Modern Poetry vs. Prof. Lewisohn [Answer to Lewisohn's 'Problem of Modern Poetry,' *Bookman* (XLVIII, 550–57, January 1919)], *Bookman* (XLVIII, 558–66)
February	After How Many Years [FFT] Calligraphy [FFT] Emperor's Return, The [FFT] Evening Meeting, An [FFT] From the Straw Hut, I & II [FFT] Inn at the Western Gate, The ['Inn at the Mountain Pass, The,' FFT] } *Poetry* (XIII, 233–242) On Seeing the Portrait [FFT] On the Classic [FFT] One Goes a Journey [FFT] Palace Blossoms, The [FFT] Recluse, A ['Hermit, The' FFT]
February 1.	Broken Fountain, The [PFW], *Tout le Monde*, p. 38
March 9.	Generations [PFW], *N.Y. Tribune*
March 23.	*New England Album, A [Review of Edward Waldo Emerson's *Early Years of the Saturday Club*], *N.Y. Times*
March 30.	Road to the Mountain, The [uncollected], *N.Y. Tribune*
April.	*Casual Reflections on a Few of the Younger English Novelists, *Bookman* (XLIX, 173–81)
April.	*Jean Untermeyer's Book [Review of *Growing Pains*], *Poetry* (XIV, 47–51)
April 18.	Gargoyles [PFW], *Reedy's Mirror* (XXVIII, 242)
April 20.	*Look: We Have Come Thru! [P&P] [Review of D. H. Lawrence's book], *N.Y. Times*
May.	Dried Marjoram [L], *Atlantic Monthly* (CXXIII, 636–43)

May.　　　　　　On the Mantelpiece [PFW], *Bookman* (XLIX, 267)
May　　2.　　Violin Sonata [PFW], *Boston Transcript*
May　　3.　　*Letter [Dated April 23, in reply to Mrs. Florence Howe Hall's letter in regard to the Saturday Club, April 13, 1919] *N.Y. Times*
May　　5.　　Correction of misprint in 'Violin Sonata' [published May 2], *Boston Transcript*
May　　31.　　Coq d'Or [PFW], *Dial* (LXVI, 549)
May　　31.　　Entente Cordial [PFW] ⎫
　　　　　　　Spectacles [PFW]　　⎬ *Independent* (XCVIII, 327)
　　　　　　　To Winky [PFW]　　　⎭
May　　31.　　*Pioneering in Poetry [Reprint from introduction to *Tendencies*], *Independent* (XCVIII, 326)
June.　　　　　To Two Unknown Ladies [BFS], *North American Review* (CCIX, 837–42)
June.　　　　　Weather-Vane Points South, The ['Weather-Cock Points South, The,' PFW], *Vanity Fair* (XII, 33)
June　　1.　　*Letter on Whitman and Emerson [Dated May 25. Replying to J. L. Hervey's letter on the Saturday Club, May 25, 1919], *N.Y. Times*
June　　15.　　*Convention and Revolt in Poetry [Review of John Livingston Lowes's book], *N.Y. Times*
July.　　　　　Quincunx [BFS], *Harper's* (CXXXIX, 255)
July.　　　　　*To the Editor of the *North American Review* [Letter dated May 22, 1919], *North American Review*
August.　　　And Pity 'Tis 'Tis True [EW], *Touchstone* (V, 369–72)
August.　　　At the Bookseller's [PFW], *Youth* (I, 107)
August.　　　Frimaire [PFW], *Scribner's* (LXVI, 192)
August　7.　　Chopin [PFW], *Reedy's Mirror* (XXVIII, 528)
September.　Artist, The [PFW]　　⎫
　　　　　　　Autumn [PFW]　　　　⎪
　　　　　　　Balls [PFW]　　　　　⎬ *Poetry* (XIV, 310–13)
　　　　　　　Bookshop, The [PFW]　⎪
　　　　　　　Good Gracious [PFW]　⎪
　　　　　　　Peach-Colour [PFW]　⎭
September.　Constancy [PFW]　　　⎫
　　　　　　　Daimio's Oiran, A [PFW]⎪
　　　　　　　Frosty Evening [PFW]　⎬ *Touchstone* (V, 500)
　　　　　　　Temple Ceremony [PFW]⎭
September.　Panel, A ['Gold-Leaf Screen,' PFW] ⎫　　*Century*
　　　　　　　Poet's Wife, A [PFW]　　　　　　⎬
　　　　　　　Spring Longing [PFW]　　　　　　⎭　(XCVIII, 616–17)
September　6.　Night Before the Parade, The [PFW], *Independent* (XCIX, 316)
September 20.　To Li T'Ai Po ['Li T'Ai Po,' PFW], *Dial* (LXVII, 241)
September 24.　PICTURES OF THE FLOATING WORLD
October.　　Little Ivory Figures [PFW] ⎫　North American Review
　　　　　　　Trees in Winter [PFW]　　⎭　　　(CCX, 560–61)
October.　　*Modern Poetry: Its Differences, Its Aims, Its Achievements [Abstract of lecture, June 9, 1919, to Massachusetts Library Club and Bay Path Library Club], *Massachusetts Library Club Bulletin* (IX, 8–10)

October	19.	*In Memoriam [Tribute to Mrs. Helen Bullis Kizer], *N.Y. Times*
November.		Memorandum Confided by a Yucca [L], *Bookman* (L, 273–85)
November	8.	*What I Read As a Child, pp. 14–20 in *What I Read As a Child* by Witter Bynner, Joseph Hergesheimer, Rupert Hughes, Stephen Leacock, Amy Lowell, and Hugh Walpole [Pamphlet reprinted from the Wednesday book page of the *Chicago Daily News*, Nov. 8, 1919]
December	7.	*John Masefield's Ballad of the Hunting Field [Review of Masefield's *Reynard the Fox* [P&P], *N.Y. Times*

1920

January.		*Some Musical Analogies in Modern Poetry, *Musical Quarterly* (VI, 127–57)
January	24.	Once Jericho [WOC], London *Nation* (XXVI, 570)
February.		One! Two! Three! [BFS], *Anglo-French Review* (III, 68)
February	8.	*Considerations of a Modern Painter [Review of Charles Woodbury's *Painting and the Personal Equation*], *N.Y. Times*
March.		Legend of Porcelain [L], *North American Review* (CCXI, 371–86)
March.		Summer Night Piece [WOC], *Anglo-French Review* (III, 154)
Easter.		Carrefour [BFS] ⎫ *Coterie* (No. IV, p. 58)
		Granadilla [BFS] ⎭
April.		Night Clouds [WOC] ⎫ *Voices* (III, 100–01)
		Stalactite [BFS] ⎭
April.		Shower, A [PFW], *Century* (XCIX, 755)
May.		Merely Statement [WOC], *Bookman* (LI, 297)
May	16.	*Parody or Permanence [Review of Vachel Lindsay's *Golden Whales of California*], *N.Y. Times*
June.		Gavotte in D Minor [L], *Dial* (LXVIII, 709-10)
June.		*Sevenels, Brookline, Mass., *Touchstone* (VII, 210–18)
July.		*Article concerning 'A Keats Memorial' [The Wentworth Place letter forwarded by her, with appeal for contributions], *Poetry* (XVI, 231–32)
July.		Old Examination Hall, China [BFS], *Unpartizan Review* (XIV, 34)
August.		Many Swans [L], *North American Review* (CCXII, 250–66)
August.		Water Stair, The [BFS], *Romance* (II, 36)
August	22.	*Voice Cries in Our Wilderness, A [P&P] [Review of Lawrence's *Touch and Go*], *N.Y. Times*
September.		Basket Dance [BFS] ⎫
		Flute Priest's Song [BFS] ⎪
		Prayer for a Profusion [BFS] ⎪ *Dial* (LXIX, 247–51)
		Prayer for Lightning [BFS] ⎬
		Women's Harvest Song [BFS] ⎪
		Women's Song of the Corn [BFS] ⎭
September.		Funeral Song for [L] ⎫
		Meeting House Hill [WOC] ⎪ A Miscellany of American
		New Heavens for Old [BFS] ⎬ Poetry, 1920 [with three other
		Old Snow [BFS] ⎪ poems previously published]
		Wind and Silver [WOC] ⎭

September 18. Lilacs [WOC], *Literary Review, N.Y. Post*
September 18. *That Bookcase, *Literary Review, N.Y. Post*, pp. 1, 2
September 29. If I Were Francesco Guardi [WOC], *New Republic* (XXIV, 117)
October. Palazzo Contarini [BFS], *Romance* (II, 112)
October. *Weary Verse [P&P] [Review of *Georgian Poetry, 1918–1919*], *Dial* (LXIX, 424–31)
October 6. Morning Song with Drums [WOC], *New Republic* (XXIV, 147)
October 10. *Louis Untermeyer: Critic, Parodist, Poet [Review of *The New Adam*], *N.Y. Times*
October 24. *Poetry and Propaganda [P&P] [Review of Sandburg's *Smoke and Steel*], *N.Y. Times*
November. Day That Was That Day, The [EW], *Poetry* (XVII, 59–67)
November. *Preface to Annie Shepley Omori and Kochi Dori's *Diaries of Court Ladies of Old Japan* (Boston: Houghton Mifflin, 1920), pp. xi–xxxiii
November. *Preface to Winifred Bryher's *Development* (N.Y.: Macmillan Co., 1920), pp. ix–xvi
November 14. *Mirage of Experience, A [Review of Elizabeth Shepley Sergeant's *Shadow Shapes*], *N.Y. Times*
November 20. Rhyme Out of Motley, A [WOC], *Literary Review, N.Y. Post* (p. 1)
December. *Preface to Hilda Conkling's *Poems by a Little Girl* (*N.Y.*, c1920), pp. vii–xix
December 29. Grave Song [WOC]
House with the Marble Steps [EW] } *New Republic* (XXV, 140–41)
Texas [WOC]

1921

January. Threnody [BFS], *Unpartizan Review* (XV, 42)
February 23. *Last Letter of Keats, September 22nd, 1819, The [Transcribed and edited by Amy Lowell], *The John Keats Memorial Volume*, issued by the Keats House Committee (Hampstead, London and N.Y.), pp. 115–20
March. Enchanted Castle, The [WOC], *The Enchanted Years*, p. 26 [Anthology, dedicated by poets of Great Britain and America to the University of Virginia on the occasion of its 100th anniversary. Edited by John Calvin Metcalf, James Southall Wilson. N.Y.: Harcourt Brace & Co., 1921]
April. Afterglow [WOC]
Dimension [WOC] } *Bookman* (LIII, 146)
April 16. *Stocktaking [P&P] [Review of J. G. Fletcher's *Breakers and Granite*], *Literary Review, N.Y. Post* (p. 1)
May 14. *Miss Lowell Explains [Letter to editor answering W. L. Werner's complaint (April 30, 1921, p. 24) against her review of J. G. Fletcher in *Stocktaking* (April 16, 1921, p. 1)], *Literary Review, N.Y. Post* (p. 14)
May 20. LEGENDS
June. Twenty-four Hokku [WOC], *Poetry* (XVII, 124–27)
July. Autumn River Song [FFT]
Battle to the South of the City, The [FFT] | *North American*
Parrot Island [FFT] | *Review* (CCXIV,
Songs of the Marches [FFT]

July.   *Poems of the Month, The, *Bookman* (LIII, 404–06)
August.   Footing Up a Total [WOC] } *Dial* (LXXI, 146–49)
                    Swans [WOC]
August.   Miniature [BFS], *Century* (CII, 529)
August.   *Poems of the Month, The, *Bookman* (LIII, 531–33)
August   3.   To Carl Sandburg [WOC], *Nation* (CXIII, 124)
August   20.   Sorrel Horse [FFT], *Literary Review*, N.Y. *Post* (p. 1)
Autumn.   Paradox [BFS], *Tempo* (I, 3)
September.   Doll [EW], *North American Review* (CCXIV, 354–59)
September.   Lonely Wife [FFT], *Bookman* (LIV, 56)
September.   Prime [WOC], *Atlantic Monthly* (CXXVIII, 375)
September   28.   *Marionettes of Fate [Review of Aiken's *Punch*], *New Republic*
                    (XXVIII, 139–40)
October.   City of Stone (Nanking), The [FFT] } *Dial* (LXXI, 438)
                    Retreat of Hsieh Kung, The [FFT]
October.   *Foreword to Mrs. Lucy Gibbons Morse's *Breezes* (Boston,
                    1921), pp. vii–ix
October.   *From Amy Lowell [Message to the Poetry Society of South
                    Carolina], *Year Book of the Poetry Society of South Carolina*
                    (p. 17)
October.   Terraced Road of the Two-Edged Sword Mountains [FFT]
                    Asia (XXI, 848)
October.   White Currants [WOC], *Century* (CII, 834)
October   23.   *Miss Lowell on the *New York Times* [Letter, dated Sept. 1,
                    1921, on the 25th anniversary of the *Times*], N.Y. *Times*
November.   Book of Stones and Lilies [BFS], *Scribner's* (LXX, 560)
November.   Lilacs [WOC], *Broom* (I, 41)
November   27.   Unfortunate Interlude, An [P&P] [Review of J. Masefield's
                    King Cole], N.Y. *Times*
December.   Perils of the Shu Road, The [FFT], *Chinese Students' Monthly*
                    (XVII, 114)
December   3.   *On Criticism, *Literary Review*, N.Y. *Post* (pp. 217–18)
December   14.   FIR-FLOWER TABLETS

1922

January.   Katydids [WOC], *Dial* (LXXII, 16)
January.   New Year's Card [BFS], *Century* (CIII, 470)
January   21.   *Second Chapter, The [Reviews of *Dreams Out of Darkness* by
                    J. S. Untermeyer, *Hymen* by H. D., *Songs for Parents* by
                    John Farrar, *Wampum and Old Gold* by Hervey Allen],
                    Literary Review, N.Y. *Post* (p. 364)
February.   *Bird's Eye View of E. A. Robinson [P&P] *Dial* (LXXII,
                    130–42)
February.   House in Main Street [EW], *Century* (CIII, 549–62)
March   25.   *'Fu' Discussed, The [Letter to the editor in answer to Arthur
                    Waley's review of *Fir-Flower Tablets* (*Literary Review*, N.Y.
                    Post, Feb. 4, 1922, pp. 395–96)], *Literary Review*, N.Y. *Post*
                    p. 538
March   26.   *Breaker of Moulds, A [Review of Sackville-West's *Dragon in
                    Shallow Waters*], N.Y. *Times*
June.   Sisters [WOC], *North American Review* (CCXV, 785–89)

June   7. Aquatint Framed in Gold [BFS], *Nation* (CXIV, 687)
July.   Purple Grackles [WOC], *Bookman* (LV, 458–60)
July   2. Revenge [BFS], *New Republic* (XXXI, 191)
August   12. *Is There a Reaction?, *Literary Review, N.Y. Post* (pp. 865–66)
September.   Immortals [BFS] ⎱ *Century* (CIV, 790–92)
                In Excelsis [WOC] ⎰
September.   Ronde du Diable, La [WOC] ⎱ AMERICAN POETRY, 1922; [with
                Vespers [WOC]   ⎰ five other poems previously
                                             published]
September 15.   CRITICAL FABLE, A
October.   Chill [BFS], *The Reviewer* (III, 615–16)
October.   Easel Picture [BFS] ⎱ *Dial* (LXXIII, 392–94)
                Orientation [WOC]   ⎰
October.   Red Knight, The [WOC], *Dial* (LXVIII, 392–94)
October   7. On Reading a Line Underscored [WOC], *Literary Review, N.Y. Post* (p. 81)
November.   Grievance [BFS] ⎱
                Portrait [BFS]   ⎬ *Harper's* (CXLV, 800)
                Song for a Viola d'Amore [WOC] ⎰
December.   Charleston, South Carolina [WOC] ⎱
                Magnolia Gardens [BFS]   ⎬
                Middleton Place, The [WOC]   ⎬ *Poetry* (XXI, 117–24.
                South Carolina Forest, A [BFS]   ⎬
                Vow, The [WOC]   ⎰
December.   Congressional Library [WOC], *International Book Review* (I, 18). [Corrected (order of verses), Jan., 1923 (I, 75)]
December.   *Miss Lowell on Translating Chinese [Reply to Eunice Tietjens], *Poetry* (XXI, 167–72)
December 22.   *Tribute to E. A. Robinson on his 50th Birthday, A, *N.Y. Times*
                Silhouette with Sepia Background [BFS], *Year Book of the Poetry Society of South Carolina*

                                1923

January.   And So, I Think, Diogenes [BFS], *Yale Review* (n.s., XII, 286–87)
January.   Dissonance [BFS], *Rhythmus* (I, 4)
January   20. Accolade [BFS] ⎱
                Cut Shadow, The [BFS] ⎬ *Independent* (CX, 48)
                Green Shadows [BFS]   ⎬
                Lustre [BFS]   ⎰
Jan.–Feb.   Heraldic [BFS], *Prairie* (I, 9)
February.   Nuit Blanche [WOC], *Double Dealer* (V, 46)
February.   Rosebud Wall Paper [EW], *North American Review* (CCXVII, 218–31)
March.   Fact [BFS], *Scribner's* (LXXIII, 305)
April.   Primavera [WOC], *Bookman* (LVII, 249)
June.   Dracula of the Hills [EW], *Century* (CVI, 173–85)
August.   Eleanora Duse [uncollected], *Poetry* (XXII, 234–36) [Written at the age of 28]
August   Pastime [BFS], *Forum* (LXX, 1800–1801)
August   1. Watershed [WOC], *New Republic* (XXXV, 253)

August 18. Attitude Under an Elm Tree [WOC], *Literary Review, N.Y. Post* (III, 905)

October. Autumn and Death [WOC], *Atlantic Monthly* (CXXXII, 482–83)

October. View of Teignmouth [WOC], *North American Review* (CCXVIII, 497–503)

December. Evelyn Ray [WOC] } *Poetry* (XXIII, 117–27)
Green Parrakeet, The [WOC]

December. Sultry [WOC] } *Dial* (LXXV, 561–64)
Time's Acre [WOC]

December 5. Exercise in Logic [WOC] } *New Republic* (XXXVII, 39)
Fugitive [WOC]

December 5. *Two Generations in American Poetry [P&P], *New Republic* (XXXVII, 1–3)

1924

January. 'Plum Blossom' Concubine, The [BFS], *The Reviewer* (IV, 106)

January 16. Alternatives [BFS], *New Republic* (XXXVII, 206)

March. Pantomime in One Act [WOC], *Harper's* (CXLVIII, 446)

April. 30. Eleanora Duse [WOC], *New Republic* (XXXVIII, 261) [six sonnets]

May. Humming Birds [WOC] } *Bookman* (LIX, 277)
Sand Altar [WOC]

May. Paper in the Gate-Legged Table, The [EW], *Century* (CVIII, 45–51)

October. Conversion of a Saint [EW], *Bookman* (LX, 139–47)

October. East, West, North and South of a Man [WOC], *Harper's* (CXLIX, 608–12)

1925

*Preface to Vol. VI of *The Works of Stephen Crane*, edited by Wilson Follett (N.Y.: Alfred A. Knopf, 1925), pp. ix–xxix [Signed: Amy Lowell, Brookline, Mass., Sept. 1924]

February 10. JOHN KEATS

February 14. On-Looker [WOC], *Saturday Review of Literature* (I, 52)

February 21. *Open the Door [Protest against review of Grace Conkling's *Ship's Log*, Jan. 25], *Saturday Review of Literature* (I, 550)

April 19. Ambassador, The [BFS]
Fête at Caserta [BFS]
From Nice to Oneglia [BFS]
Lime Avenue, The [BFS] } *(N.Y. Herald Tribune) Books* (II, 7)
Santa Settimana [BFS]
Stable, The [BFS]
Villa Capouana [BFS]

May 17. Anniversary [WOC], *N.Y. Herald Tribune*

June. In a Powder Closet [WOC], *Harper's* (XV, 59)

June 6. Slippers of the Goddess of Beauty [WOC], *Saturday Review of Literature* (I, 801)

July. Fool o' the Moon [WOC], *Atlantic Monthly* (CXXXVI, 47–49)

July.	Poetic Justice [BFS] Time Web [WOC] } *Bookman* (LXI, 552)
July 15.	Preface to an Occasion [WOC], *New Republic* (XLIII, 199)
August 25.	WHAT'S O'CLOCK
October.	Apotheosis [BFS] Communication, A [BFS] Mesdames Atropos and Clio [BFS] Sibyl, The [BFS] } AMERICAN POETRY, 1925 [with one other poem previously published]
October.	Folie de Minuit [WOC], *Harper's* (CLI, 546–47)
October 7.	To a Gentleman [BFS], *New Republic* (XLIV, 175)
October 17.	To a Lady [BFS], *Saturday Review of Literature* (II, 207)
October 25.	In the Campagna [BFS], (*N.Y. Herald Tribune*) *Books* (VI, 2)
November.	To Eleanora Duse: In Answer to a Letter [BFS], *International Book Review* (III, 806)
December.	Madonna of Carthagena, The [BFS], *Poetry* (XXVII, 117–29)
December.	Points of View [BFS], *Bookman* (LXII, 383)

1926

January.	Behind Time [BFS], *Yale Review* (n.s., XV, 246–53)
January.	Gravestone [EW], *Century* (CXI, 283–90)
January.	Hippocrene [BFS], *Atlantic Monthly* (CXXXVII, 47–48)
March.	On Looking at a Copy [BFS], *Atlantic Monthly* (CXXXVII, 323–25)
April 10.	Who Has Not, Cannot Have [BFS], *Saturday Review of Literature* (II, 695)
May.	Epithalamium in a Modern Manner [BFS], *Double Dealer* (VIII, 322)
June.	Real-Estate Agent's Tale [EW], *North American Review* (CCXXIII, 345–52)
August.	EAST WIND
August.	Mid-Adventure [BFS], *International Book Review* (IV, 555)
Sept.–Oct.	Rode the Six Hundred [BFS], *The Harp* (II, 1)

1927

April.	*Walt Whitman and the New Poetry [P&P], *Yale Review* (n.s., XVI, 502–19)
September 16.	BALLADS FOR SALE

1928

	*Foreword to *A Symposium on His* [Percy MacKaye] *Fiftieth Birthday*, 1925 [Tribute delivered at Authors' Club dinner, March 16, 1925] (Hanover, N.H., 1928), pp. xi–xii
April.	SELECTED POEMS, ed., John Livingston Lowes

1930

May.	POETRY AND POETS [Selection of prose articles. 'Emily Dickinson,' an extract from a lecture, 'Imagism Past and Present, I, March 20, 1918, had not been published previously.]

INDEX

INDEX

INDEX

PRINTED IN U.S.A.